Contents

Preface

For those of you who read (and much more importantly to me, bought) the first and second editions, you will recall that I described the task of collating the material and writing a book like this:

'The task has been similar to that circus act – you know, the one where the man and his assistant (who I suspect of being both his daughter *and* the lovely Rosetta, tightrope-walker, 'all the way from Romania') make two hundred plates spin on top of canes. They have to keep sprinting around making sure that the two hundred plates are all staying on, and of course there is always one that is about to wobble off.
Well, the same with the contents of this book. I race from computer file to computer file, desperately slipping new information into "Community Care" or "Social Security" to keep up to date and spinning away.'

Well, eight years have passed since I wrote that, and yet I don't think that I can describe the process as having changed much, for this, the third edition – surely, a case for *The Guinness Book of Records*?

Actually, I am lying, for I can describe the process as having changed – the damned 'plates' have multiplied in number to seemingly thousands, I have to spin them ever faster and, even worse, I have to keep changing them in mid-spin! So, instead of just me and my mythical 'Rosetta' (a rather shadowy, but sensuous figure in my imagination), we are now a circus troupe (as you can see from all the additional credits), madly rushing past each other, as we balance our own set of plates and I run amok amongst them all, causing chaos and playing, I suspect increasingly, the role of the clown!

I think I may have carried the metaphor of the circus as far as it will go, so let me just make the point that I have tried to encompass the diversity of debates and issues which make the subject matter of social policy so topical and interesting, and to keep the book as up-to-date as possible. However, even by the time the book is published, I am sure that some things will already have changed. But, believe me, we are busy adding things and updating until the very last possible moment.

I hope you find the book as useful as the previous editions and, of course, that you buy lots of copies!

Acknowledgements

I would just like to reiterate that the book has become more of a team effort, as the sheer size of the area to be covered has begun to defeat me. Peter Scourfield was his usual helpful self. Stevie Sinclair was his usual clever self. Richard Davis leant me his knowledge of mental health and learning disabilities. Sarah Burch and Bryan Wendon, true friends and colleagues, leapt in to help me at a very late stage, despite enormous workloads of their own.

Stephen Moore
August 2001

Introduction

This book provides a detailed and, I hope, dynamic introduction to the major issues regarding the provision of health and welfare in the UK and also to the criminal justice system.

It is intended to serve the needs of a variety of students who are specialising in social welfare or, more commonly, who are following a course which includes an examination of health, welfare and criminal justice.

When writing the book I tried to bear in mind the needs of students who were following professional courses, such as nurses and social workers, and aimed to provide them with the information which they would normally be expected to learn as part of their courses. I also spent some time examining undergraduate courses which contained an element of social policy – these including law, housing, health studies, public administration, economics and politics. It seemed to me that there are many modules where students are expected to gain an overview of the structure of the Welfare State and to have an understanding of some of the debates and problems facing health, welfare and criminal justice in the contemporary UK. I think that you will find that you will certainly have an adequate understanding of these issues by the time you finish this book.

There has been a rapid increase in vocational courses in social care in FE and recently an AS-level in Social Policy was introduced. Though I have not set out to cover the syllabuses as such, I have read all the syllabuses, and I have tried to incorporate as much relevant information and activities as I can. Anyone using this book will find much of relevance here and I would expect that using this book would certainly provide all necessary information for the social policy part of the syllabus.

The new Sociology A and AS syllabuses have substantially increased the amount of what I would term 'social policy' content, so debates on the poverty, the Welfare State, theories of welfare and criminal justice are all covered in considerable depth.

The range of this book, as can be seen from the chapter titles, is extensive, and I have attempted to cover most areas of relevance to the Welfare State. However, I have tried, successfully I hope, to combine breadth of coverage with the appropriate depth and, most importantly, to bring an interesting subject very much alive. You will find that this book contains information on the majority of the Acts and government commissions and also covers the wider social, economic and political contexts, as well as looking at what actually happens in the agencies which provide the welfare services.

However, most of all, I hope that you will find the book exciting and 'alive' as well as informative. Social policy is an extremely important and exciting subject with direct relevance to the life of every person in the UK. I hope that some of this dynamism and relevance emerges from the following pages.

Acknowledgements

The author and publishers wish to thank the following for permission to use copyright material:

- Philip Allan Updates for material from D Marsland, 'Face to Face', *The Social Studies Review* (Nov. 1989); B Jordan, 'Face to Face – The Case Against', *The Social Studies Review* (Nov.,1989); M Banton, 'The Culture of Poverty', *The Social Studies Review* (Jan.,1990), N Jewson, 'No Place Like Home', *The Social Studies Review* (March,1989) and S Arber, 'Class and the Elderly', *The Social Studies Review* (1989)
- Cambridge Newspapers Ltd for material from various editions of Cambridge Evening News
- Cambridge County Council for an extract from 'The County Budget Explained' (2001) and information forms from 'Charges for Services', Social Service Dept., CHAD 14, 19
- Causeway Press Ltd for figures, 'The Scottish Parliament' and 'The Welsh Assembly' from R Bentley et al, *British Politics in Focus*, 2nd. ed. (1999) p. 98
- Child Poverty Action Group for material from *Poverty: Journal of the Child Poverty Action Group*, Issues 106 and 107 (2000)
- The Editor of Community Care for material from 'Adoption facts', *Community Care* (10–16 August 2000), 'What life is like caring for Daniel', *Community Care*, (6–12 July, 2000), Moraz Minefield, 'Principles are one...', *Community Care*, (13–19 July, 2000), and Bob Holman, 'Charity should begin nearer home', (16–22 Sept., 1999)
- Equal Opportunities Commission for material from EOC Factshheet, pp. 4, 5
- Guardian Newspapers Ltd for material from various issues of *The Guardian/The Observer*. Copyright © The Guardian/The Observer
- Health Service Journal for material from 'Private Wings, Ruffled Feathers', *Health Service Journal*, (2 Nov., 2000)
- The Controller of HMSO and the Queen's Printer for Scotland for Crown copyright © material reproduced under Class Licence No: 001 W0000195
- The Independent for material from various issues of *The Independent*
- IPPR for data from J Micklewright, 'Child well-being and social cohesion', *New Economy*, 7:1 (2000) pp. 18-23
- JMH Publishing Ltd for material from Chris Ham. 'The Organisation of the NHS', pp. 7, 8, B Marsden, 'Financing the NHS', p. 117, 'Factfile', pp. 276, 280 in *Wellards NHS Handbook* (2000/2001)
- Claire Laurent for material from 'Putting gender on the management executive', *Health Service Journal*, 15.8.91
- Jayne Mooney for tables from *The North London Domestic Violence Survey*, Middlesex University (1993)
- National Association of Citizens Advice Bureau for an extract from 'Falling Short: The CAB Case for Housing Benefit Reform' (1999)
- The Policy Press for material from Philip Leather and Kerry Revell, *The State of UK Housing* (2000) Fig. 5.17, Table 5.2
- Policy Studies Institute for material from R Berthoud, 'Incomes and Standards of Living', Tables 5.2, 5.6, and J Nazroo, 'Health and Health Services', Table 7.1, in T Madood and R Berthoud, *Ethnic Minorities in Britain: Diversity and Disadvantage* (1997)
- ROOF, Shelter's Housing Magazine, for material by Louise Casey, *ROOF* (Jan./Feb. 2001) and S Lowe et al, 'Twilight Zones', *ROOF* (Jan./Feb. 1999)
- Routledge for material from J Mack and S Landsley, *Poor Britain* (1985); A Oakley and A. S Rigby, 'Are men good for the welfare of women and children', Table 4.7, in J Popay et al, eds., *Men, Gender Divisions and Welfare* (1998); and Jean Conway, *Housing Policy* (2000) Fig, 2.1 and p. 24, Gildridge Press (2000)

- Joseph Rowntree Foundation for 'A Modern Day Absolute Model of Poverty' from *Social Policy Findings*, 31 (Nov. 1992), and 'The changing population in social housing in England', *Housing Research,* 202 (Feb. 1997)

- Telegraph Group Ltd for material from Richard Downie, 'People with special needs 'live in fear'', *The Telegraph*, 21.6.99. Copyright © Telegraph Group Ltd 1999; 'Celia Hall, 'Concern over sterilization for handicapped', *The Telegraph*, 12.9.97. Copyright © Telegraph Group Ltd 1997; and Alice Thompson and Rachel Sylvester, 'Care in the Community is scrapped', *The Telegraph*, 17.1.98. Copyright © Telegraph Group Ltd 1998

- Times Newspapers Ltd for material from various issues of *The Sunday Times*. Copyright © Times Newspapers Ltd:

We are grateful to the following for permission to reproduce illustrations and for providing logos and other material:

- Bupa, advertisement (page 156)
- Hulton Picture Library, photos (pages 179 and 247)
- Plaid Cymru – The Party of Wales, logo (page 9)
- Robert Harding Picture Library, photos (pages 5 and 131)
- Rough Sleepers Unit, photo (page 128)
- The British Red Cross, leaflet (page 250)
- The Conservative Party, logo (page 8)
- The Department of Social Security, leaflet (page 356)
- The Family Holiday Association, Gift Aid leaflet (page 246)
- The Labour Party (New Labour), logo (page 8)
- The Liberal Democrats, logo (page 8)
- The National Council for Voluntary Organisations, logo (page 252)
- The Scottish National Party, logo (page 9)

Every effort has been made to trace the copyright holders but if any have been inadvertently overlooked the publishers will be pleased to make the necessary arrangement at the first opportunity.

Chapter 1

THE POLITICAL AND ADMINISTRATIVE CONTEXT

Chapter contents

- ### The European Union
  The European Union is becoming increasingly important in influencing and, in some cases, determining UK social policy. Any understanding of UK policies must therefore take the European Union into account.

- ### Devolved governments within the UK
  Perhaps the biggest shake-up in UK politics in recent years has been the formation of devolved governments. The power to decide social policies has now been handed over to the Scottish Parliament and there is considerable autonomy also for the Northern Ireland and Welsh Assemblies. We note the importance of this for the future.

- ### Central government
  For the bulk of the UK population, the central government at Westminster still retains the major powers of the State, and even the Scottish Parliament only has very limited tax-raising powers. Funding for social services and health, as well as all other areas of policy, lies in the hands of central government. We therefore explore the activities of central government.

- ### Political parties
  As we shall see in the rest of the book, there is no agreement on the way to organise and deliver social and health services – indeed there is bitter disagreement between political parties. In this part of the chapter we provide a very simple introduction to the differences between the parties.

- ### Local government
  Local government, by which we mean local authorities, play an important role in social services and social care. In this section we look at the role of social services and get a feel for the complex job they do.

- ### The policy-making process
  Most people are unaware of the policy-making process which influences the way that governments go about deciding which social policies should be followed and how they should be implemented. This section of the book provides a simple and clear understanding of this very complex issue.

Introduction

Health and welfare in the UK are still largely provided by and within a framework devised and controlled by the State. It is the government that pays for social security benefits, the National Health Service (NHS) and the personal social services. The government also provides the bulk of the funds for the voluntary organisations and, through the local authorities, it sets down standards of care in the private sector.

When the government chooses new policies it has an impact on all our lives. The government may decide to provide more or fewer health services, higher or lower social security benefits or pensions. It may decide to raise taxes or lower them, and to do so in such a way that poorer or richer people benefit. Indeed it is impossible to separate politics and administration from the actual provision of health and welfare in the UK.

In this opening chapter we need to gain a simple, but clear understanding of the main structure of the UK State within which social policy takes place. The differences between the main tiers of government and the roles they play in decision-making is made clear, as is the policy-making process.

We begin by looking at the four tiers of government which are of interest to us:

- the European Union (EU)
- the devolved governments of Northern Ireland, Scotland and Wales
- the central government of Westminster
- local government.

The European Union

The EU has become increasingly important. It has general powers which relate to issues such as equality of treatment of men and women and different ethnic groups, health and safety, the provision of employment and health and welfare benefits across national boundaries.

In 1997 the Labour government signed the Social Chapter of the Maastricht Treaty which introduced a range of workers' rights and was closely linked to the introduction of a minimum wage. Eventually, most observers believe that welfare and social security provision will develop along similar lines right across Europe, as economic policies become closer.

A second major influence on UK policies has been the Human Rights Act of 1998, which makes the European Convention on Human Rights part of UK law. As it only came into effect in 2000, it is too early to list the changes that are taking place. However, the Act guarantees many rights which could influence the quality of health, welfare and legal services in the UK.

The European Union is discussed in detail in Chapter 11.

Devolved governments within the UK

Definitions

Referendum – when voters are asked to decide on a particular issue (usually of great constitutional importance)

Autonomy – freedom to make decisions and act

Devolved – refers to the fact that the Welsh, Scottish and Northern Ireland governments have been granted their own power to make decisions on wide areas of policy

As a result of **referendums** held in 1997, Scotland and Wales acquired their own governments. Scotland's is more powerful and has greater **autonomy** than that of Wales. The difference is perhaps best illustrated by the fact that Wales has an elected *assembly*, but Scotland has an elected *parliament*.

Scotland

Although Westminster retains control over foreign affairs and defence, much else was passed over to the Scottish Parliament to run. Central government provides a block grant to cover most services, and then the Scottish Parliament can add to this if they wish by raising additional taxes in Scotland. How the money is spent is determined by the Scottish government.

As Scotland already had different approaches to health, welfare, education and criminal justice, there should be an ever-increasing gap growing between England and Wales, and Scotland. Indeed within only a couple of years of its existence, two huge differences emerged regarding health and welfare:

- In England and Wales care (as opposed to health care) of older, infirm people has to be paid for by the older people themselves, in the first instance. In

Scotland, the government has said that it will pay for care for all Scottish infirm older people.

- In England and Wales, university students must pay tuition fees, but in Scotland Scottish students do not have to pay fees.

The Scottish Parliament

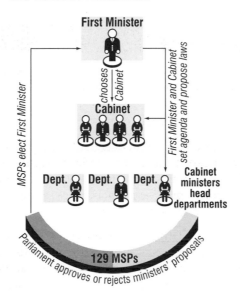

The Welsh Assembly

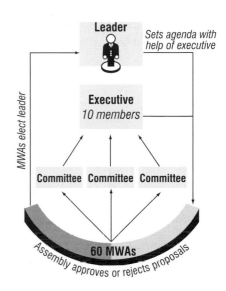

Source: Redrawn from R. Bentley *et al.*, *British Politics in Focus*, 2nd edition (Causeway Press, 1999)

Wales

The Welsh Assembly has much less power than the Scottish Parliament and is not able to vary income tax, as the Scottish Parliament can. Nevertheless, it does have some powers to vary the provision of health, education and welfare services.

Northern Ireland

The Northern Ireland Assembly has considerable powers over internal affairs, though because of the sensitive political situation there, a number of particular security and policing issues make it unusual. However, it does have power over the areas of social policy discussed in this book.

Central government

This is nationally elected, based in Westminster and it sets the laws of the country. It sets the levels of taxes in England, Wales and Northern Ireland (whilst Scotland can vary income tax levels slightly) and determines what is spent on health and welfare in England and Wales. It also determines the broad policy of all the departments dealing with the welfare and health of the population in England and Wales. It provides funding for the devolved governments of Scotland, Northern Ireland and Wales.

The UK government and administration

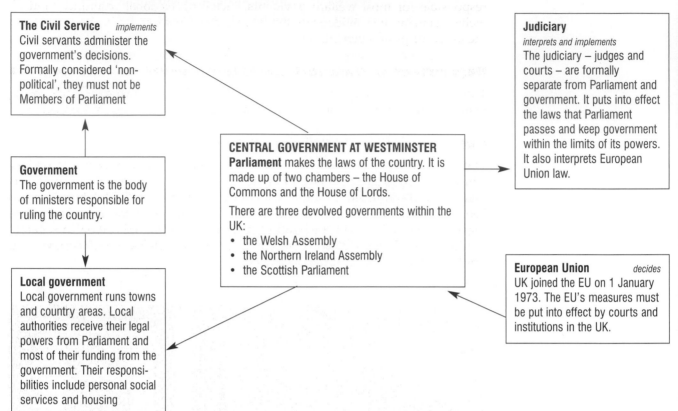

The Civil Service   *implements*
Civil servants administer the government's decisions. Formally considered 'non-political', they must not be Members of Parliament

Government
The government is the body of ministers responsible for ruling the country.

Local government
Local government runs towns and country areas. Local authorities receive their legal powers from Parliament and most of their funding from the government. Their responsibilities include personal social services and housing

CENTRAL GOVERNMENT AT WESTMINSTER
Parliament makes the laws of the country. It is made up of two chambers – the House of Commons and the House of Lords.
There are three devolved governments within the UK:
• the Welsh Assembly
• the Northern Ireland Assembly
• the Scottish Parliament

Judiciary
interprets and implements
The judiciary – judges and courts – are formally separate from Parliament and government. It puts into effect the laws that Parliament passes and keep government within the limits of its powers. It also interprets European Union law.

European Union   *decides*
UK joined the EU on 1 January 1973. The EU's measures must be put into effect by courts and institutions in the UK.

1   Which two chambers are there in Parliament?

2   What two parliaments are there in the United Kingdom?

3   Which bodies make the laws?

4   Why is local government important to welfare?

5   What is the role of the judiciary (courts and legal system)?

6   Does any political organisation have legal power to tell the British Parliament what to do?

Central government departments affecting health, welfare and criminal justice

Department of Health

The Department of Health (DoH) is responsible for all health matters. This involves making policy, and carrying out the administration of the health services and the personal social services.

• The health services are run by the NHS Executive through the NHS authorities, and the actual provision of services by the trusts (see Chapter 6).

• The personal social services are also controlled and monitored by the Department of Health, though they are actually run by local authorities who provide the services.

Department of Work and Pensions

This department, formerly known as the Department of Social Security (DSS), is responsible for most welfare payments, including National Insurance, and all welfare benefits. It is divided into two agencies — one for collecting payments and the other for paying benefits.

Department of Transport, Local Government and the Regions

This department is responsible for the control of local government, for housing matters and for many planning issues, particularly inner-city redevelopment.

Department for Education and Skills

The Department for Education and Skills is responsible for primary and secondary education, and for the overview of higher education. Traditionally, education was financed and controlled through local education authorities (LEAs), but there has been a considerable erosion of the powers and duties of the local authorities regarding education, with the shift of higher and further education to separate funding councils and the growth of grant-maintained schools, which receive their funding directly from central government.

The Treasury building (left – see page 6) is in Whitehall, London. Number 10 Downing Street (right) is the official residence of the prime minister, who leads the Cabinet (see below).

The Home Office

This department is responsible for law and order, covering such areas as the police, the judiciary, probation and prisons. It is also responsible for immigration issues, citizenship and race relations legislation. The Home Office also has responsibilities for some inner-city programmes and for government co-ordination with the voluntary social services and private agencies. Finally, it is responsible for combating the illegal use of drugs.

The Cabinet

The Cabinet consists of the ministers responsible for the departments shown in the diagram on page 6, plus a number of other senior political figures (approximately ten). All these Cabinet members have a say in the decisions of the government in areas of health and welfare. Policies are not just the decisions of the ministers responsible for individual departments.

The Treasury

The Treasury is the department responsible for looking after the finances of the State. In many ways this is the most important department of government. It is here that the amount of money that can be spent on health and welfare is decided. The person most closely involved in controlling public spending on the health and welfare services is the Chief Secretary to the Treasury, who is responsible only to the Chancellor of the Exchequer.

Each year ministers meet the Chancellor and the Chief Secretary to make their bids for spending, and after considerable discussion (in what is known as the Public Expenditure Survey Committee) the government expenditure plans are announced. These give the budget within which each department must then carry out its programmes.

Central government departments

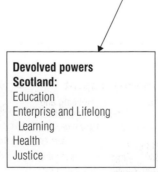

Central government

Home Office: Police, judiciary, race, immigration

Treasury: Finances all services and maintains budgetary controls

Work and Pensions: Welfare, benefits

Health: Health services, personal social services

Transport, Local Government and the Regions: Local government, housing

Education and Skills: Education, educational welfare, training

Foreign Office

Defence

Energy

Environment, Food and Rural Affairs

Trade and Industry

Culture, Media and Sport

International Development

UK departments most closely connected with areas of health and welfare

**Devolved powers
Scotland:**
Education
Enterprise and Lifelong
  Learning
Health
Justice

**Devolved powers
Wales:**
Education and Training
Health
Social Care
Crime Reduction

1 Which department is responsible for social work? Does it do this through any other agency or tier of government?

2 Which department is responsible for local government?

3 Which department gives out welfare benefits?

4 Which department determines the amount of money to be spent on health and welfare services?

The legislative process

The diagram below shows the stages that occur for an issue to develop into a government concern and finally to emerge as law.

First issues arise which the public become concerned about, usually this is the result of a public scandal, of a pressure group (see page 13) or reports in the media. Central government or the devolved governments will then seek to do something about it. Often various consultation documents are drawn up (called Green Papers) and after further discussions, a White Paper is then devised which provides the basis for a proposed law (known as a bill) which is presented to the parliament. After much debate, and if agreed, the bill is passed into law and becomes an Act of Parliament.

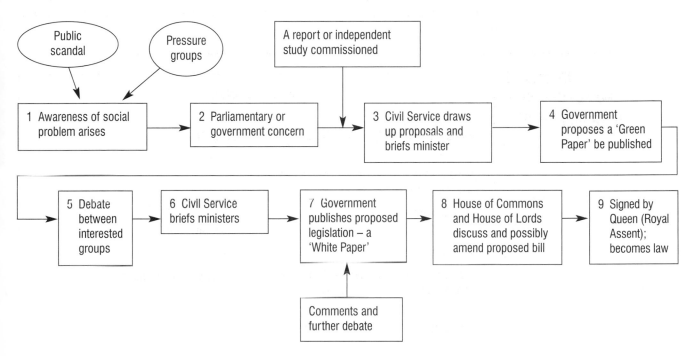

Go to the website www.doh.gov.uk and click on 'Publications'. What information can you find about White Papers and any government Acts relevant to the NHS? Can you find similar information for any other government department?

Government finance: sources and spending

These pie charts show government spending and the sources of government income planned for 2001 from the March 2000 Budget.

A Where taxpayers' money is spent

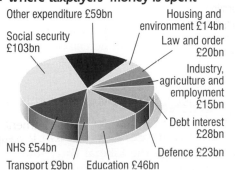

B Where taxes come from

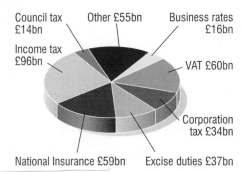

Source: HM Treasury, March 2000 Budget, www.hm-treasury.gov.uk/budget 2000

Look at **A**

1 What was the planned single biggest item of government expenditure in 2001?

2 What was the second biggest?

3 What was the projected total amount spent on health and welfare (social security, NHS, law and order)?

4 What proportion of total government expenditure does this comprise?

5 When people argue that health and welfare provision has little to do with politics and government, what reply do these figures suggest?

But, of course, the government has no money of its own, whatever it spends it takes from the population as taxes.

Look at **B**

6 Which is the single biggest source of taxes?

7 What is the second highest source of taxation?

8 Personal taxes can be divided into two main types:
- progressive – you pay more the more you earn
- regressive – fixed rates of tax which everyone must pay.

It is usually true to say that poorer people are hit harder by regressive taxes, and richer people by progressive taxes. Identify at least one example of each sort of tax in the pie chart.

Political parties

The Conservative Party

The Conservative Party is generally agreed to stand for free enterprise – that is the government should interfere as little as possible in the running of business and commerce. This idea of interfering as little as possible is also applied to the areas of health and welfare. The Conservative Party does support the Welfare State, but prefers the idea that people should look after themselves where possible, only falling back on the State when they, or their family, can no longer cope.

The Labour Party (New Labour)

The Labour Party is more closely associated with concerns over health, welfare and education in the eyes of the public. It accepts the existence of free enterprise, and indeed promotes it, but sees the government as having a greater role in monitoring and intervening in the economy than the Conservative Party does. The aim of this intervention is to bring about a greater degree of 'fairness' in terms of limiting the extremes of inequality in society.

'New Labour', first voted into power in 1997, has rather different views on the provision of health and welfare than previous Labour administrations. Although it supports the idea of a comprehensive Welfare State, it also believes that people have to make some degree of provision for themselves, if they can afford it, and it is not opposed to private, commercial companies being involved in health, welfare and criminal justice.

Liberal Democrats

The Liberal Democrats are the smallest of the three major parties. The party was formed in 1991, when the Liberal Party and the Social Democrats merged. The Liberal Party was last in government in 1915.

The Liberal Democrats also accept the importance of the State in controlling free enterprise, and are the only one of the main parties to advocate raising the level of income tax to provide higher levels of funding for education and health. They strongly support the existence of the NHS.

Scottish Nationalists (SNP)

The Scottish Nationalists were formed to press for Scottish independence from the rest of the UK. They see the devolved parliament in Scotland as a first step towards that aim. The party is extremely important in Scottish politics and has generally argued for higher taxes to fund better quality services. It pushed through the legislation which means that Scottish university students pay no fees and that old, infirm people do not have to pay for care – unlike in the rest of the UK.

Plaid Cymru – The Party of Wales

They have pressed for full self-government, but there is much less sympathy in Wales for this, so they are not as politically strong as the Scottish Nationalists. Plaid Cymru is the main opposition in the National Assembly for Wales.

Main points

- There are four tiers of government which influence social policies – the EU, central government, devolved governments and local authorities.
- The devolved governments are in Wales, Scotland and Northern Ireland.
- The central government is the most powerful, though the EU and the devolved governments are increasing in their influence.
- There are a number of government departments which are of particular importance for social policy. They include Health, Work and Pensions, the Home Office and the Treasury.
- The main political parties are Labour, Conservative, Liberal Democrats, the Scottish Nationalists and the Welsh Nationalists.

Local government

An understanding of local government is important in the study of welfare provision. For example, social services departments (which employ social workers) are run by local authorities who also manage and provide housing, administer housing benefits and are responsible for crime prevention strategies.

Local government consists of county councils, unitary authorities and district councils. They have powers given to them by central government and devolved governments. The money they have to spend is determined by Westminster (in England and Wales) or the Scottish Parliament, although they levy a local tax (council tax) to help pay for the services they provide.

Over the last 20 years, local government has lost a great deal of its autonomy and increasingly has been by-passed by central government. Local authorities used to have a great influence on the provision of health care, but this has now gone, as has much of its influence over policing. In fact, before the reforms of health and welfare in the 1940s, when the NHS and the social security system were introduced, virtually all health and welfare was provided by local government, and it wasn't until the 1980s, that local authorities began to lose their powers over housing.

A typical local authority organisational structure

Chief Executive's Unit

Stimulate partnership working inside and outside the Council, promote policy formulation, review performance and advise on the authority's forward direction

Environment and Transport Directorate

Work for an economically prosperous and environmentally sustainable county

Education, Libraries and Heritage

Promote and enable life-long learning opportunities for all the local citizens

Social Services

Secure social care, support and protection for people in need

Resources Directorate

Provide the support and resources necessary to achieve the Council's objectives and ensure the highest quality of practice throughout the authority

Fire and Rescue

Provide public protection and safety for people living, working and visiting the county

Commercial Services Board

← **Finance, IT, Property, Personnel** →

1 Arrange a visit to your local authority. Before going, draw up a list of questions to find out what services it is responsible for – focusing in particular on responsibilities for welfare services. If you cannot visit, then send off for an information pack to find out the answers to your questions or visit their website.

2 Have any local authorities any health functions?

3 Have local authorities control of policing, the courts or probation matters?

4 Do local authorities have any power over youth offending and crime prevention?

5 Find out how the finances of your local authority are organised and how much it spends on various services.

6 Depending on where you live, you may have access to a number of different councils (or you could go to the website of as many local authorities as you wish). Find out their different spending patterns and priorities.

7 Draw up a plan of the decision-making and executive structure of your local council. Do a particularly detailed one for the social services.

Changes in local government

Local government has undergone massive changes in the last thirty years, and looks set for more changes again in the near future, with the introduction of elected mayors running local authorities with a small 'cabinet' of councillors.

However, few people realise just how powerful and important local authorities used to be when it came to the provision of welfare. Historically, local government was truly local with small towns and boroughs having a wide range of powers available to them, and they used these to provide hospitals, houses, social workers, police officers and probation services. These were largely funded by local taxes.

Since 1974, there has been a gradual loss of powers and financial independence, as successive governments at Westminster tried to impose their authority on local governments.

Activity

In your local library there is sure to be a book on the history of your area, and there is probably one on the history of the council (often the council itself will produce this). Find out the changes that have taken place over the last 100 years, and the changes in the services that the council has provided – you may be surprised.

The relationship between local and central government

There are three main ways in which local government can be made to comply with the wishes of central government: advice, finance and law.

Advice

Central government departments will send 'circulars' which advise the local authorities of what they should do. These do not carry the force of law, and so local authorities will interpret them according to the views of their councillors.

Finance

This is the power most commonly used by central government. The government can send in auditors to see that the money is being spent according to the government's wishes, or they can actually control the amount of money borrowed by a local authority (as local authorities often need to borrow to finance particular projects, this is a powerful weapon).

The greatest power of all is the fact that about 80 per cent of local authority spending comes directly from the government in the form of 'government general grant', which is related to the amount of money that central government thinks a particular local authority needs (called the standard spending assessment). Local authorities are therefore very tightly controlled financially.

Local authorities also raise money through the council tax, which every household pays. Central government has the power to 'cap' this.

Law

Central government can introduce laws which simply require a local authority to act in a particular way. An example of this was the introduction and subsequent withdrawal of the community charge or 'poll tax' in England and Wales in the early 1990s. Although many local authorities were unhappy about the tax, they were forced by law to collect it and administer it on behalf of the central government.

Local government: levels and tasks

The table below shows the activities of the three levels or 'tiers' of local government.

County councils	Unitary authorities	District councils
Education[1]	District responsibilities, plus:	Housing
Personal social services	Education[1]	Environmental health
Libraries	Libraries	Local planning
Planning	Personal social services	Local parks
Highways, and traffic co-ordination		Refuse
Police		
Fire		

Note: 1 Government policies to give schools control over their own budgets (LMS) and the right to opt out of grant-maintained status means that local authorities' role in education is diminishing.

Powers of local authorities

The table above shows the different functions of the local authorities. You can see they include a wide range of duties relevant to the area of health and welfare. The most obvious are the personal social services, housing and the police. However, some local authorities may provide other services as well, for example leisure facilities, community centres, housing advice centres and transport services. Whether they provide these other services or not depends largely on the political views of the council and the financial ability to provide the services.

Local authorities therefore have two types of powers to get things done – duty and permissive power.

Duty

Duty is imposed on local authorities by laws requiring them to provide particular services. For example, community care legislation in 1990 imposed the duty on local authorities to draw up plans and provide care in the community.

Permissive power

Permissive power allows local authorities to initiate activities within certain areas. It is often the activities carried out under these powers that distinguish one authority from another. Some authorities will provide a range of leisure and youth facilities for example, while others may not see this as the best way to spend council tax budgets and may prefer to put more money into schools, the fire service or education.

Local authority spending

Local authority expenditure planned for 2001, main services

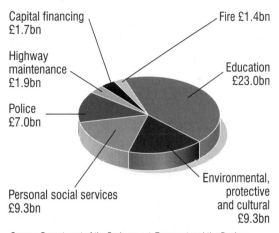

Capital financing £1.7bn

Fire £1.4bn

Highway maintenance £1.9bn

Education £23.0bn

Police £7.0bn

Personal social services £9.3bn

Environmental, protective and cultural £9.3bn

Source: Department of the Environment, Transport and the Regions

Source: *Britain 2001: The Official Guide* (The Stationery Office, 2001)

The pie chart shows just how important local authorities are in providing services for the population.

1 What was the total planned spending by local authorities for 2001?

2 What was the single biggest item of planned expenditure?

3 How much did they plan to spend on social services?

The work of one local authority social services department

Social Services
- Caring for thousands of people every day
- Protecting young people from abuse, neglect and harm
- Ensuring older people and those with disabilities receive the care they need
- Providing 800,000 hours of home care and 400,000 meals

- Providing nearly £1 million of support to voluntary organisations

It costs £12.7 million a year to provide care at home for 3,000 frail, elderly people

Source: *The County Budget Explained* (Cambridgeshire County Council, 2001)

What functions do the social services perform?

The policy-making process

Health and welfare programmes are determined by the government. However, in making their decisions and determining which policies to follow and how to spend their money, a process of policy-making and implementation is followed. The most important element influencing the decisions of government is the activity of **pressure groups**.

Definition

Pressure groups – organisations representing a particular group or viewpoint which seek to influence policy–makers

Pressure groups

The diagram on page 7 shows the importance of pressure groups in the political process in the UK. Pressure groups play the crucial role of bringing issues to the attention of the decision-makers in society. The problems raised are then addressed throughout the normal political process, as illustrated in the diagram. But even when this process is in full flow, pressure groups maintain interest and try to ensure that their viewpoint becomes law.

Types of pressure group

There are two types of pressure group:

- those which *defend* their own interests known as protective, defensive or self-regarding pressure groups, for example, in the field of health and welfare, the British Medical Association (BMA)
- those which *promote* new initiatives which they claim will improve society, or at least will improve the conditions of a particularly vulnerable group, known as promotional or pressure groups, for example the Child Poverty Action Group (CPAG).

Pressure groups are not political parties, and usually represent only one particular group or cause. They try to persuade whoever is in power to introduce or amend legislation, and rarely seek power themselves.

1 Find out what type of pressure group the following organisations are:
   a) British Association of Social Workers
   b) Howard League for Penal Reform
   c) Shelter
   d) Royal College of Nursing
   e) Royal College of Physicians
   f) Mencap
   g) Help the Aged.

2 Find out about three pressure groups operating in the area of health and welfare. Write a brief outline of their aims and activities.

How do pressure groups influence decision-makers?

There are a number of ways in which pressure groups try to influence those in power.

- **Lobbying in parliament** This involves sending representatives to discuss issues with MPs to try to persuade them of the truth of their particular argument. There are professional lobbying organisations which, for a fee, represent particular companies and interests.
- **Publicity** If you examine a quality newspaper today, you are certain to find the influence of pressure groups. Many stories which appear in the newspapers and on the television reflect the views of pressure groups which hope to galvanise the public and the decision-makers into awareness of a particular problem.
- **Direct protest** Where groups have little power and influence they may turn to the last resort, which is public protest. Public marches and demonstrations attempt to attract the attention of the media. Physically disabled people have been forced to use demonstrations in order to attract attention to their lack of rights and the way they are excluded from society.

Influencing policy

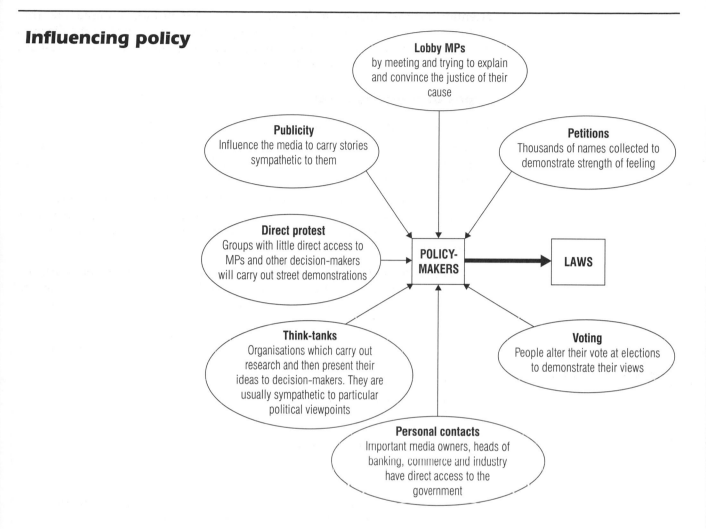

Main points

▶ Local authorities have the task of delivering much of the social care and social services rather than making policy.

▶ Local government has lost most of its autonomy in the last thirty years and is controlled by central government.

▶ Pressure groups are crucial for the policy-making process and strongly influence how decisions are made.

Conclusion

In this chapter we have gained a clear, if simple, overview of the political context in which health and social care policy is made and delivered. We have seen that different tiers of government exist and that they have different influences on the political decisions. Furthermore, we have seen that political parties differ over which policies should be introduced and which policies are effective in solving social problems. Indeed, they disagree over what are social problems. Finally, we have seen the process through which issues are raised and eventually turned into law.

1 CHAPTER SUMMARY

1   There are four tiers of government which influence social policies: the EU, central government, devolved governments and local authorities.

2   The devolved governments are in Wales, Scotland and Northern Ireland.

3   The central government is the most powerful, though the EU and the devolved governments are increasing in their influence.

4   There are a number of government departments which are of particular importance for social policy. They include Health, Work and Pensions, the Home Office and the Treasury.

5   The main political parties are Labour, Conservative, Liberal Democrats, the Scottish Nationalists and the Welsh Nationalists.

6   Local authorities have the task of delivering much of the social care and social services rather than making policy.

7   Local government has lost most of its autonomy in the last thirty years and is controlled by central government.

8   Pressure groups are crucial for the policy-making process and strongly influence how decisions are made.

Useful websites

www.scotland.gov.uk

www.wales.gov.uk

www.nisra.gov.uk: Northern Ireland Statistics and Research Agency

www.parliament.uk: the UK Parliament

www.open.gov.uk: UK government information

www.hm-treasury.gov.uk: the UK government Treasury

www.labour.org.uk: the Labour Party

www.conservatives.org.uk: the Conservative Party

www.libdems.org.uk: the Liberal Democrat Party

www.lga.gov.uk: the Local Government Association

Chapter 2

THEORIES OF SOCIAL POLICY

Chapter contents

Introduction

If you present a group of people with a complex problem, of any kind, and ask them to solve it, they will almost always set about solving it in a variety of different ways. There is rarely any single 'correct' way of solving a problem. It is exactly the same when it comes to the issues concerning welfare and health provision; there is no agreement on one 'right' way of ensuring that people receive the best health and welfare services.

Different solutions to the social problems tackled by the health and welfare services have been suggested by the competing political parties, by various academics and by a range of practitioners and professionals. The result is that a series of different 'packages of ideas' have been put forward, which claim to:

- interpret the problems
- provide answers to them.

These packages of ideas are known as *theories of social policy*.

Activity

Values and debates in social policy
The following are examples of the kinds of value/moral issue which are debated in social policy. Think through the reasons you would provide for your choice of answer in each case. Each of the theories in this chapter will provide you with differing replies to each question.

1 Which policy option should the government choose?
   A *Reduce* taxation and spend *less* on health and welfare provision (with the money people saved by lower taxes, they could be encouraged to buy their own private insurance, and the very poorest might be provided with free services).
   B *Increase* taxation and spend *more* on health and welfare provision.

2 If you had to prioritise government spending, how would you rank the following?
   Benefits for lone parents
   Reintroduction of student grants
   Retirement pensions
   Increased spending on schools
   Benefits for the unemployed
   Child Benefit for all families with children
   Increased spending on the NHS
   Benefits for disabled people
   Increased provision of social housing

3 Private medical treatment should be:
   A Abolished in all hospitals
   B Allowed in private hospitals only
   C Allowed in all hospitals

4 Do you agree or disagree with the following statements?
   - The Welfare State makes people less likely to look after themselves.
   - The Welfare State discourages people from helping one another.
   - Social security benefits make people feel like second-class citizens
   - Many people who receive social security don't really deserve help.
   - Social security benefits are too low and cause hardship.

Over time a number of theoretical approaches to social policy have emerged. These include:

- the New Right approach
- the social democratic approach
- the radical socialist approach
- the feminist approach

- the anti-racist approach
- environmentalism
- the Third Way.

The theories: a clear introduction

- **The New Right** argues that State services are inefficient and oppressive; it is much better to provide welfare through the market, by the family or through charity. Markets offer choice and encourage independence and self-reliance, and this allows people to pursue their own interests without the 'nanny state' interfering in their lives.

  New Right thinking was central to the policies of the UK Conservative governments of 1979–97, and also was influential in criticising Social Democracy and therefore encouraging the development of the new political programme called the 'Third Way'.
- **Social democracy** is a broad political movement containing several different strands. However, all of these agree that the capitalist economic and social system has many flaws and requires reform. Greater government involvement is required to regulate the economy and tackle social problems such as poverty and unemployment. It is closely linked with the traditional approach of the Labour Party
- **Radical socialism/Marxism** Until the early 1990s these were very influential theories and, although they may be less high profile than they used to be, they remain important and influential theories in social policy and social science generally. Marxists believe that the State should take complete control over industry and commerce, and should provide health and welfare as necessary.
- **Feminism** has had a very significant impact on social theory and public life since its 'second wave' emerged in the 1960s (the 'first wave' was the suffragette movement around the turn of the nineteenth/twentieth centuries).

  Feminists challenge many of the assumptions of other theories and perspectives, arguing that these are based on an unrepresentative male-dominated picture of the world.
- **Anti-racism** Like feminism, anti-racism focuses attention on a neglected issue in social policy. There is a considerable amount of evidence which shows that ethnic minorities in the UK (and in many other societies) are disadvantaged and treated unfairly. Anti-racists argue that this comes about through racist practices and attitudes which must be examined and challenged. These practices even exist within the Welfare State, and are not properly dealt with by standard policies of integration or multiculturalism. Anti-racists believe that a full-scale attack on institutional racism is required to tackle these problems.
- **Environmentalism/Greenism** The environmentalist movement has a rather different agenda from most other social theories and perspectives. Environmentalists argue that existing ideologies have led to a situation where the very future of the planet is in doubt and therefore a major rethink of our priorities is required. Instead of more economic development, environmentalist argue that we should be aiming for sustainability and protection of our fragile eco-system. This may mean that assumptions about economic and technological progress are questioned, and a more holistic idea of human welfare is developed – one which sees humans as members of a wider natural environment upon which we depend and which we must protect.
- **The 'Third Way'** is the most recent perspective to have an impact on the theory of social policy. This is the term used by the New Labour government to describe its outlook and to contrast its approach from old fashioned social democracy and also the New Right. Although not a fully developed social theory, it is possible that the Third Way may become an influential outlook in social policy in the future.

Each of the approaches described above claims that its analysis of society is more accurate than that of the others, and, furthermore, that putting into action the policies that it recommends will reduce or possibly eliminate social problems.

Before we move on to examine these approaches, we ought to be aware that there are others and, even more confusingly, different names for the same approaches!

However, if you understand the seven categories included here, you will be able to make sense of all the others you may encounter in your further reading.

The New Right approach

This approach to social problems is also known as market liberal, neo-conservative or anti-collectivist. It became very influential in the Conservative Party from the 1980s onward. Although it is called the *New* Right, many of its ideas are very old indeed. Some of its key ideas are described below.

The market

There is no need for the government to intervene in business and commerce. Indeed, by interfering it will actually cause harm. Businessmen know what they are doing, and if they are good, they will be successful. However, if they are bad, they will fail to make a profit and go bankrupt. When it comes to issues like the prices they charge or the levels of wages they pay, these will be determined by the consumers (for prices), who will decide if they think the goods are worth purchasing, and by the workers (for wages), who will decide if it is worth working for these salaries. The only time the government should intervene is if there is a monopoly, where one company becomes so large that it is effectively the only supplier of a particular article or service, and as a result may increase prices to any level it wishes.

> **Definition**
>
> **The market/market economy** – based on the idea of a marketplace or auction where the price of something is determined by what people are willing to pay. But some people have much more money than others to buy things

The result of having a **market economy**, as described above, is great inequality between the successful and the unsuccessful, because some people are successful and others are not.

The importance of the belief in the **market** is shown in the health care and community care reforms first brought in during the 1990s, which created a division between those who bought services on behalf of the public, and those who provided them. The reforms were intended to create an artificial market to increase efficiency.

Rational (wo)man

The New Right argues that everyone makes free choices according to what they think is right for them. Whatever the outcome, the person must accept it. It is similar to the saying that if you make your bed then you must lie in it. This is very important in welfare debates, for it suggests that people have no automatic *right* to welfare, whether they are unemployed, poor or a single parent they made the choice not to save for old age, they did not work hard enough to get out of poverty, they made the choice to have a child. This is important in that people are expected to plan for their old age and the possibility of illness or unemployment. Since the 1980s, both Conservative and New Labour have encouraged private pensions and have insisted that older people must pay for their own care, rather than relying upon the State.

The deserving and the undeserving

This point follows from the idea of rational (wo)man. Some people may be poor or in difficulties through no fault of their own, for example, people who are disabled or who have learning difficulties. In these cases, the New Right believes that help should be given.

However, when it comes to groups who are fit and well, such as the young unemployed, then it is argued that their situation is their own fault, and that if they tried harder they would get work of some kind. So the New Right believe no welfare provision should be given.

This has been important in affecting beliefs about health and welfare since the 1980s as successive governments have sought to distinguish those people who were less deserving of help, from those 'genuinely in need'. An example of this was the legislation in 1996 to take away the automatic right of lone-parent families to go to the head of the queue for social housing.

The case against the Welfare State

Most of the present welfare programmes should never have been enacted. If they had not been, many of the people now dependent on them would have become self-reliant individuals instead of wards of state. In the short run, that might have appeared cruel for some, leaving them no option to low-paying, unattractive work. But in the long run, it would have been far more humane …

The heart of the liberal philosophy is a belief in the dignity of the individual in his freedom to make the most of his capacities and opportunities subject only to the proviso that he does not interfere with the freedom of other individuals to do the same. Government action can never duplicate the variety and diversity of individual action. At any moment in time, by imposing uniform standards in housing, or nutrition, or clothing, government could undoubtedly improve the level of living of many individuals … But in the process, government would replace progress by stagnation, it would substitute uniform mediocrity for variety.

Source: M. Friedman and R. Friedman, *Free to Choose* (Secker & Warburg, 1980)

1 In your own words explain what would have happened if there had been no Welfare State?

2 In the main text we discuss the idea of the rational man or woman. Does this idea appear in other words in this extract?

3 Explain why government action is bad.

The family

The family plays an important part in New Right thinking about welfare. Family members owe a duty to help each other, and it is *not* the job of the State to help those who are family members. The State should only step in when there is no one to care for a particular person. This is very important when we look at issues concerning community care or the care of older and disabled people.

The New Right argues that the more the State has provided assistance and support for people who are sick, unemployed and old, the less the family has taken the responsibility seriously. Indeed one of the reasons for the decline in the family, they argue, is the increase in the role of the State in caring for people.

Charity

A good society is one in which people offer to help others, for no benefit to themselves. The more the State intervenes, the less place there is for voluntary and charity work. Charity is important as it helps hold society together by crossing the boundaries of family and class. In fact, charity work helps communities to cohere, in much the same way as the family does. Therefore the State should have very few welfare and health services and should only provide a *safety net* for those who are unable to obtain any help.

According to supporters of the New Right approach, when the State does step in, not only does it destroy charity, it also prevent people making the choice about which group of disadvantaged people they wish to help. The State makes that decision on people's behalf, and it may not be to their liking.

Dependency

> ## Definition
>
> **Dependency culture** – refers to people who prefer living off the State benefit system than working

The more the State helps some people or groups, the less they will help themselves, and eventually they will fall into a state of dependency where they will not even try to achieve anything. This situation is known as a **dependency culture**. This is closely linked in their eyes with the growth of the 'underclass' and the continuation of poverty.

The New Right argues that the only way to reduce the extent of poverty is to break the culture of dependency – by refusing benefits to those who could work if they wanted to, but prefer to live on State benefits instead.

Implications of the New Right health and welfare policies

Targeting and means testing

> ## Definition
>
> **Targeting or means testing** – people who want State services or benefits have to pass form of test to show that they deserve the service. The argument is that this targets welfare on the most deserving

Only those in real need ought to get welfare support and free health services; the rest should pay. The only way to distinguish those in need is by giving a test of income (or sometimes of disability) – a **means test**. The fewer people receiving benefit the better. Health and welfare services need to be **targeted** at those in need, and this can be achieved by setting out strict criteria as to who is eligible for any benefit.

Residual system of welfare

Linked to the ideas above of targeting and means testing is the belief that, as far as possible, there should be a private system of health and welfare, with the State only providing a 'safety-net' set of services. The State should provide absolute minimum standards and act as a safety net for those who have nowhere else to turn. The standards must be low to ensure that, given a choice, people will always prefer the private provision of welfare.

> ## Definitions
>
> **Residual welfare system** – health and welfare are provided for only the very poorest, and even then it is of the most basic standard. Everyone else should save or take out insurance
>
> **Mixed economy of welfare** – that welfare should be provided both by private companies (for profit) and by the State.

Private or mixed economy of welfare

They suggest that ideally the Welfare State should be abolished and should be replaced by privately-provided welfare. The argument is that commercial companies are efficient and can achieve better standards than the State can.

However, as this may not be realistic, they suggest that wherever possible the State should not provide services, unless there is no possibility of profit for private companies, or where a charity cannot undertake the task.

The term **mixed economy of welfare** refers to this mixture of State, voluntary and commercial provision.

Activity   Look at the questions in the activity on page 18. How would supporters of the New Right answer the questions?

Main points ▶ The New Right approach is also known as neo-conservative, market liberal or anti-collectivist.

▶ It has been very influential within the Conservative Party in particular.

▶ It believes that business should be left alone to get on with its job. Government interference harms society.

▶ People make their own decisions and should live by their success or failure.

▶ Some people who are poor are deserving, most are not.

▶ The family is the place for people to turn for help.

▶ If that fails it should be charity.

▶ There are many people who have learned to be dependent on the State.

▶ The Welfare State should be chopped back and replaced with a residual version for those few deserving poor.

▶ Private companies should be involved in delivering health and welfare and people should buy their own insurance to cover themselves against risk.

The social democratic approach

The introduction of the Welfare State came about largely through the activities of the social democrats. This approach sees the Welfare State as central to society, acting as the cement which holds it together. It is generally associated with the Labour Party, but some Conservatives and all Liberal Democrats subscribe to the general approach.

The ideas they all share are that the government should ensure the *right* of every British citizen to be free from poverty, and that they should receive health care according to need, not on the basis of their ability to pay. The causes of poverty and other social problems lie in the fact that modern society creates 'victims' – the unemployed, those with disabilities unable to compete in jobs, and those who suffer from long-term illnesses. It is the duty of society to protect and look after these people.

The ideas underlying the social democratic approach are the basis of the Welfare State, since its founding in the 1940s.

Centralised government provision of welfare

Many of the early social democrats (and in particular an influential movement within social democracy known as Fabianism) were rather **elitist and paternalistic**. This means that they believed in the ability of experts to determine what needed to be done to improve social affairs, and the right of such people to dictate policies to those who received them.

Not all social democrats were or are like this, but the 'top-down' approach was very influential in British social policy and shaped the development of the Welfare State. This is reflected in the bureaucratic nature of public welfare provision and, until relatively recently, a suspicion of private and voluntary alternatives to State services.

Definitions

Elitism and paternalism – those
in power believe that they know
what is good for others

Incrementalism – gradual change

Rather than revolutionary change, which radical socialists/Marxists want. Social
democrats believe that radical social upheaval can create as many problems as it
solves and that a slow **incrementalist** or piecemeal approach to reform is
preferable. Social problems can be dealt with and capitalism gradually replaced by
the extension of State control.

Inequality

The social democrats believe in the importance of government intervention in the
economy, to ensure that too great an *inequality* does not occur between people. The
free market harms the poor and the weak, while benefiting the powerful and
wealthy. This is because the rich have the power to exploit the poorer people,
unless the government can set limits to the inequality, and build protection for the
less well-off.

Citizenship

All members of society ought to be united by common bonds, otherwise society
will fall apart, with everyone selfishly looking after themselves.

According to writers such as Marshall, the concept of citizenship means a lot more
than just holding a passport. According to him, full citizenship is achieved through
three elements:

- *political citizenship*: the right to vote – this is seen as a right now, yet it is
  relatively new, as most people only obtained the vote in the twentieth
  century, and it was not fully extended to women until 1928
- *legal citizenship*: the right to justice under the law – probably this was the first
  of the elements of citizenship, in that the law was supposed to be imposed
  equally on all
- *social citizenship*: the right to welfare benefits – Marshall suggests that this
  remains a contentious issue, just like the campaign for votes for women in the
  beginning of the twentieth century. Nevertheless, full citizenship includes
  rights to welfare.

It is this idea which underlies much of the social policy decisions of the European
Union as it tries to extend a common citizenship across Europe.

Social democracy

The emphasis today on 'welfare' and the
'benefits of welfare' often tends to obscure
the fundamental fact that for many consumers the services used are not
essentially benefits or additions to welfare
at all; they represent partial compen-
sations for disservices, for social costs and
social insecurities which are the product of
a rapidly changing industrial-urban
society. They are part of the price we pay
to some people for bearing part of the
costs of other people's progress; the
obsolescence of skills, redundancies,
premature retirements, accidents, many
categories of disease and handicap, urban
blight and slum clearance, smoke pollution
and a hundred-and-one other socially
generated disservices. They are the
socially caused diswelfares; the losses
involved in aggregate welfare gains. We
have, as societies, to make choices; either
to provide social services, or to allow the
social costs of the system to lie where they
fall.

1 Explain in your own words, the
  meaning of the terms:
  a) disservice
  b) diswelfare.

2 Give examples of these.

3 What are the causes of disservices and
  diswelfare?

4 According to social democrats, what
  choices are there?

Source: R. Titmuss, *Commitment to Welfare* (Allen & Unwin, 1968)

The family

Families are important in the view of the social democrats, but it is not right for some people to have their lives entirely dominated by caring for a sick, old or disabled relative. The State should support and help family carers wherever possible, and should ensure that lone-parent families should have an adequate income to bring up children free from poverty.

This approach emphasises people's rights to be free from family obligations which they do not want. Looking after other members of a family should be a choice not an obligation. This is in marked contrast to the New Right who believe that the family should be responsible for caring for its members.

Private and charitable provision of welfare

Opinions vary amongst social democrats but, overall, private and charitable provision of health and welfare is acceptable as long as the State system is comprehensive (covers everybody) and is of a high standard.

People may choose private residential homes or private hospitals because they want to, not because they are forced to. Similarly, it is good for people to provide voluntary work to help others, but that should not substitute for the provision by the State.

The deserving and the undeserving

> **Definitions**
>
> **Universal benefits** – everyone has the right to State benefits and health care if they need them. It is not the job of the State to make distinctions between people (see means-testing, page 22)
>
> **Institutional model of welfare** – a high-quality welfare state, available to all who want to use the services

This approach argues that it is difficult to make decisions about who is deserving and who is not, and therefore says that welfare benefits should be easily available to all who seek them.

This means that if there is a particular category of person who is regarded as needing help, then all those in that category should be given assistance, irrespective of their apparent affluence. The best example of this is Child Benefit which is paid to all parents with young children. This is known as the provision of **universal benefits**.

Where the State provides a high standard of welfare services for all those who request them, the system is known as the **institutional model of welfare**.

Criticisms of the social democratic approach

As the approach which has dominated British social policy until the 1970s, social democracy has been criticised by all the other theoretical perspectives discussed in this chapter. Marxist, feminist and anti-racist social policy analysts do not regard social democracy as sufficiently radical. By the end of the period in which it influenced governments, critics argued that the reformist strategy has not been successful – many of the original problems of the Welfare State which were not successfully tackled remain, such as poverty, unemployment and inequalities between different social classes. It has also been claimed that the main group to benefit from the Welfare State have been the affluent middle classes who make greater use of public services, especially education, health and welfare provided by tax rebates and allowances.

Furthermore, the way in which welfare was delivered – by a Welfare State that knew what was good for people, and in which they had no influence or choice – made people who used the welfare services feel like second-class citizens. And because the people who worked in the public services knew there was no other choice, they became inefficient and unresponsive to claimants and patients' needs.

Activity   Look at the questions in the activity on page 18. How would social democrats answer the questions?

Main points ▶ The Welfare State is the result of the social democratic approach.
             ▶ This approach believes that citizens have a right to health and social care.
             ▶ It opposes radical change and want to move slowly towards a more equal society.
             ▶ The family is important but it is not right that they should be forced to look after the sick or unemployed.
             ▶ Private charity is demeaning for those who receive it and is erratic and unreliable as a system of welfare.
             ▶ It is the role of the State to provide high quality care for all those who are in need.

The radical socialist or Marxist approach

Definitions

Capitalism – the economic system based on private ownership of industry and commerce

Socialism – the economic and political system based on the state ownership and control of industry and commerce

The radical socialist and Marxist/communist approaches to welfare argue that free market economies operate to the benefit of the rich and powerful and that just tinkering with the system, as social democrats do, is mistaken. This approach argues for a take-over of private enterprise by the government, which then operates it on behalf of all members of society.

This approach has developed from the writings of Karl Marx, who lived and wrote in the nineteenth century. According to Marx **capitalism** (that is society as we know it consisting of large-scale industry and commerce, based on private ownership of property) has two classes with fundamentally opposed interests:

- capitalists or bourgeoisie – who own the industry, land and commerce
- workers or proletariat – those who work for the owners.

As the employers can only make profits for themselves by getting employees to work at as hard as possible for the lowest wages, there is inevitable conflict between the two groups.

According to Marxists, the real cause of poverty and most other social problems is the fact that a very small proportion of the population own the overwhelming bulk of the wealth. Unlike most of the other perspectives we consider in social policy, Marxism sees the only long-term welfare solution is to replace capitalism in a **socialist** revolution.

A Marxist view of welfare

One may argue that state welfare represents a *quid pro quo* or a 'bribe' offered to the working class in exchange for political quiescence and industrial peace. It captures the political importance of capitalist state welfare, which is correctly considered by working-class consumers as a 'piece of cake' sacrificed by capital to secure their wider cooperation. The Welfare State indeed exerts an important cushioning effect on working-class experience, actively diverting attention from the structure of class inequality.

1 What is the Welfare State?

2 What is the effect of the Welfare State?

3 What is the Marxist view on improving the Welfare State?

Source: N. Ginsberg, *Class, Capital and Social Policy* (Macmillan, 1979)

The State and welfare

> **Definition**
>
> **Monopoly** – only one organi-
> sation providing a particular
> service

The State should have a **monopoly** of welfare, and should ensure that there is no unemployment, no shortage of housing, and that wage levels allow everyone approximately equal standards of living. There is no place or need for charity, or State benefits.

Equality

Radical socialists believe that the ultimate goal of social policy should be equality. There should be no rich people and no poor people, and the provision of health, housing and social services should be equal for everyone.

Private property and the market

These are both evils which actually bring about misery and poverty. There would be no need for poverty, if only the wealth that exists was equally shared around and used for the common good.

The family

The family is generally regarded with suspicion. The belief is that it is a unit which corrupts as much as it helps. Why should family members be forced to look after those who are ill or disabled? This is seen as the role of the State. This does not mean there is any less love, merely that there should always be provision available for any person in need as a right for that individual, so they do not need to ask other members of the family.

The Welfare State

This approach argues that the Welfare State is actually a harmful thing, in the long run, as it prevents radical, revolutionary change. It does this by masking the great inequalities of society, and by providing just enough for people to survive on. The result is that people are grateful for the State benefits and health provision, and fail to question the continuing existence of great wealth.

 *Activity*

Look at the questions in the activity on page 18. How would radical socialists/Marxists answer the questions?

Main points ▶ The radical socialist or Marxist approach rejects the whole idea of capitalism.
▶ It develops from the writings of Karl Marx.
▶ The rich and powerful exploit the rest of society.
▶ The Welfare State merely hides this exploitation.
▶ In a society where the wealth was equally distributed there would be no need for a 'welfare state'.
▶ Marxists reject reform and want to change the entire system.

The feminist approach

Feminist approaches argue that political and economic power is in the hands of men. As a result of this, decisions about economic matters, as well as about issues of health and welfare, reflect the interests of men, and may well harm women.

For feminists, mainstream social theory has been inadequate because it has been 'gender-blind', i.e. it does not take account of the different position or experiences of men and women. Traditional social theory and social policy has been based on male assumptions and did not account for the very important differences between the men and women. Social theory pursued a **malestream** agenda in which women's interests and rights were either neglected or completely ignored. All of the different strands within feminism share this criticism of the malestream focus which puts men at the centre of the analysis and which makes women marginal or invisible.

Feminist theory is distinctive as it raises issues and studies topics neglected by the other malestream perspectives in social theory. For example, one very important concept in feminist analyses is **patriarchy**. This term is used by feminists to describe the power relationships through which men dominate women.

Some of the ways in which men control women identified by feminists include:

* the traditional male-dominated family in which men earn more money in their employment and women are dependent upon them
* gender socialisation and the construction of 'masculinity' and 'femininity', i.e. how girls and boys are taught to be different and act as women and men
* restricted educational and career opportunities for women
* male violence, including rape and domestic violence, for example.

Types of feminist theory

Liberal/reformist feminism

This theory aims to advance women's interests within the structures of the existing social order. It often focuses on establishing equal rights for women in key areas of social and public life, for example by lobbying for legislation to stop sex discrimination or sexual harassment at work.

Socialist/Marxist feminism

This theory identifies a link between women's oppression and the class system of capitalist societies, as suggested by Marxists.

Radical/separatist feminism

This theory advocates politics based on women-controlled institutions, independent from men and the State. Certain 'separatist' versions of radical feminism see men collectively as an 'enemy', who have profoundly different interests from women.

Black feminism

This theory criticises some of the alternative feminist strands for dealing exclusively with the experiences and interests of white (often middle-class) women. They identify the need for solidarity *within* ethnic groups in order to act against the different sources of oppression.

Feminism and welfare

Feminists have an ambivalent feelings about State welfare provision. On the one hand, they recognise that the Welfare State has done some good in advancing the cause of female independence. For example, benefits are provided for lone mothers which allows more women to leave unsatisfactory or violent relationships. On the other hand, feminists complain that the Welfare State may also reinforce traditional gender roles (in that it employs millions of women but tends to confine them to traditional 'women's jobs', such as nursing and teaching).

Feminist views

The organisation of these sex roles is seen to reflect not so much innate differences in the temperaments of women and men as socially-created differences in their access to scarce resources; to education and scientific training, for example, and to housing and welfare benefits. Because of these differences in access, women are more likely than men to find themselves economically dependent on others for the money they need to survive. They are, as a result, more likely to be poor. They are also more likely to be in poor health. Their higher risk of economic dependency and poverty and of ill-health (but not premature death) makes the welfare state of particular importance to women. For example, women constitute two-thirds of the elderly and two-thirds of the physically handicapped population and over half of the families on social security are female-headed one-parent families.

Despite their greater reliance on the welfare state, feminists argue that women have long been received on unequal terms to men. Welfare legislation has historically been concerned, like the wider economy, with workers, and with male workers.

Source: H. Land, 'Sex role stereotyping in the social security and income tax systems', in J. Chetwynd and O. Hartnett (eds) *The Sex Role System* (Routledge, 1978)

1 According to the author, why are women poorer and in worse health than men?

2 Why do women need the Welfare State more than men?

3 Give three examples of groups in need of welfare provision which are predominantly female?

4 What has welfare legislation been primarily concerned with?

5 What terms would we use to describe this situation? (You may need to look in the main text.)

Criticisms of the feminist approach

Feminism has been criticised for sometimes assuming that all women share the same interests. But this is only partly true as many middle-class women have a totally different experience of life that poorer women. Indeed, the liberation of many middle-class women has involved employing other women at low wages to undertake the very household tasks and child minding which they have 'escaped from'.

Look at the questions in the activity on page 18. What answers would feminists give to the questions? (You might want to distinguish between the different approaches, where you feel it is important.)

Main points ▶ Feminist approaches start from the position that power has traditionally been in the hands of men, who have exploited women.

▶ There are a number of different strands within feminist theory, all of which differ in their emphases, though they all accept the issue of males exploiting women. Their differences are concerned with how to overcome these differences.

▶ Feminists both welcome the Welfare State as having benefited them and also criticise it for relying upon and exploiting women.

The anti-racist approach

The anti-racist perspective has emerged from criticisms of racism in social policy and society more generally. Social policy has traditionally ignored questions of 'race'. However, it has long been known that people from ethnic minorities in the UK are more likely to be unemployed, low paid, poor, victims of verbal and physical abuse, victims of police harassment, and treated unfairly by State welfare institutions.

Different meanings of 'racism'

- A 'narrow' definition of racism describes it as the view that humans can be classified into a set of *distinct biological 'races'* and that some are superior to others.
- A wider definition sees it as the belief that we can distinguish groups on the basis of *physical characteristics* (for example, colour of skin), that such groups are permanently different, and that interaction between such groups is harmful in some way.
- *Cultural racism* means defining national culture (for example, 'Britishness') in a way which equates this with a dominant ethnic group and which marginalises ethnic minorities.
- *Institutional racism* refers to how the standard practices, operations and cultures of organisations can discriminate, sometimes unintentionally, against ethnic minorities.

Racism need not be intentional: the routine procedures of an organisation may be racist without any of the individuals who operate them being deliberately prejudiced. For example, it is argued by anti-racists that policing *practices* in the UK are racist, and this may be the case even if individual police officers are not racist.

It is difficult to describe anti-racism as a perspective or theory about society, as it is more a political and cultural movement and is defined almost as much by what is *opposes* as what says itself. So, anti-racism is perhaps best thought of as a set of challenges and insights directed at other perspectives and political strategies.

Welfare practices and anti-racism

The anti-racist approach is critical of two alternative approaches in British social policy which deal with issues of 'race' and ethnicity:

- assimilation (integration)
- multiculturalism.

Assimilation

Assimilation is the policy of integrating ethnic minorities into the 'host culture' by down-playing differences between them. In this policy, minority groups are encouraged to conform to the 'British way of life'.

But, according to the anti-racist viewpoint, this strategy is based on the idea of the cultural and racial superiority of the dominant (white) group and the belief that minority groups should be absorbed into this culture, and it is claimed that this leads to hostility towards any minority group which does not fit in to this ideal.

Multiculturalism

The multiculturalist approach believes that contact and familiarity with different groups will reduce ignorance and prejudice among the white population.

However, the anti-racist perspective argues that multicultural policies in the UK have only made small adjustments to welfare and health institutions, while leaving the basic 'racist fabric' of society untouched. Anti-racists therefore emphasise the need to change the attitudes, procedures and structures which allow institutional racism to go unchecked

---

Activity   Look at the questions in the activity on page 18. What answers would anti-racists give to the questions?

Main points ▶ The anti-racist approach starts from the fact that members of the ethnic minorities in the UK are likely to be poorer, in worse housing, and in lower paid jobs than the majority of the population.

▶ Members of the ethnic minorities too may not receive the sorts of appropriate services from the Welfare State, which is more attuned to the demands of the majority population.

▶ Racism comes in different forms and it may just as much be institutional and unintentional as deliberate – and the results in terms of discrimination are the same.

▶ Traditional approaches to 'race' of assimilation and multiculturalism may be inadequate to stop racism.

Environmentalism

Definitions

Sustainability – ensuring that we do not use up the planet's resources

Eco-system – a way of describing the environment which stresses the fact that the world is complex and finely balanced. Pollution and over-consumption can have drastic and unforseen effects, for example, global warming as a result of burning fossil fuels

The environmentalist or green movement has a rather different agenda from most other social theories and perspectives. Environmentalists argue that existing ideologies have led to a situation where the very future of the planet is in doubt and therefore a major re-think of our priorities is required. Instead of more economic 'development', environmentalists argue that we should be aiming for **sustainability** and protection of our fragile **eco-system**. This may mean that assumptions about economic and technological 'progress' are questioned, and a more *holistic* idea of human welfare is developed – one which sees humans as members of a wider natural environment upon which we depend and which we must protect.

Ideas of environmentalism, green politics and sustainability are now very important in public concerns and political debates. This is a sign that the green movement has had a considerable impact on social theory and politics within a relatively short time.

Unlike most other perspectives, environmentalism does not regard nature simply as a resource which is available to be exploited for human well-being. In fact, environmentalism questions the view that economic development actually represents an advance for humans or for the planet as a whole. Environmentalism broadens the idea of what counts as 'human well-being' by arguing that we must see this in the context of global ecological needs.

Environmentalists therefore draw attention to the constraints which the natural environment places on continued technological development. These constraints include such things as over-population in relation to access to resources, damage to the ozone layer, possible climate change and infections in the food chain such as BSE. All these impact badly on the health and welfare of society.

The environmentalist response to such problems is to demand a major change in lifestyles and systems of social organisations to place less strain on the eco-system. However, not all environmentalists agree on how this should be done. These differences of opinion split environmentalism into two strands:

- *radical or 'dark greens'* who want change, and they want it now. It is very closely linked to direct political action over road building and the treatment of animals
- *reformist or 'light greens'* who are less radical and seek a better balance between human and environmental needs by more careful planning and sensitivity to the environmental consequences of action.

'The politics of the Industrial Age, left, right and centre, is like a three-lane motorway, with different vehicles in different lanes, but all heading the same direction. Greens feel it is the very direction that is wrong, rather than the choice of any one lane in preference to the others. It is our perception that the motorway of industrialism inevitably leads to the abyss – hence our decision to get off it, and seek an entirely new direction.'

Jonathan Porrit, 1984

Source: Taken from V. George and P. Wilding, *Welfare and Ideology* (Routledge & Kegan Paul, 1994)

Given their preoccupation with global issues of the eco-system, environmentalists have less to say than many of the other perspectives on matters of welfare. They generally advocate a more 'holistic' idea of welfare and well-being, which involves taking a fuller view of what is needed for human development and its balance with ecological needs. However, they do have several firm policy ideas:

- *Basic income scheme:* everyone would be entitled to public support when in need without passing either a means test or contributions test (so, the claimant would not have to prove they are poor, nor prove they have paid National Insurance or taxes).
- *Health care:* they would give far greater emphasis to non-technological responses to illness, preferring, for example, preventative health preservation rather than acute health intervention after someone falls ill.
- *Subsidiarity:* they reject centralised, bureaucratic state control as the means of delivering welfare services. Instead they favour what is known as **subsidiarity**: decentralisation and greater emphasis on community and voluntary support in the family and within local areas. Environmentalists are suspicious that welfare bureaucracies and professionals exert too much control over people's lives and turn them into passive consumers. Locally based and controlled welfare services would mean a higher level of participation by citizens.

Definition

Subsidiarity – dealing with social problems at the level of the local community rather than by national government

---

Criticisms of the environmentalist approach

Critics of environmentalists argue that a distinctive 'green' perspective is neither required nor possible, as many of the key ideas are borrowed from alternative theories and political ideologies (for example, anarchism, conservatism, etc.).

Critics also argue that the environmentalist case for decentralised social policies underestimates the greater ability of central government to tackle structural social and economic problems. Anti-environmentalists also accuse greens of being irrational in their approach to technical problems, and prioritising plants and animals over human needs. This is especially dangerous in the developing world, critics claim, where the needs of expanding populations and the desire for the level of technical development achieved in the West would be denied people by environmentalists who themselves enjoy the benefits of technological advancement.

Activity

Look at the questions in the activity on page 18. How would the environmentalists answer the questions? (You might want to distinguish sometimes between the 'light' and 'dark' greens.)

Main points

▶ Environmentalism is a relatively new approach which stresses the fact that wider issues of welfare are important rather than to concentrate on traditional areas of concern.

▶ The physical world is being harmed and this will increasingly impact on our welfare

▶ Current ways of talking about improvement and well-being are mistaken.

▶ There are two different strands within environmentalism – one more radical than the other.

▶ Environmentalists have less specifically to say about the Welfare State than other approaches – preferring to redefine welfare instead.

▶ They believe that everyone below a certain income has a right to public support.

▶ They want power to be devolved down to the lowest levels.

The Third Way

The most recent perspective to emerge in politics and social policy has been described as the Third Way. This approach is claimed to underlie the policies of the New Labour government, first elected in 1997. It is still too early to describe the Third Way as a fully distinct theory, but it is different from traditional social democratic ideas, as it draws also from the New Right.

A definition of the 'Third Way'

'The "Third Way" is to my mind the best label for the new politics which the progressive centre-left is forging in Britain and beyond. The Third Way stands for a modernised social democracy, passionate in its commitment to social justice and the goals of the centre-left, but flexible, innovative and forward-looking in the means to achieve them. It is founded on the values which have guided progressive politics for more than a century – democracy, liberty, justice, mutual obligation and internationalism. But it is a *third* way because it moves decisively beyond an Old Left preoccupied by state control, high taxation and producer interests; and a New Right treating public investment, and often the very notions of "society" and collective endeavours, as evils to be undone.'

Tony Blair, 1998

Source: Taken from M. Thomas and G. Lodge (eds), *Radicals and Reformers: A Century of Fabian Thought* (Fabian Society, 2000)

The term 'Third Way' is used to distinguish this new approach from two older political traditions.

- The 'first way' is regarded as individualism and the liberalism of the New Right, as expressed by the UK Conservative Party under Margaret Thatcher.
- The 'second way' means traditional social democracy.

To supporters of the Third Way, both of these ideologies have strong points but also weaknesses, and the Third Way is represented as an attempt to combine the best elements from each.

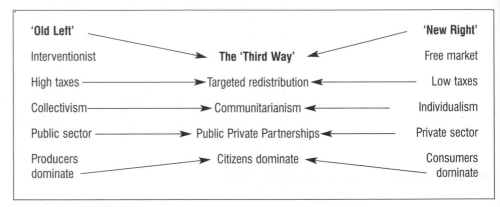

Sources of the 'Third Way'

The Third Way is described as an updated version of social democracy, which has adapted to changes in the economy and society and learned the lessons of the mistakes made by the 'old Left', for example, that high taxation does not always work and is unpopular, and that State control can be inefficient.

The Third Way stresses that the role of the government is to provide the conditions for private business to do well so that there is high employment. It sees ensuring people are in employment and receiving a minimum wage as the key to reducing poverty. Linked to this are policies to make sure that the workforce is highly educated and that anyone who is able to work should be given the opportunity – possibly even forced – to go back to work.

The traditional socialist and social democratic idea that it is the role of the State to combat all social problems has been modified, so that New Labour has increasingly argued that the State cannot do everything itself and that people have either to help themselves or each other. However, unlike the New Right, New Labour wishes to provide opportunities and funding for this self-help to occur.

Definition

Anti-discriminatory – refers to policies which ensure that people are treated equally, not on the grounds of their race, gender, disability

The Third Way also emphasises the importance of all people living in the UK to have equal rights and opportunities and so **anti-discrimatory** policies against sexism, racism and mistreatment of those with disabilities have all been introduced. The aim is to make all the population feel that they have a 'stake' in society. This is closely linked to the views on *citizenship* which we saw in the social democratic approach earlier.

Examples of Third Way policies

These include:

- *Employment and training:* Compulsory training for the unemployed and benefit withdrawal if they fail to undertake the training. Certain groups are targeted more than others – particularly the long-term unemployed, the young unemployed and never-married lone mothers.
- *State benefits:* The tax and State benefit systems are becoming more integrated, so that the State is not giving benefits through one agency and taxing the same people through another, which often led to absurd situations that people became poorer if they tried to move off benefit and into work. The level of tax paid is so gradual or non-existent that it is never financially better being on benefits than in employment. This eliminates *the poverty trap* (see page 92).
- *The Health Service:* this involves a using the private health care system to undertake the overflow work from the NHS. The Third Way is less concerned about the moral debate over private health care, as the need to eliminate waiting lists and to raise standards.

Criticisms of the Third Way

Critics regard the Third Way as little more than a term added on to a pragmatic and indistinct set of policies. A second criticism levelled against New Labour and its Third Way project from more traditional social democrats is its refusal to put the case for redistributing resources to the poor more strongly to the UK public. Such critics claim that this failure means that taxation comes always to be seen as a bad thing rather than an instrument which can be used to improve society.

Activity

Look at the questions in the activity on page 18, How would the Third Way theorists answer the questions?

Main points
- The Third Way is a new philosophy linked to New Labour.
- It has drawn ideas from across the political spectrum.
- It stresses the importance of successful business to provide the wealth for the rest of society and high employment levels.
- It also stresses a society free from discrimination on the grounds of 'race' and gender.

The following table summarises the key differences between the main perspectives on specific questions of welfare policy.

Perspectives and policies

	Health care	Social security	Personal social Services	Housing	Crime/law and order	Education
Social democracy	The NHS is one of the greatest achievements of State planning and must be protected. Reduce market involvement in NHS, and squeeze private sector which perpetuates inequality.	Collective welfare benefits are needed to reduce poverty. Benefit levels should be raised. Ideally universal benefits are best (such as Child Benefit) as this reduces stigma.	State intervention is required; monitoring families and intervention may be necessary to protect children. More trained social workers are needed to provide a wide range of services.	Private home ownership increases social division, and inheritance perpetuates inequalities. Social housing should be subsidised and allocated according to need. The rights of private renting tenants should be extended.	Much crime is caused by deprivation and unemployment. Reducing these problems is required rather than tackling the symptoms. Improved education and training can be used to reduce crime.	Inequalities and disadvantage can be combated by a universal and comprehensive State education system. Grammar schools and private education are unfair and only benefit the privileged.
Radical Socialism/Marxism	Many symptoms of ill health are caused by the exploitative and alienating capitalist system. Completely socialised public health service is required and elimination of the private sector.	Poverty is a result of capitalist inefficiency. Social security should be provided in line with Marx's principle of 'each according to his/her need'. This will never happen under capitalism.	Under bourgeois capitalism, social services are used to monitor and control the poor to ensure they conform to capitalist morality. This will not be required under socialism.	Housing must be 'decommodified', and completely removed from the market. Allocation of housing should be determined solely by need and administered by the State.	Most 'crime' is a reflection of alienation and bourgeois control of the State (for example, police concentrate their attention on the lower classes). Democratic accountability by the people of the criminal justice system is required.	Education is a system of maintaining and defending class privilege. Bourgeois parents transmit 'cultural capital' to their children which gives them advantages in 'competitive' assessment. Abolition of private sector and equality of conditions among all pupils is required.
New Right	Maximise the role of private sector: encourage more private health insurance and market discipline into public sector ('quasi-markets').	Minimise and target provision to genuinely needy. State welfare benefits encourage dependency. Should encourage more private insurance (for example, Public Private Partnerships), voluntary and domestic provision (for example, charity and family support).	Minimise interference in the private family by State officials. Care for the elderly should be provided by private insurance or the family.	Encourage home-ownership (for example, subsidies to help council tenants buy their home). Social housing should be removed from local authorities and passed over to quasi-private agencies, such as housing associations.	Tougher sentencing and more police needed. Most crime is caused by deviant individuals and cannot be attributed to social conditions. Greater deterrence is required.	Reduce local authority control of State education and give greater power to individual schools and parents. Support grammar schools and oppose comprehensives. Provide subsidies to private schools.

Liberal feminism	Women and girls are achieving more than ever in education, but still under-represented at the most senior levels (for example, head teachers, university professors). More women in science, engineering and traditionally 'male' subjects is required.	Women are treated unfairly by a male-dominated system, for example more likely to be imprisoned for first offences. Equal representation and employment of women in the criminal justice system is required to ensure equal treatment.	The equal rights of women to housing must be enshrined in law. Women's contribution as carers and home makers should be acknowledged in cases of divorce or separation. Housing provision for lone mothers should be improved.	Support for women as carers and the possibility of combining care and paid employment should be a priority.	A contributory or insurance benefit system discriminates against women who have disrupted employment record. Benefit increases are needed to reduce poverty among lone mothers and pensioners.	Special provision is required for particular female medical conditions. A freely-available health system has benefited women who were previously neglected by private health and insurance systems.
Radical feminism	Most education systems perpetuate sexist assumptions about traditional gender roles and abilities. Women and girls achieve more when educated separately and encouraged to succeed.	The police and courts are sexist institutions which serve male interests. Crimes against women (for example, rape, domestic violence) are not treated seriously. Sexist assumptions lead to unfair treatment of women victims and offenders.	Agree with many liberal feminist principles. In addition, access to housing and/or refuge shelters for women escaping violent relationships is an essential priority. Separatist feminists advocate self-help and women-only communal living.	The unpaid caring of women (for example, of children, elderly, etc.) should be recognised as equal to paid employment.	Recognition of caring and domestic labour should be included in welfare entitlement. Ultimately, wages for housework should be introduced.	Many female 'health' issues are a symptom of sexist social conditions which exploit women. A male-dominated scientific approach 'medicalises' many natural conditions (for example, childbirth). Women's labour is exploited and under-valued in health care systems.
Anti-racism	Racist stereotypes (for example, of unco-operative young black men) and under-funding inner-city schools leads to ethnic minority under achievement. Minority children suffer heavily from exclusionary systems (private and grammar schools).	The overt and institutional racism of police and courts has been proven (for example, Stephen Lawrence case) and must be tackled. More minority recruits and greater sensitivity to ethnic differences required.	Certain ethnic minorities are heavily concentrated in social housing (reflecting a history of racialised living patterns). They are also more common in the private rented sector, so improvement to these two areas would help them.	Social services 'pathologise' black families which do not conform to white norms. Racist assumptions ensure that black parents are more likely to be closely monitored than white ones, and culturally different child-rearing practices are ignored.	There is considerable institutional and much personal racism in the benefit system, for example, exclusionary effects of contribution system, lower likelihood of black claimants to receive Social Fund grants.	Conditions specific to ethnic minorities have been neglected (for example, sickle cell anaemia). NHS has exploited low paid ethnic minority labour. More 'out-reach' work by public services required to encourage minorities to use services.

	Health care	Social security	Personal social Services	Housing	Crime/law and order	Education
Environmentalism	Many illnesses are related to lifestyles and social conditions, and are better prevented than treated by scientific remedies. A more 'holistic' idea of health and medicine is required.	Support the idea of a 'citizens' income or 'basic income' scheme – where entitlement is universal and unconditional.	Support the idea of 'subsidiarity' – that care should be provided at the local level as far as possible, for example by the family first, then if necessary the neighbourhood or community, then local government, etc. This encourages mutual aid and independence.	Excessive demand for housing endangers the environment. Alternative resource-conscious lifestyles and eco-friendly living should be encouraged.	Community self-policing and strengthening neighbourhood spirit is better than technology-driven police forces. Crime can be prevented by strengthening social bonds and improved social education.	A more holistic approach to education is required. Education systems should aim to encourage socially responsible citizens and fully rounded individuals with an awareness of their relationship to their social community and the natural world.
The 'Third Way'	The public sector has achieved great things, but private resources and business management practices can be used to improve services (for example, to build new hospitals).	Work is the best route out of poverty, especially when it is made more rewarding by tax credits and a minimum wage. Improved selective benefits will be provided for those incapable of working.	Families are the main providers of care and welfare and stable families should be encouraged. However, there is an important support role for social services.	A range of housing providers will encourage best practice: local authorities have a role, but so too do social landlords (like housing associations).	People's lives are blighted by crime and anti-social behaviour and they want the government to get tough on this. However, harsher sentencing is not always best, particularly where young offenders are concerned.	An improved education system must be a priority area for government. National standards and targets must be met, but there are a range of means to achieve this. Parental involvement and choice in schools is important.

Activities

1 Draw a series of 'spider' diagrams to illustrate each of the approaches described in the table on pages 36–7.
2 Having read the theories, is there one approach which you prefer? Which one?
3 Which approaches say that we need positive action programmes?
4 What is meant by the term 'inequality'?
5 What do anti-racists say about inequality?
6 Do all radical socialists believe in the Welfare State? Explain your answer.
7 What do we mean by 'dependency culture'?
8 According to radical socialists, what causes social problems? Explain this as fully as you can.
9 According to feminists, who provides the bulk of health and social care? Who also receive the bulk of health and social care?
10 Which theoretical approach(es) fully support the NHS?
11 Why does the New Right criticise State benefits?
12 What are the advantages of the social security system, according to radical socialists, for today's capitalist society?
13 Why do the feminist and anti-racist approaches criticise the personal social services?
14 How can poverty be eliminated, according to the social democratic approach
15 Compare the views on law and order provided by the New Right, social democratic and anti-racist approaches. Are there any similarities?

Conclusion

In this chapter, we have explored the theories which underpin all discussions of welfare. Most people when discussing their attitudes towards the provision of health and welfare services may not even be aware that the views they hold can be linked to a theoretical perspective, but you can relate most people's views to at least one theoretical perspective. Many students comment that theory is boring and irrelevant. Boring is a matter of opinion, but they are certainly highly relevant, as politicians are influenced by these approaches in how they go about deciding upon, and introducing, welfare policies that impact on all our lives.

2 CHAPTER SUMMARY

The New Right

1 It has been very influential within the Conservative Party in particular.

2 It believes that business should be left alone to get on with its job. Government interference harms society.

3 People make their own decisions and should live by their success or failure.

4 Some people who are poor are deserving, most are not.

5 The family is the place for people to turn for help.

6 If that fails it should be charity.

7 There are many people who have learned to be dependent on the State.

8   The Welfare State should be chopped back and replaced with a residual version for those few deserving poor.

9   Private companies should be involved in delivering health and welfare and people should buy their own insurance to cover themselves against risk.

The social democratic approach

10 The Welfare State is the result of the social democratic approach.

11 This approach believes that citizens have a right to health and social care from the State.

12 It opposes radical change and wants to move slowly towards a more equal society.

13 The family is important but it is not right that they should be forced to look after the sick or unemployed.

14 Private charity is demeaning for those who receive it and is erratic and unreliable as a system of welfare.

The radical socialist/Marxist approach

15 It develops from the writings of Karl Marx and rejects the idea of capitalism

16 The rich and powerful exploit the rest of society.

17 The Welfare State merely hides this exploitation.

18 In a society where the wealth was equally distributed there would be no need for a 'welfare state'

19 Marxists reject reform and want to change the entire system.

The feminist approach

20 Feminist approaches start from the position that power has traditionally been in the hands of men, who have exploited women.

21 There are a number of different strands within feminist theory, all of which differ in their emphases, though they all accept the issue of males exploiting women. Their differences are concerned with how to overcome these differences.

22 Feminists both welcome the Welfare State as having benefited them and also criticise it for relying upon and exploiting women.

The anti-racist approach

23 The anti-racist approach starts from the fact that members of the ethnic minorities in the UK are likely to be poorer, in worse housing, and in lower paid jobs than the majority of the population.

24 Members of the ethnic minorities too may not receive the sorts of appropriate services from the Welfare State, which is more attuned to the demands of the majority population.

25 Racism comes in different forms and it may just as much be institutional and unintentional as deliberate – and the results in terms of discrimination are the same.

26 Traditional approaches to 'race' of assimilation and multiculturalism may be inadequate to stop racism.

Environmentalism

27 Environmentalism is a relatively new approach which argues that the physical world is being harmed and this will increasingly impact on our welfare

28 Current ways of talking about improvement and well-being are mistaken.

29 There are two different strands within environmentalism – one more radical than the other.

30 The believe that everyone below a certain income has a right to public support.

31 They want power to be devolved down to the lowest levels.

The Third Way

32 The Third Way is a new philosophy linked to New Labour.

33 It has drawn ideas from across the political spectrum.

34 It stresses the importance of successful business to provide the wealth for the rest of society and high employment levels.

35 It also stresses a society free from discrimination on the grounds of 'race' and gender.

Useful websites

www.iea.org.uk: the Institute for Economic Affairs, a right-wing 'think tank'

www.ippr.org.uk: the Institute for Public Policy Research, which influences the current Labour government

www.cps.org.uk: the Centre for Policy Studies, a relatively left-wing 'think tank'

www.socialissues.co.uk: a new site provided by the publishers Nelson Thornes covering general social policy for GCSE- and A-level students

www.atss.org.uk: the site of the Association of Teachers in Social Science, which contains some useful source material and helpful links to more specific sites

SOCIAL PROTECTION

Chapter contents

Introduction

This chapter deals with a service which is generally seen as the main component of welfare in the UK: **social protection**. Social protection is sometimes also known as **social security** or income maintenance. These all mean the same thing – the benefits provided for those who would be unable to cope financially without them. In this chapter, each of these three terms will be used to refer to these benefits. We have used the term 'social protection' as it is slightly wider than social security which most people understand as referring to the work of the

Definitions

Social security – the system of providing financial help to those in need

Social protection – the system of providing financial help to those in need, but it has a slightly wider meaning than social security, which is a term usually linked to the work of the Department of Work and Pensions

Department of Work and Pensions. Today, however, some benefits are paid through the tax system and some, like housing benefit, through local authorities.

The chapter begins with a look at the introduction and early development of social security in the UK until the late 1970s when new economic and political conditions meant that the familiar 'post-war settlement' was replaced by a rather different idea of what social protection should do. This shift meant that the 1980s and 1990s marked a new climate for social protection in the UK, so the second section of the chapter examines the main reforms which were introduced during this period and which formed the background to the system of State benefits which the Labour government inherited after the 1997 election.

Since winning the 1997 general election, the New Labour government has introduced a number of welfare reforms which have changed the nature of social protection in the UK considerably in a relatively short period of time. Many of these changes go beyond the traditional scope of social security and include changes to the tax system and new types of policy such as the Social Exclusion Unit and the National Strategy for Neighbourhood Renewal. The third section of the chapter will outline the main features of these changes, and is followed by a brief overview of the benefits available in the UK today.

The final section looks at some of the key debates relating to social security, including the choice between universal benefits and targeted or means-tested benefits. One group of writers argues that welfare benefits should be provided much more widely, with no need for claimants to prove that they should be eligible for benefits. On the other side are those who believe that there should be strict controls on the level of income people already have before they can claim benefits from the State. Each case will be discussed and considered here. We also analyse take-up rates for benefits and what affects them and finally ask if the social protection system through taxation and benefits actually succeeds in redistributing any income from rich to poor.

The introduction of social security

Social protection is big business, not only in the UK but in all modern developed societies. Around 30 million people in the UK receive some sort of social security benefit – around 70 per cent of all households. In recent years the UK government spent about £100 billion on social security benefits, which amounts to about 30 per cent of national wealth.

British government spending, 1999–2000

Social Security	£102 billion (30%)
Health	£ 61 billion
Education	£ 41 billion
Debt interest	£ 26 billion
Defence	£ 22 billion
Law and order	£ 19 billion
Industry, agriculture and employment	£ 15 billion
Housing and environment	£ 3 billion
Other	£ 41 billion
Total	£340 billion

Source: *Poverty*, 101, Spring 1999

It has not always been like this. Although social policy analysts argue about the 'beginning' of social protection, many would agree that in the UK social security is less than 100 years old. The first national government-provided benefits started in 1906 when old age pensions were introduced, followed in 1911 by benefits for some unemployed men.

However, the main elements of the social security system that we recognise today were mostly introduced between 1946–8 as part of the reforms recommended by the **Beveridge Report** (1942). Sir William Beveridge had argued that the aim of the Welfare State in the post-war period should be to defeat the 'five giants' on the road to reconstruction:

Definition

Beveridge Report – the government report, published in 1942 which provided the basis of the Welfare State

- *disease*, which was to be tackled by the creation of a National Health Service
- *ignorance*, which was to be tackled by the 1944 Education Act which created an educational system guaranteeing secondary education for all
- *squalor*, that is, poor housing, which was to be tackled by expanding local authority building programmes
- *idleness*, which meant unemployment, and was to be tackled by the government committing itself to managing the economy in such a way that there would be jobs for all
- *want*, which meant poverty, and this was to be tackled by a reformed system of social security payments.

Throughout history, repeated attempts had been made to eradicate poverty in the UK – always without success. However, Beveridge believed that he had located the basic causes of poverty in unemployment, old age and ill health. If suitable provision could be made to ensure that people in these situations received the right kind of help, then poverty could be eliminated once and for all.

Unemployment

Unemployment caused poverty because if there was no wage coming in, not only the unemployed person, but his entire family, was affected. Beveridge therefore decided that some form of unemployment benefit had to be paid, a benefit which provided enough to allow a man to support his family and keep them above subsistence level. (Please note, it was Beveridge's assumption [writing in the 1940s], not mine, that the man was the supporter of the family!)

Old age

Old age caused poverty because many people were unable to save enough during their working lives to provide for themselves adequately in their retirement. A system of compulsory saving was required, in which the State and employers would add extra funds so that when people retired there would be funds they could draw upon to provide for their needs. This became the basis for the **National Insurance** system described below.

Ill health

Illness caused poverty as it prevented individuals from earning a wage, or at least an adequate wage. Ill health included people who were injured at work or who became chronically (long term) sick, as well as people with disabilities. Beveridge therefore proposed a system of insurance for those with employment, in case they

Definitions

National Insurance – a system providing health care, unemployment and sickness benefits and pension and funded by payments made from the paypacket

National Assistance – the safety-net set of State benefits for those who were unable to pay National Insurance

should fall ill. This was to be tied into the same scheme as the National Insurance taken out against unemployment.

For those who were unable to work for health or other reasons, Beveridge proposed a 'safety net' system of benefits which would cover everybody who was unable to work but who for some reason was not covered by National Insurance. This safely net element (originally called **National Assistance**) is today known as Income Support.

Beveridge also set up various specific, means-tested benefits for people with disabilities. The modern versions of these are described in a later section of the chapter.

Related welfare provision

It is important to remember that National Insurance and National Assistance were not introduced in isolation, but were closely linked to other benefits and policies.

Definition

John Maynard Keynes – an economist whose ideas helped provide the basis of much of the economic theory underpinning the Welfare State

Full employment

It was assumed that the government would be able to maintain full employment in the post-war period, unlike the dreadful times of high unemployment experienced throughout the world in the 1920s and 1930s. This assumption was based on the belief in new economic theories developed by the economist **John Maynard Keynes**. Keynes argued that by increasing government spending in times of rising unemployment, the government could actually limit the amount of unemployment – spending on government schemes would create jobs and raise spending levels in the country, which could kick-start the economy. This theory was contrary to the economic thinking of the 1930s, which argued that it was necessary to *reduce* government spending in order to escape from economic depressions.

Health services

One of the main causes of poverty before the Second World War (1939–45) had been the illness of the main wage earner in a family (usually the man). No work meant no income. By introducing a health service that would eliminate most illness, there would be fewer people unable to work, and hence less poverty. It also meant that there would be lower demands on the social security system.

Education

A workforce of well-educated individuals would not only be more able to look after themselves by getting jobs and so limit the extent of unemployment, but this would also benefit employers and bring general prosperity to the country.

Family allowances

Closely related to the system of National Insurance was the introduction of family allowances, payable for each child, after the first child, as long as they remained in full-time education.

Definitions

Contributory benefits – State benefits based on payment of National Insurance contributions

Non-contributory benefits – safety net benefits at a lower level not based on National Insurance contributions

National Insurance and National Assistance

An important element in the development of social protection since the Second World War was the distinction Beveridge introduced between **contributory or insurance-based benefits** (known as National Insurance) and **non-contributory or assistance benefits** (known as National Assistance).

National Insurance

National Insurance was a system which was intended to offer protection for people against unemployment and medical treatment in return for 'contributions' or deductions from their wages. It also forms part of the State pension scheme. Beveridge did not invent social insurance; there had been a form of national insurance protection for unemployment, sickness and pensions in the UK as early as 1908, and this had been copied from an even earlier system in Germany. However, Beveridge argued that these early schemes covered too few people and that the benefits paid out were too low for people to have a decent standard of living. He therefore extended them to cover more conditions and claimants.

Compulsory National Insurance is a system whereby people pay into a common fund, along with their employers and the government. In the event of unemployment or illness, and during retirement, every person who has made enough payments has a right to claim the relevant benefits through the National Insurance system.

The National Insurance system which Beveridge introduced was based on a number of principles which he felt were very important. These included:

- *Comprehensiveness*: The scheme was to cover as many people as possible, and as many risks as possible. However, Beveridge realised that a scheme which required contributions over a long period of time would not be appropriate for certain groups in the population, for example people who are long-term disabled and who could never work enough to contribute to an insurance scheme. Therefore National Assistance was developed as a supplementary scheme for those outside National Insurance protection.
- *Flat-rate benefits and contributions*: The contributions were to be paid at the same rate, regardless of earnings. Similarly, the benefits were to be paid at a flat rate.
- *Adequate benefits*: The State benefits should offer a decent minimum standard, which would allow a reasonable standard of living. Beveridge believed that the level of payments should be high enough to enable people to live free from poverty. There would be no need for any other form of supplementary payments. If some people wanted to have higher income levels in times of need, they would be free to take out their own personal private insurance on top of National Insurance.

National Assistance

National Assistance was introduced to replace the Poor Law which was a very unpopular system of welfare provision dating back to the Victorian period.

The underlying idea of National Assistance was that it was to be a 'safety net' for all those who could not be included in the National Insurance scheme, for whatever reason. Unlike National Insurance, which was a contractual right between employees who paid and the government who received, National Assistance was seen as part of the benefits of being a UK citizen. Beveridge believed that payments under this scheme would be small, and would be received by a decreasing number of people. For example, according to Beveridge, at the beginning most older people would not qualify for a State pension because they had not had enough time to build up enough contributions. At first, therefore, they should receive National Assistance. Over time, this would be phased out as the 'newer generations' of workers came to pensionable age. Eventually no one would need National Assistance as everyone would qualify for a National Insurance pensions (or be eligible because their husbands had paid). As for the sick, it was genuinely believed that the NHS would eradicate virtually all ill health in the UK and so, over time, there would be little need for National Assistance for the ill. The benefits paid from National Assistance were to be based on an assessment of the needs and the means of each claimant, in other words, they were means-tested benefits.

Summary of important legislation and administrative changes in social security 1946–79

- *National Insurance Acts 1944 and 1946:* introduced National Insurance and created the Ministry of National Insurance to run the new scheme.
- *Family Allowances Act 1945:* introduced a benefit to help families with the extra costs of dependent children (later known as Child Benefit).
- *National Assistance Act 1948:* created the National Assistance Board to administer NA benefits and formally abolished the Victorian Poor Law.
- *National Insurance Act 1959:* introduced graduated pensions, i.e. instead of everyone paying and receiving the same benefits, these became income-related.
- *National Insurance Act 1966:* introduced earnings-related benefits (withdrawn in 1982). National Assistance became known as Supplementary Benefit (SB).
- *1966:* Ministry of Social Security was created to take over the job of the National Assistance Board. Included in this was the Supplementary Benefits Commission which replaced the National Assistance Board.
- *1968:* Ministry of Social Security was renamed Department of Health and Social Security (DHSS).
- *Family Income Supplement Act 1970:* the forerunner of Family Credit and what later became the Working Families Tax Credit.
- *Child Benefit Act 1975:* Child Benefit (CB) replaced Family Allowance and Income Tax Relief for children. CB was payable for all children, including the first.
- *1978:* State Earnings Related Pension Scheme (SERPS) was introduced to give higher levels of pensions in the future.

Main points

▶ Social protection is the general term used for a range of benefits provided by the State which help its population stay out of poverty.

▶ Social protection started with various Acts giving pensions in 1906.

▶ However, the system as we know it started between 1946–8 as a result of the Beveridge Report.

▶ The Beveridge Report stated that it was important to eliminate the five giants of disease, ignorance, squalor, idleness and want.

▶ As a result the government introduced the Welfare State which provided financial benefits in the form of social security, as well as health services, an education system and the commitment of the government to maintain full employment.

▶ National Assurance was the system of benefits based upon paying an amount out in National Insurance to the government.

▶ Those who did not pay National Insurance were eligible for a safety-net set of benefits called National Assistance.

Changes in social security

1948–79

A gradual change took place in the nature of UK social security benefits between 1948–79. Most significantly, the levels of payment from National Insurance were never high enough to provide people with an adequate standard of living, and so increasingly people had to turn to supplementary benefits to top these up. (National Assistance was later renamed Supplementary Benefit, and is now known as Income Support.) What Beveridge saw as a contributions-based system in which everyone was entitled to benefits because they paid for them increasingly became a means-tested system.

There was also a growing problem of sexism in the social security system, as benefits were based on the idea of a 'normal' family, with a male breadwinner as the head of the household. As a result of this, many women were excluded from benefits or received reduced rates. The changing nature of the family also meant that there was an enormous growth in the number of lone-parent families. These women (about 90 per cent of lone-parent families are headed by a woman) and their children were forced into poverty, as the system required them to live off supplementary, means-tested benefits and effectively prevented lone mothers from working.

There was always an overlap between low paid employment and social security levels. Therefore, in the 1970s, the government introduced Family Income Supplement in which a payment was made by the State to raise low wages up to the level of pay that was thought to be necessary for a family. This was another important move away from Beveridge's principles, because it shifted social security from a system of insurance against unforeseen mishaps, such as illness and unemployment, into a form of subsidy for low paying employers.

The cost of social protection

The effect of all the amendments introduced after the reforms which Beveridge had recommended can be seen in the table below: the social security system expanded enormously in both expense and the number of people and needs it covered.

The growth in social security spending, 1949–2002

	1949–50	1979–80	1996–7	2001–2 (forecast)
£ million cash	598	18,777	92,212	105,549
£ million at 1998–9 prices	12,201	51,648	97,182	98,253
Index of spending in real terms, 1949 = 100	100	423	797	805
Spending as a % of GDP	4.7%	9.1%	12%	11.2%

Source: *The Changing Welfare State* (Department of Social Security, 2000)

1 At 1999 prices, what was the spending on social security in 1949–50 and 2001–2?

2 What proportionate increase is that (look at 'index of spending in real terms')?

3 How has spending on social security increased in terms of cost to the economy as a whole (GDP)?

4 Why do you think governments are keen to lower social security spending?

Until the mid-1970s, most of the growth in spending was due to the introduction of new benefits or the extension of existing ones. After the mid-1970s, a rather different dynamic took over. By the mid-1970s many felt that the social security system which Beveridge had designed for the post-war years was out of date, and in practice many of his principles had been virtually abandoned. Around the same time, a global economic recession meant that public expenditure cutbacks were imposed and ideas for a more drastic overhaul of the social protection system began to emerge. Some of these ideas were especially appealing to the

Conservative Party which, under Mrs Thatcher, had taken on a new radical free-market outlook. When the Conservatives won the 1979 general election, the British social security system entered a new phase.

1980–97

In 1979, a Conservative government was elected with very clear views about the future of social security. In their view, the system had drifted away from its original aim of providing help for those who were unable to find work or who were unable to perform work because of ill health or disability. Instead they believed that social protection had become a wasteful bureaucratic structure that actually discouraged people from working.

The initial aims of the government in 1979 included ensuring that:

- less money was spent on social security
- State bureaucracy was cut back
- the most needy should be targeted for help
- a new enterprise and self-help culture would be created to replace what they believed was a 'culture of dependency'
- private business, such as private insurance companies, could do a better job of providing pensions and certain other welfare benefits than the State.

Although the Thatcher governments were not successful in achieving all of these aims (as can be seen from the table on page 48 they did not manage to reduce spending), the attempt to change the social protection system had a lasting impact.

Activities

Ideologies and policies

1 Look at Chapter 2. Which theoretical approach did the objectives of the Conservative government relate to?
2 Select three objectives, beliefs or policies described in this section of the chapter which characterise the theoretical approach you have identified.

At first, the new Conservative ideas were put into effect by means of what initially appeared to be small alterations to the benefits system. However, some of these had very important long-term effects. For example, the government broke the link between increases in benefits and increases in earnings, and instead linked benefit rises to increases in prices. As price increases are usually lower than wage rises, the long-term result was a significant saving in public expenditure but also that welfare benefits, including pensions, fell much further behind average wages.

Does social security create 'dependency'?

Universal welfare provision works its damaging effects on everyone, not just the poorest. The expectations that society, the State, the government, 'they', will look after our problems tricks us into abdicating from self-reliance and social responsibility. This is a major cause of escalating crime, the collapse of the family, inadequate schools, and health care, and economic decline. Despite what universal welfare provision pretends, it is down to each of us, individually and in voluntary co-operation.

We should encourage those at the bottom of the pile to aspire and struggle to improve their lives. Universal welfare provision instead locks them tight into under-caste dependency. For example, it offers incentives for staying unemployed, or underemployed, though work is the major source of independent dignity.

By ridiculing competition and excellence, it deprives the children of the welfare-dependent under-class of self-improvement through education – in the past the salvation of even the most disadvantaged.

Source: Adapted from D. Marsland, 'Face to face', *Social Studies Review*, November 1989

We have devalued all of the things you have to do to get out of poverty, like hard work, personal responsibility, getting married and taking care of family, staying in school, and we have valued all the things that if you're poor and you do them, you'll stay poor forever, like ... dropping out and not being serious about work.

Source: Myron Magnet, *The Dream and The Nightmare: The Sixties Legacy to the Underclass* (Encounter Books, 1998)

1   What theoretical viewpoint do Marsland and Magnet support?

2   What kind of welfare provision are they criticising?

3   What causes a 'culture of dependency' to develop, according to Marsland and Magnet?

4   What are those who live in a culture of dependency doing which is wrong, and what ought they to be doing?

5   What does Marsland mean when he says that there are incentives for staying unemployed or under-employed?

6   What kind of reforms to social protection do you think that Marsland and Magnet might recommend?

7   Do you agree or disagree with Marsland's and Magnet's analyses? Give reasons for your answer.

8   What evidence might you need to test their opinions?

1986 Social Security Act

Reforms introduced in the 1986 Social Security Act (which came into force in 1988) brought about some of the most significant changes in UK social protection since the 1940s. This legislation included:

- *Income Support*, for the unemployed with no entitlement to unemployment benefit (now partially replaced by Jobseeker's Allowance)
- *Family Credit*, which replaced Family Income Supplement and was a payment to encourage people who had families back into work (This has since been replaced by Working Family Tax Credit.)
- the *Social Fund*, which replaced a previous system of allowances which people had a right to, for such things as help with bills, purchasing items such as clothes or household goods (for example, cookers) and other necessities. Unlike the previous system where people had a right to help in emergencies, the Social Fund only provided help at the discretion of DSS officials. Also, most of the Social Fund was made up of loans which had to be repaid, and there were very few grants which were available only to a few priority cases. (The Social Fund continues today.)

These reforms were only one part of a much wider programme of change which started in 1979 and significantly altered the UK system of welfare provision. There were many other significant changes.

Pensions

In 1978, an all-party agreement brought about a change in the pension scheme, to a system called the State Earnings Related Pension Scheme (SERPS). Under SERPS, State pensions would be paid at different levels according to how much people had paid into the system over the years (those on higher salaries were to pay in more than those on lower salaries).

The Conservative government in the 1980s was concerned that the increase in the number of pensioners would make SERPS impossible to finance, as population projections showed that there was likely to be a threefold increase in pensioners in the following forty years. As a result, future earnings-related pension levels were substantially reduced and employees were encouraged to take out private pensions, either occupational schemes (i.e. which come as part of a job) or personal (i.e. individual) ones. Pensions therefore moved from a State benefit to a private arrangement.

One problem which has since emerged with this policy, however, has been the so-called 'mis-selling' of personal pensions. In the mid-1980s, many people were persuaded by private insurance companies to abandon their State or occupational pension in favour of a personal pension. Unfortunately for many people this was a bad deal and they would have been far better off staying in the State or their occupational scheme. By 1998 the total cost of this mistake was estimated to be £11 billion in terms of compensation and lost income.

The Labour government elected in 1997 introduced further pension reforms several of which continue the trend of making pensions a private arrangement; in fact it is estimated that although currently 60 per cent of pension costs in the UK is carried by the public sector and only 40 per cent by the private sector, by 2050 these figures will be the other way round (i.e. 40:60 public:private sector). These main changes introduced by the Labour government in pensions and other areas of social security are described later in this chapter.

Child Benefit

Child Benefit was introduced after much delay by the Labour government in 1977 (the legislation had been passed two years before). It is sometimes described as an example of a 'universal' benefit, because it is paid to every household with dependent children no matter how well-off the family may be. Strictly speaking, however, it is not really 'universal' as it is not paid to everyone, only people with children to care for.

Despite the fact that several campaign groups (such as the Child Poverty Action Group, women's groups and representatives of lone-parent families) had campaigned for child benefits, they have never been very popular in the UK. Child Benefit was introduced because it was believed that families should not have to bear the full cost of raising children without some financial help from the government, as children are the country's future and everyone who reaches old age will depend on them to produce and provide services. However, not everyone takes this view, and Child Benefit has been criticised as expensive and indiscriminate – giving too little to low income families which really need help and a little unnecessary extra money to better-off families who do not need any help (see the discussion of universal and targeted benefits later in this chapter).

Child Benefit was not directly affected by the reforms of 1986–8, but it was frozen during the mid-1980s in order to save money, and the government's intention was to phase it out altogether in the 1990s. However, the Conservative government never got around to this as Child Benefit still has some very high profile supporters. To this day it remains the centre of major debate in UK social security.

Housing Benefit

Housing Benefit was introduced in its current form in 1982 and was intended to simplify what one previous government minister had described as the 'dog's breakfast' of housing support payments which had developed since the Beveridge Report. The New Housing Benefit system was to be administered by local authorities and help low income households to meet their housing expenses. Following the reforms of 1986–8, the levels of benefit declined, and new restrictions and methods of working out entitlement were introduced. In 1996, further strict new rules were introduced to limit the amounts payable, in particular to control the amounts paid to single, young people.

Main points ▶ The social security system did not change as fast as society, so that soon people could see that some of the assumptions about the nature of the family and the role of women for example were outdated.

▶ A poverty trap was created because of the overlap of low wages and State benefits.

▶ The Welfare State came to be seen by many as too expensive and too bureaucratic.

▶ In 1979, the newly elected Conservative government began a series of significant changes in the social security system.

▶ They wanted to cut back on social security, making people less dependent on benefits amongst other things.

▶ Some of the changes they introduced were very important, for example the link between the rise in wages and pensions was broken. This meant that pensions increased in their worth more slowly than the general rise in the standard of living. This made older people relatively poorer.

Summary of important legislation and administrative changes in social security 1980–97

- *Social Security Acts 1980*: introduced a range of cut-backs in social security, and a considerable 'tightening up' of the rules on discretionary benefits so that they were more difficult to get. Most earnings-related supplements for benefits were also abolished

- *Social Security and Housing Act 1982*: introduced Housing Benefit and shifted responsibility for paying it to local authorities.

- *Social Security Act 1986*: introduced the most significant changes to social security since 1948. The changes included the introduction of Income Support in place of Supplementary Benefit, Family Credit instead of Family Income Supplement, and the Social Fund instead of emergency needs payments which were additional to SB. The improvements to pensions which were introduced with the creation of SERPS in 1978 were severely 'watered down' and people were encouraged to take out private pensions.

- *1988*: Department of Health and Social Security split into two – the Department of Health (DoH) and the Department of Social Security (DSS).

- *Child Support Act 1991*: came into effect in 1993. The Act required absent parents (usually fathers) to contribute to the maintenance of their children.

New Labour and social protection

The Labour government which was first elected in 1997 has been very active in the general field of social policy and welfare reform, and has introduced over 100 new polices in this general areas in its first two years. Its activities can be classified into four main categories:

- *preventative measures*, such as the 'Sure Start' scheme, action to reduce teenage pregnancies, NHS reform, and so on. Here the idea is to prevent social problems occurring

- *labour market measures* – various 'New Deals' for young people, older unemployed people, single parents and disabled people; the national minimum wage. Many of the ideas here derive from the previous Conservative government and concern themselves with trying to get as many people back to work as possible

- *neighbourhood measures*, such as the New Deal for Communities and the National Strategy for Neighbourhood Renewal. These are policies designed to attack the decline in neighbourhoods which occurred during the 1980s and

1990', as industries were closed down and many industrial and coal-mining areas were devastated

- *social protection measures* – these include the various changes to social security, such as pension reforms, which try to eliminate poverty.

Who benefits from social security?

Distribution of benefit expenditure by beneficiary, 1998–9

People over working age	46%
People with a long-term illness or disability	24%
Non-disabled working age people	21%
This is made up of...	
Families	11%
Unemployed people	5%
People with a short-term illness, widows and others	5%
Children	8%

Source: *The Changing Welfare State* (Department of Social Security, 2000)

1 Which group has the highest percentage of social security spending? What is the next group?

2 Some commentators have talked about 'the deserving poor and the undeserving poor', referring to people who need help because they are unable to help themselves, and those who simply don't want to help themselves. What comment can you make about that idea, looking at the figures here?

Joined-up government

The Labour government has emphasised the need for what they call 'joined-up' government. By this they mean better co-ordination of policies so that policies in different areas (such as crime and education) support and strengthen each other and do not pull in opposite directions. One effect which this has is to complicate discussions of social protection as there are now many more areas which have an effect on benefits and income maintenance than simply the support offered through the Department for Work and Pensions. For example, the Inland Revenue and the Treasury have become very important providers of welfare through the expansion of tax credit schemes as an alternative way of delivering social protection, and the development of employment and training programmes to lift people out of poverty. In addition, new organisational structures like the Social Exclusion Unit have developed policies also have an impact on income levels of social protection.

Social security reforms

Among the main welfare reforms introduced by the Labour government are:

- Working Families Tax Credits which replaced Family Credit – this is intended to guarantee a minimum weekly income (April 2001 £200) for full-time working families with children
- Children's Tax Credit – which from 6 April 2001 replaced the Married Couples Tax Allowance and provides income tax rebates (up to £10 per week in April 2001) for people with children under 16
- the welfare reform proposals published in March 1998 – *New Ambitions for our Country: A New Contract for Welfare*

- pension reform, including a new stakeholder pension to be offered by employers and other non-state organisations, and a Second State Pension (SSP) for those on lower incomes.

The government claims that these measures plus others, such as increases to Child Benefit (up 25 per cent since 1997) and Maternity Grants, have lifted 1.5 million people in the UK out of poverty (including 700,000 children) and made the poorest fifth of the population £1,000 per year better off. Tony Blair pledged to eradicate child poverty within 20 years, and in April 2001 the government promised to introduce new *child endowments* ('baby bonds') as another measure to achieve this objective – where each child was to be 'given' £500 which parents could add to, and the accumulated amount could be spent on a such things as education when they are 18.

Continuity between Labour and Conservative policies

These policies tell us a lot about the New Labour approach to social policy and social protection. Tony Blair has argued that 'Some things the Conservatives got right. We will not change them', and several measures which the Labour government introduced continued trends set by the previous Conservative government. Important examples of this include:

- the retreat from universal State-funded provision towards more targeted support (as in pensions)
- the shift from Welfare-to-Work, and describing the objective of welfare reform being to 'rebuild welfare around the work ethic'
- arguing that entitlement to benefits for many groups has to be earned rather than granted as a right – this was shown in Labour's 1997 general election manifesto which insisted that 'rights and duties must go together'
- reducing certain benefits during the first two years of the 1997 government – most notably the cuts to lone parents' benefits in December 1997.

On the other hand, the Labour government is also different from its predecessor in important ways:

- The Labour government publicly recognises that there really is such a thing as poverty and it has committed itself to reducing it.
- It has introduced increases in benefit levels which were higher than increases in prices, including increases in Child Benefit and Income Support.
- There has been some **redistribution** of resources to lower income groups, although this has often been 'by stealth' and not always apparent to those who have benefited from them or who would support such moves.

Definition

Redistribution – movement of income from richer to poorer

Social protection and the labour market

One of the most significant examples of the New Labour approach to social protection has been its 'active labour market' policies where it has attempted to reduce poverty and increase incomes by various programmes to encourage employment. Because they are so important and central to the Labour strategy, these measures deserve special consideration.

Welfare-to-Work

The Welfare-to-Work programme, or the New Deal, was announced by the government in 1997 and took effect in January 1998. Initially it focused on four main groups who are seen as having particularly severe problems in obtaining employment:

- 18–25-year-olds who had been unemployed for six months or more (This began in March 1997, and cost £1,480 million, or 57 per cent of the 'Windfall' tax money allocated until 2002.)
- lone parents on Income Support whose youngest child is in primary school (This began in October 1998 and cost £200 million, or 8 per cent of the Windfall tax.)
- long-term unemployed people who are over 25 (This began in June 1998, accounting for £600 million, or 23 per cent of the Windfall tax.)
- people with disabilities in long-term unemployment.

Work: New Labour's solution to poverty

... ministers have now abandoned hope of pruning DSS spending – 30 per cent of the government total – in the short term.

They do argue that benefits expenditure is rising far less quickly than under the Conservatives. Commenting on the annual report, Alistair Darling, Social Security Secretary, said: "Social security spending is under control and will grow at an annual rate of less than 2 per cent across this parliament, less than half the annual rate of the last parliament."

This, however, ignores the fact that the new working-families tax credit, which could be costing £5 billion a year by the next election, will come under the Inland Revenue budget, whereas family credit, which the new credit is replacing, has been under the DSS.

... To achieve long-term reductions in benefits spending, the Government must address claimants other than the available-for-work unemployed. This is why there is such stress on the New Deal for lone parents and on pilot schemes, starting next week, giving incentives for disabled people to find work.

Latest New Deal figures show that 7,311 jobs were obtained by lone parents under the scheme between July 1997 and the end of February this year. Almost 42,000 lone-parent claimants have joined the voluntary scheme: six times as many have been invited to do so. It is slow progress, as Darling seemed to admit in saying "many will need time and support to prepare for work".

Source: *Guardian Unlimited*, 7 April 1999

1 Why is the New Deal extended beyond the 'available-for-work' unemployed?

2 What is the New Deal take-up rate amongst lone parents?

3 Why do you think that the government is increasing the pressure put upon lone parents and disabled people to find work?

4 What is the Working Family Tax Credit?

5 Why does it lower social security spending (though not government spending)?

6 What percentage of all government spending is taken up by the (then) Department of Social Security?

18–25-year-olds

The programme for 18–25-year-olds offers work experience and skills training and provides organisations with a subsidy (£60 per week in April 2001) for employing young people who have been unemployed for six months or more, in order to give them experience of employment.

The scheme offers young unemployed people the choice of working for:

- a private sector company
- a voluntary organisation
- an environmental task force
- on-going training for 12 months.

There is a 'gateway' scheme in which all young, unemployed people will be provided with education and social skills training to enable them to keep a job.

The rules state that those who refuse to join the scheme, or who drop out without good reason, lose two weeks of benefit. If they continue to refuse to join the scheme, they will lose a further four weeks of benefit. This can go on indefinitely if they will not work. In practice, it is sometimes possible for people to avoid this penalty for a long time by withholding information and not co-operating with the programme.

Lone parents

Lone parents with children over the age of five are offered 'individualised, case-managed assistance' to help them find jobs. This includes help in searching for work, advice and training. An important aspect of the New Deal is that lone parents may also receive help with childcare through after-school clubs and childcare network funded by National Lottery money. As part of the work available for young, unemployed people, there will be 50,000 new places made available for trainee childcarers. Financial help with childcare for lone parents in low-paid employment is also available. Lone parents with more than one child are allowed to pay up to £100 per week for childcare without losing any entitlement to Family Credit.

Long-term unemployed people

People who have been unemployed for more than two years qualify for a different Welfare-to-Work programme. The government provides £75 per person each week for six months to employers to take these people into work.

People with disabilities

People who are disabled and those receiving Incapacity Benefit are offered a specialist training and job training programme to help them into work.

Criticisms of Welfare-to-Work

The government's programme has not gone ahead without strong criticism, including the following points.

Are the jobs created really new?

The Welfare-to-Work programme subsidises employers to take workers on for a period of six months. But many commentators argue that many of these employers would have employed people anyway, so the subsidy is a gift to employers for doing what they were intending to do. Secondly, other workers may be laid-off because, by replacing them with 'new' workers from the Welfare-to-Work scheme, they will gain a subsidy.

What happens when the job subsidies end?

The subsidy lasts for six months, and at the end of that time employers may choose to lay-off the person on the scheme and replace them with another unemployed person. The six-month employment does not mean that there will be a job at the end of the period.

What happens to those who refuse or do not want to work?

The scheme is not voluntary. People who refuse to undertake employment or training lose their personal benefit (although benefit to dependent children continues). Presumably those who lose their benefits will have to turn to crime to support themselves or, at the very least, to the informal economy.

Why are they unemployed in the first place?

People who are long-term unemployed are often in that situation for a variety of reasons which are not tackled by Welfare-to-Work. These include:

- *personal reasons* – they may not have the qualities which employers want, they may be disabled or incapacitated, or they may not wish to work in the types of employment available
- *structural reasons* – the area where they live may have few opportunities for anyone, because of a lack of industry or commerce in the area.

It is unclear how the training programmes and subsidies available under the Welfare-to-Work programme will significantly change these conditions on their own. Previous schemes, including the Youth Opportunity Programmes, Youth Training Schemes, the Training Education Councils and Employment Training for adults, have all attempted to provide the opportunities to help overcome the 'personal' reasons for not getting work, with only limited success. The 'structural' reasons for unemployment will not be altered by giving a subsidy to employers. If there are few employers, there will be few opportunities to subsidise employment.

The government gives with one hand and takes with the other

Although the government is committed to spending £3.5 billion on the various New Deal programmes, it has also introduced stricter rules regarding people's right to refuse training. Benefit is taken away from those who do not accept places in subsidised employment or in training.

Unemployment has fallen considerably in recent years, including among groups who have been targeted for the various New Deals. However, whether this is due to the success of Welfare-to-Work in tackling the causes of unemployment or because of a period of sustained growth in the national economy is open to debate. One of the first evaluations of Welfare-to-Work, which concentrated on the New Deal for Lone Parents, concluded that it had not been a great success: less than 1 in 10 single mothers contacted had gone on to find a job one year after the scheme started.

Initial results of the New Deal for Lone Parents

	Total no.	%
Target group	40,000	100
Number contacted	22,401	56
Number interviewed	5,832	26
Number who agreed to participate in New Deal	5,235	23
Number who found work	1,678	8

Source: J. Hales and A. Shaw, *Evaluation of the New Deal for Lone Parents* (Department of Social Security, 1998)

Main points
- New Labour first came into power in 1997 and began a wide range of new policies.
- Social security was closely linked to other changes and any understanding of social security changes need to be seen in a wider context.
- Labour's policies were centred on four areas: preventative measures, the labour market, neighbourhood developments and social protection.
- Many of the policies of the previous Conservative government were still carried on – or at least the ideas underlying them were.

▶ One of the most important ideas was of Welfare-to-Work. This was the belief that a lot more could be done to 'encourage' groups who were living on benefits to enter the labour market.

▶ A whole series of new policies were organised and new forms of benefits paid.

▶ For those in work, some of the benefits were paid through the inland revenue taxation system, rather than social security.

▶ Many people criticise the Welfare-to-Work programme for its coercive nature (people feel forced to do it) and for the fact that many of its payment simply subsidises low-paying employers.

▶ Although unemployment has decreased this may be reflecting the change in the economy, not the success of the Welfare-to-Work programme.

Summary of social protection reforms since 1997

May 1997: Harriet Harman is appointed as Secretary of State for the Department of Social Security (DSS), Frank Field is appointed as Minister for Welfare Reform with the responsibility to carry out a fundamental review of social provision.

June 1997: Government announces a 'New Deal for Young People' – a national scheme for tackling unemployment among young people aged 18–24, funded by £3.5 billion raised by taxes on privatised services.

November 1997: National Minimum Wage Bill is published.

December 1997: Social Exclusion Unit is launched.
120 Labour MPs sign a motion in the House of Commons condemning the government's proposal to reduce social security for lone parents.

January 1998: The New Deal for Young People (aged 18–24) is launched in twelve pilot areas

March 1998: The results of the government's review of social protection is published as a Green Paper: *New Ambitions for our Country: A New Contract for Welfare.*

April 1998: The Welfare-to-Work programme is launched nationally.

June 1998: New Deal for Long-Term Unemployed (aged over 25) launched.

July 1998: Lone Parents Benefit abolished.

September 1998: New Deal for Disabled People launched – £195 million for advice and assistance to help unemployed disabled people into work.

October 1998: New Deal for Lone Parents launched – £190 million devoted to advice and assistance to help unemployed single parents into work.

February 1999: New Deal for Partners of Unemployed People – £60 million devoted to advice and assistance to help people into work.

April 1999: National Minimum Wage introduced. £3.60 per hour for those aged over 22.

April 1999: Minimum Income Guarantee for pensioners – no retired person should have an income below £75 per week (£116.60 for couples). This figure will be increased annually in line with rising prices. In order to get this level, lower income pensioners will have to claim Income Support, as the basic state pension will not be increased above the rate of inflation.

October 1999: Working Families Tax Credit replaces Family Credit. This includes a new Childcare Tax Allowance which provided 70 per cent of the costs of childcare for working parents.

October 1999: Disabled Person's Tax Credit replaces Disability Working Allowance.

April 2001: Disability Income Guarantee introduced.

June 2001: Department of Social Security renamed Department of Work and Pensions (DWP).

Social protection: benefits in the UK today

Definition

Means-tested benefits – benefits which are paid out on a scale depending upon the savings and income that the claimant has

Despite the many changes which have been made over the years, it is still possible to classify the British social security system in terms of the following main types of benefits:

- contributory benefits
- non-contributory benefits
- **means-tested benefits**.

Although social security is still mainly the responsibility of the Department of Work and Pensions, there are now two semi-autonomous 'agencies':

- the Contributions Agency, for collecting National Insurance
- the Benefits Agency, for the payment of benefits .

Contributory benefits

Contributory benefits are those paid for through National Insurance payments, which are automatically deducted from pay packets in much the same way as Income Tax. This is the State's way of making us pay for insurance against redundancy and assurance against our old age.

The right to receive National Insurance benefits are related to the amount of time someone has paid into the scheme. An important feature is that, like private insurance schemes, the person receives the money no matter how much income she or he has from another source. For instance, if a person becomes unemployed and has paid enough contributions, then she or he receives Jobseeker's Allowance, even if she or he is also receiving a large income from investments.

Non-contributory benefits

These are benefits from the State for which individuals do not have to have paid National Insurance contributions. They are generally targeted at those who have very clear physical needs, such as disabled people or young children. These are not means tested (that is income is not taken into account when giving these), entitlement depends on whether the person falls into the appropriate category.

Means-tested benefits

These are given to those whose income falls below a certain level, and claimants need not have paid National Insurance contributions to obtain them. In other words, there is a test of your means (income) before you can receive such payment. No matter what their income, however, certain groups are not eligible for means-tested benefits at all, for example students.

Benefits for different types of claimant

Benefits can also be classified by which groups and individuals are eligible to claim them. As we can see, different members of the same group may be able to claims different types of benefit – some will qualify for contributory benefits, others for non-contributory benefits, and some will only be able to claim means-tested benefits, which are generally set at a lower rate. There are also overlaps between different types of claimant (especially between older people and the disabled), but to keep things simple, we can distinguish the following five groups and benefits.

Benefits for older and retired people

Benefits for older and retired people are by far the largest component of social protection, making up 46 per cent of expenditure. In 1998/99 pensions cost £35.6 billion (37 per cent of all public expenditure). 10.8 million people received the basic State pension – over half of them also receive SERPS.

State pensions

These have declined in real terms over the last 20 years. Before 1980, they were linked to rises in wages, but they are now linked to rises in the cost of living, and as wages generally have risen faster than the cost of living, the relative value of pensions has fallen: retirement pensions now stand at about 17 per cent of average male salaries and the government has more or less committed itself to keeping pensions at a low level. On the other hand, the Labour government has also introduced a minimum income guarantee for pensioners so that even though they are falling behinds average living standards, no pensioner will receive less than £75 per week

The new Second State Pension which will be phased in over several years is also intended to improve the incomes of lower earners, the long-term sick and disabled, and those who cannot get a job because they care for others. The government claims that the SSP will eventually double the pension of some people from among these groups from the level which SERPS would have provided.

Tax concessions for private pension schemes

The Conservative government in 1986 introduced incentives for people to enter private pension schemes. Contributions to such schemes are deducted from a person's income before tax is assessed, so that less income tax is paid.

Income Support

Older people are covered by the government policy of minimum income guarantee and so for those on State pensions only, they may receive additional payments via Income Support to bring their income up to the Minimum Income Guarantee.

Benefits for the unemployed

Jobseeker's Allowance

This replaced both Income Support and Unemployment Benefit in October 1996. It has two strands:

- a *contribution-based* allowance – this element of Jobseeker's Allowance replaced Unemployment Benefit. If a person has paid enough National Insurance contributions they will receive Jobseeker's Allowance irrespective of their own savings or a partner's earnings. However, no additional allowance is given for dependants. Contributory Jobseeker's Allowance lasts for a maximum of six months
- an *income-based (or means-tested)* allowance – this element of Jobseeker's Allowance is for people who have not got enough National Insurance payments or have been unemployed for longer than six months.

How much is given depends upon a range of factors including:

- age (18 to pensionable age)
- number of dependent children
- partner's earnings
- amount of savings.

The underlying idea of the Jobseeker's Allowance is to ensure that the person who is unemployed is actively seeking work and doing everything in their power to obtain some form of employment. This is intended to distinguish between those who are uninterested in employment and those who are genuinely keen to find work. The idea is that the more rigorous conditions of Jobseeker's Allowance might deter some of those who were claiming social security but had no intention of working, and also put off people who were (illegally) working and claiming benefits at the same time. In 2000–1 there were about one million Jobseeker's Allowance claimants, 25 per cent of whom were women

Benefits for families with children

For the families of lone parents and low paid people, the government has a number of policies to help combat poverty.

Child Benefit

This is a flat-rate payment for all families with children. Despite recent increases, its real value has declined over the last thirty years.

Working Families Tax Credit (WFTC)

This was introduced in October 1999, to replace Family Credit. Like its predecessor, WFTC provides financial support for people in low paid employment and who have dependent children.

Income Support and Jobseeker's Allowance

People with families can obtain additional income under the Income Support and Jobseeker's Allowance schemes in the form of premiums. These are described above.

Eligible for what?

1 A woman, Mrs A, is unemployed because the company for which she worked has gone bankrupt. She has been paying her National Insurance contributions for the last three years. Her husband is in full-time employment. What benefit can she claim?

2 Her friend, Ms P, is in exactly the same situation except that she left the company two weeks before it closed as she said she could no longer stand the rudeness of her boss. What is she entitled to?

3 A third woman, Ms C, who is now unemployed as a result of the company going bankrupt, only started work nine months ago, after she left college. What is she entitled to?

Benefits for sick and disabled people and their carers

Spending on people with a long-term illness or disability takes up about 24 per cent of the social protection budget (about 2.8 per cent of GDP).

There are two types of benefit for this groups:

- *income replacement benefits* – these include Incapacity Benefit, Severe Disablement Allowance and Income Support
- *benefits to pay for extra costs* – these include Disability Living Allowance and Attendance Allowance.

As in the case of retired people, there is also a minimum income guarantee for people with disabilities who are dependent upon benefits.

Income replacement benefits

- *Incapacity Allowance* In general, this is an allowance paid to those unable to work through physical or mental injury who have been off work for more than 28 weeks, although in certain circumstances it is payable before that time. Incapacity Benefit has short-term and long-term elements.
  Under the Welfare-to-Work scheme for disabled people, there is a £200 million programme for training and individual employment counselling for people receiving Incapacity Benefit.
- *Disabled Person's Tax Credit* This is for people of working age in employment, and is paid through their wage packet.

Extra cost benefits

- *Attendance Allowance* This is the benefit paid to people under the age of retirement who are severely disabled (mentally or physically) and can prove that they need to be looked after for six months or more. It costs £2.7 billion per year.
- *Severe Disablement Allowance* This is a benefit for those of working age, who cannot get Sickness or Incapacity Benefit because they have not paid adequate National Insurance payments. It is effectively a flat-rate benefit.
- *Disability Living Allowance* This is for people under 65 with very significant disabilities who need help with personal care in such things as washing, dressing or using the toilet, either because they are ill or because they are disabled. DLA can be paid to people who do not actually have anyone looking after them. There are special arrangements for the terminally ill. There are two components of Disability Living Allowance: a care component and a mobility component. They are assessed separately, and paid at different rates.
- *Invalid Care Allowance* This is available for carers rather than for the person with disability. It is a flat-rate payment to those looking after the severely disabled in receipt of Attendance Allowance. The carer must not earn more than £30 each week (after 'reasonable expenses' have been deducted from earnings). Invalid Care Allowance is not available to wives of disabled people.
- *Income Support and Jobseeker's Allowance premiums* These schemes offer additional payments for people with disabilities – the extra amount depends on the severity of the disability.

Benefits for mothers, widows and parents

Statutory Maternity Pay

This is a payment for women who have been with the same employer for 26 weeks prior to 'the 15th week before the baby is due', and have paid National Insurance contributions. The level is linked to earnings for the first six weeks, followed by a flat rate payment.

Maternity Allowance

Women who do not qualify for the Statutory Maternity Pay receive a flat-rate payment. It was reluctantly introduced by the government in response to the European Union Pregnancy Directive of 1994.

Widow's benefits

There are three benefits for different categories of widows:

- widow's bereavement payment – a one-off payment for those with National Insurance contributions
- widowed mother's allowance – for widows with dependent children
- widow's pensions – available for those aged 45–65. Widows may receive husband's earnings-related pension.

Child Benefit

This is available to every family with dependent children. The first child has a higher rate of benefit than other children. Child Benefit is not taxed and does not affect rights to other benefits.

One Parent Benefit

This is additional Child Benefit paid to single parents (not co-habiting couples). It is a flat-rate payment which the person receives no matter how many children she or he has. However, no new claims for this benefit are to be accepted and it will eventually 'die out' as the children currently receiving it grow up.

Income Support

Income Support is a general, means-tested benefit which covers not only the unemployed but a number of other groups too. For example, in 2000–1, there were about 3.8 million Income Support claimants, two-thirds of whom were women, and 25 per cent of whom were disabled.

Income Support is in effect a range of benefits for those:

- whose incomes are below a certain level
- who are not working 16 hours a week or more, and do not have a partner in full-time employment either
- who are not required to be available for work because, for example they are sick or disabled, a lone parent or aged 60 or older.

Income Support is a means-tested benefit, which means that other family income is taken into account. For example, if a woman is unemployed, and her husband is working, then his income will generally mean that she is not eligible for Income Support.

Income Support for young, single people is particularly low, as there is a special lower rate for 18–24-year-olds. Those aged 16–17 years are not eligible for benefits at all, unless they are engaged on a job training scheme.

IS allowance comprises of several parts:

- a personal allowance for the person claiming and the partner, as well as for children
- a premium for people with 'special needs', such as families with children, people with disabilities and those over 60.

The premium for lone-parent families is being phased out, with no new premiums being allocated to this group since December 1997.

Since 1980, benefits for the unemployed have decreased in value (although they have remained the same in relation to prices):

- 1980 – Unemployment Benefit was worth about 18.5 per cent of average earnings; by 1996 it was approximately 13 per cent
- 1982 – the earnings-related supplement to Unemployment Benefit was abolished
- 1984 – children's additions for Unemployment Benefit were abolished
- 1988 – under-18s were no longer eligible for Income Support. If they did not have a Youth Training Scheme place or were in extreme hardship, they received no help from the State. Lower rates of benefit were also introduced for under-25s
- 1996 – Unemployment Benefit was abolished and replaced by contributory Jobseeker's Allowance. Unemployed claimants are only eligible for the non-

means-tested element of the benefit for only six months, compared to one year previously.

Jobseeker's Allowance is worth only 13 per cent of average male earnings, yet 20 years ago it was worth 17.5 per cent.

According to the Unemployment Unit, people aged 18–24 have been the worst affected by the cuts in support to unemployed people, with a reduction in benefit from £2,633 to £1,880 in their first year of unemployment since Jobseeker's Allowance was introduced.

Activity

1 Calculate your own eligibility for Jobseeker's Allowance or Income Support, and how much benefit you would receive (if any).
2 Compare this to you weekly expenses and see what you could afford if you lived on either Jobseeker's Allowance or Income Support (don't forget to include your housing expenses in your budget).
3 What links can you find between the increase in young beggars on the streets of British cities and changes in benefit entitlements?

The Social Fund

This is a system whereby people on low incomes, almost always on Income Support, can apply for either grants or loans. The grants are severely restricted, and so usually the payment takes the form of an interest-free loan, which is then directly subtracted from Income Support at source (that is before it is handed over to the individual). The entire Social Fund for each DSS office has a fixed budget, which the official responsible (the Social Fund Officer) cannot exceed.

It has been estimated that the level of payments under the Social Fund is 80 per cent less than it would have been if the previous system of cash payments had continued. Many families have found the costs of paying back loans from the Social Fund a considerable hardship. In a survey of Social Fund recipients by York University:

- 70 per cent said the repayments left them with insufficient money to live on
- 35 per cent said that they had to cut back on food, clothing or paying bills
- 20 per cent borrowed money from other sources to cope. (These 'other sources' were often illegal money lenders who charged extortionate rates of interest.)

Recently it has been suggested that the government may reform the Social Fund so that it becomes a more general source of credit for low income households (including those who have jobs) but who are not attractive to most banks and might turn to 'loan sharks' to borrow money.

Housing Benefit

This is a payment, made through the local authority housing departments, to cover the costs of rents and local government tax. It is available to those on Income Support, and to other low income individuals or families. The calculations for Housing Benefit are extremely complicated, and it is claimed that even the officials who calculate the amounts have trouble understanding. However, the principle of working it out is similar to that used in Income Support. The various 'needs' of an individual or family are worked out according to government guidelines and the total cost is called the 'applicable amount'. The income of the individual or family is then totalled and if this falls below the applicable amount, payments are made. The higher the income, the smaller the payment. Students do not qualify for Housing Benefit.

Too poor to be helped

The House of Commons social security committee recently published its report on the social fund. Unfortunately, it has copped out of a recommendation that could improve the lives of poor people.

Prior to 1988, claimants depending upon welfare benefits long term were entitled to grants for essential domestic items such as fires and cookers. In a cost-cutting exercise, the then Conservative government devised the social fund. The fund retained some grants, called community care grants, for people leaving institutions or to prevent them having to enter institutions.

Other grants, however, were replaced by loans. Budgeting loans were for "irregular needs" – such as when a family's cooker blows up – while crisis loans were for emergencies. The loans were repaid by automatic deductions from weekly incomes. They were interest free and could take up to a quarter of the debtor's weekly income.

In opposition, the Labour party vehemently condemned the changes. But once in power it retained them. It is to the social security committee's credit that it decided to investigate the workings of the social fund, and its report provides a thorough and critical analysis.

The report points out that despite constant demand, the number of community care grants has dropped from 294,000 in 1993–94 to 219,000 in 1999–2000. Four in 10 applications for budgeting loans and nearly three in 10 (27%) for crisis loans were rejected. The applicants might well be eligible and in desperate need but under the social fund system each district has a fixed and inadequate budget. So when that budget runs out, no more is available.

Extraordinarily, some applicants for loans have been refused because they were considered too poor to make repayments. In other words, the very poorest were denied help. Those receiving loans could purchase one essential item but, the committee found, the weekly repayments left them in absolute poverty.

Both those refused loans and those repaying them then often turned to commercial lenders who charge interest rates of up to 150%. ...

Last week a lone mother told me how her daughter had spilt a drink on, and ruined, her only fire. She has already had an application to the social fund refused. Does the committee advise her to get money from a loan shark or just to stay cold?

As a voluntary neighbourhood worker in the Easterhouse estate, Glasgow, I have seen 50 families in financial distress over the last two years. So what is my way forward? I propose that every long-term claimant be given a £500 annual bonus.

It would be up to them to decide whether to use it to buy furniture, Christmas presents or a holiday. The community care grants would have to remain, as often the costs of people taking up residence in the neighbourhood after years in an institution are more than £500.

But the loans would be abolished and, with them, their expensive administration. People on low incomes would have £500 as an entitlement and so be spared the humiliating experience of trying to convince officials that they need a loan.

Source: *The Guardian*, 17 April 2001

1 What replaced loans for essential items (for most people at least)?

2 Why was this done?

3 What percentage of loans were rejected?

4 What is the reason for this?

5 What proposal does the writer of the article make?

6 Which term would best describe the proposal that the writer makes – universal or means tested?

7 Do you agree with the writer?

There has been very considerable tightening of Housing Benefit rules since 1995, when the annual costs of £8.8 billion was considered too much by the government. Instead of paying the full costs of rents for housing, the 'local reference rate', which is the average rents for the area, will be paid.

Council Tax Benefit

Council tax is the payment people make for local government services. Benefits are available to help pay this. Most people on Income Support or Jobseeker's Allowance are eligible and the same rules for eligibility apply as those for Housing Benefit.

Activity

1 Which form of payment is the most difficult to obtain? Collect and compare the different application forms for the benefits described above – how easy would they be to complete properly?

2 Contact your local DSS office. Ask whether you can interview a Social Fund Officer. Find out how they decide whether to refuse or allow a claim.

Social security spending

Social security spending, 1994–2002 (real terms at 1999–2000 prices) (£ million)

	1994–5	2000–1 plans	2001–2 plans
Retirement Pension	33,220	37,707	38,710
Job Seeker's Allowance	–	3,316	3,275
Incapacity Benefit	–	6,629	6,592
Income Support	18,938	12,871	13,346
Child Benefit	7,067	8,344	8,401
Family Credit	1,665	–	–
Total benefit spending	98,059	98,883	101,249

Source: *Social Security Statistics* (Department of Social Security, 2000

In 1994–5, 44 per cent of benefit spending was devoted to retired people, 25 per cent to the unemployed, and 23 per cent to those with long-term illnesses or disabilities. In 1999–2000, 48 per cent went to retired people, 25 per cent to those with long-term illnesses or disabilities, and 19 per cent to unemployed people of working age. This change was mainly due to a fall in unemployment, rather than any reductions in benefits to unemployed people or increases to other groups. Spending on the unemployed varies with the state of the economy – during a recession when unemployment is high, more people claim benefits; for example, spending on the unemployed was 12.5 per cent of total social security expenditure in 1992–3, but only 6 per cent in 1998–9.

1 What changes, if any, took place, in the percentage of social security spending going to different groups between 1995 and 2000?

2 Why did this occur?

3 What affects the amount of money spent on the unemployed?

4 Explain why you think the government is very keen to promote Welfare-to-Work.

5 What was the overall spending on social security in 2001–02?

6 Does this represent an increase or decrease on earlier years shown in the table?

7 Identify the areas which accounted for this change in expenditure.

8 Does the total level of spending on a group mean that they receive higher benefits? What other factors might influence to total amount spent, and why might the total spending vary over time?

Debates in the provision of social security

There are a number of key issues which reappear in debates on social security provision. These include targeting (or selectivity) versus universalism, levels of take-up and the poverty trap (discussed in Chapter 4).

The death of universalism

Not many Labour Ministers could wipe £7 billion off their budget over three years without provoking a political bloodbath. Even fewer Ministers could do it if they were in charge of a tinderbox such as Social Security.

Yet Alastair Darling, by dint of lower than expected unemployment figures and some barely understood reforms in last week's Welfare Bill, has achieved this remarkable feat.

The old insurance system, he argues, had broken down because it was designed by Beveridge for males in full-time continuous employment. The woman's job was to stay home, caring for children and the elderly. Mass unemployment, fractured families, women in employment and greater labour mobility have destroyed the basic premise on which the post-war welfare state was built.

Income disparity has also widened considerably in the past 20 years. If social security is to survive for the next 30 to 50 years radical reform directed at the poor is the only option.

In reply to the accusation that his reforms are a retreat from the principle of universalism, Darling is unapologetic. Given the scale of the task, he says, there is simply no sensible, or affordable, alternative.

This analysis frees him to require almost all those on benefit to attend repeat interviews to see if they can be helped to find work, including the disabled and single parents. ... importantly, it has led him to aim benefits at the poorest, especially those with children, in the process necessarily extending means testing and hitting the middle class. ...

The single biggest political coup so far is the reform of disability benefits, especially Incapacity Benefit, which is paid to those with a work history who become too sick to work. ...

In future, those with an occupational pension of more than £50 a week will gradually lose IB entitlement above this income level. This saves £750m in a full year and channels help to the poorest, especially those disabled young who go on to lead lives of desperate poverty.

Darling sees the old IB as a classic piece of British welfarism – masking unemployment by putting the elderly jobless on to a benefit until retirement. In future, IB claimants will face more rigorous tests.

But the reforms also make a dramatic break with the principle that those who have paid their National Insurance are entitled to a benefit if they fall ill, regardless of other income.

Another move away from the principle of universality is the plan to tax child benefit, favoured by Darling and Chancellor Gordon Brown. ...

The final strand in Darling's reforms to date is pensions. His pensions Green Paper, again largely reflected in last week's Bill, contained one truly radical change: the abolition of the State Earnings Related Pensions Scheme (Serps) and its replacement with a State Second Pension (SSP).

The SSP will be paid at a flat-rate to those earning below about £9,000 a year. Those earning more will be expected to provide for themselves, albeit with generous rebates. Serps was explicitly designed to appeal to the better off, by ensuring that those who earn more get more on retirement. The SSP, worth proportionately much more to the very poorest, inverts this principle.

Labour will not means test the basic state pension, as they constantly remind us. Instead they are creating a second basic pension, and means testing that (though on the basis of earnings during working years, rather than income on retirement).

Source: *Guardian Unlimited*, 14 February 1999

1 What had broken down in the old Beveridge-based welfare system, according to the Minister?

2 What does the article mean by talking about a 'retreat from universalism'?

3 What system of allocating benefits is increasingly happening?

4 What is Incapacity Benefit (check main text) and what is happening to it?

5 How is this an example of the changing nature of the social security system?

6 What is SERPS?

7 Explain the problem with SERPS, and what changes are taking place in pensions?

Targeting and means testing

'Targeting' is the term used to describe a system of welfare provision that aims benefits at particular groups in the population – usually those who are identified as most in need. The very concept of 'most in need' usually has a moral element in it that says these people are the most deserving, as opposed to others who, if forced to, could escape from their poverty by their own efforts. One example of targeting which was introduced in the 1986 Social Security Act is the exclusion of young people under 18 from Income Support. The arguments underlying this are that it is up to the parents of these young people to support them, and that they ought to be on a work experience programme. Critics of this policy argue that it has led to cases of significant hardship, although the benefit rules do provide for payments to younger people in certain exceptional circumstances.

Targeting is closely linked to the idea of means testing. The policy of means testing has a long history in the provision of social benefits. Means testing is a system of awarding benefits on the basis of comparing the actual income of a person or family against what the State thinks they need in order to have an adequate standard of living. The person or family have then to prove that their income is so low that they cannot manage, and then the State makes up the difference between actual income, and the official estimation of what is required. Claimants therefore become eligible for certain benefits not just because they fall into a certain category, such as pensioners, disabled people, etc., but because they fall into this category and are also poor.

The advantages of means testing

Means testing has certain useful features, which is why so many UK social security benefits are provided in this way.

- It targets help to the most needy, and does not give money or services to those who could afford to pay and who would otherwise be supported unnecessarily by the rest of the population. Without means testing it is possible that some people who do not receive benefits could actually be worse off than those who do. For example, free travel is given by some local authorities to pensioners, yet many of these pensioners may, in fact, be well off, while other people, paying the full fares, could be earning lower wages.
- Providing help to selected groups usually costs much less to the State, as fewer people should receive benefits.
- The savings made could be spent on providing better services for those who receive the benefit, or these savings could be used by the government to lower taxes or spend on other services.

The disadvantages of means testing

However, there are certain problems with means-testing which critics argue make it unsuitable in helping low income households.

- Means testing is complex and requires a large bureaucracy to administer it, and this costs a great deal of money. Much of the 'savings' which means testing involves would not return to the government but would be used up in higher administration charges. This is precisely what happened with the Community Charge, or 'poll tax' as it was known, and was one of the reasons why it was soon replaced by the Council Tax.
- As targeting is complex, it means that quite often mistakes are made by those giving out the benefits. For example, it was found that almost half of the initial calculations for Child Support carried out by the Child Support Agency (CSA) were mistaken.
- People are often confused as to what they are entitled to have, and so the complexity of the system acts as an obstacle to claimants (this relates to the discussion of take-up rates below).
- It is claimed that people often fail to take up means-tested benefits because they feel embarrassed to ask (they feel 'stigmatised') or because they are ignorant of what they might claim.
- As income rises, State benefits decline, and this can lead to what is called the 'poverty trap', whereby people actually lose more in benefits than they gain from the increase in income they receive when they get a job or a pay rise. This problem is described in more detail in Chapter 4.

Universalism

The alternative to targeting through means testing is to give benefits to everybody who falls into a particular category. These are known as 'categorical' benefits. Retirement pensions, for example, are not means tested. Every retired person who has paid enough National Insurance contributions receives a pension – even though some may not need it. Similarly, everyone who has a dependent child receives Child Benefit.

When everyone in a particular category receives benefits, then the benefit is sometimes described as 'universal'. Those who argue for universalism claim they are defending the true principles of the Welfare State, yet very few benefits available since the Welfare State began are truly universal. The overwhelming majority of State benefits are means tested.

Advantages of universalism

Supporters of universalism argue that:

- it eradicates the poverty trap – people can receive wage increases and do not lose any benefits as a result
- it ensures that everyone who is in need obtains the benefits, and no one is excluded through their ignorance of the benefits available or through fear of stigma
- it is cheap to operate because there is no expensive bureaucracy involved in working out entitlement through means testing
- where everyone gets a benefit there is more public support for it and pressure to maintain its value and the quality of service. In contrast, it has often been said that services which are only provided for poor people tend to become poor services.

Disadvantages of universalism

Critics of universalism dismiss these points, claiming that it is highly expensive because so many people receive benefits unnecessarily. Money is wasted, which could go to other more needy groups. Critics also argue that giving people benefits which are not really needed encourages them to rely on the State rather than on their own resources.

Distribution of social security spending

Distribution of social security expenditure	
Retirement Pension	37.2%
Income Support	12.3%
Housing Benefit	11.7%
Child Benefit	7.6%
Incapacity Benefit	7.6%
Disability Living Allowance	5.6%
Jobseeker's Allowance	3.7%
Attendance Allowance	2.8%
Council Tax Benefit	2.6%
Family Credit	2.5%
War Pension	1.3%
Others	5.1%

Source: *The Changing Welfare State* (Department of Social Security, 2000)

1 Which benefit has the highest percentage of social security spending?

2 Which has the least? Why do you think that is?

3 Choose any three of the benefits and explain what they are.

4 Identify one 'universal' benefit.

5 Identify two means-tested benefits.

6 Which of the benefits has now been replaced by Working Family Tax Credit?

For and against Universalism

An argument against universalism

Universalism has many harmful consequences. By multiplying public expenditure, it distracts finances from productive investment which would raise the general standard of living. By creating huge centralised bureaucracies, it weakens the vitality of the family, the local community and voluntary associations, which are the natural arenas of genuine mutual help. It fails to get help to those who most need it. The disadvantaged lose out to more sophisticated, better organised fellow citizens. It gradually reduces the capacity of the population for personal autonomy by schooling them to welfare dependency.

Source: D. Marsland, 'Face to face', *Social Studies Review*, November 1989

The case for the principle of universalism

The alternative to universal provision for education, health and social security is not independence but selective provision. If these things are left to markets and families, then a substantial minority will not be able to afford them. This means a choice between leaving them to die, and providing selective 'targeted' services for those who can prove they are in serious need of state provision.

Selective 'targeted' services really do create a kind of one-way dependence, ... excluding [people] from the opportunities and incentives enjoyed by their fellow citizens. For example, if a person who is unemployed can get free education, free health care and means-tested benefits, while a person in paid work must pay for schools and [medical] treatment, and food out of [their] wages, then many unskilled and partially disabled people will not be able to afford to work. If people with low wages get benefits and services which they lose as their earnings rise, they have no incentives to improve skills and increase earnings. And if savings disqualify people from getting benefits and services, poor people won't try to save.

Source: B. Jordan, 'Face to face: the case against', *Social Studies Review*, November 1989

1 Marsland rejects universalism and puts forward four objections to it. Explain what he means by 'distracting finances from productive investment which would raise the general standard of living'.

2 In what way could it be argued that public welfare bureaucracies weaken the family, the local community, etc?

3 Explain what Marsland means when he argues that 'the most needy lose out to the better organised'.

4 Explain the meaning of the concept of 'welfare dependency'.

5 Jordan defends the principle of universalism. What does he mean by 'selective provision'? Why is selective targeting bad, in his opinion?

6 What positive arguments does Jordan make for universalism?

7 Which argument do you find most persuasive? What reasons would you offer for this selection?

Take-up rates

A considerable number of benefits have low take-up rates, by which we mean that many people who are entitled to the benefits simply do not apply for them. The table below summarises the DSS estimates of take-up in 1998–9.

Take-up rates, 1998–9 (% of eligible claimants who apply)

Income Support	79%–89%
Family Credit	66%–70%
Housing Benefit	91%–97%
Council Tax Benefit	91%–97%
Jobseeker's Allowance (Income-Based)	68%–82%

Source: *Social Security Statistics* (Department of Social Security, 2000)

The reasons for low take-up rates

- Lack of knowledge: potential claimants may be ignorant of the benefits available, as most people do not have an awareness of the entire range of benefits which exist.
- Complexity: application forms may be so complex that they discourage potential claimants from completing them.
- Too little benefit: the complexity of the form, the amount of time spent finding out about the appropriate benefits, the time spent waiting in benefits departments might all add up to a major commitment by claimants in comparison with what they are likely to receive. This is more likely to be true if the person imagines that the situation of need will be short-lived, for example if they are likely to get a job.
- Stigma and embarrassment: many people find it embarrassing for others to know that they are claiming benefits. This is particularly true for Income Support and Housing Benefit. Older people feel that there is a stigma attached to asking for help from the State.
- Consequences: some of the consequences of claiming some benefits, particularly Housing Benefit, may dissuade people from putting in the claim in the first place. For example, landlords may not want their rent known to the tax authorities.
- Language and literacy: there may be a language barrier which prevents the person claiming, although the main benefits are explained in Bengali, Chinese, Gujarati, Hindi, Punjabi, Turkish and Urdu, as well as English. People may not be literate and may be unable to read the forms.

Why some people don't claim benefits

Attitudes to means tests vary widely both among those subjected to them and among those who administer them, but it is extremely difficult to avoid altogether their stigmatising effects. To claim Supplementary Benefit [now Income Support] is to admit that one is poor, and this is in itself a major barrier to overcome in a society which tends to equate poverty with failure if not moral defects.

Source: C. Walker, *Managing Poverty* (Routledge, 1993)

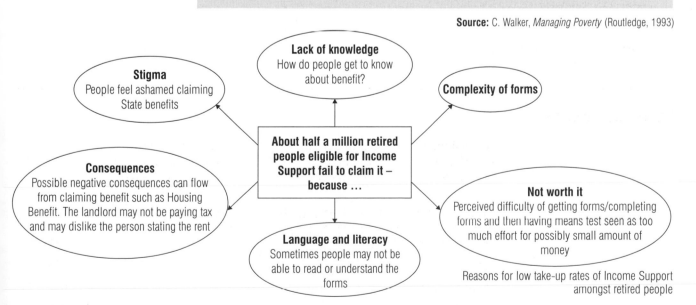

Reasons for low take-up rates of Income Support amongst retired people

1 What do you think is meant by 'stigma'?

2 How does it affect the desire to apply for benefits?

3 Do you think it is true that there is a stigma to collecting benefits today?

Redistribution

One other major debate between social policy academics is the extent to which government action actually succeeds in redistributing some income from richer people to the poor. Many critics have argued that the State is so inefficient that it actually fails to redistribute wealth and that all the money taken in taxes from the rich actually gets eaten up in bureaucracy and ineffective government programmes.

However, there is strong evidence that the State does succeed in redistributing wealth.

Taxation and redistribution

Taxes and benefits make things fairer
% share of total UK household income

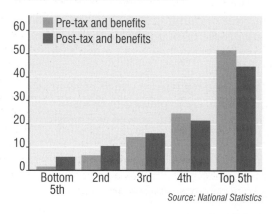

Source: National Statistics

The Tories are right: Labour has taxed and taxed again. Since 1997, tax rose as a share of national income by nearly 3%. And better-off people pay a lot of it: the top 1% of households in the income distribution pay 21% of income tax, and the top 10% pay 50% – a remainder, says Andrew Dilnot of the Institute for Fiscal Studies, that top people do most of the earning.

Income inequality rose under Thatcher, declined somewhat under Major (thanks to the Tories' policy-induced recession) and has been rising again since the mid 1990s. Past history would indicate that with earnings rising as they have been, the gap between haves and have-nots would go on growing. Unless the government intervenes.

Unlike lots of things the government does, state manipulation of incomes does work. Before taxes and benefits are taken into account, the ratio between the average income of the top and bottom fifth of households is about 19 to one. After the taxman calls and social security and pension cheques are paid, the ratio is cut to four to one... In 1999, income tax cost households £90bn; cash benefits paid them some £99bn. But better-off households paid the former while poorer households received the latter.

Source: *The Guardian*, 26 April 2001 (original source: www.statistics.gov.uk)

1 What percentage of income tax do the richest 1 per cent pay?

2 What percentage do the 'top' 10 per cent of the earning population pay?

3 What would happen to the gap between the 'haves' and 'have nots' if the government did not intervene?

4 How much in total did the poorer households receive? How much did the better-off households pay?

5 The extract refers to a number of social security benefits. List them and explain what they are.

6 Look at the table. In your own words, explain what it is telling you about pre-tax and post-tax incomes.

Main points ▶ There are a number of debates over how best to allocate State benefits to people. One group of writers argue that targeting benefits on a smaller group of needy people is best. Another view is to give benefits to all the people who might need it.

▶ Means-testing is closely linked to targeting. It means checking people's income to see if they really need the State benefit.

▶ There are many advantages and disadvantages to each approach.

▶ Means testing (and targeting) is usually cheaper – but there are still high costs of actually administering the benefits and many people who should get the benefits miss out.

▶ Universalism is very expensive, but everyone gets the benefits, so no one misses out.

▶ Many people who are entitled to benefits fail to apply for them. This is known as low take-up.

▶ Low take-up rates are linked to lack of knowledge of benefits, complexity of the forms to fill in and stigma, amongst other things.

▶ Government taxation policies do redistribute income from richer to poorer.

Conclusion

In this chapter, we have explored the range of provisions provided by the government. Because the benefits provided come from departments and agencies other than the Department of Work and Pensions, we have used the term 'social protection'. We have seen that the original Welfare State was set up to tackle the problems of poverty, poor housing, unemployment, sickness and lack of education. Fundamental to all this were the problems of poverty caused by sickness, disability and old age. The system of social security was set up to tackle these. Over time the changes have been quite profound, as the State realised that the sheer cost of trying to support a decent standard of living for the unemployed, disabled people and older people was arguably beyond its means – or at least beyond its desires to provide. The shift has therefore been to a much more 'disciplinary' system of social protection in which people are encouraged to work and are given training and financial benefits to do so. The system of social protection is becoming one where the role of government appears to be that of getting as many people into work as possible and then topping up low wages to ensure that the people are living above the poverty level. As for retired people, the decline in the relative value of the State pension is such that it is clear that this is to be seen only as a safety-net and that everyone is now expected to make their own provision for retirement.

3 CHAPTER SUMMARY

1 Social protection is the general term used for a range of benefits provided by the State which help its population stay out of poverty.

2 Social protection started with various acts giving pensions in 1906.

3 The system as we know it started between 1946–8 as a result of the Beveridge Report.

4 The Beveridge Report stated that it was important to eliminate the five giants of disease, ignorance, squalor, idleness and want.

5 As a result the government introduced the Welfare State which provided financial benefits in the form of social security, as well as health services, an education system and the commitment of the government to maintain full employment.

6 National Assurance was the system of benefits based upon paying an amount out in National Insurance to the government.

7 Those who did not pay National Insurance were eligible for a safety-net set of benefits called National Assistance.

8 The social security system did not change as fast as society, so that soon people could see that some of the assumptions about the nature of the family and the role of women for example were outdated.

9   A poverty trap was created because of the overlap of low wages and State benefits.

10   Between 1948 and 1979, the Welfare State came to be seen by many as too expensive and too bureaucratic.

11   In 1979, the newly elected Conservative government began a series of significant changes in the social security system.

12   They wanted to cut back on social security, making people less dependent on benefits amongst other things.

13   Some of the changes they introduced were very important, for example the link between the rise in wages and pensions was broken. This meant that pensions increased in their worth more slowly than the general rise in the standard of living. This made older people relatively poorer.

14   New Labour first came into power in 1997 and began a wide range of new policies.

15   Social security was closely linked to other changes and any understanding of social security changes need to be seen in a wider context

16   Labour's policies were centred on four areas: preventative measures, the labour market, neighbourhood developments and social protection

17   Many of the policies of the previous Conservative government were still carried on – or at least the ideas underlying them were.

18   One of the most important ideas was of Welfare-to-Work. This was the belief that a lot more could be done to 'encourage' groups who were living on benefits to enter the labour market.

19   A whole series of new policies were organised and new forms of benefits paid.

20   For those in work, some of the benefits were paid through the inland revenue taxation system, rather than social security.

21   Many people criticise the Welfare-to-Work programme for its coercive nature (people feel forced to do it) and for the fact that many of its payment simply subsidises low-paying employers.

22   Although unemployment has decreased this may be reflecting the change in the economy, not the success of the Welfare-to-Work programme.

23   There are a number of debates over how best to allocate State benefits to people. One group of writers argue that targeting benefits on a smaller group of needy people is best. Another view is to give benefits to all the people who might need it.

24   Means testing is closely linked to targeting. It means checking people's income to see if they really need the State benefit.

25   There are many advantages and disadvantages to each approach.

26   Means testing (and targeting) is usually cheaper – but there are still high costs of actually administering the benefits and many people who should get the benefits miss out.

27   Universalism is very expensive, but everyone gets the benefits, so no one misses out.

28 Many people who are entitled to benefits fail to apply for them. This is known as low take-up.

29 Low take-up rates are linked to lack of knowledge of benefits, complexity of the forms to fill in and stigma, amongst other things.

30 Government taxation policies do redistribute income from richer to poorer.

Useful websites

www.dwp.gov.uk: the Department for Work and Pensions

www.jrf.org.uk: the Joseph Rowntree Foundation, a research institution

www.rightsnet.org.uk: for social security rights

www.cabinet-office.gov.uk/seu: the Social Exclusion Unit

Chapter 4

POVERTY

Chapter contents

Introduction

There are at least two ways in which poverty is at the very heart of health and welfare.

- The development of modern State-organised welfare services came about largely because more and more people realised that poverty was not a natural condition, nor always the result of laziness or poor budgeting. Once it became accepted that poverty was a bad thing and that it could be tackled by government, we began to see the development of the modern Welfare State.

- Related to this new thinking about poverty, studies suggested that poor health, bad housing, and anti-social activities are all related in different ways to poverty, and that to tackle them effectively meant that attention had to be paid to the income needs of ill, badly housed and criminal groups. Measures to deal with poverty are among the oldest parts of the Welfare State. The 'starting date' for anti-poverty policies is disputed but certainly the old age pensions introduced in 1906 count as among the first national welfare measures in the UK (see Chapter 3).

Definition

Disputed concept – when experts disagree over the meaning and significance of something

The study of poverty is also important because it demonstrates a central feature of social policy: that it is not always a question of facts but of debates, argument and interpretation. Many people agree that poverty is important, but they do not always agree about what they mean when they say this, as poverty is a **disputed concept**.

What is poverty?

Here are three definitions of poverty taken from a social survey on British attitudes:

- 'Poverty is not having enough to eat and live without going into debt.'
- 'Poverty is having enough to eat and live, but not to buy other needed items.'
- 'Poverty is having enough to buy the things you really need, but not enough to buy the things most people take for granted.'

Activities

1   As a group, decide which of these three statements you agree with (you can agree with only one, or all if you wish). If you disagree with one or more, give your reasons. If you agree with all three, give a definition of what constitutes *not* being in poverty.
    For the findings of the survey, turn to page 108.
2   The quotes make references to 'needed items' or 'necessities'. As a group, come to a unanimous agreement on what you consider these needs to be.
3   As a group, use these three statements to find the views of a sample of people. This will involve questioning a random sample of people (perhaps in the road outside your college). Which is the most popular definition of poverty? You might ask them what they consider 'necessities' to be.

Even if you are quite certain in your own mind about what poverty is, the same cannot be said about everyone else who studies and writes about social policy! The problem arises because there is no agreement about how to define poverty and therefore how to measure it (so to say whether poverty is increasing or reducing is also disputed).

It may sometimes appear frustrating that different ideas exist and that there is no agreement about what might seem straightforward questions, but this is a common feature of many political issues. Concepts such as poverty are not natural or neutral, they are based on values and beliefs about what ought to be the case. Some people believe that it is enough for everyone just to have enough to live on and survive, others argue that people need or deserve more than this. These two viewpoints would 'see' different levels of poverty in the same society. We don't offer here an answer to the question: Which viewpoint is the 'correct' one? It is a matter for individual judgement, but it is necessary to understand that people might not always mean the same thing when they argue about 'poverty'.

Definitions

Absolute poverty – not having the very basic means to live adequately

Relative poverty – a measurement of poverty based on working out the income needed to attain the accepted standard of living in a society

Consensual poverty – a definition based upon whether or not people can afford a series of items which most people, when questioned, regard as 'necessities'

Social exclusion – being shut out of the economic, political and cultural systems which make up social life; excluded people are no longer integrated in society and do not feel that they are a full members of society

Main approaches to studying poverty

To clarify the debate about poverty we can reduce the various different viewpoints to four broad alternative approaches:

- the **absolute approach**
- the **relative approach**
- the **consensual approach**
- the newest approach – **social exclusion**.

We shall look at each of these in turn.

Absolute poverty

In the 1890s, a social reformer, Seebhom Rowntree, set out to prove to a very sceptical public that there was a lot of poverty in the UK. Rowntree's aim was not just to research the extent of poverty, but to force Parliament to do something about it. He reasoned that if he could define a level of poverty so low that nobody could dispute it, then when he produced his figures on the extent of poverty, people would be so shocked that they would insist the government tackle the problem. Rowntree therefore devised a poverty line, which he described as the minimum level of provision needed to maintain health and working efficiency. His poverty line was pitched deliberately low, so that nobody could argue that his definition of poverty was too generous, and therefore dispute the necessity of doing anything to combat the problem.

Rowntree argued that there were three essential elements of expenditure that every person makes. These are:

- *food* – he devised a basic diet which would be enough keep people healthy
- *clothing* – he calculated the minimum necessary clothing for a person to keep warm and dry
- *housing* – he took the average rents paid by working-class people at that time.

He then totalled the amounts of each of these expenses, and this level of income required to pay for them equalled the poverty line.

Rowntree then distinguished between what he called *primary poverty*, which was an income lower than this basic level and *secondary poverty* which was an income high enough to afford the basic necessities of life, but 'misspent' on non-essentials such as a newspapers, food and clothes other than the most basic kinds.

Modern versions of the absolute definition of poverty

The idea that poverty can be measured by the strict calculation of biological necessities remains an attractive idea for many. The Conservative governments of the 1980s and 1990s supported the absolute definition of poverty, and argued that the aim of social security should not be to improve the living conditions of the poor, but to make sure that the 'least well off' in the population could afford the basic necessities of life.

Definitions

Low cost budget – an absolute measure of poverty based upon the cost of a very basic range of food, services and goods

Modest but adequate budget – an absolute measure of poverty based upon the cost of a basic range of food, services and goods

More recently, social researchers have attempted to update Rowntree's work by calculating what a basket of essential items would cost in contemporary society. This 'budget standard' approach does not necessarily believe that poverty can be fixed at an absolute level, but it does agree with Rowntree's idea of calculating the cost of basic items. Two such budget standards have been created: a **low cost budget** which includes only the very cheapest items, and a **modest but adequate budget** which allows for some things above the basic necessities. These two measures can then be compared to benefit levels or average living standards in society to see how much different types of household need.

A modern-day absolute model of poverty

Low cost budget		Modest but adequate budget	
Examples of items included	Examples of items excluded	Examples of items included	Examples of items excluded
Basic furniture	Antiques	Basic designs, mass-manufactured furniture	Handmade or precious household durables
First aid kit and basic medicine	Prescription and dental charges	Prescription and dental charges	Spectacles, private health care
Fridge, washing machine, lawn mower and vacuum cleaner	Freezer, tumble-dryer, shower, microwave	Microwave, food-mixer, sewing machine	Tumble-dryer, shower, electric blanket
Basic clothing (cheapest prices at C&A)	Secondhand, designer and high fashion clothing	Basic clothing, sensible designs	Designer and high fashion clothing
TV, video hire, cassette player, a basic camera	Hi-fi, children's TV	Basic music system and camera	CD player, camcorder
Public transport, children's bikes	Car, adult bike	Secondhand five-year-old car, secondhand adult bicycle, new children's bike	Second car, caravan, camping equipment
Clocks, watches	Jewellery	Basic jewellery	Precious jewellery
Day trip to Blackpool	Annual holiday	One week annual holiday	Holiday abroad

Source: Joseph Rowntree Foundation, *Social Policy Findings*, 31, November 1992

What is your view? Which of these two absolute models is a better measure of poverty in the UK today?

Advantages of the absolute definition of poverty

- Absolute definitions of poverty are very clear and unambiguous.
- Relative definitions of poverty (described below) become absurd at a certain point, for in rich societies (such as the UK) people who have far more than the necessities of life, by any definition, can still be classified as 'poor'. For example, a former Conservative Minster for Social Security in 1988 pointed out that according to a relative definition of poverty 'in a rich community, where most people have three cars, the people with only one car are poverty stricken'!

Disadvantages of the absolute definition of poverty

- It is extremely difficult to define 'necessities' or 'minimum standards of living'. (This is demonstrated more clearly when we consider the consensual approach to defining poverty later.)
- Even those who support an absolute definition of poverty tend to relate 'necessities' to their own society. For example, even Rowntree accepted that the choice of food to make up a person's diet was related to the cultural expectations of food in a society, not just any mixture of vitamins, calories, etc.

Relative poverty

Supporters of the relative definition of poverty argue that it is impossible to isolate what counts as poverty from the general expectations of people in society, or from everyday living standards. Expectations change over time, and of course they vary from one society to another. Consider the case of televisions: in the 1950s, having a black and white receiver was considered as a luxury; then, as television ownership increased and became accepted as normal, colour televisions signified affluence; next came video recorders, then satellite dishes. Today, over half of all homes in the UK have video recorders, and over 3 million homes receive satellite broadcasts. Supporters of the relative definition of poverty would say that people who are unable to afford these items are poor.

Relative definitions of poverty stress not so much necessities, but exclusion from the normal patterns of life in a society, due to a lack of income. This approach is associated with Peter Townsend who developed it most fully in his 1979 study *Poverty in the UK*. According to Townsend, people are in poverty if they do not have the things that most people take for granted, because this means that they are not able to participate as equals in social life.

Questions

1   Relative definitions stress that poverty can only be measured by comparing one person's standard of living against another's. Therefore, there is no such thing as an absolute and fixed level of poverty. But can this be true? If it is, how can poverty ever be eliminated? What implications does this definition have for people who are 'poor' in the 'Third World'? Is their poverty comparable to not having a television in the UK?

2   The gap between the rich and the poor in the UK has widened in the last twenty years, but the actual standards of living of many of the poorest people in the population have risen steadily during this time. The poor are better off now than poor people were in 1960. Does this mean that poverty is decreasing, increasing, staying the same, or is it impossible to compare poverty at different times?

How the poverty line is measured in relative definitions

There are two main ways of measuring poverty according to the relative definition.

Definitions

Low Income Families statistics – a measure of poverty which says that poverty equals 140 per cent of Income Support

Households Below Average Income (HBAI) – a measure of poverty based on a certain percentage (usually 50 per cent) of average income

- The first is to take the government's own level of Income Support (plus an allowance for housing, etc., which adds up to approximately another 40 per cent of the Income Support) as a guide to poverty. The reasoning behind this is that Income Support reflects the minimum level of income the government itself believes it is reasonably possible to live on. So poverty equals 140 per cent of Income Support. The figures are based on the **Low Income Families statistics**, published by the Institute of Fiscal Studies.

- An alternative method of measuring poverty in relative terms – the method which came to be used by the UK government in the **Households Below Average Income (HBAI)** – is to say that having less than 50 per cent of average income, adjusted for family size (after housing costs), is an approximate guide to poverty. This, of course, means that there is no way that poverty can ever be eliminated because as average incomes increase, so too will the poverty line, as shown in the following table.

The 'poverty line' in 1994 and 1999 (at February 2000 prices)

	1994–5	1998–9
Single adult	£71	£79
Couple with no children	£129	£144
Couple with 3 children (aged 3, 8, 11)	£215	£241

Source: Department of Social Security, *Households Below Average Income: 1994/95–1998/99*
(Government Statistical Service, 1999)

Advantages of the relative approach

- It relates poverty to expectations in society generally.
- It gives a realistic picture of deprivation within modern society.
- It broadens the idea of what poverty is, from basic necessities to a range of other needs that people in a society have, and which make life bearable.

Disadvantages of the relative approach

- Taken to its extreme, this approach means that as long as there is inequality there is poverty.
- It could be argued that simply because someone does not have the 'extras' which others enjoy this does not make them poor. As long as people are fed, housed and clothed then they have all that is needed.
- If we go beyond the biological necessities, who is to say what should count as something which everyone ought to have?
- The relative approach can lead to people ignoring the differences across societies. The approach seems to say that someone who is not starving in a developing society is not poor, because expectations are so much lower in that society.
- Why should we look at half average incomes, why not one-third or three-quarters, or some other point?
  In addition, the average is a mid-point measure and often creates the false idea that the average is also typical. However, averages of anything can be distorted by the effects of a relatively few high or low values, and this happens in income measures where high earners raise the average. The top 10 per cent of earners in the UK receive almost one-third of total national income, and this pushes up the average to £21,000. But two-thirds of UK earners are actually below this figure.
- If Income Support is used as the measure of poverty, the absurd situation occurs that the higher the level of Income Support, the more people counted who are in 'poverty'!

The language of poverty

The UK government use the measurement of less than 50 per cent average income to differentiate between the poor and those better-off. However, in the 1980s and 1990s it became rare for the then Conservative government to use the term 'poor'. Instead, terms such as 'lower income families' or 'below average income household' were used. The current Labour government prefers to speak about the 'socially excluded' rather than 'the poor' (the term 'social exclusion' is discussed later).

This refers to the very real battle which often goes on between governments and pressure groups interested in the issue of poverty about whether we should continue to use the terms 'poverty' or 'the poor' at all. These disputes reinforce the point that there is no agreement over what the term 'poverty' should mean.

The consensual definition of poverty

We have seen that there are a number of problems with both the absolute and the relative approaches to defining poverty. In defining poverty in absolute terms, the problem is knowing exactly what a 'necessity' is in any particular society. A problem associated with the relative approach is that the definition is generally based on levels of income. Yet a person's standard of living does not always reflect the amount of money coming into a house. For example, one disabled person may be on Income Support, but have a pleasant house in a decent area of town, with a large garden, supportive relatives and efficient social services, yet another in the same town may have none of these things. In this case, their incomes do not reflect their different living standards or levels of deprivation.

To overcome such problems, a third measure of poverty has been suggested – the consensual approach. This method was first devised in 1985 for the television programme *Breadline Britain* and then used (with slight modifications) in follow-up studies in 1991 and 1999. In the consensual approach, a sample of the public are asked to rank in order of importance what they consider to be necessities for life in contemporary Britain. Any item which more than 50 per cent of respondents selected was included in the definition of poverty. In fact, in the initial 1985 study, thirty-seven items were included in this consensual estimate of poverty, and the researches counted as 'poor' anyone who could not afford three or more of them.

Measurement of the poverty line according to the consensual approach

Below is the list that researchers of the most recent Breadline Britain survey (now called the Poverty and Social Exclusion Survey) used when they asked the 1999 sample to assess what counts as a necessity of life in contemporary Britain.

Ability to replace or repair broken electrical goods	Daily newspaper	Living/bedroom carpets	Small amount to spend on self weekly
Access to internet	Damp free home	Meat, fish or vegetarian equivalent every other day	Telephone
An evening out once a fortnight	Deep freezer/fridge freezer	Microwave oven	Television
Annual holiday away from home (not with relatives)	Dictionary	Mobile phone	Two meals a day
Appropriate clothes for job interviews	Dishwasher	Outfit for social occasions	Two pairs of all-weather shoes
Attending weddings and funerals	Dressing gown	Prescribed medicines	Video
Beds/bedding for all	Fresh fruit and vegetables daily	Presents for friends and family once a year	Visiting friends or family in hospital
Car	Having friends or family around for a meal	Refrigerator	Visits to friends or family
Celebrating special occasions (e.g. Christmas)	Heating for living areas	Regular savings of £10 a month	Visits to school (sports day)
Collect children from school	Hobby or leisure activity	Replace worn-out furniture	Warm, waterproof coat
	Home in decent state of decoration	Roast joint/vegetarian equivalent, weekly	Washing machine
	Insuring home contents		

Source: J. Mack and S. Landsley, *Poor Britain* (1985)

1 Tick the items which you think were regarded as a necessity by 70 per cent or more of people questioned.

Compare your answers with those on page 108, where you will find the results of the survey.

2 Compare the list above to the items included in the low cost and modest but adequate budgets provided earlier. What differences are there? Do you agree or disagree with the experts who decided what should be included?

Social exclusion

A new term which has recently emerged in discussions of poverty is 'social exclusion'. In many ways it is similar to the relative definition of poverty, but it involves much more than looking at income, as it includes many other factors which shape life chances, such as health, education, security and general participation in society. Social exclusion means being shut out of the economic, political and cultural systems which make up social life, so that excluded people are no longer integrated and do not feel that they are a full member of society. The term is also used to express the idea that deprivation is a dynamic process: 'the poor' or excluded are not a fixed group stuck in a permanent condition, many of them go through different phases where they are able to participate in social life for a while before becoming excluded again (for example, they find a job for a while before becoming unemployed).

For these reasons, social exclusion cannot be measured only by looking at income levels and it cannot be summarised by a figure in the same way that a poverty line can. For example, the New Policy Institute's assessment of exclusion involved over fifty different indicators covering the whole lifecycle, ranging from the weight of newborn babies to the pension levels of retired people. The government's report on social exclusion involves twenty-four separate measures across nine areas which apply to both individuals and neighbourhoods. These are intended to provide an annual calculation of social exclusion so that the success or failure of government welfare policies can be measured.

Government indicators of social exclusion

1 **Income**
  - proportion of people on low income
  - proportion of people dependent upon benefits for a long time

2 **Fuel**
  - proportion of children and older people in households which struggle to pay fuel bills

3 **Finance**
  - proportion of people contributing to a non-State pension
  - amount contributed to a non-State pension

4 **Employment**
  - proportion of people in employment number of people who live in households where no one is in employment
  - employment rate for disadvantaged groups in comparison with average rate

5 **Housing**
  - proportion of children living in poor housing
  - proportion of households in poor housing with someone aged 75 or over
  - proportion of older people being helped to live independently by public service
  - number of homeless rough sleepers

6 **Environment**
  - proportion of older people who live in fear of crime

7 **Health**
  - proportion of low weight births and serious injuries in deprived areas
  - number of children's injuries
  - level of illegal drug use among younger people
  - proportion of adults smoking
  - suicide rate
  - healthy life expectancy at age 65

8 **Education**
  - educational achievement of 7-, 11- and 19-year-olds in deprived areas
  - proportion of working age people with at least one qualification
  - levels of truancy and school exclusion
  - proportion of 16–18-year-olds not in education or training

9 **Teenage pregnancy**
  - number of conceptions among those under-18 and proportion of teenage parents in education, training or employment

Source: Department of Social Security, *Opportunities for All: Tackling Poverty and Social Exclusion* (The Stationery Office, 1999)

Different definitions of poverty

A

[Poverty] is defined by reference to the actual needs of the poor and not by reference to the expenditure of those who are not poor. A family is poor if it cannot afford to eat. ... A person who enjoys a standard of living equal to that of a medieval baron cannot be described a poor for the sole reason that he has chanced to be born into a society where the great majority can live like medieval kings.

B

The picture which emerges is one of constant restriction in almost every aspect of people activities ... The lives of these families ... are marked by the unrelieved struggle to manage with dreary diets and drab clothing. They also suffer from what amounts to cultural imprisonment in their home in our society in which getting out with money to spend on recreation and leisure is normal at every other income level. ...

C

It is not just money that decides how people live – it is access to resources that makes the difference between drowning in poverty and managing just to keep your head above water. To measure poverty only by income is inaccurate – what facilities people have and what social activities they are able to engage in, are the real indicators of poverty.

Source: All quotations from R. Lister, *The Exclusive Society* (CPAG, 1990)

1 These three quotations reflect different approaches to defining poverty. Indicate which of the approaches to the definition of poverty discussed earlier you think underlies each quotation.

2 Which of the quotations do you feel is the most acceptable?

Defining and measuring poverty

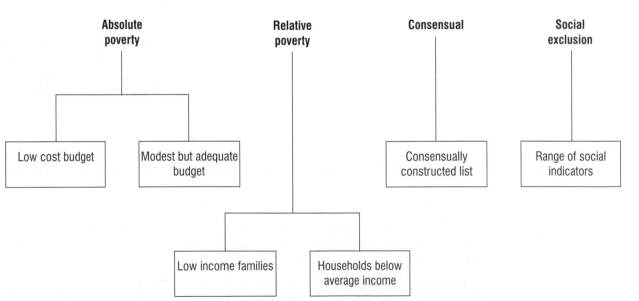

Explain in your own words what each of the definitions means and what each of the measurements are.

Main points ▶ There is considerable dispute over how to define and measure poverty.

▶ Social policy analysts have suggested that there are several different ways to define poverty. These are: absolute, relative, consensual and social exclusion.

▶ Each of these is linked to different forms of measurement.

▶ The different definitions and measurements will produce different figures as to the numbers in poverty and the extent of the problem.

The extent of poverty

The number of people living in poverty depends upon how poverty is defined. If we take the absolute definition then there are very few poor people in the UK. Only those who are really destitute would count, which only includes a few thousand people.

However, if we use a relative definition of poverty, such as that used in the Households Below Average Income statistics, then we reach a very different estimate, as the table below shows.

Recent trends in poverty in the UK

Individuals in UK households below 50 per cent of average income (after housing costs), 1979–1997/98

Year	% of population	Number (millions)
1979	9%	5.0
1994/95	24%	13.3
1997/98	25%	14.0

Source: *Poverty: Journal of the Child Poverty Action Group*, Issue 106, Summer 2000. Data – Crown copyright ©

1 How many people were living in poverty in 1997/98, according to the official statistics?

2 What is the increase in numbers since:
   a) 1979?
   b) 1994/95?

3 What percentage of the population are living in households with an income of below 50 per cent of average income?

Almost three times as many people lived in poverty at the turn of the twenty-first century compared to the late 1970s. According to the Treasury, inequality in the UK also increased by one-third over the same period.

Average incomes increased by 44 per cent between 1979 and 2000, but among the poorest 10 per cent of the population there was a fall of 9 per cent in real income after housing costs, while among the richest 10 per cent there was an increase of 73 per cent.

Groups in poverty

It is quite clear that poverty is more likely in some types of household than others.

Who are at risk of poverty?

A **% of group in poverty, 1997–8**

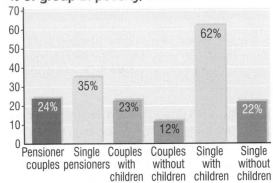

Look at A.

1 Which family type had the highest percentage of people in it in poverty? What percentage of that family type was in poverty?

2 Which group has the second highest proportion of its members in poverty? What percentage was it?

3 Which family type has the lowest percentage of its members in poverty? What is the percentage?

Look at B.

B **Number in poverty (% of total), 1997–8**

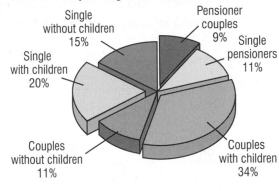

4 Which group formed the biggest percentage of people in poverty? What percentage is that? How many people is that?

5 Which group forms the second biggest percentage of people in poverty? What percentage is that? How many people does it comprise in total?

6 Which group provides the smallest percentage of the poor? What percentage is that? How many people does that comprise in total?

Source: Adapted from *Poverty: Journal of the Child Poverty Action Group*, Issue 106, Summer 2000 Data – Crown copyright ©

Composition of poverty and risk of poverty

> ### Definitions
>
> **Composition of the poor** – who makes up the poor at any one time
>
> **Risk of poverty** – which social group's members have a higher risk of becoming poor

It is important not to confuse the **composition of the poor** (i.e. the different groups who together make up the poor) with the **risk of poverty** faced by different types of household. For example, although lone-parent families make up 20 per cent of the poor, they are at a much higher risk of being poor: 63 per cent of lone parents lived in poverty in the UK in 1997/98, which was the highest proportion of any family type. However, the largest group in poverty were actually couples with children, who made up 34 per cent of the total in 1998–9. Unlike, lone parents, however, most couples are not in poverty.

The categories of people living in poverty only tell part of the story, however. Certain groups of people are more likely than others to be in all or most of the family and household types which are most at the greatest risk. Women, for example, form the majority of older people, disabled people, lone parents and the low paid – all groups which are prominent among the poor. Similarly, people from the African-Caribbean and certain British Asian communities are disproportionately represented amongst the poor. We discuss the position of women and of ethnic minorities in more detail in Chapter 14.

Families move in and out of poverty over time, depending upon the financial demands they face. There are movements in income and poverty through finding new jobs, skill enrichment and promotion. This is illustrated in the following extract. Remember, however, that people go down into poverty too as the result of such things as redundancy, illness and divorce.

It is fallacious [a mistake] to think of the poor as a desperate, unchanging underclass forever mired in poverty. An analysis tracking the national insurance and tax returns of men aged 25–45 in 1978 found that there was a great deal of "churning", with work statuses and earnings changing over time.

The study found that only 16% of the men in the bottom tenth of the earnings league were still there by 1992/3, and only 4% remained in the lowest groups for the whole period.

Source: *The Guardian*, 28 April 1997

The lifecycle and poverty

When we talk about 'the poor', it gives the impression that there is a fixed body of people, separate from the mainstream society, who live in poverty all their lives. This is true for some people, but the majority of the poor are people who live on the margins of poverty and who are more likely to be in poverty for certain periods of their lives, and to climb out of it during other periods.

For example, people who have young, dependent children and a low wage will probably be in great financial difficulties because of the financial burden of having children. They will, therefore, be likely to go into poverty – and of course their children will be poor too. Later, as the children are able to do part-time work or later enter full-time employment, then the parents may well move out of poverty (just!). However, as they grow old and their incomes decline again, and with little money saved, they may fall back into poverty.

Poverty and the lifecycle

The unemployed and the insecurely employed

Changes in the economy

The number of people who are out of work changes with the overall situation of the economy. There have been very significant changes in the UK economy over the last twenty to thirty years, including increasing automation in industry, increasing productivity and the general decline of UK manufacturing because of foreign competition. The result of these developments has been that fewer workers are required in traditional sectors of the economy and employment growth is highest in services and information technology.

This trend is significant for poverty levels because the sectors which are expanding are rather different from traditional areas of employment which are in decline.

The expanding service and information technology sectors require different types of skill and are less likely to offer the traditional security of a life-long career. Only 40 per cent of the UK workforce were employed on full-time and long-term contracts, so although the UK in the early twenty-first century is going through a period of almost full employment in terms of the *numbers* of people who have jobs, many more of these jobs than ever before are insecure.

In 2001, over 27.5 million people in the UK were in work – an all-time high, 1.8 million more than five years earlier – and unemployment was below one million.

Different definitions and measures of unemployment

Officially recorded unemployment: This means the number of people out of work and claiming benefit. This is sometimes known as the 'claimant count'.

The International Labour Organisation measure: There are actually more people who do not have jobs than calculated by the claimant count, for example, disabled people and lone parents who do not have to claim Jobseeker's Allowance. The ILO counts as unemployed everyone who says they want a job even if they do not qualify for benefits. It has been estimated that if these people were added to the claimant count, the total figure of unemployed people in the UK would be 3.5–4 million.

However, despite this apparent economic success, there are still problems of poverty and unemployment in the UK. Certain groups in the population are more likely than others to be made unemployed.

The concentration of unemployment

Research ... has found out that Britain is now split between work-rich and work-poor households and that new jobs tend to be snapped up by the partner of somebody who is already working. Almost 20% of households with a person of working age has no wage coming in. Three things have helped to entrench poverty. First, unemployment has been much higher in the 1980s and 1990s than in the first 30 years after World War Two. Second, the jobs taken by the unemployed pay far less well than they did in the past. Third, income mobility (the chance of increasing income over time) is less now than it was in the 1970s.

Source: *The Guardian*, 28 April 1997

1 What division is there in Britain today?

2 What happens to new jobs?

3 What percentage of households in Britain with a working age person has no income coming in?

4 a) What three things have helped to entrench poverty, according to the extract?

   b) One of these is no longer true. Which one is it (see main text)?

Insecurely employed

The first problem with the recent growth in employment is that many of the jobs that have been created are insecure. There has been an increase in casual employment, self-employment, part-time work and contracts which can be ended by employers at short notice and without any compensation to employees. There were more than 5 million part-time workers in the UK in the late 1990s, over 80 per cent of whom were women, and 2 million of these worked less than 16 hours per week. Part-time, self-employment and temporary work grew from 15 per cent of total male employment in 1986 to 25 per cent in 1996, and for women it grew from 50 per cent to 53 per cent.

This can make such workers vulnerable and also reduces their ability to build up savings or sustain contributions to State or private welfare services, such as pensions or insurance. When these workers retire, therefore, they may find that their pensions are too low and they are forced to supplement these with means-tested Income Support benefits. Also when some of the unemployed do find work it is often part-time or insecure, so that their lives consist of unemployment interspersed with periods of insecure or part-time employment.

Employment insecurity

So far as the unemployed flow as a whole are concerned, they tended to work in low paid, low skilled and manifestly insecure jobs. They lost them with little notice and little or no compensation. Despite the fact that being in work furnished them with little or no rewards, they found that being out of work was so much worse that they were generally prepared to take the first job offered to them, however unsatisfactory, simply to be back in work. Again, although they tended to be low paid in their previous jobs, they took a pay cut, on average, in order to return to work. Moreover, and perhaps most importantly, for those who found new jobs relatively quickly, those new jobs proved to be only temporary in most cases.

Source: W.W. Daniel, *The Unemployed Flow* (Policy Studies Institute, 1990)

Describe what happens to unemployed people.

The least skilled

Many of the jobs which these people would have performed in the past are now carried out by automated machinery. Unemployment levels for unskilled manual workers can be as high as six times that of professional workers.

Those living away from the south and south-east of England

The south-east of England has a number of advantages for employers, including a more skilled workforce, its proximity to mainland Europe, and a large and more affluent population to buy goods or products. This is reflected in higher wages and living standards in the south of England than other parts of the UK.

Average household income in the south-east is 18% higher than the national average. A major reason for this is that wages are far higher in this region than elsewhere. The southern part of the country has therefore benefited far more than elsewhere in the creation of new jobs: 53% of all new service jobs created since 1976 were located in the south east.

Source: C. Oppenheim and L. Harker, *Poverty: The Facts* (CPAG, 1996)

Ethnic minority groups

Partly as a result of racism, and partly because educational and skill levels tend to be lower among African-Caribbeans and some British Asian communities, there are significantly higher levels of unemployment and low pay amongst the ethnic minority groups in the UK. It is estimated that twice as many British Blacks and Asians are unemployed as are Whites. Disadvantage in unemployment holds true even if a black or Asian person has the same educational qualifications as a white person.

African-Caribbeans and Asians are also more likely to earn lower wages than white people, and to be employed in the lower paying sectors of the economy (although African-Caribbean women earn more on average than white women).

> Every indicator of poverty shows that black people and other ethnic minority groups are more at risk of high unemployment, low pay, shift work, and poor social security rights. Their poverty is caused by employment patterns which have marginalised black people and other ethnic minority groups into low-paid manual work, direct and indirect discrimination in social security and the broader experience of racism in society as a whole.

Source: R. Skellington and I. Morris, *Race in Britain Today* (Sage, 1992)

Long- and short-term unemployment

A distinction should be made between long- and short-term unemployment, as those who are unemployed for a long-time face much greater problems than those out of work for a limited period. These problems include a lower level of income, as a result of the way benefits are worked out (see Chapter 3), exhaustion of savings, and a gradual running down in the condition of clothing, furniture and general possessions. One government study in 1990 found that, after three months of unemployment, the average disposable income of a family dropped by 59 per cent. Longer periods lead to even more serious falls in living standards and tougher barriers to overcome. Also, the psychological effects of lack of confidence, stress and depression are more acute for the long-term unemployed.

Because of this, Robert Walker distinguishes between three types of poverty in terms of duration:

- the 'transient' or the 'fleetingly poor' – such as students who can expect an upturn in their fortunes in the future
- the 'recurrent' poor – 'who move through a revolving door of unemployment and low pay throughout their lives'
- the 'permanent' poor – about 20 per cent of the total number of poor people at any one time; the majority of them have no employment, no educational qualifications and live in rented accommodation.

Activities

1 Which groups are the most likely to become unemployed?
2 Why are unemployment levels higher amongst some of the ethnic minorities?
3 Why is there greater concern over those unemployed for a long time?
4 From your library, obtain copies of the most up-to-date editions of *Social Trends* or *Economic Trends*. Find the extent of unemployment and the different levels of unemployment by category.
5 a) If possible, use a copy of *Regional Trends* (if not available at your college, then certainly to be found in your central library) to find the unemployment statistics for your area. (You should be able to obtain the statistics if necessary from the local office of the Department of Work and Pensions or from its website – see page 108).
    b) Is your region above or below the national average?
    c) Name three factors which explain why some parts of the country have higher unemployment levels than others.

The effects of unemployment

Families

If a man becomes unemployed, it is likely that his wife or partner will also have to give up work as well, because the benefit system works in such a way that what she earns he loses from Jobseeker's Allowance. By the time travel costs and other expenses are taken into account, the family becomes worse off if the wife continues to work. As a result, a two-earner family can rapidly become a no-earner family.

Unemployment can lead to problems of stress as families are forced to live 'on top of' one another, and this becomes serious if unemployment continues for a long time.

> You end up pulling your hair out because you can't ever get away for a night out like working people ... Tensions build when you can't get a bit of time on your own.

Source: R. Cohen et al., *Hardship Britain* (CPAG, 1992)

Individuals

Unemployment has powerful effects on an individual's mental state too, which can help trap him or her in poverty. When people are made unemployed, they may lose their self-esteem, and of course this affects their ability and willingness to seek a job. Someone who has been unemployed for twelve months is four times less likely to find work than a newly unemployed person. This is partly because long-term unemployed people can become resigned and discouraged, partly because their skills may become rusty, but also partly because of negative attitudes by employers who may be suspicious about their ability and motivation.

The stress resulting from lack of employment affects people's health, and standards of health amongst the unemployed are significantly lower than the population in general. The risk of premature death is 25 per cent higher amongst unemployed men than those in work. This becomes another reason why they are less able to take on employment. And so a cycle begins, preventing the person getting employment and thereby escaping from poverty.

> I think the real problem of being on the dole is it destroys your self-esteem, you know, and your ability to provide for yourself ... I said lack of self-esteem but I mean also like a lot of apathy. If you're on the dole for a long period of time you tend to get ... quite apathetic in many ways.

Source: R. Cohen et al., *Hardship Britain* (CPAG, 1992)

Communities

As we saw above, poverty and unemployment is more likely to occur amongst certain groups and in certain areas than others. When these problems become concentrated in particular areas or neighbourhoods then a spiralling decline can begin. Without adequate income, people cannot afford to maintain their accommodation, they cannot afford to shop or to purchase decent leisure services. The result is a lack of shops and leisure amenities, high crime levels and a general dowdiness in the area, which, in turn, puts off employers and new businesses. Thus a downward cycle begins, leading to yet more poverty and further decline in the area.

The low paid

> ### Definition
>
> **Low pay** – less than two-thirds of the male average hourly wage

Although general wage levels have increased over the last fifteen years, there has been a widening of the gap between those in secure, higher-skilled and professional employment and those who are in jobs requiring little skill or who have skills that are no longer in demand. This has contributed to an increase in inequality mentioned before. In the early 1970s, the incomes of the richest 10 per cent were three times higher than the poorest 10 per cent, but by the turn of the century they were four times higher, and over half of all the wealth in the UK was owned by this richest 10 per cent of the population.

The increase in **low-paid** employment is demonstrated by the fact that the risk of poverty for households where only one partner works or where both are engaged in part-time work doubled between 1979 and 1999

The extent of low pay

> ### Definition
>
> **Poverty trap** – where entering employment means that the person will receive less than from remaining on State benefits

The Low Pay Unit (LPU) estimates that 45 per cent of UK workers are in low-paid jobs. This figure is composed of 78 per cent of part-time workers (mainly women) and 29 per cent of full-time, adult workers.

Low-paid workers are particularly vulnerable to the **poverty trap**, which is when an increase in earnings means the loss of means-tested benefits so that they may be no better off. In the mid-1990s, over 430,000 people in the UK were caught in this 'trap'. The poverty trap occurs in situations where a person (or family) receives a number of means-tested benefits from the State when they are unable to obtain work; if the person then finds employment, their gains in income from employment may well be lost, because the Department of Work and Pensions (formerly the Department of Social Security) withdraws some or all of their means-tested benefits. The person (or family) is therefore no better off in employment, and may even be poorer than when they were living only on welfare benefits.

The poverty trap

The low paid with children

A high proportion of those living in poverty comprise the low paid and their children. In recent years, there has been a relative increase in the standards of living of many older people who previously were a large proportion of the poor. However, with the growth of low-paid and part-time employment, particularly for lower skilled workers and families headed by women, the income earned from employment is increasingly inadequate to pay for the very significant extra costs of having children. Although benefits are available for families with children, these have been too low to pay for the additional food, housing, clothing and leisure costs involved in raising a family.

> The children are always asking for things – they say their friends have this and this we have to say no, so the children get upset and we feel upset.

Source: R. Cohen *et al.*, *Hardship Britain* (CPAG, 1992)

The minimum wage

In 1998 the government introduced a national minimum wage. By doing so, it hoped to eliminate low pay as one of the causes of poverty. Initially, the Conservative Party was opposed this, as it believed that a minimum wage would increase the costs of employing people and would result in fewer jobs. Instead of low-paid workers, there would be unemployed people receiving State benefits. (Interestingly, a similar type of argument was put forward to oppose the abolition of slavery, as it was argued that paying wages to slave workers would lead to economic disaster.) Minimum wages exist in most European Union countries, although the levels vary.

The minimum wage was introduced at a level lower than recommended by the trade unions and an even lower rate applies to younger workers. Its impact on the level of poverty is debatable – far more significant has been the general continued fall in unemployment, and supporters of the minimum wage argue that this proves that a basic wage level does not lead to fewer jobs. The Conservative Party are no longer opposed to the minimum wage, but arguments about what level it should be at occur every year when the government has to decide how much to increase it by to match rising prices.

Children

A higher proportion of children are living in poverty in the UK than adults. According to the government's report on poverty and exclusion – *Opportunity for All: One Year On* – the number and proportion of children in poverty has fallen in recent years, but the figure is still higher than twenty years ago and also higher than it is in many other countries.

Number of people and children in poverty in the UK (including self-employed)

	People			Children		
	Total population (millions)	Number in poverty (millions)	% of total population	Total population (millions)	Number in poverty (millions)	% of total population
1979	54	5	9%	13.8	1.4	10%
1998/99	56	14.3	25%	12.8	4.5	35%

Note: the figures for 'people' include children

Source: *Poverty*, 107, Autumn 2000 Data – Crown copyright ©

Over two million children in the UK lacked at least two basic necessities (18 per cent of all British children) and approximately 4 million children (34 per cent) lacked at least one essential item. More specifically:

- 21.8 per cent went without a holiday away once a year
- 1 in 25 went without celebrations on special occasions, educational games and meat, fish or vegetarian equivalent at least twice a day
- 1 in 50 did not have new, properly fitted shoes, a warm waterproof coat or daily fresh fruit and vegetables.

Half of the children in households which were classified as poor were not deprived of anything because the parents sacrificed their own needs.

The UK has a higher percentage of poor children per household than any other European Union country. The left-hand column in the table below indicates the relative wealth of the country while the right shows the proportion of poor children. As can be seen, despite being the tenth richest country in the EU, the UK has the highest proportion of young children in poverty. The table also shows that a country need not be very wealthy to reduce child poverty – compare the situations in Sweden and Ireland.

Children in poor households

Children aged 0–5 in poor households in the UK and other EU countries

	GDP per head as % of EU average[1]	Children 0–5 in poor households
Austria	106	fewer than 1%
Belgium	113	15%
Denmark	115	5%
Finland	93	fewer than 1%
France	106	12%
Germany	108	13%
Greece	65	19%
Ireland	100	28%
Italy	105	24%
Luxembourg	169	23%
Netherlands	105	16%
Portugal	68	27%
Spain	77	25%
Sweden	97	fewer than 1%
UK	99	32%
EU average	100	20%

1 The higher the number, the wealthier the country

Source: IPPR

1 Which three countries had the lowest levels of child poverty?

2 Which country had the highest?

3 Do British people believe this? Choose five countries, including the UK. Ask people to rank the countries in the order they think is correct for the percentage of children living in poverty.

Reasons why children are in poverty

The causes for the high levels of poverty in the UK include:

- the high number of low income lone-parent families
- the high number of households where no one is in employment – until very recently, almost 20 per cent of British children lived in families where no one had a job
- larger families are also at greater risks of being poor – 20 per cent of children living in families with three or more children are poor even if these families include full-time adult workers.

> **Definition**
>
> **Cycle of disadvantage** – poor parents are unable to help their children to get out of poverty. They in turn live in poverty, and are unable to help their children

On 18 March 2000, the Prime Minister Tony Blair pledged that the Labour government would eliminate child poverty in the UK by 2019. He said: 'Poverty should not be a birthright. Being poor should not be a life sentence. We need to break the **cycle of disadvantage** so that children born into poverty are not condemned to social exclusion and deprivation.'

The proportion of children living in workless households has fallen from 17.9 per cent in spring 1997 to 15.8 per cent in 2000 and, over the same period, there were 300,000 fewer children living in families claiming out-of-work benefits. This means that in 2001 there are 2 million fewer people in poverty in the UK, and that the number of children in poverty has fallen to 3.5 million. However, this is still twice the level of child poverty that existed in the UK in 1979

Women

Although both males and females are affected by poverty, the majority (56 per cent) of the poor in the UK are women, and the risk of poverty is also much higher for women than men. There are many reasons for this. Earlier we categorised the poor in the UK into the several groups, including: the unemployed, the low paid, lone parents, the sick and disabled and older people. Each one of these groups has a majority of women, except perhaps the unemployed (and there is a fierce debate about this too, as it depends upon how we define unemployed). For example, 71 per cent of the low paid are women, as are 90 per cent of lone parents.

Reasons why women are more likely to be in poverty

Family responsibilities

Women are more likely to be in low-paid jobs because they are restricted by family responsibilities (whether married, co-habiting or single) from pursuing a full-time and life-time career. It is generally regarded as the woman's role to take primary responsibility for the care of the family.

Childbearing

Childbearing disrupts the continuity of employment, which is necessary to gain promotion and higher salaries, and is also necessary to build up savings and benefit entitlements.

Low pay

Approximately 6.5 million women are low paid according to the Council of Europe's decency threshold. Women comprise 64 per cent of all people in the UK on low pay. Low pay is closely linked with part-time work which is more common for women than men. This is one reason why women's average earnings remain below those of men: in 1997 women's wages were still less than 75 per cent of men's on average despite Equal Pay legislation being passed in the UK in the early 1970s.

Ineligibility for non-means-tested benefits

The disruption of a woman's working life caused by childbearing and family responsibility prevents her from building up enough contributions for non-means-tested benefits. This means that when she needs State assistance she almost always has to turn to Income Support. In 1995, 95 per cent of lone parents on Income Support were women, and over three times as many women over pensionable age were receiving Income Support compared to men.

> Women are ... less likely than men to be receiving the superior contributory benefits and more likely to be receiving the inferior non-contributory equivalents. Many women are entitled to neither (leaving aside benefits for children) and are therefore reliant on means-tested income support or on a man for economic support.

Source: R. Lister, *Women's Economic Dependency and Social Security* (Equal Opportunities Commission, 1992)

Sharing family income

Within the two-parent family, it is usually the woman who goes without if there is any shortage. So although the family may not be poor, the woman often is.

Caring

Women are expected to care not only for their children, but also for older people and for disabled partners or relatives. There are almost 4 million women 'carers' in the UK today, of whom about half spend more than 50 hours a week in unpaid caring. The average cost for a middle-aged woman who gives up her employment to look after someone is approximately £12,750 per year in lost wages.

> I hadn't anticipated giving up work. ... But the thing was in the summer days she came out to meet me, her petticoat round her top. She'd got changed during the afternoon. My heart nearly broke when I saw her ... and then twice she ran after me as I was getting on the bus – didn't want me to go. The time had come to stop work.
>
> *(Mrs Grey, who gave up her job as a child welfare clinic clerical officer several months after her mother came to live with her.)*

Source: C. Glendinning, *The Costs of Informal Care*

Activity

Just what is life like for women who are caring for others? Approach your local Crossroads Group, or if there is not one, then your local Council for Voluntary Activities, and ask them if they can put you in touch with women who would be prepared to be interviewed. Devise a small interview, finding out why they care, who else could do it, what the effects are on their lives, who they are looking after. You could also use this information for your studies on community care.

It might be useful to record the interviews and play them back to the group as a whole. If you do decide to record an interview, remember the following points:

- Ask permission of the person to be interviewed – either record the person giving permission, or ask them to sign an agreement/permission form.
- Warn the interviewee if you think there is anything personal in the interview which may be embarrassing, and let them decide whether this should be edited out of the recording.
- Ask the interviewee whether they want their name revealed.

Lone-parent families

Poverty is not something that occurs to particular individuals, but rather to individuals in particular situations. Therefore, someone who is low paid but who manages to live adequately, or who has been married and is then abandoned by her partner, can be pushed into poverty by, for example, the extra burden of supporting children.

As we saw above, one of the more common causes of poverty derives from the high costs of having children, and this is particularly severe when it is combined with lower incomes because of limited earning opportunities. This 'double whammy' describes the situation of many lone-parent families. Sixty-two per cent of lone parents live in poverty, and they are likely to be the poorest of the poor: 40 per cent live on incomes below 40 per cent of the national average and 70 per cent are below 60 per cent of the national average (in contrast, only 7 out of 20, or 35 per cent, of couples with children live below 60 per cent of the average). Of the 1.3 million lone parents in the UK, just under a million are on Income Support and only 40 per cent were in paid work, mainly because of the problems in getting affordable childcare provision and the disincentive of the 'poverty trap' described earlier.

Since the 1970s, there has been a rapid increase in the number of lone-parent families in the UK. Today, more than one in every six families is headed by a lone mother. This is caused mainly by the growth in the divorce rate and by the increase in lone parenthood (that is women having and raising children on their own). Between 1971 and 1995, the number of divorces in England and Wales doubled from 74,000 to 155,000 a year – after having doubled during the 1960s. By 1995, 22 per cent of families with dependent children had only one parent in the home, compared to 8 per cent in 1971. The result of these trends is that 20 per cent of families are now headed by a lone parent: almost three times the proportion 25 years go.

However, the table below shows that there is no necessary connection between lone parenthood and poverty: Sweden has the highest proportion of lone parent families in Europe but very low rates of childhood poverty, while there are few lone parents in Ireland but a much higher level of child poverty.

Child poverty and lone parenthood

Child poverty and lone parenthood

	Child poverty: % living below poverty line	% of lone parent families
Sweden	2.6	21.3
Australia	12.6	14.1
Ireland	16.8	8
UK	19.8	20
US	22.4	16.6

Source: *The Guardian*, 23 August 2000

1 Which two countries had the highest rate of child poverty?

2 Is there a link between the numbers of lone-parent families and the number of children in poverty?

3 Draw a diagram to illustrate why children are likely to be in poverty.

Poverty among children in lone-parent families is avoidable if policies exist which help single mothers to get jobs and benefits to families with children (such as Child Benefit or the Working Families Tax Credit in the UK) are well designed (see Chapter 3).

Sick and disabled people

According to government statistics, there are over 8 million adults and 500,000 children in the UK who suffer from one or more disability. Their economic situation is not very good:

- 64 per cent of households with a sick or disabled person received no income from employment
- 7 per cent of households with a sick or disabled person received all their income from benefits, compared to 10 per cent of households without a sick or disabled person
- 83 per cent of sick and disabled persons living alone had a gross weekly income of under £200, compared to 41 per cent of all households.

For people under pensionable age, the average income for an adult with a disability is 72 per cent of the average income of non-disabled people. Many people with disabilities are unable to work, or are limited to particular kinds of employment, usually that which is low paid. Of all the people who are registered as disabled, 5.1 million are willing to work, but 59 per cent are 'economically inactive' (not working) compared with 15 per cent for the population as a whole.

One poll of employers' attitudes towards disabled people in the UK found that:

- 75 per cent of employers said they would not discriminate against disabled people
- 25 per cent might discriminate against disabled people
- 6 per cent would not employ disabled people under any circumstances
- 13 per cent would only employ them for certain jobs
- only 4 per cent would actively encourage applications from disabled people.

When disabled people do find a job, they are more likely to be in low-paid, low-skilled and low-status work than the non-disabled: only 12 per cent of disabled people are employed in professional/managerial positions, compared to 21 per cent for non-disabled workers, and 31 per cent of disabled people are in low-skilled manual work compared with 21 per cent of non-disabled people. The result of these patterns is that 34 per cent of all people with disabilities are living in poverty.

A person with a disability not only has problems obtaining employment, but also has greater expenses than a fully able person. Approximately 8 per cent of disabled people's incomes goes on expenses related to their disability. The Disablement Income Group estimated that the extra costs of disability in 1995 was £69.20 per week, i.e. the additional expense of special diets, adapting homes for wheelchair access, transport needs, etc.

There have been significant increases in the number of people with disabilities. This is mainly as a result of people living longer and therefore being more prone to disabilities in old age, and also because improvements in medicine have led to higher rates of survival of younger people and infants with disabilities.

Older people

Approximately 18 per cent of the population is over retirement age. Currently there are about 12 million people in the UK aged 65 or over, 65 per cent of whom are women. This figure will grow by 43.6 per cent over the next 30 years, as life expectancy continues to increase. In 1996 life expectancy for men was 74.6 years and for women 79.8 years. By 2021, life expectancy will be 78.1 years for men and 82.5 years for women.

This trends are not confined to the UK – Europe's population generally is ageing as the following table shows.

Population in Europe: percentages over 65 years old

1950	13%
1985	18%
2000	21%

By 2025 there will be 133 million pensioners in the European Union and soon there will be more retired people in the EU than there are children.

Most older retired people are dependent on pensions for their income. However, in the UK, State pensions have been pitched so low that anyone living only on them will automatically be in poverty. The State pension is less than 20 per cent of the average male weekly earnings. Although, a 'minimum income guarantee' has recently been introduced in the UK (see Chapter 3), unlike the case for children, there is no government commitment to abolish poverty among older people or even restore the value of the State pension to what it was in the late 1970s.

Poverty in old age is not something that happens to all pensioners – rather, old age poverty reflects divisions in employment, income and fringe benefits that exist throughout a person's employment. Inequalities between pensioners have been widening in recent years so that life expectancy at age 65 is much higher for better-off pensioners, particularly the 60 per cent of pensioners who now have private occupational pensions and do not need to rely on State support. As was pointed out above, those who are poor in old age are most likely to have been those who earned least during their working life. Therefore, the groups we looked at before are all likely to be poor in their old age, i.e. low-paid people, lone-parent families, sick and disabled people, those who have been unemployed for some time, and women.

Questions

Consider the following statements about poverty. Do you think they are true or false?

1 Poverty doesn't exist in the UK anymore as everyone has become better off.
2 Poverty could be solved by everyone having a job.
3 Women are more likely to be in poverty than men.
4 The levels of many welfare benefits in the UK are too low to pull claimants out of poverty.
5 Poverty means not having enough to eat to survive.
6 The main group in poverty are older retired people.
7 The scale of poverty in the UK has been reduced by the introduction of a minimum wage.

The answers are on page 109.

Groups in poverty

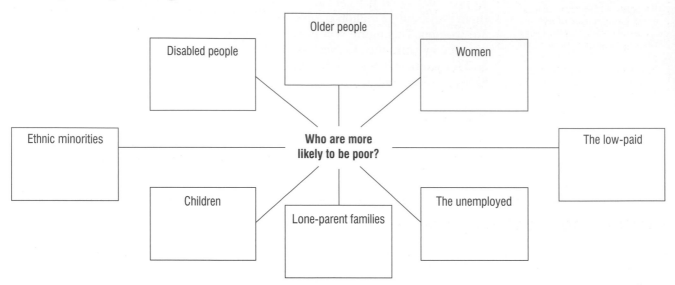

Copy the diagram and complete it by adding the reasons for the higher chances of each group being in poverty.

Main points ▶ There are about 14 million people living in poverty according to the Households Below Average Income measure.

▶ Some groups are much more likely to have a percentage in poverty than the rest of the population.

▶ These groups with higher than average proportions likely to be in poverty are: the unemployed, the low paid, children, women, lone-parent families, sick and disabled people, older people.

▶ It is important to remember however, that within these groups there will be great variation, with many rich and affluent as well as poor people. It is just that there is greater likelihood of people in these groups living in poverty.

▶ Each group is not separate, they overlap, so that women for example may be in all of these groups (girls for the children group).

▶ The reasons for these groups being more likely to live in poverty vary according to each group. However, low pay and low levels of benefits are two common themes running throughout.

Explaining the causes of poverty

Definitions

Dependency explanations of poverty – the poverty is the result of a fault in the poor person

Exclusion explanations of poverty – the poverty is the result of the society and the way it is organised

There are two different types of explanation for the causes of poverty. The first group of explanations stresses process of **dependency**, and the second type tends to stress the process of **exclusion**. We shall look at each in turn.

Dependency approaches

Explanations which centre on the concept of dependency stress that people who are poor are in that state because of some deficiency either in themselves or which has been passed on to them through the group to which they belong in society (for example, through their family or their community sub-culture). Such people have become dependent on the State, and have no desire to work or to cope with the

Definitions

The culture of poverty – groups of people who share certain values which effectively prevent them 'getting on' in the world

The underclass – a particular group of people who prefer living off benefits than working

problems of budgeting, as the bulk of the population has to do. This idea has considerable similarity to nineteenth-century views on poverty.

Within this overall approach to explaining the causes of poverty, we can distinguish three categories:

- the individual
- the 'underclass'
- the culture of poverty.

The individual

Here the stress is placed on the failure of the individual to achieve through his or her own efforts. People who are poor are lazy and should try harder.

Contrasting views on poverty

Compare and contrast the two following opinions about the causes of poverty and the nature of poor people by answering the questions that follow.

A

The £58bn spent annually by the Department of Social Security to relieve or prevent poverty is being poured into a black hole and neither the Government nor the poverty lobby care how families spend the money, according to a report published today.

Dr Digby Anderson ... suggests that 'domestic incompetent economy' has as much to do with hardship as low income.

He says the biggest weekly outlay is on food, accounting for a third of families' budgets. 'However, there is little sign that most take much time and trouble to shop well or to cook well,

although clearly they are not short of time.

'They buy expensive convenience foods, designed for people who do not have time; tinned pies, tinned hamburgers, tinned carrots, packets of shepherd's pie, ready prepared stuffing, soups, sauces, fish fingers ...

'They do not buy breasts of lamb and bone, stuff and roll them or mince them.' Dr Anderson says poverty is prolonged or made worse by inadequate budgeting, inefficient spending on food, patterns of borrowing and the allocation of money between husband and wife.

Source: From an article by Celia Hall in *The Independent*, 5 August 1991

1 According to the author of this article, is social security money being spent sensibly? Explain the reasons for your answer.

2 Whose fault is poverty?

3 What form of policy do you think Dr Anderson would support to eradicate poverty?

4 What criticisms would be made of this approach by other viewpoints?

B

... poverty is not a problem of poor a sad but inevitable consequence of misfortune, inadequacy or fecklessness. On the contrary, poverty can only be understood as a feature of society as a whole,

disfiguring and diminishing the lives of some as a result of the way we organise our collective way of life.

The institutional injuries inflicted by punitive social security regulations, racist and sexist welfare legislation, or increasingly

differentiated educational provision, deny large numbers of people their full social rights.

There are major costs imposed by the requirements made by a society increasingly organised around consumption and market values. ...

Poverty does not make people a group apart from society so much as victims of the injustice and incivilities of the social order of which they are very much a part. ...

Source: R. Lister, *The Exclusive Society* (CPAG, 1990)

1 Which perspective(s) on poverty does this extract support?

2 What implications for social policy would emerge if we accepted this argument?

3 What criticisms would Dr Anderson make of Lister's viewpoint?

The 'underclass'

This is a development of the explanation concerning the individual, but is more 'sociological' in orientation. The argument, which was first developed by the American writer, Charles Murray, centres on the existence of an 'underclass' of people who are lazy and who make no effort to work or look after themselves. They prefer to live off the State. Murray argues that three features can be used to identify such an underclass:

* high level of illegitimacy and single parenthood
* lack of commitment to work
* high crime levels, particularly violence and theft.

From this perspective, the underclass are a product of declining moral standards and generous welfare provision which have combined to create a *dependency culture*.

It is important to remember that the underclass refers only to those poor people who make no effort to help themselves. Murray accepts that there are poor people who are in this state through no fault of their own, including some old age pensioners and disabled people. Nevertheless, the bulk of poverty (especially among the unemployed) is caused by those who do not make the effort to earn a living, and/or squander what they do have.

Descriptions of the 'underclass

The underclass spawns illegitimate children without a care for tomorrow. ... Its able-bodied youths see no point in working and feel no compulsion either. They reject society while feeding off it, giving the cycle of deprivation a new spin. ... No amount of income redistribution or social engineering can solve their problem.

Source: Editorial in *The Sunday Times*, 26 November 1989

... increasingly, low incomes are associated with behaviour such as irresponsible sexual habits and unstable family formation, lack of commitment to work ... and failure to save or spend prudently.

Source: D. Anderson, *The Sunday Times*, 29 July 1990

The idea of a separate 'underclass' of poor people has been severely criticised. Many sociologists reject the idea, and argue that the only thing which really distinguishes the so-called 'underclass' is their low income and the fact that they have been blamed for social problems (such as juvenile delinquency, crime, welfare dependency and benefit 'scrounging') which are not their fault, and often exaggerated by critics of State welfare.

Criticisms of the 'underclass' idea

The existence, even the creation, of a group identified as the poor serves to set them apart from the rest of the population. The result is not just ... that the working class is divided and thereby weakened. Rather, the use of the poor as a reference group persuades those sections of society (which are neither wealthy nor poor) that their lot in terms of status, resources and power is acceptable. Consequently, the possibility that they will strive to change the position of the elite is reduced. Further, they (the poor) act as a warning. They demonstrate the fate of those who do not conform to prevailing work and social standards. Their plight is needed to reinforce the will of others to work for low returns in unpleasant and even degrading conditions from which the economic output gives a disproportionate financial reward to a minority of existing resource holders. Not least, those in poverty act as scapegoats, a vulnerable group on whom the blame for social problems can be placed, so diverting attention away from that minority which has some control over social affairs.

Source: R. Holman, 'Another model of poverty' in F. Butterworth and R. Holman (eds), *Social Welfare in Modern Britain*, 1975

In our view the concept of the underclass is a set of ideological beliefs held by certain groups among the upper and middle classes. It helps them sustain certain relations of domination of class, patriarchy and race towards the unemployed, single mothers and blacks through the formation of state welfare policies.

Source: P. Bagguley and K. Mann, 'Idle, thieving bastards? Scholarly representations of the underclass', *Work, Employment and Society*, 6 (1), 1992

1 How would you test to see whether an 'underclass' really exists? Design a research strategy which outlines the evidence you would need and how you might go about collecting this.

2 Why do some critics of the 'underclass' idea claim that it serves the interest of powerful and wealthier groups in society?

3 What social and welfare policies would the critics of the 'underclass' idea recommend, do you think?

The 'culture of poverty'

This approach stresses that the way people act is the result of how they are brought up by their family. It differs from the underclass explanation because it does not see poverty as a fault of the person, rather individuals are brought up in such a way that they never have a chance to escape the poverty of their parents.

Cultures develop to give people a guide as to how they should behave. In different societies people behave differently because they learn different cultures from their parents. Usually a particular culture develops because it enables people to cope with their surroundings. Cultures are always changing, but the broad outlines are passed on from one generation to another by parents and others who influence people when they are young.

The culture of poverty argument was first developed by Oscar Lewis when he studied very poor communities in Central America. Lewis argued that the values and behaviour (in other words, the culture) of these poor people was significantly different from the majority of the population. Lewis concluded that this was because these particular values enabled the very poor to cope with circumstances which would otherwise lead to despair and hopelessness.

A culture of hopelessness and despair

A

The culture of poverty is both an adaptation and a reaction of the poor to their marginal position in a class-stratified society. It represents an effort to cope with feelings of hopelessness and despair which develop from the realisation of the improbability of achieving success in terms of the values and goals of the larger society. ...

On the level of the individual, the major characteristics are a strong feeling of marginality, of helplessness, of dependency and of inferiority. ... Other traits include a high incidence of maternal deprivation, of orality, of weak ego structure, confusion of sexual identification, a lack of impulse control, a strong present-time orientation with relative little ability to defer gratification and to plan for the future, a sense of resignation and fatalism, a widespread belief in male superiority, and a high tolerance for psychological pathology of all sorts.

Source: O. Lewis, *La Vida* (Random House, 1969)

Definition

Cycle of poverty – poverty continues from one generation to the next

A development from the culture of poverty argument is the claim that a **'cycle of poverty'**, or a cycle of 'transmitted deprivation' exists. This idea was developed in the 1970s by a former Secretary of State for Health and Social Services, Sir Keith Joseph. His view of transmission, however, ignored the way in which the culture of poverty was supposedly a response to intense deprivation and a certainty that the person had no future. Instead Joseph alleged that some low income parents failed to help and support their children. In Joseph's view, therefore, a different culture and up-bringing was a cause of poverty rather than a product as Lewis believed.

A cycle of poverty?

B

The Economic and Social Research Council commissioned a review of evidence about transmission of deprivation. *Cycles of Deprivation* – the review by Rutter and Madge – concentrates upon longitudinal studies, like the National Child Development Study, which follow the progress of a cohort of individuals, gathering information about them and their circumstances at regular intervals. ... 'With respect to intelligence, educational achievement, occupational status, crime, psychiatric disorder and problem family status there are moderate continuities over two generations' ... yet 'Over half of all forms of disadvantage arise anew each generation'.

... At least half of the children born into a disadvantaged home do not repeat the pattern of disadvantage in the next generation.

Source: M. Banton, 'The culture of poverty', *The Social Studies Review*, January 1990

Look at A.

1 In what circumstances is it claimed that a 'culture of poverty' arises?

2 Go through each of the traits of the 'culture of poverty'. Explain each term.

3 The 'culture of poverty', or variations of it, has been very influential in social policy, especially in the USA. Do you find these traits convincing? Would you argue, however, that people who are poor (some/all/a majority?) hold different values from the rest of society?

Look at B.

4 Does this support or undermine the culture of poverty thesis?

The causes of poverty

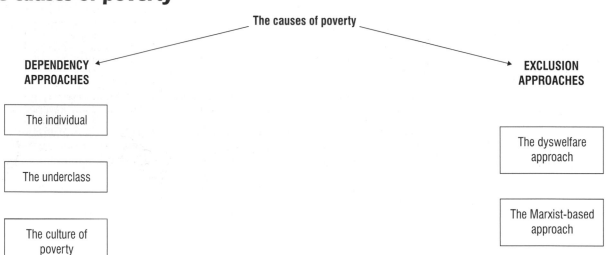

When you have finished reading this section about the causes of poverty, copy this diagram and complete the boxes by noting the main points of each approach.

The exclusion approach

Definitions

Dyswelfare approach – poverty is the inevitable, but unintended outcome of industrial society

Marxist-based approach – poverty is inevitable in contemporary 'capitalist' society

The second set of explanations for poverty is based on the idea of exclusion, meaning that the poor are in that situation because they are squeezed out of a decent standard of living by the actions of others. This relates to the concept of social exclusion described earlier in the chapter.

This approach stresses differences in power between the various groups in society. Those who lose out – disabled people, older people, women, people from ethnic minorities and, of course, children – have significantly higher chances of living in poverty.

Within this explanation, we can distinguish two approaches: the **dyswelfare** view and the **Marxist-based** approach.

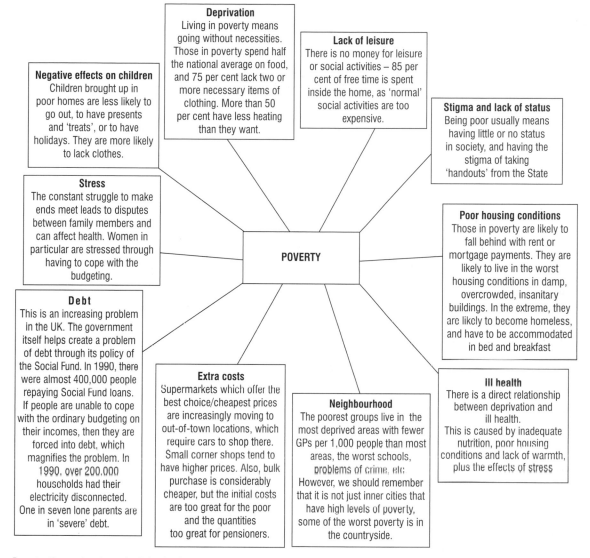

Poverty: the centre of a web of deprivation

Deprivation
Living in poverty means going without necessities. Those in poverty spend half the national average on food, and 75 per cent lack two or more necessary items of clothing. More than 50 per cent have less heating than they want.

Lack of leisure
There is no money for leisure or social activities – 85 per cent of free time is spent inside the home, as 'normal' social activities are too expensive.

Negative effects on children
Children brought up in poor homes are less likely to go out, to have presents and 'treats', or to have holidays. They are more likely to lack clothes.

Stigma and lack of status
Being poor usually means having little or no status in society, and having the stigma of taking 'handouts' from the State

Stress
The constant struggle to make ends meet leads to disputes between family members and can affect health. Women in particular are stressed through having to cope with the budgeting.

POVERTY

Poor housing conditions
Those in poverty are likely to fall behind with rent or mortgage payments. They are likely to live in the worst housing conditions in damp, overcrowded, insanitary buildings. In the extreme, they are likcly to become homeless, and have to be accommodated in bed and breakfast

Debt
This is an increasing problem in the UK. The government itself helps create a problem of debt through its policy of the Social Fund. In 1990, there were almost 400,000 people repaying Social Fund loans. If people are unable to cope with the ordinary budgeting on their incomes, then they are forced into debt, which magnifies the problem. In 1990, over 200,000 houscholds had their electricity disconnected. One in seven lone parents are in 'severe' debt.

Extra costs
Supermarkets which offer the best choice/cheapest prices are increasingly moving to out-of-town locations, which require cars to shop there. Small corner shops tend to have higher prices. Also, bulk purchase is considerably cheaper, but the initial costs are too great for the poor and the quantities too great for pensioners.

Neighbourhood
The poorest groups live in the most deprived areas with fewer GPs per 1,000 people than most areas, the worst schools, problems of crime, etc. However, we should remember that it is not just inner cities that have high levels of poverty, some of the worst poverty is in the countryside.

Ill health
There is a direct relationship between deprivation and ill health. This is caused by inadequate nutrition, poor housing conditions and lack of warmth, plus the effects of stress

The dyswelfare view

Dyswelfare refers to the process in which some people lose out in complex industrial societies through no fault of their own. They are the casualties of industrial and social change. The 'victims' of dyswelfare include physically or mentally disabled people, lone parents, and so on. The points to emphasise here are that their poverty is blameless and is the result of changes in the nature of society. Secondly, a society does not deliberately discriminate against any group (compare this view with the following Marxist-based approach), but it is inevitable that some people will lose out in any form of society.

It was this explanation for poverty that largely underlay the foundation of the Welfare State.

Marxist-based approach

The final and most radical explanation for the continuation of poverty comes from those who argue that society is a competition between various groups. Some groups have considerably more power than others and are able to impose their will on the rest of society. Power and wealth generally go together, as do poverty and powerlessness. The groups in poverty are largely formed from the powerless, in particular women, children and people from ethnic minorities. Low pay and poor State benefits result from the view that to pay more would be harmful to the interests of those who are more affluent.

This approach contrasts with the dyswelfare explanation, because it says that poverty is the direct result of the intended development of modern Western society.

The three causes of poverty

Poverty in the UK is largely determined by three factors – access to the labour market, extra costs and the failure of policies to deal with them.

Access to the labour market depends upon a number of factors – among them class, gender and race. … Getting a job is not necessarily the way out of poverty if that job pays paltry earnings, entails long hours and has poor working conditions – the poverty of unemployment is simply translated into the poverty of work.

Extra costs often come with changes in the life cycle. For example, the extra costs of a child, combined with being out of the labour market, brings poverty to families with children and in particular to lone mothers. Disability and sickness also bring extra costs, but at the same time less or no opportunities to be in paid work. And finally, old age carries a high risk of poverty because it is a time of life when there are few earnings and as old age progresses, no earnings at all.

Source: C. Oppenheim, *Poverty: The Facts*, 3rd edition (CPAG, 1996)

1   How does the first sentence of this extract illustrate the process of social exclusion?

2   How is it that people can be in work and poor?

3   Give some examples of extra costs which people have which may push them into poverty.

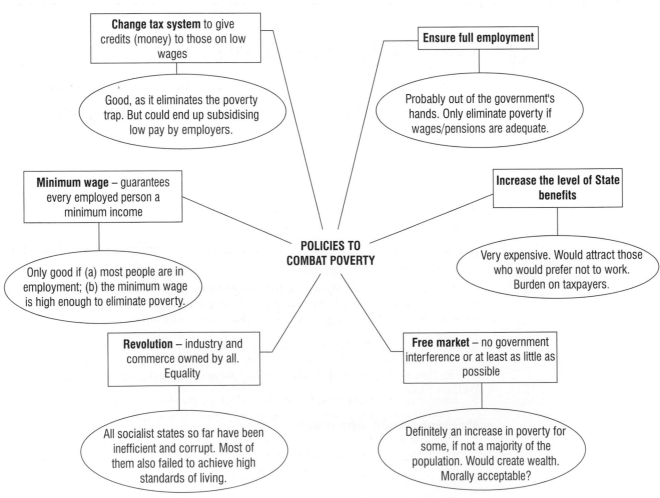

Policies to combat poverty

Main points ▶ Social policy analysts do not agree on the causes of poverty.

▶ Explanations which have been suggested fall into two main categories: dependency approaches, exclusion approaches.

▶ Both of these approaches then have separate strands within them.

▶ Dependency approaches include explanations stressing the individual, the underclass, the culture of poverty.

▶ Exclusion approaches include explanations stressing dyswelfare, Marxist-based criticisms of capitalism.

▶ All of the explanations suggest different policies to combat and eliminate poverty.

Conclusion

In this chapter we have examined the extent and causes of poverty in the UK. We have seen how difficult it is to define poverty and that there are important consequences in terms of policy of the different definitions and explanations. Poverty does not strike randomly across the population, some groups are much more likely to be in poverty than others.

4 CHAPTER SUMMARY

1 There is considerable dispute over how to define and measure poverty.

2 Social policy analysts have suggested several different ways to define poverty: absolute, relative, consensual, social exclusion. Each of these is linked to different forms of measurement.

3 The different definitions and measurements will produce different figures as to the numbers in poverty and the extent of the problem.

4 There are about 14 million people living in poverty according to the Households Below Average Income measure.

5 Some groups are much more likely to have a percentage in poverty than the rest of the population.

6 These groups with higher than average proportions likely to be in poverty are: the unemployed, the low paid, children, women, lone-parent families, sick and disabled people, older people.

7 It is important to remember, however, that within these groups there will be great variation, with many rich and affluent as well as poor people. It is just that there is greater likelihood of people in these groups living in poverty.

8 Each group is not separate, they overlap, so that women for example may be in all of these groups (for example, girls for the children group).

9 The reasons for these groups being more likely to live in poverty vary according to each group. However, low pay and low levels of benefits are two common themes running throughout.

10 Social policy analysts do not agree on the causes of poverty.

11   Explanations which have been suggested fall into two main categories: dependency approaches, exclusion approaches.

12   Both of these approaches then have separate strands within them.

13   Dependency approaches include explanations stressing the individual, the underclass, the culture of poverty.

14   Exclusion approaches include explanations stressing dyswelfare, Marxist-based criticisms of capitalism.

15   All of the explanations suggest different policies to combat and eliminate poverty.

Useful websites

www.dwp.gov.uk: the Department of Work and Pensions

www.cabinet-office.gov.uk/seu: the Social Exclusion Unit

www.jrf.org.uk: Joseph Rowntree Foundation – a major source of funding for social policy research and a site where many project findings are summarised

www.lapa.org.uk: Lothian Anti-Poverty Alliance – a good overview of recent trends in poverty and exclusion

www.lowpay.gov.uk: the Low Pay Commission

www.nmss.org.uk/cpag: the Child Poverty Action Group

Answers

Page 77

The following figures represent the percentage of people who responded positively to each statement as their preferred definition of poverty:

- 'Poverty is not having enough to eat and live without going into debt.' – 95%
- 'Poverty is having enough to eat and live, but not to buy other needed items.' – 55%
- 'Poverty is having enough to buy the things you really need, but not enough to buy things most people take for granted.' – 25%

Page 82

Item	% who say items are necessary	% who cannot afford them
Beds/bedding for all	95	1
Heating for living areas	94	1
Damp-free home	93	6
Visiting friends or family in hospital	92	3
Two meals a day	91	1
Prescribed medicines	90	1
Refrigerator	89	0.1
Fresh fruit and veg. daily	86	4
Warm, waterproof coat	85	4
Ability to replace or repair broken electrical goods	85	12
Visits to friends or family	84	2
Celebrating special occasions (e.g. Christmas)	83	2
Home in decent state of decoration	82	14
Visits to school (sports day)	81	2

Item	% who say items are necessary	% who cannot afford them
Attending weddings and funerals	80	3
Meat, fish or vegetarian equivalent every other day	70	3
Insuring home contents	79	8
Hobby or leisure activity	78	7
Washing machine	76	1
Collect children from school	75	2
Telephone	71	1
Appropriate clothes for job interviews	69	4
Deep freezer/fridge freezer	68	2
Living/bedroom carpets	67	3
Regular savings of £10 a month	66	21
Two pairs of all-weather shoes	64	6
Having friends or family around for a meal	64	6
Small amount to spend on self weekly	59	13
Television	56	1
Roast joint/vegetarian equivalent, weekly	56	3
Presents for friends and family once a year	56	3
Annual holiday away from home (not with relatives)	55	18
Replace worn-out furniture	54	12
Dictionary	53	5
Outfit for social occasions	51	4

Among the items omitted from the study because fewer than 50 per cent of the sample agreed that they were a necessity were:

- a car
- a dressing gown
- a daily newspaper
- an evening out once a fortnight
- a microwave oven
- a video
- a dishwasher
- a mobile phone
- access to Internet.

Page 99

1 If you use the definition of relative poverty, it does. If you don't, it is probably very rare.

2 Yes, as long as the wages were of a high enough level, and the gap between the richest and the lowest paid was not too great.

3 True.

4 True.

5 No, this is destitution.

6 It was true once, but no more – depends on how you define poverty – but probably lone parents.

7 I shouldn't have asked this question – the answer is too complex! Yes, the minimum wage has had a very small impact on poverty, but it is set too low to really change things.

Chapter

5

HOUSING

Chapter contents

- **Historical background**

  We explore the development of housing as a social issue and look at the work of charitable organisations and local authorities as they battled to provide adequate housing. We also see how housing came to be accepted by the government in the late 1940s as a key part of the Welfare State. We also see how legislation gradually transformed that.

- **Tenure**

  Here we briefly clarify what the different types of tenure are and how they have changed over time.

- **Local authority housing**

  We explore the development and eventual decline in local authority housing provision and in particular we look at the impact of the right-to-buy legislation which effectively removed a huge proportion of local authority housing from public control.

- **Housing associations**

  These have existed for over 150 years, but they came into prominence with the decision by the government in the 1980s to try to squeeze out local authorities from providing homes. Successive governments have favoured them as the best way to deliver housing needs. We explore their success.

- **Private rented tenure**

  At the turn of the twentieth century, this was the most popular form of tenure. By the end of that century it was only a marginal provider of housing. We chart this decline and look at who lives in privately rented accommodation today.

- **Owner-occupancy**

  Owner occupancy has been the huge winner in the race between the types of tenures. Over 70 per cent of householders are now purchasing or own their own homes. We examine the rise of the homeowner and the implications for those left out.

- **The significance of housing as a social issue**

  Housing is more than bricks and mortar. In this section we look at the impact it has to our lives and relationships.

- **Homelessness**

  We take a detailed examination of homelessness, exploring who becomes homeless and why, what can be done for homeless people and if the provision is adequate. We take an especially close look at young homeless people and rough sleepers.

- **Housing quality and regeneration**

  It is not just the numbers of houses but the condition of those houses which is important. We look at the quality of housing and what is being done to improve them and to regenerate areas of rundown housing.

- **Financial benefits for housing**

  Here we take a look at the Housing Benefit and examine how it is delivered and what problems there are with it. We also look at help for owner-occupiers in financial difficulties.

- **Equal opportunities**

  This final section explores an all too familiar story of discrimination. Some groups in society live in worse quality housing than others. We look in detail at the issues of equal opportunities, ethnicity and gender.

Introduction

Housing was one of the central elements in the original idea of the Welfare State when it was first envisaged by Beveridge. The provision of good quality, low rent, local government accommodation was certainly as important as a National Health Service in the original plans for a Welfare State. This chapter explores housing as a social issue, illustrating its relationship to the health and welfare services.

We begin the chapter by focusing on changes in housing policy. The policies which the Conservative government introduced after 1979 are in striking contrast to those of the period immediately after the introduction of the Welfare State. Probably the most important changes during the period since 1979 have been the decline in local authority housing and its partial replacement by housing associations and, secondly, the growth of home ownership.

The impact of some of these 'reforms', such as the opportunity for tenants to buy local authority housing and the consequent growth in home ownership, will continue to have an impact for many years to come.

Recognising that housing is a key element of the Welfare State, the next section of the chapter looks at the importance of housing to people, and at the relationship of housing to other social issues, such as poverty and ill health.

The greatest contemporary problem regarding housing is the fact that there is not enough of it available at prices which the lower paid sections of the population can afford – either to buy or to rent. So, in the next part of the chapter, we move on to look at homelessness, analysing its causes, measuring the numbers of people without adequate housing, and discussing the government's response to this problem.

We then explore the quality of housing in the UK today and concern ourselves less about the numbers of houses and more about the quality.

After a brief look at the State benefits available to those renting property, and the more generous benefits for people purchasing their own homes, the chapter ends with an examination of the issues surrounding gender and race in the context of housing.

Historical background

In the nineteenth century, inadequate housing and town planning had been clearly linked, on the one hand, to poverty and, on the other, to such things as poor health and other social problems. So, from about 1840 onwards, numerous charitable organisations began to set up housing schemes to try to provide better housing conditions for the working class. Schemes such as those known as 'philanthropy at 5 per cent' (referring to the 5 per cent rate of interest investors would receive for lending money to the charitable housing associations) had some success.

However, without government involvement, there was little possibility of seriously tackling the problems of homelessness, overcrowding and sub-standard housing, which were rife. Although an Act in 1866 allowed charities to borrow money cheaply from the government for the construction of new homes for the poor, it was not until the early part of the twentieth century that local government became involved in a serious way in providing houses for the less well off. By the 1930s, an average of 50,000 homes were built each year for local authorities to rent out.

After the Beveridge Report in 1942 (see Chapter 3) and the end of the Second World War, there was general agreement that everyone had a right to a home, as well as to free health care and decent employment. Indeed, squalor – by which he meant substandard housing – was one of Beveridge's five evils, which the Welfare State was committed to eradicate. Both Conservative and Labour governments supported large programmes of local authority rented housing, while also encouraging home ownership through the use of tax relief on mortgages.

By the 1960s, however, local authorities were beginning to recognise that they were unable to keep up with the demand for housing and were looking at cheaper ways of providing accommodation for those with lower incomes. The result was the developments of high-rise apartment blocks in all the major cities in the UK, even though it emerged later that these flats could actually cost up to 70 per cent more than the low-rise buildings!

Definition

Right-to-buy – the rights given to local authority housing tenants to buy their properties at a discount, in the 1980 Housing Act

---

By the end of the 1970s, with the UK economy entering a period of stagnation, it became apparent that the traditional mix of public and private housing was not going to satisfy the demand for housing, and more radical approaches were needed. The Conservative government which came into power in 1979 was ideologically committed to cutting back on the role of the State, and in particular local authorities. They therefore introduced the right of local authority 'council house' tenants to buy their own homes (**right-to-buy**), and they prevented local authorities from building new homes. They also loosened planning controls to enable a huge increase in private homes to be built. The lower paid who could not afford to buy property were catered for by charitable 'housing associations'.

A summary of recent housing legislation

* *Housing Act 1980*: introduced the right for council house tenants to buy their own homes. The Act took away some rights of tenants renting from private landlords.

* *Social Security and Housing Benefit Act 1982*: introduced Housing Benefit payable by the local authority rather than by social security.

* *Housing and Planning Act 1986*: made the purchase of council property easier.

* *Housing Act 1988*: ended the control of the privately rented sector with a resulting loss of security for tenants and increases in rents. Possibility of transfer of entire council estates to private interests or to housing associations. It allowed the creation of local organisations (Housing Action Trusts) to take over and improve run-down council estates.

* *Local Government and Housing Act 1990*: prevented local authorities from subsidising the rents of their tenants. Controls placed on the income from sales of council housing under the 'right to buy' scheme. This has led to a great increase in rents.

* *Housing Act 1996*: restricted access to Housing Benefit; took away the obligation on local authorities to offer homeless people permanent housing by going to the top of waiting lists.

* *Homes Act 2001*: Made buying and selling homes easier and placed a duty on local authorities to develop policies to monitor homelessness and develop policies to prevent it. Also amended parts of the 1996 Act regarding the provision of permanent housing to the homeless, by introducing set of priorities laying down who should have the highest priority in obtaining housing.

By the end of the century, the UK had largely become a home-owning (or at least a home-buying) society, with about 70 per cent of households purchasing or already owning their own homes.

Tenure

Tenure is the term used to describe the ownership patterns of housing. A person can be buying, already own or be renting from a private, State or not-for-profit organisation. There are three main types of tenure:

- *owner-occupancy*, where the person living in the property is buying or actually owns the property
- *privately rented*, where the person living in the property is paying rent to the owner, who is renting the property simply to make money. The property can be rented with furniture or without
- *social housing*, where the person living in the property pays rent to the owner. The owner however is providing the property as a social service, rather than for profit. There are two main providers of social housing:
  - *local authorities*, which provide what people traditionally call 'council housing'
  - **registered social landlords (RSLs)**/*housing associations*, which are private, not-for-profit organisations.

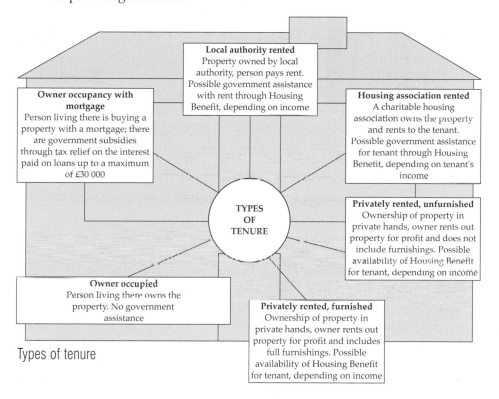

Types of tenure

Changes in tenure

From the 1930s, there had been a broad agreement between all political parties on the importance of maintaining a balance between local authority housing programmes and private house building. This was broken in 1979 when the Conservative government decided that local authority provision of housing was wrong, and the emphasis shifted to encourage the growth of rented accommodation (from both private landlords and housing associations) for those who could not afford to buy, while for the majority of the population the chance to own a home was strongly encouraged. This policy was highly popular, and, as we saw earlier, home ownership has now increased to over 70 per cent of the population through a combination of subsidised sales of council properties to tenants and the encouragement of the private sector to build new houses for sale.

Housing associations have also received funding to build 'affordable housing', which consists of housing which people can buy up to a maximum of 80 per cent ownership (this means that the price is cheaper).

On the other hand, as there is now no subsidy for social rented housing, rents are much higher than in the past.

Changes in tenure

A Housing tenure in England and Wales 1914–97

☐ Owner-occupied ◼ Local authority ◼ Private rented
◼ Housing association/Registered social landlords

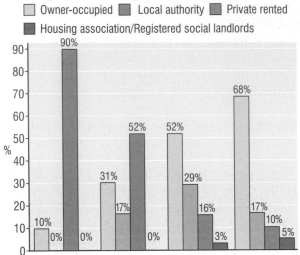

Source: J. Conway, *Housing Policy* (Gildredge Press, 2000)

B Transfers from local authorities to housing associations in England, 1988–2000

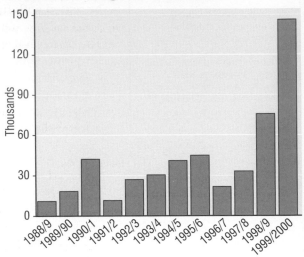

Source: M. Walsh, *Social Policy and Welfare* (Nelson Thornes, 2000)

Look at A.

1 What was the most common form of tenure in 1914?

2 Which two forms of tenure did not exist then?

3 What changes had taken place by 1951? Using the main text, explain these changes.

4 In 1997, what was the most common form of tenure? What had happened to the tenure which you gave as your answer for question 1?

Look at B.

5 What do you think has been happening to the pattern of tenure since 1997?

Local authority housing

At the beginning of the twentieth century, most people could not afford to buy their own homes and would rent from private landlords. However, the conditions were so appalling that in 1919, the Housing and Town Planning Act allowed local authorities to build homes for rent. This was later expanded in the 1924 Wheatley Act. By 1939 and the outbreak of the Second World War, half a million, high-quality houses had been built. Although today, social housing caters for the poor, and there is some stigma attached to living in social housing estates, in the 1930s the local authority homes were relatively expensive to rent and were regarded as being very prestigious.

After the Second World War, the desire to rebuild and house the population was blocked by a lack of government funds. The result was that poorer quality housing was built and few facilities were provided. Private builders were strongly encouraged and there was a rapid growth in owner-occupancy.

By the 1960s, living in local authority housing started to be associated with poverty and increasingly became the housing safety net for those who could not afford to buy.

In 1980, the then Conservative government's right-to-buy scheme was introduced, which allowed tenants living in a property for three years or more the right to buy that property at discounts on the market value of between 30 and 50 per cent.

Since 1980, 2.27 million flats and houses have been bought under this scheme. Most of the properties bought were the better quality ones, meaning that increasingly council stocks are of poorer quality. It also means that the supply of council housing available for rent has effectively disappeared.

The Conservative government objected to local authority provision of housing, because:

- *of an ideological 'belief in the market'* – the Conservative government of the 1980s believed that housing was best left to 'the market', in other words to a system known as *laissez-faire.* Under this principle, the best way of rationing things is to see how much people are prepared to pay. The government believed that local authorities drive out private landlords, and dissuade people from saving their money and eventually buying their own house
- *self-help* – the government believed that people should look after themselves and 'stand on their own feet', and not rely on the State to provide things
- *unresponsive bureaucracies* – the government argued that bureaucracies are unresponsive to the real needs of people. Rather than serving people, they are intent on looking after themselves. Local authority housing departments were good examples of bureaucracies, according to this view.

(For a more detailed discussion of New Right thinking, see Chapter 2.)

The issue of residualisation

> **Definition**
>
> **Residualisation** – housing that nobody wants, usually because of social problems

As we have just read, originally local authority housing was very prestigious accommodation and only the better-off, stable working-class families with good employment were allowed to live there. However, since the 1960s the reputation of local authority housing estates has changed, as have the tenants who occupy them. Increasingly, social housing is the preserve of those who have social problems of one kind or another. This has been termed **residualisation**.

However, despite all these problems and the shift to housing associations, local authorities are still responsible for 3.2 million homes.

Housing associations

In order to limit the role of local authorities in providing and running housing, the 1980s Conservative government increasingly switched its funding to housing associations/registered social landlords (RSLs).

The advantages of RSLs are that, being in the private sector, they can raise private finance for new schemes and for investing in stock transferred from local authorities outside the constraints of government financial controls. There are over 2,000 RSLs that together own about 1 million homes. The largest 200 RSLs own 90 per cent of the stock. Five per cent of all housing stock is owned by RSLs and they have raised £10 billion in private finance.

The Labour government has not been as strongly opposed to local authority housing as the previous Conservative governments, but has still continued the policy of transferring local authority housing stock to RSLs. So, for example, in 1999–2000, 116,000 properties were transferred from local authority stocks to housing associations, bringing the total of properties transferred between 1980 and 2000 to 474,000 properties.

In 1999–2000, local authorities built in total 100 houses compared to the RSL's 17,000 new properties.

RSLs are co-ordinated and receive funding through an organisation known as the Housing Corporation, which was established by Parliament in 1964 to promote voluntary non-profit-making housing associations and co-operatives. Since 1974 it has been the major provider of finance for RSLs.

Housing associations (RSLs)

Rise in grant rate keeps rents down

The proportion of public money allocated to new housing association homes has reached its highest level for seven years, reflecting the increasing focus on keeping rents low.

Housing associations, which now provide the vast bulk of new social housing, fund new development from a mixture of public grant administered by the Housing Corporation, their own resources and private loans.

In the mid-1990s the proportion of public grant allocated to new schemes decreased as housing associations became more reliant on private finance. This allowed the associations to build more homes but at the cost of higher rents to repay loans. The proportion of public grant used on schemes is therefore seen as a key barometer of the trade off between building more homes and ensuring that rents are affordable.

Source: *The Guardian*, 2 March 2001

1 Which organisations produce the bulk of social housing today?

2 How are these organisations funded? How is this different from private landlords and local authorities? (You will have to work this out by reading the main text.)

3 Who administers the funds?

4 If the rents are kept down, as the headlines suggests, what happens to the numbers of homes being built?

Private rented tenure

At the beginning of the twentieth century, the most common form of tenure was of privately rented property. There were many problems associated with this sort of tenure, most notably the lack of security of tenants who could be evicted easily and the poor quality of the properties, which were built simply to make as much money as possible.

In 1915, the situation was so bad that a series of rent strikes took place right across the UK. As a result, the government introduced the Rent Act which imposed rent controls on private landlords, and in 1924 the Protection from Eviction Act which gave tenants some security.

However, the outcome of this was that landlords began to sell off properties and to halt even the small amount of investment in maintenance which had previously occurred. It was in response to this that the great growth in local authority housing took place in the 1920s. This growth in local authority housing further decreased the supply of privately rented accommodation.

After the Second World War (1945), and in response to the housing crisis, the government tried various schemes, including getting rid of controls on the prices of rentals (1957), and then in the 1960s and 1970s introducing greater tenant security and 'fair rent' schemes. None of these schemes seemed to revive the private rented market, and controls were loosened in 1988 and have remained so since then. Today, about 12 per cent of tenures are privately rented accommodation.

Housing: an indicator of Social divisions?

Household type: by tenure, 1998–9, United Kingdom   **Percentages**

	Owned outright	Owned with mortgage	Rented from social sector	Rented privately[1]	All tenures
One person	35	22	31	12	100
Two or more unrelated adults	25	20	18	37	100
One family households[2]					
Couple					
No children	42	39	12	7	100
Dependent children[3]	6	72	15	8	100
Non-dependent children only	37	51	11	2	100
Lone parent					
Dependent children[3]	6	27	54	13	100
Non-dependent children only	35	29	32	4	100
Multi-family households	18	49	29	4	100
All households	28	41	22	9	100

Source: General Household Survey, Office for National Statistics, Continuous Household Survey, Northern Ireland Statistics and Research Agency

1 Includes rent-free accommodation.
2 Other individuals who were not family members may also be included.
3 May also include non-dependent children.

That tenure of housing also varies with the age of the head of household in part reflects people's life cycle transitions. In 1999–00 almost half of households headed by someone under 25 in England were living in privately rented accommodation, which was more than three times the proportion for those aged 25 to 44 and far greater than for any other age group. Private renters in furnished accommodation were particularly likely to be young, male and single. Heads of households aged 65 and over were most likely to own their property outright, as by the time they retire many will have repaid their mortgage in its entirety. A third of all social sector renters in England were aged 65 or over compared with a quarter of owner-occupiers.

Source (table and text): *Social Trends 31*
(The Stationery Office, 2001)

1 Explain the difference between renting from the social sector and renting privately.

2 Explain the difference between owned-outright and owned with a mortgage.

3 Which social group is most likely to rent from the social sector? Suggest reasons.

4 Which social group is most likely to rent form the private sector? Suggest reasons.

5 Which social group is most likely to own outright? Suggest reasons.

6 What does the term 'life cycle's transitions' mean and what relevance might it have for understanding tenure? Give examples from the table to illustrate your explanation.

Owner-occupancy

Owner-occupancy is the main type of tenure in the UK, and has been growing since the 1920s. The growth over time is the result of a number of factors:

- the lack of rented accommodation
- the availability of mortgages to buy properties
- the increasing affluence of the population
- the right-to-buy legislation of the 1980s which allowed local authority tenants to purchase their homes at a discount.

The modern development of owner-occupancy occurred after the 1923 Housing Act, which provided subsidies and discounted loans for builders to construct cheaper homes and to guarantee building society mortgages. This meant that within ten years, 20 per cent of all new homes were constructed as a result of these subsidies.

During the 1930s a number of financial and planning abuses took place, which brought private house builders into disrepute, but the Act which resulted from the scandals (the 1939 Building Society Act) later provided the financial structure to finance the building boom of the 1950s onward.

In order to extend owner-occupancy in the 1960s, the government introduced tax relief on the money borrowed to pay for a house. So, owner-occupancy was government subsidised. The tax relief was only abolished in 1999.

Perhaps the most radical change in owner-occupancy was the right-to-buy legislation (1980) which we discussed earlier, whereby local authority tenants could purchase their own properties. This has resulted in two and a quarter million properties shifting from local authority rented to owner-occupancy.

Tenure 'flows'

It is important to remember that tenure types are not fixed, and that people are constantly moving between one tenure type and another. The diagram gives a picture of this flow in the mid-1990s.

Numbers of households moving in and out of social housing in 1993/4

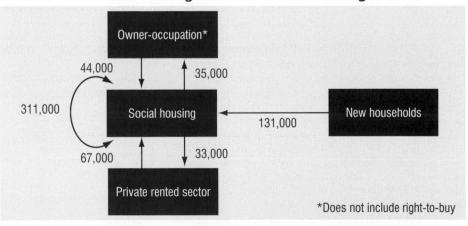

Source: www.jrf.org.uk/knowledge/findings/housing/h202.asp, taken from 'The changing population in social housing in Britain' in *Housing Research*, 202, February 1997, Joseph Rowntree Foundation

1 Where did people come from who moved into social housing?

2 Was there any movement within social housing? How many was this?

3 Suggest reasons why people might want to move within the social housing sector.

4 How many people left the social housing sector to the private rented sector?

5 How many people changed from social housing tenure to owner occupancy? Can you suggest any reasons for this (see main text)?

6 How many people left owner-occupancy for social housing? Suggest why this might happen.

Main points ▶ Cheap housing was first provided by charitable associations in the nineteenth century.

▶ Local government first became heavily involved in house provision in the early part of the twentieth century.

▶ Housing was recognised as one element of the five evils identified in the Beveridge Report.

▶ There are three main types of tenure: owner-occupancy, private renting and social renting.

▶ Gradually during the 1960s there was a shift away from renting houses to owner-occupancy.

▶ Today, the majority of householders are buying their homes.

▶ A huge increase in home ownership took place in the 1980s when the Conservative government introduced the right-to-buy legislation.

▶ Rented housing is increasingly being run by housing associations.

▶ Privately rented tenure has decreased greatly. Now it is the very rich or the very poor who use this form of tenure.

The significance of housing as a social issue

Housing cannot be seen solely in terms of bricks and mortar. People live in the houses, and invest much of their income in buying them, or renting them. They also put something of themselves into their houses, in the way they decorate and treat the property. Houses also have meaning for the people who live in them, as they have come to represent a private sphere where the individual and their family can relax and express themselves.

Poor housing can affect people's health and well-being, and can have a destructive effect on family relationships too.

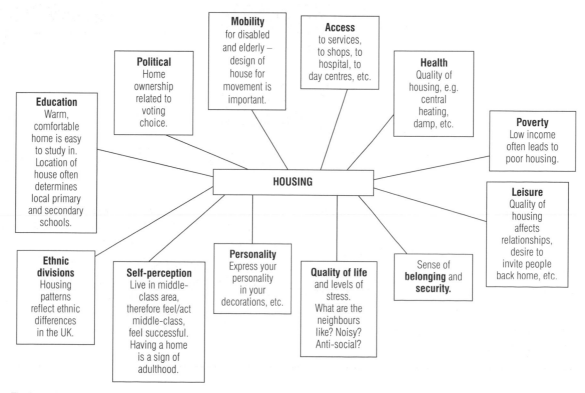

The importance of housing

The significance of housing

Housing is a critical source of material and emotional comfort, protection and health. Both the quality and quantity of life are connected with accommodation (see below).

Where somebody lives also plays a major role in determining access to a wide range of other goods and services – such as health care, education, transport, leisure facilities and retail outlets.

Furthermore, the home and its immediate environment are very widely regarded as a source of personal identity, of self-expression and social status. This is reflected in high levels of expenditure on items such as furnishings, fittings, decor, gardening and the like.

For the young, acquiring a home of one's own is an important step in attaining adult status; for the old, losing it is often experienced as a painful erosion of social standing and independence.

The home both reflects and shapes gender divisions. It has also been argued that political support is influenced by housing. Thus a property-owning democracy is sometimes said to be more likely to vote for political parties of the right (such as the Conservatives).

For most people, housing represents the single most expensive thing purchased over a lifetime. For some, this means that housing becomes a valuable asset … for others it represents a major drain on their financial resources.

Location in the housing market is closely connected with location on the labour market.

Source: Adapted from N. Jewson, 'No place like home,' *Social Studies Review*, March 1989

1 How many of the points shown in the diagram 'The importance of housing' on page 119 can be found in the extract above?

2 Are there any other points you can find showing why housing is so important as a social issue?

3 What does the author of the extract mean when he says that the home 'reflects and shapes gender divisions'?

4 Explain why certain groups in society find housing a 'major drain on their financial resources'. If this is the case, what possible consequences can come from this?

Housing, health and poverty

Numerous studies have indicated the close link between poor housing conditions and premature death or chronic illness. Damp, infested homes cause ill health and, of course, as it is usually the poor who live in bad housing, they are already disadvantaged by inadequate heating, poor diets and general deprivation.

The mental health of children and their parents is so often closely intertwined.

Children are sensitive to the moods of their carers and a child exposed to a parent depressed about their living conditions will undoubtedly be affected.

A depressed mother who is breast feeding may find her milk dries up; a parent out of work because of their problematic housing situation may become frustrated and take his or her aggression out on the children; a whole family living in one room

are likely to affect each other's mental state, with no privacy, constant noise and no space for the children to play.

Respiratory infections are the most common cause of death in children between the ages of one and 14 years.

Recent research from Edinburgh University, appears to confirm that children living in damp conditions are more likely to suffer respiratory problems such as persistent coughs, wheezes, running noses and are more susceptible to infections causing

fevers, sore throats and headaches. The housing studied had poor ventilation and heating, contributing to mould and damp.

This study is perhaps one of the most important in relating poor health to poor housing as, unlike many others, it has taken into account most other variables such as low income, overcrowding and smoking.

Other studies make similar findings as well as showing the effects of living in certain urban environments. Freeman demonstrated links between living

in high rise flats or on run-down estates with some psychiatric conditions. A North Manchester Health Authority report supports these findings showing that the mental health of adults improves when they move out of tower blocks.

More recent research from Edinburgh University shows that children living in environments internally polluted by damp and mould are more likely to experience poor educational and intellectual performance as well as suffering more emotional distress.

Source: Adapted from Annette Furley, *A Bad Start in Life: Children, Health and Housing* (Shelter, 1989)

1 What are the most common causes of death for children between one and 14 years of age?

2 In what way(s) can this be linked to housing?

3 Explain the relationship between mental health and housing.

4 In your opinion, and drawing upon the extract, is poor housing the **root cause** of the physical and mental illnesses mentioned? Explain your answer.

Neighbour disputes

One of the most rapidly escalating problems in housing is that of disputes between neighbours. This ranges from racial harassment to general 'anti-social behaviour', which refers to behaviour that ruins a person's right to enjoy and use their own home in a reasonable manner.

The main complaints against neighbours include noise levels, disputes over gardens, abuse, damage to property (often by young people), dogs, physical intimidation and car repairs.

Residualisation

The increase in neighbour disputes, particularly in the social housing market, is related to the changing nature of social housing. We saw in an earlier part of the chapter that originally local authority housing was high status, and reflected quite a wide section of society. However, as owner-occupancy has become the norm in UK society, social housing (and in particular, older stocks of local authority housing) have increasingly been the place for the poorest, the most vulnerable and the socially excluded. The result has been a complex mix of those who are people most likely to be victims and those who are most likely to engage in anti-social behaviour. This process is known as residualisation (see also page 115).

Standards of housing

A second contributory factor has been an overall decline in the standards of housing in the social sector. Until recently, houses were built with an eye to cheapness and quantity rather than quality. There is poor noise insulation, high density, low levels of maintenance which have helped give a run-down appearance and few communal facilities.

Dealing with disputes

Most social landlords arrange mediation – a trained and independent official who will try to generate calm discussion between tenants to see if an agreement can be reached. There are a number of powers which local authorities have over those causing disturbance. These include the Noise Act 1996 which states that it is an offence to commit excessive noise at night, and the Protection from Harassment Act 1997 which provides for civil or even criminal remedies for victims of harassment.

In cases of intimidation or violence, the victim has traditionally been rehoused if possible. However, since the 1998 Crime and Disorder Act, new powers have been granted to local authorities and other social landlords to place the focus on those engaging in anti-social behaviour, and it is now the perpetrators who will be moved out of the house – in extreme cases they can be refused housing.

Homelessness

Defining homelessness

Until 1977, the definition of homelessness used by the government was of families who had been placed in temporary accommodation by the 'welfare authorities'. The local authorities were not obliged to place people in temporary accommodation, and more people were turned away than accepted.

In 1977, following immense pressure, the Housing (Homeless Persons) Act was passed. This provided a wider definition homelessness and imposed on local authorities the legal obligation to provide accommodation for certain 'priority' groups and to provide 'advice and assistance' for other groups.

In 1996, the government changed the priority list as a result of complaints that it gave unfair advantage to single mothers who 'jumped the queue' ahead of homeless families who were lower down on the housing list as they were not regarded as top priority.

The Homes Act 2001 abandoned the idea of a housing list altogether, and replaced it with priority groups whom the local authority must house. From 2001, local authorities must house the following priority groups in 'suitable accommodation', if they are unintentionally homeless:

- families with dependent children or someone who is pregnant
- people who are vulnerable in some way (for example, old age, or mental or physical disability)
- people who are homeless as a result of a disaster such as flood or fire
- homeless 16- and 17-year-olds (except those for whom a council have responsibility under the Children (Leaving Care) Act 2000)
- care-leavers aged 18–21
- people the council consider to be vulnerable as a result of fleeing domestic violence or harassment
- people the council consider to be vulnerable as a result of an institutionalised background (for example, those leaving care, the armed services or prison).

In 1999, 105,000 'households' in England and Wales were homeless (according to the official definition). This covers over a quarter of a million people, about half of which are children.

However, the official definition of homelessness is disputed by many who point out that about 1,000 households each day approach local authorities claiming that they are homeless, but over half are turned away as they do not fit into the official definition of homelessness. Shelter (a housing pressure group) estimated that the real extent of homelessness in the UK may well be over one and a half million.

Who are the hidden homeless?

These hidden homeless people are in a variety of circumstances and include those sleeping rough, squatting, staying in hostels, lodgings or insecure private lets, women living with violent partners, travellers and people living in caravans and boats, and people sharing with others who wish to live separately. ... Among those who use hostels and bed and breakfast hotels are increasing numbers of young people and a disproportionate number from ethnic minorities. ... A high proportion of single homeless people have spent some time in an institution such as a children's home, hospital, prison or remand centre, with perhaps a quarter having been in the armed forces.

Source: J. Conway, *Housing Policy* (Gildredge Press, 2000)

1 What do we mean by 'the hidden homeless'?

2 Give three examples? In your opinion are these people 'homeless'?

3 Who are those more likely to be using bread and breakfast accommodation and hostels?

4 What backgrounds do a high proportion of single homeless people have? Suggest reasons why this should be so.

5 The extract was published in 2000, a year before the Homes Act. How might the new Act help the 'hidden homeless'? (See main text above.)

Homelessness and health

Families in temporary accommodation	Single homeless people
Poor diet – convenience foods, inadequate cooking facilities	Chronic chest and breathing problems caused by infections and high rates of smoking
High rate of infectious illnesses – because of overcrowding and poor living conditions	Malnutrition – cannot afford food and unable to cook
High levels of accidents to children – overcrowding, poor safety levels	Infestation of lice and a variety of skin problems, caused by few toilet facilities
Poor child behaviour as a result of stress and conditions	Dental problems – no access to a dentist
Symptoms of depression and stress	Eyesight problems – no access to an optician
High miscarriage rates	High risk of violence and assault
Babies born with low birth weights and poor infant health	High levels of mental health problems

Source: Information drawn from J. Conway, *Housing Policy* (Gildredge Press, 2000)

Causes of homelessness

In looking at the main causes of homelessness, we can make a distinction between:

- immediate causes
- structural causes.

Immediate causes

The immediate causes of homelessness are the final, specific 'precipitating' reasons which force a person or family to seek help from the local authority or housing association. These include:

- parents/families/friends no longer willing or able to provide accommodation
- partners separating
- the loss of the rented property through disputes with landlords
- inability to pay the mortgage
- rent arrears.

Why homeless? Some of the reasons people become homeless

People become homeless because they cannot find accommodation which is suitable for them, and which they can afford. There are many reasons which explain how people become homeless, among them:

Parents/families/friends no longer will or able to provide accommodation: 40%
Many young people in particular become homeless because they are no longer able or willing to live with their parents. Some people have to leave their homes because they find they are unable to share accommodation with friends.

The loss of rented property through disputes with landlords: 15%
About one in eight people who become homeless do so because they are forced to leave their privately rented homes. Landlords have the power to evict tenants after their agreed tenancy period has finished.

Construct a diagram which illustrates the link between the immediate causes of homelessness above with the structural explanations which we discuss in the main text.

Partners separating: 18%
The second most common cause of homelessness is the break down of marriages or relationships. When a couple splits up, one or both partners are often left with no home.

Inability to pay the mortgage: 9%
The fastest-growing group of homeless people comprises those who have lost homes which they owned themselves. Owner-occupiers are vulnerable because of high interest rates, which have pushed up their mortgage repayments. In 1995 more than 50,000 properties were repossessed because their owners fell behind with their mortgages.

Structural causes

The immediate causes we looked at above focus on the specific problems of the individuals and seem to suggest that it is the fault of the individual or their family or landlord that has led to the situation of homelessness.

An alternative way of explaining homelessness is to put the immediate causes within a wider context. For example, why is it that people cannot afford to repay their mortgage? One (immediate cause) explanation is that they must have made a miscalculation over how much they could afford, and now have to suffer the consequences. An alternative (structural) explanation is that as governments have failed to provide an adequate supply of 'affordable' houses to rent or buy, families have been forced to take on very high mortgages in order to obtain accommodation. The 'blame' should therefore be placed on the government rather than the family.

Structural causes of homelessness include:

- *Lack of affordable homes:* There has been a decline in the numbers of affordable homes to buy or rent, as builders prefer to construct larger houses which give greater profit. However, even small houses in the south of England are too expensive for many.
- *Right-to-buy:* This policy, introduced in 1980, gave local authority tenants the right to buy their own homes at a discount. In all, over 2.3 million homes have been sold. Traditionally, these homes were the ones are available for rent to the lower paid sections of the community.
- *Benefit changes:* The government has lowered State benefits, including Housing Benefit, for those under 25 and tied benefits for the under 18s to attendance on the New Deal programme. Only in exceptional circumstances will they be awarded Housing Benefit to enable them to live away from home.
- *Decline of the private rented sector:* Today only about 12 per cent of homes are privately rented. Traditionally, apart from local authority housing, private landlords provided the accommodation for the lowest paid.
- *Poverty:* Perhaps surprisingly, there is no housing shortage; there is enough accommodation for those who want it. The real problem lies in the fact that up to three million people in the UK simply cannot afford to pay the rents or to purchase a home. The issue could therefore be regarded as one of poverty, rather than homelessness.
- *Employment pattern:* House prices and rents are lowest in the north of England and Scotland. This is precisely where unemployment rates are at their highest. In order to find work, people are forced to move to the south-east, where rents and house prices are at their highest.
- *Changing nature of the family:* The increase in lone parents and the decline in the stability of relationships mean that there are far more people seeking accommodation.

Groups more likely to be homeless

Homelessness is more likely to occur to some groups of people than others

Lone parents
Lone parents are ten times more likely than chance to be homeless. Lone parents comprise over 60 per cent of households with children applying for housing.

Low income
Those with the lowest incomes are least likely to be able to afford accommodation. Over 80 per cent of those applying for housing are on State benefits.

Larger families
Larger numbers of children means the need for a larger home, which costs more. Larger families are also over-represented amongst the poorer families.

THE HOMELESS

The unemployed
Sixty per cent of those applying for housing are unemployed or not in full-time work.

Young people
Young people are more likely to be homeless than the rest of the population. This is because they tend to be poorer and to have a higher proportion of lone parents. About 40 per cent of those applying for housing are under 25, and 75 per cent are under 35 years of age.

Temporary provision for the homeless

Definition

Temporary accommodation – the range of cheap hotels and basic hostels used by local authorities to house people who are homeless

One of the responses of local authorities to the housing crisis has been to house homeless people in **temporary accommodation**. Often the conditions are reminiscent of the nineteenth century. The accommodation includes bed and breakfast, hostels, shelters, refuges and short-life tenancies in poor quality accommodation which no one else wants.

Bed and breakfast accommodation

With the decline in council housing availability, local authorities have increasingly turned to placing the homeless in bed and breakfast accommodation. Today, this form of accommodation provides for about half those accepted as homeless and placed in temporary accommodation. The next largest provision is in the form of 'short-life' tenancies' (see page 127).

Usually bed and breakfast accommodation is in run-down hotels which no longer attract tourists or, increasingly, in private hotels (invariably of a poor standard) run especially to take in the homeless.

Looking after the homeless?

Homeless households in temporary accommodation, Great Britain

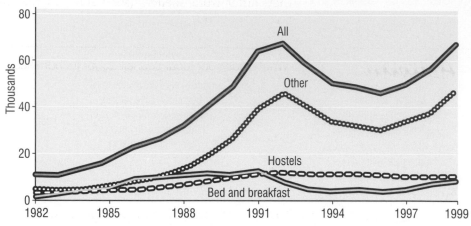

Source: Department of the Environment, Transport and the Regions; National Assembly for Wales, Scottish Executive

Source: Social Trends 31 (The Stationery Office, 2001)

Households in temporary accommodation, 30 June 1998

	B&B	Hostels	Other	Total
North East	90	200	540	830
Yorks and Humberside	50	480	640	1,170
East Midlands	10	350	1,020	1,380
Eastern	120	1,170	1,930	3,220
Greater London	3,360	3,460	18,880	25,700
Rest of South East	770	1,580	5,780	8,130
South West	410	570	2,510	3,490
West Midlands	80	510	1,150	1,740
North West	70	760	940	1,770
Merseyside	10	230	220	460
England	**4,970**	**9310**	**33,610**	**47,890**
Wales	**140**	**134**	**540**	**814**
Scotland	**476**	**157**	**3,387**	**4,020**

Source: London Research Centre Housing Update, No.19, 1998

1 In which two years, according to the graph, did the number of homeless households in temporary accommodation peak?

2 How many were in bed and breakfast accommodation in 1998?

3 What has happened since 1997 to the numbers in bed and breakfast accommodation?

4 What sort of accommodation does 'Other' refer to do you think?

5 Which place in England and Wales had the highest rate of people in temporary accommodation?

Hostels

These are run either by local authorities or by voluntary organisations. Generally, they differ from shelters (see below) in that they provide rather longer-term accommodation.

What does your local council do for its homeless?

Contact your local council and request a representative to come to your college for a question and answer session. Perhaps, through the local housing department, somebody who is or has been 'homeless' can also be asked to come to talk.

Shelters

These are increasingly being provided and run by charitable organisations such as St Mungo's, Centrepoint and the Salvation Army. Shelters provide a place to sleep overnight, somewhere to wash, and sometimes food. They could not be described as 'home', or even a substitute for home.

Women's refuges

These are provided for women who are the victims of male violence. They are generally local authority aided, but are run as independent charities. Since 2001, women escaping from male violence have been classified as unintentionally homeless and qualify for rehousing.

Short-life tenancies

Where properties are about to be demolished, or their condition is so poor that most people will not accept living there, local authorities use them on a temporary basis for those accepted as homeless. They are the second most common form of accommodation offered to those accepted as homeless by local authorities.

Rough sleepers

Definition

Rough sleepers – homeless who sleep out at night, or may use a night shelter offered by a charity

The term **rough sleepers** is used to describe those who sleep on the streets. In a series of night counts throughout England in 1999, it was estimated that there were about 2,000 sleeping out on any particular night – but that there were possibly as many as 10,000 rough sleepers in all.

The majority are white males aged between 25 and 60, though there has been an increase in those aged 18–20 in recent years, so that they now form about 25 per cent of all rough sleepers. Most of the men are sleeping rough as a result of a relationship breakdown which led to them leaving home. Over half of them have been in prison at some time, and they are also likely to have been in local authority care as children. About 20 per cent of all rough sleepers have been in the armed forces.

Apart from their homelessness, rough sleepers have a range of physical and mental health problems – one-third suffer from some kind of mental illness, 50 per cent have a serious alcohol problem and anything up to 40 per cent misuse drugs.

To try to eliminate the rough sleeper problem, the government has funded a variety of initiatives since 1991, usually involving funding hostels, additional winter shelters and day centres.

Is there really such a thing as homelessness?

There are 21 million 'dwellings' in England, of which 762,700 were empty in 2000. There were 105,000 households homeless in the same year These alone would provide enough places for all the homeless.

However, even of those homes which are not 'empty', some are second homes, some people live in homes which are too large for them, some are homes located in one part of the country and the demand is in another, some are homes which are too expensive for poorer people to rent or buy.

1 What is your opinion? Do you think people should be banned from owning second homes?

2 Should people renting social housing which is too large for them (for example their children have left home) be required to move to smaller properties?

3 What would you do about empty homes?

How best to help the homeless?

In 2000, the Rough Sleepers Unit, a government organisation, started a campaign asking people to stop giving change to beggars and to donate the money instead to a project to help rough sleepers to escape from their predicament, by providing drug counselling, education and training opportunities, plus some form of accommodation.

The reality of life on the streets is that drug misuse is widespread. The 'need' of someone begging is often to sustain a drug habit. Research shows that almost half of those begging regularly use heroin and one third use crack. We must do all we can to help people in dangerous and damaging situations, including asking whether giving money directly on the streets is an effective response ...

... around half of those begging are rough sleepers and a further third are in hostels and night centres.

Source: Louise Casey, Head of the Rough Sleepers Unit writing in *Roof*, January/February 2001

1 Many people object to the government trying to stop people giving change to beggars. What is your opinion?

2 Look up the website for the campaign mentioned above: www.changealife.org.uk

3 If you live in a town where there are beggars, ask a sample of people if they ever give money to beggars, how much they give and on what basis they decide to give (or not give) the money

Young people and homelessness

One particular growing problem is that of homelessness amongst young people. The main reasons for homelessness amongst young people include:

* *decline in the provision of rented accommodation* both by local authorities and the private sector for single people
* *lack of employment* – young people have some of the highest unemployment rates compared to older groups
* *low pay* – young people are more likely to be receiving the minimum wage, and below 18 there is an lower tier minimum wage.
* *cuts in State benefits for young people:*
  1985 Strict limits imposed on bed and breakfast payments
  1988 Social Security Act cut benefit levels for those under 25
  1989 Changes in regulations concerning exactly what Housing Benefit and Income Support would pay for in hotels and bed and breakfast accommo-dation (would no longer pay for 'services' such as rates, fuel, cooking, food,

cleaning, laundry). This meant that bed and breakfast accommodation became too expensive for many young people. Introduction of the Social Fund and the difficulties in obtaining it has meant that few homeless young people are able to borrow the deposit required by many private landlords.

- *abuse* – *a* high percentage of the young homeless have left home after experiencing physical or sexual abuse. Almost 20 per cent of the young homeless claim to have been abused
- *leaving care* – less than 1 per cent of all children go into local authority care. However they form 1 in 4 of all the young homeless
- *leaving custody* – about one-third of all young people leaving custody are homeless or 'at risk of becoming homeless'.

The foyer movement

Youth homelessness is a particularly complicated issue, in that homelessness is often linked to other factors, which may actually be greater problems than the lack of accommodation. Traditional approaches to homelessness provided somewhere to live, but regarded the solution to other problems as lying in the hands of other agencies.

The **foyer** movement provides a range of services linked with either short-term or long-term accommodation. Foyers vary enormously, but are usually drop-in centres with a range of facilities, including the provision of basic education, an advice desk, counselling, employment and skills training advisory services. The movement is growing rapidly.

> **Definition**
>
> **Foyer** – hostels for young homeless people which provide a range of training and leisure facilities

---

An example of the foyer approach to homelessness

Wakefield accommodation project			
Barnardo's, Wakefield Metropolitan District Housing and Social Services Department provide a service for young people who are homeless or threatened with homeless. It provides drop-in sessions, a newsletter, individual work and	a housing and advice service. There is also a supported lodging scheme with 14 providers, shortstop and night stop provision for assessment or one night stays only and links with the local authority and housing associations to access	long-term housing. Young people are helped to plan their future housing and support needs by attending the Housing Panel where the partnership agencies are all present.

Source: Donnehy, Smith and Harker, *Not To Be Ignored* (CPAC, 1997)

Runaways and homelessness

'It's so cold on the streets and so frightening,' says Marie, from Birmingham, now a 20-year-old student who ran away from a care home just before she was 16. ... because the stepfather who had sexually abused her as a child, which led to her going into care in the first place, kept following her.

'In the end, I couldn't stand it and felt the only thing I could do was run away.'

She finished her GCSEs, took a job washing up in a restaurant for three weeks to save enough money for a train ticket to London, and then ran.

'The worst thing was that no one would listen to me,' she recalls. 'I was scared and nervous when I got on the train, but I felt I couldn't go back to the situation I had left behind. Kids will only run away if the situation they are in is so bad that living on the streets seems like a better option. Something has got to be really wrong to make a young person do a thing like that.'

Marie was so terrified when she arrived at Euston station that she simply walked the streets for three days too frightened of what might happen if she lay down and closed her eyes. 'I felt so alone in the world,' she says. 'Nobody in my care home bothered to report me missing. The streets are full of homeless young people crying out for love.'

Marie was one of an estimated 129,000 young people who run away each year. The commonest reasons for children taking flight include desperation at not being listened to, rows with parents over the amount of freedom they are allowed, bullying at school, and drug problems or abuse.

While, Marie, who have been in care, make up a large proportion of runaways (approximately four in 10), the report[1] finds that 21%

are fleeing stepfamilies, and 13% one-parent families, compared to 7% who live with both birth parents. But, contrary to stereotype, poverty was found not to be a significant factor leading to young people running away: those from leafy suburbs are just as likely to flee as those from deprived inner-city areas. The majority of runaways are aged between 13 and 16 and are more likely to be girls than boys (although boys tend to run away earlier and more often). It is not only a problem of troubled adolescence: an estimated 18,000 children under 11 also run away each year, of whom about a third are under eight. Shockingly further 18,000 children a year thrown out by their parents.

1 *Consultation on Young Runaways* (Social Exclusion Unit, 2001)

Source: *The Guardian*, 28 March 2001

1 What are the reasons cited here causing young people to run away?

2 How many young people run away each year?

3 What percentages are running away from:
a)   step families?
b)   lone-parent families?
c)   both birth parent families?

4 How old are the majority of young runaways?

5 Are they eligible for State benefits? (You may have to investigate this.)

6 How many are thrown out by their parents?

Main points ▶ Housing is extremely socially important in people's lives.

▶ Housing is linked to levels of stress, of health and of poverty, amongst other things.

▶ One of the fastest growing problems is that of neighbour disputes.

▶ Local authorities now have powers to intervene and to evict troublesome tenants.

▶ There is still a considerable amount of homelessness.

▶ There are two groups of explanations for homelessness: structural and immediate causes.

▶ Structural causes refer to the wider issues about lack of adequate housing and differences in income to obtain housing.

▶ Immediate causes refer to such things as personal relationships breaking down which cause someone to have to leave a household and then become homeless.

▶ Some social groups are much more likely to become homeless than others.

▶ Homeless people are generally housed (at first) in temporary accommodation, which is of poor quality.

▶ There are still about 10,000 people who sleep rough on the streets at night on regular occasions.

▶ Young people who become homeless are especially vulnerable to a range of social problems, but receive only limited help.

Housing quality and regeneration

Quality of housing

According to the 1989 Local Government and Housing Act, housing is unfit for human habitation if it is lacking in:

• piped water
• wash basin with hot and cold water, fixed bath or shower and an internal WC
• drainage and sanitation facilities
• facilities for cooking and food preparation
• adequate light, heating and ventilation

and if it is not:

- free from damp and condensation
- structurally stable and in adequate repair.

At the turn of the twenty-first century, there were 1.7 million dwellings which were considered as unfit for human habitation, of these 207,000 lacked a basic amenity such as a bathroom, sink, basin, hot and cold water or an indoor toilet. Twenty per cent of homes in England and 30 per cent in Scotland suffered problems of damp, condensation or mould growth.

About 7 per cent of homes are 'unfit', and this figure has dropped only slowly from 9 per cent in the mid 1980s. Older housing tends to be in the worst condition, particularly terraced housing and converted flats. The majority of homes in poor condition are owner-occupied, but the private rented sector has the highest proportion of unfit homes. However, the growth in unfit homes is in the local authority sector, as little money is made available to local authorities to upgrade their housing stock.

Those who live in the worst conditions tend to be:

- older people
- younger people
- people in ethnic minority groups.

Cycle of neighbourhood decline

Regeneration

The government provides a range of grants to upgrade housing, for owner-occupiers and for the private rented sector. However, in recent years there has been a realisation that providing individual grants is not adequate, as it is often whole areas with poor housing which have contributed to a movement out of the area of better-off families and a movement in of people with various social problems. The result is that poor housing and community problems have become inextricably linked.

Successive governments have therefore sought to **regenerate** the most deprived urban areas, starting in 1979 with the *Priority Estates Project*, a pioneering approach which involved the tenants in particularly deprived social housing developments in planning the redevelopment of the estates.

A much broader programme known as *Estate Action* was introduced in 1985, which again focused on social housing estates. It involved trying to create a broader mix of families living in the estates and partially handing management control of the estates to tenant organisations. It was wound down in 1998 after improving 450,000 homes.

The *Single Regeneration Budget* was introduced in 1993 and received EU funding. It was a very wide programme to tackle unemployment, social disorder and educational improvements, as well as tackling housing.

Since 1998, the *New Deal for Communities* has provided funding for the most deprived neighbourhoods. It is competitive, in that local authorities and residents must put forward bids which will help tackle a range of social and physical problems in the area. The bids include measures to combat:

- welfare dependency, including improving the skills needed for employment
- health problems
- crime and disorder
- housing other physical improvements.

The argument for the introduction of New Deal for Communities and the disbanding of earlier programmes was that it was necessary to tackle the problems which caused the need for regeneration in the first place, and the major cause was poverty. The current government believes that the key to eliminating poverty is to ensure that as many people as possible are in employment. Thus the new emphasis on 'employability'.

Criticisms of regeneration projects

Critics have pointed out that the small-scale nature of the projects can have very little impact on the wide-scale deprivation and poverty which leads to poor housing. They argue instead that a much broader and ambitious anti-poverty programme is needed which will eliminate poverty and then lead to people being able to afford better housing conditions.

Low demand areas

Low demand or unpopular housing, which people simply do not want, is now one of the major housing problems in the UK, with almost one million homes affected, and includes two-thirds of all local authority housing stock, and 375,000 of privately rented properties.

Many of the areas which are in need of regeneration are **low demand areas**, that is areas which have many more houses than people want to live in. The areas of low demand are mainly in the north of England and some areas of Scotland, and reflect the changing economic structure of the UK. These are the inner-city areas of large industrial towns and cities where there are few jobs. A vicious cycle takes place as properties become vacant when people move away in search for employment and older people die, but too few people want to move into these areas. Those who do are often the socially excluded, the poorest and often the most anti-social. The neighbourhood changes, with increases in crime, vandalism and drug dealing. Remaining families who can move out do so, leaving behind the older, poorer residents and a mix of single people, lone parents and the poorest of families.

Low demand and neighbourhood decline

Not enough attention has been paid to the traumatic effects on communities and households afflicted by the consequences of low demand. … There seems to be an element of randomness in this, with one or two boarded-up dwellings creating a kind of contagion which spreads with alarming speed. Corner shops close down, people that can choose to do so drift away and housing abandonment intensifies. Property values quickly ebb away and rental housing becomes difficult to let. Crime, often associated with drugs, soon colonises the streets.

The irony of this is that those households remaining can move more easily round the area. Paul Keenan's study in Newcastle shows how hundreds of people – often single people, single parents or childless couples move sometimes two or three times in a year, going perhaps from a social housing let to the private sector or to live with relatives or friends and then back into public housing. When social stability breaks down in this way it becomes more difficult to conduct stable relationships, and the social 'glue' that holds communities together begins to dissolve. These people are not exercising some new found freedom to move when housing market conditions are ripe They are escaping abusive relationships, running from debt, from overbearing and fraudulent landlords, and from disruptive neighbours. Pimps and criminals are never far behind and a twilight world soon settles like an autumn fog, soulless and menacing.

Source: S. Lowe, P. Keenan and S. Spencer, 'Twilight zones', *Roof*, January/February 1999

1 What do we mean by 'low demand housing'?

2 Who leaves the area?

3 What are the consequences?

4 Who move around the area with greater ease?

5 What are the reasons for their movements?

6 What or who settle like an 'autumn fog'?

7 What methods is the government using to regenerate run-down areas?

Financial benefits for housing

Housing Benefit

Housing Benefit is paid to people who are on low incomes or who receive Income Support. If the person is already a council tenant, their rent is automatically reduced by the appropriate amount. If the person pays rent to a private landlord, then the Housing Benefit can either go directly to the tenant or to the landlord.

As we have seen, Housing Benefit is means-tested (see Chapter 3), so that anyone with, for example, savings over a certain level has to have them taken into account. Basically, you are more likely to receive Housing Benefit the lower your income and the greater your family responsibilities, although factors such as disability and age are also taken into account.

- Private sector tenants receive full benefit only on a 'local reference rent' set by the rent officer as the mid-point range of local market rents.
- Local authorities are required to follow the Rent Officer's determination in paying benefit.
- Housing Benefit is paid four weeks in arrears.
- All single people under 25 have Housing Benefit restricted to rent of a 'bedsit' only.

There are a number of problems with Housing Benefit:

- *persuading all those who are eligible to apply for it*: it is estimated that between 5 and 10 per cent of those eligible simply do not claim
- *fraud*: no one knows the true extent of Housing Benefit fraud, however there were 120,000 proven cases of false claims uncovered by the Department of Social Security (now called the Department of Work and Pensions) in 1999/2000
- *delays*: Housing Benefit is complex to administer, and the government has recognised that the local councils who carry out this work appear to administer it badly. One requirement is that all claims are processed within fourteen days. However, one-third of new claims are not processed, with the result that people often lose their accommodation.

Housing Benefit

On what was only its second birthday, in 1984, a leader in the Times dismissed it as "the biggest administrative fiasco in the history of the welfare state". Next month, the fiaso otherwise known as housing benefit will be 18 years old – but the bureaucratic nightmare that began at its birth has only worsened.

Thousands of claimants are in debt, with delays in payment forcing them into rent arrears. Others are at risk of eviction.

Intended to help the most vulnerable, Britain's crumbling housing benefit system appears to be doing the very opposite.

… A report, *Housing Benefit – No Cause to Celebrate*, reveals that 1.5m of Britain's 4m housing benefit claimants, are owed money – totalling up to £1.6 bn. [and delays can last up to five months].

A Commons social security select committee report last year blamed the chaos on privatisation and red tape. The volume of claims overwhelms contractors who run housing benefit services. In Lambeth, south London, a backlog of 40,000 claims last year forced the Labour council to spend £1.5m helping its contractor, Capita, to process paperwork.

The system [also] suffers in-built problems. Where housing benefit is paid direct to the landlord, it is paid four weeks in arrears. This automatically puts the tenant in arrears, since their tenancy will usually require rent in advance.

Another complication arises when a claimant's employment situation changes – even if it is just a few hours' work – and the claim has to be adjusted. In some cases, housing benefit stops completely; in others, benefit is paid as before and, months later, the claimant is told they have been overpaid.

Source: Adapted from *The Guardian*, 14 March 2001

1 When was Housing Benefit first introduced?

2 Why are claimants in rent arrears?

3 How many people claim Housing Benefit?

4 How many people are owed money and how much does this total?

5 How long can delays last?

6 What did the House of Commons blame these problems on?

7 What two problems does the article point out?

A CAB [Citizen's Advice Bureau] in Kent reported a 19 year old who had claimed benefit in May 1998. In July he came to the CAB concerned that he had not received any benefit and his landlord was threatening to evict him. His parents had paid his rent for the first month and he had paid the last two weeks' rent out of his giro but he now had only £2 to live on until his next giro. The CAB established that the housing benefit office had not received the NHB1, and they agreed to send him a further form and an application for backdating. However two weeks later the landlord turned him out because no benefit had been paid. When he next returned to the CAB in September he had been sleeping in a friend's garden and wanted help in finding accommodation.

Source: Citizen's Advice Bureau report on Housing Benefit

Benefits for those with mortgages

Housing Benefit is not available for those who fall behind in their mortgage repayments. Private insurance is available to guard against redundancy and sickness, but there have been many complaints that the insurance companies find reasons not to pay out.

State help distinguishes between those with mortgages taken out before 1995 and after:

- For those with mortgages before 1995, borrowers in arrears receive no help for the first 8 weeks on their mortgage interest, half the 'eligible' interest for 18 weeks and then full help after 26 weeks.
- Lone parents and carers receive this level of help no matter when they took out their mortgage.
- Those with mortgages taken out after 1995 receive no help for 39 weeks and then receive the 'eligible' interest payments after.
- People over 60 years of age get immediate help.

All these payments are for the interest on the amount borrowed, not to help actually repay the mortgage.

Equal opportunities

Housing and gender

In recent years concern has been expressed over the provision of housing for women. The Housing Act 1988, it is argued, considerably worsened the situation for women.

As we have seen, Conservative governments 1979–97 shifted the emphasis and financial support away from local authority housing towards property ownership (with a mortgage). The benefits therefore accrue to higher income families who can afford to purchase their own homes, and receive tax relief.

Of female-headed households, over 42 per cent rent from local authorities and only 11 per cent are buying their own homes. This compares with 43 per cent of male-headed households buying their own homes, with only 25 per cent renting from the local authority. The gap revealed by these figures between men and women will almost certainly grow in the future.

Women are less likely to be buying their own homes, because they earn relatively low wages compared to men. We know, for example, that women earn a little more than 75 per cent of males' wages on average.

When women do become owner-occupiers in their own right, the statistics show us that they are likely to inhabit the older, cheaper properties in less desirable positions with few amenities. More than one third of women buy property built before 1919, compared to less than a quarter of men.

Women tend to concentrate in council property; indeed, over half of all divorced, separated and widowed women turn to the local authority for housing.

The control by men of the income coming into a house, and therefore the payment of the rent or mortgage, has far-reaching repercussions for women (and children). Women accept violence by their partners for an average of seven years without leaving, mainly because they have nowhere else to go.

The 1988 Act limits the right of succession for local authority and private tenants. In other words, the automatic right to take over the tenancy from the parent is denied. One in five women over the age of 40 are caring for a sick, disabled or older person. When that person dies, then the carer is faced with new tenancy agreement (or none at all), which will probably have a significantly increased rent.

Housing and ethnicity

Ethnic minorities have quite different tenure patterns from each other and from the majority white population. At its simplest, those of African-Caribbean origin are more likely than other groups to be in local authority housing, whilst Asians have the highest levels of owner-occupation of all three of these groups.

However, when it comes to *quality of housing* measured by amenities or overcrowding, it seems that the white, majority population emerge well ahead. The explanations for these patterns are not difficult to find.

Quality of housing

Housing reflects the divisions in society in general, as we saw with the situation of women and housing. Asians and those of African-Caribbean origin are less likely than Whites to be in well-paid employment. They are therefore less likely to have housing of as good a quality. The reasons for those of African-Caribbean origin and Asians earning less than Whites is partially due to discrimination, a fact of life that affects all areas of their lives, not just housing tenure. (Chapter 14 discusses the issue of discrimination in more detail.)

Owner-occupation

The high levels of owner-occupation amongst Asians represents a reflection of their culture and a response to racism.

Reflection of culture

Amongst many of the Asian communities in the UK, there is a belief in the value of owning property, and family groups will club together to purchase housing. The reason for the higher density of people living in Asian households is a reflection of the strength of the extended family, and of this mutual aid to buy property. Living together gives them the economic power to purchase property.

Response to racism

When African-Caribbean and Asian migrants first came to the UK in large numbers in the 1950s, they were excluded from most forms of housing. Their housing conditions were appalling. Asians responded by purchasing property through extended family networks. Blacks did not have their family network, and were anyway less culturally interested in the purchase of property. As a result they suffered for many years from some of the worst housing conditions. They began to enter local authority housing because their accommodation was so poor, gaining points on the housing lists for this reason.

It is interesting to note that people of African and African-Caribbean origins and Asians who have council accommodation are heavily over-represented in the worst council properties.

Racial harassment

One of the major problems faced by Asians, and to a lesser extent those of African-Caribbean origin, is that of racial harassment. The 1998 Crime and Disorder Act contained a specific section which allowed the termination of a tenancy and eviction for those engaged in racial harassment.

Housing and ethnicity

Change in tenure by ethnic group, 1977/78–1994/97

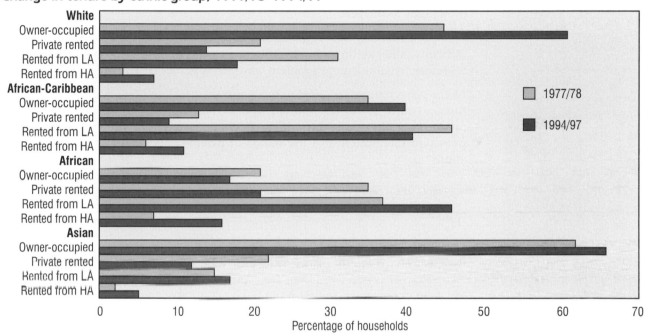

Source: E. Howes and D. Mullins, *Dwelling on Difference* (London Research Centre, 1999)

1 In 1994/97, which ethnic group was most likely to live in:
a) owner-occupied housing?
b) private rented?
c) local authority housing?

2 List the three most noticeable changes between 1977/78 and 1994/97 in housing tenure shown in the chart.

Main points
▶ There are still a large number of homes in the UK which are unfit or of poor quality.

▶ Certain groups of people – older people, younger people, ethnic minorities – are more likely to live there.

▶ The government provides a range of grants for regeneration of areas with large amounts of unfit housing.

▶ Often unfit housing is linked with low demand for housing and neighbourhood decline.

▶ Those in need can obtain Housing Benefit.

▶ There are a number of problems in the claiming and payment of Housing Benefit.

▶ Owner-occupiers who get into financial problems receive only limited help from the benefit system.

▶ Housing reflects the same issues of discrimination as other areas of social life.

▶ Ethnic minorities and women seem to have worse housing conditions.

Conclusion

This chapter has explored the way that housing came to be seen as a social rather than a private issue. This led to the growth of local authority provided, rental accommodation which reached its peak in the 1960s. From then on, and particularly under the stimulus of right-to-buy legislation in the 1980s, owner-occupancy took over.

However, this has left significant groups of people on the outside with great difficulty either getting a home or having one of suitable standards. Homelessness therefore remains a great problem, and this is particularly acute for young people.

As the government has come to recognise the problem of inadequate housing and homelessness, it has handed the task of helping over to housing corporations rather than the local authorities. It would seem that the future of housing provision therefore lies in the hands of private developers and housing associations.

5 CHAPTER SUMMARY

1   Cheap housing was first provided by charitable associations in the nineteenth century.

2   Local government first became heavily involved in house provision in the early part of the twentieth century.

3   Housing was recognised as one element of the five evils identified in the Beveridge Report.

4   There are three main types of tenure: owner-occupancy, private renting and social renting.

5   Gradually during the 1960s onwards there was a shift away from renting houses to owner-occupancy. So that today, the majority of householders are buying their homes.

6   A huge increase in home ownership took place in the 1980s when the Conservative government introduced the right to buy legislation.

7   Rented housing is increasingly being run by housing associations.

8   Privately rented tenure has decreased greatly. Now it is the very rich or the very poor who use this form of tenure.

9   Housing is extremely socially important in people's lives and is linked to levels of stress, of health and of poverty, amongst other things.

10 One of the fastest growing problems is that of neighbour disputes, though local authorities now have powers to intervene and to evict troublesome tenants.

11 There is still a considerable amount of homelessness.

12   There are two groups of explanations.

13   Structural causes refer to the wider issues about lack of adequate housing and differences in income to obtain housing.

14   Immediate causes refer to such things as personal relationships breaking down which cause someone to have to leave a household and then become homeless.

15   Some social groups are much more likely to become homeless than other.

16   Homeless people are generally housed (at first) in temporary accommodation, which is of poor quality.

17   There are still about 10,000 people who sleep rough on the streets at night on regular occasions.

18   Young people who become homeless are especially vulnerable to a range of social problems, but receive only limited help.

19   Certain groups of people – older people, younger people, ethnic minorities – are more likely to live in poorer quality housing.

20   The government provides a range of grants for regeneration of areas with large amounts of unfit housing.

21   Often unfit housing is linked with low demand for housing and neighbourhood decline.

22   Those in need can obtain Housing Benefit.

23   There are a number of problems in the claiming and payment of Housing Benefit.

24   Owner-occupiers who get into financial problems receive only limited help from the benefit system.

25   Ethnic minorities and women seem to have worse housing conditions.

Useful websites

www.housing.dtlr.gov.uk: the Department of Transport, Local Government and the Regions

www.dtlr.gov.uk/rsu: the Rough Sleepers Initiative

www.regeneration.dtlr.gov.uk: regeneration

www.shelter.org.uk: the housing pressure group, Shelter

www.housinguk.org: the Housing Resource Guide

www.demon.co.uk/hcorp: the Housing Corporation

www.homelesspages.org.uk: homelessness

Chapter 6

THE HEALTH SERVICE

Chapter contents

- ### The development of the NHS
  The chapter begins with an exploration of health care as it was before the NHS and the reasons for the introduction of the NHS. We look at the way that doctors were actually opposed to its introduction and fought a long and bitter battle against it. We then look at the financial crises faced by the NHS and the eventual move to a split between purchasers of health care and providers of health care.

- ### The NHS today
  Here we examine the way the NHS is organised today in order to make it efficient in providing health care. In particular we look at the way that health care is commissioned by local health authorities and increasingly by GPs and other professionals through the new primary health care trusts.

- ### The economics of health care
  The cost of health care has always been extremely high and places a great burden on the taxpayer. Despite this, there is a great groundswell of support in the UK for a decent health service and politicians have continued to spend billions of pounds each year on providing 'free' health care. We look at where the money comes from and where it goes, and ask whether the money spent does improve standards of health. In recent years a number of ideas have been put forward to ease the financial burden, or at least shift it from the taxpayer, and we look at a few of the more practical ideas.

- ### Private health care
  Despite the existence of the NHS since 1948, there has continued to be a private health service in which people pay for their health care. In the 1980s there was a very significant growth in this area, paid for by companies as a benefit to their employees. Many people took out private insurance against possible health problems. We examine the importance of the private health care sector and look at debates about the morality of private health care.

- ### Rationing health services
  The demand for health care has always outstripped the ability of the government to provide adequate services. This is caused mainly by economic constraints, though lack of trained staff has also been a handicap. In this section, we discuss the way that rationing has been introduced both on a formal and an informal basis. In particular, the use of waiting lists.

- ### Quality in the NHS
  Traditionally the main debates over the NHS have concerned its funding problems and how long people have to wait for operations. What has not been discussed until recently has been the quality of the services provided by the medical staff. In this section we look a the initiatives introduced recently to ensure that the NHS achieves the highest possible standards.

- ### Inequalities in health
  The NHS is only one factor influencing our health. Other factors such as stress, housing and income also have a great impact. Because we live in an unequal society, when it comes to quality of life, we also discover that health and illness directly reflect this inequality.

- ### Access to health care
  In the previous part of the chapter we looked at the way that health standards reflect the inequalities of society, but inequalities of health are also caused by different use of the health service by different groups in society. So use of screening programmes and consultations with GPs, amongst other things, varies according to ethnic groups, sex and social class.

- ### Combating ill health: new initiatives
  There has been increasing recognition by government that the health service can no longer remain a reactive service, waiting for people to become ill and then seeking to cure them. The NHS today forms part of a wider attack on ill health which recognises that poverty and under-use of health services have had a significant impact on the health of the population. This section explores the new initiatives intended to raise the standards of health of the population as a whole.

Introduction

The National Health Service (NHS) is the largest employer in Western Europe. It forms, in most people's eyes, the most important service of all those provided by the government. The ideal of a 'free' health service providing high standards of care to all people as a right still commands almost universal respect and admiration. Yet the complexity of financing and providing adequate health is quite staggering.

The chapter opens with a look back at the history of health provision and how the NHS developed, following the changing structure of the NHS since its creation in 1948. Over the last ten years, the government has moved towards giving local trusts and now GPs much greater freedom to spend as they wish. This chapter tackles these issues, describes the changes that have taken place and assesses their impact, in particular by examining the restructuring of the health service, with the move away from central control to local power-holding by primary health care trusts.

One of the major issues has always been how to balance the demands for health care, which seem inexhaustible, with the funds available from government, which are limited. The chapter takes a look at the issue of finance and of the rationing of health services, and how the government achieves reasonable spread of finance across the country.

It is no use worrying about health service organisation, if the point of providing high quality health care is missed, nor the moral argument that access to health care should be available equally to all. These issues are discussed in the context of inequalities in the standards of health in the population.

In a typical week:
- 1.4 million people will receive help in their home from the NHS
- more than 800,000 people will be treated in NHS hospital outpatient clinics
- 700,000 will visit a NHS dentist for a check-up
- NHS district nurses will make more than 700,000 visits
- over 10,000 babies will be delivered by the NHS
- NHS chiropodists will inspect over 150,000 pairs of feet
- NHS ambulances will make over 50,000 emergency journeys
- NHS Direct nurses will receive around 25,000 calls from people seeking medical advice
- pharmacists will dispense approximately 8.5 million items on NHS prescriptions
- NHS surgeons will perform around 1,200 hip operations, 3,000 heart operations and 1,050 kidney operations.

Source: NHS website: www.nhs.co.uk

The development of the NHS

Health provision before the NHS

In the nineteenth century, hospitals were used only by poor people, as they were dangerous places where it was far more likely that the patient would end up dying rather than being healed. This is because there was little awareness of hygiene, and the standards of care were very low.

The affluent paid for a doctor to visit them at home, and had a noticeably higher chance of survival. At the time this was regarded as the result of the work of doctors, though now the higher survival rates are understood to be as result of better diet, housing and work conditions.

Friendly societies

Insurance companies, or friendly societies, developed amongst the regularly employed working class, often organised by trade unions. They paid doctors a fixed amount per subscriber to provide health care. By 1900, over half the working class were covered by such insurance.

State intervention

During the Boer War (1899–1902), a third of all recruits were judged to be physically unfit to serve because of illness (which was generally caused by malnutrition). In a time of empire and imperial armies, this caused serious concern to the government. Social reformers used the information as evidence of the need for the government to provide better health and welfare services than those that existed at the time.

The government was also concerned about the possibility of serious social unrest, and were looking at ways of undermining support for the radical elements in the Labour movement. A limited amount of health reform would help do this. An example of how limited State provision served to dampen tension was provided by Germany. Its Chancellor, Bismarck, had introduced a social insurance system which covered a range of issues including accidents at work, disability and old age pensions.

Health insurance

This was introduced by the government in 1911 and covered workers between the ages of 16 and 65, who earned a range of incomes. (Agricultural workers were omitted because they earned too little to afford to pay the contributions!) This provided access to doctors at home and cash benefits for sickness, accidents at work and for disability. The scheme did not cover any hospital treatment. The group of doctors who provided the medical treatment were paid a fixed amount by the agencies running the scheme, and they were generally referred to as 'the panel'.

All the dependants of workers were excluded. As most workers were male, this meant that the majority of women and children received no automatic right to medical care.

The reasoning behind this was simple: the wage earner was the male in the majority of households and therefore if he could not work the family would fall into poverty. By keeping the male well, or by tiding the family over in the short periods in which he was ill and unable to provide (as employers did not give sick pay), the family would not become poor. The worker would therefore be able to afford to pay for health care for the rest of his family.

By the beginning of the Second World War, in 1939, over 40 per cent of the working population had coverage giving them access to a GP (or family doctor).

The introduction of the NHS

In 1939, the outbreak of the Second World War forced the government to intervene in the provision of medical services, as it had to organise health care for the armed forces and the civilian casualties. The Emergency Medical Service (EMS) was established, which consisted of hospital bed provision, a national blood transfusion service and an ambulance service.

As we saw in Chapter 3, the Beveridge Report (1942) isolated five 'giants' which blemished the lives of ordinary people: disease, ignorance, squalor, idleness and want. The report argued that the government after the war would have to tackle these problems, and so 'disease' was placed on the political agenda.

A third factor leading to the introduction of the NHS was the desire of the government to maintain the morale of the population during the war, and to provide them with a vision of a bright future, including free health care if Britain won the war.

The National Health Service (NHS) was formally brought into being in 1948. However, the route to the establishment of the NHS was not an easy one, as GPs and consultants demanded high incomes and limited government control. Indeed, it was the opposition of doctors to the National Health Service that delayed its introduction by almost three years. When the NHS was finally started, the doctors gained considerable advantages from it:

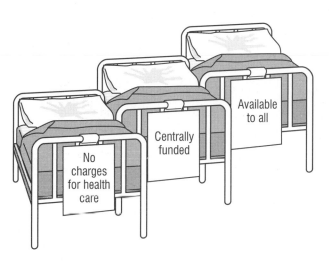

The founding principles of the NHS

- GPs remained independent practitioners who were self-employed and received a fee from the government for the work they did
- consultants could work part-time for the NHS and part-time in private practice
- consultants were offered special 'merits' awards, which were extra payment for selected consultants
- private patients (of consultants) could use NHS facilities
- doctors were to have considerable power in the running of the NHS at all levels.

Local authorities, which had previously run hospitals, were given only a minor role in running the NHS. The structure of the NHS has changed on a number of occasions since then, so that, after more than fifty years of being reorganised, the NHS of today is dramatically different from that of 1948. Nevertheless, doctors still remain very powerful and the latest reforms have put a great deal of power back into their hands, which they had gradually been losing over those fifty years.

The NHS 1950–90

The NHS developed in a way that the founders would not have believed possible. The belief of the founders was that there was an enormous backlog of ill people who had been denied health care because of the cost. Over time the numbers of people in this pool had grown massively – but once this backlog was tackled, there would be a much smaller number of people coming forward for treatment. Therefore although the initial costs of the NHS would be huge, over time it would decrease as the numbers of people coming forward for treatment declined.

Unfortunately, this belief was to be proved completely inaccurate. Numbers of sick people *increased*, rather than decreased. The reason for the increase is that the definition of what is an acceptable level of health alters over time. Once people saw what could be done, they demanded higher and higher standards of health care. Linked to this was the fact that as technology advanced and new drugs developed, medicine really was increasingly able to tackle health problems seen as incurable only twenty years earlier. The problem though was that all this cost huge amounts of money.

The period from the 1950s onward was therefore characterised by increasing numbers using the NHS and by a very great growth in the costs of providing health care – far beyond anything that the original founders had ever imagined. The result was that the NHS lurched from one financial crisis to another.

1990: The purchase/provider revolution

The NHS has had many different structures over the its history, but the biggest shake-up occurred in 1990, with the NHS and Community Care Act. Before this organisations known as **health authorities** had run all hospitals and community services in their areas. The government gave each authority an amount of funding from taxation and the authorities were expected to provide all the health needs of the population.

There were huge problems with this, which had finally reached crisis point in the late 1980s. There were no incentives for health authorities to save money, so they wasted it. The health authorities and hospitals had no reliable accounting procedures, for example they did not actually know how much particular surgical operations cost. The government at the time felt that the more efficient practices of business should be applied to the NHS and they therefore split the health service into two – **purchasers** and **providers**.

Health authorities as purchasers

In future, health authorities had the job of finding out the health needs of the local population and then purchasing these from hospitals and community health services.

Trusts as providers

Hospitals and community health services were to become independent **trusts** and were to provide health services on a competitive basis. These were the providers.

GPs were encouraged to become 'fundholders', which meant that they were given budgets to purchase a range of health care services directly from hospital trusts.

Although fundholding has now been replaced by community care groups, and competition between trusts has been phased out, this purchaser/provider split provides the basis of the current system, which we will look at next.

The NHS today

Department of Health (DOH)

This government department is responsible for:

- public health
- social care.

The DOH:

- *negotiates* resources from the Treasury and then
- *allocates* them to the NHS authorities.

The NHS Policy Board exists within the DOH, and is broadly responsible for the 'strategic direction' of the NHS. It is chaired by the Secretary of State for Health.

Health authorities

Health authorities cover populations varying from 125,000 up to a million. These
are the organisations which receive the funding from the Department of Health to
purchase health care. The health authorities:

- *assess the health needs* of the people in their areas
- *purchase hospital and community health services* for these people (in collaboration
  with the **primary care groups** (see page 146) from the NHS trusts, and from
  private providers of care and medicine
- draw up *health improvement plans* which give clear targets about what needs to
  be achieved and how this should be done
- *monitor the quality* of the care provided.

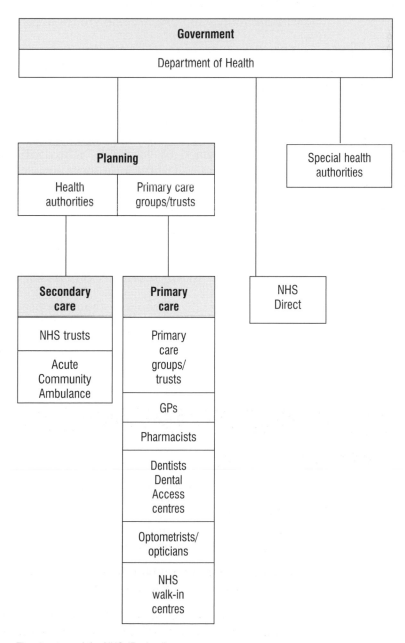

The structure of the NHS (England)

NHS trusts

Trusts were first developed in 1991 as part of a major shake-up in the NHS. There are currently 374 trusts in England providing 95 per cent of all health services in the country. A trust can be:

- a hospital
- a service providing community health services
- an ambulance service

or all of these things combined.

Trusts are independent organisations but are still part of the NHS. Trusts are the organisations that actually *provide* the health services to the population and receive their funding for doing so from the health authorities and primary care groups, which are the *purchasers* of these services. The trusts do not receive money directly from the government, but only through the contracts agreed with the health authorities and primary care groups to provide health care.

Primary care groups/trusts

Definitions **Primary health care** – health care provided by GPs in their practices **Community health care** – health care provided for the community by nurses, doctors, psychiatrists midwives and community mental health nurses **Primary care trusts (PCTs)** – a more complex form of primary care group, not only do they commission health services from hospitals, but they also run a range of community health services

These are new and very powerful groups which were first introduced in 2000. Each PCG or PCT covers a population of about 100,000 people. The PCGs are organisations formed by local GPs who (with some representatives of the community nurses and of the local social services on their boards) are gradually taking over most of the responsibility from the health authorities for purchasing health care from the hospital and community trusts.

The next step in the process is that the primary care groups will begin to take over the roles of community trusts, so that they will provide all primary and community health services and purchase other services from local hospital trusts. They will then be known as **primary care trusts**.

The belief is that GPs know more about the needs of local populations, because they are the people who deal directly with the public.

The primary care groups have now completely replaced the previous 'fundholding' system where individual GPs were given grants to purchase health care for their own patients.

NHS Scotland

There is a Health Department of the Scottish Office with the Chief Executive being responsible for fifteen health boards who purchase health services in their areas. There are forty-seven Scottish health trusts. Unlike England, there is a Common Services Agency which provides services such as ambulances, building and legal advice, central purchasing and blood transfusion.

Local health co-operatives advise the boards on which services to buy, but do not purchase them directly as in England.

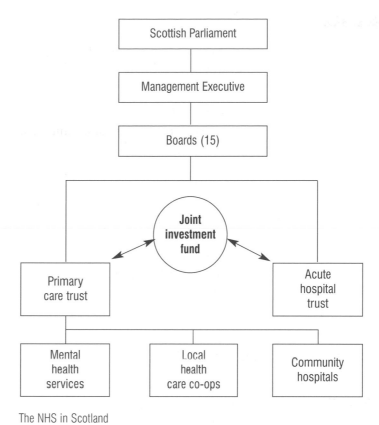

The NHS in Scotland

Source: *Wellard's NHS Handbook 2000/01*

NHS Wales

Here there are five authorities and sixteen trusts with a Welsh Common Services Authority, providing similar services to the Scottish one. Twenty-two *local health groups* have recently been introduced to undertake a similar job to that of the PCGs in England, but they are more directly controlled by the health authorities than in England.

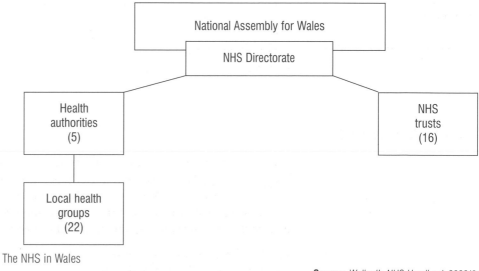

The NHS in Wales

Source: *Wellard's NHS Handbook 2000/01*

Northern Ireland

The service is slightly different in Northern Ireland. In particular, the social services are fully integrated into the health services. Four health boards are responsible for assessing the needs of the population and purchasing from the nineteen health and five social services trusts. Fundholding still existed in Northern Ireland in 2000.

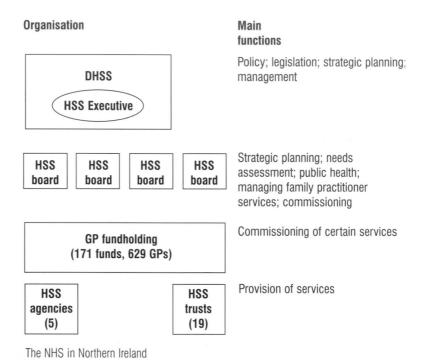

Organisation

Main functions

DHSS — HSS Executive — Policy; legislation; strategic planning; management

HSS board | HSS board | HSS board | HSS board — Strategic planning; needs assessment; public health; managing family practitioner services; commissioning

GP fundholding (171 funds, 629 GPs) — Commissioning of certain services

HSS agencies (5) | HSS trusts (19) — Provision of services

The NHS in Northern Ireland

Source: *Wellard's NHS Handbook 2000/01*

The economics of health care

How the NHS is funded today

The NHS seems to be in a permanent crisis of under-funding, yet the government actually spends about £62 billion on providing health care. The overwhelming majority of the funds to support the NHS comes from general taxation, with about 12 per cent coming from National Insurance contributions which all employed people must pay, and only 2 per cent from charging people. Charges are made for certain medical appliances, for prescriptions and for dental check-ups and eye tests – though about 85 per cent of the population are actually exempt from paying any of these.

Over the last fifty years, health care spending by the government has increased by about 3 per cent per year, though in the last few years, this has risen to 3.7 per cent.

The amount of money spent on the NHS each year is not a reflection of the demand of people for treatment, but is determined by negotiations between the Treasury and the Department of Health. Each year, a Spending Assessment is published which says how much the government intends to spend on all its

Where the money comes from

The NHS is often claimed to be free. It is not. We do not pay directly for services when we receive them, except for those in employment who pay for prescriptions. But we do pay indirectly. Health services consume about 5 per cent of total public expenditure. The diagram shows where funding for the NHS comes from.

NHS sources of finance, 1997–8

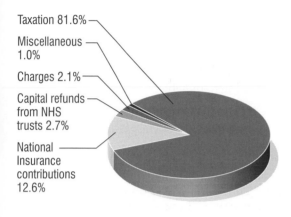

Taxation 81.6%

Miscellaneous 1.0%

Charges 2.1%

Capital refunds from NHS trusts 2.7%

National Insurance contributions 12.6%

Source: *Wellard's NHS Handbook 2000/01*

1 What percentage of NHS funding comes from general taxation?

2 What proportion comes from National Insurance?

3 What percentage of the NHS comes from 'charges'? Give one example of something which the NHS charges for.

4 What is National Insurance? Who pays it?

5 By how much each year has the NHS spending increased? (You may need to look in the main text.)

6 What is the single most expensive item in the NHS? (See the main text.)

services. Currently, the NHS accounts for between 13 and 14 per cent of all government expenditure. Within the NHS, about 70 per cent is spent on hospital and community services and 25 per cent on primary health services. The most expensive items are drugs, followed by GPs, dentists and opticians.

The private finance initiative (PFI)

<table>
<tr><td>

Definition

Private finance initiative – a policy whereby private companies fund the building of new hospitals and other health care initiatives. The NHS then leases them back. Often known as Public Private Partnerships

</td></tr>
</table>

Before 1991, all funding for new buildings had to be gained direct from the government. Since then, however, trusts have had much greater freedom to buy and sell property. They have also been encouraged to go into partnership with private companies, including private hospitals, to build new facilities. Under the PFI arrangements (often also called *Public Private Partnerships*), the private companies build the hospitals and then the NHS leases them back.

By 1997, 14 new hospitals were co-funded under this initiative and, by 1999, £3 billion worth of projects were in place.

Why does the cost of health care keep rising?

The assumption underlying the introduction of the NHS in 1948 was that there was a large number of ill people who needed to be cured, but that once this had been achieved the role of the NHS would consist mainly of keeping people in good health and dealing with emergencies. This view was based on two ideas:

• that there was an objective, fixed standard distinguishing good health from poor health

- that the entire range of welfare initiatives, including council housing, social security payments and full employment, would ensure that the diseases caused by poverty would never return.

In both these assumptions, planners were proved to be wrong.

Standards of health

Health is not a fixed, objective thing but, in a similar way to poverty, it varies depending on the expectations of the population of a society. Therefore, illness and disease that would have been accepted as normal or at least bearable for one generation could to be regarded as insupportable by another. Once free health care became available, people wanted to use it, and expectations of health rose. The healthier people became, the more aware they were of symptoms that previously they had accepted as natural or unchangeable.

Therefore, contrary to what the planners had expected, usage of the NHS increased through the 1950s and afterwards, and did not decrease as they had thought.

Technology

Linked to the changing views on health standards was the introduction of new technology. Previously, people had accepted that there was nothing to be done about certain diseases, but the rapid increases in technology – both in machines and in drugs – have revolutionised the capabilities of medicine. The problem is that these new developments are highly expensive, and add to the costs of health care.

Role of welfare initiatives

As we shall see later in the chapter, there are very close connections between poverty and ill health. Despite well over 50 years of the Welfare State, great inequalities still exist in society, and these are reflected in the continuing poor health of much of the population. However, there is also a great success story to be told. The Welfare State in general has created the conditions in which people now expect to live longer – and older people account for a high proportion of NHS costs.

Health costs and age

A Long life or healthy life

Life expectancy and healthy life expectancy, at birth, Great Britain, 1994

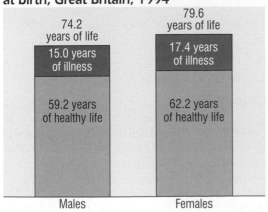

Source: *Our Healthier Nation* (The Stationery Office, 1998)

B Health costs of older people

Hospital and community health service expenditure, by age of recipient, 1998–9, England

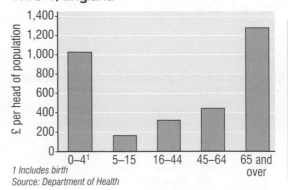

1 Includes birth
Source: Department of Health

In 1998–99, nearly two-fifths of hospital and community health service expenditure in England, around £10 billion, went towards people aged 65 and over.

Source: *Social Trends 31* (The Stationery Office, 2001)

Look at A.

1 What is the expectation of life of:

a) females?

b) males?

Look at B.

2 Identify the two groups who have most spent upon them?

3 What is the cost of this per head of population?

4 Explain why these groups have the greatest proportionate expenditure.

5 How many 'years of illness' might each sex expect to have?

6 What are the implications for health care?

<table>
<tr><td>Definition

Chronic illness – a long-term illness</td></tr>
</table>

The NHS has also been the victim of its own success too. Through advances in medicine and care, it has succeeded in prolonging the lives of people with **chronic illnesses** and also through advances in care allowed many children to survive who would previously have died in infancy.

Combined, all of these have added considerably to the costs of health care.

The causes of rising health care costs

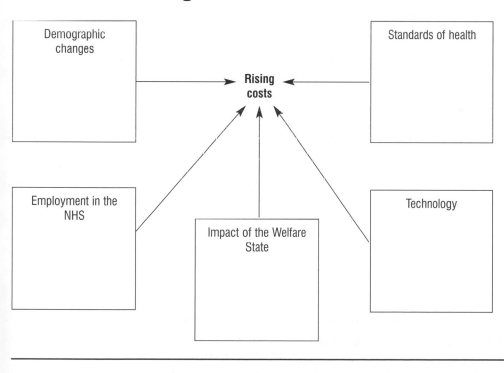

Copy the diagram and complete the boxes, explaining each reason for the causes of rising health care in your own words.

The efficiency of the NHS

One common argument is that the NHS is inefficient in the way it is organised – the costs of the bureaucracy used to deliver health care are too high.

As long ago as 1953, the Ministry of Health was so concerned that it ordered an inquiry into health care costs – but the committee that reported on this (the Guillebaud Committee) actually recommended an increase in funding for the health service.

In recent years this debate has re-opened and since 1997 there has been an increasing pressure on the NHS to become more streamlined and more 'efficient'. This has been achieved by the government setting very clear health care targets and efficiency savings for NHS trusts.

Spending on health and standards of health: is there a link?

Comparing health costs: is the NHS expensive?

A

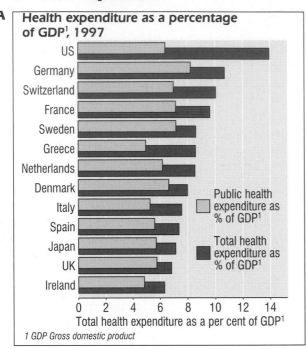

Health expenditure as a percentage of GDP¹, 1997

Public health expenditure as % of GDP¹

Total health expenditure as % of GDP¹

Total health expenditure as a per cent of GDP¹

1 GDP Gross domestic product

Source: *Wellard's NHS Handbook 2000/01*

Comparing life expectancy and mortality

B Life expectancy and infant mortality in selected countries

	Infant deaths (per 1,000 live births)	Male life expectancy	Female life expectancy
United States	8.9	72.0	78.3
Germany	6.8	72.6	79.0
Japan	4.4	76.0	82.1
UK	7.4	72.8	78.6
France	8.3	72.5	80.6

Look at A. It shows the proportion of the wealth of a country (GDP) which is spent on health care each year.

1 Which country spends the most on health care in total? Approximately what percentage of GDP is this?

2 Which country has the highest percentage of public (government) spending on health care? Approximately what percentage of GDP is this?

3 Which country spends the most on private health care (i.e. total health care minus public health care spending)?

4 Which country spends the least proportion on private health care?

Look at B which gives information on infant deaths and life expectancy.

5 Which country has the longest expectation of life for both males and females?

6 Which country has the lowest life expectancy for both males and females?

7 How do these statistics relate (if at all) to the spending patterns on health care?

In 1949, £444 million was spent on the NHS; in 2000, the figure was approximately £61 billion. However, the NHS is an efficient, cheap means of providing health care compared to alternative models used by other countries. In fact, the NHS spends less on administration than any other advanced health care system.

Funding debates

The present NHS receives virtually all of its funding from taxation, but there are many critics who argue that there are other ways of paying for the NHS. These include:

- **hypothecated taxes**
- social insurance
- medical savings accounts.

Definition

Hypothecated taxes – the government identifies exactly how much of a person's tax is spent on each government programme

Hypothecated taxes

In surveys, the public usually states that it is prepared to pay higher taxes for better health care, but not for some other public services. This results in political parties avoiding policies which would result in high taxes and thus health care suffers. One way out of this is hypothecated taxes. This simply means taxes which are earmarked for a particular purpose. So, the government will say that a particular element of income tax is going to go on health care. The public might well then be prepared to vote for higher taxes, as they know what it will be spent on.

Critics argue that it is more complicated than this. Once hypothecated taxes are introduced for health care, it would be necessary to introduce it for everything – and this could lead to major problems. Areas of government spending which are not popular, but may well be essential, might receive no funding. Areas to lose would be overseas aid, funding for better conditions in prisons and benefits for the unemployed.

Social insurance

This is common in mainland Europe. Health care is paid for by a tax on employees' wages, with an additional contribution from the employers. The State would make up the contributions of those not working. In fact, this was what National Insurance payments in the UK were originally intended to be.

But, the system has been found to be very expensive to administer, with all the work going into the collecting of taxes and then paying out to the doctors and hospitals which have to claim for each patient.

Medical savings accounts

This system is used in Singapore and is being trialled in the USA. This is a compulsory savings scheme for which the saver earns interest. The person pays for his or her health care out of the savings plus interest. For those who are unemployed, or have used up their savings, there is a very basic government safety-net health care system.

Individuals can dip into their savings, if they wish and spend the money on other things apart from health. For those with an income which allows them to save, the system is a great improvement on the NHS system which is funded by general taxation. However, for those who have little or no savings, the standards of care are lower. This contradicts the principle of the NHS – that the treatment should be based on need not on ability to pay.

Main points ▶ The first form of government health provision was in 1911, when a very limited cover was provided for workers aged 16–65.
▶ The NHS was inaugurated in 1948 in the face of opposition from the majority of doctors.
▶ The NHS was the result of the social changes which took place during the Second World War.
▶ The NHS has had major financial problems for most of its existence, but the current system of purchaser/provider was introduced in 1990.
▶ The NHS is funded by the government from taxation and is run locally by health authorities which have the role of ensuring that the local population get the health services they need. This is done by buying health care from trusts (such as hospitals and community care organisations).
▶ Over the next ten years new organisations – primary care trusts – will take over much of the work of the health authorities. These are run by GPs and other health professionals.

▷ Health care costs continue to rise, as a result of changing standards of health, rising costs of drugs and developments in new technologies and surgical procedures.

▷ The NHS is funded by taxation, but critics have suggested other ways of funding the NHS, in particular three suggestions have been made: hypothecated taxes, social insurance and medical savings accounts.

Private health care

The NHS is a State-funded health service in which every UK (and EU) citizen has the right to appropriate health treatment, free of charge. However, people can choose to have private health care. There are various reasons as to why a person may opt for private health care. These include:

- choice of consultant and hospital
- belief that a better standard of medical and nursing care is given in the private sector
- desire to avoid waiting lists
- wish to have better control over treatment and to be consulted
- desire for private room
- company offers private medicine as a 'perk' of the person's employment.

Before the NHS, health care was based on voluntary and private provision. With the introduction of the NHS in 1948, the private health care market collapsed, as people realised that they could obtain high standards of care without payment. Only 230 small, poorly equipped hospitals remained outside the NHS. In the 1950s, most commentators on the NHS argued that private medicine would disappear. However, private medicine remained and even managed to grow slowly. In the late 1970s, there was a faster rate of growth in the numbers of people using private medical services, and this increased rapidly in the 1980s. The majority of the provision was through medical insurance companies such as BUPA (British United Provident Association) and PPP (Private Patients' Plan).

The growth in private health care

A People insured by private medical insurance, United Kingdom

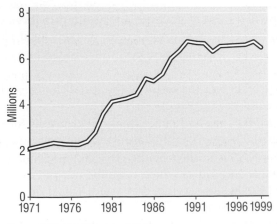

Source: BUPA, PPP, WPA, Laing & Buisson

The numbers of people covered by private health care insurance in the UK in 1971 was 2.1 million, by 1990, this had increased to almost 7 million. Since then, the figures have stabilised and remain at about 11 per cent of the population covered. The private health care industry is huge, with about £1³/₄ billion paid out by health insurance companies.

Source: *Social Trends 31* (The Stationery Office, 2001)

B

Acute
General Healthcare Group, BUPA and Nuffield Hospitals account for nearly 60 per cent of the independent acute hospital markets.

BUPA, which also has a separate private medical insurance wing, and runs nursing homes, has 36 UK hospitals with 1,908 beds. In 1999 the BUPA Group saw a £31.8m pre-tax operating profit.

General Healthcare Group has 43 hospitals (trading as BMI Healthcare) with 2,346 beds. It made £23.3m pre-tax profit in 1999.

Nuffield Hospitals is a registered charity, and clocks in with 40 hospitals and 1,651 beds. It made £16.1m last year.

NHS pay beds account for about 17 per cent of the market. According to DoH figures, in 1998–99, the NHS received £290m for the treatment of private patients.

Acute psychiatric
The top three providers are Partnerships in Care Ltd – owned by General Healthcare Group – which made £9.9m profit last year, Priority Healthcare, which is owned by Westminster Health Care and made £3.1m, and St Andrew's Hospital, which saw a £2.3m profit.

Long-term care
The major operators are BUPA Care Homes, with 16,625 beds in 233 homes, Ashbourne (8,326 beds in 145 homes) and Westminster Health Care with 5,897 beds in 91 homes, (Laing and Buisson figures for October).

Source: *Health Service Journal*, 2 November 2000

Look at A.

1 Overall, what has happened to the numbers of people taking out private medical insurance?

2 What has happened since 1991?

3 How many millions of people have private medical insurance in the UK?

Look at B.

4 Which are the three main organisations which provide private acute facilities?

5 How many hospitals do they have in total? Do they make a profit?

6 Does the NHS provide private medical facilities?

7 What other forms of private health care provision are there?

The growth in private medicine has been influenced by a number of factors, including the following.

- There was a change in people's attitudes in the 1980s, in that it became acceptable to pay for health care; whereas in the 1950s and 1970s there was a common view that it was somehow immoral to 'jump queues' for health care by paying.

- Employers began to provide employee purchase schemes for private health cover as a part of the normal employment package, along with company cars and sometimes assistance with school fees. In fact the growth in private health care was mainly through these schemes, rather than through individual subscribers.

- Public debate about the state of the NHS and the problems that were beginning to emerge, of under-funding and long waiting lists, began to worry people. Because of the growth in prosperity since the 1980s, many more people and companies were prepared and able to pay into private insurance schemes.

- The private health care companies were able to play on people's fears in advertising campaigns.

- A further development, that was both a result and a cause of the growth of private health care, was the rapid growth in small, local private hospitals. This meant that people could have private treatment without having to travel to London or another big city – making it far more accessible

- The government too has contributed to the growth of private medicine by paying for private treatment for NHS patients from 1999, in order to reduce the waiting lists.

Activity

Draw a diagram illustrating and explaining the reasons for the growth of private medical insurance.

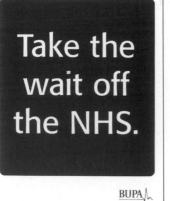

The growth in private health care has not been just in hospital beds (the acute sector), but also in private residential care homes and in private nursing homes. The residential homes have increased their bed numbers by nearly 500 per cent in the last twenty years, and the private nursing homes by over 300 per cent.

Arguments for and against private health care

In favour of private health care	Against private health care
As there would be a number of competing health care organisations, this would drive the cost down and the quality up.	There would be a growth in the bureaucracy involved in invoicing patients and collecting fees from individuals and insurance companies.
People would be able to make choices about where and when they were looked after.	It is true that the better-off and the insured would have a choice, but the poor would have to use the poorly funded, safety-net, government hospitals, as they do in the USA.
Because there is a cost to health care, people would be more careful about visiting their doctor for minor illnesses.	Poorer people would not visit the doctor in order to save money. Many serious illnesses would go undiagnosed.
Health care is no different from buying any other service, for example holidays. Why should those who pay more taxes subsidise the health care of the rest of the population. Besides, if State health care was abolished, taxes would be lower.	Health care would be divided between those receiving high standards because they can afford to pay and those who receive little or no health care, because they are too poor to pay. Surely, health care is a right?
It is the job of the government to provide education and training. Everyone who employs people who go to State schools, colleges and universities could be called 'parasitic'.	Private health care is 'parasitic', as it uses doctors and nurses who have been trained (and the training paid for) by the NHS.
Private health care relieves the pressure on the NHS, thereby making waiting lists shorter for a wide range of operations.	Private care is only interested in short-term health intervention and cannot provide long-term care for the 'chronically ill'.

Health care for sale or health care as a right?

My mother has been in severe pain for the past several years with a form of arthritis and can now walk only with considerable difficulty. It is very distressing to see her in this state every day. She has now been told that her condition can be considerably alleviated by a hip replacement operation. She recently went to see the consultant surgeon in the NHS hospital in Newcastle who told her that this is correct. He then told her that she can either remain in pain and semi-crippled for the next 12 to 18 months or she can pay more than £5000 and he will do the operation straight away.

Some people might call this choice but from my mother's position it feels very like blackmail. She is in pain. The pain can be relieved, but only if you have a lot of money. This is a condition which primarily affects the oldest and weakest members of society. Is it right that they be offered the 'choice' of 12 months pain or parting with their savings? She is very brave but the pain often reduces her to tears.

David Brazier, Jesmond,
Newcastle upon Tyne

1   Critics of the NHS argue that because there are no limits to treatment, people make demands which they would not do if they had to pay for them. In reply, supporters of the NHS argue that free health care is a human right, and that it is wrong for anyone to suffer simply because they cannot afford to pay. What is your view?

2   Since the letter was published, the government has provided funding for the NHS to pay private hospitals to carry out a number of surgical interventions such as hip replacements, in order to shorten the waiting lists. Do you think this is a good thing – or are there some disadvantages to doing this?

Rationing health services

In the UK, most health services are provided free-of-charge. As a result there is no constraint on people making demands on the service and there is usually greater demand for health and welfare services than there is the supply available. In fact, doctors often complain that many of those who make appointments with GPs have very minor complaints which do not merit a doctor's attention.

In most commercial situations this high level of demand would not be a problem, as the suppliers of the services would simply raise their prices until there was a balance between the numbers of people able and willing to pay the price asked, and the amount of services available. But the health and welfare services are provided because people are in need. The services are not commercial. This means that generally other means of controlling demands for services have developed.

Free health care for all?

... Many operations now conducted frequently on the NHS apparently have little scientific evidence of clinical benefit. Extraction of wisdom teeth, insertion of grommets for glue ear, removal of tonsils, many hysterectomies, even coronary artery bypass surgery can be considered of doubtful benefit. Considerable spending covers procedures conducted on otherwise healthy individuals. Family planning, sterilisation and termination of pregnancy are provided to a differing extent from district to district already. Cosmetic surgery is another example.

Health authorities could choose to be more stringent in buying these services of doubtful medical value, and do so only if there is a clear health need. ...

It is also worth looking at ailments which are clearly self-inflicted. Tobacco and alcohol-related conditions account for a high proportion of total health service spending. After many years of publicity, few smokers and drinkers can be unaware of the risks they run to their health. Yet, damage to a minority of self-indulgent individuals is being repaired at a considerable cost to the majority. ... (and the money) ... spent on treatment of smoking-related disorders could be better used in additional hip replacement operations, more intensive care facilities and more incubators for sick children. Perhaps the treatment cost of self-inflicted conditions should be met instead from a specific tax on cigarettes, beer or spirits.

Similarly, treatment of sports injuries should not be a burden on the taxpayer. Instead, all sports clubs should be required to carry private insurance to cover the risks of their members' sporting activities. ... In placing these sensible restrictions on the cover provided through our state health insurance system, the government would still guarantee that patients with clinically signi-ficant conditions will receive their approved treatment without charge and without undue delay.

Source: Anthony Byrne, *Health Service Journal*, 9 July 1992

1 What is the difference at present between the provision of health care by the private sector and by the NHS?

2 Why should the NHS begin to copy some of the approaches of the private sector?

3 What sort of activities would the author of the above article like to see curtailed by the NHS? Do you agree?

4 In the state of Oregon in the USA, legislators have decided that the only way to reflect public opinion in the rationing of health care is to present people with a list of 500 ailments and ask them to rate them. Those that come highest get more money and those that come lowest get the least. In the UK, at least one health authority has conducted research on similar lines, in order to try to reflect the public's opinion on health matters. Do you think this would be the way to solve the problems of finance in the NHS?

5 a) Conduct a small survey. Below is a list of well-known medical conditions/situations. (Add some more or alter them if you wish.) Ask a small sample of people to rate these in order of importance, i.e. the most important should have the most money spent on it, and so on. It would be helpful to ask people to explain to you very briefly their reasons. You could then summarise these at the end of your research.

Improvement in abortion services
More equipment to help premature babies survive
More equipment for the treatment of cancer
Better facilities for AIDS patients
Nursing homes for older people
Hip replacements
Dialysis machines
Hospital accident and emergency units
Better facilities for the mentally ill
Heart transplants
Improving treatment for serious burns
Speech therapy

b) Are there any conclusions you can draw about the priorities people have for medical care? Do you think this would be a good/equitable method of deciding on priorities? If you do not think so, then how would you decide on the priority of spending for health?

Techniques of rationing

How then can the NHS ensure that people receive the health services they demand, when there is inadequate finance to cater for these demands? The answer is to **ration** the delivery of services in some way. One basic division needs to be made between:

- **formal rationing** where the agency involved (such as the NHS) deliberately and formally sets out to use a particular technique, for example, waiting lists
- **informal rationing**, where the individual or agency uses techniques which are not formally acknowledged, such as the activities of the receptionist in a surgery, who decides who should be seen first by the doctors and who should have to wait for their appointments.

Waiting lists: an example of formal rationing in practice

If someone is involved in an accident, then they can expect to be treated immediately in a UK hospital, and about half the people who are admitted to hospital do not have to go on a waiting list.

However, those who require treatment, but who are not in desperate urgency, are put on to a waiting list. The length of time people have to wait is often the subject of great controversy.

In 2001, there were just over 1 million people on the waiting lists of hospitals. Twenty-five years earlier, there were around 600,000 people waiting at any one time. Although waiting lists are longer now than in the past, it is important to note that the numbers of people being treated have actually increased.

Question

Waiting lists today are longer than they were twenty-five years ago, yet more people are being treated. Can you explain this apparent contradiction?

The length of time that people have to wait is not related necessarily to the actual illness or condition, it is just as likely to be related to the financial situation of a health authority.

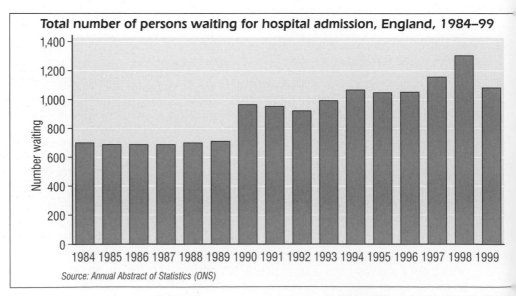

Total number of persons waiting for hospital admission, England, 1984–99

Source: Annual Abstract of Statistics (ONS)

Source: *Wellard's NHS Handbook 2000/01*

The Labour governments elected in 1997 and 2001 were committed to shortening waiting lists and have introduced a range of initiatives to shorten them. These include guarantees that everyone who is suffering from certain types of cancer will see a specialist within two weeks, and paying private hospitals to undertake certain routine operations. They are also funding the building of new specialist surgical centres which will undertake a range of routine operations and which will

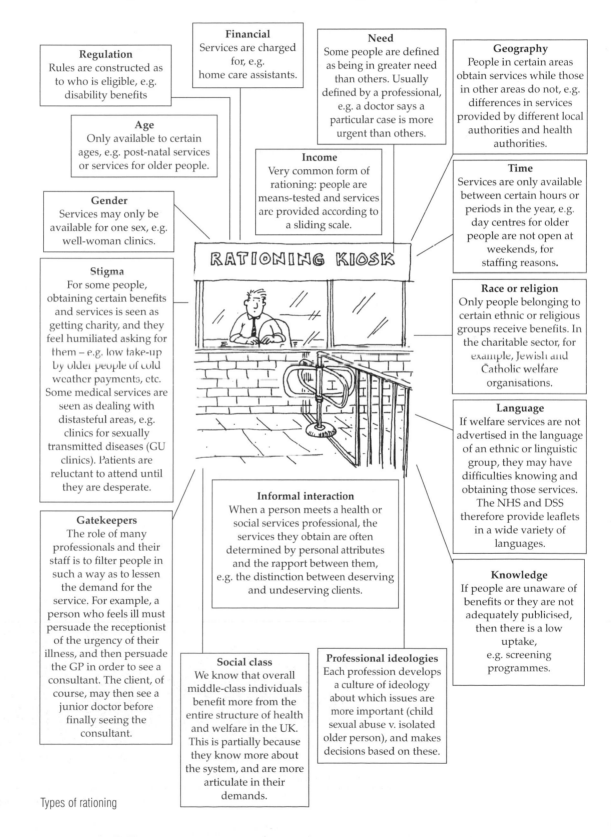

Types of rationing

run independently of the hospitals. However, critics point our that waiting lists will continue, as people's expectations of the NHS continue to rise.

Informal rationing

Waiting lists are an example of formal rationing. However, this is only one of many types of rationing which are less explicit. The diagram 'Types of rationing' on page 159 shows just how many forms of rationing there are. Rationing in its various forms is not necessarily any fairer than payment, as people do not necessarily receive treatment by the NHS simply on their need. So, older people may not be placed high on up on the list for transplants, whilst others may be excluded because the medical professions regard the particular group as not being worth treatment, for example alcoholics or heavy smokers.

Techniques of rationing

Authorities throughout Britain are employing all five of the available techniques to ration services:
    ... in Cambridge and Huntingdon, in order to fund an expansion of services to pay for the growth in emergency care and mental health needs, we have *denied* women access to infertility treatment; we have *deterred* people accessing out-patient services at their local community hospital by centralising them on the district hospital site; we have deliberately induced treatment *delays* by lengthening waiting times; we have *deflected* costs on to other public agencies and the private individual by continuing to disinvest in long-term NHS care; and we have witnessed a continued *dilution* in the quality of services as local hospitals cut nurse staffing levels to cope.

Source: Adapted from *The Guardian*, 2 July 1997

Draw a diagram showing the five available techniques of rationing mentioned and illustrate each one using the diagram on page 159 to help you.

Quality in the NHS

Traditionally, issues of quality in the provision of health services were based on the assumptions that the medical professions and hospital management were 'doing their best'. Few people questioned if their 'best' was good enough, and fewer suggested ways of measuring quality.

However, the quality of services has become one of the more important issues facing the NHS. This search for quality has resulted in the government paper *A First Class Service* in 1998, which led to the introduction of:

- NICE
- National Service Frameworks
- Commission for Health Improvement
- clinical governance

all of which have contributed to an improvement in the quality of medical provision.

Quality in the NHS

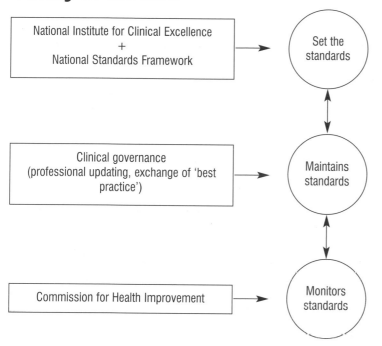

1 Explain in your own words what is meant by 'clinical governance'.

2 Explain the role of:
  a) NICE
  b) the Commission for Health Improvement.

You will need to read the main text.

National Institute for Clinical Excellence (NICE)

This began to operate in 1999 and it provides formal advice for all health professionals and managers in the NHS on the clinical and cost effectiveness of the new and existing technologies used in the health service – medicines, diagnostic tests and surgical procedures.

NICE was needed because the huge increase in new technologies and pharmaceuticals available to the NHS was far more than it was able to afford. Decisions were being made locally by different trusts and health authorities over what they would purchase. This led to the development of what was known as 'post-code prescriptions', meaning that in certain areas of the country, drugs were available on prescription to combat a particular disease, but in other areas of the country, the health authorities had decided not to fund the drugs.

NICE appraises new drugs and technologies (and some existing ones) and then says whether or not the costs involved are worth the results in terms of improved health.

National Service Frameworks

The NHS has always been based upon giving as much 'clinical freedom' to the doctors to provide what in their opinion is the best health care available for their patients. Yet, as we mentioned earlier, there was rarely any clear way of measuring what was best practice. Throughout the UK different patients would receive different treatments and standards of care. In an effort to have similar high standards, the government introduced National Service Frameworks. This is a series of set national standards which define what is expected of doctors and other care staff, and provides examples of the best practices across the country for a range of particularly serious and common illnesses. At present there are NSF's on cancer, mental health, coronary heart disease, diabetes and the treatment of older people.

Commission for Health Improvement

This was launched in 1999. It is an independent body which is accountable to the Health Secretary (the government minister responsible for the NHS), and it monitors the existence and quality of health care throughout England and Wales. It has the power to intervene in hospitals if it thinks that the quality of the care is not high enough.

In Scotland, there is a similar body, known as the Clinical Standards Board.

Clinical governance

The Department of Health adopted the idea of 'clinical governance' in 1999 and defines it as 'a framework through which NHS organisations are accountable for continuously improving the quality of their services and safeguarding high standards of care by creating an environment in which excellence in clinical care will flourish'. What it means, in practice, is that there needs to be a change in the culture of the NHS, so that all the professionals and management attempt to provide the very highest standards possible, and that it is the duty of all the health organisations and professionals to develop routine procedures which ensure that the highest standards are met. This can partly be done by following the advice of NICE and conforming to the standards set by the Commission for Health Improvement. But it also requires regular updating and retraining for medical staff and management of trusts.

Main points ▶ Private health care grew rapidly in the 1980s up to the mid 1990s. Since then it has remained constant. Many people have moral objections to its existence – though the government uses it to shorten waiting lists by paying for operations to be performed by the private sector.

▶ The demand for health care outstrips the NHS's ability to provide it, so there are various forms of rationing used. The most common form of rationing is that of waiting lists. Over one million people are on these lists, waiting for medical attention.

▶ In recent years there has been a number of initiatives to improve quality in the NHS. These include NICE, National Service Frameworks and the Commission for Health Improvement.

Inequalities in health

Apart from some well publicised links between, for example, cancer and smoking, most people believe that health and illness are 'natural states', and that is a person is unlucky or genetically predisposed when they fall ill. However, all the research indicates that health and illness are not random: certain groups in the population are far more likely than others to be ill and to die at a younger age than normal.

In 1979, a government report was commissioned to try to uncover these clear variations in health between groups in the population. The study, known as the Black Report, showed shocking differences between the social classes, and the remedies it suggested were so expensive that the government ignored its conclusions. Almost twenty years later, the newly elected Labour government in 1997 commissioned a similar report (*Independent Inquiry into Inequalities in Health*, 1998). This found that overall people's health had improved over the last twenty years, but that the 'health gap' between the poorest and the richest had actually widened.

The main differences in health are related to:

- geographical location
- social class
- gender
- ethnic group.

Geographical differences

In a recent study by Shaw *et al.* (M. Shaw, D. Dorling, D. Gordon and G. Davey Smith, *The Widening Gap*, Policy Press, 1999), the researchers looked at all the MP's constituencies in the UK and gathered information on the health of the people living there. They then compiled tables showing these differences, in which they compared the one million people living in the constituencies with the very worst health records and compared them with the one million people living in those constituencies with the very best health records. The gap between these groups surprised even the researchers themselves.

Comparing the million people living in the worst health areas with the one million living in the best health areas in the UK:

- Children under the age of one year are twice as likely to die.
- There are ten times more women under the age of 65 who are permanently sick (including disabled).
- Adults were almost three times as likely to state that they has a serious 'chronic' (long-term) illness or disability.
- Adults have a 70 per cent greater chance of dying before the age of 65.

These geographical differences generally reflect differences in income and levels of deprivation. However they are not simply a reflection of these, because poorer people living in affluent areas tend to have higher standards of health. It seems that where there is a high proportion of a local population living in poverty, the quality of life is generally lower and the health standards are much worse, so a sort of snowballing effect takes place which exaggerates the differences between richer and poorer areas.

Definition
Mortality – refers to death

But also, people in different areas of the UK have different eating patterns and leisure lifestyles, and live in very different levels of pollution, and have varying standards of housing quality. All these overlap with poverty and inequality to create the differences in health and **mortality** between areas.

Social class

Mortality

Over the last twenty years, death rates have fallen for both men and women in all social classes. But they have fallen faster for those in the higher social classes. So the difference in rates between those in the higher and lower social classes has actually grown. For example:

- In the early 1970s, the death rate among men of working age was almost twice as high for those in class V (unskilled) as for those in class I (professional). By the early 1990s, it was almost three times higher.
- Men in social class I can expect to live for almost nine years longer than men from social class V, whilst women can expect to live six years longer than their social class V counterparts.

The geography of death

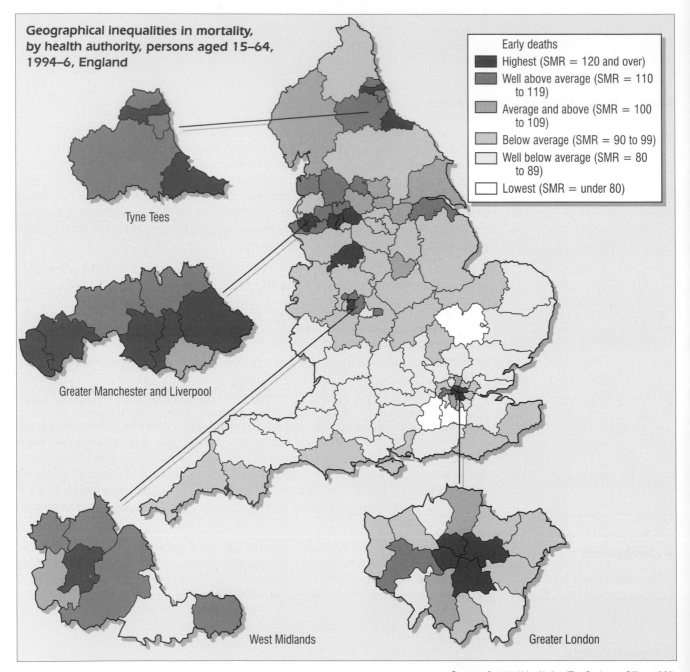

Geographical inequalities in mortality,
by health authority, persons aged 15–64,
1994–6, England

Early deaths

Highest (SMR = 120 and over)

Well above average (SMR = 110 to 119)

Average and above (SMR = 100 to 109)

Below average (SMR = 90 to 99)

Well below average (SMR = 80 to 89)

Lowest (SMR = under 80)

Tyne Tees

Greater Manchester and Liverpool

West Midlands

Greater London

Source: *Our Healthier Nation* (The Stationery Office, 1999)

1 Which four areas in England had the highest proportion of early deaths?

2 Which had the lowest?

3 What is the situation where you live?

4 In your opinion, and reading the text, what reasons are there for this geographical variation?

- Men and women in social classes I and II are roughly 16 per cent more likely to state that they have good health than those in classes IV and V.
- Premature mortality (that is people dying before the age 65) is also linked to social class. For example, if all men had the same death rates as those in classes I and II, it is estimated that there would have been over 17,000 fewer deaths each year.

The growing gap in mortality

A **The widening mortality gap between social classes, men of working age, England and Wales**

Standardised mortality ratios indexed to 1930-32

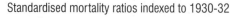

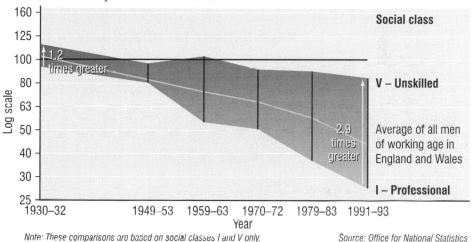

Note: These comparisons are based on social classes I and V only.

Source: Office for National Statistics

Source: *Saving Lives: Our Healthier Nation* (The Stationery Office, 1999)

B **Life expectancy by social class, males at birth, England and Wales, 1972–91**

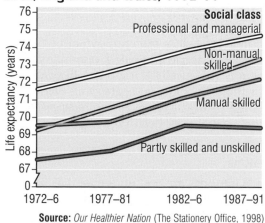

Source: *Our Healthier Nation* (The Stationery Office, 1998)

Look at A. In the diagram the lower the figure, the lower the chance of dying before retirement age.

1 What is the gap between the professional employee and the unskilled employee in terms of mortality?

2 What has happened to this gap since 1930–32?

Look at B

3 What age can a professional/managerial employee expect to live to?

4 What age can a partly skilled/unskilled worker expect to live to?

5 On average what has happened to men's mortality rates since 1930–32 in all social classes?

6 What statement can you make which summarises all this information?

Morbidity

Among the 45–64 age group, 17 per cent of professional men reported a limiting long-standing illness compared to 48 per cent of unskilled men. Among women, 25 per cent of professional women and 45 per cent of unskilled women reported such a condition.

In adulthood, being overweight is a measure of possible ill health, with obesity a risk factor for many chronic diseases. There is a noticeable social class gradient in obesity which is greater among women than among men, so about 25 per cent of women in class V were classified as **obese** compared to 14 per cent of women in class I.

Another indicator of poor health is raised blood pressure, which can lead to strokes and heart attacks. Here again there is a clear social class differential among women, with those in higher classes being less likely than those in the manual classes to have hypertension – 17 per cent of women in class I and 24 per cent in class V had **hypertension**.

Explanations for differences in the social classes

The following approaches have been suggested to explain these differences in mortality and morbidity along class lines:

- artefact
- social selection
- behavioural and cultural
- materialist explanations.

Artefact

This approach suggests that the statistical evidence is giving a misleading picture. It is agreed that overall health has improved, and that the gap between the lowest social classes and the rest of the population has grown. However, the argument continues, there are far fewer people in the lowest social classes because of the changing nature of employment in the UK. Therefore, in reality, the vast bulk of the population are actually in good health – it is only this small, and declining social class group which has poor health. However, the report *Independent Inquiry into Inequalities in Health* (1998) shows that even when the classes were regrouped to include classes IV and V together, very great differences remained, for example early death rates are 68 per cent higher among men in classes IV and V compared with those in class I.

Social selection

This explanation suggests that it is not social class and employment which causes poor health, but poor health which *leads* to people being unemployed and in worse jobs. For example, if a person is chronically (long-term) ill or disabled in some way, it is usually difficult for them to obtain a secure, well-paid job. Once again, the statistics paint a misleading picture. However, *the Independent Inquiry into Inequalities in Health* found evidence that poor health is a result of poverty, not a cause of it.

Behavioural and cultural explanations

The approach argues that individual lifestyles are best understood as the result of the cultural choices made by different groups in the population. For example:

- *Cigarette smoking:* Whereas over 40 per cent of males and 35 per cent of females in social classes IV and V regularly smoke, about 12 per cent of males and females in social class I smoke.

- *Diet*: Working-class people are more likely to eat white bread, less fresh fruit and vegetables and more sugar. So manual workers consume twice as much white bread, have higher sugar consumption and eat less fresh fruit, for example, than professionals. Alcohol consumption is higher amongst the working-class.
- *Lifestyles:* Middle-class people are more likely to take exercise and undertake social activities, which reduce levels of stress, and maintain a higher standard of health.

Sex, class, cigarettes ... and cancer

Levels of smoking have fallen more quickly in professional classes (men and women aged 65 and over, Great Britain)

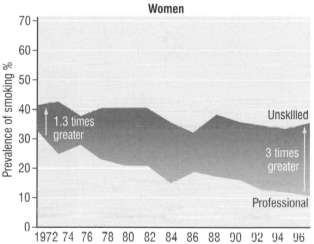

Source: Office for National Statistics

Source: *Saving Lives: Our Healthier Nation* (The Stationery Office, 1999)

Mortality from lung cancer by social class, men aged 20–64, England and Wales, 1991–3

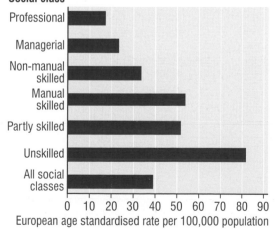

European age standardised rate per 100,000 population

Source: *Our Healthier Nation* (The Stationery Office, 1998)

1 Which social class is most likely to die from lung cancer?

2 What is the rate per 100,000 of the population?

3 Which social class is most likely to smoke cigarettes?

4 Which sex is more likely to smoke cigarettes?

5 Overall, do more or less people smoke cigarettes today than in 1972?

6 What has happened to the differences between the social classes over time?

7 Why do you think that (a) males and (b) working-class people are more likely to smoke cigarettes?

There is a particular weakness however in this approach, in that it fails to ask *why* groups have these poor diets and high alcohol and cigarette consumption. The answer for many social scientists, and one which has begun to influence government policy is the 'materialist' or 'structural' explanation.

Materialist explanations

The final explanation comes from those who see a direct relationship between differences in health and the unequal nature of UK society. This approach agrees with all the points made about behavioural differences pointed to earlier, but argues that this behaviour has to be seen within a broader content of inequality in UK society. Supporters of materialist explanations point out that many apparent 'free choices' which poorer people make are a result of factors over which they have little control. For example, poor diets are often the result of being unable to afford decent food, and smoking is a way to cope with the depressing life circumstances.

Hidden killers?

Unequal risk of heart disease death at different employment levels in the public sector: even after allowing for risk factors

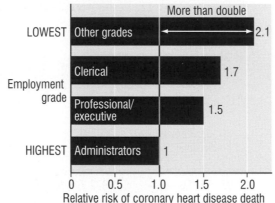

Controlling for age, smoking, systolic blood pressure, plasma cholesterol concentration, height and blood sugar

Source: *Saving Lives: Our Healthier Nation*
(The Stationery Office, 1999)

1 Which grade of civil servant had the lowest chance of dying from heart disease?

2 Which grade of civil servant had the highest chance of dying from heart disease?

3 What does the diagram tell you about the relationship between job and heart disease?

Poverty, housing and health

Asthmatics are two or three times more likely than the general population to live in damp properties (residents of Glasgow, 1991–3)

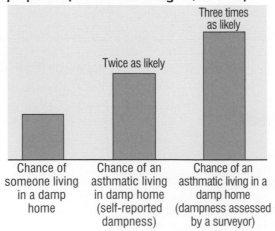

Source: *Saving Lives: Our Healthier Nation*
(The Stationery Office, 1999)

1 What are the chances of an asthmatic person living in a damp home?

2 What does this imply about the relationship between low income and asthma?

This approach highlights a number of key factors which affect wealth. These include:

- *Poverty:* Poorer people have worse diets, worse housing conditions, are more likely to be unemployed and generally to live a more highly stressed, lower quality of life.

- *Employment:* Certain types of work are more dangerous than others, apart from the obvious ones, such as mining. Research on civil servants has shown that routine clerical workers are much more likely to die young than those of higher grades. Comparing the lowest to highest grades, those in the lowest grades are actually three times more likely to die before reaching the age of 65.

- *Unemployment:* According to Moser's long-term study of the relationship between income and wealth, unemployed men and their wives were likely to die younger than those in employment (K. Moser, P. Goldblatt, J. Fox and D. Jones, 'Unemployment and mortality' in P. Goldblatt (ed.) *Longitudinal Study: Mortality and Social Organisation,* HMSO, 1990).

Unemployment and health

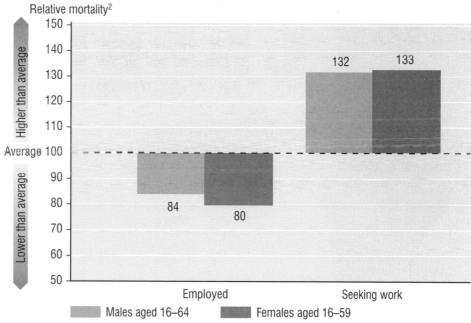

Employment, unemployment[1] and mortality, by sex, England and Wales, 1981–92

1 Unemployment = People currently unemployed but seeking work. The chart does not include those who are permanently sick or disabled, or inactive for other reasons.

2 Standardised mortality ratios (SMRs) from all causes by economic activity status at 1981 Census (deaths occurring between 1981 and 1992)

Source: *Our Healthier Nation* (The Stationery Office, 1998)

Look at the definition of SMR on page 166.

1 What are the SMRs of (a) males and (b) females who are unemployed and looking for work?

2 What are the SMRs of (a) males and (b) females who are employed?

3 What does this tell you about death and employment?

4 What reasons can you suggest for this relationship?

This approach has the advantage of explaining why there are cultural differences in behaviour between various groups in society. The argument advanced by those who support the structural or materialist approach is that people may make choices about their behaviour, but that the circumstances within which they make their choices are strongly affected by the extent of inequality existing in the UK.

Gender and health

Women live longer than men, but are more likely to visit their GPs for treatment and they also have higher levels of mental illness.

Sex differences in health

A **Self-reported restricted activity[1], by gender, Great Britain**

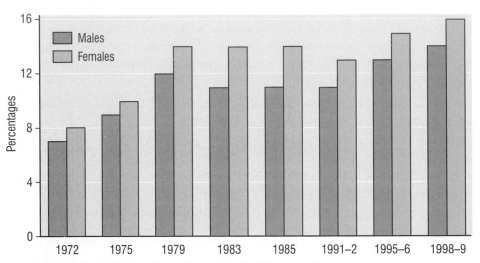

1 Percentage of people of all ages reporting restricted activity in the 14 days prior to interview

Source: General Household Survey, Office for National Statistics

Look at A.

1 What percentage of females had restricted activity in (a) 1972 and (b) 1998–9?

2 What percentage of males had restricted activity in (a) 1985 and (b) 1998–9?

3 Which sex has higher levels of restricted activity?

4 What explanations have been offered for this?

B **Prevalence of treated depression: by type of area and gender, 1994–1998, England & Wales**

Rates per 1,000 patients[1]

	Males	Females
Deprived industrial areas	34	77
Mature populations	29	67
Metropolitan professionals	28	60
Industrial areas	27	71
Lower status owner-occupier	26	62
Rural fringe	23	56
Established owner-occupier	23	58
Rural areas	23	57
Inner/deprived city	23	53
Middling Britain	22	58
Prosperous areas	22	57
Suburbia	21	55
All areas	25	61

[1] All ages.

Source: Office for National Statistics: Medicines Control Agency

Source: Social Trends 31 (The Stationery Office, 2001)

Look at B.

5 Overall, which sex has higher levels of depression? What are the figures?

6 In which areas of England and Wales are people most likely to be depressed? What are the figures?

7 Suggest any reasons for these differences.

The reasons for health differences between the sexes include:

- *Biology:* There is some evidence to suggest that women are biologically stronger than men (for instance female foetuses are less likely to die than male foetuses) and have a greater biological possibility of living longer.
- *Risk-taking behaviour:* Women are less likely to engage in violence, to be involved in serious road accidents, and to consume excess alcohol or smoke cigarettes. They are therefore less at risk of deaths as a result of these.
- *Poverty:* Women are more likely to be living in poverty than men and this is likely to cause chronic illness and mental disorder (as a result of the consequent stress).

Ethnicity and health

Members of minority ethnic groups are more likely to define themselves as having poor health, than the majority population, with just under 50 per cent of ethnic minority members described themselves as having fair or poor health compared to just under 30 per cent of the majority population.

Overall, health levels are worse and life expectancy lower than the majority population, but all ethnic minority groups have lower levels of deaths from cancers than the majority population. However, ethnic minority groups have a shorter life expectancy than the majority population.

Patterns in the causes of death vary across ethnic groups, with, for example:

- those from the 'Indian subcontinent' having the highest levels of coronary heart disease
- those from the 'Caribbean Commonwealth' having the lowest levels of death from coronary heart disease and suffering higher levels of strokes.

Reasons for the differences in ethnicity and health include:

- *Poverty:* The higher levels of morbidity and higher early mortality rates can partially be explained by their relative social deprivation.
- *Racism:* some analysts argue that the experience of living in a racist society can place great stress upon people and this may impact upon health levels.
- *Lifestyle differences:* Differences in terms of diet and lifestyle may influence health, with some diets causing ill health. For example, this may partially account for the high levels of heart disease amongst those of Asian origin.

Factors influencing an individual's health

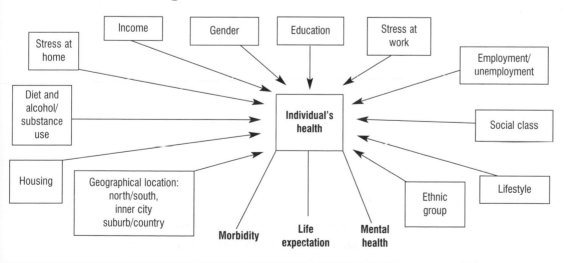

Copy the diagram and complete each box, explaining why these factors are important in influencing health.

Access to health care

Variations in the provision of health care

Health service provision varies according to:

- geographical differences
- the decisions of the medical professions
- variations in the competence of health organisations.

Geographical differences

Different areas in the UK receive different levels of funding per head of the population. London, for example, receives far more than most other areas of the country.

Funding to each health care region is decided by the government on the basis of a formula which takes into account such things as the size of the population, the age and sex of the population and a variety of socio-economic factors, so that more money should go to poorer areas and less to richer areas. But unfortunately, this has never worked out in quite the way it should as poorer areas have never seemed to get the funding that they ought. The reasons include:

- *Historical precedence:* Certain areas of the country have historically received more money for a variety of reasons and despite the intentions of governments, they have continued to receive the funding, despite the original reasons for the funding having disappeared.
- *Specialist teaching hospitals:* These receive particularly high levels of funding. They are usually located in the richer areas of the country (such as London).
- *Political pressures:* It is extremely difficult for governments to cut back on an area's funding, as this would lead to a huge outcry. Politicians are very concerned that this might lose them votes. London, for example, receives more than its 'fair' share of funding, yet each attempt to cut back on funding has led to a massive campaign against it, so the government has given in.

The medical professions

Different areas of health care have lower or higher status amongst health professionals. Paediatrics and surgery have high status, while geriatrics and chronic illness have low status. The influence of the medical professions is such that the funding follows very much their views.

Hospitals and competence

Despite all the guidance from the Department of Health, it would appear that, irrespective of funding, the organisation of hospitals and the competence of doctors vary. A study by Janner, for example, in 2000 showed that comparing the worst with the best hospitals in the UK, and taking account of all factors such as age, sex and diagnoses, seventeen people were likely to die in the worst hospitals for every ten in the best.

Demand for health care

Our discussion so far indicates that although the population's health has increased overall, the gap between the various social classes has grown, and that there are significant differences between the health of ethnic groups and the sexes.

Much of the explanations for these differences lies in the lifestyles and income levels of these groups, but also it is important to realise that there are many barriers which the less privileged groups in society face in obtaining health care.

Use by social class

Despite the fact that members of the working class are more likely to be ill and to have accidents, they are actually less likely to attend doctors' surgeries. They are also less likely to undertake any form of *screening programme* (such as that for breast cancer, for example). But they do make greater use of accident and emergency services, often because health problems have been left to such a stage that they become an emergency.

The reasons for this lack of attendance is that there are more *barriers* to them accessing health care.

- They are less likely to be able to afford to take time off work, especially if they are hourly paid.
- It is more difficult for them to get to GPs' surgeries because of the costs and time using public transport. This is a particular problem, as GP practices are more likely to be in affluent areas
- Working-class people are less likely to consider their symptoms serious enough to warrant a visit to the GP's surgery, than a middle-class person.

Use by gender

Women are more likely than men to visit a doctor and to make use of medical services. But given the higher levels of illness, both mental and physical, suffered by women, it has been argued that women under-use the health services compared to their actual needs.

Since 1988, there has been a national screening programme for breast cancer and since 1995, one for cervical cancer. However, the take-up rates have been approximately 75 per cent, and the poorer the social group the less likely they are to attend. Attendance rates vary by ethnicity and rates of attendance are particularly low for women of Bangladeshi and Pakistani background.

Use by ethnicity

Ethnic minority groups have a significantly lower take-up of health services. The reasons for the lower levels of use of health services include:

- *Language barriers:* There are limited translation facilities, or information available to publicise the NHS in minority languages.
- *Cultural differences:* Many Asian women are unwilling to be seen by male doctors, for example.
- *Poverty*: As ethnic minorities contain a high proportion in poverty, the problems over travel and taking time off work apply to them.

Use by age

Although older people are those who are most likely to use the health services, they under-use them relative to their needs. Older people are more reluctant to use GP services and to see themselves as 'wasting the doctor's time' if they consider that they are consulting the doctor unnecessarily.

Geriatric medicine (the health care of older people) is seen by the medical professions as an area of low prestige, so relatively few services are provided.

Ethnicity and smear tests

Women in some ethnic groups have low uptake of potentially life-saving cervical cancer smears (women aged 16–74 by ethnic group, UK 1992)

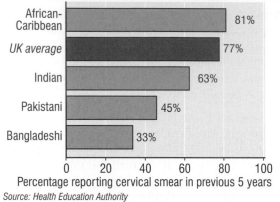

Source: Health Education Authority

Source: *Saving Lives: Our Healthier Nation*
(The Stationery Office, 1999)

1 What is the average take-up of cervical cancer smear tests?

2 Which group has an above-average take-up? By how much?

3 Which group has the lowest take-up rate? How much below average are their rates?

Access to health

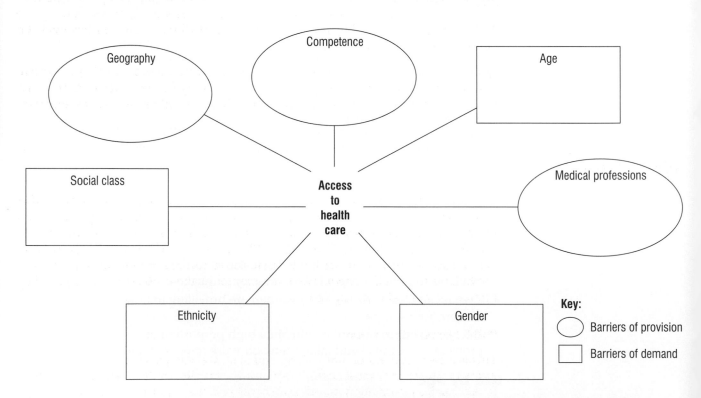

Copy the diagram and complete the boxes, explaining how each factor affects the demand or provision of health care.

Strong evidence exists to support what might be called the 'Inverse Prevention Law' in primary care in which those communities most at risk of ill-health have least access to a range of effective preventive services including cancer screening programmes, health promotion and immunisation ...

Source: D. Gordon, M. Shaw, D. Dorling and G. Davey Smith, *Inequalities in Health* (The Policy Press, 1999)

Combating ill health: the new initiatives

Since 1998, the government has introduced a range of initiatives which are part of a general process of modernising the NHS. The aim of each of these is to improve access to health services for those people who have under-used existing health services. The new initiatives include:

- health action zones
- NHS Direct.

Health action zones (HAZs)

In 1998 the government launched the health action zones, and from 1999, twenty-six of these were set up in areas of underprivilege, where the health status of the local population was particularly low. The HAZs are based on the principle that combating poor health is not just the work of the NHS. Instead the local HAZ brings together a number of different agencies such as local government housing departments and social services, as well as GPs and local trusts.

For example, damp and cold housing is closely linked to asthma, so one HAZ introduced a scheme to improve the health of asthmatic children by improving central heating, insulation and damp-proofing in council and private housing where children are affected. The advantage was that by improving the health of the children there was a reduction in hospital admissions (therefore saving the NHS money) and a reduction in days off school (thus helping to improve the children's educational performance).

HAZ activities are divided between what is known as *upstream* work, to improve health and reduce health inequalities by intervening in the wider factors which cause poor health, and *downstream* work which consists of improving the access to, and quality of, health services.

NHS Direct

A good example of downstream work is another health development – NHS Direct. This is a telephone-based helpline for people to contact if they are unsure of what to do about a health problem. The helpline is staffed by nurses who provide advice on how to treat the problem. The aim of NHS Direct is to make health advice much more accessible, but it also saves the NHS money as those who might have made a GP appointment for a minor health problem can be advised by phone – a much cheaper option.

NHS Direct On-Line

This is a development of NHS Direct and is an website which provides a self-care guide for the twenty most common symptoms of callers to the telephone helpline. It also carries information on other diseases and the contact numbers for a range of health care organisations.

NHS walk-in centres

These are health centres which are located in shopping precincts, supermarkets and alongside Accident and Emergency Units in hospitals. They are open long hours and at weekends to deal with a variety of minor health problems and to provide advice. The centres are staffed by nurses.

Main points ▶ There are very great inequalities in health between social classes, the sexes and ethnic groups. Although overall the standards of health have improved, there is a growing gap between these various groups.

▶ Social scientists do not agree on the exact causes, but there is agreement that poor health is related to wider inequalities in society.

▶ The different groups in the population also have different rates of use of the NHS, with certain groups – particularly the poor and certain ethnic minority groups – failing to use the services of the NHS.

▶ In the last five years, there have been a number of initiatives to combat the wider causes of poor health. These include health action zones, health improvement plans and NHS Direct.

Conclusion

In this chapter we have examined the changing nature of the NHS. The problems it faces now are far different from those faced by the original NHS in 1948. The main differences are that today expectations of what the NHS ought to provide for people are so much higher, whilst at the same time the range of services which it is able to provide has increased substantially – aided by advances in technology and medication. The response to these changes has been to alter the structure, by dismantling the rigid centralisation of the traditional NHS, by setting up quality councils and by trying to control the explosive growth in the pharmaceutical bill.

A much more contentious issue has been the move towards a partial privatisation of the NHS through contracts with private hospitals and other health corporations. However, what we have also seen is that health inequalities are caused by wider factors than those which the NHS can deal with, so that any strategy to improve health, also has to improve the wider quality of life of the population.

6 CHAPTER SUMMARY

1 The first form of government health provision was in 1911, when a very limited cover was provided for workers aged 16–65.

2 The NHS was inaugurated in 1948 in the face of opposition from the majority of doctors.

3 The NHS was the result of the social changes which took place during the Second World War.

4 The NHS had major financial problems for most of its existence, but the current system of purchaser/provider was introduced in 1990.

5 The NHS is funded by the government from taxation and is run locally by health authorities which have the role of ensuring that the local population get the health services they need. This is done by buying health care from trusts (such as hospitals and community care organisations).

6 Over the next ten years new organisations – primary care trusts – will take over much of the work of the health authorities. These are run by GPs and other health professionals.

7 Health care costs continue to rise, as a result of changing standards of health, rising costs of drugs and developments in new technologies and surgical procedures.

8 The NHS is funded by taxation, but critics have suggested other ways of funding the NHS, in particular three suggestions have been made: hypothecated taxes, social insurance and medical savings accounts.

9 Private health care grew rapidly in the 1980s up to the mid 1990s. Since then it has remained constant. Many people have moral objections to its existence, though the government uses it to shorten waiting lists by paying for operations to be performed by the private sector.

10 The demand for health care outstrips the NHS's ability to provide it, so there are various forms of rationing used. The most common form of rationing is that of waiting lists. Over one million people are on these lists, waiting for medical attention.

11 In recent years there has been a number of initiatives to improve quality in the NHS. These include NICE, National Service Frameworks and the Commission for Health Improvement.

12 There are very great inequalities in health between social classes, the sexes and ethnic groups. Although overall the standards of health have improved, there is a growing gap between these various groups.

13 Social scientists do not agree on the exact causes, but there is agreement that poor health is related to wider inequalities in society.

14 The different groups in the population also have different rates of use of the NHS, with certain groups – particularly the poor and certain ethnic minority groups – failing to use the services of the NHS.

15 In the last five years there have been a number of initiatives to combat the wider causes of poor health. These include health action zones, health improvement plans and NHS Direct.

Useful websites

www.nhs.uk: the National Health Service

www.doh.gov.uk: the Department of Health

www.ohn.gov.uk: Our Healthier Nation

www.audit-commission.gov.uk: the Audit Commission

www.who.org: the World Health Organisation

www.ash.org.uk: Action on Smoking and Health

Chapter 7

PERSONAL SOCIAL SERVICES: SOCIAL CARE AND SOCIAL WORK

Chapter contents

The origins of social care and social work

The beginnings of social care

Philanthropy and mutual aid

What we now call social care or social work mainly developed as a response to poverty and unemployment. In the nineteenth century, conditions in the large industrialised towns had become appalling for enormous numbers of people, and their plight was painfully obvious to the more affluent living in those towns. The response from the better-off sections of society was mixed. Many regarded poverty and the problems associated with it as the fault of the individuals concerned. It was regarded as a sign of laziness or moral degeneracy, such as a desire to drink or gamble their money away. As a consequence it was generally felt that any attempt to give help to the poor would make the problem worse as this would encourage dependency and reinforce bad habits. However, the nineteenth century saw the beginnings of various types of social research that tended to bring out the fact that much poverty was caused by social and economic factors beyond the control of the individual. Over and above all this there was a growing concern about the welfare of children who, by dint of their lack of years, were exempt from much of the moral condemnation that adults faced.

During the nineteenth century, various initiatives developed to combat poverty and the problems associated with it. On the one hand, the workers themselves combined together in friendly societies and later trade unions to try to improve working conditions and provide themselves with some basic forms of health and welfare benefits. This is called **mutual aid**. On the other hand, the more affluent began to develop **philanthropic** (charitable) organisations that, in their eyes at least, would alleviate some of the greatest problems of the poor. By the middle of the nineteenth century, a large number of such organisations existed, offering assistance of one kind or another. Generally help tended to be given to those who were thought to be morally deserving of it.

Charity Organisation Society

In 1869 the Charity Organisation Society was set up partly to create some order amongst the proliferation of different charitable bodies. This organisation took a strong moral approach. It set out to distinguish between people who were poor or needy through no fault of their own, and the rest of the poor. The society then undertook to work with individual families to improve their situation. In order to discriminate between the 'deserving' and the 'undeserving' poor the COS developed the method of visiting people in their own homes and investigating in detail how they led their lives, what their problems were, and so on. It formed the basis of what was later to become social casework. Today it still exists as the Family Welfare Association and whilst the casework approach is still used, the Victorian morally judging dimension has gone.

Social work emerges

Also in the nineteenth century in London, Octavia Hill, a housing reformer, organised the purchase and building of blocks of flats for the poor, where they were encouraged to follow particular patterns of behaviour that she believed would help alleviate their poverty.

These were the beginnings of social work, as we would define it today, that is, a consistent, organised approach to the social problems of individuals, which focuses on enabling them to change their situation and to help themselves.

The first probation officers also emerged at this time, when magistrates began to 'bind people over', instead of sending them to prison. The person had to report to a clergyman or someone appointed by the court, who would ensure that the person behaved in a lawful way.

Finally, hospitals began to appoint almoners or medical social workers, whose job developed into assisting patients and their families.

It is not difficult to see how social work, apart from being motivated by the impulse to 'do good', also has a long tradition of 'social control' which many argue is a characteristic of social care and social work that continues to this day.

Throughout the early part of the twentieth century, the belief grew that there ought to be some form of State provision of social work for certain needy groups – ideally to be provided through the local authorities. An example of this is the establishment in the 1920s of services for physically and mentally disabled people by local authorities with grants from central government.

The first half of the twentieth century also saw the development of the relatively new social and behavioural sciences and the psychoanalytic theory of Sigmund

---

Definitions

Philanthropic – doing good for others

Mutual aid – people in a similar situation helping each other

Freud. These new ideas were beginning to change people's understanding of the nature of human problems.

However, these beginnings have only limited links with modern social and probation work, as the real beginnings of the modern form of social work can be traced back to the period after the Beveridge reforms of 1948 (see Chapter 3).

Social services from 1948 onwards

By 1948, three different sets of personal social services had developed:

- children's departments
- health services
- welfare departments.

Children's departments

In 1946, the Curtis Report recommended the setting up of departments of local authorities which were responsible for fostering and adoption, child care, family casework and children's homes. Gradually the powers of the children's departments were extended, so that by 1952 they were given the power to investigate cases of abuse and, in 1963, they were given powers to undertake preventive action.

Health services

Various health services which were related to existing or possible social problems were also provided by local authorities under the power of the Medical Officer of Health. These services included health visiting, occupational therapy, mental welfare officers, hospital social workers and day nurseries.

Definition

Generic social work – where a social worker is trained and employed to work with all client groups whether they be adults or children. The opposite of specialist

Welfare departments

Welfare departments of local authorities covered a wide range of responsibilities and activities that the other two omitted. These included residential care for older people, assistance for homeless families and services for disabled people. In 1962, they had their powers extended to provide meals, a range of social services (such as day centres) and recreational facilities.

The first **generic social work** course was established at the London School of Economics in 1954.

The Seebohm Committee

This was set up in 1965, and reported in 1968. The result was the structure of the social services which basically still exists today.

Seebohm recommended that the various different elements of personal social services should be unified into one organisation, which would be run by local authorities. In 1970, as a result of the Local Authority Social Services Act, the new local authority social services departments were set up. The health departments were broken up, with some of the responsibilities handed over to the NHS, including health visiting and much of the occupational therapy work.

The welfare departments and children's departments formed the basis of the new personal social services departments. Medical social workers joined later in 1974. The importance of the social services departments also increased at this time with the passing of two Acts (the Children Act 1969 and the Chronically Sick and Disabled Persons Act 1970) which placed greater responsibilities on the shoulders of the local authorities regarding children and the long-term sick and disabled.

As a result of the changes, the new social workers were to be 'generically trained', by which it was meant that they would not have a narrow specialism, but would be able to deal with the problems of a range of different groups. It was argued that, in the past, social workers could only deal with a very narrow range of problems, and that when the problems went wider than this, more social workers would have to be brought in. This wasted time and energy and often led to poor co-ordination and duplication of effort. Today, whilst most training is broadly generic, most social work and social care practice has reverted to being more specialised.

The Barclay Report

In 1980, the Barclay Report argued for a radical rethink of social work and in particular pushed for the community approach. Peter Barclay, the author of the report, argued that the bulk of assistance was provided by family, friends and neighbours (nowadays known as the informal sector), rather than the statutory (i.e. government) or voluntary organisations. Therefore, he argued, the task of social workers should be to try to build up this community, so that it could care for its own. In order to do this, the report recommended that small groups of social workers should be attached to a neighbourhood or 'patch' to foster good community relations and to help weld the community together.

This idea of helping a community to help itself has been influential, but it never really became part of mainstream social work in the way that Barclay intended. Perhaps because, as the one dissenter on the Barclay Committee, Robert Pinker, argued, such moves were unrealistic, would erode the professionalism of social workers and possibly bring them into conflict with their employers.

Nevertheless, the desirability of 'networking' with local voluntary groups, the need to work in partnership with families, the importance of recognising the needs of carers and supporting them has been the basis of much social policy in all areas of social care in the last decade.

The Children Act 1989

The Children Act 1989 brought changes in working with children and families, particularly with the need to work more in partnership with parents, to take more account of the child's wishes and to use court action more sparingly but more decisively when needed.

The NHS and Community Care Act 1990

The National Health Service and Community Care Act 1990 had a significant influence on the role of social services departments in that they are now less the providers of services to clients, particularly in the field of community care for adults, and more care planners and commissioners of those services.

The coming into force of both these major pieces of legislation has meant that most local authority social services departments now tend to be organised along the lines of broadly separate Children's Services and Adult Services divisions.

Modernising social services

In 1998 the Labour government produced a major **White Paper** *Modernising Social Services, Promoting Independence, Improving Protection*. Its key messages, many of which have been translated into legislation, are:

- improving standards in the workforce
- improving inspection systems
- improving partnerships with other agencies
- establishing a greater level of consistency and fairness in social care
- improving delivery and efficiency.

Main points ▶ Social work emerged as a response to poverty and unemployment in the nineteenth century.

▶ There were many early initiatives by workers themselves, but also a tradition of philanthropy developed amongst some sections of the middle class.

▶ The first recognisable social work programme developed from the work of the Charity Organisation Society

▶ Gradually a role for social work emerged which was based on helping individuals who were believed to be morally worthy of help.

▶ In the twentieth century, influenced by a range of social and psychological theories, social work developed as a distinct profession.

▶ After the end of the Second World War, a number of services within the Welfare State employed professional social workers.

▶ In 1968, the Seebohm Committee set up the organisational structure of the social services and this structure remains largely the same today.

▶ *Modernising Social Services* will introduce many changes to social work.

The legislative context of social work and social care

The personal social services are those services which are intended to meet the social (as opposed to health) care needs of certain vulnerable groups in society such as children in need, older people, people with mental health problems, people with learning disabilities and people with physical disabilities. The services are provided by local authorities or by voluntary and private organisations of various kinds. However, the organisation which has the majority of statutory responsibilities in this area is the local authority social services department. Set out below are some of the more important pieces of legislation which guide the work of social services departments in terms of *who* they should work with and *what* they should do.

National Assistance Act 1948

This Act was subtitled 'An Act to terminate the existing Poor Law'. It still underpins much of what social services departments do today. For example, under Part Three (Section 21) local authorities are responsible for arranging suitable accommodation for persons who, through age, illness, disability or for any other reason, are in need of care and attention otherwise not available. Section 29 gives local authorities the power to promote the welfare of all people with disabilities, such as people with mental disabilities.

Chronically Sick and Disabled Act 1970

As its name implies this Act covers people who have disabilities. The Act gave local authorities the duty to establish the numbers of disabled people in their area, to assess and determine their needs, compile a register of all such people and publicise relevant services. The local authority is supposed to use the register as a tool to help plan provision and raise awareness of the problems of disability.

Adoption Act 1976

Matters relating to the adoption of children are still covered mainly by the Adoption Act and also by Part 1 of Schedule 10 of the Children Act 1989. Adoption law is complex and there are many areas under review. Legislation in this area is due a complete overhaul but social services departments will continue to have an important role to play. (See Chapter 8 for more about adoption.)

Mental Health Act 1983

This Act sets out the rights of people suffering from a mental disorder. Under this Act local authorities have responsibilities for securing care and treatment for people suffering from a mental health problem.

Disabled Persons (Services, Consultation and Representation) Act 1986

This Act consolidates and builds on the Chronically Sick and Disabled Act 1970 by extending rights to services and information about services to disabled people. Advocates are acknowledged. The needs of carers are to be taken into account.

Children Act 1989

The Children Act 1989 came into force in October 1991. It represented a major overhaul of the existing legislation regarding children. The Act brought about many changes in the practices and organisation of social services departments. Basically, it gave more 'rights' to young people and their wishes. (See Chapter 8 for a fuller discussion.)

NHS and Community Care Act 1990

This Act has probably had the single biggest impact on social services departments since they were created. It is discussed in more detail in Chapter 8, page 215. Even more so than the Children Act, the NHS and Community Care Act 1990 has radically changed the organisation, functions and practices of social services departments. It is just for adult groups; children do not come under its scope and provisions. The Act:

- places great emphasis on people being cared for in the community
- makes a distinction between *providers* of care (hospitals, nursing homes, etc.) and *purchasers* of care (social services departments, GPs, etc.)
- emphasises the importance of the care planning process as the key to services.

Criminal Justice Act 1991

This Act came into force in 1992. It established Youth Courts and affected the way young people up to the age of 17 are dealt with in the criminal justice system. Following the Act's implementation many social services departments have set up specialist Juvenile Justice or Youth Justice teams. The Act placed a greater emphasis on the social services' role in the prevention of offending.

Carers (Recognition and Services) Act 1995

This Act came into effect from 1 April 1996. It requires local authorities to assess the circumstances of a carer providing substantial care on a regular basis to an adult in need or a child with a disability, at that carer's request. The carer has no right to the provision of services, but the local authority must acknowledge the carer's circumstances in any care plan.

Community Care (Direct Payments) Act 1996

From 1997 social services departments could offer people with a disability under the age of 65 cash instead of arranging community care services for them. Following the publication of the White Paper, *Modernising Social Services*, this option has been made available to over 65s as well. To receive the money, social services must still first assess that the person is eligible for services under the NHS and Community Care Act 1990. The person must also be able to show how they will use the money to meet their care needs.

Crime and Disorder Act 1998

Under this Act, social services departments are required to produce annual youth justice plans. They also have to establish special youth offending teams whose membership is made up from the police, social services, the probation service, health and education authorities. Their job is primarily to prevent offending and reoffending by young people.

Care Standards Act 2000

This Act was passed in 2000. It overhauled the way social care and early years services are inspected and regulated. A key development was the creation of a National Care Standards Commission (due to be established in April 2002) whose role is to regulate and inspect the range of care services in England from care homes to fostering and adoption. This Act also established a national Children's Rights Director for children in the care system. Another consequence is the setting up of the General Social Care Council whose main function will be to regulate all social care workers.

Carers and Disabled Children Act 2000

This Act contains measures to help carers of disabled children. For example, they will be entitled to direct payments from local authorities for the services they provide, and an assessment in their own right of their community care needs.

Children (Leaving Care) Act 2000

This introduces new rights for care leavers and duties for the local authority. Greater support for care leavers is also part of the government's bid to combat social exclusion. Traditionally care leavers are a group vulnerable to poverty and social exclusion.

Health and Social Care Act 2001

Under this Act, residents in old people's homes are entitled to free nursing care. Care trusts will integrate the commissioning of health and social services provision – particularly for older people – in a single organisation. Some argue that this Act could signal the end of separate adult social services departments.

The role of social services departments today

Structure of a typical social services department

Social work tasks

Social services departments have to have a strategic (overall, planning) view of all the sources of care available in their area. Direct provision of care by the local authorities is only be one of a number of forms of provision purchased from a mixed economy of care (use of statutory, independent and informal care). In fact the most important role of the social services is no longer the provision of care, as in the past, but:

> **Definition**
>
> **Service providers** – term used to mean any/all health and social care services

- assessment of clients' needs
- planning care provision
- stimulating service provision where it is missing
- assessing **service providers**' ability to deliver services

- contracting with service providers
- monitoring and evaluating services against contract
- registration and inspection of services.

Who uses the services of social work departments?

Social services departments have a wide range of tasks including care and support for:

- older people
- physically disabled people
- people with mental disorders
- people with drug and alcohol problems
- people with learning disabilities
- families
- children in need of protection
- children in care homes, fostering and adoption
- young offenders.

What do social work departments do

Access to social care

Gaining access to social services usually requires some form of *referral* being made. This will involve either writing, telephoning or calling in a person to bring a situation of need or concern to their attention. In the latter two cases this will usually go through the duty social worker.

There are three types of referral:

- *self-referral*, when the person themselves makes the contact. In order to self-refer the person must know who to contact, be aware of what's available and be able articulate (explain) their own needs. It must not therefore be taken for granted that someone in need of a service will be able or willing to refer himself or herself for it
- *referral by a professional*, when, for example, a GP, district nurse or health visitor makes contact on behalf of one of their patients
- *referral by a member of the family or community* (sometimes called a *third-party referral*), when, for example, a son is concerned about his frail, ageing parents' ability to manage on their own.

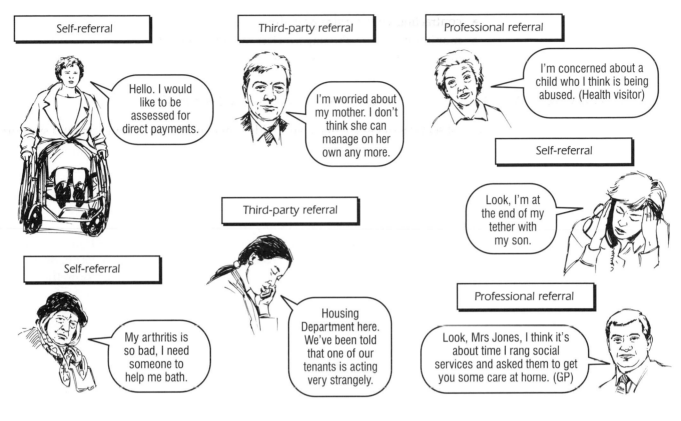

Types of referral

Main points ▶ There have been a wide range of Acts passed to regulate social work and to define its role.

▶ The first Act which provided the basis for modern social work was the National Assistance Act of 1948.

▶ Since then, there has been legislation to cover children, crime, disabled people, carers, adoption, mental health and a range of other groups.

▶ Today, social services departments have a range of tasks which largely consist of assessing people's needs, planning for the delivery of appropriate services and then monitoring the quality of those services.

▶ People come into contact with social services departments through a process of referral.

▶ Social work departments deal with a wide range of people – from children to older people, young offenders, people with drug problems and even entire families.

The social work task: theories of social work

Social workers, as we have seen have a number of tasks to undertake, often in difficult circumstances. Social workers almost always have to sort out problems which most people find difficult to handle.

It is important, however, to be aware that not only are there several different views about *how* these activities should be carried out, but also *what* exactly is being carried out. Before looking at some of these different views, we must first acknowledge that when we talk about 'social care' and 'social work' these two terms are not exactly interchangeable. It is actually quite difficult to make clear distinctions between the two terms. However, *social care* is the broad term used to cover the range of activities involved in looking after people. *Social work* is often considered to refer to the more professionally trained, theory-informed practices which qualified social workers carry out.

Question

'... there is no such thing as the social work task; it is not even certain that there is any such activity as social work.'

Source: Martin Davies, *The Essential Social Work*er (Heinemann, 1981)

What does the author mean by this statement, do you think?

Whether there is something identifiably unique called social work as an activity is obviously open to argument. Notwithstanding this point though, it is important to understand that there is no one correct way of going about the process of social work. There is disagreement amongst social workers as to exactly how they can best carry out their tasks. Theories of psychology, sociology and even politics have been adopted and adapted to provide often conflicting guidelines on how social workers should undertake their role. There are several quite different theoretical approaches to how social work should be practised.

The psychodynamic approach

This approach broadly stems from the psychoanalytic ideas develop by Sigmund Freud in the early twentieth century. It was an approach to social work that was particularly influential in the 1950s and 1960s. It places emphasis on the working of a person's unconscious mind and how the mind, often unconsciously, influences behaviour.

An important idea in this approach to helping people is that our personalities and behaviour can be understood by analysing our early childhood development and upbringing. A social worker working within the psychodynamic tradition would be keen to help their client develop insights by getting them in touch with their deeper feelings and talking about them. Because of this it is important for social workers using the psychodynamic approach to establish a strong relationship with their clients. They would encourage their client to 'ventilate' (open up about) their feelings such as anger or anxiety. A social worker would use this 'therapeutic relationship' to help the client gain insight into their situation and to move them on from whatever is 'blocking' them from dealing with their problems. If social workers experience resistance from their clients (which is not uncommon) Freud's ideas about 'defence mechanisms' such denial, projection or regression enable the social worker and their client to better understand what is going on and why.

This is an approach that aims to examine beneath the surface of problems, expose inner conflicts and emotional blocks and basically help the client understand how past experiences and relationships can affect subsequent behaviour and current relationships.

This approach is not as influential as it once was. However, many of the ideas and terms have passed into everyday usage within social work. The psychodynamic approach is considered to be strong on talking and feelings but less useful in practical ways such as changing behaviour. It is also criticised for 'pathologising' clients (treating them as sick individuals) rather than looking at social or environmental factors as being the main causes in people's distress. It is also less favoured as an approach because has also been a reaction in recent years away from the idea that 'social worker always knows best'.

Crisis intervention and task-centred models

Crisis intervention and task-centred models of social work focus on the individual rather than wider society. They have this common with the psychodynamic approach. However, unlike the psychodynamic approach, the task-centred approach in particular does not focus on a person's feelings and the unconscious motivations for behaviour. Therefore gaining insight is not that important as long as the person moves on. There is instead an emphasis on changing behaviour often through practical tasks. These approaches use contracts or 'specified agreements' between the worker and the person as the focus of the work. There is no one dominant theory. Usually the person who requires help has to be prepared to identify areas for change and work with the social worker to achieve centre targets within an agreed timescale.

Although not the answer to all problems, these approaches have been popular over many years.

Cognitive-behavioural theories

This approach has several variants but basically it developed from behaviour therapy and has added the key idea that changing the way people actually think can not only help change their mood but also their behaviour. The approach is based on cognitive and learning theories from psychology. The individual rather than society or other wider factors are the focus for change. Techniques are used to enable someone to question the 'automatic thoughts' they have about themselves or their situation, change their mental outlook and then learn more suitable forms of behaviour. So, for example, someone who is depressed might have a very poor self-concept and always see the negative side of situations. The more things don't work out for them the more they will blame themselves and think, irrationally, that there is something about them personally which means the worst will always happen.

Definition

Cognitive – relating to the way we think and perceive the world

---

A **cognitive**-behavioural approach seeks to challenge this negative and fatalistic appraisal, demonstrating, for example, that there are things they can do which are successful. By carefully setting up situations that challenge someone's irrational beliefs, a more balanced view of the world together with a more positive set of core beliefs can follow. The approach has been criticised for being rather too controlled, specialist and technical for many social workers to carry out properly.

Questions have also been raised as to who social workers are to judge which thoughts and behaviour are maladaptive (unsuitable). Could it be them simply wanting their outlook to prevail? That said, this is an approach, which, if carried out well, has shown itself to be very effective not only for depression but also stress management, anger management, anxiety and several childhood disorders.

Empowerment/Advocacy

The concept of 'empowerment' has become deeply ingrained in thinking about social work since the 1980s. Partly, it is based on the recognition that 'clients' of social services usually start off with little control over their lives and this is reinforced and made worse by social workers 'solving' their problems for them – leaving them even more dependant. Like the Marxist/radical approaches, this approach to social work also sees social oppression behind individual problems. The social worker's role is to enable people to overcome obstructions caused by organisations or by society at large and take control over their own lives. The approach draws on both sociological and social psychological explanations of oppression.

There are different ideas of what actually empowerment is. To some it is allowing people to be involved in their own care planning, to others it means people taking complete control over whether and how they are cared for. In broad terms, people can become empowered by having a 'voice' in what happens to them, by exercising 'rights' to services or by having the power to 'exit' one form of care and choose an alternative. Generally speaking, to empower someone is to work towards them becoming fully independent and able to take control over their own lives despite the restrictions or obstacles they may face. The idea of maximising the power of service users creates problems for social work because it has traditionally been social workers holding the power, making decisions and so on. Some have argued that power can't be given to people, they have to take it, so that the idea of 'empowering' someone is a contradiction in terms.

> **Definition**
>
> **Advocacy** – speaking on someone's behalf so that their views are heard and their point of view is represented

Advocacy is not the same as empowerment but it shares with it the aim of allowing those without a voice to have their rightful say about what happens to them. So, for example, historically adults with learning disabilities have often been treated as children – usually with the best of intentions – as workers make decisions about how their lives should run. Advocacy recognises that while speech or communication in general might be difficult with this group of people, every effort must be made to seek their views and to have their wishes carried out. This can often involve the use of dedicated and independent volunteers acting on the person's behalf.

Both views are about shifting the traditional power balance away from the social worker and towards the person needing help.

Anti-discriminatory and anti-oppressive perspectives

Anti-discriminatory and anti-oppressive perspectives are derived from several theoretical positions. Feminist thinking in its many forms has been very influential, as have theories on race and sociological analyses of how power is exercised in society by certain groups at the expense of others. This approach is in the tradition of radical thought that questions the predominantly able-bodied, middle-class, male and heterosexual *status quo* that exists in society. It criticises a social system wherein certain groups of people suffer inequality, injustice and exclusion and inevitable the distress that these 'oppressions' cause.

Groups such as disabled people, ethnic groups, gays and lesbians as well as women and the poor are seen as those likely to be victims of oppression and discrimination. This approach recognises that membership of more than one 'minority' group can increase the oppression experienced. So, for example, to be a black disabled person places you in a doubly disadvantaged position in our society.

Which approach?

Yes, the childcare is not brilliant. I told Geraldine not to make it worse by blaming herself though. Put anyone in that grotty high rise flat on Income Support and they would struggle as well. We'll write to the council to get her rehoused. I've given Geraldine the name of her local councillor to put pressure on there as well.

Darren has got things completely out of perspective. I have asked him to complete a 'thought-catching' diary. Every time he starts to feel anxious I have told him to write down exactly what's going through his mind. Then we can work on looking how realistic his thoughts are.

This is the third time that Jim has got angry and hit Jason for not eating his food. I need to draw up an agreement with him on how we're going to break this problem down and deal with it step-by-step so that Jim can see the pattern emerging and change his behaviour. I'll start by doing a problem specification exercise with Jim.

Kevin has decided he would like to opt for Direct Payments. I am going to put him in touch with the Rowan Foundation. They'll give him the necessary support to make sure it works.

The problem is that Veronica failed to bond with her mother when she was younger. She has a very poor self-image. This comes out in aggression. I need to do therapeutic work to build up her ego strength.

I am not happy with Mr Khan's placement at the Cherry Trees Day Centre. The staff are quite friendly but they make absolutely no provision for his cultural needs. One of the workers also referred to Mr Khan as an immigrant – that is an offensive term. I am going to speak to the manager and make sure that the centre changes its ways.

Match each one of the above with one or more of the theoretical perspectives used by social workers (described on pages 188–93).

Definition

Anti-discriminatory practice (ADP) – describes how workers take account of structural disadvantage and seek to reduce individual and institutional discrimination particularly on grounds of race, gender, disability, social class and sexual orientation

Anti-discriminatory perspectives acknowledge that despite the good intentions and helpful motivations of social workers, social services are powerful institutions of the State dominated by able-bodied, heterosexual, white, male values and as such can reinforce the powerlessness of the users of their services. Therefore social workers need to be trained to see the world from the position of other groups' perspectives. They need to avoid using language that oppresses, discriminates or excludes others and they must make every attempt to empower service users and promote their dignity, self-respect and independence. They must also work transparently and in partnership with their clients. All current training courses within social care are committed to **anti-discriminatory practice (ADP)**.

Radical social work

This approach stresses that most of the social problems that bring people to the attention of social services are the result of an unjust political and social system. Often, but not always, the theoretical basis for this approach comes from socialist (predominantly Marxist) views. Social workers who adopt this approach point out that poverty, exclusion and society inequality are the main causes of social problems such as child abuse, mental illness or drug abuse. They argue that if these structural problems were eliminated then many of the social problems of society would no longer exist. Here the role of the social worker is to help challenge the unfairness of society, often through raising their clients' political consciousness, and by encouraging them to participate in collective action, for example by forming a pressure group (see page 13). Radical social workers are enthusiastic supporters of community action and welfare rights approaches. Radical social work assumes that people have the capability to generate their own solutions to their problems. Social workers setting themselves up as experts with 'special knowledge' actually 'disable' people rather than enable them.

Martin Davies, though, questions whether social workers who are employed by the State can 'have their cake and eat it', that is denounce and undermine their own employer while being paid by them to carry out a certain set of responsibilities.

In contrast to the psychodynamic approach very little, if any, emphasis is given to allowing an individual to talk about their emotions. The emphasis is much more on encouraging collective action to change society.

Radical social work of this kind enjoyed its greatest level of support in the 1960s and 1970s. Since then it has been criticised for over-concentrating on social class divisions and failing to take into account other forms of oppression, for example that experienced by black people or by gays and lesbians. The chief criticism has tended to be that as an approach it is not very helpful in a practical way for people who are having emotional problems, family crises or are not having their personal needs met for whatever reason.

Main points

▶ There is considerable debate over how it is best to go about the task of social work.

▶ This debate is reflected in the range of theories which suggest how best to undertake social work.

▶ Psychodynamic approaches stress working to help the client to come to terms with personal problems by opening out and exploring their feelings.

▶ Crisis intervention and task-centred models emphasise changing the behaviour of the client so that they can solve their problems.

▶ Cognitive-behavioural theories are psychological in character and try to get the person to explore their attitudes and find out what causes their problems.

▶ Empowerment/Advocacy argues that the role of the social worker is to help the person to stand up for their own rights.

▶ Anti-discriminatory perspectives. Many groups believe that they are treated unfairly by society and that this unfair treatment is the cause of their problems. The role of social work is to promote their dignity and self-respect.

▶ Radical social work argues that the cause of the problems faced by most people is actually society and so the role of social work is to confront society, changing it, rather than the client.

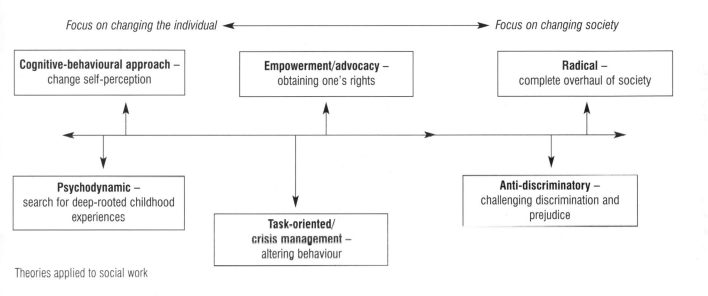

Theories applied to social work

Case study

Violet Harrison (57) and Michael Harrison (59) came to the UK from Jamaica in 1962. They have three children: Errol, 29; Jasmine, 26; and Llewellen, 24. Llewellen has moved out, but Errol and Jasmine are currently living with their parents. This is because Errol is a diagnosed schizophrenic. He has found it practically impossible to get any form of employment or cope on his own. He has had periods in hospitals and has also been arrested several times by the police over the years on charges of threatening behaviour and breach of the peace. Currently, the family are made very tense by Errol's severely withdrawn and agitated behaviour.

Jasmine has a 5-year-old daughter Serena. She is struggling in school. She appears to have learning problems and exhibits emotional and behavioural difficulties at times. Serena's father only has intermittent contact. When he shows up, there is generally conflict and abuse. Violet has had a big part in looking after Serena and as Jasmine has become quite tearful and depressed more recently, Violet is questioning her daughter's ability to cope.

The situation in the home has been made worse recently because Michael has lost his job as gas fitter. He is unlikely to get another job. This has made him anxious and irritable. Jasmine poured all her troubles out when invited into the school by a teacher. The teacher suggested that a referral be made to Social Services to help the family with their problems.

Take each theory outlined on pages 188–93 in turn.

a) Identify how the problems the family faces would be analysed.

b) Suggest how a social worker working within that approach might suggest ways of helping.

Finances and the social services

Where the money comes from

Each year approximately £10 billion is spent funding personal social services.

The beneficiaries of social service spending

Local authority personal social services gross expenditure by client group, England, 1996–7

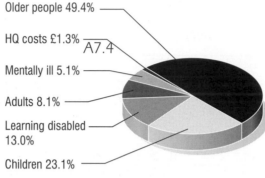

Older people 49.4%

HQ costs £1.3% A7.4

Mentally ill 5.1%

Adults 8.1%

Learning disabled 13.0%

Children 23.1%

Total: £9.3 billion

Source: Department of Health, *The Government's Expenditure Plans 1999-2000*

1 Which group of people receive the largest amount of government spending on social care?

2 Give two reasons why this should be so.

Local authority social services departments are funded in three main ways:

- *Grants from central government*: The majority of local authority funds come from the government. The exact amount is based on the Standard Spending Assessment, which is how much the government thinks the local authority ought to spend.
- *Council tax and local business rates:* Roughly speaking, revenue from the council tax makes up about a third of local authority funding.
- *Revenue from charging for services:* Legislation permits social services departments to charge for domiciliary (home-based), day and residential (live-in) services. Each local authority social services committee decides which services it will charge for and how much the charges will be.

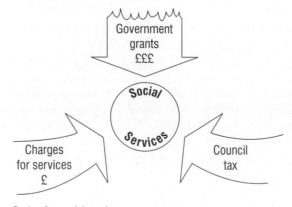

Government grants £££

Social Services

Charges for services £

Council tax

Paying for social services

Paying for social services

Since the 1990s, there has been a gradual but widespread introduction of charges for various welfare activities. Charging has become a topical issue and closely relates to the debate on long-term care for older people.

Why charge for social services?

There is more to this question than you might think, as charging for health and social services had several purposes other than simply raising revenue. The charges that are made are often less than the sum needed to cover the full cost of the service – in other words, they are subsidised. So why make a charge that does not relate to the full or economic cost of what's being provided?

The reasons suggested are:

- *Cost reduction*: It reduces costs to the general taxpayer by raising some revenue from users. It also signals to the general taxpayer that their contributions are not simply being given away. People may be less reluctant to pay taxes.

- *Reduced demand*: If something is completely free, there is often a desire to demand without realising the cost implications. Charging makes people think whether they really want the service.

- *Avoids cuts in services*: Charging can make it possible for certain services to be maintained even if government funding is cut back.

- *Encouraging quality:* When a service is free, it difficult for users of the services to express dissatisfaction – after all 'they're getting it for free'. Charges makes service users think and act more like customers who want value for their money.

- *Symbolism*: People shouldn't be made to feel that they are accepting charity. This is **stigmatising**. Therefore, even a small or token charge helps maintain people's self-respect. The service provider has a different relationship with the service user rather than if it were just giving services for free. The service user feels they have more rights.

Definition

Stigmatising – the process whereby someone feels ashamed of using a service

---

To charge or not to charge?

The principle of charging for domiciliary, day and residential social care has been around since the Welfare State was first established. However, only since the 1980s onwards has it become such a controversial issue.

More recently the Royal Commission on Long-Term Care and several reports from the Audit Commission have highlighted the inconsistencies and variations in charging around the UK. Historically, local authorities have had the freedom to make their own policy on charges. Domiciliary and day care has seen the greatest differences. Whilst some local authorities provide all non-residential care for nothing, others have increased charges to the point where the service user is paying close to the full cost. Between these extremes the Audit Commission has pointed to a 'bewildering array' of methods used by councils to determine how much service users should pay. Pressure groups like Age Concern and Help the Aged together with the Coalition on Charging have campaigned against the unfairness of charging people for care particularly when charges vary so much from one authority to another.

Activity

This is a list of services commonly provided by social services or purchased by them from other agencies:

- home care
- day care for older people
- a meals delivery service
- respite care in a residential home
- foster care
- day care for adults with learning disabilities
- transport to day centres.

1 Contact your local social services department and find out what the charges are for each of the services listed above. Find out whether it is for the full cost of the service or whether social services subsidise the cost to the user.

2 Less money coming from central government could well require the social services to double the existing charges for home care and meals delivery service. What effect would this have on:
   a) the users?
   b) their carers?
   c) other services?

RESPITE CARE

Respite Care for adults and older people covers:

- short term temporary residential care
- respite care provided in a person's own home
- respite care provided in the home of a carer (e.g. the Adult Link and Family Break schemes).

Respite Care Charges 2001/2002

If you do not wish to provide information about your capital or benefits, you will pay £201.20 per week.

If you have capital with a value in excess of £18,500 and:

	YOU PAY:
• you receive High Rate **Attendance Allowance** (£55.30) or High Rate **Disability Living Allowance Care Component** (£55.30)	£201.20 per week.
• you receive Low Rate **Attendance Allowance** (£37.00) or Middle Rate **Disability Living Allowance Care Component** (£37.00)	£190.90 per week.
• you do not receive **Attendance Allowance** nor **Disability Allowance Care Component**.	£170.30 per week.

If you have capital with a value less than £18,500 and:

	YOU PAY:
• you receive High Rate **Attendance Allowance** (£55.30) or High Rate **Disability Living Allowance Care Component** (£55.30)	£95.80 per week plus extra income support (see below).
• you receive Low Rate **Attendance Allowance** (£37.00) or Middle Rate **Disability Living Allowance Care Component** (£37.00)	£85.50 per week plus extra income support (see below).
• you do not receive **Attendance Allowance** nor **Disability Living Allowance Care Component**.	£64.90 per week plus extra income support (see below).

Extra Income Support (minimum income guarantee)

Sometimes you can get extra income from the Benefits Agency, whilst you are in respite care. In this case you would pay the charge shown above plus any extra money you are entitled to claim. Your Care Coordinator or Financial Assessment Officer will help you claim this extra money.

Please Note Even if you choose not to claim this income support (minimum income guarantee) you will be charged as if you had claimed.

An example of one social services department's charges for respite care

The Royal Commission on Long-Term Care concluded that 'personal care' should be free but that it would be reasonable to charge for meals, lunch clubs and domestic help.

The government did not fully accept this point and instead has accepted that whilst 'nursing care' should be free (because this essentially is a health service), charges should remain for personal care. It has pledged to set up a national system of charging. How this will work in reality when social care is still basically delivered by local authorities remains to be seen.

Case study

Social services committee: cuts in the budget

In the financial year 2000/01 Careshire Social Services need to find £1,000,000 worth of cuts. This is because the money they receive from central government has been limited and they are not in a position to raise Council Tax levels sufficiently to make up the shortfall.

The decisions before the committee are where to cut back services and whether to impose or increase charges. The committee has to ensure that the department's statutory commitments are met. A research team has raised the following possibilities:

1 Do not fill five vacant social worker posts across the county. Saving £110,000.

2 Close down the Elms Old People's Home. Move residents to other private and voluntary homes. Saving £250,000. Sell building and site for £250,000.

3 Add £1 per hour to home help charge for all users. Total estimated extra revenue £160,000.

4 Cut grants to the Taurus Project, a drop-in centre for people with mental illness. This will mean the centre can no longer open five days a week (9.00 a.m. to 5.00 p.m.), but only three days (10.00 a.m. to 3.00 p.m.). Saving £80,000.

5 Scale down operations at the Hartsfield Family Centre which provides assessment and help for parents who are having problems coping. The centre would only be able to take four families at a time instead of seven. Saving £100,000.

6 Close down the social services-run Padley Day Nursery for 'at risk' children. Total

saving £150,000. Paying for children to go to other less specialised nurseries would cost £60,000. Net saving £120,000.

7 Discontinue the respite care bed at the Croft Old People's Home. Saving £60,000.

8 Increase the cost of respite care for old people from £80 per week to £100 per week. Estimated increase in revenue £50,000.

9 Ensure that all users (older people and adults with learning difficulties) of social services transport pay an extra £1.25 per day. Total extra revenue £75,000.

10 a) Add 60p to all meals delivery charges. Total revenue £70,000.
   b) Add £1.80 to all meals delivery charges. Total revenue £210,000.

11 Cut three staff at Merryfield Social Education Centre for adults with learning disabilities. This means they have to reduce intake from 60 to 34 a day. Saving £55,000.

12 Cut back on training. Reduce numbers of trainers from six to three. Saving £80,000. This will mean an eight month longer wait for new staff to receive training on child protection, care planning, etc.

13 Raise eligibility criteria for home care services so that in future only personal care tasks are carried out and that all people definitely need to be high-risk groups to be eligible for services. Saving £150,000.

14 Change policy in occupational therapy department. No small aids or to be loaned. Instead people encouraged to buy their own equipment privately. Saving £100,000

1 Decide how you could make the £1,000,000 worth of cuts.

2 Explain the rationale behind your decisions and explain any likely consequences due to the cuts you have made.

Main points ▶ Around £10 billion a year is spent by the personal social services.
▶ This comes from central government and local taxation as well as charges to the people receiving some of the services.
▶ There is some disagreement over whether people should pay for social services or not.
▶ Those who support paying point out that it stops people wasting services because there is a fee. It also reduces demand slightly and it can help raise the standards. Most importantly it does not seem as if it is charity.
▶ However, many people may not be able to afford to pay and they pay different amounts for services in different areas.
▶ Despite the Royal Commission on Long-Term Care suggesting that personal care should be free, the government has not accepted this in England and Wales. It is free in Scotland.

Conclusion

In this chapter we have explored the development and nature of social care and social work in the UK. We have seen that it developed out of a desire by middle-class groups to help poorer and less fortunate groups in society, who were perceived as not being able to help themselves. A wide range of Acts have been passed which have clarified the role of social workers and social services departments so that the tasks set down for social workers are clear. However, how to go about this, and the long-term aim of social care and social work is clearly a matter of dispute – the theories which form the core of the chapter show what a diverse range of approaches exist.

Finally, we have looked at issues of funding and payments for social services – would we be better off just giving disadvantaged groups more money and letting them get on with buying their own services, rather than having social workers organise things for them?

7 CHAPTER SUMMARY

1   Social work emerged as a response to poverty and unemployment in the nineteenth century.

2   There were many early initiatives by workers themselves, but also a tradition of philanthropy developed amongst some sections of the middle class.

3   The first recognisable social work programme developed from the work of the Charity Organisation Society

4   Gradually a role for social work emerged which was based on helping individuals who were believed to be morally worthy of help.

5   In the twentieth century, influenced by a range of social and psychological theories, social work developed as a distinct profession.

6   After the end of the Second World War, a number of services within the Welfare State employed professional social workers.

7   In 1968, the Seebohm Committee set up the organisational structure of the social services and this structure remains largely the same today.

8   There have been a wide range of Acts passed to regulate social work and to define its role.

9   The first Act which provided the basis for modern social work was the National Assistance Act of 1948.

10 Since then, there has been legislation to cover children, crime, disabled people, carers, adoption, mental health and a range of other groups.

11 Today, social services departments have a range of tasks which largely consist of assessing people's needs, planning for the delivery of appropriate services and then monitoring the quality of those services.

12 People come into contact with social services departments through a process of referral.

13 Social work departments deal with a wide range of people – from children to older people, young offenders, people with drug problems and even entire families.

14 There is considerable debate over how it is best to go about the task of social work.

15 This debate is reflected in the range of theories which suggest how best to undertake social work.

16 Psychodynamic approaches stress working to help the client to come to terms with personal problems by opening out and exploring their feelings.

17 Crisis intervention and task-centred models emphasise changing the behaviour of the client so that they can solve their problems.

18 Cognitive-behavioural theories are psychological in character and try to get the person to explore their attitudes and find out what causes their problems.

19 Empowerment/Advocacy argues that the role of the social worker is to help the person to stand up for their own rights.

20 Anti-discriminatory perspectives. Many groups believe that they are treated unfairly by society and that this unfair treatment is the cause of their problems. The role of social work is to promote their dignity and self-respect.

21 Radical social work argues that the cause of the problems faced by most people is actually society and so the role of social work is to confront society, changing it, rather than the client.

22 Around £10 billion a year is spent by the personal social services.

23 This comes from central government and local taxation as well as charges to the people receiving some of the services.

24 There is some disagreement over whether people should pay for social services or not.

25 Those who support paying point out that it stops people wasting services because there is a fee. It also reduces demand slightly and it can help raise the standards. Most importantly it does not seem as if it is charity.

26 However, many people may not be able to afford to pay and they pay different amounts for services in different areas.

27 Despite the Royal Commission on Long-Term Care suggesting that personal care should be free, the government has not accepted this in England and Wales. It is free in Scotland.

Useful websites

www.nisw.org.uk: National Institute for Social Work

www.ccetsw.org.uk: Central Council for Education and Training in Social Work

www.doh.gov.uk: the Department of Health

www.community-care.co.uk: *Community Care* magazine

www.jrf.org.uk: the Joseph Rowntree Foundation

Chapter 8

INSIDE SOCIAL WORK: THE CONTEXT AND PROVISION OF CARE TO ADULTS AND CHILDREN

Chapter contents

Part 1: Children's services

- **Who works in children's services?**

  We set out the principal workers and professionals involved in social work with children. This section also aims to create an understanding of exactly how key professionals spend their day and the kinds of issues they have to contend with.

  Towards the end of the twentieth century children's homes gained a very bad reputation in some quarters. This was linked to stories of abuse and neglect. Successive governments have ordered enquiries and reports to be made. In this section we discuss two of the main reports to be published in recent years.

- **Where does social work with children take place?**

  There are a range of settings where social work with children takes place: the child's own home, schools, residential homes, and so on. This section describes these settings in more detail.

- **Child protection**

  Child protection is one of the most important areas of work within the personal social services for children. In this section we put child protection in its historical, social and legal context. The systems used by local authorities together with the role of professionals are explained in detail.

- **Substitute care: fostering and adoption**

  Another important task of social workers working with children is to arrange substitute care for those who need it. We set out the variety of ways that substitute care might be used and explain the difference between fostering and adoption. We also discuss some of the issues raised in the complex area of work.

- **Social work with children with disabilities**

  It is often overlooked that social services departments have a statutory obligation to children with disabilities. This section goes into more detail and outlines some of the issues that can emerge when caring for disabled children.

- **Recent government initiatives**

  This part of the chapter concludes by looking at what the government is proposing to do at the start of the twenty-first century.

Part 2: Adult services

- **Adult services: organisation, clients, staffing and settings**

  We note the way that social services for adults are organised within local authorities, the huge range of services which these organisations must provide, and the diversity and numbers of their client groups.

- **Community care**

  This is overwhelmingly the largest sector of social work operations today. Community care is rather difficult to grasp as it has many different forms, but it has become accepted as the best way to deliver care to the majority of people. We look at the legislation which has brought this about, the factors that persuaded the government that community care was the best, and the principles underlying community care.

- **The role of the professionals: care management**

  This part of the chapter takes a detailed look at the tasks of social workers, and the way in which they go about the process of care planning and assessment. We examine the problems they face, and the way that there is increasingly a move by the client groups to demand that rather than be assessed and provided with services, social workers should restrict themselves to an enabling role, providing resources and letting the clients chose what services they want.

- ### Residential care
  Although residential care has declined, it remains a very important part of social care provision. We examine the advantages and disadvantages of residential care and the changes the government has introduced to raise standards.

- ### Carers
  Most care is provided informally by members of families. Until recently, the carers have received limited help from the social services. The focus has always been on the ill or disabled person. From the early 1990s this has changed, and increasing attention has been paid to the rights and financial problems of carers.

Introduction

This chapter explores in some detail how social workers go about their tasks, and the policy environment in which it takes place. Social work is generally split between adult teams and children teams, so to reflect this, the chapter is divided into two parts and we explore them separately.

Of course, many of the issues which social workers face are relevant to both types of teams, and where this is the case these shared concerns will be examined only once. We will look at exactly what social workers do, how their departments are organised and what their clients expect of them.

But not only does social work take place with different client groups, it also takes place in different settings – in residential accommodation and in the community. Most qualified social workers operate in the community, so you will find this examined in rather more detail. However, much social care is provided in residential homes, and social workers must have full knowledge of what goes on there too.

The final group of people whose position we look at, is that of the unsung heroes of care – the informal and unpaid carers who do the overwhelming bulk of caring work. We look at their position and how policy changes have slowly come around to recognising their importance.

Part 1: Children's services

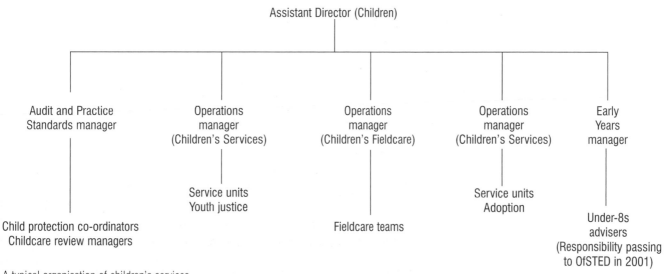

A typical organisation of children's services

Who works in children's services?

Types of social worker

There are two main types of social worker: field social workers and residential social workers.

Field social workers

These are social workers who work in teams and who are generally based in social work offices in the community. The approach to their work is often described as multi-disciplinary. This involves liaison and collaboration with other agencies and professionals, such as GPs and health visitors, to provide a service to protect vulnerable children and promote the child's welfare. Their work often involves visiting individuals or families in their homes. Some situations require work with the whole family; others can involve direct work with the children concerned. Where children are being looked after or accommodated by the social services, the social worker will also work with the substitute carers.

The field team manager usually decides whether and how to allocate cases to the various workers in his or her team. Not all referrals can be dealt with immediately – they are prioritised in terms of seriousness. A referral about child abuse would automatically be dealt with as a matter of urgency; other less urgent cases might have to wait for a longer period before someone takes them up.

The qualification route for field social work is through the Diploma in Social Work. Field social workers can specialise in different areas of childcare work, for example, child protection, fostering, adoption, family therapy or youth justice. Most but not all social workers work for local authority social services. However, there are many voluntary agencies such as NSPCC, the Family Welfare Association and independent adoption agencies that also employ qualified social workers.

A day in the life of Baldish Sahota, social worker in a fieldcare team

9.00 a.m. Arrive in the office. Check messages and e-mails. Many are from other professionals such as health visitors, from clients or foster carers.

9.30 a.m. Attend a Core Group Meeting on Jason Wilcox. These meetings take place roughly every six weeks. They are for children whose names are on the Child Protection Register (see page 206). The group consists of the key people involved with Jason. In this case it is his parents, GP and headteacher. The purpose of the group is to review how things are going and identify work to be done. Baldish is encouraged by the progress being made.

11.00 a.m. Following the meeting Baldish must write up the minutes. But first there are more messages! One needs to be responded to urgently – it is from a school concerned that one of Baldish's cases, Lisa aged 7, has become very tearful again. Baldish contacts the school and makes a few other phone calls. Her manager has e-mailed her to rearrange tomorrow's supervision session – she can't make it because she has to go to court.

12.30 a.m. Baldish makes a home visit to Kim, a young single parent with a toddler. Baldish is trying to arrange community childminding for Kim's daughter firstly to give Kim a break but also to give her the opportunity to attend the Drugs Dependency Unit (DDU) which is part of the agreement Baldish has with Kim. Kim is a bit wary at first but after a while they are able to make some plans.

2.00 p.m. Baldish is back in the office. She has to record the visit and arrange the childminding. Baldish will also need to fax a referral to the DDU. There are more messages to take, letters to write and phone calls to make on her other cases.

4.15 p.m.   This is Baldish's last visit of the day. It is a statutory visit to Kevin. Kevin is a 12-year-old 'looked after' child who is in long-term foster care. By law a child like Kevin would need to be visited at least every six weeks during their first year in the placement. Baldish's job is to see how things are going and to check out with Kevin whether there are any issues he wants to talk about.

5.50 p.m.   The visit is ended and Baldish will make her way home pleased that she has no evening calls to make that night. Tomorrow she will need to write up the statutory visit and place this on the file.

Residential social workers

These traditionally have had a much lower profile than field social workers and have been less likely to be qualified. Although the work of residential social workers requires a high level of skill and ability, this branch of social work has tended to have had lower status than field work. However, in recent years, particularly in response to concerns that have emerged, official reports have recommended raising the profile of residential childcare work through better pay and training. The work in residential care has a greater emphasis on working directly with clients, attending to personal care, the forming of close relationships and, especially with older children, helping to develop life skills.

These days many residential units offer 'outreach' work. That is to say, they will continue to work with their clients outside the residential home either when they are back home or with foster parents as part of a care plan.

Residential social workers can work for social services or one of the many providers of residential care in the independent sector.

Reports on residential social work

The Utting Report

In November 1997, the Utting Report was published. This reviewed the provision of residential care for young people. The review was extremely critical of care in the past, saying that those young people who had suffered abuse in care had generally not been believed when they complained of sexual or physical abuse in care and had even been sent back to the institution where the abuse was happening.

The report's main proposals included the following points: homes taking fewer than four children had to be formally regulated, and that in general large residential institutions should be provided so that they could offer a full range of services. The Health Secretary should have powers to investigate boarding schools. However, the report also covered fostering and suggested that there were weaknesses in the current system as well, such that physical and sexual abuse could take place.

The Waterhouse Report

The Waterhouse Report was published in 2000. Sir Ronald Waterhouse was asked to lead an investigation into the widespread physical, emotional and sexual abuse that took place in North Wales children's homes over many years. Disappointingly it showed that the messages from Utting had not been fully heeded. Waterhouse identified a lack of skilled staff and good professional leadership, lack of good quality placements, misuse of power and lack of respect for children. Following Waterhouse there will be a closer scrutiny of staff when it comes to recruitment, improved training and a new Director of Children's Rights who will be an officer of the National Care Standards Commission.

Where does social work with children take place?

Family home

A lot of social work takes place in the family home. It is the philosophy of working with children and families that, wherever possible, children are best looked after in their own families. Social workers use a range of techniques such as working with the whole family or directly with children to ensure that whatever is causing the problem is either resolved or at least managed better.

Substitute homes

Field social workers have a legal duty to visit children while they are in foster homes. This could be to monitor the placement, work directly with the children, to supervise contact with natural parents, or to respond to any issues that crop up.

Schools

Sometimes social workers see children and interview them or work with them at their school. For children in care, residential social workers can often liaise very closely with schools. However, a field social worker cannot usually visit a school and see a child without first gaining the parent's consent. Exceptions can be made when there are important child protection considerations.

Children's homes

Over recent years there has been a deliberate policy to reduce the number of children placed in children's homes (sometimes known as community homes). Generally if a child goes into residential care it is as a 'last resort'. However, many would argue that it would be wrong to stereotype residential care in such a negative way and that it can provide a valuable resource for children at key times. Nevertheless, wherever possible, children are looked after by foster carers, as a family is considered to be a more desirable environment for children to grow up in. It is sometimes the case that children in residential homes display forms of behaviour which are very possibly too difficult for foster carers to cope with. Working in children's homes therefore can involve working with seriously emotionally and behaviourally disturbed children, children, for example, who have been through several different foster placements. Research has shown that children in residential units are more likely to show, amongst other things:

- chaotic behaviour and poor impulse control, including being prone to harming others or destroying property
- a sense of being lost, of having no one and having no future.

Residential social workers must walk a very narrow line between providing warm and reassuring relationships for the children, and yet dealing firmly with those in their charge. They need to have a very good understanding of what children need to develop properly and skills to interpret children's behaviour.

Day settings

The range of day care opportunities has developed considerably. Different authorities have been quite innovative in this form of social care. As a result more opportunities are opening up for skilled care workers in this area. Family centres and specialist nurseries employ social workers, together with other workers such as nursery nurses, to observe, assess and advise on child development, child behaviour and parenting issues. Such centres usually require families experiencing difficulties to attend over a period of time.

Hospitals

Definition

Multi-disciplinary team – a team of workers drawn from more than one discipline (area of expertise), for example from psychology, nursing, occupational therapy medicine, and so on

Some social workers, whilst still being employed by social services departments, work within health settings such as hospitals. Here they form part of a **multi-disciplinary team** made up of doctors, nurses, occupational therapists, and so on.

Field social workers carry a case-load of different individuals and families who they are working with. In some teams it is common for social workers to 'joint work' some cases (i.e. where two colleagues work the case together).

Question

Tracey, aged 3, and Jason, aged 6, have come to the attention of the social services by a telephone call from a concerned neighbour. She has told the duty social worker that both children's care is being seriously neglected. The parents often go away for long periods, leaving them locked in the house on their own. Jason is frequently asking neighbours for food. Both children look unhappy and physically malnourished.

Which other professionals or agencies would a field social worker work with in this case?

Child protection

The first specific piece of legislation to deal with child abuse was the Prevention of Cruelty and Protection of Children Act 1889. Since then many different laws have been passed with the aim of increasing and improving the protection of children against abuse and promoting the welfare of needy children.

Definition

Child protection – the branch of social work that is concerned with the investigation and prevention of child abuse in its many forms

Definitions

Child Protection Register – a list of all the children whom social services know are at serious risk of abuse. If a name is put on the register, a Child Protection Plan must be made, recommending how to help the child

Key worker – the social worker who puts the Child Protection Plan into action and monitors it

Court order – the court can make an order to help protect a child. It can only do this if there is evidence, or facts, about what has happened to the child, and only if it thinks this is the best way to help a child. There are different types of court order

After the creation of the Welfare State, the primary statutory responsibility for child protection was given to the newly created children's departments. With the passing of the Local Authority Social Services Act in 1970 the prime statutory responsibility has been with social services departments.

Unfortunately, despite the legislation, all has not gone smoothly for social services in the field of **child protection**. Four examples illustrate this:

- There have been several high profile cases where children already known to social services have died. Maria Colwell and Jasmine Beckford are too notable cases. Subsequent reports criticised social services for not taking enough action and not communicating with other agencies.
- There was a situation in Cleveland in the 1980s where widespread sexual abuse was suspected, action taken and then followed by a period of disagreement over the real extent of the abuse and the appropriateness of the action taken. Many thought that in this case the social services had over-reacted and had been too influenced by one particular form of medical investigation.
- Over the last thirty years several instances have come to light where 'institutional' child abuse has taken place *inside* the care system. Leicestershire and North Wales are two such areas where this is known to have taken place.
- What constitutes child abuse has never been exactly settled over this period. For example, it was commonplace in the 1950s, 1960s and 1970s for teachers to give 'naughty' children some form of corporal punishment, for example a slap, the cane or slipper. These days, if a teacher slippered a child, a child protection enquiry would be likely to be initiated. There is currently a public debate about whether parents should be able to smack their children at all (it has been outlawed in Sweden for over 25 years).

These points and others illustrate just what a complex area child protection can be. Guidelines, policies and procedures are constantly under review.

Current official guidelines stress the need for inter-agency co-operation in child abuse cases. Hence each locality has an Area Child Protection Committee (ACPC) made up from senior representatives from health, social services, education, probation and the police. One of their responsibilities is to produce comprehensive guidelines for all those working with children on what to do if any kind of child abuse is suspected. Another important function of the ACPC is to oversee the local **Child Protection Register** (CPR). A Child Protection Register is a list of children where concern about their welfare is such that they are the subjects of specific inter-agency plans for their protection. Each child on the CPR needs to have a **key worker** and a child protection care plan. It is the role of social workers to be the key worker and to draw up and monitor the care plan.

Questions

1 Look at the diagram opposite. Which other agencies apart from social services can be contacted if you think a child is being abused?
2 Are all children on the Child Protection Register officially 'in care'?
3 How are parents involved in the child protection process?
4 Which other workers would you expect to attend a Child Protection Conference if:
   a) the child was seven?
   b) the child was one?

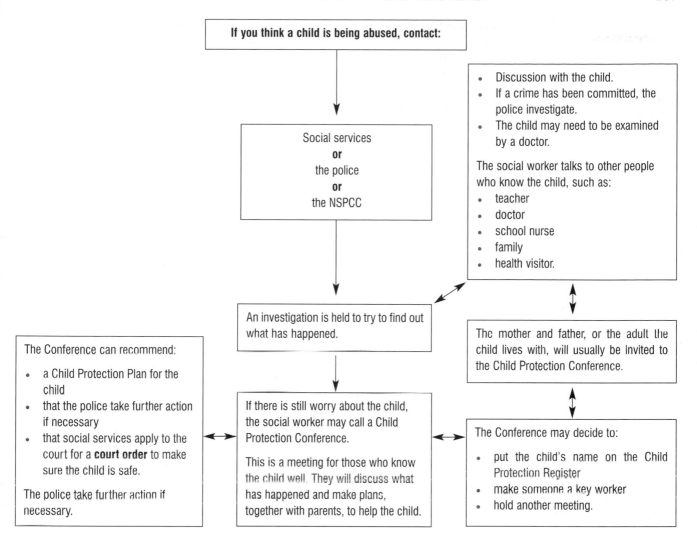

If you think a child is being abused, contact:

Social services
or
the police
or
the NSPCC

- Discussion with the child.
- If a crime has been committed, the police investigate.
- The child may need to be examined by a doctor.

The social worker talks to other people who know the child, such as:
- teacher
- doctor
- school nurse
- family
- health visitor.

An investigation is held to try to find out what has happened.

The mother and father, or the adult the child lives with, will usually be invited to the Child Protection Conference.

The Conference can recommend:
- a Child Protection Plan for the child
- that the police take further action if necessary
- that social services apply to the court for a **court order** to make sure the child is safe.

The police take further action if necessary.

If there is still worry about the child, the social worker may call a Child Protection Conference.

This is a meeting for those who know the child well. They will discuss what has happened and make plans, together with parents, to help the child.

The Conference may decide to:
- put the child's name on the Child Protection Register
- make someone a key worker
- hold another meeting.

Substitute care: fostering and adoption

Children in the care of local authorities

Children looked after by local authorities, by type of accommodation, 1994 and 1998, England, Wales and Northern Ireland

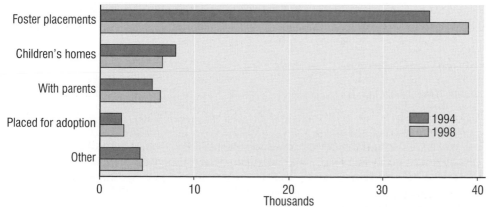

1 Approximately how many children were being looked after in foster placements in 1998?

2 Identify any trends from 1994 to 1998 and suggest reasons behind them.

Source: Department of Health; National Assembly for Wales; Department of Health and Social Services, Northern Ireland

Source: *Social Trends 30* (The Stationery Office, 2000)

Social services play a major part in arranging **substitute care** for children. There are several reasons why children are looked after by foster parents.

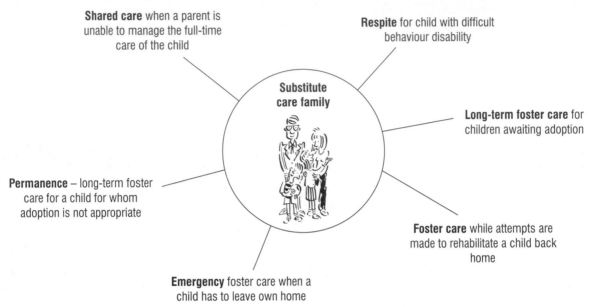

Shared care when a parent is unable to manage the full-time care of the child

Respite for child with difficult behaviour disability

Substitute care family

Long-term foster care for children awaiting adoption

Permanence – long-term foster care for a child for whom adoption is not appropriate

Foster care while attempts are made to rehabilitate a child back home

Emergency foster care when a child has to leave own home

Types of substitute care

Adoption is the process whereby a court transfers legal responsibility for a child from their birth family to the adoptive family. To all intents and purposes, the adopted child is then the same as if they were born to the parents. Adoption work is complex and all the more so these days as most children who come up for adoption are not newborn babies but older children who often have several years of 'history' behind them. The Department of Health approves different organisations to act as adoption agencies and carry out the process of recruiting and vetting adopters, matching children to families and other related tasks such as post-adoption counselling. Social services departments act as one of the main adoption agencies throughout the UK. The government believes that encouraging more adoptions is the best way of removing those children from the care system who cannot be returned to their own families for whatever reason.

Adoption facts

- Of the 52,000 children looked after by local authorities at any one time about 70 per cent will go home to their families.
- The number of adoptions from care has remained stable for the past 30 years at about 2,000 children a year. England has one of the highest rates of adoption from care in Europe (4 per cent) although not as high as the US. In Australia and New Zealand fewer than 1 per

cent of children are adopted from care and most of those are babies. In Scandinavia adoption is not viewed as an option in child welfare policy.
- Studies indicate that about one adoption in five breaks down within five years, leaving the child back in local authority care.
- The most stable and successful long-term placements for children are with members of their own network – relatives,

or others already well known to them including their existing long-term foster carers.
- Adoption breakdown rates are strongly linked to the child's age at placement. Five per cent of children placed as infants, 10 per cent of those placed at age five, 20 per cent of those aged seven or eight and nearly half of 11 to 12 year olds will experience breakdown of their placement. Breakdown rates for

adoptions are similar to those for long-term foster placements when the age of the child is taken into account.
- More than 80 per cent of looked-after children are over five years old, although the average age of looked-after children is falling.
- An analysis of children referred to British Agencies for Adoption and Fostering (BAAF), by local authorities which had

been unable to find placements for them, found that:
40 per cent had learning difficulties, physical impairments or medical problems;

20 per cent had been sexually abused;
25 per cent had special educational needs;
One in four were from minority ethnic backgrounds, the

majority of them of mixed ethnic parentage.
• A study of birth mothers who lost their children through adoption from care found that a substantial proportion were

mentally ill, had alcohol or drug problems, or had learning difficulties. One in four mothers had lost their child because the child was abused by a male partner.

Source: *Community Care*, August 2000

1 List anything which surprises you about the facts on adoption given here?

2 Why do you think that placements could not be found for some children?

3 What reasons were there for mothers losing their children through adoption from care?

Social work with children with disabilities

Under the Children Act 1989 (s.17 [10]) children with disabilities are classed as children 'in need' and therefore social services have a general duty to:

'promote the upbringing of such children by their families, by providing a range and level of services appropriate to those children's needs.' Children Act 1989 [s.17 (1)]

Most social services departments have set up separate Children with Disabilities Teams. Often a prime task is to ensure that respite care is available and that the children's primary carers are supported. The Carers and Disabled Children Act 2000 introduces a duty on local authorities to provide services directly for the carer to meet their assessed needs. Carers should be able to receive services, such as counselling and training, in their own right independent of the child they are caring for. The Carers and Disabled Children Act 2000 is part of the National Carers Strategy, which recognises the stresses of caring and aims to promote better ways of relieving these stresses (see page 237).

What life is like caring for Daniel

Julie Davies is volunteer co-ordinator for Contact a Family in Warrington, Cheshire. She has three sons and one of them – eight-year-old Daniel – is severely disabled. Daniel has cerebral palsy and severe learning difficulties. He suffers from hydrocephalus, epilepsy and unpredictable breathing rhythms.

Daniel goes to school when he is able to, but is often too ill with chest problems. Julie gave up a part-time nursing job because of the unpredictability of his health, and her husband works shifts. The Davies family has the support of a paediatric nurse 20 hours a week, plus three hours' help from a carer from Crossroads, an organisation that provides respite care for carers, funded by the social services

department. "Because Daniel has a lot of breathing and other problems during the night I try to get as much of the 20 hours during the night as I can. Some nights we're up and down the whole time.

"One problem is we get a lot of different nurses, often from an agency, and it's really hard having people come into your home when you don't know them. We tried for a long time to manage, but in the end just could not cope with so little sleep.

"The Crossroads carer has been coming for ages, and I've taught her to look after Daniel myself. She comes to get him ready for school three days a week while I'm helping the others. But now social services are saying they don't want to pay for carers to

carry out medical procedures, so we're not sure what is going to happen. Daniel is fed by tube and if he coughs up anything you have to suck it out of his mouth, which they say is a medical procedure."

Ironically as the local authority was deciding to stop funding carers to undertake nursing tasks, the health trust has decided that the paediatric nurse can be replaced by trained non-nurse carers. But the problem for families is often the anxiety that a service they rely on is going to be withdrawn.

Julie explains: "A woman rang me recently who had been told by social services that they would not pay for her Crossroads carer to tube-feed her son any more, and she was extremely worried and

upset. Then they had a review meeting and decided that because health paid for part of their package, they could shuffle the money around and work it out between them.

"I think they should have sorted out the solution before they bothered her with the details of who should be paying for the service. They don't realise how worrying little things like that can be – they can tip you over the edge."

Daniel goes to a Frances Hose children's hospice in Didsbury, Manchester, for one weekend every two to three months, but July explains that she and the rest of the family prefer to stay there with him. "I have difficulty leaving him. He has never cried, and I am concerned that people won't notice when he's uncomfortable or unhappy. But we go out for days together when he's there, and the hospice is very good with siblings."

Despite Julie's close bond with Daniel, she sympathises with parents who feel they can no longer cope with the full-time care of a severely disabled child. "There are more children with complex needs at home now. Years ago parents used to be advised to institutionalise their children but now I know parents who want residential care for their child and find it impossible to get. One friend of mine fought hard to get her daughter into a weekly residential school, but she was made to feel very guilty for asking. Now there's talk of closing the school so she's very anxious.

"Sometimes families just can't cope any more. And the child must pick up those vibes, and suffer for it."

Source: *Community Care*, 6–12 July 2000

1 Write a list of all the difficulties that Daniel's parents face.

2 What services do they receive from various sources?

3 Are the carers' needs being properly met?

4 If you were the social worker for the family, what other options do you think you could feasibly explore?

Recent government initiatives

Changes in inspection

Until 2001 children's services were inspected and regulated in two main ways:

- Under 8's Advisers had the responsibility for any Early Years services or children's day service where there are children under eight years of age, such a nursery, crèche, childminder, playgroup, and so on.
- The Registration and Inspection Unit had the responsibility for children's residential care.

Since 2001 OfSTED (Office for Standards in Education) has taken over the function of the Under 8's Adviser. Under the Care Standards Act 2000, the task of inspecting residential homes now falls to the newly created regional Commissions for Care Standards (see page 41 of *Commissions for Care Standards*).

Quality Protects

The Quality Protects programme was launched by the Department of Health in 1998. The purpose of this initiative was to improve both the standards of care given to children looked after by social services and others not necessarily looked after but who require social work intervention such as disabled children. The programme was mainly a response to the growing concerns during the 1990s about children's social services ability to protect children and promote their welfare adequately. In particular, the concern was that there were great inconsistencies across the country. As is common with many government programmes, a series of national targets were set for social services to meet within a three-year period. Special grants were given to help make the programme successful. A typical objective was asking local authorities to:

'reduce by 10 per cent, by 2002, the proportion of children who are re-registered on the child protection register, from a baseline for the year ending March 1997.'

So what this means is that social services need to work hard to reduce risk factors in known child protection cases. Another target is:

'To reduce to no more than 16 per cent in all authorities, by 2001, the number of looked-after children who have three or more placements in one year.'

This suggests that local authorities should try to minimise disruption in children's lives by better planning. Failure to meet the targets could mean that a particular social services department could be put on 'special measures'.

Adoption

The adoption system was criticised as being too slow and bureaucratic, leading children to be left too long in the care system. This led the government to draw up a White Paper, *Adoption: A New Approach* (2000), which introduced new measures to improve and speed up the process, including greater provision of information on the children for potential adopters; an increase in funding; an adoption register and a decision within six months.

Main points	▶	There are two main types of social workers working with children: field social workers and residential social workers.
	▶	Social work with children takes place with the following settings: their family home, substitute care homes, schools, children's homes and hospitals.
	▶	One of the chief responsibilities of local authority social services departments is that of child protection. There have been several high profile child abuse cases where the work of social services departments has been criticised.
	▶	Child protection systems are continually monitored.
	▶	Multi-disciplinary Area Child Protection Committees produce guidelines and supervise child protection work in an area.
	▶	Foster care is generally preferred to residential care and can be used for a variety of purposes.
	▶	Adoption is a permanent form of substitute care.
	▶	Reports have shown that abuse has been evident in certain children's homes. They have recommended that better training be given to residential social workers and that the inspection of homes be improved.
	▶	The responsibility for inspecting under-8s facilities has been passed from social services to OfSTED.

Part 2: Adult services

Adult services: organisation, clients, staffing and settings

Organisation

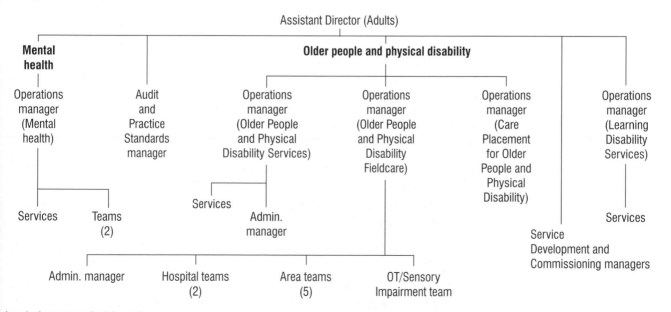

A typical structure of adult services

Clients

It has been estimated that there are well over ten million people in the UK who need someone to help them to look after themselves. The overwhelming majority of these people receive adequate levels of help from members of their own family or friends (informal care). However, there are many whose needs are so great that they cannot be satisfactorily looked after by friends, neighbours and family members, or else it could be that they have no family to look after them and are socially isolated.

There are nearly 11 million people in the UK over the age of 65 and over 1 million over the age of 85, many of whom are receiving care from one source or another. In 2001, about 3.4 million people were sufficiently disabled to be eligible for either Disability Living Allowance or Attendance Allowance. Over 600,000 people are referred to psychiatric services each year.

For many of these people, the State intervenes to arrange care. State intervention takes many forms, but they all fall between the two 'extremes' of residential care and community care. For example, of these groups, about 260,000 are in residential care (in hospitals, nursing homes, older persons' homes, etc.). In England alone in 1995 a total of over 600,000 day-care places were purchased or provided for adults, in addition domiciliary services (such as home care and meals-on-wheels) were delivered to well over million households.

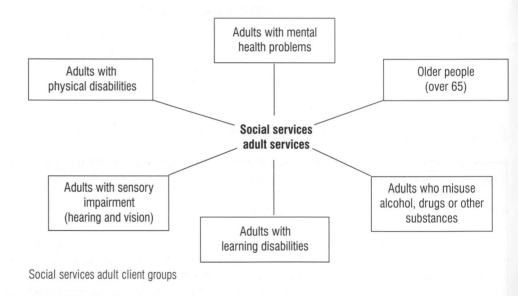

Social services adult client groups

Who works in social care for adults?

Each local authority decides how to organise its department in order to provide these services. Typically, adult services is made up from the following teams:

- *Older People/Physical Disability Team* – usually staffed by a team manager, care co-ordinators, administrative and reception staff
- *Learning Disability Team* – usually staffed by team manager, social workers, administrative and reception staff. These teams are often joint funded with the NHS and contain some NHS workers such as learning disabilities nurses
- *Mental Health Team* – usually staffed by team manager, social workers, administrative and reception staff. These teams are also often joint funded with the NHS and contain some NHS workers such as community psychiatric nurses and occupational therapists. There is usually input from a psychiatrist

- *Sensory Impairment Team* – usually staffed by specialist workers such as social workers with the deaf and social workers for visual impairment
- *Occupational Therapy Team* – usually staffed by occupational therapists, occupational therapy aides, administrative and reception staff
- *Health Team* – usually staffed by hospital social workers, administrative and reception staff
- *Drugs and Alcohol Service* – usually staffed by social workers, administrative and reception staff. This sort of team can also be joint funded with the NHS.

Where do social work and social care with adults take place?

The settings in which social care takes place are described as:

- *domiciliary care*, where people are visited in their own homes
- *day care*, where people attend some kind of centre for either part of or the whole day
- *residential care*, where people actually live away from their own homes, either temporarily or permanently, and receive care in an institution.

The move towards community care has led to more social care being provided in domiciliary and day settings and less in the residential sector.

Residential social work

Residential social work takes place in a variety of settings, and with a range of groups. Therefore the skills required of residential social workers very much depend on which particular client group they are working with, and the aims of the residential programme. Residential social work settings include the following.

Older people's homes

Traditionally only the managers or senior staff in residential care have held a recognised care qualification. However, more and more residential care staff at all levels are training to the appropriate NVQ/SVQ standards. Government concern about standards – outlined in the Care Standards Act 2000 – will mean that more staff will need to be trained up to the correct level. The aim of residential care is to ensure that older people, who are unable to be cared for in their own homes, are able to live with as much comfort and dignity as possible, as well as being safe. With the introduction of community care, only the most dependent of older people suffering from the problems associated with ageing, such as **dementia**, are admitted into residential care on a permanent basis. In line with the NHS and Community Care Act of 1990, the majority of older peole's homes now operate within the independent sector.

Homes for people with severe physical disabilities

Where possible, people with severe physical disabilities are looked after in their own home, especially since the introduction of community care. However, there are still those whose needs are so great that they need constant attention, either in special housing schemes or residential units. Much of this provision is run by the independent sector, although social services will often help with finance.

Homes for people with learning disabilities

Homes and hostels for people with learning disabilities (often combined with some physical disabilities) are more common than those for people with only physical disabilities. Since the 1990s there has been an expansion in group homes and other supported living schemes. These are usually run by registered social landlords – mainly this means housing associations – or by voluntary organisations like Mencap. It is not uncommon for the care workers to work for a

---

Definition

Dementia – the name given to conditions where the brain loses functions because of irreversible brain cell damage. The sufferer can experience memory disturbance, change of personality and loss of other mental and physical skills

separate care organisation from that managing the housing. Social care workers (often called 'project workers') working in this setting will spend their time working closely with their clients. Their main aim is to create as normal a living pattern, and as wide a range of choices and activities, as possible. The job usually ranges from giving personal care and counselling to helping with the development of independent living skills.

Homes for people with mental illness

There is a move towards providing shared flats and houses, rather than larger institutions. Usually, care workers are attached to a number of these. They spend their days (and often nights) helping people who are mentally ill to cope with a normal pattern of life. Very often, these shared houses and hostels are regarded as 'half-way-houses' in that they take people who have been undergoing therapy in a hospital and who are considered to be ready to begin the process of adjustment to living independently again. Many group homes for both this client group and for adults with learning disabilities are now run by the independent sector. Others are often jointly run by social services and the NHS. The emphasis of the work is much more on forming relationships and providing emotional support than on personal care.

Probation hostels

These are for people who have not been placed in custody by judges or magistrates, but instead are required to be supervised by a probation officer and for whom a 'condition of residence' order has been made. The senior warden will most likely be a qualified social worker and will have the responsibility of ensuring that the legal requirements of the court are met, whilst at the same time attempting to develop the life skills and employment skills of the people in her or his charge.

Day care

Day care is growing in scope and diversity and is moving away from its old image of bingo for older people and menial contract work for people with learning disabilities. Day care and the workers who provide it are seen as an ever important part of the continuum of care.

Day-care centres

These cater for any of the adult client groups mentioned above for anything from one to seven days a week. The clients mainly live at home and attend the day-care centre for social and therapeutic activities. Other medical and personal services are usually provided. Day care is usually part of a care package designed to meet the needs of a specific individual. Like residential care, it can often play an important respite function.

A range of care settings

Types of care setting	Institutions	Institutional care in 'the community'	'Community care' in the institution	Domiciliary care by statutory and voluntary organisations	Domiciliary care by friends neighbours and family
	◄—— Care **in** a home ——►		Care **from** home	◄—— Care **at** home ——►	
Examples	Hospitals Clinics 'Asylums'	Hospital hostels Hostels Rest homes Nursing homes Children's homes	Respite care Day care Day hospitals Luncheon clubs Travelling day hospitals	Health visitors Community psychiatric nurses GPs Home helps Social workers	Many forms of care including: bathing toileting feeding cooking

			Bed and breakfast accommodation Sheltered housing	Occupational therapy Industrial therapy Physiotherapy Out-patient treatment	Care attendants Meals on wheels Sitting services 'Tucking-in' services	leisure shopping dressing
Types of solution	Residential and caring (with services)	Residential and usually caring, with services	Caring, with services, but not usually residential	Caring, with services, but not residential	Caring and not residential	
Length of stay	Often short-term and temporary	Often long-term and permanent Some short-stay	Often long-term and regular but part-time	Often long-term and regular but part-time	Long-term regular and often full-time	
Volume of care to dependent groups	Approx. 3.5% of total		Approx. 15%		Approx. 80%	

1 Give two examples of 'institutions'.

2 What is the difference between 'institutional care in the community' and 'community care in the institution'?

3 Give four examples of domiciliary services provided by professionals.

4 Who does the bulk of the caring?

5 When the government says it wishes to see more caring in the community – is it clear what this means?

6 Commentators (and textbooks) often make clear distinctions between residential or institutional care and community care. What comment can you make as a result of the above table?

Main points ▶ Adult services usually cover the following groups of service users: people over the age of 65, people with mental health problems, people with physical disabilities, people with sensory impairments, people with learning disabilities and people who misuse alcohol or drugs.

▶ Most social services departments have specialist teams to cover each of these groups.

▶ Social work/care with these groups can take place in a variety of settings. Typically this can be in the person's own home, in a day care setting or in a residential home.

▶ There is a 'continuum of care' providing a good deal of overlap between the settings.

Community care

Community care is the approach which provides care in the person's home, if possible. There are considerable variations within this definition, however, as individuals may be living in a group home, where three or four people share accommodation (often used when moving mentally ill people out of long-stay hospitals), or it may be that the person lives in accommodation which is watched over by a warden (such as sheltered housing). Ideally, community care has the following characteristics:

• The person is living at home and has privacy.
• There are no staff living in.
• Normal living routine is determined by the individual as far as possible.
• The individual receives services from outside.

Principal elements of community care

'One door'

In the past, community care had been provided by a number of different agencies, with the main two being the health service and the local authority social services. With the implementation of the 1990 NHS and Community Care Act, however, the *local authority* was given the major responsibility for social care of older people, people with physical disabilities and people with learning disabilities. The idea here is that people know exactly where to go for their requests for help in caring for relatives, friends or for themselves. This meant a significant change in the role of social workers. Social workers in adult services have become more care co-ordinators and they have had to develop skills in commissioning care from providers. The relationship between social and health care has not been a 'seamless service' despite the intention of governments. This led the government through its NHS 2000 plan to insist that health authorities and local government work together. Today, integrated services are regarded as quite normal.

Distinction between health and social needs

A clear distinction was made between a person's health needs and social needs. Where a person's needs were concerned with their health, they would be provided for by the GP (or hospital). It was decided that people with mental illness clearly fell into the category of having health needs, and so, for these people, the health authority was the 'one door'. This has led to some confusion over the exact dividing line between health and social needs. Who is responsible for the services for older people who are at home and who have both social needs, such as isolation, and also physical/mental heath problems? How the continuing care needs of older people are managed once they have been discharged from hospital has become a considerable topic for debate. As we have seen, the NHS Plan 2000 tries to address this thorny problem by forcing social services and the NHS to come together with new agreements to pool resources. The NHS-run primary care trusts (created by the Health and Social Care Act 2001) have the responsibility of commissioning health and social care in a single organisation.

Planning

One of the major flaws of traditional approaches to community care had been the failure to transfer good intentions into practice. As a result of this, the government placed a duty on local authorities to work with health authorities to produce and publish clear plans for community care in their areas.

Originally, the entire community care programme was to be introduced in April 1991, but the Conservative government was concerned about the electoral consequences of introducing a community care programme which was calculated to add at least £15 per head to the already unpopular community charge, or 'poll tax' as it was known. They therefore suggested a timetable, with full implementation of the community care programme complete by April 1993. The major advantage of the delay was to allow good planning, although the local authorities maintained they would have been ready in 1991.

Under traditional systems of care, the client was regarded as a member of a category, such as 'elderly', 'physically disabled', etc. Many social services departments and most health authorities had teams which specialised in these categories. The result was that services were developed for these particular categories, and when a social worker or district nurse went to assess an individual, they would have a package of services for the particular category of person. The assessment would consist of deciding which of these was most suitable in terms of its appropriateness and availability.

Care planning is supposed to create a situation where the person is assessed for what they need as an individual. As long as the person's needs are considered significant enough to meet any eligibility criteria laid down, the care co-ordinator would then assemble an individual care package.

The easiest way of understanding the new approach to providing care is to remember that Sir Roy Griffiths, author of the Griffiths Report, was managing director of the Sainsbury's supermarket chain. The traditional method of the social services department deciding what services they could fit people into seemed as absurd to him as the supermarket cashier deciding what food people ought to have.

In truth it would be a fair analysis to say that whilst local authorities have reorganised in the spirit of the 'needs-led assessment', in reality lack of resources has led to a lack of genuinely 'needs-led' care packages in many cases.

From 2001, both health and social services staff will use a 'common assessment tool' to help integrate services.

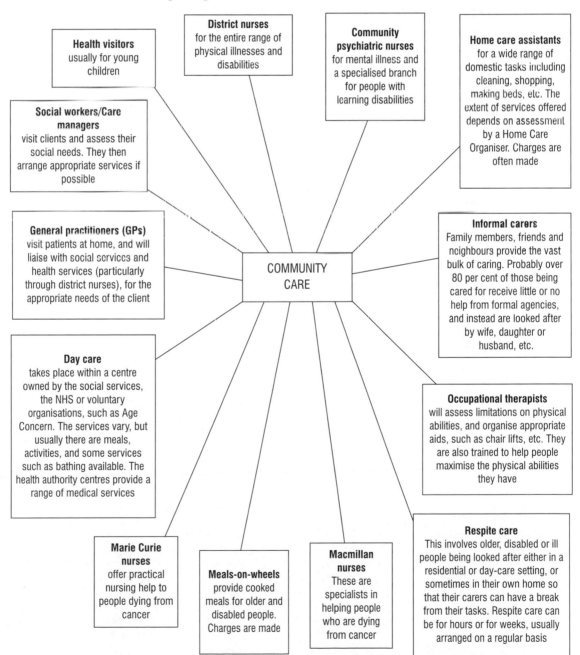

Enablers, not providers

The idea that welfare is the monopoly of the local authority social services departments has long been abandoned. Instead, private, charitable and voluntary organisations (the independent sector) are being used as much as possible.

Social services 'enable' people to live as independently as possible by use of the necessary services. The expansion of 'direct payments' means that more independence again is being given to service users.

Maintaining standards

The local authorities originally had the duty to maintain the quality of local provision. This was to be done through the regular inspection of all residential institutions in the area. Registration and inspection units were required to be set up by local authorities and operate at 'arm's-length'. In other words, although they might well be inspecting their own local authority-run provision they could show no favouritism. They had to act as if they were a completely separate body and operate the same standards as if they were inspecting an independent provider. This system was felt to be too patchy so the Care Standards Act 2000 has introduced bigger, independent Regional Care Standards Commissions to replace the local authority units (see page 41 of Commissions for Care Standards).

However, local authorities still need to be seen to be pursuing quality assurance. They all work within the governments 'Best Value' programme which is designed to improve the delivery of all local government services.

Ethnic minorities

Traditionally, it has been assumed that the needs of people from ethnic minority backgrounds were no different from any others. However, more recently, there has been an awareness of the importance of recognising that different ethnic groups may well have their own problems and their different needs.

This should mean that social workers should try to look at the needs of someone as a member of the ethnic minorities, rather than trying to fit them in to already existing provision, which is usually angled towards the servicing of the majority white population.

'Race' and community care

In the book 'Race' and Community Care, the editors Waqar Ahmad and Karl Atkin argue that:

> The introduction of the current community care reforms cannot be divorced from the existing disadvantages facing minority ethnic communities, especially since evidence suggests that community services do not adequately recognise and respond to the needs of people from ethnic minorities.

They identify the following three themes that have emerged since the beginning of community care:

First, community service provision often ignores the needs of black and minority ethnic the service being provided.

Second, racist attitudes on the part of service providers have been reported in a number of studies in health and social services. Health and social service professionals exercise considerable discretion and their views about users and carers can influence the nature of service provision. Local authorities often list black people as 'high risk' clients, 'uncooperative' and 'difficult to work with'. Similarly, stereotypes of minority ethnic group patients, as 'calling out doctors unnecessarily', 'being trivial complainers' and 'time wasters', are common. These racist attitudes deprive minority ethnic communities of their full and equal rights to services.

Second, community care services often misrepresent the needs of ethnic minorities … (and) … blame the potential client group for either experiencing specific problems or not making 'appropriate' use of services, rather than examine the relevance of the service being provided.

Despite the current restructuring of community care provision, there remains widespread uncertainty, puzzlement and ignorance about what should be done to meet the community care needs of minority

| ethnic communities. Policy remains underdeveloped, comprising little more than bland statements of racial equality, while the | mechanisms that might achieve race equality, and the principles that underlie them, remain unexplored, the mixed economy of | care and the enabling role of social services do little to acknowledge, let alone alter, the unequal structuring of opportunities | and are, therefore, unlikely to deal with the fundamental disadvantage faced by ethnic minorities. |

Source: W. Ahmad and K. Atkin (eds), *'Race' and Community Care* (Open University Press, 1996)

1 Why don't the needs of ethnic minorities get addressed?

2 Who is meant to change, according to the social service providers?

3 What is the 'mixed economy of care'?

4 The final paragraph reflects the theoretical views of the authors. Go back to the section on theory (pages 187–193) and see if you can identify which theories seem to be underlying the final paragraph.

Background to community care

The modern concept of providing care in the community can best be traced back to the early 1960s with the publication of the White Paper, *Health and Welfare: The Development of Community Care*. In this, the government proposed the setting up of district general hospitals to replace the large variety of smaller hospitals then existing. These new DGHs were to focus on acute (immediate and short-term) illnesses. The chronic illnesses, the problems of older people, mentally ill people and people with learning difficulties would all be dealt with in the community.

The part of the plan concerning the creation of district general hospitals was carried out, but no moves were made to introduce community care. Indeed, even though other reports and White Papers (such as *Better Services for Mentally Handicapped People*, 1971, and *Better Services for the Mentally Ill*, 1975) continued to call for the run-down of residential institutions, it was not until the Audit Commission Report of 1985 that the truth emerged. (Audit Commissions are investigations by government-appointed accountants and experts who see whether the government is getting value for money in its services.) There had been no move forward in the provision of community care for those in need, rather things had taken the worst possible turn for some groups. For example, there were 37,000 fewer mentally ill and 'mentally handicapped' patients in hospitals in 1985 compared to 1975, yet there had been no corresponding increase in community care provision. Even worse, there was no knowledge of what had happened to these 37,000 people.

Moves towards community care were slow for various reasons:

- There was a lack of funds available to local authorities from local government, which they could use for community care.
- The National Health Service was not willing to hand money over to local services to provide community care for some of its patients.
- There was a 'perverse incentive', as the Audit Commission called it, for local social services to place people in institutions rather than look after them at home. If the social services provided community care, then they had to pay for that out of their income. However, if they placed people in institutions, then social security paid the cost. This meant that it was cheaper to put people in institutions than to care for them in the community.

The main factors leading towards community care

There were three main factors causing the government to take the issue of community care seriously:

- cost
- demographic changes
- ideological beliefs.

Cost

By 1986, the government was spending approximately £6 million in the area of community care. At the beginning of the 1980s the cost of social security benefits for people in residential accommodation was approximately £20–25 million, by the late 1980s it had risen sharply to £1 billion, and this was continuing to rise. By the early 1990s, the DSS was paying out over £1.6 billion. Such sustained rises in this area of social security spending had big implications for levels of public borrowing and taxation. A financial 'crisis' was being openly discussed.

Demographic changes

There are about 4 million people over the age of 75 (16 per cent of the population), and 1.25 million people over the age of 85, compared to 700,000 in 1986. This figure is important, because it is at around this age that older people need substantial assistance from the State.

However, not only was there likely to be a growth in the number of dependent older people, there was also a similar growth in the numbers of severely disabled people. In 1999, it was estimated that there were just over one million severely disabled people living in the UK (although remember the numbers of older and disabled people overlap considerably). In 2000 approximately 6.2 million people in the UK had a physical disability of some kind. The majority of these are of pensionable age.

Ideological beliefs

The Conservative government of the mid 1980s was dominated by the ideas of the so-called New Right (see page 20), whose members believed strongly in 'traditional' values, such as self-reliance, independence and the family. In particular, the government asked why it was that the State was having to care (in institutions) for people who could (and the implication was *should*) have been looked after by family members. A strong belief of the New Right is that the family has a duty to look after its members, and that wherever possible the State should encourage people to do so.

A further consideration was that there were already 6 million people (6 out of 10 of whom are women) caring for others in the community, and of these up to 1.5 million were acting as unpaid carers for more than 20 hours a week. These people were doing exactly what the New Right believed in and so it was argued that the government had a duty to provide some support.

The countdown to community care

- *Mental Health Act 1959:* set out to establish a community care service for people who were mentally ill not requiring hospital treatment.
- *1963* White Paper, *Development of Community Care*, but no Act followed.
- *1975* White Paper, *Better Services for the Mentally Ill*. This planned for the growth of local authority social services departments to deal with mentally ill people in the community, and for the medical treatment to be provided by psychiatric units of local hospitals.

- *1977 Joint Finance introduced*: health authorities were required to earmark funding for joint services with local authorities.

- *1986 Audit Commission Report*: a very influential official government study of the costs of institutions, and the inadequate provision of community care. Urged a radical rethink.

- *1988 Griffiths Report:* the most influential report on community care, which decided that the role of local authorities must change. They should take on the role of purchasers of care for those in need of community-based assistance, instead of the traditional role of provider of care.

- *National Health Service and Community Care Act 1990*: this was largely based on the Griffiths Report, and shifted the emphasis on care for older people, mentally ill people and people with learning difficulties away from institutional provision to community care provision. It also provided funds to local authorities to undertake the bulk of the caring work for people without medical needs.

- *April 1993*: full implementation of the 1990 Act. Social security funds are transferred to local government

---

Main points
- ▶ Since 1993 the UK has officially embraced the concept of community care.
- ▶ Community care has the following characteristics: the person lives in their own home thus promoting privacy and independence, a range of services are used to maintain the person in their own home. Whilst social services departments are responsible for arranging the care, it is mainly provided by independent care providers.
- ▶ Community care has meant a deliberately encouraged growth of the independent sector (private and voluntary providers).
- ▶ The reasons for community care being officially introduced are complex but three main reasons stand out: the rising costs of institutional care, the huge projected increase in the elderly population and changing attitudes to the role of the State in social welfare.
- ▶ Studies show that the advent of community care has not been without its problems. Certain groups in society are not necessarily having their needs met; some members of ethnic groups and people with severe mental illness have attracted particular attention in this respect.

The role of the professionals: care management

With the implementation of the 1990 NHS and Community Care Act, the main role of social workers working within community care is *care management*. The central elements of this are:

- assessment
- care planning:
  - implementation
  - monitoring
  - reviewing.

As we have seen, the role of social workers in particular has changed – at least in theory. They no longer assess individuals in terms of what services are available (a 'service-led' assessment). They start from what the person actually needs.

The first step is to carry out a full *'needs-led' assessment* of the person. Following this, the social worker then commissions the necessary care package which will best meet the person's needs within the budget constraints imposed upon them (a bench-mark figure). Authorities record any shortfalls between the 'ideal' care plan and the actual package offered for future planning purposes.

Next, the social worker *monitors the quality of care* being given. Clear specifications or standards of care are now laid down. If they are not met by providers then contracts can be terminated or switched elsewhere. In certain situations of severely substandard residential care, social services have the power to stop the particular home from continuing by terminating their registration.

Assessment

Question

Part III S.47 (1) of the NHS and Community Care Act 1990 states:
'where it appears to a local authority that any person for whom they may provide or arrange for provision of community care services may be in need of any such services, the authority:

a) shall carry out an assessment of his needs for those services; and
b) having regard to the results of that assessment, shall then decide whether his needs call for the provision by them of any such services.'

Is the local authority obliged to provide services? Explain your answer.

It is the role of the care manager/care co-ordinator to assess the needs of the client. The assessment will include taking into account the wishes of the client, their carer(s), the level of funding available and the care manager's professional views of what is in the best interests of the client. The final decision about how to proceed with community care provision is based on whether the person meets certain laid-down eligibility criteria. A set of typical eligibility criteria used by a local authority in 2000 is shown in the table opposite.

In order for a person or household to receive a service purchased by social services, their assessed needs must put them in risk groups 4, 5 or 6 on the eligibility criteria matrix. If their assessed needs fall only into categories 1, 2 or 3, they are eligible for advice or information and are redirected to alternative organisations providing appropriate services in the independent sector.

Case study Using the eligibility criteria opposite, consider the following case study.

Ted Mackenzie is 75. He has suffered from Parkinson's disease for many years. This has left him in a severely dependent state. He is very immobile and practically housebound. He falls period-ically and needs help to get up again. He often requires help with personal hygiene and food preparation. At the moment his sole carer is his 75-year-old wife June. She is just about managing. However, she has a history of heart problems. The couple live in a three- bedroomed house. June has become very stressed by the situation. She deals with this by going out and leaving Ted on his own for long periods. This, in turn, creates guilt and tension between the two.

1 Would you feel that Ted meets the eligibility criteria? Explain your decision.

2 What care package would you consider most appropriate in this case?

Eligibility criteria for services

Needs	Degree of risk					
	1) Low/little immediate impact	2) Limited impact	3) Some concerns	4) Major concerns	5) Major risk of harm	6) Immediate/very high risk of harm
a) Physical safety of individual and others			Some concerns about physical safety. Risk slight.	Daily support required in view of continuing risk of harm.	High risk to physical safety.	Cannot be left alone.
b) Physical health/ disability of individual and others		Some concerns about physical health. Reduced quality of life due to disability.	Possible risk of deterioration in health/quality of life without support.	Requires daily support to prevent deterioration in health/maintain quality of life.	Requires assistance several times a day. Carer under severe stress.	Requires continuous care from others. Carer at risk of collapse.
c) Mental health of individual and others		Some concerns about mental health.		Temporary or recurring depressive or anxiety state affecting ability to care for self or relate to others. Severe depression or delusional condition affecting ability to care for self or relation to others.	Likelihood of self harm/neglect or harm to others, although not detainable under the Mental Health Act.	Likelihood of self harm/neglect or harm to others with history of detention under the Mental Health Act.
d) Independent living skills	Unable to fulfil potential due to limited skills.	Reduced quality of life due to limited skills. Requires minimal help.	Requires support from others (several times a week) in order to remain at home.	High level of support required (daily) due to loss of skills.		
e) Opportunities for social interaction	Limited opportunity for social contact	No contact outside immediate family/neighbours.	Very isolated	Rejected by neighbourhood or carer.	Rejected by neighbourhood and carer.	Rejected by professionals, neighbourhood and carer.

The assessment generally involves finding out the following information from the individual.

- *Biographical details:* The following information is required: name, age, marital status, religion, and so on.
- *Self-perceived needs:* The assessment should always start with the views of the individual and his/her wishes.
- *Self-care:* What the person can do for him/herself, such as washing, cooking, dressing, etc. An important point here is that the potential of the person should also be taken into account. For example, an older widower may have been used to being looked after by his wife. When assessed, he makes little effort to do anything for himself. The care manager must decide what the appropriate level of help for him is, given his own capacities and the resources available.
- *Physical health:* This is crucial, and a proper assessment of the person's health will be undertaken by a health professional, most probably the GP. Health problems often require both medical and social services, as ill health may prevent a person from performing self-care adequately.
- *Mental health:* Again, an assessment by an appropriate health professional is required, probably the community psychiatrist. The mental health of the individual may effect his/her perception of needs and the ability to perform a number of routine daily activities.
- *Use of medicines:* Many people need regular medication, and a common problem is the inability to self-administer this. Problems resulting from inadequate medication may affect the broader lifestyle of the person and their ability to achieve an adequate standard of self-care.
- *Abilities, attitudes and lifestyle:* Each person is unique in their views, abilities, lifestyle and personal range of family and friends upon whom they can rely. The assessment must take this into account and must not simply stereotype an individual, for example as an older person with arthritis living alone.
- *Race and culture:* The assessment must include an awareness of race and the cultural wishes that spring from this. The impact of racism on people's lives should also be considered.
- *Personal history:* Any relevant information that the individual provides which may help to understand their present needs, for example, the death of a partner, or past involvement with health or social services which they regard as unsatisfactory and which affects their attitude to the current assessment, should be taken into account.
- *Needs of carers:* These have been more formally addressed by legislation. (See the section on carers, page 234). Where there is currently someone providing care, his or her views also need to be taken into account. The individual being assessed, and the care manager, may make false assumptions about the wishes and attitudes of the carer.

  Regarding the carer, the following points should be covered in an assessment:

  - relationship to the individual being assessed (for example, wife or daughter)
  - care provided
  - expressed needs for support
  - wishes and preferences
  - nature of the relationship (warm/distant).

- *Financial assessment:* The financial assessment looks at the person's income and savings in order to see how much, if anything, the person has to pay for services. The local authority has traditionally decided its own rules for domiciliary, day and short-term (respite) care; for permanent care in residential or nursing homes they must follow nationally laid down rules. Below are guidelines on respite care issued by one council.

How much you pay

COUNTY COUNCIL SOCIAL SERVICES
NOTES ON SHORT TERM RESIDENTIAL (RESPITE) CARE CHARGING QUESTIONNAIRE

HOW MUCH YOU PAY FOR SHORT TERM RESIDENTIAL CARE

You can estimate how much you are going to pay for your short stay by answering the following questions:

QUESTION A — **Do you have more than £16,000 capital and receive High Rate Attendance Allowance or High Rate Disability Living Allowance Care Component?**

| YES | You will pay £195.34 per week |
| NO | Go to Question B |

QUESTION B — **Do you have more than £16,000 capital and receive Low Rate Attendance Allowance or Mid Rate Disability Living Allowance Care Component?**

| YES | You will pay £185.35 per week |
| NO | Go to Question C |

QUESTION C — **Do you have more than £16,000 capital and are not in receipt of Attendance Allowance or Disability Living Allowance?**

| YES | You will pay £165.35 per week |
| NO | Go to Question D |

QUESTION D — **Do you have less than £16,000 capital and receive High Rate Attendance Allowance or High Rate Disability Living Allowance Care Component?**

| YES | You will pay £93.00 per week **plus*** |
| NO | Go to Question E |

QUESTION E — **Do you have less than £16,000 capital and receive Low Rate Attendance Allowance or Mid Rate Disability Living Allowance Care Component?**

| YES | You will pay £83.00 per week **plus*** |
| NO | Go to Question E |

QUESTION E — **Do you have less than £16,000 capital and are not in receipt of Attendance Allowance or Disability Living Allowance?**

| YES | You will pay £63.00 per week **plus*** |

*plus any gain in entitlement to Income Support as a result of respite care (including RCA)

Please note: **Even if you choose not to claim Income Support, you will still be charged on this basis.**
If you receive respite care for part of a week you will be charged one-seventh of the weekly charge for each night of care. Periods of less than one day will be charged at one-seventh of the weekly rate.

---

1 Under what conditions would the person pay £185.35 per week?

2 Under what conditions would a person pay £83.00 (plus)?

3 If the person has respite care for less than seven days, what will they pay?

4 Briefly summarise what factors are taken into account when determining how much someone should pay?

5 What reasons might someone have for going into residential care on a short-term basis?

The care plan

There are three stages to the care plan, once assessment has taken place:

- implementing
- monitoring
- reviewing.

Implementing the care plan

Implementing the plan consists of achieving the objectives of the care plan with the least intervention necessary. This means using the fewest services and personnel possible. This is to ensure that the individual understands the plan, and there is not a complexity of wasteful, overlapping providers.

Monitoring the care plan

The aim of monitoring the care plan is to confirm the achievement of set objectives over a period of time, and to change the plan in line with the differing needs of the individual. The extent of monitoring depends on how complex the community care provision is. Monitoring specifically and formally checks that the implementation has been effective and as set down in the care plan. It records the reasons for objectives not being met, and leads to the final part of the care manager's role-reviewing.

Reviewing the care plan

This is the formal process which occurs at regular intervals (usually every six months), where the service user, care co-ordinator and other relevant parties meet to reassess the needs of the person and make any necessary revisions. Many local authorities employ separate review officers to carry out this task once a care package has settled down.

Community care: an evaluation

Ideal versus reality

The ideal of providing every person with all the services they require, while allowing them to choose to live in their own home, is something that (virtually) everyone agrees with. However, the job of actually carrying this out is extremely complex and expensive. The gap between reality and ideals emerged when the government delayed the full introduction of the 1990 community care legislation from 1991, when it was originally scheduled to come into effect, until April 1993.

Care in the community?

I am 80 years old and live alone. I was briefly in hospital for an operation on my hand and was visited by social services who asked if there was any help I would need when I went home. Yes, I replied, someone to bathe me and clean the house. These things are not possible, she said. They are not insured for bathing clients and cleaning was limited to "dusting to tops", no furniture could be moved. How awful it must be to be disabled and dependent on social services – never to have a bath, and never to have the dust cleared out from behind your chair or under your bed.

Do people realise what care in the community amounts to?

Source: Letter to *The Guardian*, 23 August 2000

1 What is your immediate response to the letter?

2 Earlier we talked about needs-led assessment. Does this letter suggest that social services really are 'needs-led'?

3 In the letter writer's position, what options, if any, does she have?

Funding

The cost of providing adequate community care was originally believed to be less than the cost of running residential institutions. However, we now know that this is not the case. In fact, it is probably more expensive to provide the required personal and health services in the community than it is to have them available in hospitals and social services institutions. With governments of any persuasion reluctant to raise taxes, this calls into question how much people are prepared to 'top up' what they can get from the State by paying for it themselves. If they cannot or will not, there are likely to be shortfalls in the services they get.

Inequality of provision

Community care is provided mainly by local authority social services departments, GP surgeries and by local community health units. There are very great differences in the resources that these agencies put towards community care.

Co-ordination

The single biggest providers are local authorities, yet the government did not say what they must spend on community care. This means that 'good' councils provide greater funds, while 'bad' councils may prefer to spend the money on other activities. This is a particularly important point, because old mentally ill and disabled people are very often the least powerful groups in society and have few means to persuade local authorities to devote greater resources to them.

With the fragmentation of services, there is greater difficulty in enforcing uniform standards of quality across the country – something that has been recognised by the passing of the Care Standards Act 2000.

Community care requires close co-ordination between GPs, community health units and local authority social services departments. The evidence in the past shows that despite official guidelines to work in partnership, they were never able to achieve the necessary levels of co-ordination. In acknowledgement of this the government introduced the NHS Plan 2000 which more or less forces health and social services to work together.

The carers and the community

The basis of community care is that the social and health services support the existing (and increasing) networks of support for people in need of help. Yet the evidence shows that the community simply does not exist. Help is overwhelmingly given by family members, usually the spouse or the daughter. The 'community' of friends and neighbours provides only a tiny proportion of assistance. The older one gets, the less likely one is to have a network.

Resistance

Some groups, such mentally ill people, and even those with learning disabilities, produce feelings of fear and resentment amongst residents in areas where the health or social services wish to purchase group homes. The attitude of most people is to support the idea of community care as long as no 'abnormal' people live near them.

Potential danger

The introduction of care in the community has seen the deaths of more than ninety people at the hands of psychiatric patients over a ten-year period. This includes the murder of a commuter on the London tube and a machete attack on primary schoolchildren in 1996, both by people with schizophrenia who were not taking their medication and were not being closely supervised. This has brought discussion about the viability of caring for such a potentially high-risk group in the community. Compared to other hazards in modern society, the risk posed is comparatively small. However, media coverage has built it up in the public minds to the extent that government is reviewing mental health legislation with a view to restricting the liberty of those considered to be a serious risk. Ironically those most likely to suffer from gaps in community care are mentally ill people themselves. The system failing to provide for them can lead to vagrancy, violence from others, self-harm, poverty and even suicide.

Support

People who have spent a long time in institutions become **institutionalised**, and experience great difficulty coping with life 'outside'. Unless significant support is provided by the social services, the experience of living in the community can be too much and the person needs to return to the institution. (This unfortunate state of affairs is often referred to as a 'revolving door'.)

There is evidence that mentally ill people who have been discharged are likely to end up in prison, and it is believed that about 3 per cent of all prisoners are actually mentally ill. In recognition of this problem in 2000 the government introduced the Supporting People programme designed to improve the quality of support services to vulnerable people by separating their delivery from the provision of accommodation.

Definition

Institutionalisation – the process whereby living in an institution affects the mind and behaviour of the individual. The individual loses independence, dignity and self-respect

Main points

▶ Community care is based around the practice of care planning which has clearly laid down stages.
▶ The needs of carers are an important part of the care planning process.
▶ Most social care for adults is charged for by local authorities. Each local authority has its own policy on who gets charged and how much they pay.
▶ Community care is based on the reality that most care is carried out by informal carers and that an important function of care in the community is to 'care for the carer'.
▶ There is an ongoing debate about whether community or residential care is the most appropriate form of care, especially for certain very dependent or vulnerable groups of people.

Residential care

By residential care, we generally mean care in institutions such as nursing homes or homes for older people. The individuals being cared for in these institutions live there permanently – eating, sleeping and having their leisure there (24-hour care).

Many residential institutions are characterised by the following:

• They are usually run by the State, by charities, or by profit-making companies.
• Individuals live in the institution, receive their services within it and rarely have to leave the buildings.
• Individuals living there have limited privacy.
• The staff are often trained, and almost always paid a salary.
• There are usually clear-cut rules of behaviour and formal routines for activities such as eating.
• Because of organisational needs, the institutions generally limit individual choice and freedom.

Who provides residential care?

The three main providers of residential care are:

- local authorities
- voluntary organisations
- the private sector.

Local authorities

The provision of residential care dates back to the setting up of workhouses in the nineteenth century, when those who were totally 'destitute' were forced to live in institutions where they had to work in extremely harsh conditions. The aim was to ensure that only those who were truly desperate would stay in. The workhouses took not only poor people, but older people and ill people as well.

Modern residential accommodation dates from 1948, when the National Assistance Act placed a duty on every local authority to 'provide residential accommodation for persons who by reason of age, infirmity or any other circumstance are in need of care and attention which is not otherwise available to them'. Ironically a lot of the residential accommodation that was used in the early days of the Welfare State was converted workhouses. Some are still being used to this day!

In the Mental Health Act 1959 a further duty was placed upon local authorities to provide residential care for people with a 'mental handicap' or mental health problems. By the late 1980s, there were approximately 16,000 places for people with learning disabilities, and 5,000 for people who were mentally ill.

Since the advent of community care the percentage of residential homes run by local authorities has decreased as can be seen in the chart below. This trend continues with many local authorities transferring the ownership of their homes to the independent sector.

Places in residential and nursing homes for the elderly, 1997, England

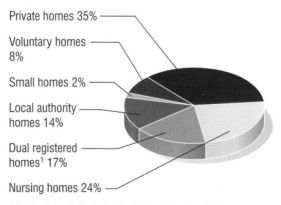

Private homes 35%

Voluntary homes 8%

Small homes 2%

Local authority homes 14%

Dual registered homes[1] 17%

Nursing homes 24%

1 Dual registered with the local authority and health authority
Source: Department of Health

Source: *Social Trends 30* (The Stationery Office, 2000)

Voluntary organisations

The Community Care Act has given impetus to the growth of the voluntary sector in the provision of community homes for a wide variety of clients. Voluntary organisations have often been chosen by local authorities to take over their residential homes which they have largely been obliged to give up under the funding arrangements which have come into force since the early 1990s.

Apart from being involved in the general care of older people, voluntary organisations are also involved in residential care for younger people who are physically disabled, learning disabled or older people from specific religious or cultural backgrounds. More recently, there has been a substantial shift towards residential accommodation for people with mental or severe physical disabilities.

Private organisations

This sector has grown enormously since the late 1970s, although the period around the turn of the century appears to be one of slight decline in numbers. With government encouragement of the private sector in the 1990 Community Care legislation it has become the largest provider of residential care. Its growth reflects the profits that can be achieved, the increasing number of older people, and the guarantee that for those without sufficient funds, financial support is available from the government.

The market for private residential and nursing homes is expanding. Almost one in five men and one in three women over 65 are likely to spend their final years living in residential accommodation. The turnover of the private residential care 'market' is in excess of £12 billion each year.

A checklist of good practice in residential care

✓ *High standards of physical needs:* There should be good food, a pleasant environment and comfortable rooms.

✓ *Independence:* Clients should be encouraged to do as much for themselves as possible.

✓ *Choice:* There should be genuine choices between alternatives, for example with meals, bed times, and so on.

✓ *Self-esteem:* Individuals should be encouraged to value themselves and to view their achievements positively, however 'small' these may appear to an outsider.

✓ *Privacy:* Each person has the right to a degree of private space and, should they wish to be alone, this too is their right. This is of particular importance in view of the way in which many residents are forced to share a room.

✓ *Confidentiality:* Each person has the right to keep personal information private or, at least, limited to those who must know.

✓ *Individuality:* Every person must be encouraged to express themselves, as long as they do not harm others in the process.

Local authority registration and inspection units

One of the effects of the NHS and Community Care Act 1990 was that each local authority social services department was required to set up 'arms length' registration and inspection units whose chief function was to inspect and register the residential accommodation in their area. They would be checking for health and safety, standards of care, and so on. The government White Paper *Modernising Social Services* criticised this arrangement saying that 'the present regulatory arrangements are incomplete and patchy'.

As a result when the Care Standards Act 2000 came into effect new regional Commissions for Care Standards (CCSs) were brought in, and a National Care Standards Commission established.

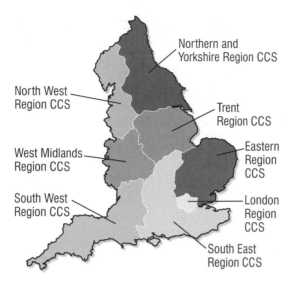

North West Region CCS

Northern and Yorkshire Region CCS

Trent Region CCS

West Midlands Region CCS

Eastern Region CCS

South West Region CCS

London Region CCS

South East Region CCS

The regional Commissions for Care Standards

Source: White Paper, *Modernising Social Services* (The Stationery Office)

The CCSs are more independent than the former local authority units and they have a much wider scope. They are responsible for regulating the following services:

- residential care homes for adults
- nursing homes
- children's homes
- domiciliary social care providers
- independent fostering agencies
- residential family centres
- boarding schools.

Residential care: an evaluation

Institutionalisation

Living within an institution is fundamentally different from normal life in the community. In normal life, individuals make decisions for themselves, wear the clothes they choose, eat at the times they want, and are usually living in their own home. The majority of people under retirement age also go out to work each day, meet people, commute and have a range of stimuli. In addition, many people can have leisure activities of their own choosing.

Living in an institution takes all these things away from individuals, and therefore deprives them of what most people would consider a decent quality of life.

Perhaps even worse is the fact that individuals in institutions have their daily lives controlled by others, such as staff members, who make decisions for them. This can be a humiliating and dehumanising experience. Institutions vary enormously but even those run by the most enlightened staff inevitably have aspects of what Goffman called 'batch living' where the needs of the institution come before the needs of the individual. With limited numbers of staff, residents have to be 'processed' (for example, fed, toileted, washed, etc.) in batches. Attitudes to risk, health and safety generally involve the values of the institution prevailing as well. For example, a resident who wanted to smoke when and wherever they liked (as they might do in their own home) would be constrained in how freely they could do this.

Abuse

Abuse can take place in any care setting. Caring is often a thankless and stressful task. Institutions can be more cut off from the outside world. It is not always staff who abuse, it can be other residents. Because of the imbalance of power in the institution, with residents being expected to do what they are told, and because of the lack of control over the activities of the staff, many examples of abuse of residents have been uncovered over the last years.

Alzheimer's sufferers 'mistreated' in homes
One in 10 carers of people with Alzheimer's Disease say their relatives have been mistreated in residential or nursing homes, according to a survey published today.

The mistreatment included restraint, rough handling, bruising, neglect of personal hygiene, poor standards of feeding and a lack of stimulation. Relatives were also concerned about over-use of sedatives. ...

Poor staffing ratios were cited as the main reason for inadequate care. ...

One carer from Hampshire wrote: 'I asked staff many times to help him dress and take him to the toilet and shave him. I visited my husband almost daily to wash and dress him, feed him, toilet him and shave him. Many times I found him with urine-soaked trousers. He was locked in a chair for hours. I was scared to say too much in case they took it out on my husband.'

Source: *The Guardian*, 28 May 1997

Nursing home boss jailed for abuse
A nursing home director, who ran two private care centres for people with learning disabilities 'like an army camp', was jailed for two and a half years yesterday for abusing residents in her care.

In the centres ... residents were slapped, had their hair pulled and jugs of water poured over them.

She also denied them toilet paper and essential toiletries and made one woman with Down's Syndrome ... eat her meals outside, even in the rain.

Source: *The Guardian*, 14 June 1997

Arguments in favour of residential care

However, the arguments for residential care are also quite strong. In certain cases there is little alternative to institutional care, for example, where a person is so enfeebled by age, or so seriously mentally ill, that he or she simply cannot continue to have an acceptable standard of life without constant care or supervision. Secondly, there is no reason why, *necessarily*, people's lives should come under the control of members of staff. It is quite possible to organise democratically-run institutions, where, as far as possible, residents can enjoy significant power sharing with staff. Thirdly, if the buildings are old and of poor quality, it is not residential care that is being criticised, but the lack of resources available for improving it.

Residential care is something which is always seen as inferior to living with a family. However, there are often situations in which it is better, for both the carer and the person with disabilities, if the person goes into residential care. Discussions about residential care mustn't ignore the fact that some people actually want to live in residential care rather than in the community. This could be because they are scared or anxious living on their own or they feel isolated and neglected or it could be that they prefer the residential environment.

Reports on residential care for adults

The Wagner Report

In 1988, the Wagner Report (*A Positive Choice*) was published. This highlighted the demoralised state of the residential social services, and uncovered what it called 'disturbing evidence of insensitivity ... and examples of cruelty' in residential care establishments. The report itself was largely ignored, because the move towards community care was beginning in earnest and the Griffiths Report on this subject attracted much greater interest.

The Department of Health did, however, set up the Caring in Homes initiative in order to build upon Wagner's recommendations. Finally, in 1992, *Take the Initiative* was published. This showed the extent of the advances resulting from Wagner for all groups in residential accommodation, including older people and people with learning disabilities and physical disabilities.

These are some of the findings and recommendations of the Wagner Report:

- *Positive choice:* The report said that people ought to want to enter residential homes, and not have it forced upon them. Homes therefore need to provide detailed information about themselves and the alternatives available.

- *Monitoring*: Staff need to carry out regular monitoring of the quality of life in the institutions, both as regards the individuals living there and the staff themselves. There should, as part of this, be a way for residents to express their discontent and feelings in an open way. 'We came across one woman who had been living in a home for 23 years and no one had discovered that she didn't like the food.'
- *Part of the community*: In the past, residential homes were cut off from the general community outside. There need to be as many useful links as possible between residential homes and the communities in which they are based.
- *Co-operative planning*: The aspirations of the individuals in the institutions, and of their carers/relatives, need to be part of the planning, delivery and monitoring of the services.
- *Friendly environment:* Residential homes often have a particular look and impersonal feel about them. This can be remedied by changing their appearance and the general environment.
- *Adequate training:* Staff in residential establishments were traditionally poorly trained. The report recommended that specific training was needed.

Activity

Institutions can be unwelcoming and unfriendly. They can give negative messages through their pictures, smell and general appearance. Is this true?

Arrange to visit three local institutions. After your visit, write down your impressions. If your impressions were negative, what do you suggest could be done to change the environment? Why do you think the institutions are like they are?

No Secrets

In 2000 the Department of Health published *No Secrets: Guidance on Developing Multi-Agency Policies and Procedures to Protect Vulnerable Adults from Abuse*. It was produced out of the recognition that over the years many vulnerable adults have been exposed to different types of abuse whether this be from staff, carers or other service users and in any care setting. Unlike with child abuse where there are clearly laid out procedures for all those involved to follow, the abuse of vulnerable adults has had much less research carried out into it and much less in terms of guidelines to practice. The aim of *No Secrets* is to ensure that key local agencies particularly the health service, social services and the police, work together to protect vulnerable adults from abuse by developing local multi-agency policies and procedures.

Royal Commission on Long-term Care

One of the most contentious issues in social care is how to arrange and pay for care in old age. The current generation of older people grew up as adults believing that the State would provide for them in their old age. This is the generation that went through the Second World War and greeted the Beveridge Report with such enthusiasm. Since then it has become apparent that the State is not providing for them as well as they had thought. Not only has the State pension diminished in value, but if people need to go into residential care then they are expected to mainly pay for themselves even if this means selling their houses to do so. Only when the total value of their capital reduces to £16,000 can they approach social services for help with funding. Nursing homes, which used to be provided free on the NHS, have become a thing of the past and have been largely replaced by privately-run nursing homes charging anything from £400 to £600 per week, more in some places. Unlike with mental health or learning disability, just about everyone can identify with the care problems of old age so the issue has become part of mainstream politics.

In 1997 the Labour government set up a Royal Commission on the funding of long-term care for older people. The Commission's report, *With Respect to Old Age: Long-Term Care – Rights and Responsibilities*, was published in 1998. It considered a wide range of proposals, some were advocating that all care should be free; others felt that at least nursing care should be free. Some wanted the capital disregard (£16,000 at the time) abolished; others wanted it raised much higher.

Its final recommendations included splitting the costs of long-term care between living costs, housing costs and personal care and establishing a National Care Commission. The government took a long time considering the recommendations but didn't adopt them completely.

Several key changes were implemented with the passing of the Health and Social Care Act in 2001. From April 2001 the value of a person's home has been ignored for three months. The £16,000 capital limit was raised to £18,500 with the agreement that it would be uprated annually. From October 2001 nursing care in whatever setting became free (though 'care' has to be paid for). A new grant will also be available to local authorities to enable them to make a loan (recoverable on their death) to older people going into care. The NHS Plan 2000 pledged a budget of £900m to keep older people out of hospital and residential care by, for example, beefing up home care. The Care Standards Act 2000 introduced binding statutory guidance to local authorities on charges for non-residential social services. Despite these policies the government is looking for ways of developing private insurance and insurance to pay for long-term care – recognition that the cost to the taxpayer of covering most long-term care costs would be huge.

Main points
- Residential care has declined in the last ten years.
- Residential care has its advocates and critics. Its critics point to the risk of institutionalisation or abuse taking place.
- There have been a range of reports and government commissions on residential care for adults, all pointing to the need for higher standards.
- Inspection systems for social care have been overhauled by the introduction of National Care Standards Commission.
- People in long stay residential accommodation receive free nursing care, but must pay for 'care'.

Carers

Definition

Carer – anyone who spends time and energy looking after a friend, relative, neighbour or spouse who is ill or disabled

Informal **carers**, that is to say relatives, friends and neighbours who care on a non-professional basis, are the mainstay of the care system. The health and social services only care for a tiny proportion of those in need of assistance – probably about 10 per cent at the very maximum. A large proportion of community care is provided informally. According to an official survey published in 1998, one in eight adults was providing informal care and one in six households contained a carer. 'Carers' were defined as people who were looking after or providing some regular service for a sick, handicapped or older person living in their own private household.

'When my wife was in hospital, it took four nurses to lift and turn her; now she's at home, I have to do it all on my own. Is that what they call community care?'

Source: J. Pitkeathley, *It's My Duty, Isn't It?* (Souvenir Press, 1989)

How many, how long?

In the UK today, over 6 million people are caring for sick, disabled or older people on a regular basis. Over half of all carers carry the entire burden of care alone, and about a quarter of them do so for at least 20 hours per week – there are approximately 1.5 million people in this category. Indeed, of this quarter, almost two-thirds of them (800,000 people) spend at least 50 hours each week caring. It has been estimated that if the State had to pay people to undertake these duties, then it would cost approximately £24 billion each year to the taxpayer.

There is going to be an increase in the numbers of carers in the next 20 years, as the older population (particularly those aged 85+) continues to grow, and as the effects of the switch towards community care begins to become apparent.

An overdue act of compassion

'Do you know, she's been a carer for over 50 years!' I must have looked surprised, so they explained. Vera first became a carer at the age of 20, when her mother died on Good Friday, 1945. She had to leave the WRNS to look after her father and her sister, who had a mental disability. She still cares for her sister. In between times she cared for her husband when he became mentally ill and an elderly aunt.

So Vera has been a carer ever since the development of modern social policy – the days of Beveridge and Bevan. This gutsy one-woman welfare state providing all this care, with little support from the formal welfare state.

It was just one of many such experiences from numerous meetings last year with carers throughout the country. They made me determined that my tenth place in the political lottery of the private member's ballot should not be squandered. I was convinced that my Carers' Bill must get on the statute book. Carers deserve legal recognition, practical help, not some grand backbench measure that would go down to glorious defeat at second reading.

The Carers' Act comes into force this week and does two things. It requires social services authorities, when requested by the carer, to undertake an assessment of their needs, and it says that these needs must be taken into account, alongside the needs of the cared-for person, when the care package is devised. It is not much to ask for. Yet it contrasts starkly with the experience of all too many carers. 'I've had two visits in 16 years from the social services department'; 'No one ever asks, how are you?'; 'Other people can just switch off when they finish work'.

Government and Parliament have been slow to recognise that these are people who put the word care into community care. Yet the numbers involved are truly colossal. One adult in seven is a carer and for the middle-aged this is the experience of one in four people. Among Britain's estimated 6.8 million carers, some 1.5 million provide care for more than 20 hours each week. That is a larger labour force than the NHS and social services combined.

Within these numbers there are some special groups. About 400 000 carers are supporting a relative or friend with dementia. and of the 360 000 children with disabilities, virtually all, 98.5 per cent, are cared for by their parents at home. Then there are children themselves, some very young, who find themselves prematurely taking on adult responsibilities, often caring for a disabled lone parent.

One searches in vain to find any recognition of these carers in our national arithmetic. They are not, of course, in the employment statistics, despite many working longer hours than most employees, and they apparently contribute nothing to our national wealth, as they are not included in the conventional definition of gross domestic product. Yet they are worth at least £30 billion each year, according to modest estimates of their value.

Carers' needs are varied and that's why the assessment of needs has to be a sensitive, individualised exercise. Not some uniform, clipboard response designed merely to satisfy the requirements of a new Act. But it is the need for respite – the need for a break – that stands out when you ask carers what they most want: the chance to go out occasionally, knowing that someone at home is looking after their relative; or the chance to take a summer holiday. That is how the Carers' Act should work in practice. But will it? Without an increase in resources to support implementation, many local authorities are being understandably – if regrettably – cautious in their approach.

But social policy should play to strengths and not just compensate for weaknesses. And carers are a strength. The Carers's Act recognises their work and their worth. The Government will not encourage it, but carers must now be made aware of their new rights and seek assessments should they wish to do so. Britain's carers are forgotten and silent. Over the past 10 years, not least due to the sterling work of the Carers' National Association which supported the Carers' Bill, they have become more widely recognised. That recognition must now move from rhetoric into practical support.

The author of this article, Malcolm Wicks, is Labour MP for Croydon NW and sponsor for the Carers' (Recognition and Services) Act of 1995.

Source: *The Guardian*, 3 April 1996

1 Put in your own words the sorts of experiences that persuaded Malcolm Wicks that he should sponsor the Carers' Bill.

2 What is it that carers are said to want above all else?

3 Why did the writer think that the government of the time would not encourage carers to be made aware of their new rights?

Who are the carers?

Of the nearly 7 million carers, well over half are female. In fact, over a quarter of all females aged 45–64 are carers, compared to 16 per cent of males. Apart from the differences in the proportion of males and females, carers are otherwise a typical cross-section of the community, reflecting the differences in class and education in the population at large.

There are an estimated 1.5 million carers who spend at least twenty hours a week caring, without any payment. When it comes to who looks after whom, and what the carers do, then the crucial importance of the family emerges, with the overwhelming bulk of caring being undertaken by family members. A large number of carers are looking after an elderly spouse or partner and are themselves elderly and often in poor health. The majority of carers are women, but a substantial minority are men.

Young carers

Over 10,000 carers are young people aged 18 or under, generally caring for a parent.

In 2000 a study was carried out by Deardon and Becker looking at the experiences of young people caring for a parent with a long-term illness or disability. The authors pointed out that:

- a large proportion of young carers had educational problems and missed school. Many failed to attain any educational qualifications
- leaving home was difficult for many young carers, particularly if they had a parent who required considerable help and support
- some young people reached crisis point and left home prematurely, sometimes to be taken into care
- many families received no or inadequate social care services. Where services were provided they were sometimes inappropriate, intrusive, or too costly
- many young carers were lonely and isolated, with little or no social life.

Until the passing of the Carers and Disabled Children's Act 2000, local authorities were not obliged to recognise and respond to their needs, however now 16- and 17-year-old carers will, by law, have to be assessed by local authorities and their needs met.

Activity

Conduct a small survey in your college. Using the definition above, find out how many students are either carers themselves or have a family member who is. What do your findings suggest about what type of people become carers and how widespread caring is?

In a study of older people, Evandrou found that nearly all the needs of the older respondents were met by spouses or other family members. For example, 91 per cent of those needing help to get in or out of bed, 84 per cent of those needing meals and 71 per cent requiring help with the laundry received it from their spouse or a member of the household. When it came to the other most common needs, help with shopping, walking outdoors and bathing, these were overwhelmingly provided by (adult) children, followed by other relatives. The activities performed by friends and neighbours ('the community'?) consisted of help with walking, unscrewing jars and bottle tops, and shopping – hardly a positive confirmation of the existence of community care!

There were only three areas of life in which the medical and social services made a significant contribution: 70 per cent of those receiving help with their toenails had them cut by one of these services, while 23 per cent of those receiving help with bathing were provided for by these services, and a further 20 per cent received help getting in and out of bed.

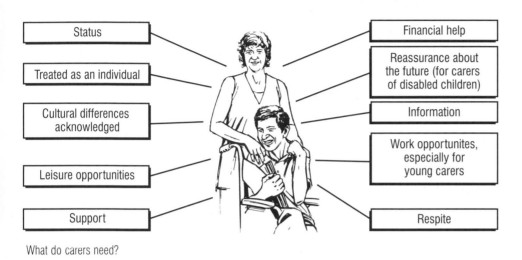

Status	Financial help
Treated as an individual	Reassurance about the future (for carers of disabled children)
Cultural differences acknowledged	Information
Leisure opportunities	Work opportunites, especially for young carers
Support	Respite

What do carers need?

'I didn't know about the incontinence service until I went to the carers' group and someone there mentioned it. I suppose they worry that too many people will want it if they publicise it.'
   'Caring has made me a physical and mental wreck, totally unable to relax and without a clue how to even try to think of myself.'

Source: J. Pitkeathley, *It's My Duty, Isn't It?* (Souvenir Press, 1989)

Support for carers

There was no special provision in the 1990 Community Care legislation for extra help for carers, even though the success of the entire community care programme depends very much on the increasing efforts of carers. The Carers' National Association, with others, campaigned vigorously to rectify this. In 1995, the Carers' (Recognition and Services) Act was passed. While being welcomed by carer's organisations, many felt that it did not go far enough. Subsequently the government has introduced Caring About Carers, a national strategy for carers. This is largely about providing better information to carers but extra money was set aside so that more support and care was available for carers. Special measures were introduced for carers in employment and young carers.

Under the Carers (Recognition and Services) Act 1995 carers were given the right to an assessment of their needs if they wish. This can be done when the person they care for is being assessed for community care or their care is being reviewed.

The Carers' Assessment provides an opportunity for carers to talk about their needs, their experience of caring, their circumstances and views and whether they wish or are able to continue caring. All of these points should be taken into consideration when looking at the support available to the person the carer is caring for. However, services will depend upon the level of need. Benefits of such an assessment could be practical help, information and advice, recognition of the role being played, and an opportunity to share feelings and experiences.

In 2000, the Carers and Disabled Children's Act took this a step forward and allowed carers to receive direct payments for the services they receive. It also allowed the provision of vouchers for disabled people to purchase the services themselves.

Other schemes

Each area will have its own smaller schemes for carers. Most will get some funding from social services, particularly since the introduction of the National Carers Strategy. Of the national voluntary organisations, Age Concern provide a range of services, and there is also the Crossroads Scheme, which consists of volunteers who will 'sit' with the older/disabled person so that the carer can have a break, go shopping, etc.

Contact your local social services and find out what help they can offer to:

a) an elderly wife looking after her disabled husband
b) a young carer looking after a disabled parent
c) the parents of a disabled child.

Who do you think gets the best service? Give your reasons.

Cash benefits for carers

There is only one benefit specifically for carers – Invalid Care Allowance (ICA). This is available for people spending at least 35 hours a week looking after an ill or disabled person who is receiving a recognised disability benefit such as Attendance Allowance, or the middle or highest rates of the care component of Disability Living Allowance.

The conditions of eligibility for ICA are that the person is of working age (16–64) when they first claim. ICA was £40.40 in April 2000. It can be backdated for fifty-two weeks. In addition if you receive ICA you are entitled to National Insurance credits which will count towards State pension. There is a Carer's Premium (an additional sum of money) if you qualify for ICA *and* you are in receipt of Income Support, Housing Benefit or Council Tax Benefit. There is no State assistance targeted specifically at carers who spend less than 35 hours a week caring.

Main points ▶ There are nearly 7 million carers in the UK. They have many needs that need to be met. Legislation states that local authorities must offer carers their own assessment.

▶ The bulk of care is provided by families through informal networks.

▶ These include many young people caring for parents

▶ There has been a move away from provision of services, to vouchers and funding for carers and disabled people to purchase their own care.

Conclusion

This chapter has explored the wide range of social care available to adults and children, and the two main settings in which they take place. The majority of care today is in the community (although the definition of this remains unclear), while a lesser, and declining, proportion is in residential settings. We have looked in particular at the role and work of social workers and how they tackle their jobs within these settings. Furthermore, we have discussed the legal and policy constraints and opportunities which provide the framework in which social workers operate.

Finally, we looked at the role of carers and the problems they face – and how only recently there has been a recognition by governments of the importance of their work.

8 CHAPTER SUMMARY

Children

1   There are two main types of social workers working with children: field social workers and residential social workers.

2   Social work with children takes place with the following settings: their family home, substitute care homes, schools, children's homes and hospitals.

3   One of the chief responsibilities of local authority social services departments is that of child protection. There have been several high-profile child abuse cases where the work of social services departments has been criticised.

4   Child protection systems are continually monitored.

5   Multi-disciplinary Area Child Protection Committees produce guidelines and supervise child protection work in an area.

6   Foster care is generally preferred to residential care and can be used for a variety of purposes.

7   Adoption is a permanent form of substitute care.

8   Reports have shown that abuse has been evident in certain children's homes. They have recommended that better training be given to residential social workers and that the inspection of homes be improved.

9   The responsibility for inspecting under-8s facilities has been passed from social services to OfSTED.

Adults

10   Adult services usually covers the following groups of service users: people over the age of 65 years old, people with mental health problems, people with physical disabilities, people with sensory impairments, people with learning disabilities and people who misuse alcohol or drugs.

11   Most social services departments have specialist teams to cover each of these groups.

12   Social work/care with these groups can take place in a variety of settings. Typically this can be in the person's own home, in a day care setting or in a residential home.

13   There is a 'continuum of care' providing a good deal of overlap between the settings.

14   Since 1993 in the UK we have officially embraced the concept of community care.

15   Community care has the following characteristics: the person lives in their own home thus promoting privacy and independence, a range of services are used to maintain someone in their own home, whilst social services departments are responsible for arranging the care it is mainly provided by independent care providers.

16   Community care has meant a deliberately encouraged growth of the independent sector (private and voluntary providers).

17   The reasons for community care being officially introduced are complex but three main reasons stand out: the rising costs of institutional care, the huge

projected increase in the elderly population and changing attitudes to the role of the State in social welfare.

18   Studies show that the advent of community care has not been without its problems. Certain groups in society are not necessarily having their needs met; some members of ethnic groups and people with severe mental illness have attracted particular attention in this respect.

19   Community care is based around the practice of care planning which has clearly laid down stages.

20   The needs of carers are an important part of the care planning process.

21   Most social care for adults is charged for by local authorities. Each local authority has its own policy on who gets charged and how much they pay.

22   Community care is based on the reality that most care is carried out by informal carers and that an important function of care in the community is to 'care for the carer'.

23   There is an ongoing debate about whether community or residential care is the most appropriate form of care, especially for certain very dependent or vulnerable groups of people.

24   Residential care has declined in the last ten years

25   Residential care has its advocates and critics. Its critics point to the risk of institutionalisation or abuse taking place.

26   There has been a range of reports and government commissions on residential care for adults, all pointing to the need for higher standards

27   Inspection systems for social care have been overhauled by the introduction of National Care Standards Commission

28   People in long-stay residential accommodation receive free nursing care, but must pay for 'care'.

29   There are nearly 7 million carers in the UK. They have many needs that need to be met. Legislation states that local authorities must offer carers their own assessment.

30   The bulk of care is provided by families through informal networks.

31   These include many young people caring for parents.

32   There has been a move away from provision of services, to vouchers and funding for carers and disabled people to purchase their own care.

Useful websites

www.nisw.org.uk: National Institute for Social Work

www.doh.gov.uk: the Department of Health

www.jrf.org.uk: the Joseph Rowntree Foundation

www.nspcc.org.uk: NSPCC

THE INDEPENDENT SECTOR

Chapter contents

Introduction

When we talk about the independent sector we mean the **non-statutory** providers of welfare. The sector is called 'independent' because, although it is usually

Definitions

Statutory – health and welfare organisations established by law with specific tasks to perform, for example local authority social services departments

Non-statutory – health and welfare organisations which are not established by law

regulated in some way by the State, it is not controlled and run directly by the government. There are two types of independent provider of welfare:

- voluntary – non-profit-making organisations
- private – privately-owned, profit-making or commercial organisations.

In this chapter we explore the nature and role of the voluntary sector in providing welfare services. The idea of voluntary organisations to help those in need is very much a British tradition and the voluntary and charitable organisations have continued to play an important role, even with the existence of the Welfare State. In recent years the government has shown particular support for the voluntary sector, to the extent that it has insisted that the bulk of local authority spending on community care services must go to the voluntary (and private, profit-making) organisations. So 'voluntarism', rather than being a historical leftover of charity work from the nineteenth century, has taken the central place of the government as the way forward to provide care.

The chapter begins with a brief definition of the voluntary sector, and then continues to look at its history, with some comments on the reasons behind its rise and decline, before the present growth as a result of government policies. Following this is a brief section on fundraising and the various types of charitable and voluntary organisations that exist.

Many professionals are critical of voluntary organisations, as they claim that they get in the way of properly funded and organised State services. This is hotly disputed by the voluntary sector, and this debate is discussed here.

Whenever there is a large number of individuals or organisations working in the same area of welfare provision, there is always the possibility of confusion, overlap and a waste of resources. However, the voluntary organisations have developed a national council to co-ordinate their activities, and we examine the activities of this council.

We turn to look at the new role of voluntary organisations in government thinking and, in particular, their importance for community care. The government is particularly keen to encourage a mixture of welfare provision instead of having a monopoly provided solely by the local authorities, and so it is switching funding away from local authorities. The term used by social policy analysts to describe this move towards a mixture of central government, local authority, private and charitable welfare provision is the mixed economy of welfare. We examine the reasons for this move and its perceived advantages and disadvantages.

Lastly, we look at the growing private, or 'for profit', sector and examine some of the important issues created by the increased privatisation of care

The voluntary sector

State and local government social services are only a part of the provision of organised help that people in difficulties receive. Another significant element of formal care is that of the voluntary or charity organisations. In 2000 the voluntary sector employed in the region of 485,000 people with an additional 3 million volunteers making a regular contribution, and 17 million more people helping on a less regular basis.

Charitable voluntary organisations

There are approximately 400,000 voluntary organisations in the UK, of which about 40 per cent are officially defined as charities. In 2001 about 163,000 voluntary organisations were registered as charities. This status allows them gain exemption from some forms of taxation. The official definition of a charity is an organisation which 'benefits the community in some way, but does not engage in political activity'. Charitable organisations typically 'advance education, religion or relieve poverty'.

According to this definition of a charity, however, the organisation must not have any political or pressure group activity. A group such as the Child Poverty Action Group, which attempts to influence the public and the politicians to combat poverty more effectively, is therefore not a charity. If it confined itself to raising money for poor people, it would be. On the other hand, public schools (because they advance education) do have charitable status.

Non-charitable voluntary organisations

The majority of voluntary organisations *do not* have charitable status. As we have seen, CPAG is one example. They still operate on a 'non-profit-making' basis – they raise money from a variety of sources which is then ploughed back into the running of the organisation. A significant group within the non-charitable voluntary organisations are housing associations (sometimes known as registered social landlords). One of the main purposes of registered social landlords within the UK's social welfare system is to provide affordable accommodation for vulnerable or disadvantaged groups, such as young single parents, adults with learning disabilities or people with mental health problems. These groups would probably find it extremely difficult to purchase their housing in the housing market. Often the accommodation will come with extra care support.

Both charitable and non-charitable voluntary organisations are described as voluntary, not because they are staffed by volunteers (although some will be) but because unlike statutory organisations they don't have to exist in law. They have usually been created to fill a social need or to pursue a particular issue.

Define each of these terms:
a) private organisations
b) charities
c) independent organisations
d) voluntary organisations.

Funding of voluntary organisations

The charitable sector makes up a considerable part of the economy. The combined annual income of registered charities in England and Wales in 2001 was just over £23 billion.

Over three-quarters of these organisations had an annual income under £10,000, accounting for only 2 per cent of total charities' incomes. The financial wealth is concentrated in a few very big charities. The main ones in the field of social welfare are Oxfam, the Salvation Army and Barnado's.

The top ten richest charities

Income and expenditure of the top fund-raising charities 1998–9

£ million

	Voluntary income	Total income	Total expenditure
Oxfam	106	170	155
National Trust	100	221	190
Imperial Cancer Research Fund	96	118	102
Cancer Research Campaign	80	89	88
Royal National Lifeboat Institution	79	94	60
British Heart Foundation	78	88	93
Salvation Army	66	83	79
Help the Aged	60	67	63
Diana Princess of Wales Memorial Fund	59	97	20
Barnardo's	59	110	125

Source: Charities Aid Foundation

Source: *Britain 2001: The Official Guide* (The Stationary Office, 2001)

1 a) Which charity has the top total income?

b) Which charity has the top voluntary income?

2 Which charity spends the highest proportion of what it collects?

3 How do you think the differences between the voluntary amount and total amount are made up? (Take a walk down a local high street for one idea!)

4 Are there any charities here which surprise you?

There is a wide range of sources from which voluntary organisations receive income. The diagram below shows the main sources.

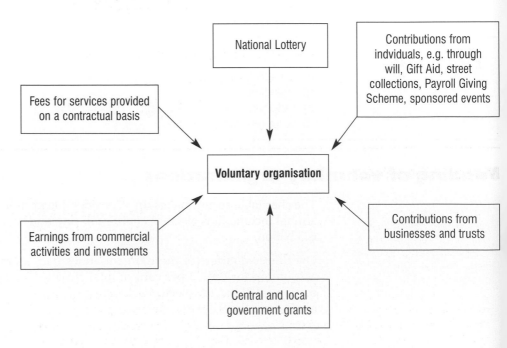

Sources of income for voluntary organisations

The National Lottery

The introduction of the National Lottery in 1993 has had a mixed effect on voluntary organisations. Whilst several have benefited directly from Lottery funds being given to them, there has been concern expressed that money spent by the public in playing the lottery has had a serious effect on the amount of money donated to charities – see the letter to the Guardian below, for example.

The Lottery's net losers

Yet again Camelot seeks to convince the public that buying National Lottery tickets will help good causes, as the full page advertisement (*Guardian*, November 16) purports to say. The reality, never mind the demeaning imagery, however, is somewhat different.

Whilst a few hundred charities will be very fortunate net benefi-ciaries as recipients of grants from the National Lottery Charities Board, thousands if not tens of thousands more will be net losers as a result of £100 million per week being spent on the lottery.

Contrary to John Major's view that is not 'additionality' [sic] but a huge substitution of spending some of which (£339 million per annum according to the latest NCVO research) would have been given to charities. For arts and heritage organisations these grants may well constitute new money – they are not the ones out on the streets seeking support from the general public. For many charities a real decline in spontaneous, discretionary donations has already happened and even a grant from the NLCB may not compensate them for that loss of income.

The Lottery continues to be, just that; and any message from Camelot to the contrary is, to say the least, pretty suspect.

The writer of this letter, Peter Maple, is Director of Communications and Fundraising for Arthritis Care, a charitable organisation

Source: *The Guardian*, 18 November 1995

According to the writer, has the introduction of the National Lottery been of benefit to the voluntary sector as a whole? Give reasons.

How each £1 spent on the National Lottery is allocated

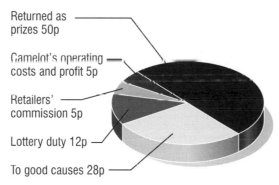

Returned as prizes 50p

Camelot's operating costs and profit 5p

Retailers' commission 5p

Lottery duty 12p

To good causes 28p

Total raised for good causes by 2001 = £10.6 billion

Source: National Lottery Commission

Source: *Britain 2000: The Official Guide* (The Stationary Office, 2000)

1 How much did the retailers and Camelot (who run the Lottery) get?

2 How much did the government get?

3 How much do 'good causes' get?

4 What does it mean by 'good causes'?

Moral minefield

Principles are one thing – money is quite another. In recent months charities have come under fire for using what some consider to be "tainted" money.

Staff at NCH Action for Children protested, and one staff member even resigned, at the charity's attempts to bring in sponsorship from the UK's largest arms manufacturer BAe Systems. The charity was in line for £600,000, but staff complained it was unethical for a charity whose purpose is the welfare of children to enter into partnership with such a company.

Besides the direct injury done to children and young people in strife-torn countries by these arms, the charity's staff argue that accepting this money would run contrary to the charity's central values as an empowering Christian-based organisation.

NCH Action for Children's case is not new. Many of the UK's most prominent charities have found themselves investing tens of millions of pounds in the arms trade, genetically modified crops and petrochemicals, issues they may directly oppose, via their staff pension funds.

Oxfam, which has £25 million invested, and Christian Aid, which has about £9 million invested, are among the 3,500 charities with pension schemes run by the Pensions Trust. The company specialises in pensions for voluntary and charitable organisations and, as such, assumptions have often been made about where it invests its members' money. Its main portfolio, however, has always been run on a market rather than an ethical basis.

And therein lies the dilemma. Market forces almost never equate with ethics. Charities have a legal obligation to maximise their charitable investments and perhaps a moral obligation to provide the best-performing pensions for their staff.

The Charity Commission, in regulating the sector, states: "Trustees of a charity should decline to invest in a particular company if it carries out activities which are directly contrary to the charity's purpose and, therefore, against its interests and those of its beneficiaries.

"For instance, a charity for the relief of cancer sufferers would be justified in avoiding investment in tobacco companies, or temperance charities in breweries.

"However, trustees may not exclude, to the financial detriment of the charity, a particular range or class of investments in order to give effect to some moral or political belief held by the trustees but not directly related to the interests of the charity and its beneficiaries."

For this and other reasons NCH Action for Children felt it was not betraying its principles, Christian or charitable, to go for sponsorship from BAe Systems.

Source: *Community Care*, 13–19 July 2000

Why might some charities face dilemmas about how they raise funds? Should there be any restriction on how charities raise revenue or invest their money – because, after all, they are doing it for a good cause, aren't they?

Gift Aid

The Gift Aid scheme provides tax relief on any donation provided that the donor is a taxpayer and is paying an amount at least equal to the donation in tax.

20p a day is all it takes to give a kid a break

The reasons our children need holidays are varied but what they all have in common is the desperate need for a break: a chance to be carefree, to splash in the sea, run through fields and simply recapture the innocence and joy of childhood.

By becoming a **Friend of the Family**, you can help us give a kid a break for as little as £5.85 a month. That's just 20p a day – **less than the price of a first class stamp.**

Please complete the details overleaf and return this entire form to FHA in the FREEPOST envelope provided. *Thank you so much.*

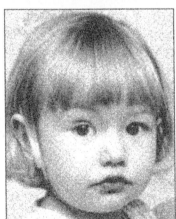

£5.85 a month

It costs less than 20p a day to Give a Kid a Break if you Gift Aid your donation, so do please complete the details overleaf so that another family in need can start looking forward to the first holiday they will have probably ever had.

What is Gift Aid?

The Inland Revenue will refund the tax you have already paid or will pay in this tax year on your donations to the Family Holiday Association (FHA). The following points are for your guidance and to ensure that FHA is able to collect this tax refund properly.

- Please let us know if you change your name/address.
- If you decide you no longer want us to reclaim tax on your donations (for example, if you become a non-taxpayer), please let us know.
- You must be paying an amount of income tax/capital gains tax at least equal to the tax that FHA reclaims on your donations in that tax year up to the basic rate of tax. If you pay tax at a higher rate you can claim further tax relief in your Self Assessment tax return.
- If you are unsure whether your donations qualify for Gift Aid, please contact Andy Grout at FHA on 020 7436 3304. Or you can ask your local tax office for leaflet IR113 Gift Aid.

Data Protection:
Selected organisations will send information about FHA to their supporters if in return, we tell you about them. If you do not wish to share in this cost-effective fundraising method, please tick. ☐ Family Holiday Association – Registered Charity Number 800262

1 What work does the Family Holiday Association do?

2 How does the Gift Aid scheme help the development of the voluntary sector?

3 Why would a government choose to support voluntary organisations?

History of the voluntary sector

There have always been charities and voluntary activities, especially those organised by religious groups. By 1869, the Charity Organisation Society (today the Family Welfare Organisation) had been founded with the aim of uniting the 640 charities that were operating in London. During the middle of the nineteenth century, some large organisations emerged which influenced the structure of many modern forms of voluntary organisations, for example the founding of Dr Barnardo's Children's Homes (1870) and the National Society for the Prevention of Cruelty to Children (1884).

There were various reasons for the emergence of such a large number of charitable organisations at this time. Some of the principal reasons are listed below.

Social surveys

Role for women

Growing democracy

Control of the poor

Ideological beliefs

Octavia Hill (1838–1912) felt strongly about the lack of adequate housing. She campaigned vigorously for improved housing and open spaces for working people

Growth of mutual aid

Victorian philanthropy

Growth of organisations

Reasons behind the development of the voluntary sector

Awareness of problems

People had always been aware of poverty, but the sheer scale and extent of social problems were proved and publicised by a small number of academic researchers and political reformers, such as Mayhew, Booth and Rowntree.

Ability to influence

The emerging democratic structure of British society meant that pressure groups were able to influence the politicians who were beginning to take into account the views of the voters. Remember, though, that the right to vote was limited throughout the nineteenth century to a minority of the adult population, for example, women did not fully attain the right to vote until 1928!

Beliefs

The dominant ideology or belief system at the time was of *laissez-faire*, which meant that the government was not supposed to interfere in society, rather its role was to defend the country and to maintain law and order within it.

A second belief was that the financial position that people found themselves in was largely a result of their own hard work and good fortune. If people were poor, it was generally because they did not work hard enough, or they had personal failings.

Victorian philanthropy

<table>
<tr><td>

Definition

Philanthropy – active effort in promoting the welfare of others

</td><td>

In the second half of the eighteenth century, certain sections of the better-off, the urban middle class, were becoming aware of the inadequacy of the existing Poor Law to deal with the extent of poverty and its related problems. A common response of the socially concerned middle and upper classes was to dispense private charity and to promote 'good works' among the poor – as long as they were considered deserving! It was regarded as a social duty which had to be done and, for many, had to *be seen to be done*. Such actions, doing good out of a sense of duty and conscience, are called **philanthropy**. Notable philanthropists from this period include: William Booth, founder of the Salvation Army; Octavia Hill, a pioneer of social housing; and Dr Barnardo.

</td></tr>
</table>

Organisations

Today, we accept the idea of organisations based on rules and bureaucratic procedures. If you are studying this book, you will probably be at a college or in employment where there is a complex organisation making specific demands. This way of undertaking tasks is a relatively new form of activity, however, and one which profoundly influenced industrialised societies – including the way of organising to combat social problems, as opposed to the unco-ordinated efforts of individuals.

Rising power of the working class

<table>
<tr><td>

Definition

Mutual aid – ordinary people clubbing together to help themselves

</td><td>

The nineteenth century saw the organisation of the working class into unions and friendly societies (the influence of organisation again) to further their own interests. These unions and societies organised charitable self-help groups. This is often described as **mutual aid**.

</td></tr>
</table>

Social control

We noted earlier that the role of the government was to defend the country and to maintain law and order. Part of law and order involved ensuring that the demands of the working class and the poor were not met, as that would disturb the living standards and the political power of the rich. Charities formed a very useful way of doing this. Help to the poor was given, not as a right, but as an exercise in charity for which the poor had to be grateful. This strengthened the moral superiority and right to rule of the rich.

The role of women

The nineteenth century saw a rise in the status of men and the imposition of their views as 'normal' in society. Undoubtedly women were repressed in a way that would shock most people today. Poor women were often forced into the roles of servants, and many were driven by desperation into prostitution. The wives of rich men were excluded from taking an active part in business affairs, no matter how capable they were. The only acceptable outlet for their drive, intelligence and energy was charitable work.

Statutory and non-statutory services

A subsidiary but important part of the drive towards statutory social services represented a deliberate move away from voluntary provision, not least within the Labour Party. Faith was invested in statutory services as a way of guaranteeing provision that was comprehensive and universal, professional and impartial, and subject to democratic control. The immediate post-war implementation of social policies marked an attempt decisively to move away from social policies that were partial in scope, socially divisive in action, and socially controlling in intent.

Voluntary organisations were regarded with not a little suspicion in the process. While readily acknowledged for their pioneering contribution and their highlighting of social problems, voluntary organisations were also seen as ill-organised, amateur and fragmented and unevenly distributed. With the rapid secularisation of British society between the wars, the voluntary organisations were no longer rooted in significant social groupings in a way that the mass of people could identify with.

They were, in a society that continued to be riven with class divides, identified with middle-class patterns of patronage and charity.

In the construction of the new social service state we turned our backs on philanthropy and replaced the do-gooder by highly professional administrators and experts. From the 1920s on, the normal left-wing attitude has been opposed to middle-class philanthropy, charity and everything else connected with do-gooding.

Those of us who became socialists grew up with the conviction that we must in this point ally ourselves with the professionals and trades unions and discourage voluntary effort particularly since it was bound to reduce the number of jobs available.

Source: M. Brenton, *The Voluntary Sector in British Social Services* (Longman, 1985)

1 Why was it believed that statutory social services were the way forward after the Second World War, when the Welfare State was first set up?

2 What were the perceived disadvantages of the voluntary services?

Charitable and self-help organisations were in the forefront of providing help to people in ill-health and to disabled, older and poor people, until the introduction of the Welfare State in the 1940s, when many believed that there would be no further need for voluntary groups. However, it is interesting to note that William Beveridge, who many regard as the architect of the Welfare State, wrote a paper in 1948 called 'Voluntary action'. In it he anticipated that voluntary aid would continue to play a role in welfare provision, which it did, although it was a much diminished role.

By the end of the 1970s disillusionment had begun to set in with the idea that State welfare could meet all society's needs and problems. In 1978 the Wolfenden Committee, which was financed by voluntary groups, wrote a report on the future of voluntary action. It identified four sectors of 'social helping' at work in the UK. They were the *informal*, the *commercial*, the *statutory* and the *voluntary* sectors.

Definition

Mixed economy of welfare – the system in which social welfare services are provided through different organisations in the statutory, private and voluntary sectors. Some would add to this the need to include the informal sector of social helping

Wolfenden described this situation as *welfare pluralism* (though it is now known more as the **mixed economy of welfare)**. The report argued a case for the voluntary sector to play a more significant role than it had been in previous decades.

Since then, the ideas of the Wolfenden Report have been taken further by the conservative New Right (see Chapters 1 and 2) and Conservative government policy actively promoted the growth of both the voluntary and commercial (or for profit) sectors. New Labour has continued to endorse the need for a strong independent sector. (See the section on mixed economy of welfare, page 256.)

The variety of voluntary groups

The 1960s saw an increase in the number of voluntary organisations which had rather different methods and aims from the traditional ones. These organisations developed to fill the gaps in the Welfare State that had become apparent twenty years after it was set up. The groups developed in different ways and for different purposes:

- *political pressure groups*, for example, the Child Poverty Action Group (poverty) or Shelter (housing)
- *self-help groups*, for example, Alcoholics Anonymous, Gingerbread (for lone-parent families) – this has been the fastest growing type over the last thirty or so years

- *non-profit-making providers*, for example, housing associations (known as registered social landlords) – these now play a major part in the provision of social housing supported living schemes, and so on
- *education*, for example, AIDS charities such as the Terrence Higgins Trust (although education is only part of its activities)
- *direct assistance*, for example, Help the Aged, Children in Need
- *advice and counselling*, for example, Citizens' Advice Bureaux, Relate (marriage guidance)
- *religious*, for example, the Salvation Army – although this organisation runs a variety of schemes which provide practical help as well.

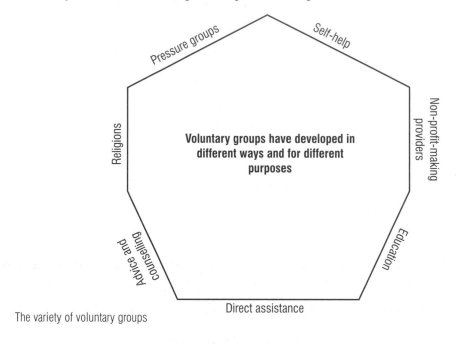

The variety of voluntary groups

The Red Cross: an example of a non-statutory agency

British Red Cross
Caring for people in crisis

Helping patients return home

Home from Hospital Service

Would you like to help?

The British Red Cross welcomes people who can work within the Home from Hospital Service. Please contact the Community Services Manager at your local British Red Cross Branch Headquarters.

The British Red Cross Home from Hospital Service complements and enhances the care provided by statutory agencies to people needing practical assistance or personal care following in or out patient treatment.

The service operates as part of the planned discharge procedure and works with other service providers to minimise disruption and ease the adjustment between one environment and another for patients and their informal carers.

The key objective of the service is to ensure that people do not remain in hospital longer than they need to once medical and nursing requirements have been fulfilled.

Home from Hospital provides a very flexible, patient-centred, response using trained and skilled volunteers working in their own communities, and managed by a paid co-ordinator who can access professional advice as needed.

These are some of the tasks Home from Hospital volunteers can undertake:

- *Prepare the home*
- *Shop*
- *Welcome the person home*
- *Help with meals*
- *Build confidence*
- *Help with mobility*
- *Collect prescriptions*
- *Relief for carers*
- *Support self-care*

1 In your own words, explain how the Hospital at Home service works.

2 Is it meant to replace statutory services?

3 The service is free to users but what costs does the Red Cross have to cover in order to run the services?

4 What methods does the Red Cross use to raise funds?

Charity begins at home

When the communist states of Eastern Europe collapsed in the early 1990s, Western experts were appalled at the conditions that orphans and disabled people lived in. Yet there seemed little concern by the local populations to try to improve the conditions of these people. The main reason for the inactivity of the Eastern European populations was that they had no concept of voluntary work. The State had taken over all responsibility for individuals' lives, and people were simply unused to initiating help for those with needs.

'I hate them … the way they treat me as if I am some sort of beggar or something. Just because I'm here [in this state] … it doesn't mean I'm … worth less than them … life's been unfair … I mean I've been unlucky. As far as I am concerned they were born with money and I wasn't. It is the government which should help me, not these … Lady Muck busybodies.'

Questions

1 Is it true that voluntary workers act as superior to their clients? What are the motives of those who are volunteers – to help or to fill in their spare time?
2 Would it be better if the State were to run all caring activities – as they effectively do with health care?
3 Or would it be better to limit the role of the State to providing offices and some funding for charitable organisations?

An evaluation of voluntary organisations

The advantages of voluntary organisations

Social integration

The giving and receiving of gifts (including our services) helps the integration of society by creating bonds between different groups of people, and entails them in mutual obligations. Those who give may lose their time or money, but they benefit from feeling they have been generous. Those who receive benefit directly through goods and services, but pay by demonstrating their gratefulness.

Meeting of specific needs

Very often the specific needs of groups in society cannot be catered for by the huge and impersonal health and welfare services. Voluntary groups can fit into this gap in provision.

Responsiveness

The voluntary sector can respond quickly to new needs that arise or new concerns of society. The growth in AIDS organisations occurred long before the government began to respond.

Less bureaucracy

Voluntary organisations, especially the smaller ones, are less bureaucratic in the way they operate. They are less bound by official rules and regulations, guidelines and procedures. They can therefore be more flexible and creative in what they do.

Personal commitment

The health and caring services are staffed by professionals whose job it is to provide a good service, but who are trained to distance themselves from individual clients as a means of coping and treating all clients fairly. Voluntary organisations can often provide people who are personally committed to the particular group or charitable activity.

Experience

Often, and especially in self-help groups, the carers are those who have themselves been through the particular problems and can therefore understand the issues and needs of the clients.

Expertise

Often the real experts on a particular issue may not be the statutory services but the voluntary groups. For example, the problems of prisoners and their wives are better known by NACRO (the National Association for the Care and Resettlement of Offenders) than by the authorities.

Stigma

This is a particularly difficult issue. However, it is claimed that there is less chance of being 'labelled' when voluntary organisations, and particularly self-help groups, are involved.

Disadvantages and criticisms of voluntary organisations

Welfare is the duty of the State

Many people are critical of the voluntary services because, they argue, it is the role of the government to ensure that all citizens have a decent standard of living. They claim that when charities and voluntary organisations provide welfare, the State steps back from providing these services. In some cases, the argument continues, the quality and coverage of the voluntary services are not as comprehensive as those of the State (or local authorities), and so overall the quality of services declines. The greater the intrusion of charities into health and welfare, the more the government retreats from its responsibilities.

Patchwork

Voluntary services provide an uneven spread of services. The areas best covered are those which are attractive (looking after children), while others attract little interest (older people). The more effective an organisation is at gaining publicity and public sympathy, the more the resources are given to its particular client group. Also, geographical variations can occur, where one place has better provision, because there is a more enthusiastic group based there.

Lack of skills and training

Professional social workers and health care employees are trained to undertake a particular task and have the relevant knowledge and skills. A misguided, enthusiastic amateur can actually do more damage than good.

Inadequate funding

When a voluntary organisation has to rely on charity, then the flow of funds can be uneven or inadequate. This results in an insecure service, with inconsistent standards. Government funding ought to guarantee long-term planning.

Duplication

The tasks which a voluntary organisation sets out to do may also be performed by a statutory agency, and some confusion can result, unless close co-operation is undertaken. Agencies like the NSPCC (child protection) need to co-operate closely wherever possible with the Children and Young Persons Team of social work departments.

Lack of proper accountability

Many voluntary organisations are subject to less public scrutiny and are less accountable for their actions than statutory ones. This can mean that any unsatisfactory, inefficient, or dubious practices are less likely to be spotted and rectified. It is harder for users to call to account the people who are running the services.

Putting people out of jobs

Social workers and health care professionals are trained for their work and undertake this as their employment. When volunteers perform these duties, they run the risk of taking jobs away from the professionals.

Professional ethics

Part of the training that social workers undertake is in ethics and standards of behaviour. Those operating in the voluntary sector may also have this training, but if they are unqualified they may not operate to the same exacting standards of professional behaviour.

It is important to remember that voluntary organisations range from small groups of people who have no training at all to those which employ highly trained professionals. Therefore, the above criticisms regarding standards and training may well not apply. Indeed, it is argued by the bigger voluntary agencies that they do a better job than the local authority agencies.

Activity | Decide what you consider to be the three biggest advantages and the three biggest disadvantages of voluntary organisations.

Co-ordination of voluntary organisations

Earlier we saw that the huge number of charities existing in London in the 1860s necessitated a new organisation to co-ordinate them. In 1869, there were 640 charities; at the end of 2001 (as we saw earlier), there were over 163,000 in England and Wales alone!

In 2000 the government introduced Compacts in England, Scotland, Wales and Northern Ireland with the purpose of providing a general framework for better relationships between the government and the voluntary sector. Partly this was to do with the fact within the voluntary sector there are so many different organising and co-ordinating bodies they, themselves, need co-ordination!

voice of the voluntary sector

The National Council for Voluntary Organisations (NCVO) could be described as an 'umbrella organisation'. It is one of the main national co-ordinating bodies in England, providing links between voluntary organisations, government bodies, local authorities, the EU and the private sector.

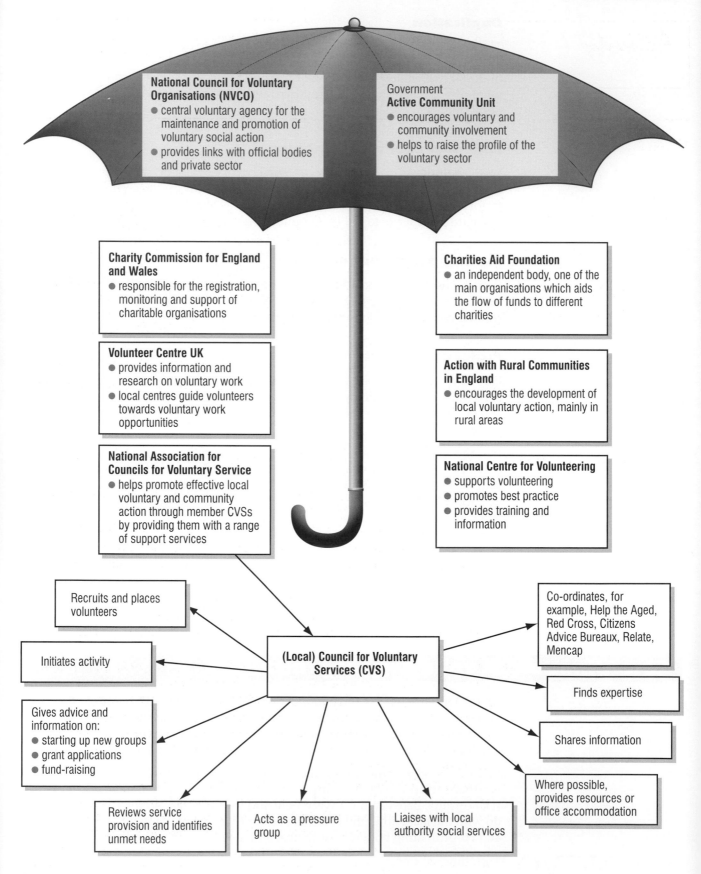

National Council for Voluntary Organisations (NVCO)
- central voluntary agency for the maintenance and promotion of voluntary social action
- provides links with official bodies and private sector

Government
Active Community Unit
- encourages voluntary and community involvement
- helps to raise the profile of the voluntary sector

Charity Commission for England and Wales
- responsible for the registration, monitoring and support of charitable organisations

Charities Aid Foundation
- an independent body, one of the main organisations which aids the flow of funds to different charities

Volunteer Centre UK
- provides information and research on voluntary work
- local centres guide volunteers towards voluntary work opportunities

Action with Rural Communities in England
- encourages the development of local voluntary action, mainly in rural areas

National Association for Councils for Voluntary Service
- helps promote effective local voluntary and community action through member CVSs by providing them with a range of support services

National Centre for Volunteering
- supports volunteering
- promotes best practice
- provides training and information

Recruits and places volunteers

Initiates activity

Gives advice and information on:
- starting up new groups
- grant applications
- fund-raising

(Local) Council for Voluntary Services (CVS)

Co-ordinates, for example, Help the Aged, Red Cross, Citizens Advice Bureaux, Relate, Mencap

Finds expertise

Shares information

Where possible, provides resources or office accommodation

Reviews service provision and identifies unmet needs

Acts as a pressure group

Liaises with local authority social services

The co-ordination of the voluntary sector

Arrange an interview with your local CVS (Council for Voluntary Services). Find examples of each of the functions shown in the diagram opposite? Are there any other functions not shown.

Charity should begin nearer home

The Children's Promise, the Millennium Final Hour Appeal, is a great idea. Employees are encouraged to donate their final hour's earnings of the Millennium to the cause and it is expected to raise millions of pounds with the proceeds distributed to charity. Marks & Spencer is covering the operating costs.

Distributed to whom? To five very large charities; namely Barnardo's, the Children's Society, the NSPCC, NCH Action for Children and ChildLine. I have worked for two of them and I know that they all do valuable work. But they are rich charities. Barnardo's, for example, has an annual income of £109 million and net assets of £196 million. The

decision of the Children's Promise to work with the big boys will reinforce the trend of the rich voluntaries getting richer, while the poor ones get even poorer.

One part of the voluntary sector is ignored completely – neighbourhood groups, which are small, locally controlled projects, usually in deprived areas. They are important

because they constitute an alternative approach to both statutory and large voluntary agencies. Staff tend to live in the area and take modest incomes. Services reflect what residents need because decisions are made by committees elected from the neighbourhood. Just as importantly they are valued by local people.

Source: *Community Care*, 16–22 September 1999

What evidence is there, in the extract, that there is 'substantial disparity' (great inequality) in resources within the voluntary sector? What is the writer's viewpoint?

Main points ▶

- The independent sector is made up from the voluntary sector and private sector.
- The voluntary sector is an umbrella term for a range of different voluntary organisations, some national, some local, some big, some small.
- About 40 per cent of voluntary organisations are registered as charities.
- Voluntary organisations get their funding from a range of sources ranging from individual donations, through charges for services, to grants from government.
- The voluntary sector has roots going back beyond the nineteenth century. However, from the mid/late nineteenth century the voluntary sector of social welfare grew significantly for a range of social, ideological and political reasons.
- Many thought that the creation of the Welfare State in the 1940s signalled the end of the voluntary welfare sector in any meaningful sense. However, despite the expansion of statutory services it continues to play a key role.
- Voluntary groups have different reasons for being in existence. Some, for example, emphasise self-help, others campaign and act as pressure groups, others offer direct assistance whilst others are more about education and the dissemination of information.
- Opinions differ over whether voluntary organisations have a proper place to play in modern welfare. Some see voluntary organisations as a positive improvement on what the State has to offer, whilst others believe that voluntary organisations are a poor substitute for State-run provision.
- Several bodies (most recently Compacts) have been created in order to co-ordinate the many and various organisations working in the voluntary sector.

The mixed economy of welfare

A serious concern of governments in the 1980s and 1990s was the way in which the State had seemingly taken over many of the caring responsibilities which politicians argued were the role of families, neighbours, friends and communities. The argument has been that when the government steps in and takes responsibility for the welfare of its citizens, then the social fabric of society – which consists of individuals giving and taking – is shredded. Gradually the attitude of dependency develops amongst those in difficulties, so the argument is that 'the government ought to do something'. On the other hand, those who are in a position to give through charity, or to help directly by shopping for a neighbour, no longer regard it as being their business.

Welfare pluralism: the four sectors

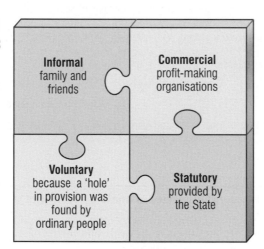

Give two examples of organisations in each of the following sectors:

a) commercial
b) statutory
c) voluntary.

In many ways this is simply a reflection of a debate that has gone on throughout history on the extent to which the State should take responsibility for others. In Victorian times, it was quite clear that the majority of affluent people regarded social welfare as something to be performed by the family, the church or by neighbours. The role of the government was to provide a very basic form of welfare which no one would turn to unless they were desperate. The role of the affluent was to select worthy causes to give their money or energies to.

The 1980s in the UK saw a shift back to the philosophy that the State should intervene only when absolutely necessary, and when it did so, it should help those who were really in genuine need. Recent governments, then, have attempted to move away from a single provider – the State – towards a wide range of providers of welfare, drawn from the public, voluntary and private sectors. This system of mixed provision using charitable organisations, volunteers, private agencies, State provision and non-profit-making organisations is known as the mixed economy of welfare or sometimes as welfare pluralism.

The Labour government, which first came into power in 1997, continued this policy of welfare pluralism.

The table opposite illustrates how the four sectors of the mixed economy of welfare provide services for older people.

Welfare sectors and community care provision for older people

Service	Statutory	Commercial/private	Voluntary	Informal
Personal care	Home care assistants, community nursing	Private nurses, private home care, live-in carers	Voluntary agencies	Relatives, friends and neighbours doing what they can
Other social care	Day care, occupational therapy, care call alarms, respite care, meals, mobility aids (loaned), house adaptations, mobile wardens	Private home care, private meals service, private respite and day care, privately purchased mobility aids, adaptations	Voluntarily run home care, day centres (for example, by Alzheimer's Disease Society), sitting services, lunch clubs, meals-on-wheels (WRVS), dog walking, mobility aids (Red Cross)	Relatives, friends and neighbours, community networks doing what they can
Domestic assistance	Home care assistants	Private domestics, cleaners, housekeepers, laundry services, gardeners, window cleaners	Voluntarily-run domestic services, for example Age Concern, locally-run schemes, for example Garden-Aid	Relatives, friends and neighbours doing what they can
Nursing, medical, health input	District nursing, GP, NHS dentist, occupational therapy, physiotherapy, chiropody, specialist nursing, for example incontinence adviser, Parkinson's nurse, etc.	Nursing agencies, for example BNA, private dentist, chiropodist, physiotherapist, osteopath, etc., private medicine, health insurance	Hospital at Home (Red Cross), joint schemes with NHS such as Macmillan and Marie Curie	Limited because of lack of specialist training
Financial	Pensions, Attendance Allowance, Income Support, other benefits	Private and occupational pensions, annuities, savings and investments	Charitable grants	Financial support from relatives
Housing	Local authority housing, for example sheltered schemes, extra care units, residential homes	Privately owned or rented houses, flats, sheltered schemes, private nursing or residential homes	Housing associations sheltered housing, voluntarily-run nursing or residential homes, for example Sue Ryder, Red Cross	Accommodation provided, granny annexes or flats, living with relatives
Transport	Ambulance service, social services transport, subsidised schemes, for example bus passes, taxi cards, etc.	Taxis, buses, own car	Voluntary driver schemes, car service (Age Concern), day centre transport	Relatives, friends and neighbours doing what they can

Using the table on page 257, and the main text, identify areas where:

- the statutory sector plays the greatest role in the provision of services
- the informal sector plays the greatest part
- the independent sector plays the major role
- the private sector plays the major role.

Debating the mixed economy of welfare

Supporters of the mixed economy of welfare

Supporters of the mixed economy of welfare argue the following points in its favour.

Sense of community

When the State takes over complete control of the provision of welfare, then the mutual obligations and sense of community of society weakens. By removing the dominant role of the State, more people will be drawn into welfare and there will be a regrowth of a sense of belonging and community.

Higher quality of services

When the State is the monopoly provider of services, there is little incentive to provide high standards. By having a range of welfare agencies, there will be competition to provide better quality. Furthermore, a number of providers will create a range of types of welfare provision, and encourage new initiatives.

Flexibility

The range of different welfare agencies will allow greater flexibility in that each welfare provider will offer different approaches to care and therefore there is greater likelihood of suitable provision for all needs.

Choice

The greater the number and type of providers, the wider the choice (in theory at least) for those in need the consumers.

Reduced costs

By using charities and voluntary organisations, the costs of providing services are lowered.

Public preference for charities

The introduction of a mixed economy of welfare is linked to attempts to lower the costs of public services in general, and to cut taxes. With the extra money available to taxpayers, they can decide to give more money to the charity of their own choosing. This applies in particular to companies which can give to charity and improve their public image. This supporting of charities is often done through corporate trusts.

More focused role of social services

The social services perform a very wide range of welfare functions. Some argue this range is simply too wide and complex for all the activities to be provided at a high standard and to be well co-ordinated. The community care changes, which came into effect in April 1993, began to clarify the role of the social services as a purchaser of services for a number of its adult client groups such as those with disabilities and older people.

Critics of the mixed economy of welfare

Critics of the mixed economy of welfare put forward the following objections.

Dismantling of the Welfare State

The mixed economy of welfare is one way of bringing about the end of the Welfare State. The greater the independent sector grows, the more this will leave State welfare as a residual service only for the very poor and needy.

Lower quality

The move away from public provision, with its moral basis of caring for people as citizens, to one based on charity or profit-making (as in the private sector) would actually lower the standards of care, as profit rather than public service becomes the overriding motive.

Lack of choice

The move towards the mixed economy of welfare will lead to a narrowing of choice as the public sector loses its (legal and financial) abilities to provide care. The only remaining providers of care will be the profit-making companies and a patchwork of charitable organisations.

Increased costs

It will actually cost more money than at present, because the private homes and services (such as home care assistants) need to make a profit.

Stigma

There will be a move back towards clients being seen as receiving charity or too poor to pay for their own welfare. This means a degree of stigma.

Haphazard provision

As there will be no statutory body providing services in each local authority the extent and the quality of services will vary from place to place.

Unreliability

However badly resourced or run State organisations may be on occasions, they are never allowed to go out of business or disappear. This can happen to private or voluntary organisations – and often does.

Main points ▸ The mixed economy of welfare refers to the system of social welfare which is based on using the statutory, voluntary, private sectors. The adoption of this principle in the 1980s represented a shift away from the view that the government (State) would have a virtual monopoly on provision.

▸ Supporters of the mixed economy approach say that, among other advantages, it offers an increased choice and flexibility of services together with reduced costs.

▸ Critics argue that in reality a mixed economy has led to patchy and erratic services that are not necessarily cheaper and that the system is less fair and more complicated.

The private or 'for profit' sector

The **private sector**, that is those services which operate on a profit-making basis, has a long history. For example, private health care long pre-dates the National

Definition

Private sector – those organisations that operate for profit, and are run as a business

Health Service, as does private residential and nursing care. Needless to say such provision has only been available to those wealthy enough to afford it! The private organisations together with voluntary organisations make up the independent sector of social welfare.

With the creation of the Welfare State the need for private care provision of any kind was greatly reduced. However, the 1980s and 1990s saw an increase in the use of private services. During the early 1980s there was a huge growth in the number of private residential care homes (from 1981 to 1985 the number of such homes more than doubled to well over 5,000). This was, in part, to do with the availability of social security funds to pay for care. However, the rising social security bill for residential care was one of the reasons the NHS and Community Care Act 1990 was introduced, not only to promote more care in the home but also to keep the lid on care costs. The Act gave chief funding responsibility to local authorities who have to work within tight budgets. This has led to a noticeable slowing down in the growth of private residential homes. In fact many have had to close because funding has not been available.

According to analysts Laing and Buisson in 1998 the value of the care home market for older and physically disabled people was estimated at £8.5 billion. Of this, private sector operators accounted for £5.3 billion. This is a substantial share of the market.

It is not only the private residential sector that has increased in size. Since the passing of the NHS and Community Care Act 1990 there has been a vast increase in the number of domiciliary (home visiting) care agencies. People either contact them directly or, more likely, the social services commission their services on behalf of their clients in their role of care purchasers. Increasingly local authorities are confining their home care funding to personal care for people. Other elements of the traditional home help's role such as cleaning, shopping, laundry, etc. are no longer being commissioned and it is now for people to find and pay for these services themselves privately.

As more and more social care provision falls into the hands of private businesses, some argue that this is good thing because it increases choice and raises quality. Others are worried that the principle of profit will take precedence over proper care principles and that standards will fall. Critics point to the lower pay and worse conditions that exist for many private care workers.

The size of the private home care market

A Registered care homes, UK 1999, all client types

All care homes	**29,434**
Total number of places	**609,146**
Private and voluntary residential homes (4+ beds)	15,308
Small residential homes	4,581
Private and voluntary nursing homes	4,763
Private and voluntary dual registered homes	2,032
Local authority owned homes	2,592
NHS trust owned homes	158

Source: www.privatehealth.co.uk/laing/carehome

B

Counting the losses

Almost 10,000 places in care homes for elderly and disabled people were lost last year, according to figures released today by leading sector analyst Laing & Buisson (L&B). As many as 760 private and voluntary care homes closed during 2000, but the rate of closure did not accelerate – contrary to warnings from the care home sector itself that it was going into a tailspin.

L&B calculates that the independent sector (private and voluntary homes) lost a net 7,300 places, or 1.6% of total capacity. It suggests that the government will "take comfort from the fact that the percentage is not higher than it is".

Care home proprietors have complained that they are struggling to keep going on rates paid by local authority social services departments for state-funded residents. Some homes are said to manage only by cross-subsidising such residents from higher charges levied on people paying their own way

The new figures, published in L&B's Community Care Market News, show that closures last year amounted to 16,200 places in the independent sector and 2,500 in local authority homes. But 145 new homes opened and 150 repositioned in different markets, leaving a net loss of 9,700 places.

Although the closure rate nationally may have been exaggerated, and the sector may previously have had spare capacity, L&B says there is a growing number of "hot spots" with acute shortages – mainly south of a line from the Severn to the Wash.

Source: *The Guardian*, 18 April 2001

C Nursing and long-stay hospital care of elderly, chronically ill and physically disabled people, places by sector, UK 1998

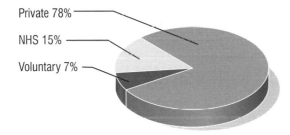

Private 78%
NHS 15%
Voluntary 7%

D Residential care of elderly and physically disabled people by sector, UK 1998

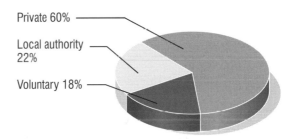

Private 60%
Local authority 22%
Voluntary 18%

Source: www.privatehealth.co.uk/laing/carehome.htm

Look at A.

1 In which of the four sectors of the mixed economy of care can each of these care homes be found?

Look at B.

2 What changes took place in the private care market?

3 How many places were there, therefore, in 2000?

4 What are care home owners complaining about?

5 What do you think 'repositioned in different markets' might mean?

Look at C and D.

6 Which of the sectors dominated the long-stay hospital and residential care provision?

The future of private provision

The private sector is expanding in the complete range of health, care and criminal justice areas and has been given a significant boost by the post-1997 Labour government which has actually increased private sector involvement in these areas. The long-term plans for the future are to continue the increase in private sector involvement.

Meanwhile, [under a variety of names] ... – public-private partnerships, private finance initiatives, best value, education action zones – the government is preparing to bring profit-seeking corporations into the heart of public health, education and other services that have so far escaped the full force of new Labour's marketing zeal. Enthusiasts insist

that users are unconcerned about who provides services. But the evidence is piling up that where private companies make cost savings, they mostly do so at the expense of the pay, conditions and jobs of public service workers, while private finance deals fail to transfer risk to the private consortia as claimed, squeeze other services and end up costing taxpayers

substantially more in the long run. What is needed is a historic reform of treasury rules to allow publicly owned bodies to borrow on their own account, removing a crucial pressure to use more expensive privately raised finance. But there is currently no prospect of the chancellor agreeing to any such loosening of central control.

Just as alarmingly, the iniquitous

health and social care bill is up for its final debate in the Lords next week. With barely a murmur of public discussion, the bill would open the way for the wholesale provision of NHS clinical services, as well as employment of doctors and nurses, by private corporations. It would also create a mechanism for health service bodies to charge for personal care for the first time.

Source: *The Guardian*, 11 April 2001

1 Find out the meaning of the terms, 'public-private partnership', 'private finance initiatives', 'best value', etc. What do they all involve?

2 What evidence is 'piling up'?

3 What does the writer suggest is needed instead of greater private involvement?

4 The Health and Social Care 'bill' is now an Act. What does this signify for the health service, compared to its original idea?

Main points ▶ The creation of the Welfare State in the UK greatly diminished private welfare services. This was especially the case with health care.

▶ Since the 1980s, due to deliberate policy changes instigated by Conservative governments, private health and social care have been encouraged. These sectors have grown.

▶ Whilst private residential and nursing care has become multi-million pound enterprises, there is still considerable uncertainty in the market. Many providers are going out of business.

Conclusion

In this chapter we have explored the independent sector, which consists of a range of non-statutory organisations providing health and social care. The motivations for these organisations varies greatly from desire for profits to desire to help others. When the Welfare State was set up in 1948, most people believed that the independent sector would wither away. It seemed to be doing so until the 1980s when, with the support of the government at that time, a huge increase in private and voluntary care took place. The New Labour government, first put into office in 1997 has carried on this move away from State provision, with great enthusiasm.

---

9 CHAPTER SUMMARY

1 The independent sector is made up from the voluntary sector and private sector.

2 The voluntary sector is an umbrella term for a range of different voluntary organisations, some national, some local, some big, some small.

3 About 40 per cent of voluntary organisations are registered as charities.

4 Voluntary organisations get their funding from a range of sources ranging from individual donations, through charges for services, to grants from government.

5 The voluntary sector has roots going back beyond the nineteenth century. However, from the mid/late nineteenth century the voluntary sector of social welfare grew significantly for a range of social, ideological and political reasons.

6 Many thought that the creation of the Welfare State in the 1940s signalled the end of the voluntary welfare sector in any meaningful sense. However, despite the expansion of statutory services it continues to play a key role.

7 Voluntary groups have different reasons for being in existence. Some, for example, emphasise self-help, others campaign and act as pressure groups, others offer direct assistance whilst others are more about education and the dissemination of information.

8 Opinions differ over whether voluntary organisations have a proper place to play in modern welfare. Some see voluntary organisations as a positive

improvement on what the State has to offer, whilst others believe that voluntary organisations are a poor substitute for State-run provision.

9 Several bodies (most recently 'Compacts') have been created in order to co-ordinate the many and various organisations working in the voluntary sector.

10 The mixed economy of welfare refers to the system of social welfare which is based on using the statutory, voluntary and private sectors. The adoption of this principle in the 1980s represented a shift away from the view that the government (State) would have a virtual monopoly on provision.

11 Supporters of the mixed economy approach say that, among other advantages, it offers an increased choice and flexibility of services together with reduced costs.

12 Critics argue that in reality a mixed economy has led to patchy and erratic services that are not necessarily cheaper and that the system is less fair and more complicated

13 The creation of the Welfare State in the UK greatly diminished private welfare services. This was especially the case with health care.

14 Since the 1980s, due to deliberate policy changes instigated by Conservative governments, private health and social care have been encouraged. These sectors have grown.

15 Whilst private residential and nursing care have become multi-million pound enterprises, there is still considerable uncertainty in the market. Many providers are going out of business.

Useful websites

www.ncvo-vol.org.uk: NCVO

http://bubl.ac.uk/uk/charities: UK registered charities

www.adviceguide.co.uk/exp/index: a list of most charities in the UK

www.nspcc.org.uk: NSPCC

www.ace.org.uk: Age Concern

www.rnib.org.uk: Royal National Institute for the Blind

www.tht.org.uk: Terrence Higgins Trust, an AIDS charity

www.redcross.org.uk: British Red Cross

www.fhaonline.org.uk: Family Holiday Association

Chapter 10

THE CRIMINAL JUSTICE SYSTEM

Chapter contents

Introduction

This chapter explores one of the most contentious activities of the government – how it goes about organising and implementing law and order. The country seems divided in its attitudes to crime, in that the majority of people constantly call for ever tougher measures against criminals, while academics and those working in the criminal justice system point out that, quite simply, tough measures do not seem to work. The chapter sets out to provide a clear picture of the criminal justice system and how it is organised and operates. We begin by noting the structure and organisation of the system and how it is funded. We then move on to explore patterns of crime. Through an analysis of the statistics, we see who commits crime and who the victims are, as well as the types of crimes committed.

We then look at explanations for crime and suggest that any policies which we develop should take these into account.

We explore the courts and the prosecution process, examining as we do so the accusations of bias against the courts. Of course, bias is something which the police force has been accused of with regard to ethnic minorities. We examine this, along with other relevant debates about policing.

Finally, we turn to look at how and why we punish people and its effectiveness.

The structure of the criminal justice system

The Criminal Justice System in England and Wales is divided into three departments:

- the Attorney General's Office
- the Lord Chancellor's Department
- the Home Office.

Attorney General's Office

Definition

Crown Prosecution Service – prosecutes offenders on behalf of the State

The main responsibility of the Attorney General's Office is the **Crown Prosecution Service (CPS)**. After the police have arrested a person on suspicion of committing a crime, the Crown Prosecution Service then decides whether there is adequate evidence for the person arrested to be taken to court. They prosecute on behalf of the Crown, that is, on behalf of the State.

The Lord Chancellor's Department

The Lord Chancellor's Department is responsible for the courts of England. The court system itself consists of **magistrates** courts, where less serious crimes are judged, and of Crown courts where the more serious cases are held. Magistrates are generally public volunteers who are not paid for their work, although there are legally qualified magistrates too. The **judges** in Crown courts are highly qualified lawyers with a background of many years practice. Crown courts usually have juries, whilst magistrates courts do not.

Definitions

Magistrates – public volunteers who are the judges in the courts dealing with less serious offences

Judges – oversee serious cases in the higher courts

Legal aid – when a person is accused of a crime in court and has no money, the State provides help to pay for legal representation (also known as public funding)

The Lord Chancellor's Department also has responsibility for controlling **legal aid** or public funding – the government provides funding for less-well-off people to obtain legal advice and representation in court.

The Home Office

This department is responsible for the running of the forty-three police forces in England, the Probation Service and the Prison Service. It is headed by the **Home Secretary**, one of the most important posts in the government.

Definition

Home Secretary – government minister responsible for all criminal justice matters (amongst other responsibilities)

The police are responsible for the maintenance of law and order. The Probation Service supervises all those people who are undergoing some form of community punishment (an alternative to prison), and those who have been let out of prison earlier than their full sentence.

The Prison Service is responsible for the 137 prisons in England and Wales. We discuss these three important departments in more detail later.

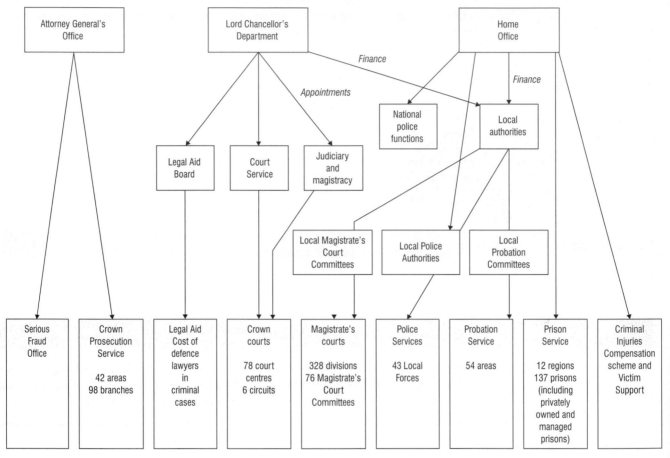

The structure of the criminal justice system

Source: www.homeoffice.gov.uk

The costs of the criminal justice system

The impact of crime on society is so great that, in an effort to combat it, the government has made the criminal justice system one of the main areas of expenditure. In 2000 over £12 billion was spent on the system:

- *The police*: Over 60 per cent of all the criminal justice system's costs are accounted for by the police force. The police force has consistently received increases in its funding from government. Between 1988 and 2000, for example, its funding increased by 33 per cent.
- *The courts*: The estimated cost of a case which is tried and sentenced at a Crown court is about £32,000 and about £800 in a magistrate's court.
- *Legal Aid*: In 2000, there were over 13,000 applications for legal aid, almost all of which were granted.
- *The Crown Prosecution Service*: The CPS costs about £330 million each year.
- *The Prison Service*: Each prisoner costs about £24,000 per year.

• *The Probation Service*: Currently local authorities must pay 20 per cent of probation costs (though there are plans to reform the Probation Service and take it out of the hands of local authorities). The cost of the Probation Service is about £500 million.

The criminal justice system: where the money goes

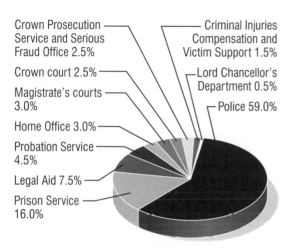

Crown Prosecution Service and Serious Fraud Office 2.5%

Crown court 2.5%

Magistrate's courts 3.0%

Home Office 3.0%

Probation Service 4.5%

Legal Aid 7.5%

Prison Service 16.0%

Criminal Injuries Compensation and Victim Support 1.5%

Lord Chancellor's Department 0.5%

Police 59.0%

Total expenditure 2000 = £12.056 billion

Source: *A Guide to the Criminal Justice System* (The Stationery Office), www.homeoffice.gov.uk

1 Which service had the highest expenditure in the criminal justice system?

2 How much was that?

3 Which had the second highest expenditure?

4 How much was that?

Crime patterns

Overall, the number of crimes recorded by the police has increased sharply over the last fifty years, although the late 1990s and early twenty-first century are showing a small decline in the number of crimes being committed.

The rising crime rate

Crimes recorded by the police

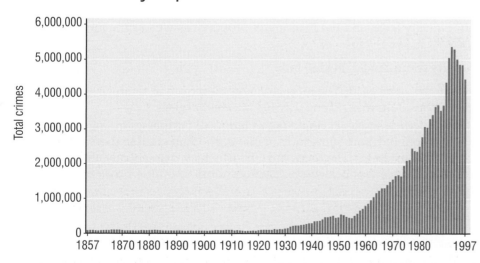

Source: *Criminal Justice Digest 4* (Home Office Research, Development and Statistics Directorate)

1 How could you best describe the crime level between 1857 and 1920?

2 Approximately how many crimes were committed in 1980?

3 In approximately what year did the level of crime peak?

4 How many crimes were committed in that year?

What types of crimes are committed?

The majority of crimes fall into two categories:

* crimes against property
* crimes of violence.

A breakdown of crimes

The pie chart below shows the numbers and relative percentages of crimes recorded by the police in 2000.

Recorded crime by offence group, 12 months ending September 2000

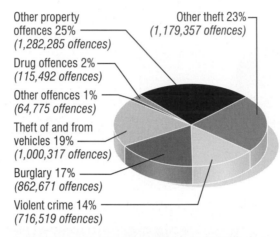

Other property offences 25% *(1,282,285 offences)*

Other theft 23% *(1,179,357 offences)*

Drug offences 2% *(115,492 offences)*

Other offences 1% *(64,775 offences)*

Theft of and from vehicles 19% *(1,000,317 offences)*

Burglary 17% *(862,671 offences)*

Violent crime 14% *(716,519 offences)*

Source: *Home Office Statistical Bulletin: Recorded Crime, England and Wales, 12 months to September 2000*

1 How many burglaries were there according to the pie chart?

2 What percentage of all crime did this account for?

3 What proportion of all offences were violent crimes?

4 What proportion of crimes were thefts of or from a vehicle?

5 Conduct a small survey of people in your college. Ask them what crimes they have had committed against them. Is the result similar? If not, can you provide any explanations as to why not?

Property crime

The overwhelming majority of crimes committed in the UK are for property offences, comprising 85 per cent of all crimes recorded by the police. Overall, since the 1990s, there has been a decrease in these sorts of crimes. The decline is generally accounted for the increased use of alarms for households and cars, better quality locks and the marking of property, as well as the increasing use of CCTV.

Property crime can be divided into:

* *theft from individuals*: The most common theft from individuals is stealing from cars, followed (a long way behind) by burglary.
* *crimes against businesses*: Eight out of ten of all businesses in England and Wales suffered from some form of crime, and half of all of these comprised theft by customers. However, not all businesses were equally affected, as about 5 per cent of businesses (mainly shops) account for over 60 per cent of all crimes.

Violent crime

Violent crime has been on the increase in recent years, but still only accounts for about 14 per cent of crimes recorded by the police. Over 75 per cent of violent crimes are, however, not very serious and only 4 per cent of violent crimes result in serious injury.

Are the criminal statistics accurate?

Definition

British Crime Survey – a survey
to find the extent of crime, which
is usually carried out every two
years and asks private
households what crimes have
been committed against them.
Usually referred to as the BCS

You will notice that all the statistics we have looked at so far are those which are reported to the police. However, it appears that a large number of crimes are not reported to the police and so escape from the official statistics. The evidence for this argument is provided by a study known as the **British Crime Survey**, which takes place every year (since 2002) and asks private households what crimes have been committed against them. This is very different from the police statistics which are based on complaints about crimes reported to them by the public.

The true extent of crime?

The chart below shows the number of crimes which are recorded by the police and later appear in the 'official' statistics. Secondly, it shows the number of crimes reported by people to the police, but the police decide that it is not serious enough to be recorded as a 'crime'. Thirdly, it shows the number of crimes which people believe are committed against them, but which they don't even bother to report to the police.

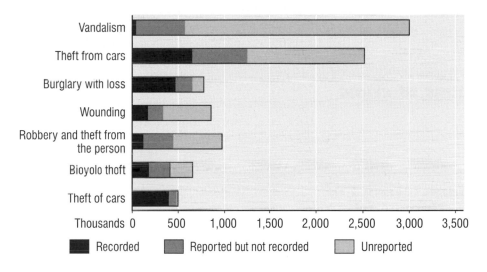

Source: *Criminal Justice Digest 4* (Home Office Research, Development and Statistics Directorate)

1 What is the most common crime, according to the chart above?

2 According to the police, what is the most common crime? (You can confirm your answer is correct by looking at the pie chart opposite.)

3 Approximately how many acts of vandalism are recorded by the police and how many do people say are committed. Why do you think so many are not reported?

4 How many cases of theft of cars are unreported? Suggest a reason for this.

5 Suggest any reasons why people would not report wounding or robbery and theft from the person. Look at the text below for help.

Why people do not report crimes to the police

As we have just seen, the police statistics on crime are considerably less than those uncovered when people are asked directly by researchers to list the crimes committed against them.

But the question remains, just why do so many crimes never get reported. The reasons suggested include the following:

- The incident is not considered serious enough by the individual to report it to the police.

- The householder thinks the police could do nothing about it.
- The victims regarded it as a private matter, within the family or friends.
- The victims wanted to deal with it themselves.
- The victim is embarrassed. This is usually when a sexual crime has been committed.

Why the police do not record all crimes

But the BCS also revealed that many complaints are made to the police which the police then fail to record as a crime. The reasons for this appear to be that the police do not:

- consider the complaint to be serious enough to record as a crime
- believe the complainant.

But some crimes are much more likely to be reported than others

However there are also some situations when the public are much more likely to report incidents to the police. This is almost always when there is an advantage to the complainant in doing so – usually because the object stolen is insured and it is a condition of the insurance that the police are notified.

Victims of crime

Each year, about a third of the population claims to be a victim of crime at least once. In 1999, for example, 9 per cent of the population claimed to have been the

---

Characteristics of victims of crime

Chart A shows the variations in chances of being victims of burglary. Note that the categories may well overlap.

A Households most at risk of burglary in 1999

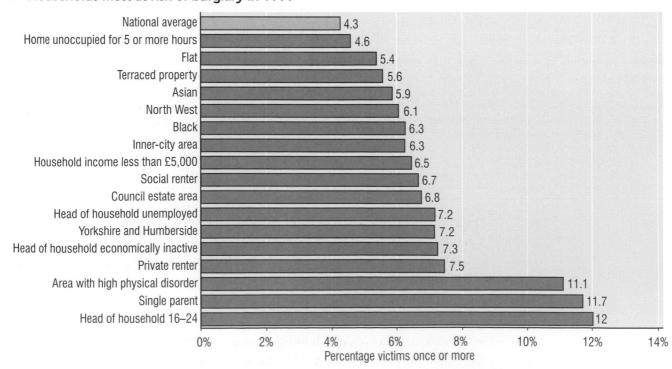

Category	Percentage victims once or more
National average	4.3
Home unoccupied for 5 or more hours	4.6
Flat	5.4
Terraced property	5.6
Asian	5.9
North West	6.1
Black	6.3
Inner-city area	6.3
Household income less than £5,000	6.5
Social renter	6.7
Council estate area	6.8
Head of household unemployed	7.2
Yorkshire and Humberside	7.2
Head of household economically inactive	7.3
Private renter	7.5
Area with high physical disorder	11.1
Single parent	11.7
Head of household 16–24	12

B Adults most at risk of violence in 1999

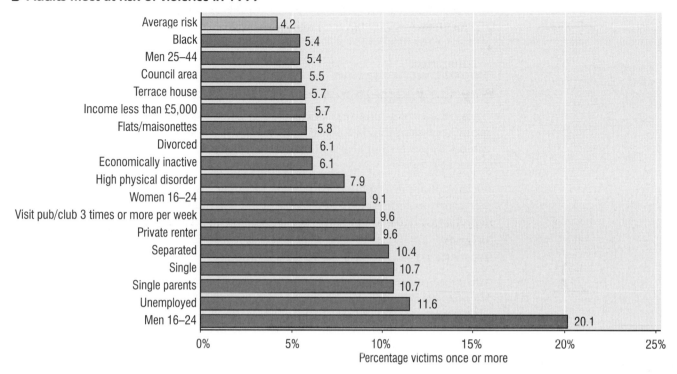

Source: *2000 British Crime Survey* (The Stationery Office)

Look at A.

1 What is the national average of people being victims of burglary?

2 Which group has the highest chance of being a victim of burglary?

3 What is the percentage difference between the two groups?

4 Are there any areas of the country with particularly high rates of victims of burglary?

5 What is the percentage of people living in privately rented accommodation who are burgled? Can you suggest any reason why their levels of burglary should be so high?

6 In the explanation of the table above, it says that some of the categories 'may well overlap'. What does this mean? Give two examples.

Look at B.

7 Which group is most likely to be victims of violence? Suggest any reason why

8 What percentage of people who visit a pub three or more times a week are likely to be victims of violence?

9 Who has less chance of being the victim of violence – men aged 25–44 or women aged 16–24? Give the percentages.

10 Construct a simple questionnaire which asks people about their experience of violence against them. Include questions on age and how often they go out in the evening. Also note their sex.

11 Does your research support the findings on victims of violence presented in the table above?

---

victim of burglary, and 20 per cent had a vehicle stolen or thefts from inside the vehicle. Twenty-two per cent of the population also claimed to be the victim of some form of violence.

These, however, are figures for the population in general, and they mask great variations in who is more likely to be a victim.

Victims of violence

On average, 4.2 per cent of adults in England and Wales were the victim of one or more violent crimes. However, some groups are much more likely to be victims of violent crimes than others, with young men aged 16–24 having by far the highest chance of being victims (over 20 per cent). Males were also much more likely to be the victims of 'muggings' (64 per cent) and of **stranger assaults** (80 per cent), while women were much more likely to be the victims of **domestic violence** (75 per cent).

Repeat victimisation

Some social groups in society are at much greater risk of being victims of crime than others. Not only that but they are more likely to repeatedly be victims of crime. For example, less than half of 1 per cent of people account for approximately 22 per cent of all burglaries, and 3 per cent of all shops experienced 60 per cent of all thefts.

Victims of domestic violence were the most likely to be victims more than once (57 per cent), and this is followed by victims of 'acquaintance violence' (31 per cent), which is violence by someone the victim knows.

Impact of crime on people's lives

Crime has a great impact on people's lives – even on those who are not victims themselves. The BCS found that almost 60 per cent of the adult population were either very or fairly worried about being the victim of burglary for example, and almost one-third of women were worried about being raped. Crime not only makes people worried, it also affects how they behave. For example, 10 per cent of all adults in Britain said that they never walked alone in their local area after dark, for fear of crime, and this increased to 16 per cent in poorer housing estates.

Help for victims of crime

Compensation

There are two sources of compensation for victims:

- *Reparation:* Here the court orders the offender to pay, or make some form of reparation to the victim.
- *Criminal Injuries Compensation Scheme*: This consists of a government fund which pays compensation to victims of crime. Any victim can claim, and the payments are based on a set tariff for each of the twenty-five categories of injury. Payments can range from £1,000 to £250,000

Criminal compensation

Nursery nurse Lisa Potts, who shielded children from a machete attacker during a picnic at school [in] 1996, yesterday called for reforms to the compensation system after she received £49,000.

Ms Potts, 25, broke down at a news conference also attended by senior officials of her union Unison, which branded the current criminal injuries compensation (CIC) process as cumbersome and unjust.

Ms Potts said that she was unable to return to the job she loved

because of psychological damage and had also been forced to pick only three of the multiple injuries she suffered to qualify for the payout. She said: "Nursery work was the job I loved and it's been robbed from me. It's totally unfair. I would have loved to have returned, but I can't."

Ms Potts was 21 when she was left with severe scarring to her arms, hands and back, chronic depression and post-traumatic stress disorder by the frenzied

attack at St Luke's school in Wolverhampton. She was awarded the George Medal for flinging herself between the children and Horrett Campbell, a paranoid schizophrenic, who was latter jailed for life on seven counts of attempted murder in 1996.

Ms Potts has undergone several operations and still has medical treatment to try to restore her grip in one hand. She also described how she had spent four years

dealing with medical examinations and injury reports as part of the compensation process.

Ms Potts' compensation, which includes £8,000 awarded shortly after the attack, divides into £28,000 for loss of earnings, £20,000 for psychological damage, £750 for partial loss of grip and £250 for scarring. Under the system, victims are limited to claims for three injuries, with 100% compensation for the most serious, 10% for the next and 5% for the third.

Source: *The Guardian*, 7 February 2001

Victim Support

Victim Support is an independent charity, partially funded by the government, which offers support and advice to victims. The advice, which is given by trained volunteers, can include things as various as emotional support to advising on financial compensation.

In 1974, the first Victim Support Scheme was set up, and today there are over 385 local schemes. Each year over 1.1 million people receive such help.

Who commits crime?

Crime is linked to sex and age. Over a half of males and a third of females admit to having committed a crime at some time. In terms of arrests, males outnumber females by seven to one.

Bad boys ... and very bad boys

A **Court appearances of males born in 1953 up to their 40th birthday**

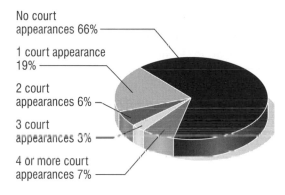

No court appearances 66%

1 court appearance 19%

2 court appearances 6%

3 court appearances 3%

4 or more court appearances 7%

Source: *Criminal Justice Digest 4*
(Home Office Research, Development and Statistics Directorate)

Look at A.

1 What proportion of males in total had made one or more court appearance?

2 What proportion had never appeared in court?

3 What proportion of males in total appeared in court more than once?

Look at B.

4 According to diagram what percentage of 14–17-year-olds committed 1–5 offences? What proportion of all offences does this comprise?

5 What percentage of boys commit more than five offences in total? What proportion of offences do they commit in total?

6 What percentage of boys commit 68 per cent of all offences?

7 Do you think there are any implications for policies to combat crime, from these statistics?

B **Distribution of self-reported offending by 14–17-year-old males in the previous 12 months**

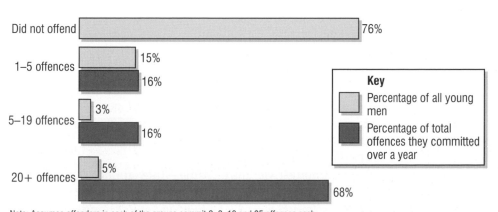

Did not offend 76%

1–5 offences 15% / 16%

5–19 offences 3% / 16%

20+ offences 5% / 68%

Key
Percentage of all young men
Percentage of total offences they committed over a year

Diagram B shows the result of a study in which young males were asked how many offences they had committed, and then these were shown as the proportion of all offences

Note: Assumes offenders in each of the groups commit 0, 2, 10 and 25 offences each.
Source of figures: Derived from J. Graham and B. Bowling, Young People and Crime, *Home Office Research and Planning Unit (Home Office, 1995)*

Source: Audit Commission, *Misspent Youth ...: Young People and Crime* (Audit Commission, 1996)

In terms of age, there is a clear pattern, with males most likely to commit crimes from the age of 14 to the mid-twenties, with a peak at 18. The pattern of crime for females looks slightly different – they start younger at about 13 and then stop in their early twenties. The age of highest offending is also about 18.

Age and crime Age of convicted or cautioned offenders by gender for indictable offences, 1997

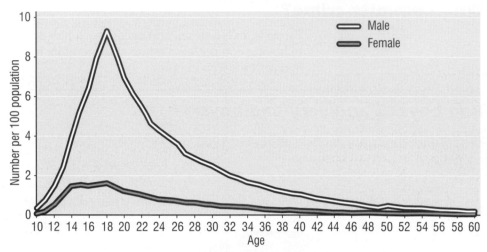

Source: *Criminal Justice Digest 4* (Home Office Research, Development and Statistics Directorate)

1 Which sex is more likely to offend?

2 What is the number of female offenders per 1,000 of the population at the ages of (a) 16, (b) 20, (c) 42?

3 What is the number of male offenders per 1,000 of the population at the ages of (a) 16, (b) 20, (c) 42?

4 Why do you think that males are more likely to commit crimes than females?

5 What reasons can you suggest for the higher levels of crime amongst young people?

Main points

▶ The criminal justice system is composed of three main government departments: the Attorney General's Office, the Lord Chancellor's Office and the Home Office.

▶ The CJS is one of the main expenses of the government, with £12 billion spent on the system.

▶ Most crimes are related to property.

▶ Violent crime is relatively low.

▶ There are two different measures of crime: the British Crime Survey and police statistics. Both have advantages and disadvantages.

▶ There are a number of reasons why people fail to report crimes to the police, and it also quite common for the police to decide not to record certain 'crimes' reported to them.

▶ There is a pattern amongst victims of crime – they are not randomly chosen.

▶ Some individuals are much more likely to be victims of crime than others.

▶ There are high rates of repeat victimisation, where the same people are likely to be victims more than once.

▶ There are organisations to help victims of crime.

Explaining crime

Without an understanding of why people commit crime, it is impossible to develop effective policies to combat it. Social scientists have suggested a wide range of explanations, which we can divide into three 'levels' or groups of explanations:

- *immediate explanations*, related to the activities of family and friends
- *contextual explanations*, based on the daily social context in which people live out their lives
- *structural explanations*, which are broader social and economic factors which help to shape the immediate and contextual explanations.

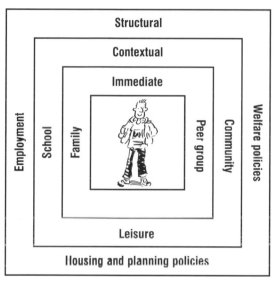

Causes of crime

Immediate explanations

Family life

Persistent young offenders, that is, those who regularly commit crime, are much more likely to have a family life which most people would regard as deficient. They are more likely to come from poor home backgrounds and to have a parent or parents who do not socialise the young person into the accepted values of society. A higher proportion than average have also experienced care proceedings or have families who are clients of the social services.

Peer group

Like most people, friendships are made with those of similar backgrounds and interests. Therefore the young people who are most deprived and who have unsettled home backgrounds very often tend to form friendship groups. Offending behaviour is more likely to occur as the group will provide mutual support in offending – essentially they encourage each other in their actions.

Contextual explanations

The behaviour of young people can only be explained by the context of their lives – that is, the broader 'space', both physical and social, in which they live their lives.

Neighbourhood and community

Young offenders are more likely to come from areas of deprivation, where there is limited community control of law-breaking behaviour and where activities like vandalism or street crime are rarely opposed by local adult residents. This may be because of fear or because the unruly behaviour is regarded as acceptable by a significant proportion of the local community.

Local authority housing policies are significant in that estates which are well-maintained, with vacant houses being retenanted quickly, with graffiti being cleaned off and broken windows rapidly replaced, contribute to a sense of worth amongst the local community.

Council allocation policies are important too. When councils allocate a disproportionate number of 'troublesome' tenants on particular estates, they find that a process of **tipping** occurs. Tipping is the process whereby, as troublesome families arrive, other families feel threatened and ask to leave, and gradually the balance of the estate

Definition

Tipping – the term used to describe how a housing estate changes in character from one with a sense of community to one with high levels of crime and disorder moves to it being a problem estate with troublesome families becoming the majority and the only other tenants living there being older people who are trapped and others who are so desperate for housing they will accept anything offered.

Schools

The relationship between truancy, school exclusion and crime is well established, as a high proportion of those truanting admit offending. Schools play a crucial role in socialising young people and providing them with the skills to enter the job market. At the very minimum, when young people are in school they are unable to offend. Ineffective schooling, poor teaching or simply the inability to cope with the disruptive behaviour of young people can lead to a reinforcement of the propensity to commit crime. When young people are excluded from schools the likelihood of them committing crime rises significantly.

Leisure

Youth is the period of life when leisure is arguably most important. Local authority provision of activities can prevent groups of young people simply 'hanging around', which causes concern to other residents. Cuts in local authority community education budgets have led to a reduction in youth services. Private facilities for young people are often too expensive for regular use.

Structural explanations

Welfare policies

There is a close relationship between deprivation and crime, so the extent and effectiveness of welfare policies to combat poverty and in creating a better quality of life is important. By supporting lone-parent families, for example, it might be possible for the parent to improve the quality of life and care for the child, as other financial pressures are eased.

Housing policies

We have already talked about housing policy at a local authority level, but overall policy comes from central government. The number and the quality of new homes for lower-income families are determined by central government who control the finances which are allocated to local authorities for spending new homes and refurbishment.

Labour market policies

This is the way the government organises and legislates on the number of jobs available and the quality of these jobs in terms of wages, hours of work and security. As most crime is committed by young males, it is particularly important that there is employment for them.

Young offenders: patterns and causes of crime

Home Office admits jobless link to crime
Unemployment is forcing a new generation of young men into a kind of 'perpetual adolescence' that leads to more crime, according to Home Office research[1] ... which underlines links between unemployment and offending ... [and] suggests that the threat of being caught and imprisoned did not deter them. ...

[The research] has found that men are no longer growing out of their offending behaviour – mainly theft and burglary – in their late teens, and are instead continuing their criminal activities well into their twenties. There was, said the report, 'little evidence that young male offenders develop a moral conscience which may inhibit their offending as they grow older'. The study concludes that young people today face more serious hazards in making the transition from childhood to adulthood in particular the availability and heavy use of drugs increasing the risk of criminal activity.

But while girls, who, between 14 and 17, offend almost as much as their male counterparts, mature out of the cycle, boys do not. A key factor is the inability to find work – traditionally one of the main ways of 'providing a sense of direction and security and bestowing the status of manhood upon young males,' the report says. ... [Researchers] found that a quarter of all juvenile crime is committed by a hard core of just 3 per cent of young offenders. Poor parenting and early truancy from school were key factors. Young people living with both natural parents were less likely, to offend than those living with one parent or in a step-family, although young men who had a particularly bad relationship with their father were particularly likely to offend.

1 I. Graham and B. Bowling, *Young People and Crime*, Home Office Research and Planning Unit (Home Office, 1995)

Source: From an article by Heather Mills in *The Independent*, 19 January 1996

1 What does the extract mean when it says that unemployment is leading to 'perpetual adolescence'? Explain how this can be.

2 What is the effect of the threat of imprisonment? What implications could this have for policies to combat youth crime?

3 Is there any difference between males and females? What explanations can offer?

4 Is regular crime committal widespread?

5 List and comment on all the factors the research links with crime by young offenders.

Criminal careers

We have seen the factors which affect whether or not people commit crime, and we have also know that the majority of those who commit crime do so only once, and about 70 per cent of all crime is committed by about 5 per cent of males. Furthermore, the majority of crimes are committed by young people, and the majority of these young people 'grow out of' their offending and become responsible adults.

The best way to picture the pattern of offending, according to social scientists is to see it as a type of 'career'. Young people are drawn into offending at a certain point in their lives, influenced by one set of factors – usually the home and the peer group, and then whether they continue to commit crime, and the sorts of crimes they commit, will be influenced by other factors such as the peer group again, gaining decent employment, entering a settled relationship, and so on.

Starting offending and then the subsequent patterns of crime can therefore be explained by different factors occurring at different times in their lives. The diagram below illustrates this.

The criminal career Becoming a professional criminal is a long and complex process, beginning with minor offending as a child and leading to crime as a way of life. There are many stages and opportunities to leave along the way.

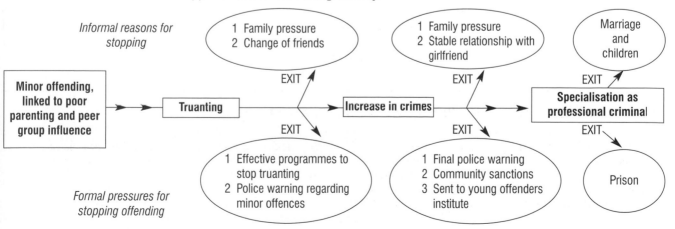

Main points ▶ There are three different types of explanations for criminality: immediate, contextual, structural.

▶ Immediate explanations centre on family and friends.

▶ Contextual explanations centre on neighbourhood, schools and housing.

▶ Structural explanations focus on the wider organisation of society.

▶ An important concept to help us understand crime is the idea of 'career', which argues that there is no single explanation for crime. But that different factors influence people at different times of their lives.

The courts and sentencing

Just how effective is the criminal justice system in combating crime? There is no easy answer to this, but we do know that of every 100 offences which are committed, only 3 per cent result in a caution or conviction for the offender and 5.5 per cent are cleared up by the police.

The chances of 'getting away with It'

Attrition: percentage of offences committed

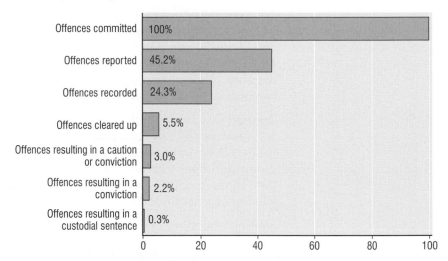

Clear-ups by offence group, 1997

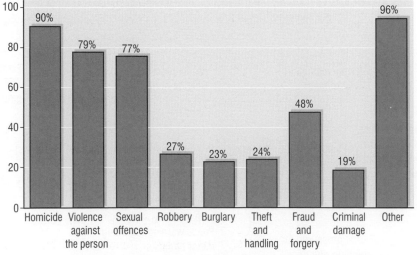

Source: *Criminal Justice Digest 4* (Home Office Research, Development and Statistics Directorate)

1 What percentage of offences committed are reported to the police?

2 What percentage are then recorded?

3 Why don't the police record all crimes reported to them (see page 270)?

4 What percentage of offences result in a caution or conviction?

5 What percentage of those convicted or cautioned receive a custodial sentence (prison, young offender institute or secure accommodation)?

6 Apart from the category 'Other', which crime is most likely to be cleared-up (solved by the police)?

7 What is least likely to be cleared up?

8 Why do you think that certain offences have higher clear-up rates than others?

The courts

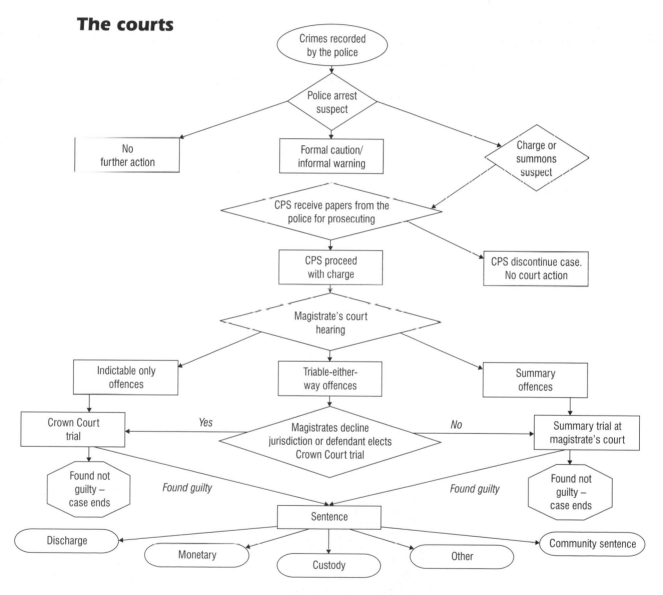

Source: *A Guide to the Criminal Justice System in England and Wales* (The Stationery Office, 2001), www.homeoffice.gov.uk

1 After arrest, what three reasons could there be for the person not to be sent on to the magistrates' court?

2 What cases go on to the Crown court?

3 Give three types of sentences which a Crown court can give.

After a person is arrested the police may decide that no further action is appropriate, or they may simply be caution them, if they admit their guilt. About 40 per cent of offenders are cautioned. No punishment follows the caution, but it does go down as part of a criminal record.

However, if the police believe there is a case to answer and it is suitably serious, they charge the person and bring them before a magistrate. At this point the prosecution is taken on by the Crown Prosecution Service, the independent agency which prosecutes 'offenders' on behalf of the State, who will decide whether to proceed with the case. The person who is charged may then be given 'bail' (conditional release before the trial) or be remanded in custody.

Types of criminal offence

- *Triable only on indictment*: These are the more serious crimes, for example rape or murder. These are always judged in a Crown court.
- *Summary*: This includes less serious offences, such as the majority of motoring offences. These are always judged in a magistrate's court.
- *Triable either way*: These offences, such as burglary and theft, may be tried at either magistrates or Crown court.

The courts

Magistrate's court

These consist of either three 'lay' magistrates (not legally qualified) or one 'stipendiary' (legally qualified, full-time) magistrate. The courts can impose a maximum sentence of up to six months in prison or a fine up to £5,000. Approximately two million people are dealt with by magistrate's courts each year.

Until 2001, in triable-either-way cases, the defendant has had the right to decide whether they wish to be tried in the magistrate's court or Crown court. About 80 per cent of defendants opt for the magistrate's court, as the maximum sentences available to magistrates are quite low. The remaining 20 per cent go on to Crown court, but of these a majority later plead guilty. The government is therefore proposing to limit the right of individuals to choose, in an effort to save the time and expense wasted by those who later plead guilty. However, many critics argue that by removing the choice of court, a fundamental right is being removed.

The Crown court

The Crown court is presided over by a judge, and trials take place in front of a jury (if the defendant pleads guilty, then the judge determines a sentence without having a jury). Crown courts deal only with the more serious cases and judges have the power to impose the impose maximum punishments as allowed by law. Just under 5 per cent of all those proceeded against are dealt with by the Crown court, and in 60 per cent of cases they plead guilty.

A jury, composed of twelve people aged between 18 and 70 who are eligible to vote in elections, decides whether defendants are guilty or not. The role of the judge is to ensure that the trial takes place fairly and according to the rules of law.

Sentencing

If the defendant is found guilty, then he/she is sentenced. Some offences have **mandatory sentences**, whereby the judge must impose that punishment,

Definitions

Mandatory sentences – where the magistrate or judge is required by law to impose a specified penalty for a specific offence

Custodial sentence – the offender is sent to prison

Community sentence – the offender is given a punishment other than imprisonment or a fine

Pre-sentence report – a report which is written by a probation officer or youth offending team worker, which gives information about the offender to the judge

Consecutive sentences – if a person is found guilty of two or more offences, the sentences are added one to another

Concurrent sentence – if a person is found guilty of two or more offences, the sentences are will run alongside each other

Mitigating crcumstances – reasons which are given by an offender to justify him/her having a less severe sentence

irrespective of circumstances, if the person is found guilty. For example, life imprisonment for murder, or a one-year disqualification for drink-driving offences. But most offences have maximum penalties, set down by law, and the judge decides the most appropriate punishment.

Sentences are of three main types:

- **custodial** – prison or young offenders institutions
- non-custodial or **community sentences**
- fines.

Before sentencing, it is usual for a probation officer to prepare **pre-sentence report** (PSR) on the convicted person to provide the judge with as much relevant information on their personality, background and the appropriateness of various sentences.

Custodial sentences

Imprisonment

Courts have the power to impose this up to a maximum or minimum amount of time as set down by Parliament. People are sent to prison only if their offences are so serious that the penalty can be justified. Otherwise they will be given a community sentence. Magistrate's courts can give a maximum of six months imprisonment.

If an offender commits two or more offences and is found guilty, then the magistrate or judge can order the sentences to run **consecutively** or **concurrently**. Consecutively means that they are added together to make a longer sentence (for example, two consecutive sentences of one year will mean a two years in total). Concurrently means that sentences will all be covered in one period of time (two concurrent sentences of one year means one year in total).

Suspended sentence

If an offence is not serious enough to warrant more than two years imprisonment, then the offender may receive a suspended sentence, which means that they do not have to serve any time in prison at all. Suspended sentences are usually given when there are **mitigating circumstances** (the circumstances of the offender or offence mean that the judge has a degree of sympathy with the offender).

Types of sentence

Death crash man loses appeal bid
A car passenger who laughed and joked about the death of an 82-year-old woman after she was struck down while crossing the

road has failed in an Appeal Court bid to cut his jail term.
Troy Whiting, 27, received a seven-year sentence at Peterborough Crown Court in

June last year after he was convicted of causing Maude Fancourt's death by dangerous driving on October 14, 1999.
His seven-year sentence was

ordered to run consecutively to a three-year term for affray and handling stolen goods, making a total of 10 years.

Source: *Cambridge Evening News*, 1 March 2001

Farmer fired rifle in row with wife
A farmer who fired a rifle to frighten his estranged wife has been ordered to do 120 hours community service.
Judge Jonathan Haworth

accepted the contents of a pre-sentence report that the incident had occurred "particular to a very specific set of circumstances" when Rains had been drinking, and was highly emotional.

In addition to the community service, he was ordered to pay £414 towards prosecution costs. The rifle must be forfeited and destroyed

Source: *Cambridge Evening News*, 20 February 2001

1   In the first extract, the offender had a three-year sentence and a seven-year sentence running consecutively. What does this mean?

2   What would have been the total length of time in prison if the sentences had been concurrent?

3   What is a pre-sentence report?

4   Who writes it?

5   What is the difference between a custodial sentence and a community sentence?

6   Go to the website of your local newspaper. See how many examples of different types of sentences you can find.

Community sentences

A community sentence is one which is served outside prison. Community sentences are actually more common than imprisonment. Community sentences include:

* *Community Punishment Orders*: Anyone aged 16 or over can be sent to do a minimum of 40 hours and a maximum of 240 hours service to the community.
* *Community Rehabilitation Orders*: These involve being supervised by the Probation Service and range from six months to three years. The offender may have to attend various courses, report for regular meetings with the probation officer or receive treatment for drug misuse.
* *Community Punishment and Rehabilitation Orders*: This is a combination of the previous two orders above. The person may have to work, be supervised by a Probation Officer and attend various courses or treatments.
* *Curfew Orders:* A person may be required to stay at a certain address. These are now electronically monitored by a tag which alerts the authorities if the person goes beyond the limits imposed by the order.
* *Drug Treatment and Testing Orders*: If a person has committed a crime because of drug misuse, they may be required to attend a course of treatment, and they will be tested regularly for drug use.

Fines

This is the most common form of punishment. The 1993 Criminal Justice Act requires all courts to impose fines based on the seriousness of the offence and the financial circumstances of the individual. People who fail to pay their fines can be sent to prison.

Are courts biased?

Critics of the criminal justice system claim that the sentences that people receive are not based entirely on the facts of the case, but that certain groups – in particular women and the ethnic minorities – are more likely to be found guilty and more likely to receive harsher sentences.

Race and sentencing

Males of African-Caribbean backgrounds:

* are more likely than Whites to be tried in Crown courts, as they are charged with more serious offences
* are more likely than average to plead not guilty and to be found not guilty
* have a 17 per cent greater chance of imprisonment than for the majority population

- have a 5 per cent higher chance of being remanded in custody than the majority population.

Males of Asian backgrounds:

- are more likely than average to plead not guilty
- are more likely than Whites to be found guilty
- are 18 per cent less likely to be imprisoned.

Statistical problems

However, the statistics are rather ambiguous. For example, those from African-Caribbean backgrounds are more likely to be tried in Crown court, but have a higher rate of acquittal. This could mean that they are discriminated against in being sent to Crown court and being charged with more serious offences. On the other hand, the higher rate of acquittals could mean that courts and juries are more lenient towards black defendants.

Gender and sentencing

Women are far less likely to appear in Crown court than men, with the majority of their cases being dealt with in magistrate's courts. When they do appear in Crown court, however, they are more likely to receive a custodial sentence, with 38 per cent of women being sentenced to custody for their first offence, compared to 10 per cent of men. This seems to suggest that women receive harsher sentences than men. However, 60 per cent of women convicted of offences were cautioned compared to 30 per cent of males, and overall women were far less likely to receive a prison sentence than males, except in drug cases.

Interestingly, when the judges or majority of magistrates are female, the female offender is likely to receive a harsher sentence.

Statistical problems

Comparing male and female sentences is fraught with difficulties, as the statistics we use compare sentence lengths and guilty findings for *apparently* similar offences, but the process of deciding what individuals will be charged with in the first place is not studied, nor is the demeanour (attitude and appearance) of the defendant, nor the list of mitigating factors in a particular case.

Sentencing

The graphs show the breakdown of sentences given in magistrates' and Crown courts for indictable offences.

Sentencing for indictable offences: magistrate's courts

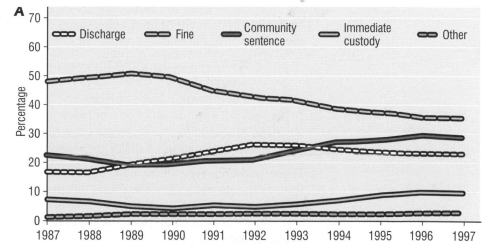

B Sentencing for indictable offences: Crown court

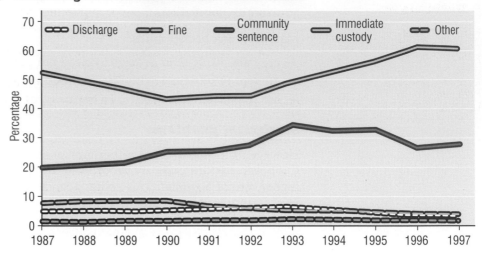

Source: *Criminal Justice Digest 4* (Home Office Research, Development and Statistics Directorate)

Look at A.

1 What is the most common sentence in a magistrate's court? What percentage of all sentences did this form in 1997?

2 What percentage were sent for immediate custody?

3 Which sentence was increasing the most?

Look at B.

4 Which was the most common sentence? What percentage of all sentences did this form in 1997?

5 Why are there many more of these sentences in Crown court than in magistrate's courts?

6 In which of the two courts were there a higher percentage of discharges?

7 What was the fastest growing form of sentence in the Crown court?

The police and policing

The history and organisation of the police

The modern police force began with the introduction of the Metropolitan Police in 1829. Before that policing duties were performed by night-watchmen, local constables employed by parishes or boroughs, gamekeepers and even private guardians for the rich.

By 1859 there were 239 police forces in England and Wales. In order to gain legitimacy in the eyes of the public, many of whom opposed the development of the police force, the founding principles of policing in Britain included:

- the enforcement of the *law* at the expense of enforcement of *order*, so that the police are not above the law and must respect people's rights
- the use of minimum force in enforcing the law and arresting suspects. This has led to the tradition of an unarmed police force
- the founding of *local* police forces, *democratically controlled* by local politicians, in contrast to a national police force responsible to the central government.

These traditions have remained largely intact today, although major changes in the organisation of the police have taken place. In 1964, the number of police forces was drastically reduced, and this process continued in the Local Government Act of 1972 when the number of police forces in England and Wales was reduced to 43 in total.

Police forces are still partially controlled by local government, though central government has taken an increasing influential role in the way that local police forces are financed and in the way that they act.

Police forces are responsible to their local police authorities which are composed of local government councillors, local magistrates and independent members of the public. Their powers included the appointment of the **chief constable** and if necessary, his/her retirement on grounds of 'efficiency'. However, all decisions of the Authority are subject to approval of the Home Secretary.

Chief constables have 'operational independence', which means, in practice, they have the right to appoint all ranks below them, and to carry out policing in the way they see best. However, all forces are subjected to inspection by **HM Inspectors of Constabulary (HMIC)** who report directly to the Home Secretary.

The funding of the police is mainly by the central government, with a smaller part coming from the local authority budget.

What do the police do?

The police in the UK have four main roles:

- *law enforcement* – investigating crimes, arresting suspects and advising Crown Prosecution Service on prosecution of suspects
- *maintenance of order* – monitoring public gatherings and demonstrations
- *traffic* – ensuring flow of traffic and dealing with traffic accidents and disruption
- *social role* – dealing with accidents and emergencies and giving advice.

Morgan and Newburn (*The Future of Policing*, Oxford University Press, 1997) found that 53 per cent of calls to the police involved crimes; 20 per cent involved social disorder; 18 per cent were for information and a variety of services; and 8 per cent concerned traffic issues.

How the police go about their work

We have seen the that the police have a number of tasks to carry out and there are different ways in which this can most effectively be done. There is considerable debate over which is the most appropriate.

Five models of police work have been distinguished:

- beat policing
- response-led policing
- zero tolerance policing
- intelligence-led policing
- problem-oriented policing.

Beat policing

This is the traditional method of policing, which involved walking around a specific area and getting to know local people. According to a study by the **Audit Commission** (*Streetwise*, The Stationery Office, 1996), police officers rarely came across crimes. In fact the study said that beat policing was highly ineffective and a poor use of police resources. In fact, it pointed out that, on average, an officer on the beat was likely to come within 100 metres of a burglary once every thirty years!

Police officers themselves dislike beat policing as they claim it is boring and tiring. Nevertheless it remains extremely popular with the public, as they like the reassurance of seeing a police officer.

Response-led policing

This style was introduced in the 1970s as patrol cars replaced police officers on the beat. Cars and personal radios allowed police officers to react quickly to events and to mobilise relatively large numbers of cars to attend any incident. This is the dominant mode of policing today, with officers responding to instructions from the central control room.

This form of police work has tended to remove police officers from the community and has isolated them. The Audit Commission also questioned its efficiency, as police officers rarely arrive at the scene of the crime while it is still taking place. Also the way it isolates police officers from the public has had the effect of limiting the amount of information they receive.

Zero tolerance policing

This model is based on the principle that small crimes if left unchecked can lead to much greater lawlessness. As a result, police officers are encouraged to crack down on any form of criminal activity, however minor. The style of policing was first developed in New York in response to very high crime rates and appears to have worked there. Although much talked about, it is not particularly common in the UK.

Police: shortage or inefficiency?

A

Police shortage 'is crime fight crisis'

CRIMEFIGHTING schemes will crumble unless they get more police support, claim Neighbourhood Watch groups.

Neighbourhood Watch coordinator Nick Goodyear said things had reached "crisis point" in the Queen Edith's area of Cambridge.

He said: "Unless something is done the whole Neighbourhood Watch network will collapse.

"It is an appalling problem. We have hardly any contact with our local policeman. He is a fine officer but his workload is too heavy.

"We haven't seen a policeman on the beat for months."

He said the group was unhappy because officers were unable to attend a Youth Forum meeting to discuss policing in Cherry Hinton and Queen Edith's

Source: *Cambridge Evening News*, 1 March 2001

B Officer deployment in a typical force

The nature of policing means that, at any one time, around 5 per cent of total strength is actually patrolling the streets.

Force establishment = 2,500 officers

minus HQ and specialist officers, e.g. CID and support functions

= 1,550 operational patrol officers

minus management and operational specialists, e.g. child protection

= 1,350 patrol constables

divided into four shifts to provide 24-hour cover

= 335 patrol constables per shift

minus abstractions, e.g. leave, sickness, training and court attendance

= 250 constables on patrol duty

minus duty time spent in the station, e.g. interviewing, paperwork, briefings and meal breaks

= 125 constables on the streets

Read A.

1 What does the local councillor want the police to do?

2 According to the headline what is the cause of the problem?

3 What is 'neighbourhood watch'? (You may have to look on the Internet by going to the Home Office home page: www.homeoffice.gov.uk and then looking at their crime reduction programme.)

Look at B.

4 What is the total number of police officers on a typical force?

5 Explain why the number of officers declines from the force establishment to 1,550 operational patrol officers?

6 Why does this then decline to 250 constables on patrol duty?

7 What percentage of police officers are patrolling at any one time? How many officers is this?

Intelligence-led policing

This is a relatively new approach which has been drawn from US experience. Traditionally, the police have responded to crime and have then sought to solve it. However, this approach concentrates on a particular problem, for example burglary, and then puts resources into obtaining intelligence on the most important offenders. Intelligence is gathered over a considerable period and then, in a series of carefully targeted arrests, the identified offenders are arrested.

Problem-oriented policing

This is a relatively new style of policing. In a particular area, an analysis is carried out of the problems which cause most disturbance to the public. The police then focus their energies on solving the particular issue – even if it not particularly serious forms of crime.

Policing and the public

In recent years a number of reports have pointed out that the police have to have the support of the local community if they are to do their job.

In 1982 after a series of riots in London, partly by members of the African-Caribbean community, a government inquiry was held by Lord Scarman who argued that only by having the active *consent*, *trust* and *participation* of the community could the police function effectively in its policing. Today the police are required to liaise with community organisations and local authorities, and to support victims of crime. However, despite attempts by the police service to do this, the actual process of policing has often been accused of racism and bias. This situation was most powerfully illustrated when a young, black A-level student was stabbed to death by a group of white youths. The police were accused of incompetence at best, and racism and possibly collusion at worst. A government inquiry led by Lord Macpherson in 1998 found that the police were 'institutionally racist', meaning that the entire process of policing in the UK was shot through with racist assumptions and practices. As a result of the Inquiry and the recommendations made by it, the police have tried to carry out a series of reforms and have been set recruitment targets for officers from the ethnic minorities.

The Macpherson Report: police, racism and policy

On the evening of 22 April 1993 two young, black youths were waiting for a bus when they were approached by five young white men who stabbed one of them, Stephen Lawrence, to death. This was inexcusable, but the police response was almost unbelievable. On arriving at the scene, no medical help was given to Stephen Lawrence by the officers and they treated the incident with a considerable degree of disinterest. During the later investigation, they ignored information given to them on the probable identity of the murderers and consistently insulted the parents of the murdered young man by their attitude and conduct. The five

presumed murderers remain free today.

As a result of the persistence of the parents a judicial inquiry, under Lord Justice Macpherson was set up in 1998 to investigate the police actions. His report accused the police of institutional racism which he defined as:

'the collective failure of an organisation to provide an appropriate and professional service to people because of their colour or ethnic origin. It can be seen or detected in processes, attitudes and behaviour which amount to discrimination through unwitting prejudice, ignorance,

thoughtlessness and racist stereotyping which disadvantages minority ethnic people.'

Perhaps a simpler definition of institutional racism would be that it describes a situation where the normal, everyday activities of police officers subconsciously incorporate racist thinking and actions.

Source: Adapted from M. Walsh, P. Stephens and S. Moore, *Social Policy* (Nelson Thornes, 2000)

1 Search the archives of the newspapers on the internet to find out as much as you can on the Stephen Lawrence case, and about the resulting Macpherson Report. What recommendations did Macpherson make?

2 Do you think that his criticism of the police was justified? Or do you think that he was not critical enough?

3 What responses have the police made to the Macpherson report?

Policing: bias and discretion

Definitions

Police discretion – there are so many laws and so many different interpretations of them that police officers have to make decisions about what is to be enforced and how to enforce it

Canteen culture – the informal values about how to go about policing which young police officers learn. This is often passed on through gossip and comments in their shift breaks – hence the term canteen culture

Working rules – the result of canteen culture; the specific guidelines which police officers follow as a result of the canteen culture

Bias – using this term suggests that the police pick on certain groups in the population more than others, treating them more harshly

Canteen culture

It is the job of police officers to uphold law and order. This seems fairly obvious, but when new police officers start the job, they are overwhelmed by the sheer amount of offences and challenges to order which they encounter. In fact, police officers cannot and do not enforce all laws – instead, they make decisions about which are important enough to warrant their time and attention. This is known as **police discretion**.

In carrying out their jobs, police officers are faced with physical attacks from sections of the public and they also face legal challenges from those they arrest, who may make complaints about the way they have been treated. As a response to the problem of how to go use their discretion effectively and how to defend themselves from sections of the public, police officers have developed a **canteen culture**, or informal set of rules which helps lower rank officers to deal with their work.

The learning process begins when the new officer is taught the 'real world' of policing and the informal **working rules** that all police officers follow. The culture teaches them appropriate attitudes towards the criminal justice system, provides explanations for criminality and how to deal with it, so new police officers learn how to distinguish criminal 'types', to recognise a worthwhile 'crime' and to ignore others.

The canteen culture will also stress the importance of supporting other police officers in any situation, whether it is assaults by an offender or in confirming their version of events when a complaint is made by a member of the public against them.

The significance of canteen culture

The canteen culture reinforces the belief amongst police officers that they are separate from the public and that their interpretation of rules is more important than strictly following the official police rules (and occasionally even following the law). This culture has been suggested as the main reason for many miscarriages of justice where police officers have believed someone to be guilty, and have bent the rules to gain evidence against them.

A white only police force?

Decline in ethnic recruits for police.

The increase in ethnic minority police officers employed by forces in England and Wales has slowed significantly, a Guardian survey can reveal.

The survey, marking today's second anniversary of Sir William Macpherson's report into the police's failings in the Stephen Lawrence case, suggests the pace of progress may be slowing on at least one crucial measure.

One of Sir William's recommendations was a rapid rise in the number of ethnic minority officers employed.

The number of ethnic minority officers increased by 155 in the past year, according to the latest figures the 43 forces in England and Wales made available to the Guardian.

The previous year the increase was 261, which itself brought into question whether the police could meet targets set by the government – an increase of around 6,000 officers by 2009. ...

The survey questions were based on recommendations by Sir William Macpherson and measures devised by Her Majesty's Inspectorate of Constabulary.

Source: *The Guardian*, 24 February 2001

1 Who was Stephen Lawrence? What was the Macpherson Report?

2 What is the HM Inspectorate of Constabulary?

3 What was the target for recruits from the ethnic minorities in the police force?

4 What were the recruitment figures in 1999 and 2000 (the newspaper article is from 2001)?

5 Does this seem likely to hit the target?

6 Do you think the ethnic origin of a police officer is important?

Canteen culture has also been linked to claims of racist and sexist behaviour by police officers. In particular, critics have argued that patterns of 'stop and search' (stopping, questioning and searching on the streets) by police officers have been heavily influenced by the 'canteen culture' belief that young, black men are more likely to involved in crime

Stop and search

Of the activities of the police, the one that appears to create the most resentment, particularly amongst young males and members of the ethnic minorities, is when police stop these people in the street and then search them. People who are stopped and searched claim that they feel humiliated, and that the police disproportionately pick on young ethnic minority males. Indeed the stop and search form of policing received particularly harsh criticism in the Macpherson Report.

The police say however that it is an effective way of preventing crime and allows them to stop people who they have suspicions about. They point out that any innocent person should be pleased to co-operate with the police, as they will have nothing to hide.

In 1999/2000, the police stopped and searched 857,000 persons and vehicles, which was 21 per cent fewer than the previous year (presumably as a response to the Macpherson Report). Arrests decreased by 11 per cent however. On the other hand, only 13 per cent of stops actually led to an arrest, and this was an increase of 2 per cent over previous years. So, there were fewer stops and searches, fewer arrests, but a higher proportion of those stopped were arrested.

These statistics support both sides of the argument. On the one hand, a reduction in stops and searches led to a reduction in arrests. On the other hand, a higher percentage of those stopped were arrested and 87 per cent of all stops did not result in any arrest.

Main points

▶ About 95 per cent of all crimes go unpunished.

▶ Less serious crimes are dealt with in magistrate's courts.

▶ More serious crimes are dealt with in Crown courts.

▶ Those found guilty can be sentenced to a custodial or non-custodial sentence.

▶ There is a debate concerning whether courts are biased or not against women and certain ethnic minorities.

▶ It is difficult to draw a conclusion because of great problems comparing cases.

▶ The police have four main roles: law enforcement, maintenance of order, traffic, social role.

▶ There are a number of very different ways of going about policing, varying from patrolling the streets to intelligence-led policing.

▶ Each different method has advantages and disadvantages.

▶ Although the public like the idea of a policeman on the beat, this is very inefficient at stopping crime.

▶ Police relations with some ethnic minority groups is poor.

▶ This has been partly the result of a method of policing called 'stop and search'.

▶ The police have been accused of racism and have had to respond with a number of initiatives including trying to recruit a higher proportion of ethnic minority offices.

Punishment

One of the bitterest debates about the criminal justice system is the question of what exactly is the aim of the system? Obviously it is to uphold the law – but once people have been arrested, tried and convicted, what is the aim of the punishment? Do we want to get revenge on them, do we want to deter them from ever committing crime again? In this case, punishment should be savage and prison conditions should be poor. But we may be setting out to rehabilitate them, making them full members of society again – will poor prison conditions be appropriate?

Five justifications for punishment have been suggested:

- retribution
- deterrence
- rehabilitation
- incapacitation
- reparation.

Retribution

Retribution is the basis of punishment from the Old Testament – 'an eye for an eye'. For those who support this justification for punishment, a person should be punished because they have done harm and society cannot simply ignore the harm. The advantage of retribution is that the penalty to be paid is usually quite clear, so for example a person who murders should be hanged.

Deterrence

By making an example of offenders, others will be deterred from committing an illegal act. This is one of the arguments put forward by those who support the death penalty, though there is no evidence that capital punishment actually deters murderers. This is because most crimes are often performed on the spur of the moment and therefore deterrence would be unlikely to be effective.

Rehabilitation

Rehabilitation starts from the view that punishment should benefit both society and the offender. It aims to bring the offender 'back into' society by changing their attitudes to offending and by providing them with new skills and opportunities. For many critics though, this means conditions in prisons are 'too good' and there are inadequate elements of punishment.

Incapacitation

This approach points out that when a person is in prison, then they cannot be committing any other offence. It is currently very popular in both the UK and the USA. As a small minority of criminals commit the majority of crimes, the claim is that by putting these in prison a high proportion of crimes can be eliminated. This has led to an increase in prison sentences for those repeatedly convicted of burglary and robbery with violence.

However, research indicates that an increase of 25 per cent in the numbers of offenders sent to prison would only bring about a cut of 1 per cent in the levels of offending. (On the other hand, if the prison population was cut by 40 per cent, it would only lead to a 1.6 per cent increase in crime.)

Reparation

This is the argument that the aim of punishment should be to somehow repair or make amends for the harm that an offender has done. Reparation is commonly used in the youth justice system.

Prisons

There are 137 Prison Service establishments in England and Wales. These may be high security, local, closed and open prisons, young offender institutions (for those under 21 years of age) or remand centres.

Types of prisons

- *Dispersal* – for long-term prisoners, who are regarded the most dangerous
- *Local prisons* – for prisoners serving short to medium sentences
- *Remand centres* – for those who are awaiting trial. These centres are usually part of local prisons
- *Training prisons* – a variety of offenders are kept here, often those coming to the end of their sentences who are being offered skills for future employment. But also many of those, such as white-collar criminals, who are not thought to be a risk to the public. Training prisons can be *open* which means that there is a lower level of security, or *closed* (higher security)
- *Young offender institutions* – for those under 21 (can be open or closed).

The Prison Service is an executive agency of the Home Office which means that it has considerable freedom in how it is run. The majority of prisons are run directly by the Prison Service, but there is a gradual move for private companies to build and run prisons.

The costs of prisons

Prisons are extremely expensive places to run – in 2000 for example expenditure on prisons was almost £2 billion and the cost of keeping each prisoner varies from about £18,000 per year to almost £40,000 per year for those in dispersal prisons, with an average cost of over £25,000 for each prisoner.

Prison numbers

In 2000 the prison population of England and Wales was just under 66,000 people, including approximately 2,700 females and 11,000 young offenders (under the age of 21), and these numbers are set to increase by about 2,500 in the next few years. This is a considerable increase over the period before 1995 when the population was under 50,000. Indeed between 1992 and 1997, the prison population increased by 24,000 people and the numbers of women inmates actually doubled. However, a smaller proportion of those committing crime are actually going to prison compared to ten years ago. So, whereas one in six people found guilty for indictable offences went to prison in 1992, it was one in four by 2000.

Does prison work?

Prison life is mostly a continuous repetition of the same day, over and over again. Finding a purpose and a meaning beyond 'punishment' can be a struggle. ... The paradox of imprisonment lies in society's expectations: the community wants retribution, but also rehabilitation. For many, sending people to prison is not enough; they must suffer while there. But only somebody who has never been to a prison would believe that jails are 'soft' places.

I remember the campaign a few years ago for prisons to be made more 'austere'. But the truth that the austerity brigade failed to grasp is that the harsher a prisoner feels himself to have been treated, the less of an obligation he will feel to abide by society's rules and the more likely new victims will be created after release. Official figures speak for themselves – more than half of prisoners reoffend within two years of release. ... Prison can work, but not if the system is overloaded and under-resourced. And if it is to work in society's interest, it is imperative that only those that really need to be locked up, are, and that all prisons work towards a positive regime where respect and dignity for inmates is not compromised for misguided reasons.

Source: *The Guardian*, 29 January 2001

1 What does the community want of prisons?

2 Why is this a paradox? (A paradox is when two things which are meant to go together are actually completely different.)

3 Are jails 'soft' places?

4 Why would a tougher, harsher jail actually increase crime?

5 What evidence does the author give for his argument?

6 What should prisons be like?

7 The writer of this article is in prison serving a life sentence for murder. Do you think that we should listen to his views?

Prison overcrowding

Definition

Certified Normal Accommodation – the numbers of prisoners the prison is officially allowed to take

Prisons have a specified number of inmates they are supposed to be able to take. This is known as the **Certified Normal Accommodation** (CNA). Over a twenty-year period from the 1980s to the late 1990s prisons routinely exceeded their CNA, sometimes by up to 70 per cent. This led to the building of two new private prisons in the late 1990s.

Prison population

A Sentenced prison population per 100,000 population and offenders: indictable offences

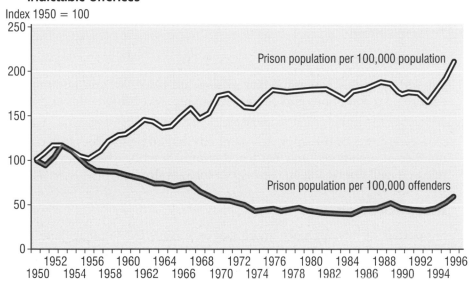

Look at A.

1 What has happened to the number of offenders since 1952?

2 Has there been a similar change in the numbers of people sentenced to prison?

3 Has it become more or less likely that when a person commits an offence, they will be sent to prison?

B Prison population per 100,000 population for selected countries on 1 September 1997 (or nearest available date)

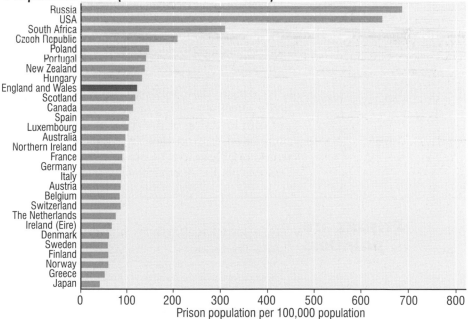

Source: *Criminal Justice Digest 4* (Home Office Research, Development and Statistics Directorate)

Look at B.

4 Which two countries have the highest proportion of their population in prison? What are their rates per 100,000 of the population?

5 Name the six countries with the lowest proportion of their population in prison?

6 Can you see any relationship between four of the 'lowest six'?

7 Where do England and Wales, and Scotland come? What are the rates per 100,000 of the population?

What are prisons meant to do?

Three aims of prison have been suggested:

- punishment
- incapacitation
- rehabilitation.

Punishment

Supporters of this aim argue that prisons are places where the inmates should endure poor conditions and be treated harshly. According to this argument, those who commit crime lose their rights to be treated as citizens.

However, critics of this approach point out that all prison does is to create a large number of embittered and hardened criminals who, when they are eventually released, will not be able to re-integrate into society.

Incapacitation

Supporters of this approach argue that as prisons fail to rehabilitate, and as it is against basic human rights to treat inmates badly, it is better simply to see prison as a place where people who regularly commit crime, or who are likely to commit serious crime, are simply kept away from society. They are placed in prison for long periods, during which time they simply cannot harm anyone. Further support is provided for this approach by the fact that over 60 per cent of crime is performed by only about 5 per cent of offenders.

This has become a particularly popular approach to the aims of prison in recent years, and laws have been introduced which mean that those who repeatedly offend receive long sentences, for example, those who commit robbery with violence, using weapons, receive a mandatory life sentence and those who commit domestic burglary three times receive a minimum sentence of three years.

Critics argue that, although this approach seems sensible, in fact it is not particularly effective. Tarling (a Home Office researcher) calculated that to achieve a 1 per cent lowering of the crime rate required a 25 per cent increase in the prison population, but on the other hand, a 40 per cent cut in the prison population would only lead to a 1.6 per cent increase in crime (R. Tarling, *Analysing Offending: Data Models and Interpretations*, Home Office, 1993).

Prisons are pointless

Chief Justice clashes with Straw on jail policy

Britain's most senior judge last night clashed with the home secretary over Jack Straw's plan for longer prison sentences for the 100,000 most persistent offenders ...

Mr Straw yesterday made plain he was prepared to see prison numbers rise to tackle the hardcore of persistent criminals who, he claimed, were responsible for nearly half of all crime.

He said there might come a time when fewer prison places were needed "but that is a long way off".

Within hours the lord chief justice, Lord Woolf, marking the 10th anniversary of the day he handed his influential report on prison reform to the then home secretary, described jail overcrowding as the "Aids virus of the prison system" and called on courts to pass shorter sentences.

He said: "The judiciary must play their part in reducing the use of custody to what is the acceptable and appropriate minimum. When a custodial sentence is necessary the shortest sentence ... should be imposed.

"Frequently one month will achieve everything that can be achieved by three months and three months will achieve everything that can be by six months and so on."

Lord Woolf made clear last night in his Prison Reform Trust lecture that the best way of cutting crime was a higher detection rate rather than an increase in the prison population of 62,000, which is already forecast to rise to more than 78,000 by 2007.

"What has to be realised, and I include the government here, is that a short custodial sentence is a very poor alternative to a sentence to be served in the community. It is far more expensive. It will do nothing to tackle the offender's behavioural problems. It should be regarded as being no more than a necessary evil whose primary purpose is to obtain compliance with court orders."

His views were in sharp contrast to those of Mr Straw, who declared that community penalties did nothing for 80% of the 100,000 hardcore of the most persistent offenders.

"Almost without exception, every persistent offender sentenced to custody has been through the mill of community sentences and has still reoffended," Mr Straw said in a lecture to the Social Market Foundation.

Source: *The Guardian*, 1 February 2001

1 According to Mr Straw (the Home Secretary in 2001), how many offenders are responsible for half of all crime?

2 What is Mr Straw's opinion of the effectiveness of community penalties for 80 per cent of these hardcore offenders?

3 What reasons does he give for his view?

4 Who is Lord Woolf?

5 Does he agree with Mr Straw?

6 What does he suggest is the best way to cut crime?

7 Why should the 'shortest sentence' be imposed, according to Lord Wolf?

8 Who do you agree with? Why?

Rehabilitation

Rehabilitation means to try to make offenders understand that offending is wrong and to think and act in a law abiding way. Most ordinary people when asked about the aims of prisons will say that they are places where prisoners are both punished and rehabilitated.

Critics point out that prisons simply do not do achieve this, with 70% of those who go into prison, reoffending within two years. This may well be a result of the fact that there is extremely limited educational and social provision in prisons, with the majority of inmates spending more time locked in their cells than doing any recreational or educational activity.

Education is even more important as approximately 60 per cent of prisoners have serious difficulties in reading and writing, and up to 70 per cent have not got basic standards of numeracy.

Prisoners spend less than four hours each week, on average, doing any form of educational, vocational or industrial training. They spend about 13 hours each week on work, and about 28 hours on recreation.

A prisoner's day

A typical daily routine for a prisoner in a closed establishment

Time	Activity
07.55 hrs	Cells unlocked; breakfast served.
08.20 hrs	Those prisoners with work or educational classes leave the wing for exercise.
09.00 hrs	Work and educational classes start. Remaining prisoners are locked in their cells.
11.10 hrs	Prisoners without work or classes are now unlocked and leave the wing for exercise.
12.10 hrs	All prisoners return to the wing and lunch is served.
12.40 hrs	All prisoners are locked in their cells and a roll call is taken.
14.00 hrs	Those going to work or educational classes are unlocked; prisoners with a planned visit are taken to the visitors room. Everyone else stays locked up.

➤

Time	Activity
16.00 hrs	Visits end.
17.00 hrs	All prisoners now locked in cells and roll call taken.
17.50 hrs	Prisoners unlocked and tea is served.
18.30 hrs	Access to television, pool tables, table-football and recreation with other prisoners begins. Some may be allowed to go to the gym.
20.00 hrs	All prisoners are now back on the wing.
20.20 hrs	All prisoners locked up for the night; final roll call taken.

Source: M. Stephens, *Crime and Social Policy* (The Gildredge Press, 2000); original source the Howard League for Penal Reform, 'A Day in the Life of a Prisoner', Factsheet No. 9, 1997

Problems in prison

Self-harm and suicide

For most offenders, going to prison is an enormous shock and a very frightening experience, as a consequence there is a very high suicide rate in prison. But, on top of this, there are many prisoners who actually harm themselves, most often by cutting and mutilating themselves. In the late 1990s, Feltham Young Offenders Institution had over 230 incidents of suicide and self-harm each year. Most of these occur in the first few weeks of imprisonment, as prisoners come to terms with the tough life in prison.

Reasons suggested for suicide and self-harm include:

- overcrowding and poor living conditions
- isolation, as they may be in prisons far away from their family
- depression brought about by long hours locked in their cells
- bullying
- lack of activity, in particular education and training.

Bullying

Bullying is a major problem in prisons and especially in young offender institutions. Unlike bullying in schools or even the workplace, the person being bullied cannot escape as they are enclosed with the bullies. This makes the situation much worse.

Bullying takes place for a variety of reasons, but reasons suggested by studies have included:

- to obtain cigarettes or additional food
- for entertainment to break the boredom
- for sexual reasons
- to enhance the status of the bullies.

In one study, almost half of young offenders and about one-third of adult prisoners had been assaulted, robbed or threatened with violence in the previous month (O'Donnell and Edgar, *Victimisation in Prisons*, Home Office Research Findings 37, 1996).

Prisons are disgusting

The full extent of the appalling conditions inside Britain's first "failing" jail is revealed in a report published today by the chief inspector of prisons. ... Brixton is already under investigation by the commission for racial equality for being "institutionally racist" but some of the findings by the chief inspector will cause even greater concern about what has been going on inside the prison.

These findings include:

• The system by which inmates contact staff in an emergency had been sabotaged by staff on more than one wing – this betrayed "a disgraceful attitude by staff towards those in their care". The excuse that the alarms were "too loud" was unacceptable, he said.

• Standards in the healthcare centre were "nothing short of scandalous" – "filth and neglect there showed a breakdown in the chain of command".

• Meals were prepared in a kitchen which had been condemned by the environmental health authorities.

• An unofficial and unlawful "reflections" system of punishing prisoners was used by staff under which inmates were locked in their cells so they could "reflect" on their misdemeanours. The inspectors wondered how long this had gone on unnoticed or condoned by managers.

• Staff on suicide watch in the healthcare centre were falsifying their entries on monitoring sheets. At 2.45pm the inspection team found observations already entered for 4pm – "a despicable practice, displaying both a lack of care and worrying certainty that no manager would check the malpractice".

• Medicines were dispensed without signed prescriptions to inmates who had not been properly identified – condemned by the report as "highly dangerous and illegal".

Source: *The Guardian*, 31 January 2001

1 Which prison was inspected?
2 Who inspected it?
3 What is meant by 'institutional racism'?
4 Why were the staff criticised for their 'despicable practice' on suicide watch?
5 What was the 'reflections' system? Did the staff have the legal right to do this?

Drug use

Drug use is widespread in prisons, with drug tests revealing that about 20 per cent of prisoners at the minimum using various forms of illegal drugs. Since 1996, mandatory (compulsory) drug tests have been used on offenders in an attempt to wipe out their use in prisons. If prisoners test positive for drugs, they will have to stay in prison longer. However drug testing has caused almost as many problems as it has solved.

Disputes over drugs have been linked to violence in prisons as inmates threaten others to obtain additional supplies. Also, drug-using prisoners argue that drugs allow them to pass the time in prison and actually calms the situation of tension and violence. This is particularly true for cannabis.

On the positive side, the Prison Service has a range of treatment programmes to support drug users who wish to give up, as well as counselling and drug-free areas in prisons where prisoners can obtain additional privileges.

The aims of the prison service

The following statement represents the official aims of the prison service.

HM Prison Service Objectives:
Protect the public by holding those committed by the courts in a safe, decent and healthy environment.
Reducing crime by providing regimes which address offending behaviour, improve educational and work skills and promote law abiding behaviour in custody and after release.

Source: *HM Prison Service Annual Report and Accounts 1999–2000* (The Stationery Office, 2000)

1 In your opinion, do you think prison achieves these aims?
2 Do you agree that this should be the aims of the prison service?
3 Would you add or take away anything?
4 Write your own aims in no more than 60 words.

The prison population

The prison population is not a mirror image of the population in general. Prisoners are disproportionately:

- *Male*: Ninety-five per cent of all prisoners are male, reflecting the different rates of crime and the seriousness of male offences compared to female offences.
- *Members of ethnic minorities*: Eighteen per cent of the male prison population are from ethnic minorities, and 25 per cent of the female prison population. Whereas the ethnic minority proportion of the population in general is just under 6 per cent. In particular, there is higher rate from those of African-Caribbean origin, with almost two-thirds of female prisoners, for example, coming from this background.
- *People with educational problems*: As we saw earlier, 60 per cent of prisoners have significant problems in reading and writing, and 70 per cent have no basic numeracy skills.
- *People with histories of mental illness*: The Home Office estimates that about 20,000 out of the 66,000 prisoners have some form of mental illness, slightly less than one-third, and about half of all those who commit suicide have been diagnosed as suffering from some form of mental illness.
- *People who have not been convicted of any offence:* This refers to prisoners **on remand**. On remand means that the offender has been sent to prison to await trial, rather than being allowed to stay at home (on **bail**). Those in prison on remand are not guilty as they have not been tried. However, they have to obey most of the prison rules and regulations. About 20 per cent of the prison population are on remand.

Definitions

On remand – some defendants are refused bail and have to wait for trial in prison. Usually this is because the police fear they will run away, or that they might present a threat to the public or witnesses

Bail – when waiting for trial or sentencing, some defendants are allowed to stay at home. If they fail to turn up in court, they will be arrested

Does prison work: recidivism rates

A Adjusted reconviction rates within two years for those released from prison and for community penalties

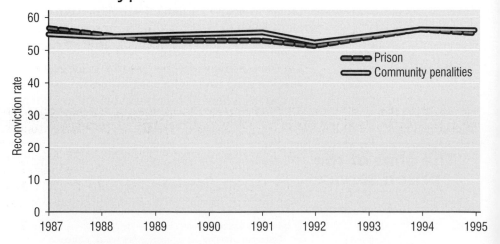

Look at A.

1 In 1995, according to the graph, what percentage of those released from prison committed another crime?

2 Has this changed much from 1987?

B **Reconviction rates by age, 1994**

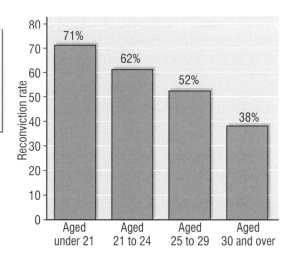

Look at B.

3 Which age group had the highest reconviction rate?

4 Which age group had the lowest rate of **recidivism**?

5 What can you say overall about the relationship between age and recidivism?

Definition

Recidivism – committing another crime after completion of punishment for a previous offence

C **Reconviction rate by previous history, 1994**

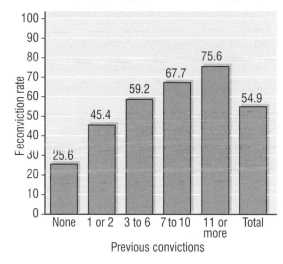

Source: *Criminal Justice Digest 4* (Home Office Research, Development and Statistics Directorate)

Look at C.

6 What percentage of those with one or two previous offences were reconvicted?

7 How many previous offences had the group with a reconviction rate of 67.7 per cent committed?

8 Overall, what is the relationship between reconviction and previous offences?

9 Make a list of possible implications for prisons and punishment of these statistics.

Probation

The Probation Service developed out of the work done by nineteenth-century church workers who volunteered to be responsible for young offenders to save them being sent to juvenile prisons. In 1907, their role was formally recognised in the workings of the courts and gradually a government probation service was formed.

Organisation

There are forty-two Probation Service Areas which align with the police authorities, and they are responsible to a National Director. This is a recent change – until 2001 the Probation Service was run by local government and local councillors appointed a Chief Probation Officer for their county or borough.

What do probation officers do?

Probation officers have a large number of different tasks including:

- *Preparing pre-sentence reports:* These are reports which give advice to judges on the background of offenders and the most appropriate sentence for them. Each year, probation officers write about a quarter of a million reports.

- *Supervising adult offenders in the community:* Most offenders are not sent to prison, but given community sentences, as we saw earlier. It is the job of a probation officer to ensure that these sentences are carried out properly. This often includes regular meetings with offenders to ensure that they are complying with the conditions of the sentence.
  Offenders who are 16 or over can be sentenced to have an electronic tag which prevents them leaving their home, except at certain times and under certain conditions. Probation officers assess whether tagging is appropriate or not.

- *Supervision after release from prison:* Offenders who have been sentenced to twelve months or more are supervised by the probation officers before and after their release from prison

- *Work in prisons:* Not all probation officers work in the community. About 10 per cent operate in prisons, working with offenders to try to prevent future offending and to ensure that conditions are right on release for them to avoid situations where they may commit crime.

Community sentences: are they tough enough?

Offenders sentenced for indictable offences, England and Wales

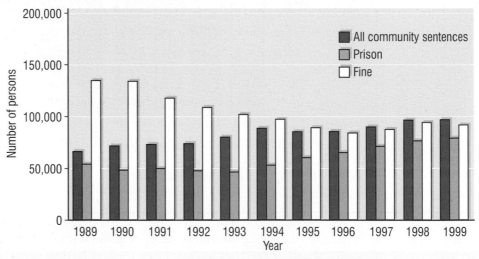

Source: *Probation Statistics* (The Stationery Office, 1999); www.homeoffice.gov.uk

1 In 1999 how many community sentences were there?

2 Was this more or less than prison sentences? How many prison sentences were there?

3 What is the third type of punishment commonly given?

4 How has the balance between the three types of punishment changed since 1989?

5 Do you think that this means that punishment in 1999 is:
   a) less harsh
   b) harsher
   c) the same as it was in 1989?

6 Do you think that community penalties are a 'soft option' compared to going to prison?

7 Which do you think would be more effective in preventing people re-offending: prison or community sentence? Look at the graph on page 298.

8 In your opinion, what does the graph show you comparing the recidivism rates of community penalties and prison?

Probation officers are responsible for a wide range of specific community penalties, but the main ones are:

- *Community Rehabilitation Order*: This is an order lasting between 6 months and 3 years for those aged 16 and over. It often has additional requirements such as living in a special (probation) hostel, and/or attending courses seen as causing the offending behaviour, such as drug, alcohol or mental problems.
- *Community Punishment Order*: This consists of between 40 and 240 hours of unpaid work.
- *Community Punishment and Rehabilitation Order*: This combines elements of the rehabilitation order and up to 100 hours of unpaid work

Electronic monitoring

Since 1999, electronic monitoring has been used by courts throughout England and Wales. By the end of 2000, over 4,000 curfew orders using electronic tagging had been made. The enforcement of the 'tagging' is done by private security firms, not probation officers. The Home Office claims a 91 per cent completion rate for tagging.

The success of the curfew orders led to the introduction of a Home Detention Curfew in which prisoners serving between three months and four years can be released up to two months earlier than they otherwise would be. At any one time, about 2,000 prisoners are completing their sentences at home.

Youth justice

Since the Crime and Disorder Act 1998, the main responsibility for dealing with offending by those aged 10–17 has been taken by the Youth Justice Board. This directs over 150 local youth offending teams (YOTs) who operate locally to combat youth crime. Youth offending teams comprise staff from social services, the police, education and health services amongst others.

Young people are tried in special courts, introduced in 1992, which deal with offenders up to and including the age of 16.

The Act which brought in youth offending teams also created a complicated raft of measures to combat youth crime, and the members of the youth offending team are required to enforce these measures. These include:

- *Final warning:* The police may decide that it is not appropriate to prosecute a young person, so they are given a final warning. The YOT worker will decide if the young person needs some form of counselling or programme to divert them from offending in the future.
- *Supervision Order*: The offender needs to meet the YOT worker regularly for three months to three years, and undertake activities set by them.
- *Attendance Centre Order*: The young offender must attend the centre for instruction in social skills and physical training. There is a maximum of twelve hours attendance.
- *Referral Order*: If a young offender pleads guilty, then he or she may be referred to a panel of experts in youth justice who will agree with the young person and his/her family a programme to address the causes of offending, and also the young person will be required to apologise to the victim.
- *Parenting Orders:* As it is commonly accepted that much offending behaviour is related to poor parenting, a new order has been introduced which requires parents of young offenders to attend counselling or guidance on parenting skills.

Crime reduction

Since 1998, one of the main ways in which crime is being tackled is through the Crime Reduction Programme. The aim is to put in place a wide series of measures which will limit crime, but these measures will be undertaken by a range of agencies under the joint leadership of local authorities and the police. Crime reduction programmes include such things as:

- Neighbourhood Watch, where the local community is requested to watch out for any potential criminal activity
- CCTV – the introduction of cameras in city centres and high crime spots
- measures to tackle truancy, as much crime is committed by young people not attending, or having been excluded from, school
- targeting policing on specific problems and specific high crime areas.

Main points

▶ A number of different justifications as to why we punish offenders have been suggested: retribution, deterrence, rehabilitation, incapacitation, reparation.

▶ The number of people being sent to prison is increasing, despite the high costs of prison, the high rates of recidivism and overcrowding.

▶ There are many problems in prisons, including bullying and drugs.

▶ The Probation Service is the agency responsible for overseeing community punishments.

▶ Electronic monitoring ('tagging') is increasingly being used to control and punish offenders.

▶ Youth justice has been dramatically reformed since 1998. Youth offending teams were created and new punishments were introduced.

▶ The government is expanding crime reduction programmes, largely through local authorities

Conclusion

In this chapter we have explored a wide range of aspects of criminal justice. We have seen that the main components of the system are the police, the courts and the agencies which look after the offenders on our behalf – the Prison Service and the Probation Service. We have also explored the type and extent of crime in the UK today. But in order to understand how to combat crime, we must know not just what crimes are committed, but *why* people commit them. We have seen that there are different explanations and those differing explanations provide very different policy implications.

When we looked at punishment too, we saw that perhaps we are rather unclear in exactly what we are setting out to do with offenders – punish them so they won't commit crime again, or rehabilitate them to the same effect. Whatever we are doing, the fact is that the majority of those who go to prison re-offend.

In our exploration of the police and policing methods, we found that the police use a range of different methods of policing to combat crime, though the public is strongly in favour of the least effective method – beat policing.

A major concern of commentators of criminal justice is that both the police and courts appear to be influenced by racism. We examined the evidence for this in the court process and also within the police force. We also looked at the work being done by the police to combat racism.

10 CHAPTER SUMMARY

1. The criminal justice system is composed of three main government departments: the Attorney General's Office, the Lord Chancellor's Office, the Home Office.

2. The CJS is one of the main expenses of the government, with £12 billion spent on the system.

3. Most crimes are related to property, but violent crime is relatively low.

4. There are two different measures of crime: the British Crime Survey and police statistics. Both have advantages and disadvantages.

5. There are a number of reasons why people fail to report crimes to the police, and it also quite common for the police to decide not to record certain 'crimes' reported to them.

6. There is a pattern amongst victims of crime, they are not randomly chosen, and some individuals are much more likely to be victims than others.

7. There are high rates of repeat victimisation, where the same people are likely to become victims more than once.

8. There are organisations to help victims of crime.

9. There are three different types of explanations for criminality: immediate, contextual, structural.

10. Immediate explanations centre on family and friends.

11. Contextual explanations centre on neighbourhood, schools and housing

12. Structural explanations focus on the wider organisation of society.

13. The concept of the 'criminal career', which argues that there is no single explanation for crime, helps us to understand that different factors influence people at different times of their lives.

14. About 95 per cent of all crimes go unpunished.

15. Less serious crimes are dealt with in magistrate's courts and more serious crimes are dealt with in Crown courts.

16. Those found guilty can be sentenced to a custodial or non-custodial sentence.

17. There is a debate concerning whether courts are biased or not against women and certain ethnic minorities.

18. It is difficult to draw a conclusion because of great problems comparing cases.

19. The police have four main roles: law enforcement, maintenance of order, traffic, social role.

20. There are a number of very different ways of going about policing, varying from patrolling the streets to intelligence-led policing.

21. Each different method has advantages and disadvantages.

22. Although the public like the idea of a policeman on the beat, this is very inefficient at stopping crime.

23 Police relations with some ethnic minority groups is poor, this has been partly the result of a method of policing called 'stop and search'.

24 The police have been accused of racism and have had to respond with a number of initiatives including trying to recruit a higher proportion of ethnic minority offices.

25 A number of different justifications as to why we punish offenders have been suggested: retribution, deterrence, rehabilitation, incapacitation, reparation.

26 The number of people being sent to prison is increasing, despite the high costs of prison, the high rates of recidivism and overcrowding.

27 There are many problems in prisons, including bullying and drugs.

28 The Probation Service is the agency responsible for overseeing community punishments.

29 Electronic monitoring ('tagging') is increasingly being used to control and punish offenders.

30 Youth justice has been dramatically reformed since 1998. Youth offending teams were created and new punishments were introduced.

31 The government is expanding crime reduction programmes, largely through local authorities

Useful websites

www.homeoffice.gov.uk: the website of the Home Office

www.prisonservice.gov.uk: the Prison Service

www.youth-justice-board.gov.uk: the Youth Justice Board

www.crimeconcern.org.uk: Crime Concern

http://web.ukonline.co.uk/howard.league: the Howard League for Penal Reform

www.nayj.org.uk: National Association of Youth Justice

Chapter 11

SOCIAL POLICY: EUROPEAN AND GLOBAL PERSPECTIVES

Chapter contents

Part 1: The European Union

- ## Origins and development of the European Union

  In this first section we get to grips with the nature and origins of the European Union. In particular we look at the reasons for its development from its beginnings after the Second World War, and then move on to explore the wider reasons pushing it forward to become a major trading bloc with very important social policy implications for the millions of people who live in the fifteen member states.

- ## Decision-making

  Decision-making in the European Union often mystifies outsiders. Here we give a very simple guide to how decisions are made with respect to social policies.

- ## The European Court of Justice

  This often appears in the press giving decisions which are binding upon the UK. Much of our equal rights legislation has emerged after decisions of the European Courts have forced the UK into accepting European legislation. This has almost always been to the benefit of ordinary people.

- ## Social policy development

  Elsewhere we have examined the overall development of Europe as a community and we have touched on specific social policy issues. In this section, we examine them in more detail.

Part 2: Comparative social policy

- ## Comparative social policy

  This part of the chapter moves more into the theoretical issue of how we go about classifying welfare states into categories and then explaining why we should want to do that. Welfare 'regimes' vary from country to country, but patterns do emerge, and by looking at these patterns we are able to categorise each country and see the reasons for their particular system. We can also look at more 'successful' and less 'successful' regimes.

- ## Why compare models of welfare?

  We show the usefulness of comparisons and classifications, pointing out how much we learn from them, and noting the complexity of the European Union's attempts to construct common social policies, as the member states start from such different sorts of welfare systems.

Part 3: Globalisation

- ## The world context of social policy

  Here we look at the reasons why we should examine the wider context of our social policies and recognise the fact that social policies are strongly influenced by world events and trading patterns.

- ## Globalisation

  This section takes us into much greater detail and examines the way that world trading patterns have impacted strongly on welfare states in a range of countries, right across the globe. We learn the reasons why and look at the role of the World Trade Organisation.

- ## Globalisation and social policy

  Finally, we move on to look specifically at globalisation's impact on welfare states and give the example of Sweden.

Introduction

This book is about the Welfare State in the UK so why have a chapter comparing European and global developments? As we will see, we should look outside the UK to Europe and beyond as the process of globalisation and European integration have dramatically transformed the world in which we live. World economic trends play a large part in affecting the wealth of any country and its ability to pay for welfare.

We start with a discussion of the European Union (EU) because it is, and will probably become even more of, an influence on the range and quality of social policies which the UK will follow. Agreements on economic and trading issues within the EU have involved agreeing to take part in certain common social policies. To be frank, these have almost all been very much to the benefit of ordinary working people in the UK.

We also introduce a fairly detailed discussion on comparative social policy. This is the attempt to categorise different welfare systems of countries into a few categories. By doing so we can see the strengths and weaknesses of different systems, but we also learn from them and take any useful policy initiatives which might improve our system. But also, we can see more clearly what influences the sort of welfare state that countries set up.

Part 1: The European Union

Origins and development of the European Union

After the Second World War, a number of European countries decided that if they were to avoid the possibility of war for a third time in the twentieth century, then they should strive to integrate their economies and political programmes.

In 1951, the European Coal and Steel Community was founded. This co-ordinated the production of coal and steel across Germany, France, Italy, Belgium, Luxembourg and the Netherlands. It functioned so well that, in 1957, the Treaty of Rome was signed, which set up the European Economic Community (the EEC, later known as the European Community or EC, and now as the European Union). The aims of the EEC were to strengthen peace, achieve economic integration and harmonious and balanced economic development, and to work towards an 'ever closer union of the peoples of Europe'.

The UK had been suspicious of the EEC, and did not join. However, the economic growth of the member states proved to be far faster than that of the UK and, after a number of failed attempts, the UK eventually joined in 1973, along with Ireland and Denmark. Greece joined in 1981, and Spain and Portugal in 1986. Later, in 1995, Sweden, Finland and Austria joined, bring the number of member states to fifteen.

However, the EU has not yet finished growing. It is likely that a number of the Eastern European countries will join the Union before long. The most likely to join are the Czech Republic, Poland and Hungary – although there is a further queue behind them which could well bring the numbers of members up to at least twenty-one.

European Union member states in 2001

What European social policy covers

Social policy is a broad field of activity of EU institutions, encompassing aspects of employment policy, free movement and social security of EU migrants, working conditions, health and safety at work, the 'social dialogue' between employees' and employers' representatives, sex equality, social protection, welfare and family policy, social exclusion and poverty, race relations, public health, training and vocational education, disability and ageing.

The need for European Union social policy

To understand the EU's role in social policy, we need to look at what the EU is really trying to achieve. The activities of the EU impact on nearly every aspect of our waking lives in one way or another – from currency and tax issues, to legislation that regulates the number of hours we can work, from food and drugs safety regulations to the single currency. The EU is a complex organisation which is involved in a wide range of activities. However, as a starting point it is useful to think about it as an organisation that has four fairly straightforward economic objectives:

1   The first stage or aim was to create a *free trade area* among the member countries. This sounds complicated but it means that in creating a free trade area, the member countries simply agreed to trade more freely with one each other which involves abolishing or reducing tariff barriers, quotas and subsidies.

2   The second stage has much more to do with protectionism than free trade. The member countries erected a tariff wall around the outside of the EU. In other words, they put a percentage charge on certain goods entering the Union from outside. This is called creating a *customs union* and its aim was to give member countries' businesses a competitive advantage over those located in non-member countries.

3   The third stage was to create a *common market* which allowed people and money to move freely within the Union. This also meant allowing people who were citizens of a member country to work in any member state. When the EU was founded back in the 1950s, it was somewhere between a customs union and common market.

4   We have now reached the fourth and final dramatic stage, *full economic and monetary union* – the single currency.

Most EU policies, but not all, can be understood in terms of the achievement of these four aims or stages. The EU's role in social policy is no exception. Most of the social policy relates to the workplace and employment in some respect.

The four stages of European economic integration

	FTA	CU	CM	EU
Free trade in goods and services	*			
Common external tariff barrier	*	*		
Free movement of labour and capital	*	*	*	
Harmonisation of currency and tax policy	*	*	*	*

Key
FTA Free trade area
CU Customs union
CM Common market
EU Economic union

Free movement of workers

In order to create a common market, workers need to be able to move freely. Over the years, the European Court of Justice (we discuss this later on page 311) has made numerous judgements in order to promote the free movement of workers – impacting on national policies in areas such as pensions, social security and health care – and the free movement of services, which have direct implications for service delivery in, for example, health care. Another example can be found in the area of educational qualifications. For citizens of member states of the EU to live and work in any part of the Union policies have been put in place to assure the recognition of educational qualifications across national boundaries.

Workers' rights

Right at the beginning in 1957, the French government argued during the negotiations of the Treaty of Rome that the social charges borne by employers were higher in France than in the other member states. The French argued that their workers had more rights (such as longer holidays, shorter hours, better pensions) which imposed greater costs on employers.

Consequently, the French argued that their employers would be at a disadvantage in the Common Market. They argued that there was a legitimate reason for government intervention in the market to 'create a level playing field'. In particular they pressed for equal pay between men and women (which had already been agreed in principle in France). These sorts of arguments about the role social policy plays in economic competition have continued between member governments ever since.

> ## Definitions
>
> **Social cost** – refers to the additional costs that employers pay on top of the wage bill, for example in pension contributions, sick pay and other work-related payments for employees
>
> **Social dumping** – a commonly used term to refer to a process of getting rid of welfare and employment rights in order to lower costs for employers

Today, there are few barriers to companies investing in any country in the EU. The expenses and laws relating to **social costs** – pensions, sick pay, redundancy payments, maternity rights, minimum wages and health and safety at work – all influence where companies choose to open and close plants. As we will see later in the section on globalisation, some claim that where there is relatively little protection for workers, companies will prefer to invest there because costs are lower. Conversely, countries which strive to provide their workforces with good conditions and high standards of rights are less attractive. In turn, some feel that this will encourage governments to practise **social dumping** and reducing workers rights to encourage investment from abroad. One of the aims of the Social Charter of 1989 was to ensure that all countries have minimum level of social rights, so that one country does not have an unfair advantage over others.

A European social model

But separately, there is a belief held by some people that all member states share a common heritage. Part of this heritage is the developed welfare state that offers citizens a right to high standards of social protection and health. This is seen by some in the European Commission as one of the key overall aims of the Union, just as important as economic success.

Industrial restructuring and unemployment

The EU is striving to make itself the dominant economic force in the world, and the majority of the member states would like it to be one of the major political forces too. But, economic developments have social costs. Europe has suffered high levels of unemployment since the 1980s caused by the enormous shift from manufacturing to services and from the use of unskilled labour to advanced technology. The EU has regional policies referred to as the Structural Funds which redirect money to the regions most affected by restructuring and unemployment.

Anti-discrimination

The EU's anti-discrimination policies have a long history. Equal opportunities policies between men and women are one of the most developed areas of EU social policy. The principle of equal pay for men and women was recognised by the Treaty of Rome. The EU has consistently supported the rights of women in terms of:

- equal pay
- equal access to training and employment
- equal treatment in social security matters
- the provision of better maternity rights and benefits, and childcare facilities.

Equal opportunities legislation

- Article 119 of the Treaty of Rome (1957) stated that 'men and women shall receive equal pay for equal work'.

- *1975 Directive on Equal Pay:* This is important because it extended and clarified the meaning of equal work. It stated that equal work meant work of equal value, so men and women did not have to be in the same job to get equal pay, but engaged in equally valuable work.

- *1976 Directive on Equal Treatment:* Insisted on equal access to employment, training, promotion and working conditions.

- *1979 Directive on Equal Treatment in Social Security*: Demanded equality of treatment from statutory social security schemes for people under retirement age. It covered equality for sick pay, accidents at work, unemployment, etc.

- *1986 Directive on Occupational Social Security Schemes*: Demanded equality of treatment for all non-State schemes provided by employers.

- *1986 Self-Employed Directive:* Ensured equal treatment between self-employed men and women.

- *1992*: Most EU member states introduced equality of rights between full-time and part-time workers. This is particularly important to women, who form the majority of part-time employees. This benefited women through an extension of sickness and redundancy rights and in many cases through pay levels. The UK did not introduce this legislation at the time. However, it was introduced into the UK after a European Court of Justice ruling.

- *1992 Directive on Maternity Rights:* Guaranteed a minimum of rights to pregnant women of 14 weeks' maternity leave and pay at the minimum rate of statutory sick pay.

- *1996 Directive on Parental Leave:* Gave a legal right to unpaid leave to look after young children.

- *1996 Proposal for a Directive on Burden of Proof in Sex Discrimination Cases:* Until now a woman who feels she has been discriminated against has needed to prove her case. The proposed Directive would partially shift the burden of proof to the employer to show that it had not discriminated.

A recent move by the European Commission in improving the position of women has been that of 'mainstreaming'. This is the process by which the impact upon the rights of women are taken into account in all the stages of devising, preparing and implementing legislation and the European Commission's activities in general.

Health and safety

This is another important area of EU social policy. A variety of directives have been introduced since 1988, the most important of which is the Framework Directive which provides the framework of rules for health and protection by specifying employers' duties and workers' rights. Employers must, for instance, assess and avoid risks, introduce preventive measures, use specialist health and safety advice, monitor potential hazards, and keep records on specified accidents and diseases. Employers also have to introduce safety training.

Decision-making

The process of making decisions in the EU is a complicated one, with different procedures for different subjects and different types of measure. Since the Treaty of European Union was signed in Maastricht in 1992, the most important participants in EU social policy-making have been the so-called *social partners*. The social partners at European level are, on the one hand, the representatives of the managers of businesses and, on the other, representatives of workers. The social partners are also referred to as 'the two sides of industry'. Management are represented by two pressure groups, UNICE and CEEP. The workers are represented by the European Trade Union Confederation (ETUC). Whilst the Commission, which is a mixture between a European civil service and a government, and the Council of Ministers, which acts like a national parliament, are involved in various ways, they have a secondary role. Basically, if the social partners agree that legislation is required, they can negotiate to produce it. If they can produce an 'agreement', it is highly likely the Council of Ministers will turn the 'agreement' into official European legislation.

Forms of EU legislation

EU legislation takes a number of forms, including:

- *regulations*, which must be enforced in the member states and have immediate effect
- *directives*, which apply to some or all member states. The EU usually sets minimum standards but national governments can decide how best to achieve these standards
- *decisions*, which apply to individual persons or member states.

The European Court of Justice

This is based in Luxembourg and has the role of ensuring that the laws of the EU are applied by its members fully and correctly. The Court has come to play a key role in ensuring individual governments grant in practice the rights which they formally agree to in their undertakings as member states of the EU. The Court often hits the headlines in the UK, where it is portrayed as 'interfering' in UK law. However, in reality it is simply ensuring that what the government has agreed to is put into effect. This has had particular importance for issues involving health and welfare in the UK.

The Court of Justice consists of fifteen judges, assisted by nine advocates-general, all of whom have two assistants who do all the research on the cases and who prepare the documents. The independence of the judges and advocates-general is guaranteed by law. Furthermore, they cannot be removed and are immune from legal proceedings against them.

The judges and advocates-general serve for six years, but may have their term of office extended. They choose a president, who allocates cases and directs the Court. The Court either sits in plenary session (for the most important cases involving member states) at which at least seven judges must be present, or in chambers consisting of three or five judges.

The Court has consistently found against the UK government on a range of social welfare issues primarily on the failure to treat women equally in terms of social welfare benefits, maternity benefits and leave from work, and equal treatment for part-time workers (usually women).

Social policy development

For the first ten years of its life, the European Commission did very little to develop its social aims. But by the 1970s a renewed interest in social conditions and the demands for equality by women's organisations led to four directives on working conditions and three on sex equality being adopted by the Council of Ministers.

In the mid-1980s, the Commission re-launched the social dimension of the EC to accompany closer economic integration, believing that economic and social progress must go hand in hand for either to be successful in the long-term. In the resulting 1986 Single European Act (SEA), the member states included the idea of 'social justice' and agreed to improve the economic and social situation of employees by extending common policies into health and safety at work. But this seemed to limited to the majority of countries and they decided to go ahead with a Community Charter of Fundamental Rights of Workers. It was adopted by eleven governments (excluding the UK) in December 1989.

Poor relations
In the next two waves of EU enlargement, the relative poverty of central and eastern Europe will bring drastic changes

The European Union has long wanted to create a single "social space" and a declared aim of the social charter incorporated into the Maastricht treaty is that Europe's social dimension be given the same importance as economics and markets. The Lisbon summit agreed earlier this year on new strategic goals for the next decade and among them was greater social cohesion.

At present about 17% of the EU's population is poor, ranging from 9.4% in Denmark to 33.3% in Portugal. Most of the poor are concentrated, not surprisingly, in the larger nations; over two-thirds of Europe's poor live in France, the UK, Spain and Germany. ... The extent and distribution of poverty affects other policies. The EU cohesion and structural funds have the goal of reducing inequality. If these funds were to be redistributed according to the extent of poverty (which is not at present the only criterion) then countries such as Greece, Portugal, Spain and the Irish Republic could lose most of what they now receive. ...

Decisions about enlarging the EU will not and should not be decided only on the basis of concerns about poverty. But they are important: how the EU develops will affect the lives of hundreds of million of people and the most vulnerable of them are those who are victims of poverty.

Source: *The Guardian*, 1 December 2000

1 What do you think the author means when he refers to a 'single social space'?

2 What was the Social Charter agreed at Maastricht?

3 Where are most poor people in the European Union?

4 What are the 'cohesion and structural funds' intended to achieve?

5 Do they do this?

The principles set out in the Charter were much more explicit and far-reaching than those of the Treaty of Rome or the Single European Act and incorporated:

- social protection for all workers, for children and adolescents, older people and disabled people
- freedom of association
- collective bargaining, consultation and participation at work
- access to vocational training
- equal treatment for men and women
- an equitable wage for workers sufficient to enable them to have a decent standard of living.

The Charter itself did not propose any binding measures, leaving it up to the member states to implement any of the fundamental rights that were not already guaranteed at national level. However, in the 1991 Maastricht Treaty, social policy was extended even further (though once again the UK opted out).

Perhaps more importantly for the future, the Treaty also set up a new route through which social policy could be developed – the social partners route. This strengthened the policy-making role of the European-level trade union confederation (ETUC) and employers' organisations of the private sectors (UNICE) and public sectors (CEEP), by guaranteeing recognition and implementation of any agreement which they might negotiate.

Though directives and regulations are the only binding policies, the Council has agreed recommendations and resolutions in the social policy field, such as on the provision of childcare, the prevention of sexual harassment at work, the guarantee of a minimum income, flexible retirement ages.

The EU also has a range of funded Action Programmes, for example those to support equal opportunities or combat poverty, and initiates campaigns to draw attention to certain issues, such as the Year of the Family and the Year of the Disabled.

Main points

▶ The European Union was set up after the Second World War to help avoid war a third time.

▶ At first it concerned itself only with economic matters, but has gradually introduced a 'social dimension'.

▶ Britain joined in 1973.

▶ The European Union now has a wide range of activities which deal with social policy in its broadest sense.

▶ EU concerns are centred around the free movement of workers, workers' rights, a new European social model, health and safety, industrial restructuring and anti-discrimination.

▶ The decision-making process with regard to social policy is based on the concept of social partners who propose the legislation.

▶ EU legislation takes a number of forms, including regulations, directives and decisions.

▶ The European Court of Justice plays a major role in ensuring that the member states implement the legislation correctly.

Part 2: Comparative social policy

Comparative social policy

Definition

Welfare regimes – groups of welfare states which share common features

This book is primarily about the welfare system in the UK. The EU is examined because it is already influencing health and welfare provision in the UK and will become increasingly significant. However, it is important to realise that the UK Welfare State is only one of many ways to deliver the provision of health and welfare to the population. All industrialised societies have some form of welfare system, either provided by the State or regulated by it. Interestingly, these apparently very different systems can be grouped together into just a few types, which share a number of key characteristics. Social policy analysts refer to these types as **welfare regimes**.

Welfare regimes

The most famous classification of welfare systems has been provided by Esping-Andersen. He suggests there are basically three types of welfare regime:

- liberal
- conservative
- social democratic.

Liberal welfare regimes

Examples of this include the USA, Australia and Canada. In these countries the belief which underlies the system is that people ought to work hard and that it is wrong to 'sponge off' the State. Influenced by this, the level of welfare benefits is very low to persuade people to take paid employment. Rules governing entitlement to benefit are very strict and those who apply for benefit tend to find the process 'stigmatising'. These types of system will always use strict means-testing (see page 59) and be carefully targeted at low-income, 'deserving' groups.

In liberal welfare regimes, private welfare schemes are encouraged, often through tax concessions, as the State benefits are so low as to provide only the most basic standard of living.

Liberal welfare regimes have a particular effect on class, or stratification, patterns of any society. The low level of benefits creates an equality of poverty among those in receipt of benefits or too poor to buy private insurance. On the other hand, those who are in decent employment and buy their health and welfare provision through private hospitals, private pensions and unemployment insurance have a higher standard of welfare provision.

Conservative welfare regimes

Examples of these include Austria, France, Germany and Italy. (The term 'conservative' here has no connection with the Conservative Party in the UK.) In these welfare states, the concern shown in the liberal regime for the free market with the private purchase of health and welfare is not so strong. In these systems, social insurance benefits are significantly more important than private insurance.

What is particularly noticeable about these regimes is that they provide very different levels of welfare according to a person's job. So, people with high-status jobs will receive higher levels of pension and higher standards of healthcare provision, for example. In the Welfare State in the UK, great importance is attached to the way the welfare system succeeds in redistributing wealth and eroding differential standards of living between people. In these regimes, there is not intended to be any redistribution.

The development of the conservative welfare regimes has been heavily influenced by the churches – particularly the Catholic Church. The result of this is that there is a strong commitment to maintaining the traditional family. This has in turn affected the types of benefit scheme which exist. Social insurance schemes may well exclude non-working wives, for example, which has the effect of making them rely on their husbands. Family benefits are usually generous too in order to encourage (married) women to have children. Finally, the principle of **subsidiarity** is important. This is the idea that the State should only ever become involved in welfare when the ability of a family or charitable organisations, or any other non-State organisations to care for people has been exhausted.

Social democratic welfare regimes

Examples include the Scandinavian countries, such as Sweden, Norway and Denmark. These sorts of welfare state have been strongly influenced by the principles of social democracy (see page 23). The belief here is that people should expect a high standard of welfare provision as a right and that everyone should have State welfare rather than private. In order to achieve this without actually outlawing the private provision of welfare, these countries have provided a very high standard of public welfare services and level of benefits.

Definition

Subsidiarity – the principle that the State should only be the very last institution to give help to those in need. People ought to help themselves and if that is impossible , they should turn to the family; if that fails to charities

All groups in society, irrespective of their income, contribute to one universal insurance scheme, with people paying more the higher their income. However, the benefits are graduated according to the normal earnings of claimants. So, they are not flat-rate benefits as in they are in the liberal regimes, but are earnings-related. The standard of welfare provision is the highest possible, so that few people find any benefit in opting out of the State system into the private market.

Whereas the conservative model places great emphasis on supporting the family, the social democratic model emphasises the rights of individuals. The State therefore looks after the welfare of children by providing child care facilities, and there is no assumption that parents (overwhelmingly the mothers) should have to be carers. The system also emphasises people's rights to welfare. There is no debate on scrounging, nor is there a stigma attached to claiming benefits.

Clearly, the costs of this form of system are very high indeed, and there is one crucial feature this type of regime needs – full employment. The very high costs involved in providing the welfare mean it is necessary to have high levels of tax of a large working population, with relatively low levels of **dependency** (see page 100).

> **Definition**
>
> **Ratio of dependency** – the balance between the non-working (and therefore dependent) population and working population, who have to provide the funding from their taxes for all the State benefits

Why compare models of welfare?

Comparative policy analysis is useful because it:

- *gives us a benchmark* against which we can judge the effectiveness and quality of our services. For example, although the UK spends about half that which is spent by the USA on healthcare, the quality of healthcare for the majority of the UK population is arguably as good as, if not better than, that in the USA. However, pensions in the UK are amongst the lowest in Europe and put most retired people into the category of the poorest people in Europe

- *provides us with different policies* which have been tried and tested. The Labour government first elected in 1997 were strongly influenced by earlier initiatives introduced in the USA

- *can help us to see what trends there are across the world.* By doing this we can begin to understand the wider economic, social and political changes which are influencing our own policies. For example, the increase in international economic competition has meant that the UK cannot automatically continue to assume that there will be high levels of employment, nor can we expect people to be employed in similar jobs for all their working lives. This means that the welfare system must be able to cope with people being routinely unemployed for short periods and perhaps facing long periods of unemployment. These problems are relatively new for western societies, and by exploring other welfare models, these may help us to solve our own problems. For example, the social democratic welfare regime has, in recent years, had great difficulties in funding and providing the high standards of welfare that it has been accustomed to give, as it relied upon high employment levels. The relatively high levels of unemployment in Sweden have meant that they have had to import elements of the liberal regime into their welfare provision.

Applying comparative models to the EU

There are currently fifteen member countries: Germany, France, Italy, Netherlands, Belgium, Luxembourg, UK, Ireland, Denmark, Greece, Spain, Portugal, Finland, Sweden and Austria. Interestingly, this means that there is an example of all three of

Esping-Andersen's welfare systems. The fact that the member countries of the EU have such different welfare systems makes the task of making EU-level social policy more difficult. When they come together to negotiate new social policies, they begin their discussions from different starting points, which of course means they find it difficult to agree on what should be done.

EU countries by type of welfare system

Welfare system	Country
Liberal	UK[1]
Conservative	Germany, Italy, France, Austria, Belgium
Social Democratic	Sweden, Denmark, Finland

1 Esping-Andersen actually thought the UK welfare system was a mixture of liberal and social democratic. However, there is general agreement that the Conservative governments of the 1980s and 1990s moved the UK more squarely into the liberal camp.

Main points

▶ Most welfare systems can be grouped into what is known as 'welfare regimes'.

▶ There are three types of welfare regimes: liberal, conservative and social democratic.

▶ The regimes vary in the extent to which they believe the State ought to be involved in supplying financial benefits and welfare services.

▶ Using comparisons of welfare states can provide us with useful benchmarks to judge the effectiveness of services; to provide us with new or different ideas on policy; to help us see what trends are happening across the world.

▶ One of the problems in creating a common set of social policies in the European Union is the fact that the welfare systems of the various countries tend to be based on different welfare regimes, so they have little in common.

Part 3: Globalisation

The world context of social policy

We have just explored the way that UK social policy is being increasingly influenced by the European Union – illustrating the fact that any attempt to understand what is happening in the UK today needs to take into account the European experience. However, even this is not enough. One of the most important influences on what form British and European social policy takes is the wider trading patterns in the world economy. There could be no welfare state in the UK if the government could not afford to pay for it. In turn, this relies upon people having adequately paid jobs and paying taxes, which in turn relies upon foreign investors setting up factories and offices, and the goods which are produced being exported to other countries. World trade then cannot be ignored if we are to understand the shape of social policy in the UK.

As a result of the agreement by 134 countries in the world to set up an organisation called the World Trade Organisation (WTO) in 1995, trading now operates on a truly global scale and it is this globalisation of industry and commerce which is having a strong impact on the shape that different welfare systems are taking in different parts of the world, as well as on the shape of our own Welfare State.

Globalisation

Goods, services and money all flow more easily between countries today than at any other time. This is partly due to technological developments, such as improvements in transport and information technology. It is also a by-product of the reduction of trade barriers brought about by the World Trade Organisation and previous rounds of free trade talks.

It is argued that, due to globalisation, a division has opened in the global economy between developing countries (the poorer nations) that carry out manufacturing and developed countries (the richer Western nations) that concentrate on the service sector. The switch of manufacturing industry away from developed countries to developing countries is said to have been a cause of unemployment in developed countries.

Big companies, like Coca-Cola, BP and Shell, that operate in a number of countries, have been around for many years. However, those who believe that globalisation is occurring argue that these transnational or multinational companies are becoming more important. Nations are becoming more reliant upon transnational companies to locate their operations within their borders in order to create jobs and wealth. At the same time, though, transnational companies close down their operation in one country and relocate to another country in order to find the most profitable locations. Some believe we are moving towards a borderless world dominated by stateless firms.

The World Trade Organisation

The World Trade Organisation (WTO) was set up in 1995 to promote and enforce *free trade* between countries. Membership of the WTO has grown to 134 countries, with thirty more countries, including China, waiting to join.

Free trade is the opposite of *protectionism*. Governments of countries are said to be protectionist when they try to protect businesses in their country from competition from businesses from abroad. Protectionism can occur in three main ways:

- *Tariff barriers*: Governments put a % charge on certain imports into their country. For example, let us imagine that a UK company made computer games machines. The UK government could seek to protect that company by erecting a tariff barrier of, say, 20 per cent. This would mean that Playstation machines which are made by the Japanese company, Sony, would cost 20 per cent more in the UK. In theory, this would give the UK machine manufacturer a price advantage and should make its product more attractive to potential customers in the UK.

- *Quotas:* The government could put a limit on the number of imports coming into the country. In our example, it could set a limit of 10,000 computer games machines coming in from Japan, thus reducing the number of Playstation and Dreamcast machines available to UK games fans

- *Subsidies*: The UK government could decide to give money to the UK machine manufacturer in an attempt to help it.

The aim of the WTO is to get members to agree to reduce tariffs, quotas and subsidies – in other words to promote free trade across the globe.

The nation state and national governments are becoming less important – they are becoming one 'actor' among many that wield influence alongside transnational companies and international and regional organisations such as the WTO and EU.

As you can see, the primary language of globalisation relates to economic issues – trade, companies and communications – but globalisation, it is argued, has dramatic and far-reaching social implications too. The Internet, email and satellite TV are changing the way people relate. We are increasingly experiencing the world as being 'one place'. The global economy never stops, it operates twenty-four hours a day with money, goods, information and images being exchanged at higher and higher speeds.

Globalisation

Clare Short, the minister responsible for overseas aid, answers questions on globalisation.

fmk: Clare Short, how do you define 'globalisation'? Is it possible for 'third world' countries to benefit from a system that simply uses them as a source of cheap labour and a location in which few environmental/human rights restrictions are imposed and most can be circumvented? Do you believe that Globalisation benefits 'first world' countries or do you believe that it makes them poorer by denying their citizens many rights?

Clare Short: Globalisation is defined in the White Paper. It has been going on since the end of the Second World War. It has accelerated recently with the end of the Cold War creating one global economy and information technology speeding the transfer of knowledge and information across the world. People talk as though it is uncontrollable. This is false. Countries that have increased their openness trade and inward investment have grown faster and reduced poverty for larger numbers of people than those that remain closed. But they vary in their degree in inequality – this is a matter of politics and choice not an inevitable consequence of globalisation. We need a positive agenda to manage globalisation so that the poor of the world will benefit and this is the whole point of the White Paper.

Meatloaf: It's not globalisation itself, but globalisation without restraint and regulation that's the problem.

Clare Short: Yes, I do agree and the White Paper makes clear that trade properly conducted will benefit everyone, particularly the poor of the world. ...

shazam2: I think there are some benefits to globalisation that will help (in the long run) the world's poor. For the less developed countries, globalisation offers access to foreign capital, global export markets, and advanced technology while breaking the monopoly of inefficient and protected domestic producers. Faster growth, in turn, promotes poverty reduction, democratisation, and higher labour and environmental standards. While globalisation may confront government officials with more difficult choices, the result for their citizens is greater individual freedom. In this sense, globalisation acts as a check on governmental power that makes it more difficult for governments to abuse the freedom and property of their citizens.

Clare Short: I agree with you. But countries must shape the way globalisation effects them. Governments must provide education and health care for all their people – not just the elites in the city. And deal with corruption and put in place proper regulation of privatised utilities. With these and other reforms outlined in the White Paper, developing countries can move forward rapidly and bring real benefits to the poor.

Source: Guardian Unlimited talk-board session, 13 December 2000

1   What does Clare Short understand globalisation to be?

2   Does she think that globalisation is a good thing?

3   What is the key thing to ensure that inequality is not widened, and benefits accrue to the people in the poorer nations ('Third World' countries)? You need to read all of her answers to reply to this.

4   How does the questioner 'fmk' think that it might harm 'first world' nations (first world refers to richer countries of the world, including the UK)?

5   List the possible benefits and harmful consequences of globalisation.

Globalisation and social policy

Globalisation is not a neutral concept, if we accept the globalisation diagnosis we have to accept that certain policy prescriptions follow. The term globalisation started to appear in discussions about social policy in the UK in the early 1990s. Those who believe that globalisation is affecting social policy argue that changes in the global economy have created economic forces that had made governments change the shape of their welfare systems. If welfare systems made employing people cost too much then international investors would go to countries where it was cheaper.

And so countries with extensive welfare provision are finding it difficult to compete economically with countries with less generous, more basic, social policy provision.

The race to the bottom

Those who accept that globalisation is a dominant influence on welfare states argue that the liberal welfare system approach to social policy (see page 314) has become more influential, and will continue to do so. They believe that the governments of social democratic and to some extent conservative/corporatist systems are being forced to change direction by globalisation.

Two pressures are felt to be particularly important:

- Firstly, in the era of globalisation, more money moves around the world from country to country and at higher speeds. If the big financial institutions and investors do not like the way a government is managing its economic and social policies they will move their money to other places to get a better profit. If a significant proportion of investors move their money out of a country at the same time the value of the currency of a country will fall, possibly creating a devaluation crisis. In a globalised world in which money moves freely, governments cannot pursue economic or social policies that will upset big investors. Thus as we have seen in previous chapters, governments cannot pursue Keynesian (see page 45), let alone social democratic (see page 23), strategies.

- Secondly, much of the bill for welfare in social democratic and conservative/corporatist systems is paid for by companies through wage bills and contributions. As global economic competition has been hotting up companies have argued that they cannot afford to sustain such costs. Many transnational companies, it is argued, have simply voted with their feet by closing plants in countries with high wage costs and relocating to countries with lower social charges and wage costs. This has put pressure on national governments to reduce taxation on companies and to reduce workers' social rights. The process by which governments compete to reduce social costs on companies is referred to in Europe as social dumping and by the American's as 'the race to the bottom'. Social dumping is the ratcheting-down of social rights by governments in order to make their country more attractive to inward investment. Some governments, the UK Conservative government of the 1980s and 1990s was good example, have actually made low employer social costs a selling point to attract outside investment from transnational companies.

Sanctions go bananas

The US has been given the go-ahead to begin imposing sanctions on European goods in the latest twist in the trade dispute over bananas.

Washington announced today that the World Trade Organisation had authorised punitive tariffs on $191 million (£120 million) worth of European goods – which could include cashmere clothes produced in Scotland.

The White House had originally sought more than double that figure in compensation but said it was satisfied by the smaller amount – still the largest trade sanctions ever authorised by the WTO.

The final list of targeted European goods will be published in a few days, US officials said. They will be selected from the original list, which ranged from Scottish cashmere sweaters and Italian cheese to French handbags and German coffee makers.

The US wants the European Union to open up its market in bananas, claiming unfair advantages are being given to former European colonies at the expense of American-backed concerns.

A thousand British jobs could be under threat after the WTO ruling. Jim Thompson, of the Hawick Cashmere Company, said the sanctions would cause major problems for his industry in Scotland.

"The Americans are unaware how polarised the cashmere industry is in the Borders," he said. "It will have catastrophic effects – if this actually goes through we are looking at most definitely a thousand jobs in the Borders."

Source: *Guardian Unlimited*, 7 April 1999

1   What is the World Trade Organisation?

2   How can it have the power to allow sanctions to be imposed?

3   Why is it important in the way it can affect the standards of living in the UK and have an impact on social policy, including government spending?

Globalisation and Sweden: an example

Advocates of the globalisation thesis frequently cite once staunchly social democratic countries such as Sweden as an example of the impact of growing economic interdependence on welfare policy.

Sweden has traditionally been given as an example of a social democratic welfare regime, with very high standards of care and benefits. However, in the 1990s under pressure from changes in world trading, the Swedish found it very difficult to continue providing such a high quality of services. The results include:

- a decrease in the value of financial State benefits
- shorter times for which people can claim the benefits
- greater waiting periods for social and health services
- tightening up of eligibility for services
- attempts to get more people back into the workforce, rather than simply paying benefits to support them
- reforms in the pensions to make them less generous.

The point is simple, that individual countries are not isolated from international economic trends and so policy-makers have to take these trends into account when providing welfare.

Main points ▶ Globalisation is the term used to describe the international patterns of trading in the world today and the social consequences which may occur.

▶ Globalisation has been increased greatly by the growth in free trade and by the activities of the World Trade Organisation.

▶ There are two main issues: those relating to the fears that globalisation will mean that the richer countries will exploit the poorer countries and those who believe that the large multi-national companies will shift their factories and production to poorer countries with few workers' rights.

▶ There does seem to be some concern that the more advanced welfare systems, such as in Sweden, have been forced to cut back on their welfare states, because of the costs of providing welfare when in competition with other countries which do not provide such a wide range of welfare services.

Conclusion

In this chapter we have studied three related areas – all having in common the fact that the British Welfare State is influenced far more by factors outside British influence than most people would think.

The EU is increasingly seeking to enlarge its 'social space' and to extend its influence in the field of social policy. There are problems to this, primarily caused by the fact that the different countries in the EU have very different systems of welfare, so there is limited common ground on which to build a common social policy.

This has caused some confusion amongst policy makers and the general public and shows the use of comparative studies of welfare. These have shown that welfare states can broadly be classified into three types of 'regimes' which have very different assumptions about the role of the family and the State in providing welfare and financial support.

The third element of our view of external factors is the importance of the newly emerging phenomenon of globalisation, where trading takes place right across the globe. The resulting trading patterns have provided both threats and opportunities to both richer and poorer nations. The impact on wealthier countries has been to make it somewhat more difficult to provide very expensive welfare systems, as the costs have the potential to scare private companies (who provide the employment) into seeking cheaper places to invest.

11 CHAPTER SUMMARY

1   The European Union was set up after the Second World War to help avoid war a third time.

2   At first it concerned itself only about economic matters, but has gradually introduced a 'social dimension'.

3   Britain joined in 1973.

4   The European Union now has a wide range of activities which deal with social policy in its broadest sense

5   EU concerns are centred around the free movement of workers, workers' rights, a new European social model, health and safety, industrial restructuring and anti-discrimination.

6   The decision-making process with regard to social policy is based on the concept of social partners who propose the legislation.

7   EU legislation takes a number of forms, including regulations, directives and decisions.

8   The European Court of Justice plays a major role in ensuring that the member states implement the legislation correctly.

9   Most welfare systems can be grouped into what is known as 'welfare regimes'.

10   There are three types of welfare regimes: liberal, conservative and social democratic.

11   The regimes vary in the extent to which they believe the State ought to be involved in supplying financial benefits and welfare services.

12   Using comparisons of welfare states can provide us with useful benchmarks to judge the effectiveness of services, to provide us with new or different ideas on policy, to help us see what trends are happening across the world.

13   One of the problems in creating a common set of social policies in the European Union is the fact that the welfare systems of the various countries tend to be based on different welfare regimes, so they have little in common.

14   Globalisation is the term used to describe the international patterns of trading in the world today and the social consequences which may occur.

15   Globalisation has been increased greatly by the growth in free trade and by the activities of the World Trade Organisation.

16   There are two main issues: those relating to the fears that globalisation will mean that the richer countries will exploit the poorer countries and those who believe that the large multi-national companies will shift their factories and production to poorer countries with few workers' rights.

17 There does seem to be some concern that the more advanced welfare systems, such as in Sweden, have been forced to cut back on their welfare states, because of the costs of providing welfare when in competition with other countries which do not provide such a wide range of welfare services.

Useful websites

www.europa.eu.int: the European Union (Europa)

www.europa.eu.int/comm: the European Commission

Chapter 12

OLDER PEOPLE

Chapter contents

- **The demography of age in the UK**

  We begin the chapter with an exploration of the numbers of people over pensionable age, looking at the similarities and differences between older people. This will help us to understand the relevance of policies which we explore later in the chapter. We also explore the issue of the so-called 'burden of dependency' and see if this is true or not.

- **The experience of old age**

  This section examines how older people actually experience old age and the way that other, younger people, stereotype them and discriminate against them. This gives us a better overall understanding of older people's lives, which we then explore in greater detail in later sections of the chapter.

- **Health and health services**

  Most older people are healthy right up to the final stages of their lives. This is often overlooked as they are seen as an expensive burden on the health service. They have routinely received poorer care, and the geriatric services have had lower levels of funding than other areas of the service. It is only very recently that this has been addressed.

- **Care for older people**

  A similar situation occurs in the provision of care for older people. The myth says that they are all in nursing homes and older people's homes. In fact the overwhelming majority of older people remain at home all their lives, or at least until near the very end. This section sets out the range of services available for those living in the community and also explores the issues of residential care.

- **Housing**

  An issue which is often overlooked is the housing conditions of older people. As is true of most of the discussion relating to older people, differences between older people are nothing to do with age, but more to do with the differences in income, housing and employment which have existed all their lives. Older people are therefore at the extremes of the housing market. On the one hand, they are more likely to own their own homes, but they are also more likely to be living in worse housing conditions than the majority of the population. We examine this situation.

- **Older people, work and leisure**

  Retirement has a profound effect on many people, who resent the loss of friendships, the decline in finance and loss of status. However, not all is gloom, relationships continue and new leisure activities are entered into. Once again, patterns of life continue – isolation, boredom and lack of leisure interests do not just appear in old age.

- **Older people, pensions and poverty**

  This section continues our theme of differences in life coming out in differences in old age. Older people are both rich and poor, but because of the lack of pension schemes for the majority of older people when they were in employment, there are significantly higher levels of poverty amongst older people. We examine this and the relevant government responses.

Introduction

In this chapter we examine the situation of older people in society and learn about the problems they face and the health and welfare services available to them. The chapter begins by looking at the increasing numbers of older people in society. As you will see, the most notable change in the nature of UK and European society has been the increasing proportion of the population over retirement age.

But why should this matter? When we talk about older people, the image conjured up is that of weak, fragile people in need of help. This is true for some older people, but the majority lead active and contented lives. We therefore examine how images of older people have been created and how they can distort the attitudes of younger people and thereby influence patterns of social care provision.

We then move on to look at the situation of older people in society, discussing issues of health, dependency, employment and poverty. We also take a detailed look at the range of health, welfare and financial issues facing older people in the UK today.

Activity   Write down five to ten adjectives or phrases which you would associate with the term 'older people'. Retain these for use later.

The demography of age in the UK

Definition

Demography – the study of population change and its significance

At the turn of the twenty-first century, there were over 10.7 million older people (over pensionable age) in the UK, comprising 18 per cent of the population. The number of people over pensionable age, taking account of the change in the women's retirement age, is expected to increase from 10.7 million in 1998 to 11.9 million in 2011, and to 12.2 million by 2021.

The last hundred years has seen a gradual increase in the length of life and the chances of reaching old age. So, in 2000, a man of 60 could expect to live for another 18.8 years and a woman of the same age for 22.6 years, and there are now 4.5 million people aged 75 and over.

An ageing population

Population, by gender and age, 1821 and 1999, Great Britain

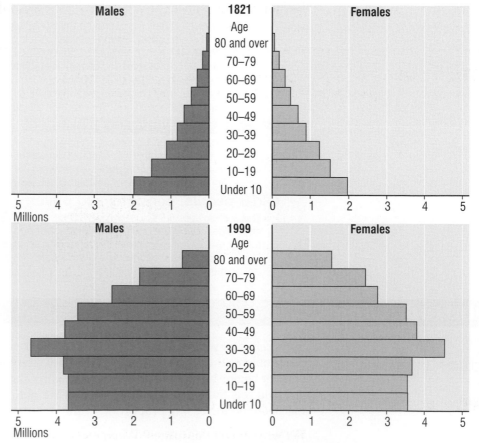

Source: *Social Trends 31* (The Stationery Office, 2001)

1 How would you describe the balance between the various age bands in 1821?

2 How had this changed in 1999?

3 Can you see any differences between older males and females in 1999?

4 What does the population distribution tell you about:

a) female life expectancy?

b) which sex is more likely to need the health and welfare services?

c) the growth in demand for health and welfare services?

Variations among older people

The distinctions of gender and ethnicity in the younger generations are also present in the older one.

Ethnicity

The numbers of older people in each ethnic minority group varies. The percentage over 60 for each ethnic group is:

- 12 per cent of Black-Caribbean people
- 3 per cent of Black-African people
- 8 per cent of Indian people
- 5 per cent of Pakistani people
- 5 per cent of Bangladeshi people
- 6 per cent of Chinese people.

Gender

Women comprise about 65 per cent of people aged 75 and 75 per cent of those aged 85 and over.

The costs of older people

Personal social services gross expenditure by client group, 1997–8

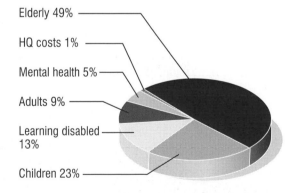

Elderly 49%
HQ costs 1%
Mental health 5%
Adults 9%
Learning disabled 13%
Children 23%

Source: *Health and Personal Social Services Statistics* (The Stationary Office, 1999)

1 Which group takes the highest proportion of personal social services expenditure?

2 What percentage is this?

3 Contact your local social services department and ask them for information on the services they provide for older people. (If possible go to the website of your local authority, you should be able to get the information from there.)

Why are the statistics important?

We need to know the numbers, gender and ethnicity of the older population, as it allows the government to work out how best to use its health and welfare resources. An older population will place greater demand on the health service, and on the caring services. A growth in the younger generation will place a greater demand on education.

Dependency

The table below shows the **dependency ratio** for the UK in terms of the numbers of working age people to those below age 16 and above age 65.

Definitions

Dependency – when a person or group relies upon others for assistance (financial, emotional or physical)

Dependency ratio – the number of children, and people over retirement age, to every 100 people of working age. The ratios take account of the changes in State pension age for women from 60 years to 65 years between 2010 and 2020

Ageism – discriminating against people on the basis of their age

Projected dependency ratios, United Kingdom

	Child dependency	Older dependency	Overall dependency
2001	33	29	62
2011	30	31	60
2021	28	30	58
2031	29	39	68
2041	28	43	72

Source: Adapted from *Social Trends 27* (The Stationery Office, 1997)

1 What was/will be the dependency ratio of (i) older people and (ii) children in:
   a) 2001?
   b) 2021?

2 Overall, what pattern is demonstrated over time in terms of the increase or decrease of the dependency ratio?

3 What is happening to the relative dependency of (a) children and (b) older people over the period shown?

4 What are the implications for health and welfare?

5 How does using language like 'burden of dependency' promote **ageism**?

The burden of dependency: accurate description?

Definition

Burden of dependency – refers to the costs of the non-working population on the working population

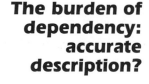

YES

Older people are more likely to:
• be unwell
• be disabled
• need caring for.

And are less likely to be:
• working
• paying tax
• contributing to the economy.

NO

Older people have paid taxes and contributed to society all their lives.

Most older people do not need care – or if they do, their families provide it.

Many older people work in voluntary organisations helping others.

Older people are consumers, buying goods and services.

Many older people care for grandchildren, allowing parents to work.

The burden of dependency

Burden of dependency is the term used to describe the proportion of people working and paying taxes in proportion to those who are not in employment (including self-employment). The larger the number of people who are not in the workforce, the greater the 'burden' of taxation on the working population, as the taxes they pay must provide the services for those who are not employed. These taxes will pay for health, welfare and criminal justice services, as well as for all the rest of government services for the population.

The experience of old age

Being physically old does not mean anything in itself, much more important is the way that we interpret age in our society. Older people are often viewed as useless, and a burden to the rest of us. The young and middle-aged look to the future with dread at the idea of being 'old'. However, this view of age is **socially constructed**. In other societies in history and even in present day China, for example, old age is seen not only as a period of physical decline, but also as a time when an individual has gained wisdom from a lifetime of experiences. In fact, the majority of retired people are physically fit and mentally alert until their death or a short time prior to this. It is only a minority who become seriously disabled, though the possibility increases with considerable old age. Using pretty much any definition of 'disabled' suggests that about 30 per cent of the over-75s can be classified as such. Only about 5 per cent of all retired people suffer from forms of confusion.

Age discrimination and legislation

Older people face discrimination in a wide range of areas:

- *social stigma* – being old involves having low status
- *employment* – compulsory retirement at 60/65
- *financial services* – insurance, assurance and certain banking services are refused
- *transport* – older people need regular medical examinations to retain their licence
- *medical treatment* – though formally denied by the NHS, geriatric medicine is seen as the least prestigious area of medicine.

Variations among older people

The underlying assumption is that the elderly are a problem for society. The growing proportion of the population who are elderly is emphasised, and particularly the burden of the 'old' elderly (i.e. over seventy-five years old) and the 'very old' elderly (over eighty-five). These two groups are seen as a burden on the State because they are high users of health and welfare services. They are also seen as a burden on women because policies of community care mean that most … care of the elderly is done by women.

The elderly are primarily seen as a homogeneous (single group with similar characteristics) group and attention is given to age relations, rather than class or gender differences among the elderly.

[They are also seen] as of low moral worth – evident from the 'social problem' focus and from the more general image of the elderly as poor, disabled, dependent and passive.

But how does social class influence these age relations? We have only to consider the Queen Mother, the House of Lords and many elderly judges and politicians to realise the sharp contrast they provide to the more general image of the elderly.

Source: S. Arber, 'Class and the elderly', *Social Studies Review*, 1989

1 What is the assumption when talking about older people?

2 What two groups of older people are seen as particularly burdensome?

3 Why is it incorrect to talk about 'the elderly' as a homogeneous group?

4 Is it true, as the writer argues, that we hold older people in 'low moral worth'? Why do you think we hold some older people in respect, as indicated in the extract, and the majority of older people as of 'low moral worth'?

5 At present, in your family, are the oldest generation contributing positively to the quality of life of the younger members of the family, or to you personally?

6 Within your group or class, how many of you would be prepared (or are now) to look after your parents should they become unable to look after themselves?

7 Whose responsibility do you think it ought to be to look after older people, if they become ill or disabled?

Code of Practice

UK governments have legislated against discrimination on the grounds of gender, religion, race and disability, but have made no attempts to do so for discrimination by age. There exists a voluntary Code of Practice against age discrimination in employment, but as this is voluntary, there are no penalties if employers ignore it and discriminate.

European Union Directive

However, despite the failure of the UK government to support age discrimination legislation, the EU has introduced a directive which will ban it by 2006.

Activity

1 Construct a simple questionnaire.
   a) Ask a sample of approximately ten younger people (aged 16–25) how they would define (in age terms) 'old people'. Then ask them for five words which they associate with old people.
   b) Next, ask a sample of people over retirement age the same questions.
   c) Compare the replies, and also include your own views expressed at the beginning of this chapter. Are there any differences?

2 Do you think there is ageism in our society? Do you think it affects the lives of older people?

Health and health services

Health

When discussing health and older people, experts tend to disagree as to exactly what 'healthy' means for older people. Although most older people suffer from various infirmities, they are also capable of a range of normal living activities and the stereotype of them as being incapacitated and in need of care is wrong.

In 1998, 40 per cent of people aged over 65 interviewed for the General Household Survey described their health as 'good', 37 per cent as 'fairly good' and 23 per cent as 'not good'. Of those aged between 65 and 74, 38 per cent and, of those aged over 75, 50 per cent said that they had a long-standing illness which limited their life style.

Definition

Dementia – mental confusion

It was further estimated that 5 per cent of the population aged 65 and over, and 20 per cent of the population aged 80 and over, suffered from **dementia**.

However, these figures point to fairly high levels of health amongst older people, with, for example, 80 per cent of the population over the age of 80 not suffering from any form of mental confusion, 50 per cent of over-75s saying that they did not have any long standing illness which restricted their activities, and over two-thirds of over-65-year-olds reporting good or fairly good health!

Health services

However, although the majority of older people are independent, they are on average less likely to be healthy than younger members of society. It is estimated that around 40 per cent of total hospital and community health expenditure is on people aged 65 and over. A person over the age of 75 costs the NHS over six times more than a person of working age. The majority of disabled people are older, as are those people suffering from some form of mental confusion. In any one year, 27 per cent of those aged 75 and over attend the casualty or out-patient department of a hospital, compared with 16 per cent of people of all ages. Eighty-four per cent of NHS GP consultations take place in the surgery, but consultations at home (the most expensive form of GP consultation) were for older people, with 25 per cent of home consultations being for those aged 75 and over. Finally, the average stay in hospital is seven nights, yet for those aged over 75, the average was just under thirteen nights.

All this means that older people cost the NHS proportionately more than younger people. However, in relation to their needs older people receive less than other groups in terms of resources from the NHS.

In response to criticisms, the government introduced the *National Service Framework for Older People*, in 2001, which promised increased spending on older people and their needs as well as outlawing discrimination on the basis of age, which had been a common problem in the NHS, where surgical interventions and other services were not provided for older people, on the basis that it 'wasn't worth it', as they had a relatively short time to live compared to younger people. In order to support the Framework, the government provided funding of £1.4 billion a year for three years (2001–2004), and appointed 200 consultants in geriatrics, introduced better conditions in wards for older people and recruited more nurses.

Use of health services

Use of health services: by gender and age, 1998–99, UK

Percentages

	16–24	25–34	35–44	45–54	55–64	65–74	75 and over	All aged 16 and over
Males								
Consultation with GP[1]	7	9	10	12	16	17	21	12
Outpatient visit[2]	12	14	13	15	20	25	29	17
Casualty visit[2, 3]	7	7	5	4	3	3	3	5
Females								
Consultation with GP[1]	15	18	16	19	17	19	21	18
Outpatient visit[2]	13	13	12	17	19	21	26	17
Casualty visit[2, 3]	6	4	3	3	3	3	3	4

1 Consultations with an NHS GP in the last two weeks.
2 In the last three months; includes visits to casualty in Great Britain only.
3 The question was only asked of those who said they had an outpatient visit.

Source: General Household Survey, Office for National Statistics; Continuous Household Survey, Northern Ireland Statistics and Research Agency

The total amount of hospital and community health services expenditure on the elderly in England was £9,927 million in 1998–99. Almost three-fifths of this was spent on acute care, spending on which rose by an average of 2 per cent per year between 1994–95 and 1998–99. One area of health that affects many elderly people is eye care. In April 1999 eye tests were made free for all people aged 60 and over. In 1999–00, around 9.4 million NHS eye tests were performed, of which more than a third were for people on the basis of them being aged 60 or above.

Source: *Social Trends 31* (Stationery Office, 2001)

1   Which age group is most likely to have a consultation with a GP?

2   Which age group is most likely to have an outpatient visit?

3   Which age groups are most likely to visit casualty? Why is this different do you think from the answers to the first two questions?

4   How much did the NHS spend on older people in 1998–9 (the last year figures were available at the time of writing)

5   What proportion of this was spent on acute care? Find the meaning of the term 'acute care'?

6   Look back to pages 58 and 68. Since 1999 NHS eye tests have been available for older people. Are these means-tested or a universal benefit?

Main points ▶ The numbers of older people in the population increased throughout the twentieth century.

▶ The proportion of older people in the population has increased too, as a result of a decline in the birth rate.

▶ This looks likely to continue far into the twenty-first century.

▶ Older people are a diverse group in terms of resources and ethnicity.

▶ There is a majority of women amongst older people.

▶ The burden of dependency is a term used to describe the costs to society of older people.

▶ Older people are discriminated against.

▶ A significant proportion of health spending is on older people.

▶ Older people until recently have not received the amount of health spending appropriate to their needs from the NHS.

Care for older people

Living alone: care in the community

In 2000, of those aged 65–74, 20 per cent of men and 34 per cent of women lived alone, and of those aged over 74, 30 per cent of men and 59 per cent of women lived alone.

The likelihood of living alone increased with age, with 43 per cent of men and 72 per cent of women aged 85 and over. 'Older' elderly people were more likely to be living with a son or daughter, rising from 4 per cent of those aged 65–69, to 8 per cent of those aged 85 and over.

Services available for those living at home include:

• *Home care:* Home care assistants are mainly employed by social services departments, although more and more these days social services might buy-in the services of voluntary organisations or private agencies. Home care assistants visit older people in their own homes and help with personal care or other domestic activities, such as cleaning and cooking. Most local authorities now charge for this service, based on a financial assessment of the person receiving the care and how much help they receive.

The importance of informal carers

Usual source of help for those aged 65 and over able to do various tasks only with help, 1998–99, UK

Percentages

	Mobility[1]	Getting in/out of bed	Walking down the road	Using public transport
Spouse/partner	57	54	46	48
Other household member	19	14	10	7
Non-household relative	11	9	25	24
Friend/neighbour	3	0	12	9
Paid help	3	2	1	1
NHS or personal social services	2	20	4	3
Other	5	1	2	7
All	100	100	100	100

1 Getting around the house, getting to the toilet, using stairs.

Source: General Household Survey, Office for National Statistics; Continuous Household Survey, Northern Ireland Statistics and Research Agency

Source: *Social Trends 31* (The Stationery Office, 2001)

1 Who is most likely to provide help for the various tasks listed in the table?

2 Which are the next two groups most likely to give help?

3 Where do the NHS or personal social services rank in the amount of help given?

4 What is the single task they provide the greatest help with?

5 What does this tell you about the nature of community care in the UK?

- *Lunch clubs:* These are for active older people who can meet on a regular basis for both food and company. These clubs are most often run by local voluntary organisations, churches or sometimes by local authorities.
- *Meals-on-wheels:* These are provided directly by local authorities or by contract, mainly with the WRVS (Women's Royal Voluntary Service). About 800,000 meals per week were served to mainly older people in their homes or at lunch clubs in England by local authorities or the independent sector in 1994.
- *Night-sitting service:* More and more it is recognised that carers need a break. Voluntary organisations and local authorities provide carers to look after older relatives at night.
- *Aids and adaptations to the home* Local authorities can pay for alterations to people's homes if this will allow them to lead more independent lives. Most common adaptations include ramps for wheelchairs, handrails for climbing stairs and grips on the bath or next to the toilet. It is usually the role of the occupational therapist to make the assessment. Much of the equipment is provided on a loan basis, but increasingly this equipment is available to purchase privately.
- *Day centres:* These are often provided by social services departments, but more and more by voluntary organisations. Some day centres exist in the NHS, but only for very dependent and sick people. Attendance at a day centre can help meet several human needs – physical, social and emotional. Day centre users are usually provided with meals, can take part in crafts,

games and other social activities, and often will be offered bathing, hairdressing and other personal services. Day centres have an important respite care function. There is usually a charge to users.

- *Medical and nursing services:* The normal range of medical services is available for older people. The most important provider of such services is the primary health care team, particularly GPs, district nurses and chiropodists who visit and maintain the health of older people.

- *Social workers:* Social workers deal with the most vulnerable people. Their main role is assessment of needs, formulating the care plan and putting together a care package.

- *Voluntary services:* Groups such as Age Concern and Help the Aged provide a very wide range of services from selling cheap insurance, acting as a pressure group, through to organising day centres. More specialised organisations, such as the Alzheimer's Disease Society or Parkinson's Disease Society, play an increasing role in support of these particular groups of older people.

Public care, private cost

My father-in law is 87. For the last two years, he has been unable to care for himself in any way and his mental faculties are deteriorating rapidly. My mother-in-law (who is 82 and has had a heart bypass operation) cares for him 24 hours a day as he cannot be left alone. They are the generation who "cope" and do not want to be separated.

Each day, carers come in to get my father-in law out of bed, wash him, attend to his basic personal needs and dress him. It takes two carers to lift and help him move. They stay for half-an-hour. In the evening, they return to reverse the process and put dad to bed. This takes 15 minutes. The rest of the time my mother-in-law, somehow, copes alone, with help

from us when possible. The carers are good, and are no doubt paid very little.

For 45 minutes of daily help, my mother-in-law pays at least £200 a month. She has just had a letter from the council to say these costs will increase by 40% shortly. …

Occasionally, dad has needed to stay in a residential nursing

home, usually following a spell in hospital. My parents-in-law have borne the full brunt of the £2,000-a-month cost. Although not wealthy, they have some savings as a result of being extremely thrifty throughout their lives.

There must be thousands of elderly people in similar situations …

Source: Letter to *The Guardian*, 18 April 2001

1 Who provides the bulk of the care?

2 Is this unusual?

3 What do the paid carers do?

4 How much did this cost, and how much is the increase?

5 Who pays for this?

6 How much does a month in residential care cost?

7 Help for older people is means tested, so those below a certain income will receive financial help. The writer of the letter argues that his parents in law have been thrifty and are being punished for this. On the other hand, many would argue why should the taxpayer pay for affluent people to receive help. What is your view?

Residential care

Definitions

Nursing homes – institutions which look after sick and disabled people

Residential homes – institutions which look after those in need of care, but who are not in need of nursing

In England there are about 200,000 people living permanently in registered **residential homes** – 35,000 are in local authority homes and 165,000 are in independently-run homes. There are a further 150,000 being cared for in **nursing homes**. However, the proportion of each age group within residential care increases quite significantly amongst the older groups in society. For every 1,000 people aged 65 to 74, six people will be in residential care, and by the age 75 the figure has risen to 49. Approximately 80 per cent of all residents in homes for older people or similar establishments will be over 75.

Of course, there is another way to look at these statistics, which is that 951 people out of every 1,000 over the age of 75 are living at home until their death (or very shortly before it).

Yet, for those who do have to enter a care institution, the effects are very great indeed. Leaving the home where they may have lived all their adult lives, where they may have raised a family and where they may have a network of friends is extremely difficult. There are three models of residential accommodation:

- *warehousing*, when older people simply have their medical, physical and accommodation needs met
- *horticulture*, in which there is an attempt to develop the skills and abilities of older people
- *normalisation*, where the aim is to make life as normal as possible for older people.

There is a greater chance of the warehousing model being used for older people as:

- they are seen as nearing the end of their lives, and no point is seen to develop their skills and abilities
- most homes are run for profit, so that the very low levels of payment provided by local authorities do not allow them to do more than provide the minimum amount of care.

The growth of private nursing homes

Places in residential care homes for elderly people, by type of care home

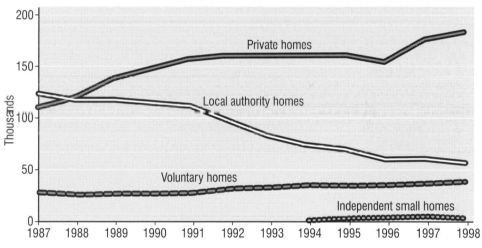

Source: *Britain 2000: The Official Yearbook* (The Stationery Office, 2001)

1 Approximately how many places in private care homes were there in 1998?

2 How many were there in local authority homes at this time?

3 How many were there in voluntary homes?

4 Overall, what pattern can be seen in the changing provision of residential care?

5 Social policy analysts have written about the 'mixed economy' of care (see page 256). What does it mean and why is it relevant here?

6 Do the majority of older people go into residential homes?

In response to a wide range of criticisms of the poor standards of residential homes, and the failure of local authorities to inspect them adequately, the government introduced the Care Standards Act in 2000. This set up the National Care Standards Commission which ensures that eleven standards are upheld in all residential settings (not just those for older people). These standards cover a wide range of issues which include such things as the management and staffing, complaints procedures, management of death and the dying, quality of food, level and quantity of social and leisure activities and standards of health care.

The unpleasant face of 'caring'

Visitors were encouraged to ring ahead when they came to see relatives at the pretty, spacious residential home near Oxford: it gave the care workers time to hide the stench of urine with room freshener and scrape faeces off the curtains.

Not that, for the most part, there was much that visitors could take exception to. After all, the 89-year-old man whose suppurating pressure sores had rotted the flesh right down to his bones was safely locked away upstairs, in too much pain to move and too much confusion to cry out. And the woman whose neck was so gnarled by age that it pressed her chin tightly into her chest only had her head violently wrenched upwards to facilitate force-feeding when no guests were present.

... . For the last four months of his life, Alec Taylor saw no one except the proprietor, Souren Ramdoo as he attempted to clean Taylor's wounds by hacking at the skin around the sores with office scissors and ripping out his rotting flesh, wearing gloves he had used to scoop faeces off the sheets moments earlier.

Staff at the home, mainly untrained and underpaid workers passing through on their way to better jobs, referred to Taylor as the 'body in the attic'. It wasn't until Ramdoo, keen to open a second home nearby, employed Andrew Barnes as the manager in July 1998 that the whistle was finally blown.

Barnes contacted the social services and Taylor was removed to a local hospital, where he died a few days later from pneumonia unconnected with his sufferings. Ramdoo was suspended from duty, the home was placed under independent control and the case progressed slowly to court.

Source: *The Observer*, 18 February 2001

The conditions here are not typical of residential homes. The vast majority are well-run and look after the people well. However, it has been estimated that as many as 10 per cent have significant failings.

What is the government proposing to do to ensure that the standards are high and this does not happen again?

Ask three residential homes near you if you could question residents about their views on residential care and what their preferences are. Do be careful not to ask provocative questions and discuss your questions with the owners/managers of the residential home beforehand. Of course, any replies from residents should be confidential.

If a residential home is unwilling to let you talk to their residents, then you ought to ask them why. After all, a good residential home should be pleased to show you examples of good practice.

Go the Department of Health Website www.doh.gov.uk and then to the Social Care page. You will find information on the national standards. Do the homes achieve the national standards in your opinion?

Care and nursing of older people: the financial issues

In England and Wales, the government has made a distinction between care of older people in residential homes and the nursing of older people in these homes. The NHS pays for all of the nursing required, but does not pay for the elements of care. This means that for those people who have to enter residential homes, which largely provide caring services, the individuals have to pay all or a proportion of the costs, until their savings (including the value of their home) fall below £10,000 – at this point the local authority takes over payments.

Although the debate has mainly been on the unfairness of payments to residential homes, it is important to remember that the people pay local authorities for their care at home as well, based on a similar sliding scale of income. Nursing and medical care is provided free by the NHS.

In Scotland, however, the full costs of care as well as the nursing tasks are met by the local authorities, depending upon the financial situation of the person.

The situation is different because of disagreements on four issues:

- over how to distinguish between what requires nursing care and what requires simply care. For example, in England and Wales people with Alzheimer's Disease are not classed as needing nursing care, despite the fact that it is a physical disease and the person needs constant attention
- over what the Welfare State has a duty to provide, given that a person may have paid National Insurance contributions and taxes all their lives. Why does the Welfare State not care for them 'from the cradle to the grave'?
- why should people who have saved all their lives have to pay for their care, when those who have spent the money and enjoyed themselves receive free care from the State?
- most people wish to pass on something, usually their home if they own one, to their children. By including the cost of the home in the calculations, this is prevented.

The reply from the English and Welsh governments is that unlimited support for older people in need of care, irrespective of their wealth, is an unfair burden on the taxpayer. It is argued the taxpayer is actually worse off than the older person in care.

Housing

Older people have rather different housing patterns and needs from the majority of the population. Older people are often living in accommodation which is of poor quality and which may not be appropriate for their physical abilities.

Older people are also more likely to actually own their own homes than younger people. For example about 60 per cent of those who own their homes outright are over 65 . However, 35 per cent of those renting from local authorities were 65 and over, and 34 per cent of those renting from housing associations were 65. Older people also have a relatively high rate of private renting. Privately rented property includes some of the very worst accommodation in the UK.

Although older people may have fairly high rates of ownership, they also have some of the poorest housing conditions of any group in society. For example, about 20 per cent of people over 75 live in poor accommodation, with twice as many homes in need of 'essential modernisation', as in the population in general.

Older people live in poorer accommodation primarily because they are poor.

Age and housing — Older households in unfit dwellings, England (1996)

Age of household head	In fit dwellings (000s)	In unfit dwellings (000s)	% in unfit dwellings
60–64	1,655	74	4.3
65–69	1,381	79	5.4
70–74	1,311	93	6.6
75–79	890	58	6.1
80–84	555	61	9.9
85 and over	270	31	10.3
All households	**18,370**	**1,273**	**6.5**

Source: K. Revell and P. Leather, *The State of UK Housing*, 2nd edition (Policy Press, 2000)

1 In total, how many people over the age of 80 lived in 'unfit dwelling'?

2 What overall pattern is there between age and percentage of unfit dwellings (there is a slight blip to this pattern)?

3 What percentage of people aged 80–84 live in unfit dwellings?

4 What percentage of people aged 85 and over live in unfit dwellings?

Definition

Sheltered accommodation –
specialist accommodation (of any
type) where facilities are available
to meet the needs of older people

In recent years, there has been a significant growth in **sheltered accommodation**. This consists of accommodation (which can vary from a room in a block to a house in a development) where a person is paid to keep an eye on the residents and ensure that their needs are met. Sheltered accommodation is provided by local authorities, housing associations and private companies. The numbers entering sheltered accommodation increases with age. At present there are about 5 per cent of people aged between 65 and 70 in this form of accommodation and it increases to 20 per cent for those over 85. More people actually live in sheltered accommodation than in residential accommodation.

Older people, work and leisure

The negative view of older people, held by some younger people, is closely linked to the fact that they are not in employment and so have limited incomes, power and status, as employment usually provides these for people. Yet there is no *natural* reason why people should retire at 60 or 65, and indeed, as recently as the 1960s over a quarter of all people continued in employment beyond retirement age, and retirement itself (on a pension) is a relatively recent innovation, only dating back to the late nineteenth century.

Retirement at a fixed age is a result of a combination of pressures from employers to slim down their workforces, from the government to decrease unemployment, and from people themselves who wish to have some time without working, before they die. But retirement has a number of important social consequences for older people. These include:

- Work provides the majority of people with social contacts. Retirement means loss of friendships.
- Status derives from employment – the terms 'retired' or 'pensioner' are terms which carry a stigma. Many people will therefore refer to themselves in terms of their pre-retirement occupation, for example 'retired head-teacher'.
- A job means a salary, and the low pension that most UK people receive means that retirement for many involves a life of poverty – and its consequences of poor health, poor housing and limited leisure.
- If a person reaches 60 years of age, they can anticipate (depending on whether they are male or female) another 15 or 19 years of active life.
- The involvement of older people in 'constructive' pastimes (such as sport, education, etc.) is quite low – of the older retired people (over 75) only two out of 100 use parks regularly and only one in 100 attends the cinema, although retired people do watch more television than most other groups.
- Their relationships, too, are rather limited:
  - one in ten never visits friends or relatives, and one-third receive no visits from friends
  - one in five is visited by relatives less than once a month
  - one in 20 never receives visits from relatives.

However, it is not all negative, as just under 25 per cent of people aged 60–69, and 15 per cent of those of 70 or older, are participating in voluntary work, for example, and about 7 per cent of men aged 65 and over and 8 per cent of women aged 60 and over remain in employment.

Overall, the majority of older people express satisfaction with their lives.

Activity

Find out about the lives of older people in your area.

Carry out a survey of charity shops in your area. How many of the volunteers are over retirement age? Ask them what they get out of doing that sort of voluntary activity. Contact other local voluntary organisations – what proportion of the people helping are retired?

What does this tell you about the continuing contribution of older people to society?

Main points
▶ The majority of older people continue living at home all or virtually all their lives.

▶ There are a wide variety of services available to them, usually provided or funded by local authorities.

▶ A minority of older people live in residential care. Most of these are 'older' old people.

▶ There have been some criticisms of residential care for failing to deliver the quality of service to older people.

▶ The government has responded by introducing national standards of care.

▶ Older people living in England and Wales must pay for their care in residential homes. It is free in Scotland. This is a direct result of devolution (see page 2). Nursing is free everywhere.

▶ Older people tend to live in poorer quality accommodation.

▶ Older people are at risk of greater loneliness and isolation, although the majority of older people are not in this situation.

Older people, pensions and poverty

Pensions

The main income for older people, as we said earlier, is their retirement pension. In addition to their pension roughly 20 per cent of pensioners claim extra help through Income Support, known as the Minimum Income Guarantee. It is likely that many more are eligible, but either through ignorance or through the desire not to accept charity and to remain independent, they do not submit a claim.

Old age pensions were first introduced by the Liberal government in 1908. They were non-contributory, and available for all people over the age of 70, providing their income from other sources was below a set amount. In 1925, a contributory pension scheme was introduced for those aged over 70, and included widows and orphans.

The Beveridge Report of 1942 (see page 44) recommended a pension scheme in which people paid the same amount irrespective of income. This was to be invested for 20 years, and then the proceeds would be paid out on a flat-rate basis (that is the same for everyone) with a 50 per cent contribution from the government.

However, in 1946, the government introduced the National Insurance Act, which included a pension scheme based on the idea of 'pay as you go' – meaning that people paid contributions but there was no fund that was invested. The contributions people make today pay for the pensions of retired people today. The assumption was that there would always be enough people in employment paying their National Insurance to fund the numbers of older people in retirement at a particular time. By the 1990s, however, this was been found to be a doubtful assumption, as the numbers of older people increased and the number of younger people in the population declined relatively (see *Burden of dependency* on page 326). In 2000, there were 3.4 people of working age for every person of pension age, but by 2040 there will only be 2.4 people for every one person of retirement age.

In 1975, the pension system was reformed to bring in a relatively generous earnings-related pension system known as SERPS (State Earnings Related Pensions Scheme). However, the sheer costs of providing a reasonable pension scheme for the whole of the population proved too much, in the eyes of the government. So, in 1986, the Social Security Act limited the amount of the government's contribution and consequently the value of the benefits for most employees. It also encouraged people to switch to private pension schemes, which are based on a 'funding' principle. This means that the money is invested in stocks and shares and then the money earned is distributed, after the fees of the insurance company have been deducted, to the pensioners. The result of successive governments' encouragement has been the deposit of over £630 billion in private pension assets in the UK financial markets, but even this will be inadequate to meet future needs.

The value of pensions can still be considered too low, but the effect of the gradual intervention of the government in forcing people to have private or State pension schemes has been to reduce the extent of poverty for older people.

Between 2000 and 2003, the government introduced further changes to the State system of pensions, with two new pension schemes introduced (to replace SERPS). These are:

- *second state pension:* A replacement for SERPS. Another earnings-related scheme for the employed (rather than self-employed) but aimed at people on low incomes, particularly those earning up to £10,000. Benefits for higher earners will be scaled down and eventually they will be encouraged to contract out.
- *stakeholder pensions*: Introduced in 2001 for people earning £10,000 or more to provide for themselves if they don't have access to an employer's scheme.

Questions

1 Pay-as-you-earn pension systems involve using the money taken in contributions from the younger age group today to pay for the pensioners today. There is no investment.
   a) There is a growing population, and plenty of work available. Is this good or bad for pay-as-you earn pension schemes?
   b) There is a declining or static population with an increase in the numbers of older people. Is this good or bad for pay-as-you-earn pension schemes? Explain your answers.

2 The proportion of people receiving pensions will increase relative to the employed population by the end of the century to 2.3:1.6. What does this mean, and what are the possible implications?

Pensions

The basic pension has risen in line with prices rather than earnings since the early Eighties, when the Thatcher government scaled back state provision. The effect was gradual, but two decades on pensioners are feeling the pinch.
...

Many adults still think the state will provide for them. Forty-three per cent of those in the Barclays survey expected their living standards in retirement to be better than at work. A third had no private pension. ...

The reality for people already living on pensions was very different, Barclays found. Forty per cent of them were living on less than £10,000 a year, while 57 per cent wished they had planned better.

... the charity Age Concern has no doubt that life for many pensioners is a struggle. It points to Government statistics showing that the median income of single pensioners after housing costs two years ago was £88 a week , or £4,576 a year, and £195 a week (£10,140 a year) for couples. This compared with average full-time earnings of £384.50 a week (£19,994 a year).

Elderly people have begun to get militant about the state pension. ... But the Government refuses to restore the link between pensions and average pay.

Age Concern says if the basic state pension had kept pace with average earnings a single pensioner would be looking forward to a weekly income of £101.15 from April, while couples would be getting £161.70.

Instead, the Government is putting more emphasis on means testing. Its 'minimum income guarantee' ensures £92.15 a week for single people and £140.55 for couples. But the gap between the basic pension and the minimum guarantee is made up of income support, a means-tested benefit based on a person's own income and savings. This is not given automatically, and around 700,000 pensioners who are entitled to it do not receive it.

Means testing can penalise people who have saved enough to disqualify them from a state top-up, but not enough to make them significantly better off. ...

Age Concern asks whether it is worth people on low incomes saving for retirement if this just disqualifies them from state help.

Rhian Beynon, an official of the charity, says: 'Ideally everyone should be saving for the future but it may be that you will save and still end up on income support.'

Source: Adapted from *The Observer*, 18 February 2001

Benefits for older people

In 2001, 70 per cent of pensioner households depended on State benefits for at least 50 per cent of their income. However, the Department of Work and Pensions estimates that about one-third of those of pensionable age who were entitled to claim the Minimum Income Guarantee, up to 12 per cent of those who were entitled to Housing Benefit and approximately 25 per cent of those entitled to Council Tax Benefit did not claim.

- *State Pension:* Pensions are available to all retired people as long as National Insurance contributions conditions are met. Many women who have had time out to care for children and do not have National Insurance contributions are therefore ineligible and have to claim Income Support.
- *Minimum Income Guarantee:* From 2001, all older people are eligible for the Minimum Income Guarantee. This is guarantees those over retirement age that they will have an income of £92.15 for a single person or £140.55 for a couple (April 2001). This additional top-up to the State pension is means-tested and is paid as Income Support.

The Pensions Act 1995 equalised at 65 the State pension age for both men and women. This will be phased in over a ten-year period from April 2010.

- *Winter Fuel Payment:* This is available for those in retirement to pay for the additional fuel costs. It is paid automatically before Christmas.
- *Cold Weather Payment:* This is a means-tested benefit, which is paid after seven days when the *average* temperature is below freezing.
- *Attendance Allowance:* This is for those aged over 65, who need to be looked after at home. It is means-tested.
- *Invalid Care Allowance:* This is for those who are looking after a severely disabled person for at least 35 hours a week. It is means-tested.
- *Housing Benefit:* Because of the relatively high proportion of older people who rent properties, housing benefit is an important State benefit for retired people.

- *Tax Allowances:*
  - Personal Allowance: There is a higher rate of personal allowance for those over 65 with incomes below a set level.
  - Married Couples Allowance: This is an allowance which has been phased out for most age groups but is still in existence for those married couples with one partner born before 1935.

The composition of the incomes of older people

Pensioners'[1] gross income: by age and source, Great Britain

Percentages

	Couples[2] 1998–99	Single 1998–99
Aged under 75		
Benefits	40	56
Occupational pensions	29	23
Investments	17	12
Earnings	14	7
Other	1	1
All gross income (=100%) (£ per week at July 1998 prices)	345	174
Aged 75 and over		
Benefits	51	69
Occupational pensions	29	20
Investments	15	10
Earnings	4	1
Other	–	–
All gross income (=100%) (£ per week at July 1998 prices)	275	149

1 Pensioner units – single people over state pension age (65 for males, 60 for females) and couples where the man is over state pension age.
2 Classified by age of man.

Source: Pensioners' Income Series, Department of Social Security

Source: *Social Trends 31* (The Stationery Office, 2001)

1 What proportion of the income of single people aged under 75 is made up from:
   a) benefits?
   b) occupational pensions?

2 How does this differ from couples of the same age?

3 Why do you think there is such a difference between the earnings of pensioner couples and single people? (No, not because there are two people! Look at the explanatory notes below and think about the relative ages of couples.)

4 What proportion of single people's income in the over 75 group is made up from:
   a) benefits?
   b) occupational pensions?

5 What differences are there in the composition of income between the two age groups?

6 Can you suggest any reasons for the differences?

Old age: is it all bad news?

BAD

Housing: Older people have poorer housing conditions.

Poverty: Older people form a high proportion of those living in poverty.

Burden of dependency: Older people cost us all money in our taxes.

Health: Older people are in poorer health and have higher rates of disability than the majority, younger population.

Health services: Older people receive worse care.

Stigma: Being old has low status.

Isolation: Older people are more likely to be alone and socially isolated.

Employment: Older people have to retire at 65.

Care: Older people are more likely to need residential and community care.

NOT SO BAD

Housing: Older people are more likely to own their homes.

Poverty: This is true – but not all older people live in poverty. There are variations.

Burden of dependency: Older people contribute to the economy and have done so all their lives as workers and taxpayers.

Health: Most older people remain relatively fit and active until extreme old age.

Health services: The new National Framework outlaws discrimination in health on the grounds of old age.

Stigma: True!

Isolation: Most older people remain in contact with their families. Isolation may only occur in extreme old age.

Employment: Most people are glad to finish full-time employment.

Care: The majority of older people do not receive formal care.

Poverty

Most older people rely on a private or State pension (or a combination of both). The State pension is relatively low and according to many commentators it does not enable a pensioner to reach an acceptable standard of living. In 2000 over 600,000 people aged 60 or over (single people or couples) were receiving Income Support (Minimum Income Guarantee, see page 58) because of their income was so low.

- Most older people have limited or no savings on retirement. This means that they have difficulties in paying for major purchases or repairs, as they are unable to borrow money from financial institutions.
- Many pensioners have particular costs associated with age. For example, they may have limited mobility and if they wish to go out public transport is inappropriate. These costs add to their overall higher costs of living.
- They have higher fuel bills, as they are at home all day and often need higher levels of heat than younger, more active people. The most severe deprivation is experienced by pensioners living alone who are mainly dependent on State pensions: nearly 50 per cent of their expenditure goes on housing, fuel and food. This compares with about 35 per cent for the average household. In 1998, 178 people aged 65 died from hypothermia (death from the cold).
- They are less able to do household repairs and tasks, and so require the services of professionals for which they must pay.

The result of this is that they are less likely to have a range of household goods now considered normal. For example, in 2000 of pensioners mainly dependent on State pensions and living alone:

- 80 per cent had central heating, compared to 90 per cent of all households – we have already seen the consequences in terms of spending on heating

- 13 per cent had a car, compared to 72 per cent of all households – this has serious consequences for older people, their low level of car ownership means that they may have to buy in local shops, which are more expensive. It is also more difficult to attend hospital appointments and GP surgeries. Social life too is limited
- 68 per cent had a washing machine, compared to 92 per cent of all households.

Variations between older people

Not all older people are in poverty, in fact there is a great divide between the better-off older people and the poor. The better-off tend to be younger (60–74), middle-class married couples, and the poorer are more likely to be older (75+), women and working-class couples. This is caused mainly by the fact that the younger older people have access to better occupational pensions. So, the poorest fifth of pensioner couples had an average income (1998) of £135, while the richest fifth had an income of £677.

This inequality has had an impact on government approaches to combating poverty amongst older people. Rather than providing universal benefits, the government has targeted help at the poorer older people, with its policy of minimum income guarantee and winter fuel payments. These are means-tested, with all their disadvantages (see page 60).

Main points
▶ The retirement pension has undergone many changes since its introduction in 1908.
▶ In recent years there have been concerns that the cost was too high for the government, because of the increasing numbers of older people.
▶ Recently a number of new pension schemes have been introduced which shift the responsibility more on the individuals.
▶ There is a complex range of benefits for older people, as they tend to be poorer than most of the population.
▶ There is a high rate of poverty among older people.
▶ This is caused partly by lack of company pension schemes when older people were in employment.
▶ There are variations between older people, and it is not true to say that they are all in poverty. Differences in lifetime earnings are reflected in old age.

Conclusion

In this chapter we have explored the lives of older people in our society and the services available to them. The chapter has shown that older people are negatively stereotyped and discriminated against. In terms of a wide range of services in health and social care, traditionally older people have been likely to receive lower standards of care. Only in recent years has this been recognised and attempts made to alter the balance. As the numbers of older people in the population have increased, so the issues of how to care for older people and how to pay for the appropriate level of services have come to the fore.

There are variations within older people, reflecting the differences in employment and resources throughout life, and so there are many affluent older people. However, it remains true to say that the majority of older people have fewer resources than the majority of younger people, while having greater needs.

12 CHAPTER SUMMARY

1 The numbers of older people in the population and the proportion they form of the population has been rising since the beginning of the twentieth century.

2 This looks likely to continue far into the twenty-first century.

3 Older people are a diverse group. They should not be stereotyped.

4 There is a majority of women amongst older people.

5 The burden of dependency is a term used to describe the costs to society of older people.

6 Older people are discriminated against.

7 A significant proportion of health spending is on older people, but older people, until recently have not received the amount of health spending appropriate to their needs, from the NHS.

8 The majority of older people continue living at home all or virtually all their lives.

9 There are a wide variety of services available to them, usually provided or funded by local authorities.

10 A minority of older people live in residential care. Most of these are 'older' old people.

11 There have been some criticisms of residential care for failing to deliver the quality of service to older people and the government has responded by introducing national standards of care.

12 Older people living in England and Wales must pay for their care in residential homes. It is free in Scotland. This is a direct result of devolution. Nursing is free everywhere.

13 Older people tend to live in poorer quality accommodation.

14 Older people are at risk of greater loneliness and isolation, although the majority of older people are not in this situation.

15 The retirement pension has undergone many changes since its introduction in 1908. In recent years there have been concerns that the cost was too high for the government, because of the increasing numbers of older people.

16 Recently a number of new pension schemes have been introduced which shift the responsibility more on the individuals.

17 There is a complex range of benefits for older people, as they tend to be poorer than most of the population.

18 There is a high rate of poverty among older people, caused partly by lack of company pension schemes when older people were in employment.

19 There are variations between older people, and it is not true to say that they are all in poverty. Differences in lifetime earnings are reflected in old age.

Useful website

www.ace.org.uk: Age Concern

FAMILIES AND CHILDREN

Chapter contents

- ### What is the 'normal' family?
  Ideas of the normal family influence welfare provision. The normal family is seen as a married, heterosexual couple who live together and bring up their biological children.

- ### The changing family
  Although we have an ideal of the normal family, in practice the family has changed a great deal. There are numerous different types of family. Some types, such as lone-parent families, are often seen by the State as problematic. Relationships between family members have also changed, and more women now go out to work.

- ### Lone-parent families
  The family type which has grown most rapidly has been the lone-parent type. There are particular issues which need to be examined – primarily because the adult in the family, almost always a woman, has to combine work and childcare. This has led to considerable financial problems and placed lone-parent families amongst the poorest in the country.

- ### Childcare services
  Changing roles within the family mean that there is now a greater need for childcare services. Many different kinds exist for both younger and older children, such as day nurseries and after-school clubs.

- ### The family and the Welfare State
  There are many ways in which the Welfare State supports families. One of the principal methods is by providing a range of benefits for families with children, although other provision such as health care, education and housing is also important. In this section we explore the very wide range of services and financial benefits which are available for families and children.

- ### Problems in the family
  The Welfare State also intervenes in the family by stepping in when things go wrong. Problems in the family include domestic violence, usually carried out by men against women. Another serious problem is child abuse, which can take several forms. Child protection services become involved if abuse is reported.

- ### Fostering and adoption
  Sometimes problems within the family are not solved easily. In these cases, children may be fostered with other families. A more permanent arrangement is when they are put up for adoption.

- ### Children's rights
  An important concept in recent years is that of children's rights. Decisions affecting children should be made in the best interests of the child. Children's views should also be listened to.

Introduction

This chapter looks at families and children. The family plays an extremely important role in welfare. It provides services for its members and is supported by social policy. The State may also intervene if there are problems within the family.

The importance of the family for health and welfare

The family forms the foundation for the provision of health and welfare services. Most social policy in the UK is based on the principle of the 'normal' family, which looks after its members in childhood and in old age. The family is usually seen as a private institution, which only requires State intervention when there is a breakdown in this 'normal' pattern. However, social policies also affect 'normal' families as well. In fact, when we look in detail it is quite difficult to see what a 'normal' family is – so it is simpler to think of the family as covering a very wide range of relationships. Within those relationships too, the way people behave towards each other varies – from consideration to physical and emotional violence. Those who suffer most from families appear to be women and children. Of course, at the other extreme, the family provides the bulk of care for its members.

It is this complexity of relationships from love and caring through to abuse and violence which forms the 'world' in which the health and social services operate.

The importance of the family in matters of health and welfare is summarised in the diagram below.

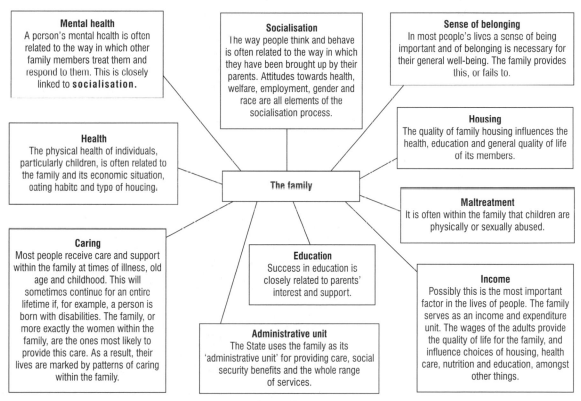

Mental health
A person's mental health is often related to the way in which other family members treat them and respond to them. This is closely linked to **socialisation.**

Socialisation
The way people think and behave is often related to the way in which they have been brought up by their parents. Attitudes towards health, welfare, employment, gender and race are all elements of the socialisation process.

Sense of belonging
In most people's lives a sense of being important and of belonging is necessary for their general well-being. The family provides this, or fails to.

Health
The physical health of individuals, particularly children, is often related to the family and its economic situation, eating habits and type of housing.

The family

Housing
The quality of family housing influences the health, education and general quality of life of its members.

Maltreatment
It is often within the family that children are physically or sexually abused.

Caring
Most people receive care and support within the family at times of illness, old age and childhood. This will sometimes continue for an entire lifetime if, for example, a person is born with disabilities. The family, or more exactly the women within the family, are the ones most likely to provide this care. As a result, their lives are marked by patterns of caring within the family.

Education
Success in education is closely related to parents' interest and support.

Income
Possibly this is the most important factor in the lives of people. The family serves as an income and expenditure unit. The wages of the adults provide the quality of life for the family, and influence choices of housing, health care, nutrition and education, amongst other things.

Administrative unit
The State uses the family as its 'administrative unit' for providing care, social security benefits and the whole range of services.

Source: Adapted from an article by Paul Barker in *The Guardian*, 4 November 1996

The importance of the family for health and welfare

What is the 'normal' family?

The 'normal' or 'traditional' family is usually seen as being made up of a married, heterosexual couple who live with and bring up their biological children. This model is often held up as an ideal, even though many people do not live in such family arrangements.

An argument for the value of marriage

The argument for promoting marriage is [strong]. And that's because it's based on solid evidence which won't go away.

The simple fact increasingly troubling government is the enormous and escalating cost to the country of family disintegration. It's adding billions of pounds to the pressures on housing, social security, healthcare, the criminal justice system. And it is storing up even more costs; increasingly solitary lifestyles and the reluctance to form permanent relationships will destroy the networks of kinship which caused generations to look after not just their children but their elderly parents, too. …

A responsible government should surely tell people the truth. "We all know that it is better for children to grow up in a secure relationship but that doesn't mean the couple has to be married," said one unnamed minister. Wrong; that's exactly what it does mean. Cohabitations break down much more frequently than marriages and also make subsequent marriages unstable.

Only 36% of children born to cohabiting parents are still looked after by both parents – even if they eventually marry – by the time the children are 16, compared with 70% of children born to married couples.

Generally speaking, children suffer permanent disadvantage if their parents aren't together while they grow up. Of course some such children emerge relatively unscathed; but to tell the public that other types of family are just as successful for children as married parents is simply a lie.

Marriage is a unique institution in which the state has a stake, because if marriages fail the state has to pick up the pieces. Value-neutral family policy means expecting the taxpayer to foot the bill for behaviour that may be ignorant or unwise, such as elective lone parenthood or cohabitation. This government is constantly telling people to live more responsibly – not to smoke, not to get pregnant in teenage years, not to be idle, not to let children truant. Yet when it comes to marriage, it gets a fit of the vapours.

The anti-marriage lobby claims that promoting marriage would stigmatise the children of unmarried parents. Well, children whose parents are convicted of crime feel stigmatised. Does anyone suggest that therefore criminal offences should be abolished?

The real misery for children in fragmented families is that they are fatherless. Often, their most powerful wish is never to do to their own children what has been done to them. Yet if nobody tells them why marriage is so important, and why it's in the best interests of everyone, they will indeed do the same to their own children.

Source: *The Sunday Times*, 19 November 2000

1 What kind of family does the writer think is best?

2 In what ways are children affected by family breakdown?

3 What are the consequences for government and society of family breakdown?

4 What are the beliefs of the 'anti-marriage lobby'?

5 Do you think the 'normal' family is always best?

The changing family

The family in the UK has been changing considerably over the last twenty-five years. The changes are twofold:

- changes in the *structure* of the family
- changes in the *relationships* of family members.

Family structure

By family structure, we mean primarily the type of bonds between people. Individuals may live in couples or alone, in large families of three generations, or simply as couples with their children. The structure of the family is thus influenced by factors such as the numbers of people who divorce, and possibly remarry, and the numbers who live alone, particularly if they have children. Therefore family structure may reflect household structure: the relationships of people who live together under one roof. However, the family can also be seen as a broader concept. People may not live together within a household, but they may still see themselves as a family and have strong relationships.

We need to know about family and household structure, as they affect the services that might be needed. For example, the more older people there are who live alone, and relatively isolated from their families, the more the State may need to arrange the provision of community care services. If there are more lone-parent families, there may be greater need for social security benefits, such as Income Support, given that it may be difficult for a lone parent to support a family without State aid.

Definitions of family types

- *Lone- (or single-) parent family*: only one parent, usually the mother. This reflects the rise in the divorce rate and the growth of childbirth outside marriage.

- *Nuclear family*: mother, father and their children. Relatively isolated from the wider family.

- *Extended family:* usually consists of three generations living close together.

- *Reconstituted family:* where the parents have previously been married (or in a long-term partnership), and join together with some or all of their children from the previous marriages.

Question

What implications for health and welfare are there for each of the following family types:

a) lone-parent family?
b) nuclear family?
c) extended family?
d) reconstituted family?

You may find it useful to list the advantages and disadvantages of each type. Issues you might want to think about include poverty, stress, isolation, violence, support, abuse, freedom, constraints, caring and appropriate housing.

Trends in marriage and divorce

Marriages and divorces, UK

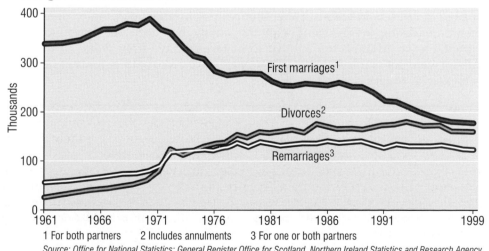

1 For both partners   2 Includes annulments   3 For one or both partners

Source: Office for National Statistics; General Register Office for Scotland, Northern Ireland Statistics and Research Agency

1 What changes can you see occurring in the number of first marriages?

2 What has happened to divorces since 1961?

3 Why have remarriages risen?

4 What implications are there for the care of family members as a result of these changes in marriage and divorce?

Source: *Social Trends 31* (The Stationery Office, 2001)

Births outside marriage

Births outside marriage as percentage of all live births, UK

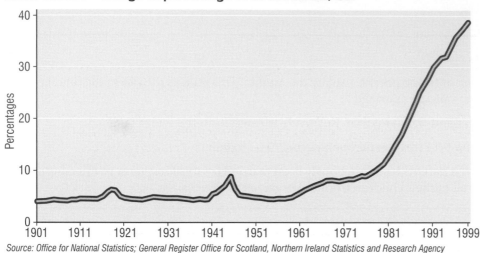

Source: Office for National Statistics; General Register Office for Scotland, Northern Ireland Statistics and Research Agency

Source: *Social Trends 31* (The Stationery Office, 2001)

1 What was the percentage of births outside marriage in 1971? What was it in 1999?

2 What social changes does this reflect?

3 Over two-thirds of births outside marriage are registered by both parents. Are there any implications of this about the relationship between the parents?

Family relationships

Traditionally, the wife stayed at home and looked after the children and the husband went out to paid employment. The male was regarded as head of the household, and the tax, social security and pension systems were all based on these assumptions. However, as we have already seen, the structure of the family has changed, with an increase in the number of lone-parent families, a growth of **serial monogamy** (that is people remarrying after divorce), and an increasingly popular preference for **cohabitation** (that is couples living together without being formally married).

Changes within the home have taken place too, which affect the way children are treated. These changes reflect the changing role of women in the wider society. There has been a move to greater equality between husbands and wives. In particular, there is a much greater acceptance by males of their responsibilities as fathers and partners. Men are now far more likely than they were 20 years ago to engage in household tasks such as shopping or housework. One recognition of men's increasing involvement with the family has been the introduction of parental leave. Mothers are entitled to maternity leave from work. In the past, fathers were not granted any leave. Parental leave gives both parents of newborn babies rights to take time off.

Parental leave

Today, expectant parents' new rights to parental leave finally come into force. ...

The impetus for these new rights is an EU directive mandating 13 weeks' unpaid parental leave per parent which Britain is finally putting into force.

... Leave is also still unpaid. ...

The measures are also not as family friendly as they appear. The right to parental leave applies only to expectant parents, not the 3.3m working parents with children under five currently in the labour market. ...

My research in the UK found that only 21% of working people under 40 would take parental leave if they have to cover the costs themselves. ...

There are other benefits: 58% of the public believe parental leave strengthens families by allowing

time and space for bonding. It could also be good for business: 53% of working people under 40 say that parental leave will make them more loyal to their employer; 46% say parental leave would reduce stress and improve productivity.

Source: *The Guardian*, 15 December 1999

1 What is parental leave?

2 Why is Britain having it?

3 Why are the 'measures not as family friendly as they appear'?

4 Do you think that parental leave will enable mothers and fathers to share childcare more equally?

5 What proportion of new parents will take parental leave? Why won't the rest?

6 What do the majority of people believe about parental leave?

Definition **Symmetrical family relationship** – both partners share household tasks equally	Some commentators have gone so far as to suggest that the relationship between husband and wife is now one of **symmetry**, indicating that they both share domestic tasks equally. However, this is probably an exaggeration.

Division of tasks in the household: evidence of a domestic family?

Oakley and Rigby conducted research to find out the extent to which men contributed to domestic responsibilities and childcare tasks and found that these areas remained much more likely to be women's tasks.

A Percentage of men helping 'rarely' or 'never' with domestic tasks during pregnancy and when children are 6 weeks, 1 year and 7 years old

	In pregnancy %	At 6 wks %	At 1 yr %	At 7 yrs %
Cooking	40	39	51	61
Housework	29	29	46	47
Shopping	18	18	31	36
Childcare (other children)	9	9	16	18

B Percentage of men helping 'rarely' or 'never' with childcare tasks

	At 6 wks %	At 1 yr %	At 7 yrs %
Changed nappies	51	50	–
Got up at night	57	62	–
Took child out on own	–	61	41
Played with child	–	8	19
Took child to school	–	–	70
Fetched child from school	–	–	73
Look after child when ill	–	–*	58

Note:
* Question not asked at 1 year

Source: A. Oakley and A.S. Rigby, 'Are men good for the welfare of women and children?', in J. Popay, J. Hearn and J. Edwards (eds), *Men, Gender Divisions and Welfare* (Routledge, 1998)

Look at A.

1 At what age of children do men 'give' most help?

2 When do they give least help?

3 What chore do they help with most?

Look at B.

4 What percentage of men, rarely or never change nappies?

5 What percentage never or rarely take the child out when they are 1 year of age?

6 Does this change at 7 years of age? Any suggestions why?

7 Do these figures suggest that family relationships are becoming 'symmetrical'?

8 Does this support the provision of paid parental leave, in your opinion?

The importance of this for social policy is that the traditional role of the wife/mother/daughter as carer continues. Women are expected to shoulder much higher proportions of childcare and domestic responsibilities, even when both partners have full-time employment. When it comes to caring for older relatives or chronically ill children or husbands, it is regarded as the duty of a woman to do this. Without the taken-for-granted work of women in families, the State would have to step in to look after the very young, the very old, the sick or disabled people, or they would be left to fend for themselves. Chapter 14 discusses the position of women in more detail.

Young carers: old lives

Not all children lead the lives we would normally expect. Relationships can often be reversed in families where a parent is ill or disabled.

A time to care

Sometimes the roles in families are turned upside down: most fundamentally when a child has to look after a mother, father or sibling. The Carers National Association, which will begin its annual awareness-raising week on June 9, estimates that there are more than 51 000 youngsters under 18 caring for a family member. In some of these families, the child may well be the only support for a disabled parent or one who has mental health problems – dispensing their medication, comforting them, lifting them or doing all the household tasks.

Lisa Johnson, now 22, who works with young carers, knows the problems only too well. She cared for her alcoholic mother, and her younger brother, as a child. 'I was on the at-risk register at eight,' Lisa says. 'But I never got any help with mum. I just got on with it. Everyone on the estate knew her because they'd see her lying in the road. But they all assumed someone else was helping, because they thought it wouldn't be left to a child to care for her.'

Lisa never approached social services for help. Like many young carers, she was frightened that if she talked about her home life, or admitted she couldn't cope, she'd be whisked into care. 'I wanted to be with my mother and brother. Even though there were times when I couldn't stand it, she's still my mum. Now I know that social services work at keeping families together, but that fear of being taken away is very common.' As a result, it is often those young carers who are most vulnerable – those in single parent families or where there are multiple problems – who keep their caring responsibilities secret. Many children go to extraordinary lengths, such as getting up in the small hours to do homework, so that no one in authority need ever guess what is going on at home. Lisa would often bunk off her last lesson to collect her younger brother from school, but no one noticed. It was only when she was doing her A-levels that she finally broke down and told a teacher what was happening at home.

For years she had mopped up when her mother threw up, picked her off the floor and dealt with the hallucinations and shakes that ensued when her mother tried to dry out. Yet despite these daunting responsibilities, she was also powerless. 'I'd be with her in casualty, knowing what medicine she needed to stop the hallucinations. But no one would listen, because I was just a kid.'

Source: The *Guardian*, 4 June 1997

Lone-parent families

In the UK, almost a quarter of all families with dependent children are headed by lone parents. Ninety per cent of lone-parent families are headed by a woman. These families are more likely than families with two parents to have substandard housing, to be poor, to have poor health and to be clients of social services departments.

There are many different ways in which people become lone parents, as the following table illustrates.

Reasons for lone-parent families

Routes into lone parenthood, 1998

	Percentage	Number
Lone mothers		
Divorced	31	536,300
Separated	20	346,000
Widowed	4	69,200
Single	35	605,500
Lone fathers	10	173,000
Total	100	1,730,000

Source: Office for National Statistics (2000 Crown copyright ©)

1 What percentage of lone-mothers are 'single'? How many parents are in this category?

2 Which is the second highest category of lone parents? How many parents are in this category?

3 What percentage of lone parents are fathers?

Low pay and lone-parent families

Families headed by lone parents are more likely than two-parent families to be low-income families, or claiming benefits. This is due to two main reasons:

- The majority of people who head lone-parent households are women. In the UK women are more likely than men to be employed in low-paid work.
- Women with families to support are unable to move to find work, and when they do find employment they have to make arrangements for childcare. Often this means that the women can only work restricted hours.

Economics of the family

A **Economic activity status of women[1]: by marital status and age of youngest dependent child, Spring 2000, United Kingdom**

						Percentages
	Age of youngest dependent child				No dependent children	All[1]
	Under 5	5–10	11–15	16–18[2]		
Not married/cohabiting[3]						
Working full time	11	18	32	51	46	39
Working part time	21	33	33	26	20	22
Unemployed	8	8	7	–	5	6
Economically inactive	60	41	28	20	28	32
All (=100%)(millions)	0.6	0.6	0.4	0.1	4.5	6.3

Married/cohabiting

Working full time	21	27	39	40	51	39
Working part time	39	49	40	38	25	34
Unemployed	3	3	2	–	2	2
Economically inactive	37	21	20	20	22	25
All (=100%)(millions)	2.4	1.7	1.2	0.4	5.3	11.0

1 Aged 16 to 59.
2 Those in full-time education.
3 includes single, widowed, separated or divorced.

Source: Labour Force Survey, Office for National Statistics

B Receipt of selected social security benefits: by family type, 1998–99, Great Britain

Great Britain   **Percentages**

	Family credit or income support	Housing benefit	Council tax benefit	Job-seeker's allowance	Retirement pension	Incapacity or disablement benefits[2]	Child benefit	Any benefit[1]
Pensioners[2]								
Couple	5	11	20	0	99	24	1	100
Single								
Male	13	29	34	0	97	21	–	100
Female	24	31	45	0	96	20	–	100
Couples								
Dependent children	11	9	11	4	–	9	98	99
No dependent children	4	5	7	2	8	16	–	28
Single person								
Dependent children	72	57	64	1	0	8	98	99
No dependent children								
Male	7	11	11	8	–	9	–	24
Female	8	9	12	5	0	9	–	23
All family types[3]	13	15	18	3	24	13	23	59

1 Incapacity benefit, disability living allowance (care and mobility components), severe disablement allowance, industrial injuries disability benefit, war disablement pension, attendance allowance and disability working allowance.
2 Females aged 60 and over, males aged 65 and over, for couples, where head is over pension age.
3 Components do not add to the total as each benefit unit may receive more than one benefit.

Source: Family Resources Survey, Department of Social Security

Source: *Social Trends 31* (The Stationery Office, 2001)

Note: Family Credit was a benefit paid to working parents. It has now been replaced by the Working Families Tax Credit.

Look at A.

1 Do you think having children has an impact on the working life of women?

2 How would you describe the patterns of women's working lives in terms of the ages of their children?

3 Are there any differences between the working patterns of mothers who are not married/cohabiting and those who are? What are they?

Look at B.

4 Does having children make people more or less likely to receive social security benefits?

5 Which type of family is most likely to receive benefits?

Lone parents and social problems

It is often suggested that children from lone-parent families both have more problems and cause more problems to society than children from two-parent families.

Fathers and crime

Having a biological father who maintained a close relationship with his son, whether or not he lived in the family home, might be crucial in preventing susceptible boys becoming criminals, research presented yesterday suggested.

But stepfathers appeared to do little to decrease the risk that a boy will turn to crime, ...

The study by the clinical psychologist Jenny Taylor looked at why a proportion of boys with all the "risk factors" associated with criminal behaviour resisted a life of crime.

Drawing on data from socially deprived areas of south London, she compared a group of "good boys", who had no criminal convictions and had caused teachers no trouble, with a group of "bad boys" at a secure unit for unmanageable adolescents, many of them persistent offenders convicted of sexual assault, theft and stealing vehicles.

All 68 boys, aged between 12 and 16, were from working class backgrounds, had lower than average intellectual ability, had similar problems with their peers and with hyperactivity, had equally large families, and in both groups 40% suffered from dyslexia.

But there was one "very striking" difference between the two groups: 55% of the "good boys" lived with their biological fathers, compared with only 4% of the "bad boys".

Almost 80% of the "good boys" spoke of being close to their biological fathers. Among these were 24% of the group who said they had a biological father living away from home who was an influence in their lives.

Only 18% said there was no one they regarded as a father figure, while 3% said they had a stepfather.

Among the "bad boys", 45% said they had no one they considered a father figure, 30% said they had a stepfather, 22% a biological father not living at home and only 4% a father living at home.

It also suggested that a father who disapproved of crime and showed an interest in his son acted as a crucial social control, countering negative influence such as criminal peers.

Boys gained a sense of being loved and approved of, and the fear of jeopardising this proved enough to deter them from crime, she said.

"It's not necessarily about them living with their biological fathers but about having someone they think of as a father who shows an interest in them and what they're doing," she said.

The research, far from providing fodder for the righting family values lobby, could be seen as a boon for single mothers, she said. "This suggests we should move away from pathologising single mums and instead see that, if there are dangers, it's due to the absence of fathers."

Source: *The Guardian*, 5 April 2001

1 What was the main difference between the 'good boys' and the 'bad boys'?

2 What was the importance of a 'father figure?

3 What does the article mean when it talks about 'risk factors'?

4 Why is this article not an attack upon lone mothers?

5 Is it just having a father that is important, according to the research?

6 How do you think the changes in the family we have read about in the main text might link to this extract?

7 Do you agree with the article?

However, it is hard to distinguish whether children in lone-parent families face problems because they do not live with two parents or because they are more at risk of living in poverty. Also, it is difficult to tell the quality of relationships from statistics. Just because a couple are separated does not mean that they are not both involved in bringing up their children.

It is not correct to see lone-parent families only in terms of problems. There are also benefits, for instance, where the mother and children have escaped from a violent or abusive father. The quality of life for the children and mother in such a case can improve quite significantly once they become a lone-parent family.

Main points ▶ The family is very important within health and welfare provision.

▶ The 'normal' family – a married, heterosexual couple raising their biological children – is seen as the ideal form.

▶ The family has been subject to many changes in recent years.

▶ Changes have mainly taken place within the structure of the family and the relationships of family members.

▶ Types of family include nuclear, extended, lone-parent and reconstituted.

▶ Problems are often associated with lone-parent families. They are frequently on a low income and require financial benefits, for example.

▶ Gender roles are changing. Men now carry out more domestic tasks, although these remain primarily women's responsibilities in most families. The introduction of parental leave reflects these shifts.

▶ More women now go out to work.

▶ Sometimes children's roles within the family may not always be what we would expect. They may care for disabled parents, for example.

Childcare services

Higher numbers of women in employment means that there is now a greater need for childcare services. This is increasingly an issue as current policies, such as the New Deal for Lone Parents, encourage parents to work rather than stay at home with their children. The National Childcare Strategy, introduced in 1997, aims to increase the number of childcare workers.

There are several different types of childcare. Often parents rely on informal carers, such as relatives. There is also a range of formal services.

Childminders
These are usually women who provide an infant care service from their own homes. They will usually only take a few children.
Childminders are required by the Children Act 1989 to be registered with local authorities and to meet certain minimum standards. In 2000, there were 370,000 registered childminders.

Day nurseries
Where children are looked after during the parents' hours of work. These can be private, run by the local authority or attached to a workplace or educational institution. In 2000, there were 260,000 day nurseries.

Playgroups
These are privately or local authority run and they usually use a local hall for morning sessions. Playgroups have to be led by individuals who hold a recognised qualification. There are places for 35 per cent of all children aged three and four. Average attendance is two to three sessions per week. In 2001, there were 390,000 playgroup places.

Nursery schools and classes
These are privately run, or may be part of a social services family centre.

Provision for under-fives in primary, special and independent schools
This provision is growing as more schools introduce reception classes.

Services for young children

The Children Act 1989 requires local authorities to review the provision of day care and other services for children to the age of eight. It also requires authorities to provide a range of services for children 'in need', including day care for the under-fives and appropriate care and supervised activities for children in need outside school hours. The Children Act also requires local authorities to take into account racial and religious factors.

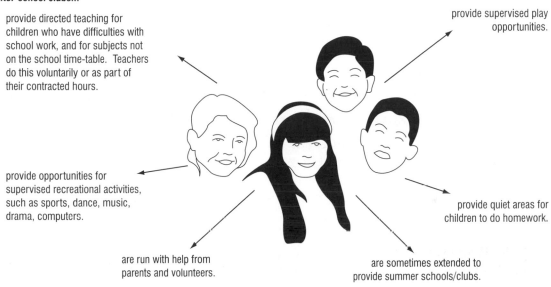

After-school clubs...

provide directed teaching for children who have difficulties with school work, and for subjects not on the school time-table. Teachers do this voluntarily or as part of their contracted hours.

provide supervised play opportunities.

provide opportunities for supervised recreational activities, such as sports, dance, music, drama, computers.

provide quiet areas for children to do homework.

are run with help from parents and volunteers.

are sometimes extended to provide summer schools/clubs.

Source: Adapted from the *Guardian Education*, 10 June 1997

Provision for older children: after school clubs

After-school clubs are an important part of New Labour's strategy to increase available childcare services. They are school-based activities for children, which effectively extend the school day to provide a place for the children of working parent(s). This particularly helps lone parents by allowing them to hold full-time employment, rather than having to pay for childcare or having to take part-time employment. The funding for the clubs is mainly from the National Lottery Commission.

The growth of nurseries

Day care places for children, England, Wales & Northern Ireland

Thousands

	1987	1992	1997	1998	1999
Day nurseries					
Local authority provided	29	24	20	19	16
Private registered	32	98	184	216	235
Non-registered	1	1	2	1	12
All day nursery places	62	123	206	236	262

Source: *Social Trends 31* (The Stationery Office, 2001)

What have been the main changes in day care nurseries provision since New Labour come to power in 1997?

The family and the Welfare State

There are a number of ways in which children and families are supported by the Welfare State. Sometimes the State will support the types of family which it considers most desirable, for example by offering benefits which make working families better off than families where no one is employed. On other occasions, the State will intervene when there are problems in the family, such as abuse.

One of the most important ways that the State supports families is by providing financial benefits. The following is an outline of the main types of benefit available specifically to families with children.

Benefits

Good News for Babies
Up to £300 for parents
on low incomes

Sure Start Maternity Grant

Expectant mothers

- *Statutory Maternity Pay:* This is paid to pregnant women by their employers, provided that they were: employed by their present employer in the fifteenth week before the baby was due; employed without a break for a minimum of twenty-six weeks into the fifteenth week the baby was due; earning an average of £67 per week.
- *Maternity Leave:* This gives women the right to eighteen weeks off work and to take the time to attend antenatal classes.
- *Maternity Allowance:* This is payable to working women who are not eligible for statutory maternity pay, for example if they are self-employed or do not earn enough to qualify.
- *Incapacity Benefit:* This is payable to women who are ill or disabled, and are not eligible for other maternity benefits.
- *Sure Start Maternity Grant:* This is payable to help parents cope with the cost of a new baby. Parents are eligible if they are in receipt of benefits, and they can receive up to £300. This grant is also payable to parents who have a child through adoption or surrogacy.

Families with children

- *Child Benefit:* This is a universal benefit, paid to all families with dependent children, regardless of the family's income. It is paid for each child under 16, under 19 and in full time study, or under 18 and registered with the Careers Service or Connexion Service for work or work-based training (Skillseekers in Scotland). £15.50 is payable for the eldest child, and £10.35 for subsequent children.
- *Working Families' Tax Credit:* This is a means-tested benefit paid in the form of reduced income tax. One- and two-parent families are eligible if they work 16 hours per week or more. An additional tax credit may also be payable towards the costs of childcare.
- *Home Responsibilities Protection:* This is a scheme whereby people who are unable to work, due to caring responsibilities, have credits made to their National Insurance record. This is important, as a National Insurance contributions record is needed to secure pension rights.
- *Jobseeker's Allowance and Income Support:* These benefits are paid to one- or two-parent families who are not in employment.

Lone parents

- *Lone Payment Supplement*: This benefit used to be payable to lone parents in addition to existing benefits. In 1998, this benefit was abolished for new claimants. Lone parents who received this supplement before 1998 do not lose it unless their circumstances change.

- *Child Support Maintenance:* This is paid to the parent with whom a child lives. It is administered by the Child Support Agency (CSA) – a government agency which works out, collects and pays maintenance. Parents who receive benefits are required to go through the CSA; parents who do not receive benefits have the option to go through the CSA. This system is designed to recover money from the absent parent towards the cost of supporting their child. Lone parents receiving benefits who refuse to name the absent parent may face a reduction in their personal allowances, unless they demonstrate that to name the parent would put them at risk of abuse.

- *Child Maintenance Bonus:* This is paid to a parent who receives child maintenance and leaves benefits to start work. It is a one-off payment of up to £1,000.

- *Guardian's Allowance:* This is payable to someone who is bringing up a child because one or both of their parents have died, or because a surviving parent cannot be found or is in prison.

- *Widowed Mother's Allowance:* This is paid to women who have at least one child, or are expecting a child, by their late husband. It is based on the husband's National Insurance contributions. It is not affected by whether the women works or not, but she will be ineligible if she was divorced, remarries or cohabits.

Child support

The Child Support Agency has more foes than friends among both people claiming maintenance and those paying it. ...

'For some people it is a good thing. For others it is going to be a nightmare and create greater inequalities than there are at present.'

The new formula, like the old, works on the basis that one parent has care of the children and the other does not. Parents without care of a child will have to pay 15 per cent of their net income to the other parent for one child, 20 per cent if they have two children and 25 per cent for three or more.

There is a ceiling on income of £104,000, so there could be an assessment to £15,600 a year for one child.

But, says Rutter: 'While the new formula sounds sensible, it is too simple. It does not take account of the income earned by the parent with care, making a

mockery of the established principle that both parents should make a financial contribution to the upkeep of their children if they can.'

Source: *The Observer*, 24 September 2000

1 What is the Child Support Agency (see main text)

2 What is the formula on which it bases maintenance?

3 Identify and explain the main criticisms of the Child Support Agency?

4 What assumption does it make about who the children will live with and who will look after them?

Benefits for children with disabilities

- *Disability Living Allowance:* This is payable for children who require more looking after due to physical or mental illness or disability. There are different rates depending on the age of the child and how much extra help they need.

- *Free milk:* This is available for children between 5 and 16 who do not attend school due to a disability.

Other benefits and services

- *New Deal for Lone Parents:* This is a service offered to lone parents on benefits who want to return to work. There are different services on offer. Its main aim is to offer individual help to parents to find work, improve their prospects through training, and to find childcare. Lone parents who take up training can receive an extra £15 per week on top of their Income Support. Parents who find work can receive help with childcare costs and have £20 of their earnings ignored when entitlement to other benefits is considered.

- *The National Health Service (NHS)*: Children and families on low incomes are eligible for free prescriptions, dental care, sight tests and glasses.

- *Education*: Most local authorities can provide free school meals for children whose families receive benefits. Parents' income is taken into account if their children go to university. If they are on a low income, they may receive reductions in fees.

- *Housing:* One- and two-parent families are given a higher priority on housing waiting lists.

- *Sure Start Initiative:* This is a programme to support parents in bringing up their children, especially in deprived areas. It is funded by the government.

Sure Start   This is the Foreword to a document about the Sure Start programme.

Sure Start is a clear demonstration of the Government's commitment to tackling complex issues in radical, innovative ways. Young children and their families are our future. Meeting their needs is in all our interests. All the evidence shows that early intervention and support can help to reduce family breakdown; strengthen children's readiness for school; and benefit society in the longer term by preventing social exclusion, regenerating communities and reducing crime. Inside the home, we want to offer support to enable parents to strengthen the bond with their children; outside it, we want to help families make the most of the local services on offer.

Our vision is an ambitious one. By the end of the Parliament, we aim to have more than 250 high-quality Sure Start programmes established in areas of deprivation throughout the country. They will improve opportunities for all families with young children in the area. Providers of services and support will work together in new ways that cut across old professional and agency boundaries and focus more successfully on family and community needs. Particular services, help and advice will often be brought together in a single place. Referral to other specialised services will be streamlined. In some cases, additional services will address unmet needs. Sure Start will work with parents to help them nurture their children and stimulate their physical, social and intellectual development. In Whitehall and at regional level, cultural change and better co-ordination will underpin local efforts.

The key principles underpinning Sure Start and the significant resources available to implement it have been widely welcomed. We are committed to basing what we do on evidence of what works, learning from those who have to deliver effectively day-by-day. There is much enthusiasm, creative thinking and good practice already. We want to make the most of this and built on it. The trailblazer approach we have adopted means that we can work with a very wide range of partners and areas to make a difference quickly but also learn how we can make the benefits of Sure Start last. The announcement of the first 60 trailblazer districts is a major step forward. Many more Sure Start programmes will follow in the months and years ahead.

We look forward to working with as many people as possible to achieve Sure Start's objectives – timely help for young children and their families to thrive and succeed.

Source: www.dfee.gov.uk/sstart/foreword.htm

1 What is Surestart? (See main text.)

2 What does early intervention achieve according to the extract?

3 What activities does the government want to do via Sure Start?

4 What are the objectives of Sure Start?

Main points

▶ More women going out to work means there is a greater need for childcare services.

▶ There are many types of services for both younger and older children, including day nurseries, childminders and after-school clubs.

▶ The Welfare State supports the family in a number of ways.

▶ A very important form of support is financial benefits. These include maternity payments, Child Benefit, payments for families where no one is in employment, and benefits for low-income families.

▶ Lone-parent families are also offered other forms of support, such as the New Deal programme.

▶ Families also receive support from areas of welfare such as education, the NHS and housing.

▶ Families in socially-deprived areas may receive additional support, such as the Sure Start initiative.

Problems in the family

Domestic violence

Definition

Domestic violence – refers to violence within the family. Usually used to refer to violence by one adult on the other

---

Domestic violence is a problem which reveals that the family is not always a place of safety, love and security. Sometimes the family can be an oppressive and damaging institution. In the past, domestic violence was seen largely as a private problem. In recent years, there has been much more awareness of this issue, and it is coming to be seen as a public health matter. However, it is still often perceived as a private trouble and not treated in the same way as other crimes of violence.

Domestic violence is usually committed by men against their wives or partners. This accounts for approximately 90 per cent of domestic violence. It is very difficult to establish just how much violence goes on in families. Women are usually reluctant to report their husbands/partners to the police for a number of reasons. These include a fear of further violence, a view that violence is a personal matter between spouses, the fact that women often blame themselves for the violence and a belief that the police are not interested. However, research studies have found that about one in four women have experienced this form of abuse.

Is violence really so abnormal?

Gill Pearce had never heard the expression "domestic violence". To her, the experience of being battered and bruised by her husband was merely a regular feature of married life.

"I called it 'being bounced round the kitchen'. I never called it 'being hit'; that was my way of dealing with it," she said. "The bruises were always to my trunk but – it'll sound silly – I used to think, 'I'm sure he's just hit me, but no, he can't have, he hasn't', because he would just carry on normally."

The beatings continued throughout the six years of Ms Pearce's first marriage but she never confronted the issue until three neighbours forced her to acknowledge something was wrong. "One day, [the neighbours] knew my parents were due to come to the house and the three of them turned up and said, 'Look, we're going to give you half an hour to tell your folks but then we're coming round and if you haven't told them, we will.' So I told them."

Only after she was put in hospital from her injuries did Ms Pearce, 37, manage to have her husband removed from the home. They then divorced and she moved to a secret location with her children.

One in four women in Britain experiences domestic violence. Incidents of domestic violence account for one-quarter of all violent crimes.

Source: From an article by Ian Burrell in *The Independent*, 10 February 2000

1 What proportion of all crimes are acts of domestic violence?

2 What proportion of women are subjected to domestic violence?

3 Do a content analysis of newspapers. Ideally this should be over a period of up to six months to one year.

Choose two examples of daily papers for each week of the year. You can either do this on the web (easier and quicker) or in your local library. (Some libraries only keep newspapers for three months, but they are also available on microfiche or CD-ROM.) Look through all the articles on murders. What is the relationship of the accused and the victim in the majority of cases?

The victims of domestic violence

These two tables are taken from a study of women in North London. Table A shows the percentage of women in the survey who have experienced domestic violence in their lifetime, and the type of violent behaviour. Table B shows who the women turned to.

A **The prevalence of domestic violence in a woman's lifetime, by type of violence**

Violent behaviours	Per cent
Mental cruelty	37
Including verbal abuse (e.g. the calling of names, being ridiculed in front of other people)	
Threats of violence or force	27
Actual physical violence	
Grabbed or pushed or shaken	32
Punched or slapped	25
Kicked	14
Head butted	6
Attempted strangulation	9
Hit with a weapon/object	8
Injuries	
Injured	27
Bruising or black eye	26
Scratches	12
Cuts	11
Bones broken	6
Rape (def. = made to have sex without consent)	23
Rape with threats of violence	13
Rape with physical violence	9
Composite violence	30

Look at A.

1 What percentage of women had been victims of mental cruelty?

2 What percentage had been threatened with force?

3 What was the most common form of violence?

4 What evidence in the table suggests the serious nature of these forms of violence?

5 What percentage of women had been raped? You should remember that the majority of these assaults were committed by their partners.

B **Reporting of the violence**

Of those experiencing violence*, the following people and agencies were informed:	Violence at any time (%)	Violence in last 12 months (%)
Friend	46	36
Relative	31	29
General Practitioner	22	17
Police	22	14
Solicitor	21	12
Social Services	9	7
Women's Refuge	5	3
Victim Support	2	1
Citizen's Advice Bureaux	2	1

Look at B.

6 Who are women most likely to contact concerning violence?

7 What percentage report the violence to the police?

8 Suggest any reason why women do not report to the police.

*Domestic violence refers to 'Composite Domestic Violence'. 10 per cent [of those] experiencing violence at any time and 6 per cent in the last 12 months said they had told another agency not specified on the questionnaire: these included the Housing Department, hospital doctor, therapist or a Court official.

Source: (both tables): J. Mooney, *The North London Domestic Violence Survey* (Middlesex University, 1993)

Definitions

Individual explanations – locate the cause of a problem in an individual or individual family

Structural explanations – locate the cause of a problem in the society itself, such as its socio-economic organisation

Explanations for domestic violence

Explanations for the causes of domestic violence vary and are to some extent contradictory. The main explanations can be divided into two categories:

- **individual** explanations
- **structural** explanations.

Individual explanations

- Alcohol seems to precipitate violence, but is not a cause.
- Violence in childhood home – evidence links violence at home to late adult use of violence.
- Deviant marital relations – male feels he is not in control of marriage or partnership and turns to violence to maintain that control.

Structural explanations

- Culture of male violence – men are encouraged to express themselves through violence and are brought up to be 'tough'. Therefore, use of violence against a partner is not abnormal.
- Fiction – images of macho men in books and stories.
- Advertising contains images similar to those in fiction.
- Childhood socialisation includes the influence of and attitudes to gender relations.
- Belief in male dominance pervades our society. Society is **patriarchal**.

Definition

Patriarchy – a society in which men have most power

Responses to domestic violence

Help and support are offered to the victims of domestic violence in a number of ways.

Women's refuges

These provide short-term accommodation and exist specifically for women and their children who are at risk of violence. The refuges are run by charitable groups and are often partially funded by local authorities. They were first set up in the early 1970s to enable women who were the victims of male violence to escape and live in a place of safety. There are more than 300 refuges, and at least one refuge in most larger towns in the UK. This is perhaps the best proof of the very widespread existence of male violence towards women.

Police and judiciary

Historically, the attitude of the police and the judiciary towards male violence to women was that of the 'threshold approach'. That is, police officers and magistrates operated on the principle that if there was no significant hurt done to a woman then the issue was relatively trivial and not worth instigating criminal proceedings. Today, the police are more likely to take complaints seriously, although women's groups argue that they still do not intervene as often as they should. The police, however, are far more likely to intervene if a child appears to be at risk. In 1996, the Family Homes and Domestic Violence Bill gave powers for violent partners to be excluded from the family home.

Intake teams

Intake teams often have to deal with instances of domestic violence. The intake team consists of social workers who first deal with enquiries from the public. They will advise the client of her rights and liaise with the police. If necessary, they will contact a women's refuge. Increasingly the impact on children is being recognised.

Children frequently witness their mothers being abused, and may be abused themselves.

Family centres

These are usually run by the local authority social services departments, or by a voluntary organisation such as the NCH Action for Children. The aim of the family centres is to teach parenting and relationship skills. Very often domestic violence is coupled with violence by the parent(s) towards the children (though it is almost always the male in the family). The main work of family centres, however, is to teach parenting skills, and usually to the mother.

Relate

This is the organisation that counsels people with marital or partnership difficulties. Couples can arrange to meet a counsellor on a regular basis to overcome their problems if possible, or if this is not possible at least to terminate the relationship in a way that minimises bitterness between the ex-partners. An incomplete or bitter ending to a relationship can often lead to further violence by the male.

The work of a local authority equalities officer

This article is written by a local authority Equalities Officer working in Tower Hamlets, London.

About four fifths of my time is spent on domestic violence issues. Tower Hamlets has 3,000 reported cases a year, 40% from ethnic minority women. Everywhere the system fails them. The better information they have, the better they're able to deal with their situations. We are working to make services better, to help women get protection and support and, ultimately, take the onus off them from having to deal with violence and abuse alone.

I have a staff of three. We coordinate an 80-strong forum – police officers, social workers, lawyers, healthcare professionals an community workers – which develops the borough's strategy to reduce domestic violence. We provide material for voluntary groups, and organise training and presentations. We're developing a team of four specially-trained community advocates to support women and we're logging complaints in a more coordinated fashion. We're always trying to broaden the issues; now we're putting more emphasis on rape and sexual assault. Forced marriage is also beginning to come on to the agenda. Last year, I wrote a 44-page domestic violence handbook for the borough.

Source: *The Guardian*, 20 March 2001

Does your local authority have a similar post? Find out if the person could come to talk to your group.

Alternatively, the police will have a domestic violence unit – ask if someone could talk to your group.

Main points

▶ Domestic violence is one of the problems which may occur in families.
▶ It is usually men who carry out domestic violence against their wives or partners.
▶ Until recently, it was treated as a private problem and the State was unlikely to intervene.
▶ Now it is taken more seriously, although most cases go unreported.
▶ Available support includes women's refuges, police intervention, local authority provision, and relationship counselling.
▶ Violent partners can be excluded from the family home.

Child abuse

Child abuse is another serious problem which may occur within families. Child abuse refers to the maltreatment of children in a number of different ways:

- *neglect* – any behaviour which results in the serious impairment of a child's health or development

- *physical abuse* – physical injury to a child which was caused deliberately or was knowingly not prevented. This can include hitting, kicking, shaking, scalding and numerous other acts

- *sexual abuse* – the involvement of children and adolescents in sexual activities that they do not fully understand, to which they are unable to give informed consent, or that violate social rules regarding family roles. This can also include exposure to sexually explicit material

- *emotional abuse* – the severe effect on the behaviour and emotional development of the child caused by persistent emotional ill treatment.

Child abuse is one of the most emotive issues dealt with by the welfare services, and child abuse intervention is certainly the most controversial of all social work activities. Whenever a child is severely harmed or dies, immense public outrage is generated. There have been several cases of children being killed by a family member which have resulted in public inquiries. Often these inquiries focus on deficiencies in the system or mistakes by professionals involved in the case. The findings of these inquiries can lead to changes in policy.

The horrors of child abuse

Anna Climbie was spirited away from her parents and her Ivory Coast home by the promise of a European education and a better life. She died a "lonely, drawn-out death" after being tied up naked in a bin bag, and left to freeze in a bath in a north London flat.

At the end of one of the worst cases of child abuse heard in a British court, Marie Therese Kouao, 44, and Carl Manning, 28, were jailed for life after being convicted yesterday of murdering the eight-year-old girl.

The 10–2 majority verdict at the Old Bailey came after 19 hours of deliberation, over four days, by a six-man and six-woman jury. The tense, emotional five-week trial, meant that the verdict, when it finally arrived, visibly moved detectives who investigated Anna's death.

"Anna has touched the hearts of all of us and will never be forgotten," said Detective Inspector Keith Niven. "It beggars belief how these two defendants could have inflicted such suffering on a defenceless child."

After months of brutal assaults and starvation, Anna finally died on 25 February 1999 with 128 injuries to her emaciated, battered body. Her legs were so deformed from her confinement in the bath – sometimes lying for days in her own waste – that they could not be straightened. A Home Office pathologist described it as the worst case of child abuse he had ever seen.

Alan Milburn, the Health Secretary, immediately ordered an independent inquiry into the case, to be chaired by Lord Laming. It will investigate how Anna fell through the net despite coming into contact with two hospitals, three social services departments and two police child protection units, during the brutal year she spent in London with Kouao, her great-aunt, and her boyfriend Manning, a gaucho bus driver.

Mr Milburn said: "Anna was murdered by her carers but undoubtedly failed repeatedly by the child protection team."

Yesterday the Metropolitan Police, Haringey social services and the Central and North Middlesex hospitals apologised for failing the girl.

Source: From an article by Mary Braid in *The Independent*, 13 January 2001

Information about severe cases of child abuse can be very distressing. However, some people argue that whilst this sort of violence is very extreme, as a society we tend to tolerate violence against children. For example, we generally see it as reasonable behaviour to smack children, even though we would not see smacking other people outside the family as acceptable. Some countries, such as Sweden, have made any form of physical violence or discipline against a child illegal.

Questions

In the UK, it is legal to hit a child provided that only 'reasonable force' is used.

1 Why is it all right for us to hit children, but not adults?
2 Should hitting or smacking children be banned?
3 Do you think that hitting children makes it easier to become more violent towards them?

A brief review of the law and child abuse

- *1868:* The neglect of children first became an offence when the Poor Law Amendment Act made it illegal not to provide food, housing or medical aid for one's child. However, the main aim was to save the ratepayers money by not having these children looked after by the local authorities.

- *1884:* Violence and poor treatment of children led to the founding of the National Society for the Prevention of Cruelty to Children (NSPCC).

- *1889:* The Prevention of Cruelty and Protection of Children Act provided legal protection for children against cruelty and permitted the removal of children to a place of safety

- *1908:* A Children's Act marked the first time when children were treated differently from adults.

- *1933:* Ill treatment and neglect became criminal offences.

- *1946*: The Curtis Report revealed the shortcomings in existing childcare provision.

- *1948*: Local authorities were given the duty to receive a child into care when the child was orphaned, or the parent was unable to look after the child, or ill treated him/her.

- *1952*: The children's departments of local authorities were required by law to investigate cases of cruelty or neglect.

- *1963*: The departments were to work with families to prevent possible abuse or neglect.

- *1969*: The Children and Young Persons' Act gave yet more powers to the local authorities, particularly in their legal rights to take children into care.

- *1989*: A major piece of legislation, the Children Act, attempted to draw together a range of existing legislation relating to the welfare of children. Guidance was produced in the form of *Working Together Under the Children Act 1989* to promote good practice and interagency collaboration.

- *1998*: The White Paper *Modernising Social Services* launched the Quality Protects programme to improve services for children.

- *1999*: *Working Together to Safeguard Children* was published. This updated previous guidance and was intended to strengthen interagency working.

- *2000*: *Safeguarding Children Involved in Prostitution* was published. This reflected the recognition that children working as prostitutes should wherever possible be treated as victims of sexual abuse, not as criminals.

The role of social services departments and other agencies

Social services departments have a statutory duty (one based in law) to look after children and protect them if they are suffering harm. Authorities are required to adopt an interagency approach to child protection. This means that social workers will work closely with health, education and specially trained police officers. Interagency working has been increasingly emphasised since the Children Act 1989. This was in an attempt to prevent mistakes being made by professionals from different agencies, who did not co-ordinate their services or communicate properly with one another. It was also designed to prevent children having to tell their stories repeatedly to different professionals.

In the majority of cases the social services intervene when abuse is reported to them, and deal with it in a number of ways, including:

- *Monitoring:* This can take the form of social workers informally visiting possible problem families and keeping an eye on the situation. However, parents have the legal right to refuse entry to their home. An alternative form of monitoring is to have the parents see the social worker at the local social services department on a regular basis.

- *Family centres:* These are centres where parents can go to have their parenting skills assessed, to develop their skills and receive counselling.
- *Referral to specialist agencies:* Social services may enlist the help of Child Guidance Clinics or other specialists in helping to understand the causes and extent of any abuse. Such centres may provide more in-depth counselling and help.
- *Child Protection Register:* Where the social workers are concerned about the possibilities of child abuse or neglect, they will instigate a Child Protection Conference which will decide whether the child should be put on the Child Protection Register for that area. This is a list of all children/families where the local social services department and/or other professionals feel there is sufficient evidence for close scrutiny of the family to be necessary, and so a formal record is kept of the condition of the child. Once included on the register, the child and their family's situation must be reviewed regularly and appropriate action taken to reduce the risk to the child's welfare. If children are seen as no longer being at risk, they must be removed from the register.
- *Legal action:* Children at risk can be taken into care, either with the parent's consent or via a Care Order. They would ordinarily be placed either with a foster family or in a residential children's home. Sometimes it is considered appropriate to make the children subjects of a Supervision Order – a formal and enforceable way of working with the family and checking on a child's welfare.

Definition

Child Protection Register – children are put on to this if there is good reason for social services to believe that they are in danger from abuse

---

The child protection register

The table below shows a significant reduction in the number of registrations after 1991. This reflects a change in how 'children at risk' were defined. Previously, a category of 'grave concern' was used. This was then dropped, as it was seen as too vague and as encouraging children to remain on the register even though there was little evidence of significant harm. An estimated 160,000 children per year are subject to child protection enquiries. Over half of them receive no further services or intervention once these enquiries are finished. About 20 per cent of children are registered more than once.

Registrations, de-registrations and numbers on the child protection register at 31 March, 1988 to 1998, England

	On the register at 31 March	Registrations during the year	De-registrations during the year
			numbers
1990	43,600	26,900	24,200
1991	45,300	28,300	26,700
1994	34,900	28,500	26,200
1995	35,000	30,400	30,200
1998	31,600	30,000	30,200

Source: Department of Health, *The Children Act Report 1995–1999* (The Stationery Office, 2000)

1 Why do you think there is an emphasis on avoiding putting children on the Child Protection Register unnecessarily?

2 Why is it important to deregister children if there is no further evidence of risk?

3 What happened to the numbers on the register after 1991?

4 Is the register static or does it change in any one year? Explain your answer.

5 What percentage of children are registered more than once?

Reasons for registration on child protection registers

Percentage of registrations to child protection registers during the years ending 31 March 1994 to 1998, by category of abuse

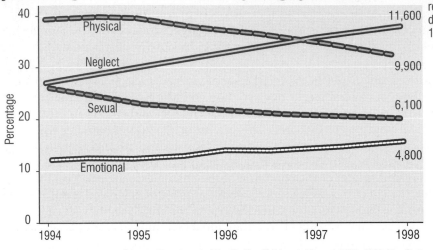

Number of children registered during 1997/98

11,600

9,900

6,100

4,800

Source: Department of Health, *The Children Act Report 1995–1999* (The Stationery Office, 2000)

1 What was the most common cause of registration in 1998?

2 What was the least common?

3 Which forms of abuse are declining and which increasing?

4 How do you think it is possible to measure 'emotional' abuse?

Criticisms of social services departments

Social services departments and other agencies have been severely criticised both for failing to intervene when necessary and for intervening too much. Commonly cited problems include:

- lack of training
- lack of communication
- an emphasis on decisions regarding registration rather than providing support to disadvantaged families
- a decline in the effectiveness of interagency collaboration once child protection plans have been drawn up
- inconsistent approaches to the use of child protection registers
- inadequate assessments
- uncertainty about how to interpret categories such as emotional abuse.

One area of concern has been the degree to which children may be repeatedly deregistered and reregistered. Although sometimes this might be appropriate if the child's circumstances change, it can also suggest that reregistration is necessary because the relevant agencies have failed to improve their family situation.

A case study

Report says Rikki case was bungled

An independent report into the Rikki Neave tragedy today condemned social services in Cambridgeshire for its handling of the case.

The Bridge Child Care Development Service was brought in to investigate the circumstances surrounding the death of the six-year-old Peterborough boy in November 1994.

Rikki's mother Ruth, 28, was cleared of his murder in October last year, but was jailed for seven years for cruelty to her son. He had been strangled.

The full version of the Bridge report was being published at midday today, but a leaked report claimed its main findings were that:

- social services failed to intervene when signs that the Neave children were being abused came to light;

- reports were often illegible and badly filed;
- staff failed to compare notes on the family and draw appropriate conclusions;
- social workers failed to connect Mrs Neave's hostility to them to her behaviour towards her children.

The report was compiled after case records were reviewed, and 17 past and present social services staff involved with the Neave family were interviewed. The Bridge report recommended a 29-point action plan including specialist training of child care staff, improved field care, monitoring the outcome of family support, investigating parents hostile to support staff, improving case management and better allocation of resources.

Ted Unsworth, Director of Social Services, said: 'This has been an in-depth and thorough investigation which identified a number of criticisms of management and practices in the period up to the tragic death of Rikki Neave.

'But we have gone through a period of considerable change since then and I am encouraged that our own internal investigation had identified the same issues as the Bridge Report has highlighted.'

He added: 'Child protection is one of the most difficult and challenging services facing local authorities. On a daily basis we are successfully looking after more than 800 vulnerable children and it is important that the public has confidence in our ability to provide services of the best quality.'

The Government Social Services Inspectorate will send a hit squad of inspectors to carry out an audit of social services in the spring giving the council three months to implement the recommendations.

Source: Adapted from an article by Julia Coffey and Glenn Thwaites in the *Cambridge Evening News*, 9 January 1997

1 Does the case outlined in the article above show that the problems of how social services deal with child abuse have been sorted out? Explain your answer.

2 Do you think there will ever be a completely failsafe child protection system? Explain your answer.

3 In small groups discuss how you would ensure that the problem of child abuse could be eliminated.

Who abuses?

It is generally the case that sexual abuse of children is the result of the activities of the father/stepfather or another male close to the child. However, the statistics of abuse are notoriously unreliable, as there appears to be widespread abuse of children by other males outside the family. The explanation appears to be that when children are asked about an act of abuse they indicate a wide range of activities which occur in public, such as indecent exposure. However, when it comes to sexual interference, then it is far more likely to be a close male relative.

Approximately 30 per cent of cases of sexual abuse are committed by young people under the age of 21. In a study by Horne in Liverpool, 34 per cent of allegations concerning sexual abuse of young children consisted of young persons abusing another child.

Reasons for abuse

It is often very difficult to determine the reasons for abuse, and it is seldom easy to single out one factor. As with domestic violence, explanations can be mainly classified as individual or structural.

Individual explanations

- Abusers are disturbed or sick.
- Abusers have poor childcare skills.
- Abusers may have problems with drugs or alcohol.
- Abusers may have been abused themselves whilst children.

Structural explanations:

- Most sexual abuse is committed by men, therefore gender roles which legitimate male power may be responsible.
- Some studies link physical abuse with poverty, suggesting that the stress of coping on a low income may lead people to take it out on their children.

How is abuse spotted?

Incidences of child abuse generally come to light in one or more of the following ways:

- *Visit to the doctor:* Doctors and nurses are trained to spot signs of possible abuse. These can include physical and behavioural signs in girls and boys.
- *Health visitors:* Health visitors are also specially trained to be aware of warning signs when visiting children and families.
- *NAI register:* Every hospital Accident and Emergency Unit keeps a Non-Accidental Injuries (NAI) register, which they pass to the social services. The medical staff will judge the type and extent of injury against the explanation offered by the parent. Most Accident and Emergency Units also keep a check on the frequency of visits of children for treatment.
- *Neighbours and relatives:* People close to the family concerned may contact the social services to voice their concerns.
- *Childline:* This is a free, direct and confidential telephone service which children can use to inform others of abuse against them (0800 1111).
- *Schools and educational welfare officers:* Abuse is often seen by teachers in school, either through physical signs or through disruptive behaviour. In particular, Educational Welfare Officers may be called in to discuss the issue with the child, and to liaise with the social services. Usually the referral would go straight to the social services.
- *Nurseries and childminders:* People who look after under-5s often notice suspicious signs in children. Guidelines require them to report child abuse.
- *The role of the NSPCC:* The National Society for the Prevention of Cruelty to Children is an independent, charitable organisation, which is recognised as having great expertise in the area of child abuse. The NSPCC is given specific independent powers to investigate child abuse, and works in harmony with the social services, whilst maintaining its independence.

Activities

1 Contact your local branch of the NSPCC. Ask a representative to visit your institution. Perhaps you could offer some fundraising activity in return. Use the opportunity to devise a list of questions about the work of the NSPCC, and about the causes of child abuse and the best way to combat it.
2 On the internet, locate Kids Zone, the children's section of the NSPCC website: www.nspcc.org.uk. Look at the contents.
    a) Why do you think children need their own section of the website?
    b) Why do you think children need their own helplines?

Main points

▶ Child abuse is another serious problem within the family.
▶ The main forms of child abuse are physical, sexual, emotional and neglect.
▶ There have been several well-publicised deaths of children which have resulted in public inquiries.
▶ There are different views on why people abuse their children.
▶ If child abuse is suspected, child protection services become involved.
▶ Although social services departments are very important within child protection, in recent years there has been a greater emphasis on interagency co-operation. This can include a range of agencies such as health care professionals and the police.
▶ If children are at risk of significant harm, they will be put on the child protection register.

▸ Families on the register must be reviewed regularly.

▸ Social services are often criticised for not providing enough support to families.

Fostering and adoption

As we have seen elsewhere, the number of children going into residential care has dropped quite significantly over the last fifteen years. Consequently, there has been a corresponding development of fostering and adoption services.

Fostering

In certain circumstances, social services departments may have to take the responsibility for the care of children. This can occur because:

● the parent or parents are unable to look after the child
● there is evidence of abuse
● there is evidence of neglect.

Traditionally, children who had family difficulties were placed in children's homes and were likely to stay there until adolescence. However, there has been a significant movement away from this. Now it is normal for these children to be looked after by **foster carers** on a short-term or long-term basis. The essence of foster care is that children are placed with carers who try to treat them as part of the family, giving them stability and affection. Foster carers receive an allowance from the social services department, which covers their expenses and a relatively small amount for their caring activities. Specialist foster carers, for example for particularly difficult and/or complex cases, are recruited and paid a greater 'wage'.

> ### Definition
>
> **Fostering** – where children are cared for by a family other than their own who are paid by the social services. It is not intended to be a long-term arrangement

Following the Children Act 1989, all children in local authority foster care are 'looked after', mainly under the following circumstances:

● accommodated (a voluntary arrangement with parents)
● in care – on a Care Order obtained from going to court
● remanded/detained on another order.

Fostering is considered superior to residential care in a number of respects:

● It does not institutionalise the child.
● It is more like a normal family situation.
● There is greater opportunity for the child to develop a personal relationship with the foster parents than with a worker in a children's home.
● The foster family is more flexible and is there all the time, as opposed to the work patterns of employees in residential accommodation, who will work in shifts.
● Foster families are considerably cheaper for social services departments.

Types of fostering

Fostering may be on either a long- or short-term basis.

● *Long-term fostering:* As implied by the name, the child lives in the foster family as if it were her/his own family. However, the child remains under the authority of the social services department, and the foster parents have no legal rights unless they adopt the child.
● *Short-term fostering:* This is an increasingly common activity. Where social workers decide to intervene in a family and take the child out of the situation, the foster carers may be asked to care for the child temporarily while the

social workers attempt to sort out the family problems. Short-term fostering includes:

— *emergency fostering*, where foster carers are able to take on children in an emergency for a short period

— *relief fostering*, where the foster carers take children in order to give the natural parents a respite from caring. This occurs in situations where the behaviour or the health of the child places particularly great demands on the parents. It does not mean that the natural parents are unable to cope, merely that they have a break.

Fostering can also be a 'bridging' arrangement. This is when a child is with foster carers prior to a move to a permanent home, either with those carers (as adopters) or others. Preparation for the permanent move is carried out during this period.

Foster carers need to be prepared to meet and work with the child's natural parents as, under the Children Act 1989, parents of children in care retain parental responsibility and should be allowed contact with their children if it is considered in the child's best interest.

Out of their families: children looked after by the State

Children looked after at 31 March by age, sex, placement and legal status, 1998

	Numbers	%
All children	53,300	100
rate per 10,000 children	47	
Sex		
Boys	29,100	55
Girls	24,200	45
Age		
Under 1	1,750	3
1–4	8,700	16
5–9	11,700	22
10–15	21,700	41
16 and over	9,400	18
Placement		
Foster placements	35,100	66
Children's homes	6,500	12
Placed with parents	5,600	11
Placed for adoption	2,500	5
In lodgings, residential employment or living independently	1,200	2
Other placement	2,700	5
Legal Status		
Care Orders	31,900	60
S20 CA 1989 (voluntary agreements)	19,200	36
On remand, committed for trial of detained	610	1
Other legal status	1,700	3

Source: Department of Health, *The Children Act Report 1995–1999* (The Stationery Office, 2000)

1   How many children were being looked after in 1998?

2   What was the most common age for children to be 'looked after'?

3   What was the most common form of placement?

4   What were the two most common grounds for children to be looked after?

Problems with fostering

Even though fostering has been seen as preferable to residential homes, there can still be problems. All fosters carers are trained and vetted before they are allowed to look after children. However, this does not prevent some carers harming the children placed with them.

Dangers even in fostering

Action to end abuse in care

The Government is to change the law to prevent children being placed in the homes of convicted sex offenders after a foster father was jailed for indecent assaults on nine boys in his care.

Roger Saint, who over 18 years was allowed to foster 19 children by six social services departments, was jailed for 6½ years yesterday at Chester crown court. He had admitted 10 charges of indecent assault. Four other charges remain on file. Two of the incidents took place when he was a residential care worker.

It emerged yesterday that four social services departments had allowed him to continue fostering children after they discovered he had a conviction from 1972 for sexually abusing a 12-year-old boy. One of those authorities, Clwyd county council, left him on its panel advising on fostering and adoption for nine years after his record came to light.

Source: *The Guardian*, 24 May 1997

If the child is not happy with the foster family, they can feel very isolated. Not all foster placements work out – 18 per cent of children will experience three or more placements a year. Sometimes children can display very difficult behaviour and foster carers cannot cope. This can result in children having many different placements, which is disruptive for them. If children cannot be returned to their families, then long-term placements are seen as best.

Adopting children

Definition

Adoption – where children from one family legally become the members of a different family

Adoption means to become the permanent, legal parents of a child, as if that child was born to the adults. The process of adopting is a complex business and usually involves fostering on a long-term basis and then, if the social services agree, they will support the legal moves to adopt.

Traditionally, couples adopted newly-born or very young babies. However, with the increase in birth control and abortion, and the increased acceptability of lone mothers keeping their babies, the number of young babies available for adoption has reduced dramatically. Today, children available for adoption are likely to be older and, quite possibly, to have some degree of behavioural problems. This means that it can be harder to find people who are willing to adopt them. Many children can be left in an uncertain position for a very long time.

Just as in the case of foster parents, there are strict criteria about who adopt children. Typically, they have to be a stable couple, who are not too old, and are in good health. Frequently, social services have tried to match children with adoptive parents from a similar ethnic group. However, recently there has been criticism of these practices. It has been argued that it is better for children to be placed for adoption than to be left in insecure situations. Therefore, there has been a move to consider each applicant on an individual basis rather than applying rigid criteria.

The Government has recently drawn up a White Paper *Adoption: A New Approach* (2000). which identifies some of the problems with adoption services and introduces new measures to improve the process. These include:

- setting a target (in 2000) of increasing by 40 per cent by 2005 the number of children being adopted

- investing £66.5 million between 2000 and 2003 in improving adoption services
- establishing an adoption register of children waiting to be adopted and of approved adoptive families
- providing adopted parents with information on the history of the children
- supporting training programmes for social workers
- placing a limit on the decision to adopt of six months.

There has also been a growing tendency for would-be adopters to look further afield for babies, for example in countries like Brazil or Romania. This practice has been clamped down on in recent years, but has not yet been eliminated.

Is it OK to buy babies?

The British couple who adopted twins on the internet have decided not to appeal against a ruling to return the babies to the US.

Mrs Kilshaw and her husband Alan claim they paid a US baby broker £8,200 to adopt the twin girls. The babies were taken by social services in January from a hotel in north Wales where the couple were staying and were placed with foster parents.

Source: *The Guardian*, 12 April 2001

1 Do you think that people should have the right to adopt a child by paying, or just agreeing with the parents to take the child?

2 Do an Internet search to find out more about the case. Do you have sympathy for the Kilshaws?

Main points

▶ Fostering occurs if children cannot be looked after by their families.

▶ It is seen as superior to residential care, so the proportion of children being fostered has risen.

▶ There are different kinds of fostering, including short-term, long-term and specialist.

▶ Long-term fostering is seen as better as it gives children more stability.

▶ If children cannot return to their natural parents, adoption may be considered.

▶ The adoption process has been criticised for imposing rigid criteria and leaving children waiting.

▶ The new White Paper, *Adoption: A New Approach*, is designed to speed up the process and make it fairer.

Children's rights

One of the biggest changes in child welfare services has been the move towards acting in the best interests of the child and listening to the child's views. This reflects an increased awareness of children's rights.

For a long time, children were not really regarded as having any rights. As we have seen, it was not until the nineteenth century that legislation was brought in to protect children. Children were considered to be the property of their parents. From the nineteenth century onwards, legislation began to protect children from cruelty and to remove them from the world of work. Increasingly, the proper place for children was seen as in the family and at school. However, this also made children very dependent on adults to look after them. We now see children as being very different from adults.

From the 1980s onwards, there was much more discussion about children's rights. One of the most important developments in this area was the UN Convention on the Rights of the Child (1989). The UN Convention consists of fifty-four articles, which cover a wide range of issues. They mainly fall into three categories:

- *Provision articles:* These recognise children's social rights, for example regarding health, social security, education, recreation, etc.
- *Protection articles:* These recognise children's rights to be protected from a range of dangers including war, abuse, exploitation and discrimination
- *Participation articles:* These recognise children's civil and legal rights, covering issues such as being consulted, freedom of speech, etc.

Almost all the countries in the world have signed and ratified the UN Convention on the Rights of the Child. Once a country has ratified the Convention, they are obliged to try to implement its principles. Two years after they have ratified it, and every subsequent five years, they have to submit a report to the Committee on the Rights of the Child. This is a UN body, which monitors countries' progress at implementing the Convention and makes recommendations.

The UK ratified the Convention in 1991. The UK argued that the Children Act 1989 meant that its obligations were fulfilled. The Children Act did go a long way towards meeting the requirements of the Convention. It contained three important themes:

- *Accommodation of children's views:* children's views should be listened to when decisions are made concerning their lives and welfare.
- *Recognition of children's capacity for independent activity:* children's views may be listened to, even if their parents disagree, provided children are seen as mature enough.
- *Provisions for older teenagers:* the more mature children become, the more they should be given a degree of independence.

However, it is also argued that the Children Act in itself did not go far enough. Problems include:

- The Children Act only applies to children who are in need or who come to the attention of the State. It does not cover all children.
- It does not extend to education, an area of welfare in which almost all children are involved.
- Although it emphasises listening to children's views, it does not guarantee that they will be followed.

Main points
- Children's rights have become an increasingly important concept in recent years.
- One of the most important policy documents was the UN Convention on the Rights of the Child in 1989.
- Its articles can be grouped into three categories: protection, provision and participation.
- The UK signed and ratified the UN Convention in 1991.
- Countries who ratify the UN Convention are expected to implement its principles. This is monitored at regular intervals.
- In the UK, the Children Act 1989 is the main piece of legislation covering children's welfare, and it reflects many of the UN Convention's aims.
- However, the Children Act only applies to children who come to the attention of the State; it does not apply to all children.

Conclusion

Families underpin much social policy. They provide the majority of welfare in society by taking care of one another. Much policy rests upon the idea of the 'normal' family as being ideal. However, in recent years the family has witnessed many changes. There are numerous types of families and households. Lone-parent families now make up nearly a quarter of all families. Relationships between family members have also changed, with traditional gender roles softening, if not disappearing. Shifts in family roles have led to greater demand for services such as a variety of forms of childcare provision.

The State seeks to encourage certain types of families in its welfare provision. For example, it rewards working families by making sure that they are better off than non-working families. However, it also has to offer support to all kinds of families. This comes not only in the form of financial benefits, but also by the provision of health care, education and housing.

The family is also a place where problems occur. Amongst the most serious are domestic violence and child abuse. Although different explanations exist for each problem, the causes are seldom simple or universal. Addressing problems within the family is a major concern of many welfare agencies, including social services departments, health professionals, the police and voluntary sector bodies, such as the NSPCC. In serious situations, families cannot always stay together, and children may be fostered or adopted by other families.

Welfare directed at the family now needs to pay more attention to the concept of children's rights, instead of treating children as simply the dependants of their parents. Children's rights were given status by the UN Convention on the Rights of the Child. This international treaty has been ratified by the UK and informs important policies towards children's welfare, although there is still progress to be made.

13 CHAPTER SUMMARY

1   The family is very important within health and welfare provision.

2   The family has been subject to many changes in recent years.

3   Changes have mainly taken place within the structure of the family and the relationships of family members.

4   Types of family include nuclear, extended, lone-parent and reconstituted.

5   Problems are often associated with lone-parent families. They are frequently on a low income and require financial benefits, for example.

6   Gender roles are changing. Men now carry out more domestic tasks, although these remain primarily women's responsibilities in most families. The introduction of parental leave reflects these shifts.

7   Sometimes children's roles within the family may not always be what we would expect. They may care for disabled parents, for example.

8   More women going out to work means there is a greater need for childcare services.

9   There are many types of services for both younger and older children, including day nurseries, childminders and after-school clubs.

10   The Welfare State supports the family in a number of ways, including financial benefits and a range of services including help with housing, education and health

11   Lone-parent families are also offered other forms of support, such as the New Deal programme.

12   Families in socially deprived areas may receive additional support, such as the Sure Start initiative.

13   Domestic violence is one of the problems which may occur in families.

14   It is usually men who carry out domestic violence against their wives or partners.

15   Available support includes women's refuges, police intervention, local authority provision and relationship counselling.

16   Violent partners can be excluded from the family home.

17   Child abuse is another serious problem within the family.

18   The main forms of child abuse are physical, sexual, emotional and neglect.

19   If child abuse is suspected, child protection services become involved.

20   If children are at risk of significant harm, they will be put on the child protection register.

21   Fostering occurs if children cannot be looked after by their families.

22   It is seen as superior to residential care, so the proportion of children being fostered has risen.

23   If children cannot return to their natural parents, adoption may be considered.

24   Children's rights have become an increasingly important concept in recent years.

25   One of the most important policy documents was the UN Convention on the Rights of the Child in 1989 and the UK signed and ratified the UN Convention in 1991.

Useful websites

www.doh.gov.uk/qualityprotects: Quality Protects

www.nspcc.org.uk: NSPCC

www.unicef.org: UNICEF

www.the-childrens-society.org.uk: The Children's Society

www.ncb.org.uk: National Children's Bureau

www.crin.org: Children's Rights Information Network

www.child-abuse.com/childhouse: Children's House, an extensive database of resources relating to children

Chapter

14

EQUAL OPPORTUNITIES

Chapter contents

- **Citizenship**

  We begin the chapter by exploring an issue of relevance to both groups discussed here – the nature and rights of citizens.

- **Ethnic minorities and ...**

  - **Racial prejudice** Here we look at the explanations offered for why people should be racist – the answer seems to lie in a combination of economic factors and false beliefs about the nature of UK society.
  - **Health** There are some differences in the health problems faced by ethnic minorities, but these are perhaps only significant in that the NHS has taken some considerable time to recognise the importance of responding to the different health care needs of ethnic minorities.
  - **Employment** There is clear evidence that ethnic minority groups are over-represented in the lower grades and lower-paid areas of employment. They are also more likely to be unemployed. This applies to society as a whole, but also within the health and caring services.
  - **Social services** The relationship between race and the social services is complex and needs clarification. Social services departments have been heavily criticised in the past for ignoring the needs of ethnic minority groups and failing to understand the cultural differences which exist in society.
  - **State benefits** Although there is no evidence that the system deliberately sets out to discriminate, it is suggested that ethnic minority households fare less well from the benefits system.
  - **Poverty** The result of prejudice and a range of other factors is that there is a greater risk that members of the ethnic minorities are more likely to live in poverty than the population in general.
  - **Housing and homelessness** Patterns of housing are extremely interesting. They show wide variations within the different ethnic minorities and between the ethnic minorities and the rest of the population. The reasons for this and the possible consequences are discussed.
  - **Harassment and violence** One frightening aspect of the UK is the existence of violence against ethnic minority members solely on the grounds of race. We look at the extent of this problem and the attempts by police and government to respond.
  - **Legislation** Finally, we explore the legislation which exists in the UK to outlaw racism.

- **Gender and ...**

  - **Caring** We explore the way that women have been expected to be carers and the implications for their lives.
  - **Poverty** A breakdown of all the groups in society reveals one common factor – women are present in a majority in all of them. This section explains why.
  - **Employment** This closely links to the previous two areas. Women have lower status jobs on the whole than men and earn less than they do. The reasons for this, and the consequences are explored here.
  - **Housing** This is a complex area, but it would seem that women are more likely to be in poorer quality housing than men.
  - **State benefits** The original Welfare State was based on the idea that women would not have careers, but would marry and be 'housewives'. This was reflected in the benefit and pension systems. Over time, this has gradually changed, but certainly for older women living on pensions the system has been unfair.
  - **Health and health services** Women live longer than men and are more likely to be the recipients of the health services. We look at the implications. We also note that although women make up a majority of employees of the NHS, they are under-represented in the senior levels of management.
  - **Legislation** Finally, we look at the legislation to combat discrimination against women.

Introduction

The concept of equal opportunities refers to the fact that certain groups are more able than others to obtain a fair share of the benefits available in society. In an unequal society, in which people compete for privilege, status and financial benefits, some groups tend to lose out more than others. These groups include most of those discussed in this book: older people (Chapter 12), disabled people (Chapter 15), mentally-ill people (Chapter 17), poor people (Chapter 4). In this chapter, we focus on two groups which are not specifically covered elsewhere in this book – people from ethnic minority groups and women.

Inequalities tend to cluster together around certain groups. We know, for example, that the overwhelming majority of poor people are women and that the overwhelming majority of disabled people are women, that women form the majority of the very old and that women are more likely to be suffering from forms of mental illness. So, if we talk about poor or disabled people, we are also talking about women.

Similarly, when we look at the situation regarding ethnic minorities in the UK, we see that they are over-represented amongst poor and poorly housed people, yet they arguably receive fewer, or at least less appropriate, benefits and social services than the majority of the population.

This chapter examines the situation of these two underprivileged groups in our society. We start by examining the concept of citizenship – the term used to describe the starting point for any discussion on why anybody should have rights to a decent standard of living or to reasonable health care. What does it mean to be a member (or citizen) of any society? Are there any grounds for women or ethnic minorities reasonably to complain that they suffer more disadvantages than many other groups in society?

We then look specifically at the problems of the ethnic minorities and examine the evidence that they really do suffer greater disadvantage than the majority of the population. The evidence is quite conclusive: ethnic minorities are more likely to be poor, in worse employment, to have specific health and social services needs and to have worse housing conditions. We therefore ask why this is so, and examine the concepts of racism and discrimination. Finally, we note the legislation that has been introduced to combat racism and discrimination.

The chapter then turns to the situation of women in our society, and you may well see the parallels with the situation of ethnic minorities. There are some differences, however. In particular, women in our society are expected to be the carers. This profoundly influences their experience of life and limits them in terms of employment opportunities. It is usually women who disrupt their careers to care for children and sick parents. The section on gender therefore includes a discussion of the caring role of women and its implications. We look at the situation of women regarding employment, poverty, health and housing, amongst other things, and our conclusions are that they still suffer significant discrimination. The chapter then describes the legislation that helps women.

Citizenship

Most people using the term 'citizen' do so with some vague idea that it is linked to the fact of being born in a particular country and having voting rights. But the question asked by social policy analysts is just what exactly does it mean to be the citizen of a country? Is the provision of health and welfare services something that a good government provides when it can, or is that provision somehow a fundamental right of each person in the same way that voting rights and the right to a fair trial are seen as absolutely central to a democracy?

If a government were to say that it had decided that only the people who paid a certain amount of money could vote in local elections in future, then there would be a national outcry as to the unfairness of it. However, if the government says that in future free health care will be restricted to certain groups, or that the State pension will gradually be withdrawn, to what extent do people regard this as an attack on their fundamental rights as citizens?

The classic starting point for the study of the meaning of **citizenship** is the work of T.H. Marshall who suggested three elements to citizenship:

- legal
- political
- social.

<table>
<tr><td>

Definition

Citizenship – the rights and duties of a person of a particular nationality

</td></tr>
</table>

The legal element of citizenship

In the UK today, everyone should have the same rights and obligations under the law. If any person is accused of an offence, the chances of a fair trial should be equal for all. Although there often appears to be a gap between practice and theory, everyone agrees that this is what should happen.

Laws apply equally to all members of society. Legal rights have developed over hundreds of years. Although Magna Carta is supposed to have enshrined the equal legal rights of people for the first time, it seems more accurate to describe the nineteenth century as the period which moved the legal element of citizenship forward most significantly. At this time, there were numerous reforms of the law in an attempt to bring greater justice.

The political element of citizenship

This refers to the democratic rights of voting and free speech. The majority of people over 18 can choose politicians to represent them. People are free to express opinions, within certain limits, and to put themselves forward for election on the basis of those opinions if they so wish. Political rights of citizenship developed through the latter part of the nineteenth and the earlier parts of the twentieth centuries, when first all men could vote and then gradually it was extended to all women.

The social element of citizenship

This is a far more contentious issue, and one which is at the heart of health and welfare provision. To what extent do people have rights as citizens to decent health services, to social security provision and to the support of the personal social services? For many commentators, particularly those from the right of the Conservative Party, people do not necessarily have rights to health and welfare in the same way that they have rights to political and legal equality.

At present there is an ongoing debate about this social element of citizenship. For most people, the right to health care seems to be fully accepted, yet the right to housing or certain social security payments seems to be much more in dispute.

The three elements of citizenship

1 What do you think – do people have a right to free health care and to welfare benefits?

2 If you think so, then why should they have rights to health care, but not to free transport (or free cars), and to free food, entertainment, etc?

3 Should only some people – perhaps the poorest – have a right to health and welfare provision?

Citizenship and equal opportunities

In a society in which all people are accepted as citizens, then there cannot be **discrimination** between different groups. Each individual will have exactly the same rights and cannot be denied them. The debate about discrimination and lack of opportunities is therefore also one about citizenship.

One point needs to be made when reading the following sections. We are not saying that *all* people who belong to ethnic minority groups and all women are disadvantaged in society (although they may face discrimination and **racism**). What the evidence suggests is that women and members of the ethnic minority groups are *more likely* to be disadvantaged in society.

The Human Rights Act

In 1998, the European Convention on Human Rights was incorporated into UK law and came into effect in 2000. The Act will gradually change much of how the UK health, welfare and criminal justice agencies approach their tasks. This is because it sets out a series of 'rights' which people have, and which are enforceable by law. The rights include the:

- right to life
- prohibition of torture
- right to a fair trial
- right to respect for private and family life
- freedom of thought, conscience and religion
- freedom of expression

- freedom of assembly and association
- right to marry
- prohibition of discrimination.

Ethnic minorities

Explanations for racial prejudice

Definitions

Stereotyping – holding negative views about an entire ethnic group

Scapegoating – unfairly blaming a minority group for social or economic problems

Cultural racism – means defining national culture (for example, 'Britishness') in a way which equates this with a dominant ethnic group and which marginalises ethnic minorities

Racial prejudice – when people are liked or disliked solely because they belong to a particular ethnic group

Racial discrimination – when people are treated differently on the grounds of their membership of an ethnic group

As we shall see reading the evidence, there is still considerable discrimination and prejudice against members of the ethnic minorities. A number of explanations have been suggested as to why people can be racially prejudiced, and the two main ones are:

- **stereotyping**
- **scapegoating**.

Stereotyping

This occurs because many white people perceive African-Caribbean and Asian people, for example, as having negative characteristics – noisy, lazy, mean, etc. All the people sharing a similar skin, culture or religion are portrayed this way. Stereotyping allows people to treat the stereotyped group in a worse way without feeling guilty about it: 'Why should I give him the job? Everyone knows those people are lazy.' Stereotyped views amongst British people derive from our colonial past, when all people from the colonies, but especially Africans and Asians were regarded as inferior. Today, such views are usually based on ignorance, but stereotyping continues in some jokes and in media images of ethnic minorities, despite it being unlawful.

Scapegoating

During periods of economic decline or social tension, people search for simple, clear answers to the problems facing them. Blaming an easily identifiable group, especially if it is powerless and can do little to challenge the way in which blame is placed upon them, is a common occurrence. When there is great prosperity, the powerless group may still be regarded as inferior, but social tensions are less. Scapegoating occurs particularly over scarce resources such as jobs, housing and education.

Ethnic minorities and health

As a result of concern about racism in the health services, the King's Fund, an independent but very influential body concerned with health issues, set up a task force to help promote models of good practice and to combat racism. However, although most health authorities and trusts have committed themselves to combat racism, according to the King's Fund, they have failed to follow this up with a programme of action.

Definition

Institutional racism – how the standard practices, operations and cultures of organisations can discriminate, sometimes unintentionally, against ethnic minorities

It has been argued that the health-providing organisations tend to assume that the provision of health care is the same for any group, independent of their background, and this indirectly assures many people from ethnic minorities a lower or inappropriate standard of service. This is an example of **institutional racism,** that is, where the normal practices of an organisation can lead to ethnic minorities being discriminated against.

Ethnicity and health

The poorer health of ethnic minority groups in the UK appears to be closely related to their higher levels of poverty and poorer standards of housing. In a study of over 500 children in inner London suffering from respiratory tract infections and gastro-enteritis, over 48 per cent were from Asian, African or Caribbean families, although these represented only 18 per cent of the population of the area.

Specific health problems of ethnic minority groups include:

- sickle cell disease, a form of anaemia which mainly affects African-Caribbean people
- rickets, which are more likely amongst Asian people
- tuberculosis, particularly amongst those with the worst housing conditions.

Ethnic minority groups also have a very low take-up of ante-natal and post-natal services.

Health and ethnicity

The diagram below shows the differences in health between the majority population 'Whites' and various ethnic groups. The short horizontal line for each ethnic group is the average and the vertical line is the spread of responses for that particular ethnic group. The higher the average the worse the health.

Relative risk of reporting fair or poor health compared with Whites (age and gender standardised)

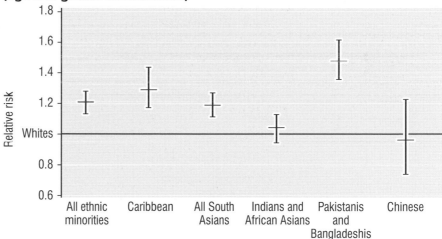

Source: T. Mamood *et al.*, *Ethnic Minorities in Britain* (Policy Studies Institute, 1997)

1 Which group consistently shows the highest levels of poor health?

2 Which ethnic minority group exhibits the best health?

3 Compared to the 'White' category, what is the level of health of the ethnic minorities?

Ethnicity and mental health

There is clear evidence to show that rates of mental illness are significantly higher for African-Caribbean-born males than for the British-born population. Rates are also higher for Indian, African, Pakistani and African-Caribbean females than for British-born females.

Of those attending hospitals as in-patients, Indian males were found to be three times more likely than British-born people to be diagnosed as schizophrenic, and African-Caribbean males and females five times more likely.

Comparing British-born Blacks against British-born Whites aged 16–19, Harrison found that the Blacks were sixteen times more likely to be diagnosed as schizophrenic. It is thought that this may be partly explained by misdiagnosis due to lack of understanding of cultural behaviour.

Ethnic minorities and employment

All studies conducted over the last twenty-five years have shown consistently that the members of the ethnic minorities are more likely to be in lower paid employment, to have lower levels of promotion and to be in lower grades of employment than their qualifications would suggest. These patterns appear across all areas of employment, and are just as true for the health, welfare and criminal justice services as they are for all other areas.

Levels of responsibility by ethnic group

Managerial responsibility of employees: by gender and ethnic group, Spring 2000, Great Britain

Percentages

	White	Black	Indian	Pakistani/ Bangladeshi	Other	All employees
Males						
Managers	23	13	17	12	21	23
Foremen and supervisors	12	11	8	–	11	12
Not managers, foremen or supervisors	65	76	75	81	68	65
All employees (=100%)(millions)	12.0	0.2	0.2	0.1	0.1	12.6
Females						
Managers	14	12	10	–	12	14
Foremen and supervisors	11	14	13	–	13	11
Not managers, foremen or supervisors	74	75	77	82	76	74
All employees (=100%)(millions)	10.7	0.2	0.2	0.1	0.1	11.2

Source: Labour Force Survey, Office for National Statistics

Source: Social Trends 31 (The Stationery Office, 2001)

1 What proportion of white males were in management?

2 Does any other group of males achieve the same levels of responsibility?

3 Which group of males had the highest levels in 'not managers' category?

4 Overall, what statement can you make about the relationship between employment level and ethnicity for males?

5 Which group of females had the highest proportion in management?

6 Which has the highest in 'not managers'?

7 Overall, what statement can you make about the relationship between employment level and ethnicity for females?

Incidentally, what statement can you make about gender and employment level?

Inequalities in employment in the NHS

Doctors

The Commission for Racial Equality conducted a study which indicated that doctors from ethnic minority groups suffered from poorer training, lower promotion prospects and lower pay than Whites. They were also more likely to be found in the lower prestige areas of mental health and geriatrics.

Nurses

African-Caribbean and Asian nurses form approximately 10–15 per cent of nurses in the UK, yet there were less than half this figure in more senior positions. Like the doctors, the nurses are more likely to be working in mental health and geriatrics.

In 2001, the government was so concerned about the situation, that it required all NHS organisations to set targets for the recruitment of staff from a number of ethnic minority backgrounds into areas of NHS employment where they are currently under-represented, and for at least 7 per cent of senior management to be from ethnic minority backgrounds by 2004.

Ethnic minorities and social services

People from African-Caribbean backgrounds are under-represented as clients receiving the preventive and supportive elements of social services provision, but over-represented in those aspects of social services activities which involve what are generally known as 'social control functions', such as supervision orders and sectioning (for mental illness).

Children in the care of social services

Furthermore, a substantially higher proportion of children from African-Caribbean backgrounds are taken into care each year compared to the majority of the population. When the reasons for the referrals to the social services departments are looked at more closely, children from African-Caribbean backgrounds are more likely to be referred because of family relationships, financial reasons and the mother's mental health problems, while white children are more likely to be referred for behavioural problems and sexual abuse.

However, it is not just that there are differences in the numbers of children taken into care and the reasons for it; evidence from a study by Barn suggests that children from African-Caribbean backgrounds are likely to enter care or receive supervision orders more speedily than those from white backgrounds, suggesting that possibly less preventive work is done here.

Ethnic minorities and State benefits

Although there is absolutely no evidence that ethnic minorities are treated any differently from other groups, there is some evidence to suggest that the way the system is designed disadvantages some members of the ethnic minorities.

State benefits tend to fall into two types – those based on National Insurance contributions and those which are more of a safety-net benefit. Members of the ethnic minorities are more likely to be receiving these safety-net benefits. The result of this is that ethnic minority households which are receiving State benefits are worse-off than white households.

Ethnicity and State benefits

Benefits received by adults in households with no earner

column percentages

	White	Caribbean	Indian/ African Asian	Pakistani/ Bangladeshi
Child benefit	14	29	31	50
One-parent benefit	3	11	2	1
Disability living allowance	8	5	10	6
State pension	43	19	12	6
Unemployment benefit	4	6	6	10
Invalidity benefit	6	7	7	5
Income support	24	44	39	50
Housing benefit	33	63	26	31
Weighted count	1700	420	426	609
Unweighted count	1111	220	221	420

Source: T. Mamood *et al.*, *Ethnic Minorities in Britain* (Policy Studies Institute, 1997)

1 Which groups receive the highest percentage of Child Benefit?

2 Child Benefit is given to all families with children in full-time education. What do you think this tells us about families of Pakistani/Bangladeshi origins? What implications might that have for the social/educational and health services?

3 Which group has the highest levels of State pension? Everyone over retirement age is entitled to this, so why is it higher for this group?

4 Which group has the highest level of Housing Benefit? (Housing Benefit is a benefit for those with low income in rented accommodation.) What does this imply for the housing patterns of this group compared to others?

5 Income Support has now been replaced by Jobseekers Allowance. Income Support was the safety-net benefit given to those who could not claim any higher paying benefits such as Unemployment Benefit. Which groups had the highest levels of Income Support claims, and what might this imply for their standards of living?

Ethnic minorities and poverty

Poverty is indirectly related to race, in that members of the ethnic minority groups are more likely to be found in low-paying occupations, to have higher levels of unemployment and, amongst African-Caribbeans, to have higher rates of lone-parent families, whilst Bangladeshi and Pakistani families tend to have higher than average numbers of children.

The low paid, large families, lone-parent households and the unemployed form virtually all the groups living in poverty. The only significant group in poverty amongst which ethnic minorities do not figure disproportionately is older people. This is because of the age structure of the ethnic minorities, which has relatively few older people compared to the general population of the UK.

Definition

Households below average income (HBAI) – a commonly used measurement of poverty

Ethnicity and poverty

The table below shows the percentage of the each ethnic group who have incomes below half the average UK income. This measure (known as **Households below average income [HBAI]**) is the most commonly used measure of poverty.

Households below average income

column percentages

	White	Caribbean	Indian	African Asian	Pakistani	Bangladeshi	Chinese
Below half average	28	41	45	39	82	84	34

Source: adapted from T. Mamood *et al.*, *Ethnic Minorities in Britain* (Policy Studies Institute, 1997)

1 Which groups had the highest percentage of people below average income?

2 Which groups had the lowest percentage of people below average income?

3 Overall, can you make any statement about the link between ethnicity and income?

Ethnicity and unemployment

Economic activity by ethnic group; Great Britain; autumn 2000, not seasonally adjusted

	ILO unemployment rate (%) all 16+
All groups	
White	4.9
All ethnic minority groups	12
Black	15
Indian	8
Pakistani/Bangladeshi	17
Chinese	*
Other origins	12

Source: adapted from *Labour Market Trends*, Vol. 109, No. 3, March 2001

1 Which two groups had the highest unemployment rates?

2 Which two groups had the lowest unemployment rates?

3 What implications might there be for receiving State benefits and pensions? (Remember the distinction between benefits based on National Insurance contributions and those 'safety-net' benefits, plus the fact that employment allows savings and private pensions.)

Ethnic minorities, housing and homelessness

The general low standards of income and disadvantage suffered by ethnic minorities is reflected in the relative quality of their housing standards. Overall, members of the ethnic minorities are more likely to live in poor quality housing and, with the exception of those from the Indian backgrounds, are more likely to rent. Ethnic minority members are more likely to live in older, terraced housing than the majority population and are more likely to live in overcrowded conditions.

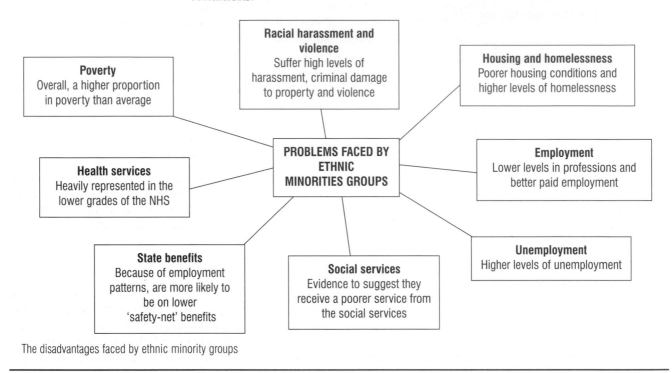

The disadvantages faced by ethnic minority groups

Ethnicity and housing quality

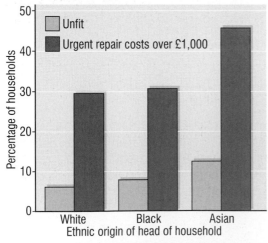

Households living in poor conditions, by ethnic origin, England, 1996

Source: K. Revell and P. Leather, *Housing in the UK* (The Policy Press, 2000)

1 In 1996, which ethnic group lived in households with the highest level of urgent repairs needed?

2 Which ethnic group were most likely to live in households considered 'unfit'? (See page 130 for a definition of 'unfit'.)

3 Look at the main text. Which groups are most likely to own their own homes and which are most likely to rent?

4 How does this bear out the claims of those who say that people from African-Caribbean backgrounds have the worst local authority housing?

Local authority housing

Traditionally local authority housing stock has been the means by which the lowest paid could obtain accommodation. However, the 'right-to-buy' legislation (see Chapter 5) has led to the sale of over one and a half million local authority houses.

This has taken away the opportunity for the poorest in society to obtain housing and, as ethnic minority groups are over-represented among the poorest, they have been particularly hard hit. Most noticeable has been the over-representation of African-Caribbeans among those in, or seeking, local authority accommodation.

Various studies by the Commission for Racial Equality (CRE) have suggested that white tenants have been given a disproportionate number of the better quality properties, and in particular, Bangladeshis were allocated the worst accommodation, and to the worst estates.

Ethnicity and housing associations

In order to combat the perceived problems faced by ethnic minority groups, the Federation of Black Housing Organisations was set up. This promotes the interests of black and Asian communities to housing organisations and monitors the extent to which housing associations cater for black and Asian tenants.

By the mid-1990s there were sixty-six ethnic housing associations registered with the Housing Corporation, as a result of the initiative mentioned earlier. These have been successful in providing specialist accommodation, catering for the specific needs of the ethnic minorities, which they can identify more easily than traditional organisations.

Homelessness

Ethnic minority groups are four times more likely than white households to become homeless. Of the young homeless, a study of a number of London boroughs found that young people of African-Caribbean origin – particularly lone-parent females – were disproportionately over-represented and in Newham (East London), for example, over 50 per cent of referrals to hostels for the homeless were for single people of African-Caribbean origin.

Ethnic minorities, harassment and violence

When a crime is committed, it is difficult to decide if it is racially motivated or for some other reason. However, 8 per cent of Pakistanis, 5 per cent of Indians, 4 per cent of African-Caribbeans and 1 per cent of Whites said they had experienced one or more racially-motivated offence.

Racial attacks and harassment

Proportion of offences seen as racially motivated, by ethnic group and type of offence, 1995

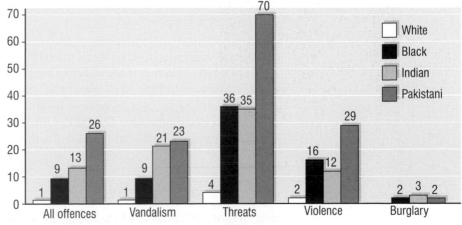

Note: The numbers for Bangladeshis were too small for detailed analysis.

Source: *Racial Attacks and Harassment* (CRE Factsheet, 1999)

1   What percentage of offences of violence against Indians were perceived as racially motivated?

2   Which group overall sees the offences against it as racially motivated?

3   Which group overall sees the lowest percentage against it as racially motivated?

4   How might the person know or guess that the offence was racially motivated? (Look at the categories of offences and at the main text.)

Combating racial crime

As a result of the increasing amount, or at least awareness, of crimes carried out because of racial hatred (increasingly known as 'hate crimes'), in 1998 legislation was introduced which made crimes of violence, criminal damage or harassment more serious ('aggravated') if they included a racial motive. A racial motive is defined as:

'Any incident in which it appears to the reporting or investigating officer that the complaint involves an element of racial motivation; or any incident which includes an allegation of racial motivation made by any person.'

A person charged and found guilty of racially aggravated crimes would receive more serious punishment for the offence.

Ethnic minorities and legislation

1976 Race Relations Act

The 1976 Race Relations Act made it illegal to discriminate directly or indirectly in the provision of goods or services to the public or in the areas of employment and housing. It also became illegal to incite racial hatred.

As part of the Act, the Commission for Racial Equality (CRE) was set-up with a range of powers. The CRE can bring people to court for cases of both:

- direct discrimination (for example, when a person is denied employment because she is black)
- indirect discrimination (where, for example, an organisation creates rules which apply to everyone, but the result of the rules is that certain ethnic groups are particularly disadvantaged).

The CRE:

- is funded by the Home Office. The Home Secretary appoints its commissioners from a wide range of ethnic groups and backgrounds. The CRE's job is to advise people who believe they have suffered racial discrimination. It also provides legal representation for them in a court or an industrial tribunal
- can take action on its own if it perceives something to be discriminatory (for example, advertisements). It can investigate organisations where racial bias might have occurred. It also advises employers, trade unions, health and local authorities about how to combat racial discrimination
- issues codes of practice on how to promote equality of opportunity and eliminate discrimination. The CRE, with the support of local authorities, also funds a network of Racial Equality Councils.

Activity

You will find that there is a Racial Equality Council in your area. Find the address through the Commission for Equal Opportunities website www.cre.gov.uk and invite a representative to visit your group to discuss issues of racism in the UK today.

In 2000, the 1976 Act was amended to become more powerful. It required all public bodies such as local authorities or the NHS, to actively promote race equality, by placing a legal duty upon them to do so.

Main points ▶ According to Marshall, there are three elements to citizenship: legal, political and social.

▶ Certain groups, including women and ethnic minorities, have not achieved their full rights as citizens.

▶ Racial prejudice can be explained by a mixture of economic factors and cultural factors.

▶ There is some evidence that ethnic minorities do not obtain equal share of resources in the NHS.

▶ Ethnic minorities have higher rates of certain illnesses, including mental disorders.

▶ Ethnic minorities are over-represented in the lower grades of the NHS.

▶ Ethnic minority members have a higher chance of being in poverty than the majority of the population.

▶ There are noticeable differences between ethnic groups and housing conditions.

▶ Ethnic minorities are the subject of racially motivated attacks.

▶ Legislation protects the rights of ethnic minorities.

Gender

The second group of people for whom there is legislation to ensure that their citizenship rights are fully met are women. Historically, men have dominated the positions of power in society, and have denied equal rights to women. The last thirty-five years in particular have seen women battling to gain equal rights, and achieving some degree of success. This success has largely been the result of the feminist movement which has argued for women's rights and pointed to the patriarchal nature of UK society.

The term 'feminism' did not really exist before the twentieth century, certainly not in everyday language. An organised women's movement first developed in the mid-nineteenth century. The first signs of this were in 1848 when a Women's Rights Convention was held in Seneca Falls, New York. This was led by female anti-slavery campaigners who felt that women were not being treated equally in this movement. This period from the mid-nineteenth to the early twentieth century is often referred to as the 'first wave' of feminism.

This first wave took its most public form in the suffragette movement which first appeared in America in the 1850s and emerged in the UK a few years later. This movement lasted in the UK until the First World War, shortly after which women won the right to vote.

When women first won the right to vote

1893: New Zealand	1919: United States of America
1902: Australia	1928: United Kingdom (for all adult women)
1917: Soviet Union	1945+: France, Italy, Ireland
1918: United Kingdom (for women aged 30 or over)	1973: Switzerland

The term 'first wave' distinguishes this earlier feminist movement from the re-emergence in feminist thought and activity which took place, particularly in the 1960s. In fact, the term 'feminism' only became part of everyday language in the 1960s, and it has only been since then that gender differences have been recognised as important. Previously, any differences between men's and women's lives that were recognised at all were assumed to be natural and unproblematic. For example, it was thought that any sexual division of labour (that is, where men and women do different jobs) was a reflection of biological differences (men were naturally stronger and more competitive than women, women were inclined to caring roles, etc.).

Feminists have pointed out many ways in which the role of women has been limited and controlled by men, and the results of these for women's lives.

Gender and caring

Throughout this book we have seen the way in which the woman's role in family is often that of carer. It is usually women who take on the role of looking after children, and older, sick and disabled people. This is largely an unpaid role, but an essential one for the family members and for the wider society. If women did not do this caring, then the State would be forced into finding alternative and expensive ways of doing it.

However, in taking on the role of carer, women generally have to give up full-time employment during the period of their lives when they are bringing up children, for example. They therefore become dependent on their husbands, their partners or the State.

The effect of caring

Thus women continue to care for the young, the old and the dependent, mainly exempting men and state services from these tasks. ... The price of such caring work is economic dependence. Looking after people is either done for no pay, within the family, or for low pay in the public sector ...

The care of most dependants has been the province of women, has belonged to the domestic arena, and has been unpaid. It thus made women dependent.

Source: G. Pascall, *Social Policy: A Feminist Analysis* (Tavistock, 1986)

1 Who does the majority of caring?

2 What is the benefit of this for the State services?

3 What is the impact for those doing the caring?

4 There are three key elements which characterise the care of dependants – what are they?

Gender and poverty

Women form the single largest group of people in poverty. This is often hidden in the way the figures are presented, by dividing the poor into categories such as pensioners, those in full-time employment, lone parents and the sick and disabled. However, all these categories are dominated by women. The only significant group in poverty which is not dominated by women is that of the unemployed. It is important to note, however, that the classification 'the unemployed' refers largely to 'heads of households', which is generally assumed to be the male (a patriarchal assumption? see page 28) and that the benefits they receive such as Job Seeker's Allowance is meant to support a family, which is highly likely to include a non-working woman. Once again, therefore, women are drawn into poverty, although the official statistics do not illustrate this.

Gender and income

The table below shows personal income by sex within each family type.

Mean individual income: by family type and gender, 1998–99, Great Britain

£ per week

	Net income[1]		Disposable income[2]	
	Males	Females	Males	Females
Single people without children	190	165	150	126
Single pensioners	155	132	140	122
Lone parents	–	166	–	142
Couples without children	307	155	263	120
Pensioner couples	203	86	193	76
Couples with children	352	147	296	97
All adults	264	144	224	112

[1] After deduction of income tax and national insurance contributions.
[2] After deduction of income tax, national insurance contributions and further deductions/additions such as childcare and travel to work costs and payments/receipts of maintenance and child support.

Source: Women's Individual Income series, Department of Social Security

Source: *Social Trends 31* (The Stationery Office, 2001)

1 Why are there no figures for the net income and disposable income for male lone parents?

2 Which two family types have the lowest incomes?

3 Which sex always receives a lower income?

4 There are two types of family where we know there is unlikely to be a male in the household. Which two are those and what are the incomes?

Income

Women's incomes are lower than men's across their lifetimes. At certain age ranges, men's incomes are twice that of females, for example, between the ages of 35 and 54, men in couples with dependent children earn about £450–£550 on average, while women in the same family circumstances earn £180–£250 per week. The gaps vary over the lifetime, and the differences are also marked between women. However, over a lifetime men's incomes are much higher than women's incomes on average.

Earnings: the gender divide

Average gross weekly individual income, 1998/99

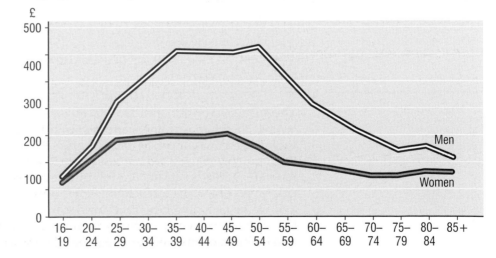

Source: *Women and Men in Britain: The Lifecycle of Inequality*, Equal Opportunities Commission (EOC) factsheet. Crown copyright ©

1 Which group had the higher income?

2 At what ages were there the smallest gaps? Suggest why this might be.

3 At what ages approximately were the largest gaps? How much were these approximately?

4 Suggest any explanations why the largest gaps should be over these ages.

Gender and employment

Women are less likely than men to be in full-time employment, and are more likely to have lower-paid, less secure positions. They are also less likely to be found in the senior positions in employment. This is just as true for areas of employment which are traditionally associated with women, such as nursing or social work.

The affluent and the poor

Highest and lowest paid occupations;[a] Great Britain; April 2000

	Average gross weekly pay (£)
Highest paid	
1 Treasurers and company financial managers	1,059.0
2 Medical practitioners	963.5
3 Organisation and methods and work study managers	812.8
4 Management consultants, business analysts	812.2
5 Underwriters, claims assessors, brokers, investment analysts	775.4
6 Police officers (inspector and above)	765.7
7 Computer systems and data processing managers	756.9
8 Solicitors	748.4
9 Marketing and sales managers	718.9
10 Advertising and public relations managers	689.9
Lowest paid	
1 Kitchen porters, hands	184.1
2 Bar staff	184.3
3 Retail cash desk and check-out operators	184.7
4 Petrol pump forecourt attendants	189.0
5 Waiters, waitresses	189.2
6 Hairdressers, barbers	190.1
7 Launderers, dry cleaners, pressers	195.8
8 Counterhands, catering assistants	196.1
9 Other childcare and related occupations n.e.c.	204.6
10 Educational assistants	211.8

Note: a Full-time employees on adult rates, whose pay for the survey period was unaffected by absence

Source: New Earnings Survey

Source: Labour Market Trends, March 2001

What does this table tell us about the situation of women in Britain? (Think about the types of job women do.)

The main reason for the differences in employment patterns (and to a large extent, therefore, income patterns) is the role of childcaring which women undertake. For example, by the age of 25–34, over 77 per cent of men are in full-time employment, so too are women without children, but only 21 per cent of mothers in this age group are full-time employees. The rest are either part-time employees or looking after children. It is during this period that careers are made, and women left out of the 'race' for better jobs suffer the consequences later. The lower pay of women as a result of this impacts upon their level of savings, and will also limit their pensions later in life (as pensions are usually related to salaries).

Women and citizenship

[regarding] ... the welfare state, women have access to fewer resources than do men because of the assumptions of female dependency that are built into the system and the way that eligibility for benefits is tied to male patterns of employment. It is that which has led feminists ... to argue that women are denied full citizenship rights because these rights are earned through participation in full-time, lifelong employment, a pattern which, until recently characterised men's but not women's working lives.

Source: N. Charles, *Feminism, the State and Social Policy* (Macmillan, 2000)

1 Do women get more or fewer resources from the Welfare State?

2 What is the system of eligibility to benefits based on?

3 Does the author believe that women are treated as true citizens?

4 How does this link to our discussion of citizenship on pages 377–80?

Gender and housing

The single biggest obstacle for women to overcome in obtaining decent housing if they are single or separated is that of income. Access to a mortgage relies upon an adequate income to repay the loan. As we have just seen, women are far more likely than men to be living in poverty, or to have a low wage. Single women are often, therefore, priced out of private housing and are not a priority in the local authority sector. Only 11 per cent of households headed by a woman can afford to purchase a house through a mortgage, compared to 43 per cent of male-headed households; and 42 per cent of female-headed households are local authority tenants, compared to 25 cent of those headed by a man.

According to a number of reports, both on housing and the state of lone-parent families, the main problem, after finance, was that of poor standards of housing. Although lone parents are a priority group for housing by local authorities, the reality is that shortage of funds for building new homes means that single mothers are often likely to be placed in bed-and-breakfast accommodation (see Chapter 5).

The sexual division of housing

Households in unfit dwellings by age and gender of household head, England (1996)

Age of house-hold head	Male headed households			Female headed households			Difference (female-male, %)
	In fit dwellings	In unfit dwellings		In fit dwellings	In unfit dwellings		
15–29	1,895	192	9.2%	723	81	10.1%	0.9
30–44	4,400	251	5.4%	962	101	9.5%	4.1
45–59	3,740	207	5.3%	825	60	6.8%	1.5
60–74	2,851	143	4.8%	1,259	87	6.5%	1.7
75+	863	73	7.8%	853	76	8.2%	0.4
All	13,748	866	5.9%	4,622	406	8.1%	2.2

Source: K. Revell and P. Leather, *The State of UK Housing* (Policy Press, 2000)

1 In 1996, what percentage of 15–29-year-old (a) men and (b) women were living in unfit housing?

2 At which age is the difference greatest between the sexes? Suggest any possible reason for this.

3 Why do you think that males are more likely overall to have better housing?

4 What are the implications of unfit housing for the health of women?

Housing has further significance for women. As it is often so difficult for women to obtain housing, they can be forced into a dependence on men in situations which are physically or emotionally difficult. One study showed that the main reason why women delayed leaving violent partners was fear of homelessness. At present, over 45 per cent of women whose marriages break up have their housing needs met through the public sector or through housing associations.

Gender and State benefits

Critics of the social security system have constantly claimed that it fails to meet the needs of women. The system was originally designed in the 1940s on the assumption that women would marry, have children and stay at home to care for them, while men were the breadwinners. Pensions, State welfare benefits and disability benefits were all based on this assumption. However, the changing nature of society, of the family and, in particular, of the role of women has left this model outdated and discriminatory against women. In recent years, many changes have taken place which have begun to provide equality of benefits for women, but problems and differences remain.

The importance of benefits to women

The chart below shows the reasons for claiming one or other of the main State benefits. These 'key benefits' are:

- Jobseeker's Allowance
- Incapacity Benefit
- Disability Living Allowance
- Income Support
- National Insurance Credit.

Claimants of key benefits, by client group, February 2000

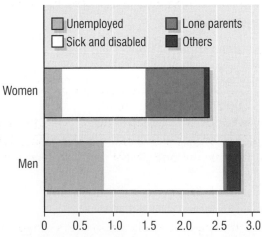

Source: *Women and Men in Britain: Pensions and Social Security*, Equal Opportunities Commission (EOC) factsheet. Crown copyright ©

1 What is the main difference between the reasons for claiming by men and by women?

2 How does this help us to understand why there is a gender issue with regard to the welfare benefit system?

3 If the government wanted to help women especially, which group might they want to concentrate on?

The result of the assumptions regarding patterns of work and marriage means that women have been discriminated against by the social security system. Women are much more likely than men to move in and out of employment as a result of their caring role in the family and the fact that they are often employed in less stable or less continuous occupations. This means that as social welfare payments are divided into contributory and non-contributory-based benefits, women are more likely to qualify only for the lower levels of non-contributory benefits. These are not just lower, they are also means-tested, which means that women are less able to build up savings of any kind. As soon as they do, they must use them to contribute to their living expenses. Over 2.5 million women are in the situation where they are not able to make National Insurance contributions and are therefore ineligible for the non-means-tested contributory benefits.

This pattern of inequality continues right through women's lives, so that even at pensionable age, over 18 per cent of all women at this age (a total of 1.2 million women) claim Income Support (to top up inadequate pensions) compared to 6 per cent of men (totalling 200,000).

There are still many examples of specific disadvantages faced by women:

- The Social Fund has a particularly powerful effect upon women. Lone parents, who are predominantly women, are the single largest group applying for this benefit. Repayments and budgeting have a powerful impact on family incomes. Even where the family has two parents, research indicates that family budgeting to repay the loans is usually the responsibility of the woman.
- Child Benefit, which is regarded as one of the most successful State benefits because it reaches all families and is paid to the mother, has fallen in real value.
- Pensions are based upon lifetime earnings, and this means that women, with their disrupted patterns of employment which we discussed above, are discriminated against.

But there have been some benefits to women:

- Statutory maternity leave will be doubled from 2003 to 26 weeks and the amount paid will be increased (to £100).
- Low income families receive Sure Start Maternity Grant.
- The National Minimum Wage benefits women workers as they occupy some of the lowest paid jobs.
- The New Deal for Lone Parents particularly benefits women, as they form the majority of lone parents.
- The Working Family Tax Credit also benefits women, as they are often caught in the poverty trap, where small increases in wages result in a drop in income because of increases in tax.
- Allowances for childcare costs are available in the Working Family Tax Credit. Childcare costs are one of the main reasons why it is financially not worthwhile for lone-parent mothers to go out to work.

Gender and health

Women live approximately seven years longer than men. However they do not necessarily do so in good health. In fact, on average they have only two years additional healthy life, that is without significant chronic illness. During their lifetimes, too, women appear to have higher levels of illness and higher rates of attendance at doctors' surgeries.

But this needs to be balanced against the health care needs of women. Women are both child bearers and have the main childcare role, both of which put great strain upon women's bodies. Feminist sociologists argue that actually women under-use the health services compared to their need.

Women in the NHS: an example of unfairness

The commission found that although women make up nearly 80 per cent of the NHS workforce, they make up just 17 per cent of unit general managers, 4 per cent of district and regional general managers and just 1 per cent of consultant general surgeons. Thirty-seven per cent of women work part-time in the NHS compared to 2.3 per cent of men, and part-time opportunities are concentrated in both the low paid jobs and lower graded posts. Female dominated professions within the NHS are lower paid than the male dominated groups, and women from black and ethnic minority groups, or women who are disabled, are further disadvantaged

Source: Article by Claire Laurent in *The Health Service Journal*, 15 August 1991

1 What proportion of those employed by the NHS are women?

2 What proportions of senior positions do they hold?

3 Are there any other groups which are similarly disadvantaged?

4 What suggestions could you make for ensuring equality of women in the NHS?

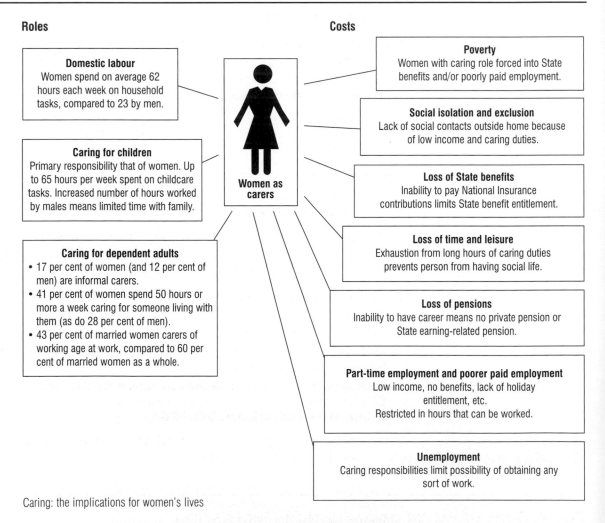

Roles

Domestic labour
Women spend on average 62 hours each week on household tasks, compared to 23 by men.

Caring for children
Primary responsibility that of women. Up to 65 hours per week spent on childcare tasks. Increased number of hours worked by males means limited time with family.

Caring for dependent adults
• 17 per cent of women (and 12 per cent of men) are informal carers.
• 41 per cent of women spend 50 hours or more a week caring for someone living with them (as do 28 per cent of men).
• 43 per cent of married women carers of working age at work, compared to 60 per cent of married women as a whole.

Women as carers

Costs

Poverty
Women with caring role forced into State benefits and/or poorly paid employment.

Social isolation and exclusion
Lack of social contacts outside home because of low income and caring duties.

Loss of State benefits
Inability to pay National Insurance contributions limits State benefit entitlement.

Loss of time and leisure
Exhaustion from long hours of caring duties prevents person from having social life.

Loss of pensions
Inability to have career means no private pension or State earning-related pension.

Part-time employment and poorer paid employment
Low income, no benefits, lack of holiday entitlement, etc.
Restricted in hours that can be worked.

Unemployment
Caring responsibilities limit possibility of obtaining any sort of work.

Caring: the implications for women's lives

The main influences on women's health include:

- *Biology:* women are biologically 'tougher' than men, and have a greater biological possibility of living longer. However, this does not mean that they are less immune to illness or to a range of health problems related to such things as reproduction and the menopause.

- *Poverty and deprivation:* standards of health are very closely related to poverty, as this determines type of food, quality of housing and levels of stress. We have already seen that women are more likely to live in poverty than men. About half of all women in the poorest households are suffering from a long-standing illness.

- *Wider material conditions,* such as poor housing and urban deprivation: again this is linked with poverty, as women have lower standards of housing than men. However, housing standards are even more important for women, because they spend so much more time at home looking after children. Overcrowding, dampness and isolation caused by high-rise housing all impact more on women (and their children).
- *Their greater length of life,* which means that they are more likely to suffer from chronic illness and disability – more than two-thirds of disabled people are women. This is because the majority of disabled people are drawn from the over-seventies age group.

Gender and legislation

Equal Pay Act 1970

This Act came into effect in 1975, and stated that where women and men are doing the same or broadly similar work, they have to be paid the same.

Sex Discrimination Act 1975

This Act made it unlawful to treat anyone less favourably on the grounds of sex. This included advertising for vacant posts. The Act also set up the Equal Opportunities Commission (EOC).

Equal Opportunities Commission

The EOC came into being in 1976 with the aim to end discrimination. Discrimination in this context means:

- direct discrimination – treating someone unfairly because of their sex
- indirect discrimination – setting unjustifiable conditions that appear to apply to everyone, but in fact discriminate against one sex.

The tasks of the EOC include:
- investigating cases of apparent or alleged violation of equal opportunities
- issuing non-discrimination notices which request employers or organisations to stop any discriminatory practices. If these are not complied with, the EOC may take the employers or organisations to court
- reviewing the workings of the Sex Discrimination Act itself.

The Sex Discrimination Act 1986

This Act extended the powers of the EOC and included a wider range of organisations which could be investigated.

The failure of equal opportunities legislation

... the [Equal Opportunities] legislation does not cover social security and taxation, areas which had been highlighted by the women's movement as discriminatory against women and in need of reform. Neither does it include consideration of child care arrangements or sexuality ... this exclusion means that all women are disadvantaged because it leaves intact domestic divisions of labour which allocate responsibility for child care and domestic labour to women. Thus men continue to be more available than are women to work full-time and overtime and can spend much more time on developing their careers.

Source: N. Charles, *Feminism, the State and Social Policy* (Macmillan, 2000)

1 What areas are omitted from the equal opportunities legislation?

2 Why is this important to women?

3 Find one example from the main text which might illustrate this point.

Main points ▶ Women have been fighting for equality for well over 100 years. Feminism is not new.

▶ Women have been expected to do the caring work and this has had a major impact on their opportunities for employment and their general standard of living.

▶ Women are more likely to live in poverty than men.

▶ Over a lifetime their incomes are significantly lower on average than men's.

▶ They are more likely to be in lower grades of employment and to earn less than men.

▶ Overall, the standard of housing that women live in is lower than that of men.

▶ Women, and particularly older women, have been discriminated against by the social security system, as a result of the way in which benefits were designed.

▶ Women have higher rates of ill health, yet live longer than men.

▶ Anti-discrimination legislation exists to protect women.

Conclusion

In this chapter, we began with an exploration of the nature of citizenship – an issue of particular importance for New Labour. We noted that a number of groups in society were discriminated against, and could not be said to have full citizenship rights. These groups include older people, disabled people, ethnic minorities and women. As we have examined the situation of disabled people and older people in other chapters, we have taken the opportunity in this chapter to explore the situation of women and the ethnic minorities. The results of our studies show us that in a wide range of areas these groups are discriminated against – whether by intention or not – and that, in order for them to attain full citizenship, the issue of discrimination must be addressed.

---

14 CHAPTER SUMMARY

1 According to Marshall, there are three elements to citizenship: legal, political and social.

2 Certain groups, including women and ethnic minorities, have not achieved their full rights as citizens.

3 Racial prejudice can be explained by a mixture of economic factors and cultural factors.

4 There is some evidence that ethnic minorities do not obtain equal share of resources as patients of the NHS.

5 Ethnic minorities have higher rates of certain illnesses, including mental disorders.

6 Ethnic minorities are over-represented in the lower grades of the NHS.

7 Ethnic minority members have a higher chance of being in poverty than the majority of the population.

8 There are noticeable differences between ethnic groups and housing conditions

9 Ethnic minorities are the subject of racially motivated attacks.

10 Legislation protects the rights of ethnic minorities.

11 Women have been fighting for equality for well over 100 years. Feminism is not new.

12 Women have been expected to do the caring work and this has had a major impact on their opportunities for employment and their general standard of living.

13 Women are more likely to live in poverty than men.

14 Over a lifetime their incomes are significantly lower on average than men's.

15 They are more likely to be in lower grades of employment and to earn less than men.

16 Overall, the standard of housing that women live in is lower than that of men.

17 Women, and particularly older women, have been discriminated against by the social security system, as a result of the way in which benefits were designed.

18 Women have higher rates of ill health, yet live longer than men.

19 Anti-discrimination legislation exists to protect women.

Useful websites

www.eoc.gov.uk: Equal Opportunities Commission

www.cre.gov.uk: Commission for Racial Equality

www.homeoffice.gov.eu.uk: Home Office Racial Equality Unit

www.womens-unit.gov.uk: Cabinet Office Women's Unit

www.csv.warwick.ac.uk/fac/soc/URER_RC/search: Centre for Research in Ethnic Relations

www.immigrationindex.org: Immigration Index

www.homebeads.co.uk: Institute of Race Relations

Chapter 15

PEOPLE WITH PHYSICAL DISABILITIES

Chapter contents

- ### Defining disability
  We begin by looking at the way that disabled people have been perceived by others and the consequences for them of the definitions of disability and disabled people which have been used. In particular, we compare the social and medical models which take very different views on the meaning of disability and how to deal with it.

- ### The numbers and composition of disabled people
  In this brief section we set out the numbers of disabled people and stress the variety of different social groups who compose the category 'disabled people'. These are a full cross-section of society, although there is a higher than average proportion of older people. But it is important to realise that there are many young people and children who are disabled too and their needs must be met.

- ### Disability and employment
  The extent of discrimination experienced by disabled people is evident in their employment situation. Disabled people are more likely to be unemployed, to have low status jobs and to work part-time. As they are a typical cross-section of the population, there is no reason for such strong differences from the employment patterns of the rest of the population.

- ### Poverty and disabled people
  High unemployment, part-time jobs and low status positions all point to another problem which disabled people live with – poverty. They have a much higher chance than the majority population to be living in poverty. This is even worse, when one considers the fact that they often have more specific and expensive needs compared to the rest of the population, for example in clothing, heating, furniture, and so on.

- ### Welfare and disabled people
  Over time, the models of welfare which have formed the basis for provision for disabled people have changed. In pre-industrial times, although poor, disabled people were largely integrated into society and economically productive. However, industrialisation meant that they were edged out of employment and the provision for many of them was the workhouse. In Victorian times and well into the twentieth century, they were put in large institutions – hospitals and asylums – where they were 'looked after' and kept away from society at large. It is only relatively recently that care in the community has become the main way in which welfare provision is delivered. However, disabled people themselves are now arguing that they don't want welfare. They want State benefits (like any other group) or employment, and they will make choices about what they want to spend it on.

- ### Stigma and disability
  We look briefly at the way in which disabled people have to deal with stigma and discrimination in their daily lives and how they manage this.

- ### The politics of disability
  This section explores the fight that disabled people have had to get their voices heard, rather than experts who talk on their behalf. Only recently have they managed to have anti-discriminatory legislation passed. However, this leaves out significant areas which impact on the lives of disabled people.

- ### Legislation
  Here we simply list the major acts and comment on them.

- ### Benefits and services for disabled people
  We list the State benefits, welfare and care services available for disabled people.

Introduction

Disability is a particularly interesting area of study as it was until recently largely ignored by researchers and academics. Disabled people were seen as 'suffering' from physical (or mental) impairments and there was little that could be done for them apart from providing adequate care and ensuring that they received State benefits. Only relatively recently, when disabled people themselves got together to complain about their situation, did 'experts' start to rethink their ideas. Rather than starting with disability and then seeing 'what could be done for them', social policy analysts now tend to ask questions more about the way that society has organised itself to exclude disabled people and has pushed them outside the boundaries of what is considered normal. Why shouldn't disabled people be able to work, shop and enjoy their leisure time, without there having to be 'special' arrangements? Why should disabled people have to accept 'experts' deciding what services and levels of care they need? Surely, argue disabled people, we know that, all we want is the money to buy it!

The chapter explores the shifting views on disability and looks at the way that disabled people have organised themselves to challenge traditional views about normality, experts and caring, amongst other things.

Defining disability

Definition

Disabled people – the correct term to use for people with impairments – not 'handicapped' or 'disabled'

There are many areas in social policy in which academics and practitioners have disagreed about terminology, but nowhere as strongly as on the issue of disability where the dispute has been long-running and sometimes bitter.

This is partly because **disabled people** themselves have joined in the debate and have linked the language used to describe them with their continuing exclusion from society. They have argued that the language surrounding disability has demeaned them (made them feel insignificant and of little value) and made them appear inferior to the wider population. This exclusion and forced inferiority has, in turn, maintained the low standards of living and low levels of social status which is the lot of disabled people.

What makes disabled people so angry is that the description 'disabled' (or 'handicapped') overshadows them being a person. So they are seen first as someone who is disabled and secondly as a person. What they want is to be seen first as a person, and then to have society provide the conditions so that their disability does not impede them leaving as 'normal' a life as possible.

Terminology

There are three terms which people commonly use in the area of disability studies:

- *impairment* – this refers to the physical dysfunction or loss of any part of the body and as such is a medically classified condition
- *handicap* – this is much less frequently used these days, but technically refers to the physical limitations which a disabled person has
- *disability* – refers to the social disadvantage faced by those people who have impairments.

Under the Disability Discrimination Act 1995, a disabled person is anyone who has a physical, sensory or mental impairment which seriously affects their day-to-day activities.

Models of disability

Definitions

Medical model of disability – a view of disability which focuses on the physical handicap and problems of the disabled person

Social model of disability – a view of disability which focuses on the way society discriminates against disabled people

The debate over definitions actually reflects a wider debate over the nature of disability which is based upon alternative models:

- the **medical model**
- the **social model**.

The medical model of disability

The medical model has been an extremely influential model of disability throughout the twentieth century and was only challenged towards the end of that century. The medical model derives from the traditional approach to medicine, which sees our bodies as something like a machine. Like a machine the body has interdependent parts which function together to work. If anything goes wrong the doctor looks for the badly functioning or 'broken' part of the body and 'fixes' it. This can be done through surgery or through the use of medication. But this machine idea is based on the assumption that there is a normal body, with only a limited range of variations. By implication, people who have impairments are somehow abnormal. Their impairment is seen as a 'problem' and, more than that, as *their* problem, not society's. The consequences for disabled people are enormous. Rather than seeing society as the problem, by discriminating against disabled people, for example, by not designing articles and buildings to accommodate them, it sees the disabled people as the problem. In this model of disability, people are encouraged to help themselves and society is seen as having to provide 'special facilities' to assist them in this.

The social model of disability

In recent years, as a result of the activities of a fairly radical group of disabled people, a different model of disability has risen which challenges the medical model and which locates the 'problem' of disability within society as opposed to on the individual. This is known as the social model. This model of disability argues that it is rarely the impairment which disables people, rather it is the failure of society to make appropriate provision for the full range of its citizens. This applies both in physical settings (such as steps which make buildings inaccessible to wheelchair users) and in terms of social attitudes to disabled people.

The social model argues that disability is located in society and that 'disabled people' are simply ordinary citizens within the normal range of physical and social variation who have a right to be treated as normal and to have all facilities designed in such a way as to incorporate their 'variation'. It also argues that social attitudes too have to be altered so that disabled people are not treated in any other way than as fully 'normal' members of society.

A different view of disability

The following extract illustrates how the social model of disability can help challenge more traditional (medical or individual) models. The writer has rephrased the questions, which were used in a survey by the Office for Population and Census Surveys (OPCS).

OPCS: 'Can you tell me what is wrong with you?'
Oliver: 'Can you tell me what is wrong with society?'

OPCS: 'What complaint causes your difficulty in holding, gripping or turning things?'

Oliver: 'What defects in the design of everyday equipment like jars, bottles and tins causes you difficulty in holding, gripping or turning them?'

OPCS:	'Are your difficulties in understanding people mainly due to a hearing problem?'		OPCS:	'Does your health problem/disability make it difficult for you to travel by bus?'
Oliver:	'Are your difficulties in understanding people mainly due to their inability to communicate with you?'		Oliver:	'Are there any transport or financial problems which prevent you from going out as often or as far as you would like?'
OPCS:	'Do you have a scar, blemish or deformity which limits your daily activities?'		OPCS:	'Does your health problem/disability affect your work in any way at present?'
Oliver:	'Do other people's reactions to any scar, blemish or deformity you may have limit your daily activities?'		Oliver:	'Do you have problems at work because of the physical environment or the attitudes of others?'
OPCS:	'Have you attended a special school because of a long-term health problem or disability?'		OPCS:	'Does your health problem/disability mean that you need to live with relatives or someone else who can help or look after you?'
Oliver:	'Have you attended a special school because of your education authority's policy of sending people with your health problem/disability to such places?'		Oliver:	'Are community services so poor that you need to rely on relatives or someone else to provide you with the right level of personal assistance?'
OPCS:	'Does your health problem/disability prevent you from going out as often or as far as you would like?'		OPCS:	'Does your present accommodation have any adaptations because of your health problem/disability?'
Oliver:	'What is it about the local environment that makes it difficult for you to get about in your neighbourhood?'		Oliver:	'Did the poor design of your house mean that you had to have it adapted to suit your needs?'

Source: M. Oliver, *The Politics of Disablement* (Macmillan, 1980)

1 How does the extract illustrate the differing views of the nature of disability?

2 What are the implications for government policy of Oliver's rewording of the questions?

3 What is your opinion – do you think that the way Oliver rewords the questions is right?

Main points ▶ There is considerable disagreement over how to approach an understanding of disability.

▶ There are two different approaches: the medical model and the social model.

▶ The medical model stresses the physical problem faced by the disabled person, and seeks to help them overcome the problem.

▶ The social model stresses the way that society limits what it regards as 'normal' to exclude the disabled person. According to this model, the disability is caused more by society than by any impairment that the disabled person might have.

▶ The language to use when discussing disability is very important. Terms liked 'the handicapped' and 'the disabled' or 'people with disabilities' can be seen as stressing the issue of disability and overshadowing the person – as a *person*.

The numbers and composition of disabled people

The numbers of disabled people in the population

The disputes over how we express and respond to disability are very important – how disability is defined and how we respond to disabled people affects a very large number of people in the UK. Estimates of the number of disabled people varies, and it depends upon the exact definition used. However, the highest estimate suggested by the government's Labour Market Survey puts the figure at

8.5 million disabled people in Great Britain – one in seven of the population (though this does include over half a million people with some form of learning difficulty or mental health 'problem'). Of these, about 5.4 million receive some form of State benefit.

The cost of disability

Social security benefit expenditure, Great Britain, 2000-01, by broad groups of beneficiaries

Total: £101.4 billion

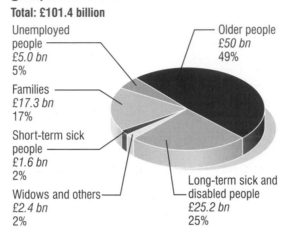

Unemployed people
£5.0 bn
5%

Families
£17.3 bn
17%

Short-term sick people
£1.6 bn
2%

Widows and others
£2.4 bn
2%

Older people
£50 bn
49%

Long-term sick and disabled people
£25.2 bn
25%

Source: *Britain 2001: The Official Yearbook* (The Stationary Office, 2001)

1 How much social security benefit was spent on long-term sick and disabled people?

2 What percentage of all spending was that in 2001?

3 Where does this in rank in the categories of social security spending?

Myths about disability

Physical disability is not one problem, but a wide range of problems of different kinds. It includes people who have lost limbs, who are blind or deaf, who have difficulty moving or walking, who are unable to sustain physical effort for any length of time, and so on. ...

The treatment of disability as if it was a single problem may mean that disabled people receive insufficient or inappropriate assistance. One of the first things to appreciate is that *most disabled people in Britain are old.* Not only are elderly people overall in the majority, with more than a third of people over 75 suffering from some kind of impairment, but they are vastly in the majority when the most serious disabilities are focused on. Relatively few chronically

sick or disabled people are under 50. Despite this, provision for the disabled is often concentrated on young disabled people, or at least people of working age.

Sheltered workshops and employment quotas have little relevance to most disabled people, as do special schools.

A second myth is that disabled people are likely to be in wheelchairs – an image encouraged by the symbol used on 'disabled' stickers. But there are probably less than 200 000 wheelchair users in the country, out of some 3 to 7 million disabled people, depending which estimate you use. And measures which are suitable for some disabled people are not necessarily appropriate for others. A public building with a large, flat floor (like Euston

station) is fine for people in wheelchairs, but a nightmare for blind people, who often prefer stairs or solid physical obstacles which make it easier for them to orient themselves. A kitchen with a low sink and cupboard is useful for some wheelchair users but may be a nuisance for anyone who has problems bending – a common complaint in 'mobility' housing. The most common cause of disability is probably arthritis, which usually limits mobility in a different way to a wheelchair.

Thirdly, there is a tendency to rely on medical evidence of disability. But functional problems are often more important than medical ones. The assessment of a social worker or occupational therapist may be far more relevant than a doctor's.

Another common misconception is that, because the cause of disability is physical, so is the solution. The problems that disabled people have in common are not so much their physical capacities, which are often very different, but limitations on their life style. Income tends to be low – partly because many disabled people are old and female, partly because they may have special income needs, and because long-term sickness late in someone's working life undermines financial security as they grow older. Socially, disabled people may become isolated, as their health declines, they struggle to manage on the resources they have, they have difficulties in visiting people, and other people find it difficult to come to terms with the disability.

Source: *Housing*, March 1986

1 Is it accurate to talk about 'the problem of disabled people'?

2 In what ways does this term cause difficulties in the provision of services for disabled people?

3 Which group accounts for the majority of disabled people? On which group, according to the author, is most provision centred? Do you agree with this focusing of provision? Explain why you agree or disagree.

4 What proportion of disabled people are wheelchair users?

S The author refers to medical and functional issues regarding disability. Explain what is meant by these two terms and the importance of the differences between them.

6 Disability has other social effects on people – what are these and what role can the State or the voluntary/social services play?

7 Ask a sample of 20 people to define what is meant by a 'disabled person' and ask them to give one example of such a person. The majority will probably talk about people in wheelchairs or with mobility problems. Ask them to name two other groups of 'disabled people' – the majority may well have difficulty thinking of any other group.

8 What are the implications for disabled people of the fact that most people think 'disability equals wheelchair'? Make a list of issues.

9 How could the stereotype be changed? What good, if any, would it achieve?

The composition of disabled people in the population

It is important not to see disabled people as one single group – to do so would be to stereotype them. There are considerable variations between disabled people

Medical conditions and impairment

Impairment can arise from a number of different causes:

- congenital (born with)
- an accident
- a previous illness which has left an impairment
- a current illness which causes an impairment.

Not all illnesses cause an impairment, many have little effect on physical performance until they are well-advanced and not all people with impairments are ill. Furthermore, those who do not have a limb since birth or as a result of an accident cannot be said to be ill. Impairments are separate from the medical conditions which might cause them.

Age

The level of disability increases with age: only 9 per cent of those aged 16–24 years have a current long-term disability compared with 33 per cent of those aged 50 to State pension age, and a further 30 per cent are over 75. However, there is an increasing number of younger disabled people, partly as advances in medicine allow disabled babies to live and secondly because of the numbers of people who no longer die from illnesses or accidents in later life.

Gender

Amongst older disabled people, there are more females – as they are more likely to live longer and therefore have higher chances of impairment. Among younger disabled people, there are slightly more male disabled people (53 per cent) than female (47 per cent).

Ethnicity

Pakistani/Bangladeshi people and older people from ethnic minorities more generally have higher disability rates than other groups.

Geography

There are regional variations in the incidence of disability which may to some extent be due to differences in the age profile of the local population. Higher than average proportions of disabled people are found in Merseyside, the North-East and Wales and lower ones in the South-East and in Outer London.

Experiencing disability

"I was meeting up with some friends in London to go to the Millennium Dome at Greenwich. The Dome was brilliant – but getting there was awful.

Our train from Birmingham broke down in north London and so we got a taxi to Euston to meet another friend as arranged on the concourse. When we arrived there was no one available to operate the lift so that delayed us for half an hour.

We had telephoned ahead to find out which buses we could use to get to the Dome. The 68 to Russell Square was brilliant – then we changed for the 'accessible' 188 to the Dome. The low floor bus seemed brilliant as we got on – there was even a space for a wheelchair user. But then we realised that the aisle to get there was too narrow – I could not get past. My friends had to carry me through, which was really undignified.

When we left the Dome we opted for the tube. We jokingly asked whether the lifts were working. They weren't! But it was OK because we went by Docklands Light Railway to Bank – but at Bank we were told that the tube station lift was not in use at the weekend. By this time we were getting pretty annoyed. Eventually we got back up to ground level and got a taxi to Euston.

It should have been a great day. I thought we had found out all the access stuff we needed to know. But with all the hassle – wrong information, poor design and dodgy lifts – the day was a nightmare."

Pippa Beilis

Source: G. Morris and J. Ford, *Left Out* (Scope, 2000)

Of course, there are many other forms of disability other than using a wheelchair. However, see if you can experience what Pippa Beilis had to endure.

Ask your local NHS trust if they will lend you a wheelchair for the day. Plan a visit to a local building or event. Go in a small group, taking turns to be the person in the wheelchair. What conclusions do you reach about having to use a wheelchair to travel.

What do you think about Oliver's rewriting of the OPCS questions which we looked at earlier?

Main points

▶ The numbers of disabled people are difficult to state exactly, because of differing definitions of disability.

▶ The figure may actually be well over 8 million.

▶ It is important to realise that the term 'disabled people' covers a huge range of different people with different impairments caused by different circumstances and which place different demands upon the disabled person.

▶ Disabled people are also a reflection of the wider population with divisions by age, ethnicity and gender, amongst other things.

▶ However, it is true to say that a high proportion of disabled people are older.

Disability and employment

Disability has an enormous impact upon working lives in terms of salaries, promotion and chances of employment. This is not a small problem either, as there are about 6.8 million people of working age in the UK who have a long-term disability or long-term illness (this includes mental disability).

Disabled people:

- are nearly seven times as likely as non-disabled people to be out of work and claiming benefits – 2.6 million disabled people in total
- have almost twice the unemployment rate of non-disabled people – 8.9 per cent compared to 4.9 per cent
- want to work – over a million of them want to work, but are unable to do so, or cannot find employment
- are twice as likely as non-disabled people to have no qualifications. This difference is consistent across all age groups
- are more likely to work part-time.

Disability and employment

Disabled people and the labour market, estimates from the Labour Force Survey, Summer 2000, Great Britain

	Long-term disabled	Not long-term disabled
All people of working age (men 16–64, women 16–59) (000s)	6,828	28,786
As a percentage of all people of working age	19%	81%
From ethnic minorities	7%	8%
Women	47%	48%
No qualifications	29%	12%
On State benefits	40%	6%
Would like work and available to start in a fortnight	6%	2%
In work	47%	81%
Working part-time	28%	23%
In a permanent job	93%	93%
Average number of years in current employment	8.6	7.4
Average gross hourly wage	£7.92	£8.84

Source: Disability Rights Commission website, November 2000 Newsletter

1 How many people were there of working age who are long-term disabled?

2 How do they differ from 'not long-term disabled' in terms of educational qualifications?

3 What percentage are on State benefits of some kind?

4 What percentage are at work compared to the not long-term disabled

5 What percentage would like to work and are available to work? Does this tell us anything about their unemployment level?

6 How do the wages of long-term disabled people in employment compare with not long-term disabled people?

Poverty and disabled people

One common problem faced by all types of disabled people is that they have a greater chance of living in poverty. Over half of all families in which the male partner was disabled were living in poverty, and only 13 per cent of disabled people could be defined as 'prosperous'. Why is this so?

Older disabled people are likely to be receiving old age pensions, and the extra State benefit they are eligible to receive does not cover the extra costs of disability.

Disabled people of working age are more likely than the able-bodied to be unemployed, so people of working age with disabilities are half as likely to be working as able-bodied people.

Causes of poverty

Older people who have been disabled throughout their lives are less likely to have been employed, or employed in well-paid employment, and therefore have had little opportunity to build up savings or to contribute to a pension scheme. They therefore must rely upon minimum State benefits.

Disabled people who are in employment are likely to be in low-paid work. On average, the earnings of males with disabilities are slightly less than 80 per cent of the average male wage in the UK. The situation for disabled women is even worse, given the differences in earnings between males and females in employment in the UK. This is despite legislation which outlaws discrimination.

Poverty and disability

As with the elderly, a high proportion of disabled people are dependent on state benefits. Fifty-eight per cent of the incomes of disabled adults comes from state benefits; ... The only group of disabled people who do not receive the majority of their income from benefits are the married non-pensioner disabled. According to Martin and White, the mean income of disabled people is 72 per cent of that of the non-disabled. They also found that a higher proportion of households with a disabled member could not afford the basic items as defined by Mack and Lansley. For example, 17 per cent of households with a disabled member could not afford to buy new clothes, compared with 6 per cent of households without a disabled member. Similarly, 15 per cent of households with a disabled member could not afford two pairs of all-weather shoes, compared to 9 per cent of households without a disabled member. Unmarried disabled people (mainly women) with children were the most deprived: 53 per cent could not afford new clothes and 50 per cent could not afford two pairs of all-weather shoes.

Source: C. Oppenheim, *Poverty: The Facts*, 3rd edition (CPAG, 1996)

1   What percentage of disabled adults income comes from State benefits?

2   What does this indicate about the level of disabled people's incomes, do you think?

3   The extract refers to Mack and Lansley's research first carried out in 1985 for the Breadline Britain programme (see Chapter 4, 'The consensual definition of poverty', page 82). Explain this research in your own words.

4   Which adults were most deprived?

Main points ▶ Disabled people face discrimination in a wide range of areas.
   ▶ One of the most important areas of discrimination is employment.
   ▶ They are more likely to be unemployed or in part-time and lower status jobs.
   ▶ One of the consequences of this is that they have relatively high chances of living in poverty, despite the fact that they often have greater expenses than the majority of the population.

Welfare and disabled people

Welfare policies towards disabled people have altered considerably over time. The type and generosity of welfare policies have been closely linked with the different models of disability discussed earlier. Until recently various types of the medical model have dominated thinking, but for the last twenty years there has been a clear development in the social model.

Before industrialisation: social integration

Before industrialisation, the position of disabled people was fairly ambiguous, in that they had a much greater chance of poverty and early death. However, there does seem evidence to suggest that in agricultural societies, there were many jobs which they could perform and that they were largely integrated into communities.

Industrialisation: economic exclusion and institutionalisation

Definitions

Social inclusion – (disabled) people are fully included in life's normal activities and rhythms

Economic exclusion – barriers exist to prevent (disabled) people from engaging in normal work and employment

Institutionalisation – where the approach to disabled people is to hide them away in institutions

Industrialisation changed this however. Employers were interested in a 'fit' workforce which could operate the machinery and those who were not productive were of little use. Early industrialisation therefore led to disabled people being **economically excluded**. The welfare response in the nineteenth century was to gather together disabled people and put them in **institutions** such as the workhouse, where they could be looked after.

Much of nineteenth century welfare was based on the importance of distinguishing between the deserving and undeserving. This means making a distinction in the provision of welfare between those who genuinely could not work and those who were lazy or indisciplined and had brought poverty on themselves. Disabled people were therefore given relatively good conditions in workhouses – though we might well be horrified at their conditions looking back from today's perspective. Gradually, however over the nineteenth century, the growing influence of the medical model saw disabled people as in need of care from medical experts, and so long-stay hospitals and sanatoriums were built. Here disabled people were brought to live – possibly for all their lives.

Welfare experts

The Boer War and the First World War brought a huge new influx of disabled people – largely men who had been left with major disabilities. The idea of putting all these men into long-stay hospitals was clearly impracticable. The result was a growth in providing compensation payments to help them remain at home. This was the continuation of a policy which had already been introduced for workers who had been disabled at work. It also saw the growth of wider welfare provision such as attempts to find work for disabled people.

By the end of the Second World War, the Welfare State saw its role as ensuring that the needs of disabled people were cared for. However, the view taken by the Welfare State was that the doctors and other welfare professionals knew what was best for disabled people. Experts decided upon the policies and then other experts, such as doctors or social workers, examined disabled people to decide what needs they had.

Citizenship and independent living

The welfare approach in which experts made decisions about disabled people began to be challenged in the 1980s by more radical groups of disabled people who pointed out that only ill people had decisions made about them by experts – everyone else made their own decisions about what they needed. As disabled people were not ill, they demanded the right to make their own decisions and to stop being treated as abnormal. Instead they argued that their 'welfare' was best looked after by having the full rights as citizens (see Chapter 14). By this they meant that they should be able to earn decent wages and to purchase what they wished. If the disability prevented employment, then the role of the State was to provide adequate financial payments so that they could spend the money on the services that they wanted, not on those that an expert decided was appropriate for them.

Stigma and disability

Stigma

The term 'stigma' is used when people with certain characteristics are regarded as inferior or deviant by many members of 'normal' society. A person with physical or mental disabilities is often not seen as a person but as a disabled person. It is often assumed that such a person does not have normal feelings, that he or she cannot or should not attempt the things that 'normal' people do. Furthermore, disabled people are often viewed with a mixture of pity and fear.

Models of response to disability

In a well-known study on the relationship between disabled people and others, Davis examined the way in which disabled and non-disabled people 'interacted' with each other in social situations (F. Davis, 'Deviance disavowal', in A.R. Lindesmith *et al.*, *Readings in Social Psychology*, 2nd edition [Dryden, 1975]). His principal findings were that there are three typical types of interaction or models of response to disability:

- *domination by disability*: The perceptions of the disabled person by the non-disabled are dominated by the disability. The disabled person is aware of the other's discomfort
- *stigma*: A second response is to express openly feelings and emotions that would normally be considered inappropriate in casual meetings. The non-disabled person would display horror, disgust, pity and fear quite readily
- *contradiction*: The third response by others to a disabled person who is acting normally is to point out the apparent (to them) contradiction, such as a disabled social worker actually helping others!

The dominance of stigma

A | Mr Miller, a young man with a progressive disabling disease went to seek the advice of a social worker about his problems. | In particular he wanted a confused social security position clarified. He returned a little bewildered. | 'I don't know really what is going on. I just wanted these forms filled in. She kept going on talking about the disease – what I | felt about it – what my wife felt about it. Coming to terms with it. All I want to come to terms with is these forms!'

Source: M. Oliver, *Social Work with Disabled People* (Macmillan, 1983)

B When teaching a group of social workers once, one student, who as a result of a car crash has great difficulty walking, told me of a visit to a new client. He got out of his car, opened the front gate, walked with the aid of two crutches to the front door and knocked. When the potential client opened the door, the student said, 'Hello, my name is John Smith from Shire Social Services,' and showed the client his identity. With a look of absolute horror, she burst out, 'Oh, my God, I didn't think they were going to send a cripple to help me!'

1 How do these two examples illustrate aspects of all three types of response to disability?

2 How do you think a social worker or medical/care professional ought to respond?

Managing the situation

Disabled people must learn to cope with the stigma placed upon them by others. They cannot be sure, for example, if assistance they are given is offered through courtesy or pity. If they are invited to a social occasion, are they really wanted or are they there because the host feels sorry for them? This makes people with disabilities face additional handicaps beyond those caused directly by the physical impairment itself. In face-to-face situations, Davis suggests that disabled people must 'manage' the interaction in some way as a means of trying to cope.

- One way of coping is to set up situations in which everyone, both with and without disabilities, pretends that all is normal. The disability is not referred to, but there is an awareness by both parties of the disability and that mention of it is deliberately being avoided.
- A second approach commonly used by disabled people is to project a particular image of themselves which stresses how 'normal' they are and how others should respond to them. The disability itself is shrugged off.
- A third approach, which usually occurs once people know each other well, but not before, is when the relationship between the disabled person comes to be based on them as individuals. The issue of disability arises only where it is relevant.

The experience of disability

This is a young disabled man speaking about going clubbing.

'I love clubbing – getting in, having a beer and having a laugh. I love the atmosphere and chatting to people, especially women. Music-wise – garage and house is what I like because you can get down to it.

Sometimes I have trouble getting into clubs – bouncers turn me away and it's really annoying because they won't give me a reason. Sometimes they tell me to come back on a quiet night. But why would I want to go when it's not pumping!

I recently went to Freedom at Bagleys in London and had a great time – it was really casual and laid back. Once inside it is quite accessible with ramps between dance floors. Getting into the club involves stairs but I had the best service I have ever had from bouncers – two guys carried me up all the stairs in my chair.

These days there are loads of good clubs, which are accessible, which makes life easier. I want to large it on the dance floor like everyone else and slowly the club scene is changing so that disabled people can party with the best of them.

May the funk be with you.'

Dave Crowl

Source: G. Morris and J. Ford, *Left Out* (Scope, 2000)

1 How does Dave Crowl 'manage' the situation?

2 If you met Dave in a club, how do you think most people would respond to him?

3 Dave says that the 'club scene is changing so that disabled people can party with the best of them'. Do you think this is true?

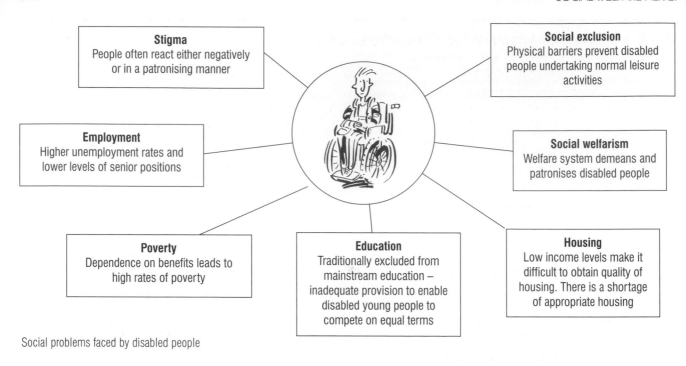

Social problems faced by disabled people

Main points ▶ Historically, disabled people have been treated very differently by different generations.

▶ Before industrialisation they were often employed and worked alongside others.

▶ During the period of industrialisation they were excluded from the factories and were 'looked after' in workhouses.

▶ Later 'care' was given in a range of residential institutions where they were cut off from the population.

▶ More recently the approach has been dominated by community care and the demands of disabled people for the right to live independent lives.

▶ In their personal lives, they still have to deal with stigma and discrimination.

The politics of disability

One of the problems which disabled people have always faced is that they have been treated almost like children, with other people – usually doctors or welfare workers – making decisions on their behalf. This had led to a lack of self-confidence and low self-esteem among many disabled people. This in turn stopped them challenging the way they were treated.

Many of the more traditional charities working for the benefit of those with disabilities accepted the position (for example, RADAR), but a range of new groups developed during the 1970s and 1980s which began to challenge these traditional ideas. More than this, they began using more radical methods of civil disobedience. What they wanted was not improved conditions or better benefits, but equal rights and anti-discrimination legislation such as that passed on behalf of women and the ethnic minorities. There had been sporadic attempts to organise disabled people to demand their rights, with limited success. One early example was the marches in London organised by the National League of the Blind and Disabled in 1920 which demanded legislation for blind people, and did attain the passing of the 1920 Blind (Education, Employment and Maintenance) Act. The more recent groups which have been demanding equal rights include the Disability Alliance, Disablement Income Group and the British Council of Disabled People.

Two models of understanding disability

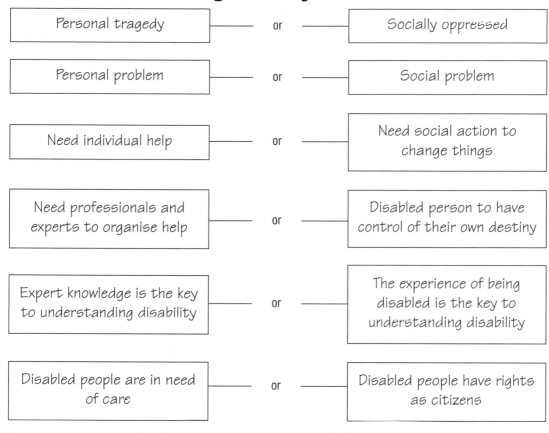

Personal tragedy	or	Socially oppressed
Personal problem	or	Social problem
Need individual help	or	Need social action to change things
Need professionals and experts to organise help	or	Disabled person to have control of their own destiny
Expert knowledge is the key to understanding disability	or	The experience of being disabled is the key to understanding disability
Disabled people are in need of care	or	Disabled people have rights as citizens

1 Explain what the two models are, in your own words.

2 Which side of the argument arc you on?

3 What are the implications for social work?

The result of their campaigns, which included every possible pressure group activity (see page 13), including direct action, led to the passing of the Disability Discrimination Act in 1995. The Act was not an unqualified success for the disability movement, but unlike earlier legislation it concentrated on preventing discrimination rather than the provision of improved services. The Act outlawed discrimination in employment and the provision of goods and services, but did not impose penalties on anyone who broke the law.

In 1999, a further Act was passed (the Disability Rights Commission Act) which established the Disability Rights Commission the following year, and which extended the provisions of the 1995 Act. However, the DRC does not have the same legal powers as the Equal Opportunities Commission or the Commission for Racial Equality to start prosecutions against people who break the law.

High fliers can't always fly

The Chairman of the Disability Rights Commission was banned from a flight to Scotland today (Thursday 19 October) because he uses a wheelchair.

Bert Massie was on his way to speak at the Directors of Social Services Conference when officials of Scotairways at London's City Airport refused to allow him to board the plane to Edinburgh.

The airline told Mr Massie that it only allowed people who could walk onto its planes and that wheelchair users were a health and safety hazard. Mr Massie, who cannot walk, offered to 'shuffle' his way up the aircraft's steps onto the plane, but this was refused.

The airline was informed that Mr

Massie was a wheelchair user and would need assistance boarding his flight. His tickets were then issued. He arrived one and a half hours before the flight departure and was then kept waiting on the runway before he was told he couldn't board the aircraft.

Mr Massie said: "I can't describe how frustrating this has been. What makes it worse is that Scotairways can get away with treating disabled people in this diabolical fashion because there's no law to cover discrimination on air travel.

"I'm writing to Scotairways' Chairman to request a meeting to review whether there are ways of overcoming its discriminatory policies.

"This case shows how much work the Commission has to do to enable disabled people to participate fully in society."

* Travel by aeroplanes is not covered by the Disability Discrimination Act of 1995.

Source: Disability Rights Commission press release, 20 October 2000

In your opinion, do the disability discrimination laws go far enough?

Independent living

A good example of the way that disabled people have moved away from dependence on experts who make decisions on their behalf, towards self-determination, has been the development of independent living. After 1993, it was possible for disabled people to reject the services offered to them by local authorities and instead take the value of these services and devise and purchase their own care plan. At first, local authorities (and the NHS) strongly resisted this move, arguing that as the experts they knew best, and that anyway without the co-ordination of the local authorities, there would be a fragmentation of care. However, further legislation in 1995 strengthened the position of those arguing for independent living, and this is becoming an increasingly common model of care.

Legislation

1601 Poor Law Act

This was the very first Act concerning disabled people, and it required the local authorities of the time (the parish) to provide support for older people, poor people and sick people.

1897, 1900, 1906 Workman's Compensation Acts

Under these Acts, payments were introduced for certain categories of workers injured at work.

1911 National Insurance Act

Once again, this Act covered sickness or injuries resulting from employment. It did not cover people born with disability, nor people who had not subscribed to the National Insurance scheme as a result of unemployment.

Many of these Acts were intended to compensate people disabled through industrial or commercial injuries. They were, however, irrelevant to the vast majority of disabled people, who were either older or unable to gain employment precisely because of their disability.

1946 National Health Service Act

This provided for free treatment and, where possible, rehabilitation.

1946 National Insurance Act

This provided weekly benefits for disabled people.

1970 Chronically Sick and Disabled Act and 1970 Local Authority Social Services Act

Under the provisions of these Acts, local authorities were obliged to ascertain the numbers and needs of disabled people in their areas. Local authorities had the power to provide a range of services, but were not obliged to provide the services in all cases. This led to a great variation in provision, depending upon the local authority.

1986 Disabled Persons (Services, Consultation and Representation) Act

This forced the local authority, upon the request of the disabled person, to decide whether the needs of the person fell under the provision of the Act.

1995 Carers (Recognition and Service) Act

This gives the legal right for the needs of carers to have their ability to provide the appropriate services assessed.

1995 Disability Discrimination Act

This makes it unlawful to discriminate against disabled people in:

- the provision of goods and services
- employment.

However, it does exclude a number of areas.

1999 Disability Rights Commission Act

This Act set up the Disability Rights Commission to work towards the elimination of discrimination against disabled people. However, it does not have the right to prosecute those who break the law.

2000 Carers and Disabled Persons Act

This Act provides further rights for carers to be assessed for their needs in helping disabled people

Benefits and services for disabled people

Benefits

The following benefits are available for disabled people.

Incapacity Benefit

This is available for those of working age who have paid National Insurance contributions. There are different levels depending upon the length of the period people are incapable of working. In order to get it, the claimant may have to undertake a personal capability assessment.

Disability Living Allowance

This is available to people under the age of 65 who have difficulty getting around – though if you are already receiving it, it carries on beyond 65. It is not means-tested. There are two levels of benefit, depending upon the level of severity of the problem of walking. The test of eligibility for the lower rate (rather unusually) is the 'cooking test', which means that the claimant is so severely disabled that they cannot prepare a cooked main meal for themselves if they have the ingredients. For the higher rate, attention is required most of the time.

Attendance Allowance

This is a non-means-tested benefit for those over the age of 65. It is paid for those who need care, and there are different levels depending whether the person needs help during the day or night, or both.

Disabled Persons Tax Credit

This is an allowance similar in nature to the Working Family Tax Credit, which tops up the income of lower paid workers. Unlike the other benefits for disabled people, it is paid through the Tax Credit Office of the Inland Revenue. To qualify the person has to work for 16 hours a week or more. It is means-tested, depending upon the level of income the person receives in wages, and the amount of savings they have.

Industrial Injuries Disablement Benefit

This is available for those who have been disabled through an injury at work. It is restricted to a those employed in certain industries.

Reduced Earning Allowance

This is payable to those who are now in lower paying work as a result of an industrial injury or disease in a previously higher paid job. This benefit is being phased out – it is only available to those who were affected before 1990.

There is also a range of benefits for carers, including Invalid Care Allowance.

Services

Local authority services

Local authorities provide the following services for disabled people:

- aids and equipment to enable disabled people to live at home
- day centres for disabled people – for both training and for social meetings
- home care
- meals-on-wheels
- parking concessions
- respite carers
- social workers and occupational therapists.

NHS services

The NHS provides aids and equipment, nursing and medical care for disabled people.

Housing authorities and associations

These provide specially adapted, newly built or renovated housing for disabled people, and approve work eligible for the Disabled Facilities Grant.

Main points	
	▶ Disabled people have formed a range of pressure groups.
	▶ These vary in their approach in obtaining the rights of disabled people.
	▶ The most radical groups are those formed by disabled people themselves.
	▶ There have been a considerable number of legislative changes to improve the position of disabled people.
	▶ Perhaps the most important was the 1995 Disability Discrimination Act which outlawed direct and indirect discrimination by commercial and public organisations against disabled people.
	▶ In 2001 the Disability Rights Commission was set up.
	▶ This, however, has no powers to prosecute companies who discriminate against disabled people.
	▶ There are also a number of important organisations which are excluded from the discrimination legislation.

Conclusion

In this chapter we have examined the way that disabled people are perceived and treated by the population and even by the 'experts'. This has resulted in disabled people being marginalised socially and economically. This marginalisation is demonstrated in the way they are treated socially by other, non-disabled people, and by the high levels of unemployment and poverty they experience.

Only relatively recently has enough political pressure been brought to bear on politicians for anti-discrimination legislation to be introduced. However, this does not give the Disability Rights Commission the same powers as the Equal Opportunities Commission, for example.

15 CHAPTER SUMMARY

1   The numbers of disabled people are difficult to state exactly, because of differing definitions of disability. The figure may actually be well over 8 million.

2   It is important to realise that the term 'disabled people' covers a huge range of different people with different impairments caused by different circumstances and which place different demands upon the disabled person.

3   Disabled people are also a reflection of the wider population with divisions by age, ethnicity and gender, amongst other things. Though a greater proportion of disabled people are old.

4   Disabled people face discrimination in a wide range of areas.

5   One of the most important areas of discrimination is employment.

6   Disabled people are more likely to be unemployed, in part-time work and in lower status jobs.

7   One of the consequences of this is that they have relatively high chances of living in poverty – despite the fact that they often have greater expenses than the majority of the population.

8   Historically, disabled people have been treated very differently by different generations.

9   Before industrialisation they were often employed, and worked alongside others.

10 During the period of industrialisation, they were excluded from the factories and were 'looked after' in workhouses.

11 Later 'care' was given in a range of residential institutions where they were cut off from the population.

12 More recently the approach has been dominated by community care and the demands of disabled people for the right to live independent lives.

13 In their personal lives, disabled people still have to deal with stigma and discrimination.

14 Disabled people have formed a range of pressure groups.

15 These vary in their approach in obtaining the rights of disabled people.

16 The most radical groups are those formed by disabled people themselves.

17 There have been a considerable number of legislative changes to improve the position of disabled people.

18 The 1995 Disability Discrimination Act outlawed direct and indirect discrimination by commercial and public organisations against disabled people.

19 In 2001 the Disability Rights Commission was set up. But this has no powers to prosecute companies who discriminate against disabled people, and there are a number of organisations which are excluded from the legislation.

Useful website

www.drc-gb.org.uk: the Disability Rights Commission website, which has a directory of links

www.disabilitynet.co.uk: Disability Net

www.rnib.org.uk: Royal National Institute for the Blind

ADULTS WITH LEARNING DISABILITIES

Chapter contents

- ### What's in a name?

  This chapter begins with a comment how society has regarded adults with learning difficulties as **different** from the general population, resulting in damaging stereotypes and a refusal to acknowledge individual potential. This is followed by a discussion about how words and labels used to describe adults with learning disabilities have changed from being stigmatising and offensive to those offering a sense of dignity.

- ### What is learning disability?

  This section clarifies the confusion some people may have between the terms 'learning disability' and 'mental illness'. It then moves on to look at the extent of learning disability in the population and how it is actually measured. Finally, the variety of causes of learning disability are described.

- ### Changing approaches to learning disability

  This is a fairly detailed discussion of the changes in the policies towards learning disabilities and how they have been linked with different academic ideas on the nature of learning disability and how best to respond to it. We note that historically people with learning disabilities were hidden away in institutions, but gradually as a result of the normalisation movement (which demanded that they should be allowed to have as normal a life as possible), there was a move towards community care. We look at the variety of community care institutions.

  In recent years more radical approaches to the position of people with learning difficulties have emerged – in particular variations on the idea of advocacy. This section includes a brief description of the movement, which gained ascendancy in the 1970s and challenged the idea of **difference** and argued for social and educational inclusion for all and encouraged patterns of daily living shared by others.

- ### Legislation

  The final section takes us through the legislation which is relevant to understanding learning disabilities and how policies have changed.

Introduction: What's in a name?

The old children's saying 'Sticks and stones will break my bones, but names will never hurt me' does not stand up when discussing the history of people with learning disabilities. If you were investigating the names and labels that have been used to describe people with a learning disability, you would quickly realise how much these names and labels have contributed to the idea of *difference* – the 'them and us' scenario. Such names and labels have encouraged stereotypical beliefs and myths about adults with learning disabilities and a recognition of their individuality, personal identity and value to society has been either ignored or rejected.

Fear and loathing: the response to people with learning difficulties

Nine out of 10 people with learning difficulties have been bullied during the past year and are in constant fear of victimisation, according to a report published today.

Nearly 1,000 people with learning difficulties, a range of conditions affecting intellectual ability, responded to a questionnaire. They complained of name-calling, threats,

harassment and assault. Two-thirds were bullied frequently and a third on a daily or weekly basis.

One woman said yoghurt and eggs had been thrown at her

windows and wire put across the gate. After a while her tormentors threatened to burn down the house. One man said: "At the bus stop, people would come up to me for no reason, call

me names, kick and push me."
  Children and young people were the most common aggressors for the 1.2 million

people with learning disabilities in the UK. When reporting instances of assault to the police, some people said officers were

dismissive or off-hand.
  Fred Hendell, chief executive of Mencap, which published the report, Living in Fear, said:

"Many people with a learning difficulty are even scared to enter public places because of their fear of such harassment."

Source: *The Daily Telegraph*, 21 June 1999

Adults with learning disabilities have often been portrayed as a 'problem', the consequences of such negativity resulting in a social policy of separation and a social practice founded on distance. In many cases, only family members and friends had experience of the day-to-day lives of adults with learning disabilities, such was the void between them and the general population.

Words like 'cretin', 'idiot' and 'imbecile' have long since passed into everyday language as terms of personal abuse, but we should not forget their origins. Some of the legislation concerning adults with learning difficulties used such definitions as 'feeble minded' or 'moral imbecile'. Being 'backward' was a common term that many people used when discussing educational ability and it was not so long ago that government departments and some educators used the term 'sub-normal'. Such terms were, and still are, offensive and cause much pain and distress. The term 'mental handicap' is still commonly used, especially if there is an identifiable medical condition, but many people find this an awkward term as it still carries an air of stigma.

Question

'I'm not handicapped, I can do things.'

Why is the term 'people with learning disabilities' preferred?

The negative career of a person with learning disabilities

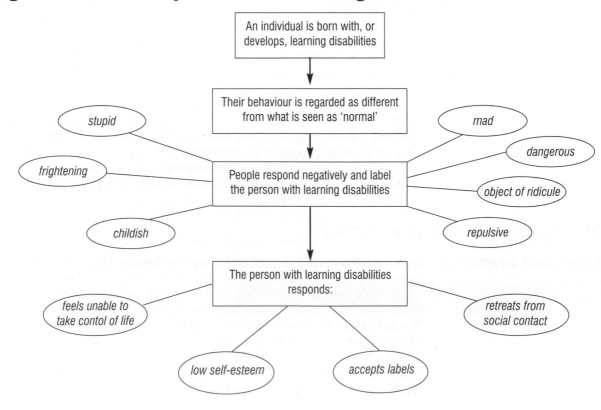

1 How do certain labels reinforce stereotyped views of adults with learning difficulties?

2 What is meant by 'stigmatising'? In what part of the diagram could the term 'stigma' or 'stigmatising' be used?

3 How does the diagram help us to understand the extract we read earlier (pages 419–20)?

The term 'adults with learning disabilities' although for various reasons unlikely to satisfy everyone (some prefer 'adults with learning difficulties'), addresses the negative image of previous terms and offers an opportunity for dignity and respect.

What is learning disability?

Definitions

Learning disability – a general term to describe a permanent condition in individuals, who for various reasons are unable to learn and understand ideas as quickly as others

Mental illness – usually a treatable condition resulting from biological/environmental and social factors. Adults with learning disabilities can suffer from mental illnesses

The term **learning disability**, often referred to as 'special needs' when used in an educational context, covers a wide range of people who for a number of reasons are unable to learn and assimilate ideas as rapidly or as thoroughly as others. Adults with learning disabilities range from those whose condition is relatively mild to those whose condition is considered severe, where, for example, the ability to communicate is a struggle and often restricted.

A learning disability is a permanent condition that has no 'cure', but with appropriate support, education and commitment from families, care agencies and politicians, much can be done to overcome the condition and encourage full integration and contribution to society.

Many people, either from lack of knowledge or prejudice, assume that learning disability (mental handicap is a common term used in day-to-day conversation) means the same as **mental illness**. It is important to make the distinction between the two terms. The central difference is that an adult with a learning disability acquires their condition either at birth or through a life event such as an accident or an illness, whereas a mental illness usually results from a change in a person's mental state arising from stress or other problems that they find difficult to control. A mental illness, for the most part, can be treated and is not necessarily a permanent condition, while a learning disability is usually a 'fixed' condition and remains throughout a person's life. This does not mean that an adult with a learning disability cannot suffer from a mental illness; psychiatrists, psychologists and other mental health professionals are aware of the possibility of 'dual diagnosis' in some individuals, who are no different from the general population in that mental illness can affect and mar their daily lives.

Measuring learning disability

Children born with severe learning disabilities, such as autism or Down's Syndrome, are usually picked up at an early stage by the authorities. Under the 1981 Education Act, such children are entitled to a statement of special educational need which will enable them to receive special education from the age of two through to the age of nineteen. During this time, they will probably receive input not only from educational psychologists and special needs teachers, but also from a range of therapists, doctors and other care workers. Parents will receive support from social services, as children with disabilities are classed under the 1989 Children Act as 'children in need'.

The method of measuring learning disability in children and adults has been
scientific, involving medical practitioners and psychologists using a variety of tests
based on the **Intelligence Quotient (IQ)** model. This model assumes that a
person's intelligence is innate and therefore can be measured. Despite being a
controversial and much debated assumption about intelligence, IQ tests are the
most common method of measurement used to assess the severity of learning
disability. Generally someone is considered to have a learning disability when they
function at a level of ability which is significantly lower than their chronological
age. For instance, a person who is twelve years old and functions at the level of
ability of a six-year-old would be said to have an IQ of 50, or half their chronological age. An IQ of 50 is often taken as the broad dividing line between moderate
and severe learning disability. It must be borne in mind, however, that the IQ as a
means of assessment is the average only and does not necessarily show up the
strengths and weaknesses of an individual. It should, therefore, be considered
with some caution.

Generally, a person with a learning disability does not develop in childhood as
quickly as other children and will not attain the full mental capacities of a 'normal'
adult.

The extent of learning disability

The proportion of people in the general population with a learning disability is
estimated at 2 per cent, and 2–3 per cent of the population has an IQ less than 70.
Of these, 1 in 10 are severely affected. The prevalence of severe learning disability
is estimated at 2–3 per 1,000 for adults and 3–4 per 1,000 for children and
adolescents.

The government estimates that this totals 210,000 adults and 1.2 million children
with severe learning disabilities.

Causes of learning disability

Learning disability is caused by a wide range of factors. Although we know there
are approximately 300 possible causes, the exact cause is known in only about
one-third of cases of children and adults with a severe learning disability in the
UK.

There are four broad reasons why learning disability can occur:

- genetic reasons (an infant is born with learning disabilities)
- illness of some kind, which leaves learning disabilities
- injuries (known as trauma), for example after a car accident
- socio-environmental factors.

Main points
▶ There has been considerable debate over the correct term to describe people
who have some permanent intellectual impairment. The term 'people with
learning disabilities' is now regarded as most appropriate.

▶ People with learning disabilities face discrimination, harassment and
stigma.

▶ It is difficult to define learning disability, but it is generally measured in terms
of IQ.

▶ There are a number of different causes of learning disability.

▶ There are 1.4 million people in England alone with learning disabilities.

Changing approaches to learning disability

Institutions

From the latter part of the nineteenth century until as late as the 1980s, people with learning disabilities were segregated from normal life. They were put into special institutions were they were 'cared for' and treated as children, being given little choice and having quite strict discipline imposed upon them. In many cases, mentally ill people and people with learning disabilities were simply put together. Indeed this confusion between the two groups remains today. Conditions in the asylums and long-stay hospitals were often quite brutal. Frighteningly, the definition of what constituted learning disability, mental illness and 'morally disapproved of' behaviour was confused, so that women who had children out of marriage (even as late as the 1920s) could find themselves placed in a long-stay hospital, having been defined as having learning difficulties. To make matters worse, the child would be taken away.

Memories   Below are two reminiscences of former 'in-mates' of institutions.

Ernest recalls:
'Patients had to be careful how they behaved in their work and on the villa or wherever they were 'cos there was strict staff in those days and any offence, they used to be up before one of the senior doctors. In the case of first offences, they were warned of the serious nature of the offence and what would happen if that or anything like it was repeated.

Then they were placed before the doctor and they lost all their privileges for a certain length of time. As far as privileges were concerned, [they] used to be going to films and concerts and in the hospital grounds, recreation hall and money included.
   Staff had their own way of dealing with minor problems. Problems such as incontinence created extra work and could lead

to punishment even when a person's physical handicaps prevented them from having control of their bladder and bowels.'
   Margaret remembers:
'If you were bursting to go somewhere and you wet yourself, you know like with me, you got punished. Say you were in a wheelchair and you couldn't talk to tell them, you still got punished

– couldn't go out, couldn't see your visitors.
   Shall I tell you sometime else – if you leave your food, you know what they used to do? If you didn't eat your dinner – leave it for your tea. And if you didn't eat it for tea, you had it for your supper and if you didn't eat it for your supper you had it for your next meal. It's true!'

Source: M. Potts, *A Fit Person to be Removed* (Northcote House Publishers, 1991)

Did Ernest and Margaret experience an institution that functioned to control them or to care for them?

Institutions for adults with learning disabilities, with few exceptions, pursued policies that resulted in segregation from mainstream society, had low expectations of individual achievement, offered little choice or opportunity to residents, acted in a patronising manner and effectively denied a person their rights and dignity. There were still 1,500 people with learning disabilities in long-stay hospitals in 2001, though these are all to be phased out by 2004.

The working life of a man with learning disabiities

For 20 years, he spent his days at a centre in Oxfordshire where people with learning difficulties sorted plastic components for things such as bicycle handles and bottle tops, work he found mind-numbingly dull. "I had an occasion where

we finished early and at lunchtime they mixed it all up and made us do it again," said Edwards, 47. He finally quit when the centre started charging members £1 per day to attend, thereby essentially asking him to pay to be bored.

Source: *Guardian Unlimited*, 14 April 2001

Normalisation

During the 1970s, in a reaction against the poor quality of care treatment of people in long-stay institutions (mainly hospitals), Wolfensberger developed the principle of **normalisation** which was aimed to promote a better quality of life for those traditionally cared for in institutions (W. Wolfensberger, *The Principle of Normalisation in Human Services* [NIMR, Toronto, 1972]). As the name implies, normalisation argues that people with any form of disability should be encouraged to live as normal a life as possible. The idea of putting people away in institutions and segregating them from the wider society, for their own protection, was, Wolfensberger argued, harmful and simply led to them being stigmatised and stereotyped. Furthermore, they never had a chance to taste 'normal' life and as a consequence their behaviour became more and more institutionalised. This made them even more different from the bulk of the population.

Normalisation derives from two beliefs:

- that people reject others because of their differences – putting them in institutions and trying to 'help' them could do nothing about society's attitudes
- that individuals have the right to be valued for themselves (as opposed to being valued as handicapped or disabled people) and, furthermore, have the right to participate in and experience all the normal activities which 'normal' people engage in.

The implications of this approach for all people with disabilities is enormous – it emphasises that the role of the social services and the health services is to help people live absolutely normal lives with the same range of choices as those without disabilities.

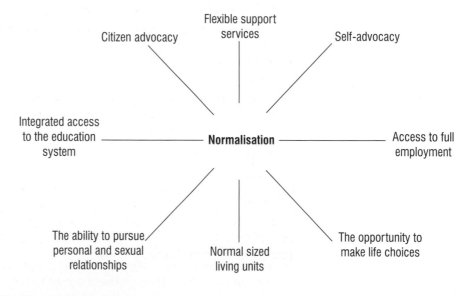

The principles of normalisation

Human rights?

Twelve cases in which parents are seeking to have their mentally handicapped daughters sterilised are being considered for court hearings, the Official Solicitor's office revealed yesterday.

A total of 89 similar cases where legal permission to sterilise had been sought, had gone to the office over the past 11 years, a spokesman said. Of these, 32 were not pursued. Of the 57 that proceeded, 48 resulted in sterilisation operations. The current cases are at various stages of legal proceedings.

Concern is growing over the numbers of applications in spite of a climate that encourages greater autonomy for people with mental illness or learning disabilities.

The charity Mencap said that the cases were unacceptable. "It is outrageous that in the Nineties any woman can be forced to have a sterilisation for social reasons," said Steve Billington, campaigns director. "People with learning disabilities must not be prevented from making their own choices. No one would dispute sterilisation for sound medical reasons, but it must be clear that it is for medical reasons only and not just for society's convenience.

"It is a fact that some parents

| want their daughters sterilised and it is right that this must go through the courts. However, this should be viewed as a last resort. | Sterilisation does not protect against disease and surgery can be dangerous to women with profound disabilities," he said. | Wendy Perez, who has learning difficulties and is a member of Mencap, said: "With the right partner and right support, women | with learning disabilities can have children and be good mums like everyone else." |

Source: *The Daily Telegraph*, 12 September 1997

1 What is your view? Do you think that people with (perhaps severe) learning disabilities should have the right to have children?

2 How does this help us to understand the concept of 'normalisation'?

Social role valorisation

In later writing, Wolfensberger saw the task of normalisation (or *social role valorisation*, as he later called it) firstly as the creation of valued roles for people who were in some way regarded as deviant (for example, being proud of themselves) and, secondly, as helping people with disabilities to develop their own skills and capabilities to the full.

The implications of this for professionals was that they should:

- ensure that individuals with learning disabilities should be seen to be present in the community and not hidden away
- encourage those with learning disabilities to make their own choices and to understand their situation
- encourage and develop the competences of individuals, so they can have confidence in their ability to function in normal situations
- enhance the respect for people with learning disabilities, so that the terms used and the status accorded them was not as second-class citizens but as valued members of society
- ensure that individuals play a full role in society, by participating and having a wide network of relationships.

The philosophy of normalisation has been very influential in policy-making since the 1970s, and in particular in the attempts to develop community services for people with learning disabilities and for those with mental illness. One can immediately see, for example, that the underlying ideas for community care spring from this philosophy.

Community care

In 1975, the White Paper, *Better Services for the Mentally Ill*, provided the policy framework for all later developments. It advocated the expansion of local authority personal social services to provide a range of support for mentally ill people, including residential, domiciliary, day care and social work support and the provision by the NHS of specialist services in the local community.

These psychiatric services are provided in district general hospitals (or trusts), which have units for both inpatients and outpatients. There are also clinics provided in the community. The teams of workers comprise psychiatrists, nurses, social workers, therapists and psychologists, and they are encouraged to work together in a co-ordinated way. By April 1991, each district had to have a fully organised care programme to provide co-ordinated care for people disabled by mental illness and living in the community.

The result of the build-up of **community care** has been the rapid run-down of the
long-term residential institutions. However, critics have pointed out that large
numbers of those being sent out from residential institutions do not appear to be
receiving help from community teams.

Advocacy

Modern thinking is very much about the promotion of choice, independence and
rights. Needless to say, this is not always straightforward among people who,
amongst other difficulties, often have communication problems. In recent years,
various forms of **advocacy** have developed to help people with learning
disabilities to stand up for their rights. Advocacy means to speak and act, persua-
sively or forcefully, on behalf of someone's rights and interests, whether these are
your own or someone else's.

Since the 1970s and 1980s, advocacy has arisen as a means by which people with
learning disabilities can be helped to say what they want and lead as independent
and 'normal' lives as possible. Three forms of advocacy have been identified:

- (citizen) advocacy – uses befrienders
- legal advocacy – a check against exploitation
- self-advocacy – encourages people to speak out directly for themselves.

Self-advocacy

Three hundred people with learning difficulties have gathered here on a muggy Saturday afternoon to participate in Express 2000, a series of discussion groups and art workshops ... at the moment they are enjoying the opening ceremony ... the final guest is introduced to the audience as "a man who has learning difficulties and has made his life work" ... He stumbles over his words. But it doesn't matter. Nearly every sentence is followed by a burst of applause.

"When it comes down to it, the only professionals who are fit to talk about what it's like to have learning difficulties are people with learning difficulties." The audience cheers.

"If something bad is happening in your life, then you need to stand up and change that." More claps and shouts.

"What's your message for people here today?" asks one of his interviewers.

"If you're not part of a self-advocacy organisation, join it. If every person with a learning difficulty across the country was part of a self-advocacy group, then that would send a message to social service professionals who think they know it all."

Lee may not look like much of a threat, but he is armed with an idea that is upending the way people understand the learning disabled. The idea is called self-advocacy. The principle behind self-advocacy is simple: people

with learning difficulties should be able to advocate for their own needs, rather than having their needs represented by others – parents, social workers, teachers, doctors.

"It's a way of people with learning difficulties getting a voice and getting their ideas across. It means they can tell people what they want and make decisions for themselves."
...

The self-advocacy movement in Britain has spent the past 20 years hammering away at that attitude. Today, people who would once have been called retards, mentally-deficient, spastic are running their own organisations, helping social workers assess health, leisure

and residential services, campaigning for increased independence, sitting on government advisory committees.

[Twenty years ago] ... people with learning difficulties were facing bigotry and prejudice as potent as racism and sexism. In Britain, most lived either in hospitals or with their families. Hospitals were large, isolated institutions, ... where disabled people were hidden from the rest of society. Overcrowded wards made privacy a scarce commodity. People shared rooms, occasionally even clothes and toothbrushes. Some people were committed as children and lived in such places their entire lives.

Source: *Guardian Unlimited*, 14 April 2001

1 What is the difference between advocacy and self-advocacy?

2 Why do they reject advocacy?

3 Do you think that people with learning disabilities can live their own lives independently?

4 Do you think that advocacy is still a form of discrimination?

WOULD YOU LIKE TO BE ONE HALF OF A POWERFUL PARTNERSHIP?

Just think …

Have there been times when someone has:

- offered you friendship?
- helped make good things happen?
- given encouragement to try something new?
- helped you change the course of events?

Most people can answer yes.

But …

Some people with learning disabilities often can't get out to meet new people and when they need someone no one is there.

So …

Could you offer someone your time and support to develop a powerful partnership and act as their volunteer Citizen Advocate?

Citizen advocacy partnerships are based on friendship and people doing ordinary things together that all friends do.

What is citizen advocacy?

- It's a powerful partnership between two people.
- It's helping someone to get themselves heard and listened to.

- It's representing the views of someone else as if they were your own views.
- It's a unique way of volunteering some time and commitment to someone new in your life.

Who can be a citizen advocate?

Advocates are ordinary local people with some free time to include someone with a learning disability in their life.

But why are advocates needed?

Many people with learning disabilities:

- are not being presented with many choices
- are not being asked to take part in making the decisions that effect their lives
- are not being asked or encouraged to join in with the local community
- are not being allowed to take any risks
- are not being listened to
- are being denied the right of equality of opportunity in every day situations, situations many people take for granted.

What do advocates do?

- An advocate enters into an equal partnership with one

person, their partner.
- An advocate makes a long term commitment to their partner and not to service providers, family, other friends, or the Advocacy Office.

One advocate researched into a particular disease which was causing her partner a lot of distress and discomfort. Armed with this information she was then able to press the institution where her partner lived to provide a suitable diet. This really made a difference to her partner's life.

Another person was introduced to a young man who lived at home with his elderly parents. He was very isolated from the local community until he was introduced to this person who became his advocate. Together they discovered some country walks, found out what was going on at the local Community College, and became great railway enthusiasts.

Another advocate was introduced to someone who had lived for 40 odd years in a long stay hospital. She had always wanted her own flat but was forever being told that she wouldn't be able to manage. She was introduced to an advocate and together they got people to listen and she is now living in her own place.

Case study

William Gadd is in his late sixties. Most of his life has been spent in institutions. Until a year ago he was living in a long-stay psychiatric hospital, where a group of older men with learning difficulties had been inappropriately placed. Before that he had lived in a hostel and in another long-stay hospital. Now he

is living in a town-based residential unit for elderly people. Adult education tutors have been involved in William's latest move, working closely with hospital staff and social services staff. William has learnt to experience choice and decision-making. Everyday experiences – visiting

supermarkets, catching a bus, making a cup of tea – have been new situations for William, who has learnt to adapt well. He has cast off his institutional clothes and has chosen for himself a set of bright new clothing. A yellow shirt and matching scarf are particular favourites. He has learnt the way to

the shops and how to buy his cigarettes. He has developed a keen interest in cookery and is learning to make new recipes of his choice. William is fond of birds and feeds them every day. He has learnt about them from books borrowed from the local library.

Source: J. Sutcliffe, *Adults with Learning Difficulties: Education for Choice and Empowerment* (OU Press, 1990)

Describe three basic life skills that William Gadd has developed since leaving an institution.

Community initiatives

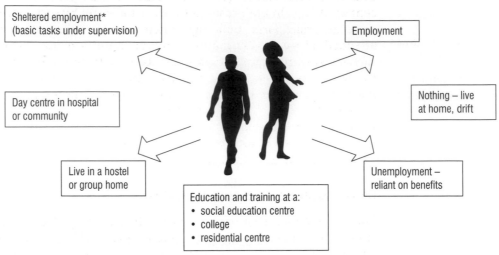

Sheltered employment*
(basic tasks under supervision)

Employment

Day centre in hospital
or community

Nothing – live
at home, drift

Live in a hostel
or group home

Unemployment –
reliant on benefits

Education and training at a:
• social education centre
• college
• residential centre

* Limited opportunities, especially in times of high unemployment

What happens to adults with learning disabilities when they reach the age of 19?

Adults with learning difficulties have not only been socially isolated by way of long-stay hospitals and institutions but also by community services such as separate transport, day centres and leisure clubs. However, community integration does take place in the form of the following initiatives, some of which have become established practice.

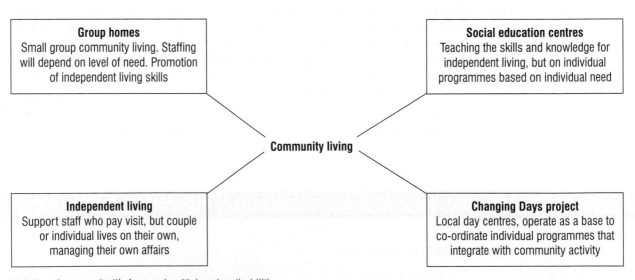

Group homes
Small group community living. Staffing will depend on level of need. Promotion of independent living skills

Social education centres
Teaching the skills and knowledge for independent living, but on individual programmes based on individual need

Community living

Independent living
Support staff who pay visit, but couple or individual lives on their own, managing their own affairs

Changing Days project
Local day centres, operate as a base to co-ordinate individual programmes that integrate with community activity

Varieties of community life for people with learning disabilities

Group homes

Group homes have become firmly established over the last twenty years as a means by which a small group of people with learning disabilities can live in the community, usually having been moved out of a mental hospital. The principle is that the residents can live with a greater degree of 'normality' and independence. Such homes are run by social services, the NHS or, more usually these days, voluntary and private organisations. The level of staffing input can vary depending on the level of need of the residents.

Social education centres

Social education centres (SECs) developed in the 1980s from the old adult training centres (ATCs). In both cases, they are usually run by social services. Whilst ATCs were generally large buildings where many adults with learning disabilities attended all week, fitting into a programme of activities such as basic personal care, cooking, routine contract work, road safety and so on, SECs have tried to be less institutionalised, building on individual personal profiles, giving individuals their own programmes based on individual need. Service users usually attend five days a week. The SEC is often a base from which other activities take place. The whole emphasis is to try to equip people with learning disabilities with the skills and knowledge for independent living. Much work of SECs is putting the normalisation principle into practice.

Independent supported living

This represents a step on from group home living. It is usually a collaborative effort between purchasing bodies (often a joint NHS/social services operation) and a private or voluntary care organisation. A 'normal' house is obtained for a small number of people with learning disabilities (it can be just one). All the relevant benefits (most commonly Disability Living Allowance, Housing Benefit and Jobseeker's Allowance) are claimed and the resident(s) are given just enough support to ensure that they can lead as independent a life as possible. With this arrangement, the keyworker or support worker visits rather than living-in.

Changing Days Project

More than 60,000 people with learning difficulties across England and Wales attend segregated day centres where opportunities for development are limited. The Changing Days Project supports the shift from services based on containment and segregation, to services centred on individual needs. It was launched in December 1994 as a partnership between the King's Fund (a social welfare charitable organisation) and the National Development Team. It was based on the belief that people with learning difficulties have the ability to become full members of their local community. The idea was to stimulate innovative and purposeful ways of providing day opportunities for adults with learning disabilities in their communities rather than being bussed to centres.

Legislation

1886 Lunacy Act

This Act addressed the needs of adults with learning disabilities with the provision of specialised institutions. Before this Act, people with learning disabilities could be found incarcerated in Poor Law workhouses, prisons and 'madhouses' (lunatic asylums).

1913 Mental Deficiency Act

This Act introduced four classifications of mental deficiency: idiot, imbecile, feeble minded and moral imbecile.

The Act was based on the belief that people who were mentally ill and people who had learning disabilities were more or less the same group of people. They were believed to be socially and morally 'degenerate', and through their irrational and immoral behaviour they were seen as dangerous threats to society. The moral element was very important indeed, and anything that was then defined as immoral, such as becoming pregnant outside marriage, was regarded as proof of mental handicap! The 1913 Act set out educational provision for handicapped children. It was, to some extent, based on humanitarian concerns. However, it was also thought that with appropriate education and training this 'burdensome' section of society could be made less of a liability.

1959 Mental Health Act

In 1957, a Commission on the Law Relating to Mental Illness and Mental Handicap reported to Parliament, and this resulted in the Mental Health Act 1959. The Act placed fairly strong safeguards on the extent to which people could be placed in institutions against their will. People with learning disabilities, up to that point described officially as 'mentally defective' or 'mentally retarded', were reclassified as 'educationally sub-normal' (ESN). IQs of under 50 were still considered ineducable; 50+ was severely ESN and 80+ moderately ESN.

1983 Mental Health Act

This Act of Parliament introduced the definitions of mental impairment and severe mental impairment and included in the definition was the guidance that only those people who showed aggressive and/or irresponsible conduct could fit the criteria of the definition. This meant that the majority of adults with learning disabilities were removed from the scope of the Act and therefore compulsory detention in a hospital was not an option for them. In short, such legal definitions prevent the 'dumping' of adults with learning disabilities into hospitals or other institutions.

1990 NHS and Community Care Act

This major piece of legislation radically changed the basis upon which health and social care was arranged. It did not start the process of moving people out of long-stay institutions, but it emphasised the needs of people with learning disabilities to be assessed and met, where appropriate, in the community.

2001 Valuing People (White Paper)

As a result of this White Paper:

- The remaining long-stay hospitals are to be closed.
- A five-year programme, costing £3 billion a year, includes a fund of £2.3 million to support an increase in advocacy rights.
- Each person with learning disabilities is to get a health professional to supervise them.
- Financial support is to be gradually shifted to the individuals and their carers, rather than funded through local authorities.
- Local authorities are to provide a wider choice of housing.

As we can see, views about people with learning disabilities have changed greatly in a relatively short period of time. The changes in thinking are summarised in the table opposite.

Deviance model (traditional view)	Rights model
'The mentally handicapped' are different, vulnerable and need protection.	Adults with learning disabilities are individuals with needs and rights like anyone else.
They should be kept apart from others (segregated).	They should be able to mix with others (integrate).
They can't cope with the everyday world we live in – and we can't cope with them.	They should have as much independence and control over their lives as possible.
They need to be looked after, supervised and controlled – treated, in respects, like children (infantilised) or even criminals.	Their lives should be as 'normalised' as possible, even if this creates risks.

Main points
▶ The policy towards people with learning disabilities has changed over time.
▶ From Victorian times until the 1970s, people with learning difficulties lived in long-stay hospitals away from society.
▶ There has been a movement towards them living in the community since then.
▶ This is partly a result of the idea of 'normalisation', which means that they should have the right and be provided with the chances to live as 'normal' a life as possible.
▶ Valorisation means to have a sense of their own worth.
▶ More recently there has been a move towards advocacy, and in the most 'extreme' case towards self-advocacy.
▶ The government has recognised the right of people with learning disabilities to live independent lives and so they have now started to obtain their rights as citizens.

Conclusion

The chapter has examined how people with learning disabilities suffer from discrimination and stigma. For many, life is very difficult. Historically, they have been excluded from society, living in large hospitals under the 'care' or, more accurately the control, of the professionals. More recently, there has been an gradual acceptance of the rights of people with learning disabilities. The long-stay hospitals have been closed down and people with learning disabilities have gradually moved into the community. They have still not won the right to lead independent lives, however, and there remains a considerable debate over the extent to which society should allow them to have freedom to make their own choices. Nevertheless, with the recent government White Paper *Valuing People: A new strategy for people with learning disabilities for the 21st century*, there does seem to be a recognition that people with learning disabilities have rights too.

16 CHAPTER SUMMARY

1 There has been considerable debate over the correct term to describe people who have some permanent intellectual impairment. The term 'people with learning disabilities' is now regarded as most appropriate.

2 People with learning disabilities face discrimination, harassment and stigma.

3   It is difficult to define learning disability, but it is generally measured in terms of IQ.

4   There are a number of different causes of learning disability.

5   There are 1.4 million people in England alone with learning disabilities.

6   Policy towards people with learning disabilities has changed over time.

7   From Victorian times until the 1970s, people with learning difficulties lived in long-stay hospitals away from society.

8   There has been a movement towards them living in the community since then.

9   This is partly a result of the idea of 'normalisation', which means that they should have the right and be provided with the chances to live as 'normal' a life as possible.

10 Valorisation means to have a sense of their own worth.

11 More recently there has been a move towards advocacy, and in the most 'extreme' case towards self-advocacy.

12 The government has recognised the right of people with learning disabilities to live independent lives and so they have now started to obtain their rights as citizens.

Useful websites

www.doh.gov.uk: the Department of Health

www.mencap.org.uk: Mencap, an organisation which supports the rights of people with learning disabilities

www.mentalhealth.org.uk: Mental Health Foundation

www.disabledliving.org.uk: Disabled Living

www.widgit.com: Learning Difficulties

www.niace.org.uk: NIACE

www.pettarchive.org.uk: Association of Therapeutic Communities

www.jrf.org.uk: the Joseph Rowntree Foundation

MENTAL HEALTH

Chapter contents

• A historical perspective: from institution to community

This chapter begins with a discussion on the changes in how people with mental disorders have been treated over time. The overall movement seems to have been first to put people with mental disorders into institutions, then when the weaknesses were identified, to try to provide community services, and more recently there has been a move back to institutions for the most severely ill people.

• Causes and responses

There is no single, unifying theory or agreement about the meaning of 'mental illness' Contemporary models of explanation suggest that genetic factors, biology, stress, vulnerability, poverty, racism, oppression, psychological trauma and a crisis of faith are all possible causes, many of them inter-related. Medication that attempts to cure or is used to control symptoms, physical treatments, individual talking therapies, group work, family therapy and self-management are some of the possible responses.

• The incidence and classification of mental disorders

The incidence of mental health problems in contemporary society is discussed, together with an explanation of the medical model used in psychiatry. There is general agreement that the medical model is seen as dominant in modern society in the explanation and treatment of mental disorders. We also note that mental health problems are spread rather unevenly amongst the population, with certain groups having higher rates than others

• Legislation

We examine the changes in the laws relating to mental disorders and focus our attention on the current law relating to mental health and the government proposals for reform. Although not unique, mental health law is unusual in that it gives powers to professionals and nearest relatives to deprive an individual of their liberty, mainly in the interests of their own health and safety, yet they may not have committed a crime or caused themselves or others harm.

• Mental health services in the community

This section provides a description of community-based, multi-disciplinary approaches to working with people with a mental disorder. The demise of institutions and the development of community care policies have encouraged innovative approaches to the care of people with mental health problems. There is a a summary of hospital, residential and community services provided by statutory, voluntary, independent and private agencies.

• Mental health and wider social problems

Mental health cannot be isolated from other issues. In this section we take just two examples – homelessness and imprisonment – and show how mental health is related to both of these.

• Empowerment

A movement has developed in recent years that questions the power of professionals and encourages service users to take more control over decisions affecting their welfare and treatment and to seek adequate representation of their circumstances by way of legal rights and participation.

Introduction

In this chapter, we explore the issues surrounding **mental health** – a topical and often misunderstood area of work in the health and caring services. We begin by looking at the changes in provision over time. This helps us to understand that views of what constitutes mental illness have varied over time and this variation has had a very significant impact on policies directed at those with **mental disorders**. We then examine just how many people in the UK have mental disorders, the various competing theories to explain the condition(s) and the different approaches taken both to define it and to deal with it.

Then we look at the changes in legislation regarding mental illness, and comment in particular on the issue of compulsory care for those regarded as having severe mental disorders.

We then move on to look at the range of services on offer and the range of professionals and their tasks. Finally, we have one more look at the **people with mental disorders.** Like other users of the health and care systems, they have begun to demand their rights and increasingly the issue of empowerment has arisen. This seems to point the way to the future.

A historical perspective: from institution to community

Concepts of mental disorder have undergone a profound change during the last two hundred years. In the nineteenth and for some part of the twentieth century, it was commonplace to find such words as 'lunatic', 'imbecile' and 'madman' used to describe individuals suffering from a mental disorder.

In the nineteenth century too, society assumed that 'madness' was incurable and resulted from either genetic factors or immoral lifestyles. Either way, the social policy that developed in this period saw the rise of large, purpose-built institutions (asylums), whose principle function was to confine and restrain 'mad' people and to keep them away from public view. People deemed 'mad' or 'degenerate' were to be segregated from mainstream society and the use of manacles and straight-jackets was not uncommon in these institutions.

The end of the nineteenth century witnessed the rise of the psychiatric profession, which challenged the notion of confinement and introduced a scientific, medical approach to the understanding of mental disorder, advocating ideas of treatment and social rehabilitation. By the beginning of the twentieth century, the medical profession had assumed control and terms such as 'psychoses' , ' neuroses' and 'personality disorders' were used to classify mental disorders within a medical framework. Combinations of biological, psychological, social and environmental models were developed to explain why people suffered from mental disorder. The idea of isolating people who were mentally ill continued until the 1970s. In the process, other groups of people were also excluded from the community and put in asylums – and the distinction between what was known as mental handicap (learning disability) and mental illness became blurred. The two groups were often put together, despite the totally different nature of their problems and their needs.

The 1970s saw the beginning of a decline in the institutionalised population. This was because:

- new drugs were developed which could allow certain categories of people with mental health problems to function more effectively
- critics pointed out the frequent cases of cruel treatment by nurses of people in mental institutions
- the costs of the institutions were much heavier than treatment in the community
- cultural changes meant that the whole concept of isolating large numbers of ill people away from the community and 'normal' life was unfair.

Definitions

Institutionalisation – putting people into institutions to live

Deinstitutionalisation – taking people out of the institutions

However, progress to **deinstitutionalisation** was painfully slow and, although the 1959 Mental Health Act was supposed to lead the way towards community-based services, by 1975, £300 million was still being spent on hospital care for those with mental health problems compared to only £16 million on community services. However, the 1990 NHS and Community Care Act finally led to a full commitment to community care.

The final twist in the history of mental disorder is that there are increasing criticisms of community care, with the argument being put forward that some people with mental disorders are so ill that they cannot cope with life in the community. This has led to the reintroduction of more residential facilities for people with severe personality disorders.

Causes and responses

While there is no one agreed cause of mental disorder, at present there are a number of models, some of them competing with one another, which are used to explain abnormal behaviour. For example, schizophrenia may have the following symptoms: the person may have lost touch with reality; may be suffering from hearing voices and may be paranoid towards those who care for him or her. Different models of mental disorder will explain this differently:

- The biological model might argue that such behaviour is the result of *biological changes* that may have a genetic or hereditary base. A physical illness, such as a brain tumour might be identified.
- Another model might suggest that unresolved conflicts in *childhood* are the root cause.
- Another might argue that *family* dysfunction leading to the breakdown of the individual is the principal factor.
- A further model might suggest academic *stress* or living on a low income as crucial. If appropriate, racism might be a major player, or that the person is experiencing a conflict of religious faith.

The table below illustrates the different models of explanation of mental disorder, and the treatment.

Models and treatment of mental disorder

Model	Theories of causation	Response/treatment
Disease/illness. Organic, medical	Physical or organic cause, identified as a result of a disorder of anatomy or physiology	Hospitalisation, physical investigations, medication and/or physical treatments, e.g. ECT
Psychological/ psychoanalytic	Individual and/or family dysfunction resulting in psychic conflict, e.g. unresolved 'loss' in childhood	Counselling, individual psychotherapy, family therapy. A variety of support networks
Religious/moral	Guilt feelings caused through sin. 'Possession' by the devil. Absence of moral code	Salvation, exorcism, moral management, e.g. health education within a family context
Social control	Delinquency, stigma, normality/abnormality, criminal behaviour	Legal controls and punishment, e.g. probation, prison
Structural factors	Psychological problems caused as a result/response to physical and social environment, e.g. poor housing, racism, stress	Political and social change, e.g. housing policy, working conditions, anti-racist policy and practice

Case study

An example of competing models of explanation occurred in the case of Albert Dryden who, in 1992, built a bungalow on a plot of land in Consett, County Durham, without planning permission from the local council. Mr Dryden had made it clear to his neighbours and especially to council officials that he would not demolish his home and that further meddling by the council into his own affairs would result in them 'running out of body bags'. He had amassed a small arsenal of weapons and explosives and had physically assaulted a council officer. Tragedy followed when Mr Dryden shot and killed a senior council official who had visited the bungalow with a demolition order. At the trial the defence counsel produced psychiatric evidence that Mr Dryden was mentally ill and had been 'commanded by voices'. Consequently he was not responsible for his actions. However, the prosecution produced a psychiatric assessment suggesting that Mr Dryden's responsibilities were 'not substantially impaired' and that he knew what he was doing. The jury agreed and Mr Dryden was given a life sentence. A recent prison hearing decided that parole will not be considered until 2004.

A full report of this can be found in **The Guardian**, 10 August 2000. Go to the Guardian website (www.guardianunlimited.co.uk) and search the archive for the story

1 Using the examples shown in the table above, identify one model of explanation that was offered to the trial judge and jury by the defence and one model of explanation offered by the prosecution.

2 List five occupations where stress levels could result in mental health problems.

3 Identify one Victorian word now used as slang to describe a person with a mental disorder.

Treating mental disorder

Adult psychiatry has taken a leading role in the explanation and treatment of mental disorders and people with mental health problems, and few would argue that the psychiatric profession is the dominant player in the mental health field. Consequently, the general public, the mass media and service users usually look to psychiatry for explanation, advice and intervention. All psychiatrists are medically trained and tend to follow the scientific approach to the understanding of mental disorder, emphasising:

- classification
- diagnosis
- treatment
- prognosis (predicting the outcome)
- aetiology (seeking the original cause).

Psychiatrists usually carry out a mental state examination to see if the symptoms presented fit a type or classification of mental disorder.

Nicola's story

One in five children is now reckoned to have some form of mental health disorder and at least 5% of teenagers are seriously depressed. ...

Nicola, now 15, received no such early intervention. "I was abused at four, I think the first one was; and if someone had tried to help me then ... but no one came to help me, you know things just got worse when I was growing up." At 10, Nicola went into foster care. At 13, she started to hear voices and, after threatening to commit suicide, was admitted to Oakham House in Leicester, one of the few residential child psychiatric units in the country.

Within months, Nicola had deteriorated so much that even Oakham House could not manage her violent and abusive behaviour. She ended up in a secure unit, where she spent over a year.

Nicola is now in a care home, and making progress. But she still takes medication three times a day: an anti-depressant, an anti-psychotic and a mood stabiliser. And when she gets angry, anxious or feels out of control, she slashes her arms. "You just want to do something to get rid of all your anger and built-up aggression and tension," she says, "so you just get something and cut away at yourself."

Source: The Guardian, 18 April 2001

1 What proportion of children are believed to have a mental health disorder?

2 What started Nicola's problems?

3 What were her symptoms?

4 Where was she cared for?

5 How does she cope now?

The incidence and classification of mental disorders

Incidence of mental disorders

It is estimated that one in four people in the UK will seek help and advice over a mental health problem during their lives. One in six will suffer a mental illness, the most common being depression and anxiety.

A study by the British Medical Journal gives some idea of the extent of mental health problems and mental disorders in the UK:

All mental disorders – 20% of adults at any time suffer mental health problems; 40% of general practice consultations involve mental health problems

Depression (including anxiety and depression) – 10% of adults depressed in a week; 55% depressed at some time

Anxiety disorders – 3-6% of adults has clinically important symptoms (about 1% each for phobias, panic disorder and obsessive compulsive disorder)

Suicide – 5,000 deaths and more than 100,000 attempts annually

Self-harm – 1 in 600 people harm themselves sufficiently to require hospital admission; 15 of these go on to kill themselves

Schizophrenia (and other functional psychoses) – 0.4% of people living at home; 1% lifetime risk; 10 patients on a typical general practice list, but 10,000 not registered with a general practitioner

Personality disorder – 5–10% of young adults

Alcohol related disorders – 4.7% of adults show alcohol dependence

Source: Adapted from T. Davies and T.K.J. Craig, *ABC of Mental Health* (BMJ Books, 1998)

Ethnicity

Members of the ethnic minorities have significantly higher chances of being defined as mentally ill than the majority, white population. This may be linked with cultural differences over what is 'appropriate' behaviour. It could also be related to the pressures and stress more commonly experienced by members of ethnic minority groups, caused partially through racism and disadvantage.

Gender

Women are more likely to exhibit behaviour defined as mental illness than men. This may be a result of women being more likely to lead stressful lives, combining careers and the responsibility for childcare, for example, and being more likely to experience poverty and poorer housing conditions.

Poverty

The poorest groups in society are more likely to have higher levels of mental illness. Some writers argue that they are poor precisely because they have lower levels of mental health, but most social scientists suggest instead that the stress of poverty is likely to bring about mental illness.

Classification of mental disorders

Classification embraces three broad categories:

- neuroses

- psychoses
- personality disorders (or psychopathic behaviour).

Each of these categories is sub-divided into specific, recognisable conditions.

Neuroses

These usually involve an exaggeration of normal life concerns and experiences. For example, feelings of depression are a normal reaction to loss. Most people will experience a degree of sadness and despair when a life event takes place that, for example, ends a relationship or involves the loss of a loved one. Many people will say they are 'depressed' to describe the lowering of mood that may be experienced in everyday life. However, when feelings of sadness, worthlessness and despair interfere with and severely affect day-to-day living, when relationships suffer and break down, when life appears futile and not worth living, psychiatrists may regard such symptoms as a mental illness and offer some form of intervention.

Other common neuroses are:

- *anxiety states*, which are characterised by heightened fear and apprehension combined with physical symptoms such as excess sweating and tension. Anxiety may be caused by stress, but becomes problematic when the severity is disproportionate to the possible cause
- *phobias*, of which there are a number of possible classifications, but essentially consist of persistent and unreasonable fear of social situations or specific objects
- *obsessions*, which can take many forms, but can be described as the symbolic repetition of certain actions or speech.

Psychoses

These are serious mental disorders.

- *Schizophrenia* is a condition with a number of psychiatric classifications, but typically a sufferer experiences a sense of unreality, may be disoriented and confused, may experience delusional ideas and be paranoid. A schizophrenic is best understood as having a fragmented, but not a 'split' personality as is sometimes portrayed by the mass media.
- *Manic depression* is an extreme form of depression characterised by excessive mood swings and behaviour. Manic depressives may be affected by suicidal thoughts.

Personality disorders

Many psychiatrists will admit that they are not always successful in treating people, often referred to as *psychopaths* in their severe form, who have been diagnosed as having personality disorders. The reason for this is that the behaviour exhibited is not seen as treatable, being characterised by a lack of conscience and concern for others, persistent criminality and social and familial upheaval. People with personality disorders often reject and disrupt psychiatric intervention.

Criticisms of traditional approaches to mental disorder

Many people are unhappy about the traditional, medical model of understanding and treating mental disorder. These critics point out that by concentrating on physical, organic and biological causes of mental disorder, psychiatry can lose sight of the social and environmental factors that may impact on a person's mental state.

The systems of classification are assumed to be applicable world wide, for example, the symptoms and consequent diagnosis for schizophrenia should be the same whether the person lives in Birmingham or Bangkok, yet cultural and ethnic lifestyles, behaviour patterns and social norms are different from one another and may not be understood or taken into account, especially if the psychiatrist and patient are from different cultural backgrounds.

Activity

Who is mentally ill?

The term 'mental illness' is usually applied when comparing a person's normal behaviour with behaviour that is regarded as untypical. This is problematic for a number of reasons, not least the concept of 'normality', which is never constant or fixed. Consequently, the term 'mental illness' can have no absolute definition, and is left to a judgement as to whether a person's behavioural patterns differ in degree to that which is considered normal in society.

Look at the cases below and decide how far they fit into your idea of being 'mentally ill'.

1 A person who believes he or she was born into the wrong sex and wants to change it.
2 A forty-year-old man who, if he steps on the cracks between paving stones, has to go back to the last lamp-post and start again.
3 A person who appears to get a kick out of upsetting other people and causing them emotional distress.
4 An old lady who forgets to light the gas stove after she has turned it on.
5 Someone who will not go to the bathroom because 'the aliens are in the water'.
6 A fourteen-year-old who attempts to burn down his school because he hates all the teachers

---

Main points

▶ Over time there has been a move away from care in institutions to care in the community.

▶ Recently there has been a limited move back to the institutions for those with severe mental disorders.

▶ There are competing models of what mental illness is and how it is caused in people.

▶ Mental disorders are widespread in the community

▶ It is difficult to define exactly the limits of behaviour which is considered to be mental illness.

Legislation

The laws on mental health over the last 150 years have reflected changing views on the nature and dangerousness of 'madness'. For the people of the late nineteenth century, right up to the middle of the twentieth century, mental disorder was something to be feared. There was a widespread belief that most people with mental disorders were actually or potentially dangerous. The result of these beliefs were that people with mental disorders were put into long-stay, residential mental hospitals, where they were expected to live out their lives as patients with few rights. Many were kept compulsorily in these institutions. The period from 1959 onward saw a change in legislation and a slow and cautious move to allow people with mental disorders to be treated in the community. However, by the late 1990s after a number of highly publicised violent incidents involving people with mental disorders, the pendulum began to swing back to custodial treatment – at least for a minority.

1890 Lunacy Act

This is seen by some commentators as the high point of custodial ideas, which protected the general public from the mentally disordered by an 'out of sight, out of mind' policy. It emphasised the need to provide care in institutions.

1913 Mental Deficiency Act

This Act enshrined the idea of 'moral management'. The Act put people with learning disabilities and people with mental disorders into the same category – they were regarded as degenerate requiring strict control over their lifestyles, and individuals showing immoral behaviour, such as pregnancy outside marriage were to be detained and cured by moral instruction!

1930 Mental Treatment Act

This Act reflected the medical model in that asylums became 'mental hospitals' and lunatics became 'persons of unsound mind', but the mental institutions remained central to psychiatric provision.

1959 Mental Health Act

This Act developed the concept of admission to hospital without compulsion, promoted the movement towards community care and, in addition to medical judgement, introduced the application for admission by mental welfare officers and nearest relatives. Much of the 1959 Act is enshrined in the current legislation.

1983 Mental Health Act

The Act stated that wherever possible people with mental disorders should be admitted to hospital on the same grounds as people with a physical illness, in that no certification is required for entry or departure from hospital or for the admission to hospital for the 'non-protesting'. So, admission (and treatment) without compulsion is a basic principle of the Act.

The Mental Health Act 1983 is extremely complex, with ten parts and 149 sections. First, it defines mental disorder in legal terms so that there are clear grounds for being compulsorily put into a mental hospital. The Act defines mental disorder as 'mental illness, arrested or incomplete development of mind, psychopathic disorder or disability of mind'. It also clearly excludes certain grounds of moral/immoral behaviour and so rejects the 1913 Act's emphasis on immoral behaviour as a sign of mental disorder.

The Act also provides clear grounds for the compulsory admission to hospital, even when the person objects. The Act gives two doctors and an approved social worker the power to admit people against their wishes initially up to a maximum of 28 days' admission (which can be extended up to six months renewable to a year). This is known as 'sectioning'. The grounds for sectioning are that the person is suffering from a mental disorder that makes them dangerous to themselves or others.

To ensure the rights of people compulsorily detained, there are Mental Health Review Tribunals, consisting of three persons – lawyer, doctor and a lay person (a member of the public) – who consider the cases of patients challenging the decisions of the medical profession.

1990 NHS and Community Care Act

This placed a duty on local authorities and the health service to collaborate in providing more community provision for people who have mental health problems. The aim was to provide less hospital-based care and replace this with care in the community.

A number of problems have occurred however, as the Act applies to those with mental disorders:

- *Targeting*: The people with the most severe problems have not received the most help. The Audit Commission says that 'community services are often focused on those with the least severe problems'.
- *Poor co-ordination*: The responsibility for mental health care lies with the local social services, but much of the expertise and funding comes from the health providers. This has led to poor co-ordination and patchy provision of community services.
- *Failure to implement the Care Programme Approach*, which consists of an organised and integrated plan for each person in the community who has a specific 'case manager' responsible for ensuring the provision of appropriate care and services.
- *Poor risk assessment:* A series of violent crimes committed by seriously mentally-ill people, including a number of killings, led in the mid-1990s to demands for greater control of mentally-ill people in the community.
- *Failure of health and social work professionals to monitor and support people who had been moved from hospital care to community care*, even where the individuals were known to be violent or have violent tendencies. This lack of supervision of people with mental disorders meant that they did not take the necessary medication required to improve their condition. The result was a number of violent assaults on members of the public, but even more common was the high incidence of suicide amongst people with mental health disorders living in the community.

1995 Supervision Discharge Orders

As a result of these concerns, in 1995 the government passed legislation to introduce a register of people discharged into the community with significant mental health problems and also introduced supervision discharge orders. These compel certain clients to live at a specific address and attend clinics for treatment or training. Failure to do so can result in the person with mental health disorders being compelled to return to hospital.

As a result, there has been an increase again in the use of compulsion and by 1997, there had been a 45 per cent increase (compared to 1991) in compulsory detention in mental hospitals.

2001 Reforming the Mental Health Act (White Paper)

The White Paper *Reforming the Mental Health Act* is an admission that the move towards community care has not been successful for all people with mental disorders, in particular those with severe personality disorders who are a danger to themselves or to others.

For people with severe personality disorders

For people who have not offended, there will be three stages before compulsory care and treatment. This will involve:

- *preliminary examination* – by two doctors and a social worker to assess the need and urgency of treatment
- *formal assessment and initial treatment* – this will involve the person being given a formal health plan and treatment for 28 days.
- *Care and Treatment Order* – after the 28 days, an independent mental health tribunal will make the decision on any continuing compulsory treatment. The tribunal will have the power to make an order for treatment which will last for up to six months initially. After that, two further six-month orders can be made.

If people with severe mental health disorders have committed a criminal offence, then it will be the responsibility of the court to make decisions on treatment, rather than the tribunal.

For dangerous people with severe personality disorder

The government estimates that there are about 2,400 **dangerous people with severe personality disorders**. They are people who are extremely dangerous to others and include people such as paedophiles who repeatedly offend. Courts can impose three orders on these people:

- *a Care and Treatment Order* – a treatment order made by the court would be for a maximum of six months. Any extension of liability to compulsory treatment after that would be through the procedures for a Tribunal Order
- *a Restriction Order* – where the clinical assessment indicates that the offender poses a significant risk of serious harm to others, or because of the nature of the current offence or previous convictions, the court will be able to add a Restriction Order to a Care and Treatment Order. This will only be applicable when the care and treatment order is based on detention in hospital
- *a Hospital and Limitation Direction* – requires the offender's detention for medical treatment in hospital until such time as the clinical supervisor advises that treatment in hospital is no longer necessary – they then may be transferred to prison.

The White Paper also provides for the creation of a Commission for Mental Health to oversee the whole area of mental disorder and which will oversee increased rights for advocacy and for the legal safeguards of those with 'long-term incapacity'.

Definitions

Severe personality disorder – people who show extreme forms of behaviour

Dangerous people with severe personality disorders – people who show extreme forms of behaviour which is likely to harm others

---

Has community care failed?

A A recent report found that one murder is committed about every two weeks by mental patients and about 1,000 commit suicide each year. The number of beds available for psychiatric patients has dropped from 150,000 in 1960 to 37,000.

The review follows growing concern over the number of patients discharged into the community following legislation introduced ... in 1990.

The Health Minister commented ...

"There are a higher proportion of people still needing some form of 24-hour residential care than the system recognises."

The Health Secretary admitted

that a return to institutional care would be expensive. ...

However, he said that the cost of the existing system was too great in non-financial terms, including "serious injury or death of some totally innocent person" as well as the "quality of life of neighbours".

He believed that care in the community had "failed a substantial number" of patients and members of the public whose lives had been made intolerable. The effort and resources have not been put into looking after people.

"Quite clearly there are a lot of people who were formerly locked up who now are getting a better life and nobody is suffering, but there are others who need a lot more attention and unless they get a lot more attention they can make other people's lives a misery."

Pressure has been growing on the Government to reverse the care in the community policy following a number of high profile cases, including the murder of Jonathan Zito, who was stabbed to death by Christopher Clunis, a schizophrenic, in 1992.

Last December, two psychiatric patients released from the same hospital were convicted of killing. Tolga Kurter, a 20-year-old schizo-phrenic, was convicted of stabbing a neighbour to death, and Martin Mursell killed his father.

Ben Bernard, then 28, who had a 10-year history of mental illness, was sent to a secure mental hospital indefinitely last year as a "danger to the public" after slashing a policeman's face with a Swiss army knife. A paranoid schizophrenic, Bernard had been released into the community only weeks before he attacked Pc Neil Maltby.

Jayne Zito, who set up the Zito Trust to campaign for reform after her husband was killed, welcomed the move. "It is very important that these changes are introduced," she said. "They have closed the old institutions without considering those people who have care needs on a long-term basis. People who are a risk either to themselves or to other people are being released into the community."

Marjorie Wallace, chief executive of the mental health charity Sane, said care in the community had been a "huge social experiment". She said that between 30 and 40 per cent of homeless people were suffering from mental illness. "Housing the mentally ill in these havens isn't Dickensian. Sending them out to beg on the streets is."

Source: *The Daily Telegraph*, 17 January 1998

B In an analysis of 35 cases where mental patients killed someone while being looked after under care in the community policies, it found that up to 57 per cent had not taken their prescribed drugs. ...

The report criticised health authorities that closed mental hospitals and discharged patients into the care of local authority social services which then passed them to the voluntary sector or housing associations to find them somewhere to live. "Many of them are housed in flats on their own and receive no face-to-face contact from the services from that point onward."

Source: *The Daily Telegraph*, 3 April 1998

1 What criticism of community care is being made here?

2 What is the health minister suggesting the answer is?

3 What percentage of the homeless people are suffering from mental illness, according to the extract?

4 What was the main reason for the violence?

Mental health services in the community

Mental health professionals

Definition

Community mental health team – a multi-disciplinary group of mental health professionals usually made up of psychiatrists, general practitioners, social workers, nurses, occupational therapists, psychologists and other specialists that work to support and treat people with mental illnesses living in the community. The voluntary sector can play an important part in this process

The **community mental health team** is composed of a group of professionals drawn from a range of services who link together to co-ordinate the provision of services to those with mental health problems. Community mental health teams have become the norm in most areas of the UK and their development has been accelerated by the decline in the number of large-scale institutions and the growth of community care policies.

Psychiatrists

Although much of psychiatric practice is influenced by the medical model, many psychiatrists realise and accept the social and psychological causes of mental illness and see the need to work in a multi-disciplinary setting alongside other professionals.

Psychotherapist/psychoanalysts

This professional group may be medically trained or lay and embrace a wide range of theoretical perspectives, including the influential work of Sigmund Freud and

Melanie Klein. This group can work within a multi-disciplinary setting, but private practitioners are commonplace, working in isolation on a one-to-one setting. Essentially, this group of professionals is interested in exploring a person's life experiences in order to understand their distress.

Social workers

This professional group are usually located within local authority social services departments and are largely influenced and guided by a legislative and community framework. Social work is equally influenced by various psychoanalytic models as well as more structural/sociological theories. Approved social workers must undergo specialist training.

Community psychiatric nurses

Since the development of community care policies, CPNs have broken away from their institutional traditions and are fast developing professional autonomy. However, much of psychiatric nursing is still heavily influenced by the medical/psychiatric model, although the social and psychological dimension is in the ascendancy in training schools.

The range of services and support that people with mental health problems need

	Acute/emergency care	Rehabilitation/continuing care
Home-based	Sector teams Sustainable out-of-hours cover Intensive home support	Domiciliary services Key workers Care management and Care Programme Approach
Day care	Day hospitals	Drop-in centres Support groups Employment schemes Day care
Residential support	Crisis accommodation Acute units Local secure units	Ordinary housing Unstaffed group homes Adult placement schemes Residential care schemes Mental nursing homes 24-hour nursed NHS accommodation Medium secure units High-security units

Source: *Funding a Place* (Audit Commission, 1994)

Activity

1 Find out about each of the services in the table above.
2 Which of these services is available in your area? You can find the information by contacting either your local NHS trust or your local health authority. These have entries in the local telephone directory. NB The provision and organisation of services may vary in different places, so you may need to amend the table to reflect this.

Specialised mental health services and community mental health teams however, cannot function well if basic necessities such as adequate income, good housing and family support are lacking.

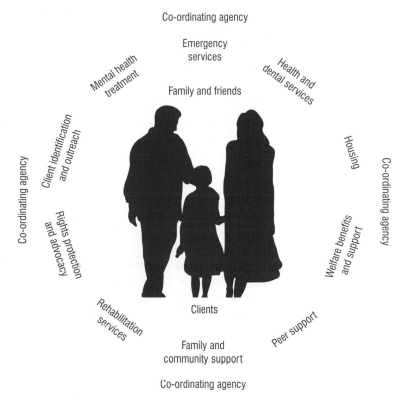

Co-ordinating agency

Emergency services

Mental health treatment

Health and dental services

Family and friends

Client identification and outreach

Co-ordinating agency

Housing

Co-ordinating agency

Rights protection and advocacy

Welfare benefits and support

Clients

Rehabilitation services

Peer support

Family and community support

Co-ordinating agency

The range of medical and social support necessary to combat mental health problems

Mental health provision in the community

Day hospitals

These are institutions which provide an alternative to full-scale hospitals, providing a place during the day. They can also provide intensive treatment for up to three months.

Crisis accommodation

This is for people who have housing needs or for whom home treatment would be difficult. These are usually rooms in mental health centres or hostels.

Acute treatment units and psychiatric beds

These provide a protective place for people who are a risk to themselves or others, and provide inpatient care for those too severely ill to be managed in the community or day hospitals. These units have taken the place of the old style asylums or psychiatric hospitals.

Community mental health centres

These are the centres from which the community mental health teams operate. The members of the team:

- assess health and social care needs
- run specialist clubs or activities
- provide adult education and training
- provide advice on a range of welfare issues.

Often these are combined with day centres which provide a range of 'drop-in' services to rehabilitate and provide a social centre for those with mental health problems who are often socially isolated.

Residential care homes

These are places where a group of people with mental health problems live and where there is staff available for all or most of the day and night. They are often based on the core and cluster model, which involves having a central residential home or hostel, which is heavily staffed, and a number of linked hostels for those with lower levels of need.

Secure units

These are generally linked to acute psychiatric units and provide care for those with extreme problems. They include, at the extreme, the special hospitals for those convicted of a criminal offence who are regarded as dangerous. There is likely to be an expansion of these according to the White Paper *Reforming the Mental Health Act*.

Specialist services

Within many of these settings, apart from the general range of services, there will also be specialist services for particular groups or disorders. For example, there will be services for children and adolescents, for older people and possibly for people with such things as eating disorders.

Voluntary organisations

A number of local and voluntary organisations provide a variety of services, including telephone advice and support, day and residential centres, counselling, befriending services and volunteers, self-help groups and charitable fund-raising. They play an important part in service delivery. These include:

- MIND
- National Schizophrenia Fellowship
- SANE
- the Samaritans.

The problems of community care

A model supported housing scheme for people who have had mental health problems has become the target of attacks that have put back its opening.

The seven-flat complex with communal facilities in Abbey Wood, south London, is designed for people who want to live independently but with a degree of practical support. The £600,000 scheme has been developed by the Bailey housing association.

Residential support worker Andrew Grieve and his partner, Jackie Henery, moved into one of the building's flats in March to prepare for the scheduled arrival this month of the first tenants.

Grieve, who is a coordinator of the charity Mind in Bexley, says the building has since come under "repeated attacks" from local young people, with scaffolding, rocks and glass thrown into the garden. Youths have broken in, causing extensive damage to the front door, and run amok inside. Henery has been verbally intimidated when near the building. ...

"It is possible the stigma and discrimination of mental ill health could threaten the building being the final stepping stone it was planned to be for people who deserve a fair chance in life."

Source: *The Guardian*, 18 April 2001

1 What sort of project is it?

2 How does this fit into the idea of community care?

3 What is Andrew Grieve's job?

4 What is MIND? Find out as much as you can about it. Do you have a local MIND branch? Invite a speaker to talk to you.

5 What does this tell us about the difficulties of community care for people with mental disorders?

6 What does it tell you 'stigma' and mental illness?

Main points ▶ There has been a range of legislation to deal with mental illness.

▶ This has often confused learning disabilities and mental illness.

▶ Until recently most legislation was moving towards an increase in community care.

▶ In recent years the concerns over people with severe personality disorders has seen the growth in residential places.

▶ There are a wide range of community services and professional carers whose job it is to deal with people with mental disorders.

▶ These include both State and voluntary organisations.

Mental health and wider social problems

Mental health is usually regarded as a problem which exists in its own right. However, increasingly people are becoming aware of the way in which it links with other social problems. Two examples illustrate this:

- mental health and homelessness
- mental health and imprisonment.

Mental health and homelessness

One-third of 'rough sleepers' suffer from some kind of mental disorder, and 50 per cent have a serious alcohol problem and anything up to 40 per cent misuse drugs, both of which are often linked to mental disorder. The problem has been exacerbated by the policy of community care which has resulted in people with mental health problems being moved out of institutions, and the subsequent closure of mental hospitals and wards. It is estimated that about 10 per cent of all residents being discharged from mental health institutions did not have a home to which to return.

There appear to be two ways in which homelessness is related to mental health problems.

- People with mental health problems are discriminated against in the housing market, such that they find it difficult to get accommodation. For example, they have been stigmatised by landlords and letting agencies, which means that, unless they are already house owners prior to their problems, they will find it extremely difficult to obtain accommodation.
- The problems are enlarged by the fact that, on the other hand, their mental health problems may be made worse by poor housing, which places greater pressure on them and prevents them from coping with the other pressures of life.

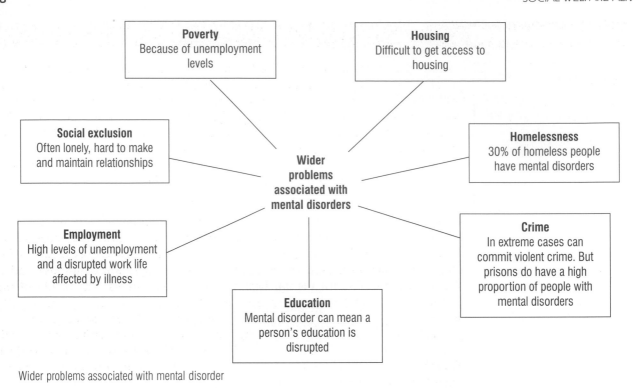

Wider problems associated with mental disorder

Mental health and imprisonment

Prisons are populated just as much by 'the socially inadequate' and those with mental problems as by people who are serious threats to society. It has been estimated that a minimum of 15 per cent and a maximum of 37 per cent (if you include the 23 per cent who have significant problems with alcohol or substance misuse) of prisoners can be said to be suffering from some sort of mental health problem. These include those who had the problems prior to imprisonment and those who may have developed them as a result of the 'pains of imprisonment'. In fact, about one-third of those with severe mental health problems had developed these after imprisonment.

Prisons and the mentally ill

Attempts to divert mentally disturbed offenders from prisons – where they constitute an estimated fifth of the population – are 'uncoordinated and slow', according to a group of health care and prison reform bodies.

Stephen Shaw, director of the Prison Reform Trust, said prisons were used as a 'dumping ground' for the mentally ill. 'The prison service has neither the skills nor the facilities to provide proper psychiatric care. The way people with psychiatric problems are treated in prison is utterly at variance with good practice in the NHS.'

Research for the Home Office by Professor John Gunn of the Institute of Psychiatry, suggests that up to one-fifth of the sentenced prison population have mental health problems and that 3 per cent of prisoners require immediate hospital treatment. The letter says there is an even higher proportion of remand prisoners with mental health problems; many of whom were in custody because of homelessness or for psychiatric assessment.

The number of mentally disordered offenders, like the homeless, is believed to have risen since the Government adopted the policy of closing down residential hospitals for the mentally ill.

Source: From an article by Terry Kirby in *The Independent*, 22 July 1991

1   What proportion of people in prison are mentally disturbed, according to the extract?

2   How many need immediate hospital treatment?

3   What reasons are given for the rise in the numbers of mentally disturbed people in prison?

Empowerment

Empowerment is an issue that has become increasingly prominent in the last ten years. The concept is particularly important for people with mental health problems. It is the argument that people with mental health problems are not just clients or patients, who need to accept that professionals know better than them what is actually good for them. Instead this approach argues that the people with mental health problems (and most other 'clients' of health and welfare agencies) are in fact consumers or service users who know what is best for them and that they should be given the power to make decisions about which services and what help they should receive.

At first this seems an odd argument – after all, aren't people with mental health problems irrational? Supporters of empowerment argue that this objection is, in fact, the whole point of empowerment – by taking decision-making away from those with mental illness, stereotypes of mental illness are confirmed and the stigma of being ill with mental health problems continues. The reality of most people with mental health problems is not that they are 'mad', but that they simply have problems which are more or less severe and last for longer or shorter periods. It has in fact been claimed that up to 30 per cent of the British population has suffered from some sort of mental health problem at some period in their life. Therefore, having a mental health problem is not unusual and can reasonably be regarded as a 'normal' risk of life.

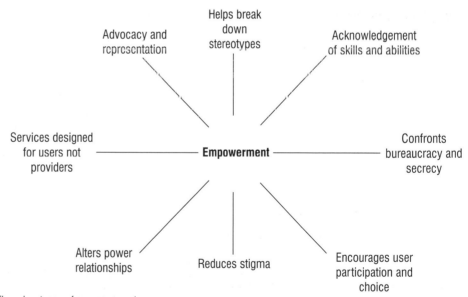

The advantages of empowerment

The empowerment debate is not restricted to mental health. It is also applied to people with learning disabilities, as well as people with physical illnesses. Supporters of empowerment argue that it:

- returns to the service user his/her rights as a citizen to make choices
- returns power to the individual over her/his own life
- helps break down the stereotyping associated with mental health problems such that they are all 'mad'
- helps to weaken the stigma attached to mental illness by showing how they can cope with help, and that people with mental health problems are 'normal' (but with a health problem)

- gets rid of an unnecessary and wasteful bureaucracy of people who decide on and allocate resources to those with mental health problems.

Although most professionals agree that empowerment is important, there are those who have some reservations, which include the views that:

- expert help is important for those with mental health problems, if they are to be cured or helped to cope with their condition
- there are a number of people with mental health problems who are in need of supervision orders and close monitoring of their medication.

New mentality: empowerment in action

A new ethos in mental health, which rejects the medical model of the illness, is being pioneered by Bradford's home treatment service (HTS). It is the first NHS service not to use psychiatric diagnoses, and uses five times less medication on its patients. It is also the first to employ a user with power to make decisions about patients.

A user for the past 35 years, Peter Relton sits alongside the team's two psychiatrists, eight nurses and three social workers at the three-weekly review meetings when clients are discussed. He has equal say on all matters – whether it be the progress of a client, how to spend the service's budget or team development.

"My position means I can make a direct impact on professionals' attitudes and the team's philosophy," explains Relton, who also serves on Bradford MIND's management committee. "Most power in mental health services lies in the hands of the psychiatrists. But, here in Bradford, psychiatrists have made the remarkable step of giving some of their power away to users."

Relton's appointment won the seal of approval from the trust because of the reputation of Bradford HTS team leader, consultant psychiatrist Dr Pat Bracken, who used to work with north Birmingham's innovative home treatment service. ... He says Relton has brought benefits to his team which all psychiatric services could learn from.

"As a user, Peter knows what it is like to be talked about by professionals. He has helped shape the team's culture away from a feeling of them, the patients, and us, the professionals. He can also communicate with patients in a way the rest of us cannot."

Source: *The Guardian*, 3 March 2000

1 What does it mean when it refers to Peter Relton as a 'user'?

2 Where does power normally lie in the NHS?

3 Why is this a fairly radical change?

4 What direct impact does it have on 'medication'? Why do you think that might be?

Main points
- Mental health is not an issue which is isolated, there are many problems associated with it.
- Homelessness is both a cause and a consequence of mental disorder.
- People in prison have a high rate of mental disorder and it may be that the pressures of prison cause mental illness.
- In recent years, people with mental disorders have started to demand some control over the services offered to them, as they feel powerless.

Conclusion

In this chapter, we have examined the way that people with mental disorders have been treated over time, and have experienced a range of policies. Historically, they have been placed in institutions – often against their will. Recently, with the development of community care and the improvements in medication available, they have managed to live their lives in the community – despite facing considerable stigma and hostility. More recently, concerns over people with severe personality disorders, some of whom are dangerous to others, have led to a limited move back towards institutions.

In noticing these historical trends we have also looked at the range of services on offer and the work of professionals, as well as finding out the way that legislation has given them a range of powers over those with mental disorders. Finally, we have also seen that there is an increasing demand by those with mental disorders to gain some control over the medical and care services.

17 CHAPTER SUMMARY

1 Over time there has been a move away from care in institutions to care in the community.

2 Recently there has been a limited move back to the institutions for those with severe mental disorders.

3 There are competing models of what mental illness is and how it is caused in people.

4 Mental illness is very widespread in the population.

5 There has been a range of legislation to deal with mental illness.

6 This has often confused learning disabilities and mental illness.

7 There are a wide range of community services and professional carers whose job it is to deal with people with mental disorders.

8 These include both State and voluntary organisations.

9 Mental health is not an issue which is isolated, there are many problems associated with it, including homelessness and crime.

10 In recent years, people with mental disorders have started to demand some control over the services offered to them, as they feel powerless.

Useful website

www.nimh.gov.uk: Institute of Mental Health

www.mind.org.uk: MIND

www.sane.org.uk: Sane

INDEX